T0223938

Lecture Notes in Computer Science   10286

Commenced Publication in 1973
Founding and Former Series Editors:
Gerhard Goos, Juris Hartmanis, and Jan van Leeuwen

Editorial Board

More information about this series at http://www.springer.com/series/7409

Vincent G. Duffy (Ed.)

Digital Human Modeling

Applications in Health, Safety, Ergonomics, and Risk Management: Ergonomics and Design

8th International Conference, DHM 2017
Held as Part of HCI International 2017
Vancouver, BC, Canada, July 9–14, 2017
Proceedings, Part I

Springer

Editor
Vincent G. Duffy
Purdue University
West Lafayette, IN
USA

ISSN 0302-9743   ISSN 1611-3349 (electronic)
Lecture Notes in Computer Science
ISBN 978-3-319-58462-1   ISBN 978-3-319-58463-8 (eBook)
DOI 10.1007/978-3-319-58463-8

Library of Congress Control Number: 2017939547

LNCS Sublibrary: SL3 – Information Systems and Applications, incl. Internet/Web, and HCI

Printed on acid-free paper

This Springer imprint is published by Springer Nature
The registered company is Springer International Publishing AG
The registered company address is: Gewerbestrasse 11, 6330 Cham, Switzerland

Foreword

The 19th International Conference on Human–Computer Interaction, HCI International 2017, was held in Vancouver, Canada, during July 9–14, 2017. The event incorporated the 15 conferences/thematic areas listed on the following page.

A total of 4,340 individuals from academia, research institutes, industry, and governmental agencies from 70 countries submitted contributions, and 1,228 papers have been included in the proceedings. These papers address the latest research and development efforts and highlight the human aspects of design and use of computing systems. The papers thoroughly cover the entire field of human–computer interaction, addressing major advances in knowledge and effective use of computers in a variety of application areas. The volumes constituting the full set of the conference proceedings are listed on the following pages.

I would like to thank the program board chairs and the members of the program boards of all thematic areas and affiliated conferences for their contribution to the highest scientific quality and the overall success of the HCI International 2017 conference.

This conference would not have been possible without the continuous and unwavering support and advice of the founder, Conference General Chair Emeritus and Conference Scientific Advisor Prof. Gavriel Salvendy. For his outstanding efforts, I would like to express my appreciation to the communications chair and editor of *HCI International News*, Dr. Abbas Moallem.

April 2017   Constantine Stephanidis

HCI International 2017 Thematic Areas and Affiliated Conferences

Thematic areas:

- Human–Computer Interaction (HCI 2017)
- Human Interface and the Management of Information (HIMI 2017)

Affiliated conferences:

- 17th International Conference on Engineering Psychology and Cognitive Ergonomics (EPCE 2017)
- 11th International Conference on Universal Access in Human–Computer Interaction (UAHCI 2017)
- 9th International Conference on Virtual, Augmented and Mixed Reality (VAMR 2017)
- 9th International Conference on Cross-Cultural Design (CCD 2017)
- 9th International Conference on Social Computing and Social Media (SCSM 2017)
- 11th International Conference on Augmented Cognition (AC 2017)
- 8th International Conference on Digital Human Modeling and Applications in Health, Safety, Ergonomics and Risk Management (DHM 2017)
- 6th International Conference on Design, User Experience and Usability (DUXU 2017)
- 5th International Conference on Distributed, Ambient and Pervasive Interactions (DAPI 2017)
- 5th International Conference on Human Aspects of Information Security, Privacy and Trust (HAS 2017)
- 4th International Conference on HCI in Business, Government and Organizations (HCIBGO 2017)
- 4th International Conference on Learning and Collaboration Technologies (LCT 2017)
- Third International Conference on Human Aspects of IT for the Aged Population (ITAP 2017)

Conference Proceedings Volumes Full List

Digital Human Modeling and Applications in Health, Safety, Ergonomics and Risk Management

Program Board Chair(s): **Vincent G. Duffy, USA**

- Andre Calero Valdez, Germany
- Eugene Ch'ng, P.R. China
- Elsbeth de Korte, The Netherlands
- Stephen J. Elliott, USA
- Afzal A. Godil, USA
- Ravindra Goonetilleke, Hong Kong, SAR China
- Akihiko Goto, Japan
- Hiroyuki Hamada, Japan
- Dan Högberg, Sweden
- Hui-min Hu, P.R. China
- Satoshi Kanai, Japan
- Noriaki Kuwahara, Japan
- Kang Li, USA
- Lingxi Li, USA
- Jianwei Niu, P.R. China
- Thaneswer Patel, India
- Beatrice V. Podtschaske, USA
- Caterina Rizzi, Italy
- Beatriz Sousa Santos, Portugal
- Nicole Sintov, USA
- Pingbo Tang, USA
- Leonor Teixeira, Portugal
- Renran Tian, USA
- Gentiane Venture, Japan
- Massimiliano Vesci, Italy
- Anita Woll, Norway
- Kuan Yew Wong, Malaysia
- Shuping Xiong, Korea
- James Yang, USA
- Chaoyi Zhao, P.R. China

The full list with the Program Board Chairs and the members of the Program Boards of all thematic areas and affiliated conferences is available online at:

http://www.hci.international/board-members-2017.php

HCI International 2018

The 20th International Conference on Human–Computer Interaction, HCI International 2018, will be held jointly with the affiliated conferences in Las Vegas, NV, USA, at Caesars Palace, July 15–20, 2018. It will cover a broad spectrum of themes related to human–computer interaction, including theoretical issues, methods, tools, processes, and case studies in HCI design, as well as novel interaction techniques, interfaces, and applications. The proceedings will be published by Springer. More information is available on the conference website: http://2018.hci.international/.

General Chair
Prof. Constantine Stephanidis
University of Crete and ICS-FORTH
Heraklion, Crete, Greece
E-mail: general_chair@hcii2018.org

http://2018.hci.international/

Contents – Part I

Smart Human-Centered Service System Design

Human-Robot Interaction

Contents – Part II

Health and Aging

Health Data Analytics and Visualization

Design for Safety

Anthropometry, Ergonomics, Design and Comfort

Developing a Rapid Assessment Method to Estimate Berg Balance Scale Score of Elderly People

Chih-Sheng Chang[✉] and Wei-Lun Chen

The Department of Product and Media Design,
Fo Guang University, Jiaoxi, Taiwan
arrowmac@gmail.com

Abstract. To prevent falls, many experts are committed to studying the balance of risk factors and assessment methods fall. Berg Balance Scale (BBS) is a clinical assessment method that most commonly used yet its characteristic of subjective and time-consuming may the consequence in different results. The purpose of this study is to use the force platform system parameters and measuring the amount of income derived factors information and related research of BBS findings and to explore the possibility of subjective and objective information to assess the assistance results. Thirty-eight elderly adults residing at the Tai Shun Senior Centre react to sit-to-stand (STS) action on the force platform with the ergonomic chair. Thereafter, 12 parameters recorded or derived from the recording of the force platforms on measured operation time and the change of force data, then assess the results of BBS for correlation analysis. The results show that the relevance of BBS and force-related parameters is lower than the relevance of BBS and time-related parameters. Whereas, Ls - seatoff (the duration from the onset of leg to the time of seatoff) has high correlation with BBS results. This achievement can be an effective initial assessment of early warning on the results of BBS elderly people's ability to, thus reducing subjective measurement results of possible bias.

Keywords: Falling · Fall risk · GRF · Sit-to-stand

1 Introduction

In terms of injury prevention, falls are one of the most ordinary accidents in the elderly. The incidence of falls will increase as age increases (Campbell et al. 1989; Alexander et al. 1991). The physical effects of aging, such as falters in vision, sensory perception, hearing, balance, muscle tone, and reaction times, in the elderly will increase falls and the resulting injuries. The external factors, such as insufficient lighting, the insufficient height of toilet seats, or uneven ground, are also possible root cause for increased falls in the aged (Spanley and Beare 1995).

In daily life, the elderly often results in reduced balance capacity and fall occurred due to the physiology of aging. Many experts are committed to studying the balance of risk factors and assessment methods fall in order to prevent falls. To decrease accidental falls in the elderly, many intervention programs have been developed. Currently, "sit-to-stand" (STS) movement is investigated using observational performance tests or

© Springer International Publishing AG 2017
V.G. Duffy (Ed.): DHM 2017, Part I, LNCS 10286, pp. 3–10, 2017.
DOI: 10.1007/978-3-319-58463-8_1

performance measures to assess the risk of falling (Bogle and Newton 1996; Rogers et al. 2003). Observational performance tests which tend to be subjective, use several assessment tools that combine measures of balance with measures of gait and mobility to determine a person's risk of falling, such as the Berg Balance Scale (BBS; Berg et al. 1992) and the Tinetti Gait and Balance Assessment (Tinetti et al. 1986).

Berg Balance Scale (BBS) is a clinical assessment method that most commonly used yet its characteristic of subjective and time-consuming may the consequence in different results by the assessment of surveying for 30 min or an hour spent. In this respect, if timely and objective measurement equipment data is offered in the BBS supplemented with comparative assessment will help in providing experts and medical personnel for determining the right balance of the elderly person. The purpose of this study was to use the force platform system parameters and measuring the amount of income derived factors information and related research of BBS findings and to explore the possibility of subjective and objective information to assess the assistance results.

2   Methods

2.1   Participants

The participants were selected from thirty-eight elderly adults residing at the Tai Shun Senior Centre. The selection criteria were over 65 years old, no acute medical illness, such as coronary heart disease, heart failure, or pulmonary infection in the past 3 months, without orthopedic diagnosis, no muscular disease, Barthel Index score ≥ 60, Mini-Mental Status Exam score >17, and Instrumental Activities of Daily Living Scale score ≥ 7. To confirm that all the participants were able to complete all the test successfully. In the end of the study, twenty-one healthy elderly participants independently completed stand up action and the BBS score in 41 or more of the elderly (12 females, 9 males; M age = 69.4 yr., SD = 3.7; BMI = 24.1; SD = 4.1) to react to STS action on the force platforms with the ergonomic chair. The study was approved by Fo Guang University ethics committee. After a full explanation of the experimental project, the Informed consent was obtained from each participant and its procedures were provided. Table 1 shows the means and standard deviation of four standard geriatric assessments.

Table 1. Means and standard deviation of four standard geriatric assessments

Variable	BBS		BI		MMSE		IADL	
	M	SD	M	SD	M	SD	M	SD
Elderly	47	3.62	95.5	3.59	29.90	0.94	7.71	0.46

2.2   Apparatus

The main aspects of the force platform system are force platforms, ergonomic chair, and a charge-coupled device (CCD) camera. The load cells detect the changes in component GRFs during the STS task. The mechanical structure consists of an ergonomic chair and two force platforms (buttock force platform, BFP and leg force platform, LFP). In this task, an experimental ergonomic chair was designed according to the suggestions of the American National Standards Institute (ANSI) and the National Standards of the People's Republic of China (GB). In addition, the angle of the seat plane and between the seat plane and back were set to be 4° backward and 100°, respectively according to ANSI. The depth and the width of the seat were set to be 40 cm and 45 cm, respectively. The height of the seat plane was adjustable, between 32 and 46 cm (GB). To avoid sliding or overturning, the ergonomic chair was fixed to the BFP (Fig. 1).

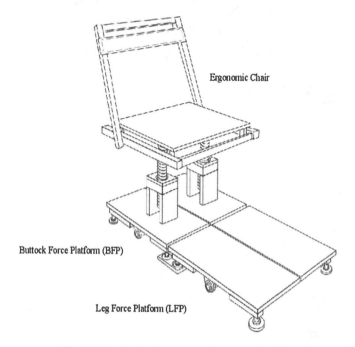

Fig. 1. Mechanical structure of ergonomic chair

In the present study, with the force platform, the GRF was defined as the force applied to the ground by the buttocks and/or the feet. Vertical GRFs were recorded from two separate force platforms (size, 500 × 500 mm; accuracy, 0.20 N) composed of eight load cells (Fig. 2). The distance between the force platforms was 10 mm. The pivot mechanism provides only one degree of freedom for the two separated plates; it was designed to prevent only three points being coplanar all because under such conditions, the boundary constraints of the remaining load cell may lead to incorrect data. Figure 2 shows the chair pivot mechanism of the force platform.

A video capture program was used to convert the video recordings of the STS movements into computer video files with a CCD camera. After force platform system data were confirmed on the video screen, the STS movements from the right side to the left and from front to back to capture images for subsequent observation was recorded by two digital video cameras. To show the movement from beginning to end, the computer video was then edited using Adobe Premiere 4.0 (Adobe Systems, San Jose, CA, USA). The layout of experimental setting is shown in Fig. 3.

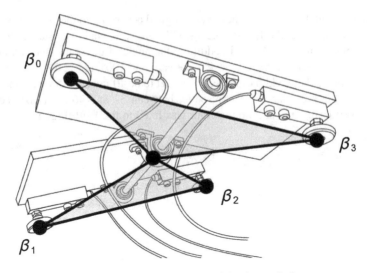

Fig. 2. Chair pivot mechanism of the force platform

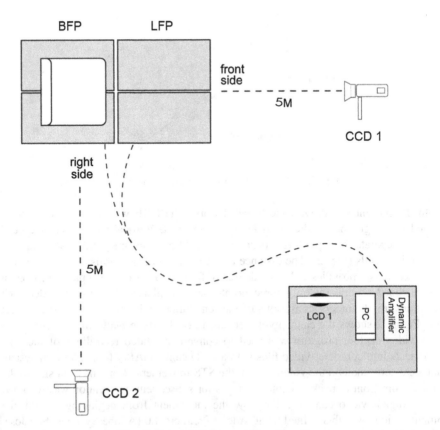

Fig. 3. Layout of the experimental setting

2.3 Procedure

First of all, participants sat on the experimental ergonomic chair on a buttocks force platform and their arms kept folded across their chest. In order to ensure that the trunk was leaning back in a standard position, the back support on the chair was used. Bare feet were positioned on the leg force platform together with the feet maintained 10° of the calf and vertical face. This sit status is the starting posture. No other restrictions were imposed on the initial position. To initiate the sit-to-stand movement, an auditory signal from the computer cued the participants. Each participant performed the task in a comfortable and natural manner and at a self-selected speed. Then, the task was performed in one trial, following two practice trials. The immediate response can be done if discomfort during the test. A registered nurse was present during all trials for safety.

2.4 Measurements

The selected ground reaction force parameters and time course of STS are as shown in Fig. 4. Two curves (Curve B, buttocks weight; Curve L, leg weight) describing the vertical GRF as a function of time were obtained from the force platforms. The sum of forces B and L showed Curve T. The time to stand up was calculated from these curves.

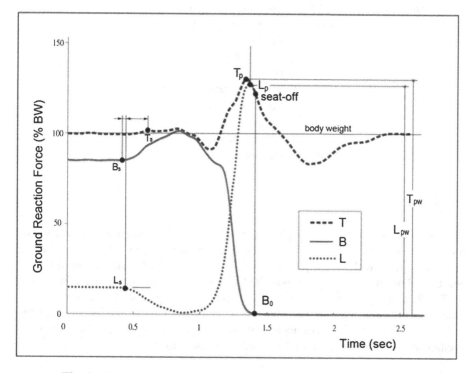

Fig. 4. Ground reaction force parameters and time course of sit-to-stand.

The onsets of Curves B (Bs), L (Ls), and T (Ts) were identified immediately after the action cue when the difference between the GRF at that time point and the previous value did not equal zero. Seatoff was defined as the time at which the thighs lost contact with the chair when the instant of Curve B was at zero (B0). Tp and Lp occurred when the GRF for Curves T and L, respectively, were maximal. Tpw and Lpw were the maximum forces of Curves T and L, respectively. The GRF oscillated following seatoff, and the sit-to-stand phase ended when the ground reaction force reached body weight. By using the moving average method, the recorded data were been smoothed before analysis (Box and Pierce 1970).

Thereafter, 12 parameters recorded or derived from the recording of the force platforms on measured operation time and the change of force data, then assess the results of BBS for correlation analysis. Each parameter is named Nomenclature as shown in Table 2.

Table 2. Nomenclature used in this study

Parameters		Description
Weight parameters	Tpw	The maximum ground reaction force of Curve T
	Lpw	The maximum ground reaction force of Curve L
Time parameters	Bs-Lp	Duration between Bs-Lp
	Bs-Tp	Duration between Bs-Tp
	Bs-seatoff	Duration between Bs-seatoff
	Bs-end	Duration between Bs-end
	Ls-Tp	Duration between Ls-Tp
	Ls-seatoff	Duration between Ls-seatoff
	Ls-end	Duration between Ls-end
	Ts-Tp	Duration between Ts-Tp
	Ts-seatoff	Duration between Ts-seatoff
	Ts-end	Duration between Ts-end

3   Results

The test results showed that among the 12 parameters that measured and derived by the force platforms, Ls-seatoff, the time-related parameters and its BBS score showed highly correlated with $-.709$ ($p < .01$). Moreover, when force related parameters Tpw and Lpw showed low correlation with BBS score, time related parameters like Bs-Lp, Bs-Tp, Bs-seatoff, Bs-end, Ls-Tp, Ls-end, Ts-Tp, Ts-seatoff and Ts-end showed significant correlation. Table 3 lists the function, mean of each independent variable including weight and time parameters of the sit-to-stand movement. The correlated coefficients of each factors and BBS score were also shown.

Table 3. The correlation of deformation parameter

Parameters	Function	Parameters			BBS score
		M	SD	P	Pearson
Tpw	$(T_{pw})^{1/4} * \sqrt{BMI}$	11.65	1.68	.078	−.393
Lpw	$(L_{pw})^{1/4} * \sqrt{BMI}$	14.25	1.67	.077	−.394
Bs-Lp	$(B_s - L_s)^{1/4} * \sqrt{BMI}$	32.20	4.44	.003	−.616**
Bs-Tp	$(B_s - T_p)^{1/4} * \sqrt{BMI}$	31.59	4.47	.005	−.593**
Bs-seatoff	$(B_s - seatoff)^{1/4} * \sqrt{BMI}$	32.63	4.39	.002	−.627**
Bs-end	$(B_s - end)^{1/4} * \sqrt{BMI}$	36.17	4.28	.002	−.635**
Ls-Tp	$(L_s - T_p)^{1/4} * \sqrt{BMI}$	31.55	4.22	.001	−.683**
Ls-seatoff	$(L_s - seatoff)^{1/4} * \sqrt{BMI}$	32.58	4.24	.000	−.709**
Ls-end	$(L_s - end)^{1/4} * \sqrt{BMI}$	36.14	4.15	.000	−.694**
Ts-Tp	$(T_s - T_p)^{1/4} * \sqrt{BMI}$	30.54	5.55	.005	−.587**
Ts-seatoff	$(T_s - seatoff)^{1/4} * \sqrt{BMI}$	31.75	5.21	.002	−.636**
Ts-end	$(T_s - end)^{1/4} * \sqrt{BMI}$	35.59	4.76	.001	−.652**

**at significant level of 0.01 (two-tailed), significant correlation.
*at significant level of 0.05 (two-tailed), significant correlation.

4 Discussion

The results of this study showed that the correlation test between the original parameter score and BBS score, that both scored mostly with low and moderate correlation. Subsequently, attempts to correlate the BMI score with the BBS score were only moderately correlated with −.452 (p = .04). However, when the BMI values are incorporated into the construction of the future parametric functions, there are different discoveries.

After the setup of each parameter function, the results show that the relevance of BBS score and force-related parameters, such as Tpw (the maximum GRF of the sum of force buttock weight and leg weight) and Lpw (the maximum GRF of force leg weight) is lower than the relevance of BBS score and time-related parameters such as Bs-end (the duration from the onset of buttock to the end of STS) or Ls-Tp (the duration from the onset of leg to the time of the maximum GRF at Curve T). Whereas, Ls-seatoff (the duration from the onset of leg to the time of seatoff) have high correlation with BBS score results (−.709, p < .01). Hence, Ls-seatoff and BBS score had the chance, through regression analysis to create regression equation.

The current assessments of clinical balance were done by experts and professional medical personnel with the BBS assessment yet it may consume more time (30 or 45 min more) to assess with individual subjective judgments, possibility on resulting deviation in rating (Chang et al. 2013). The objective and time-saving features of the force platform system can be usefully supplemented with the information, that can assist experts and professional medical personnel on the assessment of balance.

In the past, there were a lot of researches using the force platforms to measure the standing movement of the elderly (Lindemann et al. 2007; Yamada and Demura 2005), obtained the data from the objective, was used to describe the standing movement with the factors of the elderly's fall risk acquisition research. Chang et al. (2010) also through the test of ground reaction force and composition force through two force platforms, which describes more clearly on standing movements, such as Tp, Lp and seatoff key points in order to clarify the sequence, which has made a great contribution. Yet a number of high-priced force platforms may be the obstacle for universal application in the future. Figure out how to use only one piece of force platform to obtain the necessary data and information, will be the goal of the next research phase. This stage of research can be an effective initial assessment of early warning on the results of BBS elderly people's ability to, thus reducing subjective measurement results of possible bias.

Acknowledgments. This research was supported by a grant from the National Science Council (NSC-103-2221-E-431-007). The authors also gratefully acknowledge the contribution of the Tai Shun Senior Centre.

References

Alexander, N.B., Schultz, A.B., Warwick, D.N.: Rising from a chair: effects of age and functional ability on performance biomechanics. J. Gerontol. **46**(5), 91–98 (1991)

Bogle, T.L.D., Newton, R.A.: Use the Berg Balance Test to predict falls in elderly persons. Phys. Ther. **76**, 576–585 (1996)

Berg, K.O., Maki, B.E., Williams, J.I., Holliday, P.J., Wood-Dauphinee, S.L.: Clinical and laboratory measures of postural balance in an elderly population. Arch. Phys. Med. Rehabil. **73**, 1073–1080 (1992)

Box, G.E.P., Pierce, D.A.: Distribution of residual autocorrelations in autoregressive-integrated moving average time series models. J. Am. Stat. Assoc. **65**(332), 1509–1526 (1970)

Chang, C.S., Leung, C.Y., Liou, J.J.: Describing force patterns: a method for classifying sit-to-stand movement in elderly people. Percept. Mot. Skills **116**(1), 163–174 (2013)

Chang, C.S., Leung, C.Y., Liou, J.J., Tsai, W.W.: Evaluation of key points in the sit-to-stand movement using two force platforms. Percept. Mot. Skills **111**(2), 496–502 (2010)

Campbell, A.J., Borrie, M.J., Spears, G.F.: Risk factors for falls in a community-based prospective study of people 70 years and older. J. Gerontol. **44**, M112–M117 (1989)

Lindemann, U., Muche, R., Stuber, M., Zijlstra, W., Hauer, K., Becker, C.: Coordination of strength exertion during the chair-rise movement in very old people. J. Gerontol. Ser. A: Biol. Sci. Med. Sci. **62**, 636–640 (2007)

Rogers, M.E., Rogers, N.L., Takeshima, N., Islam, M.M.: Methods to assess and improve the physical parameters associated with fall risk in older adults. Prev. Med. **36**(3), 255–264 (2003)

Spanley, M., Beare, T.G.: Gerontological Nursing. Davis, Philadelphia (1995)

Tinetti, M.E., Williams, T.F., Mayewski, R.: Fall risk index for elderly patients based on number of chronic disabilities. Am. J. Med. **80**, 429–434 (1986)

Yamada, T., Demura, S.: Instruction in reliability and magnitude of evaluation parameters at each phase of a sit-to-stand movement. Percept. Mot. Skills **101**, 695–706 (2005)

A Research on Effect of Pillow Height on Pressure and Comfort of Human Body's Prone Position

Huimin Hu[1(✉)], Sun Liao[2], Chaoyi Zhao[1], Zhiyang Gui[2], and Fan Yang[3]

[1] Ergonomics Laboratory,
China National Institute of Standardization, Beijing, China
{huhm, zhaochy}@cnis.gov.cn
[2] Sport Science College, Beijing Sport University, Beijing, China
89525315@qq.com, 1498480275@qq.com
[3] School of Biological Science and Medical Engineering,
Beihang University, Beijing, China
yzyangfan@foxmail.com

Abstract. This research has explored the effects of buckwheat pillow at different heights on the body pressure distribution and comfort of women aged 44–64 years. A total of 19 women aged 44–64 years (who are healthy and have no sleep disorder or musculoskeletal disease history) were selected. The quality of sleep and the use of pillow were investigated by questionnaire survey, and subjects were guided to make subjective comfort experience evaluations on the mattresses with moderate hardness with the use of buckwheat pillows at four different heights (the pillow heights were 3 cm, 7 cm, 11 cm and 15 cm, respectively) Laboratory measurement was carried out on body shape index. The body pressure distribution in supine position was also measured. Based on the experiment results the test results of Body Pressure Distribution and Subjective Comfort Evaluation are concluded respectively.

Keywords: Pillow height · Pressure distribution · Subjective comfort · Use experience · Human body's prone position

1 Introduction

About one-third of our time is spent in sleep, so high-quality and adequate sleep is necessary for people, and the living organism maintains the body's homeostasis, immune function and its integrity through sleep. In addition, sleep also regulates the cognitive ability, ability to judge and memory needed in daily life and work [1]. According to Kyle et al, the quality of sleep is directly related to human health and living standards [2]. In sleep, pillow is an important tool to maintain the cervical vertebra's normal physiological curvature and the sleeping pillow supports the head. The right pillow is conducive to maintaining the normal physiological curve of human spine, keeping the body in a natural state and ensuring good rest and sleep of human, but in case of inappropriate pillow selected, the long-term use may cause changes in the

© Springer International Publishing AG 2017
V.G. Duffy (Ed.): DHM 2017, Part I, LNCS 10286, pp. 11–25, 2017.
DOI: 10.1007/978-3-319-58463-8_2

normal physiological curve of cervical spine, affecting the health. Therefore, how to choose a comfortable pillow for good sleep is a vital issue. In the study of bedding comfort, the research of mattress comfort has included the analyses on relationship between the prone position and the body pressure distribution and change in comfort, respectively, but the researches on pillow comfort and function are still limited. This research is aimed at exploring the effects of buckwheat pillows with different heights on the body pressure distribution and comfort of women aged 44–64 years.

1.1   Role of Sleeping Pillow

The quality of sleep at night is closely related to the sleeping posture. Specifically, incorrect cervical posture during sleep increases the biomechanical stress on the cervical spine, which can result in pain and stiffness in cervical spine, headache and pain in scapular or arm, finally leading to poor-quality sleep [3]. In heavy sleep, our neck and shoulder muscles are completely relaxed, and we maintain the normal relationship between the intervertebral structure only by the elasticity of intervertebral ligament and joint capsule. In case of the long-term use of a pillow with inappropriate height, which causes excessive flexion of the cervical spine, the ligaments and joint capsule here will suffer stretch and injury, resulting in cervical instability, joint dislocation, and then developing into cervical spondylosis [4]. If the pillow is too low, head and neck is bound to be over backward with increased lordosis, so the muscles and ligaments in the front of centrum will be too tight. For a long time, there will be fatigue and even chronic injury, accelerating degenerative changes. On the contrary, if the pillow is too high, the head and neck will have excessive antexion, which easily leads to strain of muscles and ligaments in the rear of the cervical spine.

Lavin's research on 41 patients with benign cervical pain also shows that the use of appropriate pillow can significantly reduce the pains in neck and shoulders [5]. Therefore, the selection of a pillow with appropriate height can optimize the body's sleeping posture, thereby improving sleep quality [6]. One of the key factors for a suitable pillow is the ability to support the normal physiological curvature of cervical spine [7].

The main role of pillow during sleep is to support the cervical spine and keep it in a neutral position, so as to minimize the final stage position of cervical spine motion to avoid the loss of cervical curvature and the symptoms of cervical spondylopathy in awakened state [8, 9]. In addition, proper support can increase the area of contact between neck and pillow, allowing a more even distribution of pressure on muscles [10].

Another key feature of a suitable pillow is the ability to reduce head temperature. A pillow that helps reduce core and head temperatures during sleep at night is important for deep sleep [11].

1.2   Research Status and Methods of Sleeping Pillow

In respect of pillow height, the Japanese scholar Minezaki et al. [12] used subjective evaluation method, electromyography test method and X-ray observation method to research the most comfortable pillow height for 40 20-year-old females, and the most comfortable pillow height most conducive to sleep was recommended to be 5.0 ± 1.0 cm in supine position and 6.8 ± 0.9 cm in lateral position; in terms of shape, Taiwanese scholar Chen HL et al. measured the body sizes of coronal and sagittal planes of the heads, necks and shoulders of 10 males and 10 females with an average age of 21.9 years, and designed two U-shaped pillows suitable for Taiwanese male's and female's heads respectively based on the average [10]; according to the principles and data in anatomy, physiology, pathology and biomechanics in combination with clinical experience, An [13] designed a curve heterologous pillow, applied it clinically, carried out qualitative and quantitative biomechanical analysis, and speculated that the pillow was in line with the natural posture of neck, allowing the best stress state of neck; in terms of comfort, Cheng Xiuguang stated in the Environmental Clothing Science that [14] the performance that bedding should have shall meet the physical needs of human body, such as insulation, hygroscopicity, moisture permeability and ventilation, etc., and bedding shall also be adapted to physical activities, bear reasonable load and allow good skin touch; by studying the relationship between pillow sensory evaluation and compression performance, Japanese scholar Yokura [15] carried out correlation analysis on the relationship between the subjective rating (softness, fitness and general comfort) and the compression work & compression deformation rate of pillow so as to explore the establishment of an objective assessment method of pillow comfort. Pillows with larger contact area and less contact pressure are considered to be softer and more comfortable, and pillows with the same plane shape are assessed with good consistency in terms of pillow hardness and height. Korean scholar [16] Park SJ used 3D scanning to measure adult human's head size, and the head size was classified into four types. When the head rests on the pillow, the pillow height is determined by the relationship between the pillow stiffness and the pressure distribution of head and neck on pillow, and the relationship between pillow height, shape and stiffness is found. It was found through experiment that the rule of choosing a comfortable pillow by subjects can be determined by the relationship between height, shape and stiffness of pillow, and the selected comfortable pillow is significantly correlated with the satisfaction; He [17] summarized the evaluation methods of bedding product comfort, mainly including psychological evaluation method, physiological evaluation method, objective property indicator method and microclimate theory, etc. In this paper, the psychological evaluation method based on psychological scale method and the physiological evaluation method to measure size of human body, state of spine curve and other indicators [18] were adopted to study the relationship between the pillow height the and the pressure and comfort of human body's prone position.

2 Research Subjects and Methods

2.1 Research Subjects

The subjects in this research were 19 women (healthy without history of sleep disorder or musculoskeletal disorders) of 44 to 64 years of age. Subjects were required to perform subjective comfort experience evaluation on mattresses with moderate hardness (hardness value of 1.56) in respect of pillows with four different heights (with pillow heights of 3 cm, 7 cm, 11 cm and 15 cm, respectively) with the body shape parameters and the body pressure distribution under four pillow heights were measured.

2.2   Research Methods

2.2.1   Experimental Mattress and Pillow

The mattress was brown mattress with hardness value of 1.56, and the pillow was filled with buckwheat. The pillow heights were 3 cm, 7 cm, 11 cm and 15 cm and the length and width were 55 cm × 35 cm.

2.2.2   Subjective Comfort Evaluation Scheme

Subjects experienced the comfort of 4 pillows with different heights. Subjects were free to choose pillow height and posture to use the pillow. The time of experience on each pillow was not less than 3 min. After the completion of experience, the subjective feeling evaluation form was completed with the evaluation results given on 5-level rating basis.

2.2.3   Test Program for Physiological Curvature of Human Head and Neck

In order to study the relationship between the curvature of cervical vertebrae and the pillow height comfortable for subjects, the body size of subjects in the standard anatomical position was measured with the use of Martin Measuring Scale (see Fig. 1) (Table 1).

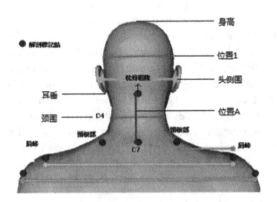

Fig. 1. Human body size test

Table 1. comparison table

解剖标记点	Anatomical mark points
耳垂	Earlobe
颈围	Neck circumference
肩峰	Acromion
颈根部	Neck root
身高	Height
位置1	Position 1
头侧围	Head side circumference
位置A	Position A

2.2.4 Scheme of Body Pressure Distribution Test Under Different Pillow Heights

(1) Test Purpose
The pressure distribution of human body under steady state of pillows with different heights was measured by Tekscan pressure transducer.

(2) Test Requirements
Subjects lying on the mattress in supine position with their head and neck completely placed on the pillow, feet naturally separated, arms placed on the chest and elbows not touching the mattress as far as possible. The test was started when the subjects lay on back in relaxed state and the pressure data was stabilized. The subjects kept still after the start of test.

(3) Testing Process
After the subjects lay down, the body weight of subjects was calibrated. After the pressure value was stabilized, the 25 s body pressure distribution test was conducted (200 frames in total, 0.125 s/frame with acquisition frequency 8 Hz). In the second half of test (after 100 frames), projections of human neck, waist and thigh on the mattress were pressed with fingers to be used as partition basis, followed by the replacement of pillows with different heights in sequence for testing. The body weight was calibrated before each test.

The body pressure was divided into the following eight areas (see Fig. 2): head, neck, trunk, waist, buttocks, thighs, shanks, feet and body. The five parameters, i.e.

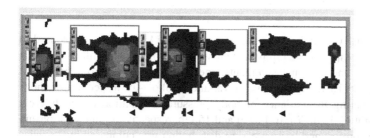

Fig. 2. Diagram of human pressure areas

pressure value (F), peak pressure value (PF), pressure intensity value (CP), peak pressure intensity value (PCP) and contact area (CA) of the eight areas were obtained. The effective average of different areas and different parameters in the whole testing process were obtained.

2.3 Data Processing

2.3.1 Raw Pressure Data Derivation

The pressure distribution data, including five parameters, i.e. pressure value (F), peak pressure value (PF), pressure intensity value (CP), peak pressure intensity value (PCP) and contact area (CA), of each subject were obtained through the BPMS Tekscan system software, and the test areas were divided into 8 partitions i.e. head, neck, trunk, waist, buttocks, thighs, shanks, feet and body according to the calibration points in testing.

2.3.2 Data Judgment and Calculation

Scripts written by Python were used to read the raw data. After excluding the outliers caused by the pressure markers during the experiment process, the mean values were selected and summed by selecting effective value range.

2.3.3 Standard Processing of Data

People with different body weights may have different pressure values. Pressure value is proportional to body weight, so standard processing was adopted.

(1) Pressure value processing: the whole body was set to 100%, with those of other part set to intensity value/body value*100%;
(2) Peak pressure processing: the maximum of partitions was set to 100%, with those of other parts set to peak pressure value/maximum*100%;
(3) Pressure intensity value processing: the maximum of partitions was set to 100%, with those of other parts set to pressure intensity value/maximum*100%;
(4) Peak pressure intensity processing: the maximum of partitions was set to 100%, with those of other parts set to peak intensity pressure/maximum*100%;
(5) Contact area value processing: the whole body was set to 100%, with those of other part set to contact area value/body value*100%.

2.4 Data Analysis

SPSS software was used to analyze the data. Spearman Rank Correlation was used to compare the relationship between pillow height and subjective comfort and that between pillow height and body measurements; one-way anova, LSD (homogeneity of variance) and Dunnett T3 (heterogeneity of variance) follow-up inspection methods were used for comparing the variance of body pressure distribution under different pillow heights (height of 3 cm, 7 cm, 11 cm and 15 cm, respectively); the relationship between subjective comfort and body pressure distribution was compared by stepwise regression; the significance level was defined as $p < 0.05$.

3 Experimental Results

3.1 Subjective Comfort Evaluation Results

Tables 2 and 3 show the results of the subjective comfort assessment for pillows with different heights (Fig. 3).

Table 2. Scores of pillow's subjective comfort experience (n = 19)

Serial no.	Head and neck comfort	Buttock comfort	Waist comfort	Shoulder comfort	Average
1 (3 cm)	3.4 ± 1.4	3.7 ± 1.2	3.5 ± 1.3	3.6 ± 1.1	3.55 ± 1.2
2 (7 cm)	3.8 ± 0.8	3.6 ± 0.9	3.6 ± 1.1	3.8 ± 1.0	3.7 ± 0.8
3 (11 cm)	2.9 ± 1.1	3.2 ± 1.2	3.1 ± 1.1	2.8 ± 0.9	3.0 ± 0.9
4 (15 cm)	1.7 ± 1.0	2.8 ± 1.2	2.6 ± 1.1	2.1 ± 1.0	2.3 ± 0.9

Table 3. Count of the most comfortable pillow selected by subjects (n = 19)

Most comfortable pillow	1 (3 cm)	2 (7 cm)	3 (11 cm)	4 (15 cm)
Count (Subject)	9	8	2	0

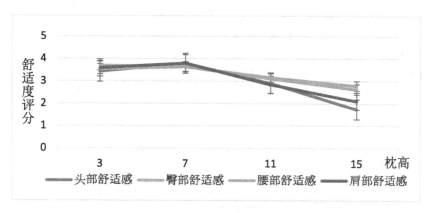

舒适度评分	Comfort score
枕高	Pillow height
头部舒适感	Head comfort
臀部舒适感	Hip comfort
腰部舒适感	Waist comfort
肩部舒适感	Shoulder comfort

Fig. 3. Main comfort evaluation scores and pillow heights

Pillow's subjective comfort evaluation results show that the subjects like 7 cm high Pillow 2 most, which was followed by 3 cm high Pillow 1.

3.2   Body Pressure Test Results Under Different Pillow Heights

All the standardized values in the tables are percentages, i.e., the percentage values standardized based on the maximum value of each subject. Tables 4, 5, 6, 7 and 8 show the results of body pressure distribution test under different pillow heights.

Table 4. Pressure values (F, %) (n = 19)

Item	0 cm	3 cm	7 cm	11 cm	15 cm
F head	7.1 ± 1.4	7.5 ± 1.6	7.2 ± 1.7	7.8 ± 2.3	7.3 ± 2.1
F neck	0.7 ± 0.4	1.9 ± 1.3	2.9 ± 2.2	3.2 ± 3.0	3.7 ± 2.6
F chest	35.8 ± 5.5	34 ± 5.9	31.5 ± 8.6	30.7 ± 8.1	29.9 ± 7.2
F waist	6.4 ± 2.1	6.7 ± 2.1	6.7 ± 1.6	7.0 ± 2.1	7.4 ± 2.7
F buttock	30.8 ± 4.5	30.2 ± 4.4	31.3 ± 5.5	30.8 ± 5.0	31.0 ± 5.6
F thigh	5.5 ± 1.5	5.6 ± 2.0	5.4 ± 1.8	5.5 ± 1.7	5.9 ± 1.4
F shank-foot	12.6 ± 2.2	13.1 ± 2.3	12.8 ± 2.3	12.8 ± 2.1	12.7 ± 2.0

Table 5. Peak pressure values (PF, %) (n = 19)

Item	0 cm	3 cm	7 cm	11 cm	15 cm
PF head	84 ± 14.8	83.3 ± 15.9	77.6 ± 16.8	76.7 ± 16.0	76.4 ± 13.6
PF neck	9 ± 4.1	25.1 ± 15.2	32.5 ± 15.4	34.2 ± 18.8	45.4 ± 25.3
PF chest	60.8 ± 18.3	64.4 ± 14.9	68.1 ± 14.7	64.9 ± 18.7	66.5 ± 15.3
PF waist	34.9 ± 16.3	38.4 ± 15.5	37.6 ± 7.9	36.5 ± 10.8	39.9 ± 16.3
PF buttock	66.5 ± 21.5	73.1 ± 20.5	80.7 ± 17.7	83.2 ± 15.7	84.2 ± 14.7
PF thigh	21.1 ± 6.1	22.1 ± 5.5	20.8 ± 4.4	21.8 ± 5.8	22.6 ± 4.8
PF shank-foot	77.7 ± 15.0	80.7 ± 12.9	80 ± 13.3	82.9 ± 13.7	81.8 ± 24.0

Table 6. Pressure intensity values (CP, %) (n = 19)

Item	0 cm	3 cm	7 cm	11 cm	15 cm
CP body	68.2 ± 7.3	70.1 ± 5.9	67.9 ± 6.9	66.7 ± 6.6	65.3 ± 5.5
CP head	82.3 ± 16.8	83.1 ± 13.8	82.4 ± 16.6	84.6 ± 14.9	83.8 ± 15.7
CP neck	26.1 ± 9.0	42.7 ± 13.2	49.3 ± 14.0	47.7 ± 19.5	56.4 ± 22.3
CP chest	79.7 ± 18.5	80.6 ± 12.9	77.1 ± 16.3	73.8 ± 14.0	71.5 ± 12.5
CP waist	53.4 ± 15.3	59.8 ± 13.2	55.0 ± 9.0	58 ± 12.7	58.6 ± 12.6
CP buttock	89.1 ± 12.0	93.4 ± 10.2	93.1 ± 10.3	93.4 ± 9.9	91.2 ± 11.3
CP thigh	35 ± 7.7	35.6 ± 7.0	33.8 ± 4.8	33.3 ± 5.0	35.4 ± 11.4
CP shank-foot	53.7 ± 15.5	54.7 ± 11.3	52.6 ± 10.4	51.7 ± 10.3	50.6 ± 10.6

With the increase in pillow height, F neck and F waist increased while F chest decreased progressively.

With the increase in pillow height, PF neck and PF buttock had an increasing trend while PF head had a decreasing trend. With pillow height less than 3 cm, the body's

Table 7. Standardized peak pressure intensity values in pressure pad test (PCP, %) (n = 19)

Item	0 cm	3 cm	7 cm	11 cm	15 cm
PCP body	100 ± 0.0	100 ± 0.0	99.9 ± 0.3	98.4 ± 6.9	100 ± 0.0
PCP head	83.9 ± 14.8	82.9 ± 16.9	77.1 ± 17.1	75 ± 17.0	76.4 ± 13.5
PCP neck	11.1 ± 3.2	26.9 ± 14.4	33.2 ± 14.3	34.9 ± 18.2	46.0 ± 24.8
PCP chest	60.7 ± 18.4	64.7 ± 14.7	68.8 ± 13.5	63.7 ± 18.2	67.4 ± 15.3
PCP waist	35 ± 16.3	39.7 ± 14.7	39.3 ± 10.1	36.3 ± 11.4	40.1 ± 16.1
PCP buttock	66.4 ± 21.6	72.4 ± 20.2	80.4 ± 17.8	84.1 ± 16.6	84.4 ± 14.6
PCP thigh	21 ± 6.2	22 ± 5.5	20.6 ± 4.5	21.5 ± 5.9	22.5 ± 4.8
PCP shank-foot	77.6 ± 14.9	80.1 ± 13.36	82.1 ± 11.6	80.8 ± 14.0	86.5 ± 16.9

Table 8. Contact area values (CA, %) (n = 19)

Item	0 cm	3 cm	7 cm	11 cm	15 cm
CA head	6.1 ± 1.6	6.4 ± 1.3	6 ± 1.3	6.1 ± 1.6	5.7 ± 1.7
CA neck	1.8 ± 0.6	2.8 ± 1.3	3.6 ± 1.7	3.8 ± 2.2	4.2 ± 1.8
CA chest	31.2 ± 3.3	29.5 ± 3.7	27.4 ± 4.2	27.5 ± 4.5	27.0 ± 4.1
CA waist	8.1 ± 1.8	7.7 ± 1.7	8.2 ± 1.6	8.0 ± 1.6	8.0 ± 1.9
CA buttock	23.8 ± 4.7	22.9 ± 4.8	23.2 ± 5.9	22.3 ± 5.4	22.4 ± 5.3
CA thigh	10.8 ± 2.8	11 ± 3.1	10.8 ± 3.0	10.9 ± 3.0	11.2 ± 2.8
CA shank-foot	16.8 ± 4.0	17.1 ± 2.5	16.6 ± 2.0	16.7 ± 2.0	16.6 ± 1.9

peak pressure appeared in the head; when the pillow was higher than 7 cm, the body's peak pressure appears in the buttocks.

In the supine lying position, the maximum body's pressure intensity appeared in the buttock area; the increase in pillow height, CP neck increased.

With the increase in pillow height, PCP neck increased, PCP head had decrease trend and PCP buttock and PCP shank-foot had increase trend. When the pillow height was less than 3 cm, the peak pressure intensity appeared in the head; when the pillow was higher than 7 cm, the peak pressure intensity appeared in the buttock and shank-foot areas.

With the increase in pillow height, CA neck increased while CA chest decreased.

3.3   Statistical Analysis Results

3.3.1   Pillow Height and Comfort

Table 9 shows the analysis results of correlation between pillow height and subjective comfort evaluation.

According to the results of Spearman rank correlation analysis, the correlation coefficient between pillow height and shoulder comfort was the highest, i.e. −0.517, which was followed by head and neck comfort, and the correlation coefficient was −0.494.

Table 9. Spearman rank correlation analysis of pillow height and subjective comfort (n = 19)

Pillow height	Correlation coefficient r	P value
Head and Neck Comfort	−0.494**	0.000
Hip Comfort	−0.284*	0.013
Waist Comfort	−0.304**	0.008
Shoulder Comfort	−0.517**	0.000

*With $p < 0.05$, the correlation was significant.
**With $p < 0.01$, the correlation was significant.

3.3.2   Most Comfortable Pillow Height and Body Measurements

Table 10 shows the analysis results of correlation between the most comfortable pillow height and the body size.

As shown by the correlation analysis results, the most comfortable pillow height and shoulder width was most relevant, in which the shoulder width had correlation coefficient of 0.463 and the correlation coefficient with shoulder width was 0.523.

3.3.3   Difference in Body Pressure Distributions Under Different Pillow Heights

Differences in body pressure distributions under pillow heights of 0 cm, 3 cm, 7 cm, 11 cm and 15 cm were compared with the use of one-way anova, LSD (homogeneity of variance) and Dunnett T3 (heterogeneity of variance) follow-up inspection.

Table 10. Spearman rank correlation analysis of the most comfortable pillow height and the body measurements

Most comfortable pillow height	Correlation coefficient r	P value
Head circumference	0.240	0.323
Side head circumference	0.024	0.921
Front head circumference	0.101	0.681
Neck circumference	0.216	0.374
From unilateral acromion to earlobe	0.259	0.284
Shoulder width	0.463*	0.046
Unilateral shoulder width	0.523*	0.022
Acromion width	0.183	0.454
Maximal shoulder width between double deltoid muscles	0.022	0.929
Height from neck bottom to head top	−0.057	0.816
From occipital bone tuberosity to C7	−0.112	0.649
Full height of head	0.129	0.597
Position of lower mandible point	0.319	0.184
Age	−0.154	0.528
BMI	0.138	0.574
Height	0.272	0.260
Body weight	0.197	0.418

*With $p < 0.05$, the correlation was significant.

Table 11. Pressure values under different pillow heights (N) (n = 19)

	0 cm	3 cm	7 cm	11 cm	15 cm
F body	586.1 ± 136.7	564.7 ± 153.2	569.5 ± 137.2	590.2 ± 164.8	582.4 ± 166.6
F head	40.9 ± 8.5	41.5 ± 11.0	40.2 ± 9.0	43.7 ± 10.0	40.3 ± 9.7
F neck	4.2 ± 2.7^{bcde}	10.3 ± 7.7^a	15.9 ± 10.3^a	19.2 ± 18.0^a	21.3 ± 14.3^a
F chest	209.5 ± 56.2	195.0 ± 74.3	181.5 ± 69.3	179.5 ± 59.8	172.5 ± 56.7
F waist	38.2 ± 16.0	38.6 ± 17.0	38.6 ± 17.1	41.5 ± 19.2	43.4 ± 21.1
F buttock	180.4 ± 49.7	169.6 ± 51.9	177.8 ± 51.4	184.1 ± 69.5	182.3 ± 66.7
F thigh	31.9 ± 12.3	31.3 ± 12.0	31.1 ± 12.9	32.8 ± 14.9	34.9 ± 13.8
F shank-foot	74.0 ± 22.6	73.3 ± 20.4	72.3 ± 20.3	75.5 ± 24.6	74.0 ± 25.3

Notes:

[a]The difference with absence of pillow (0 cm) was significant (P < 0.05);

[b]The difference with Pillow 1 (3 cm) was significant (P < 0.05);

[c]The difference with Pillow 2 (7 cm) was significant (P < 0.05);

[d]The difference with Pillow 3 (11 cm) was significant (P < 0.05);

[e]The difference with Pillow 4 (15 cm) was significant (P < 0.05).

The significance indicators of one-way anova were F neck, CA neck, CP neck, CP chest, PF head, PF neck, PCP head and PCP neck (Tables 11, 12, 13, 14 and 15).

Table 12. Peak pressure values under different pillow heights (N) (n = 19)

	0 cm	3 cm	7 cm	11 cm	15 cm
PF body	12.9 ± 5.7	11.2 ± 3.6	10.4 ± 2.6	10.9 ± 3.5	10.5 ± 3.1
PF head	10.4 ± 3.4^e	9.3 ± 3.4	7.9 ± 2.0	8.1 ± 1.8	7.7 ± 1.4^a
PF neck	1.1 ± 0.8^{bcde}	2.5 ± 1.4^a	3.2 ± 1.4^a	3.6 ± 2.3^a	4.4 ± 2.4^a
PF chest	7.0 ± 1.3	6.9 ± 1.6	6.9 ± 1.9	6.9 ± 2.3	6.9 ± 2.9
PF waist	4.2 ± 2.0	4.1 ± 1.6	3.9 ± 1.5	3.9 ± 1.4	4.0 ± 1.6
PF buttock	7.8 ± 2.2	7.7 ± 2.0	8.2 ± 2.4	8.9 ± 3.0	8.6 ± 2.0
PF thigh	2.6 ± 1.0	2.4 ± 0.7	2.1 ± 0.6	2.3 ± 0.7	2.3 ± 0.8
PF shank-foot	10.1 ± 5.4	9.0 ± 3.3	8.2 ± 2.2	9.1 ± 3.4	8.7 ± 3.7

Notes:

[a]The difference with absence of pillow (0 cm) was significant (P < 0.05);

[b]The difference with Pillow 1 (3 cm) was significant (P < 0.05);

[c]The difference with Pillow 2 (7 cm) was significant (P < 0.05);

[d]The difference with Pillow 3 (11 cm) was significant (P < 0.05);

[e]The difference with Pillow 4 (15 cm) was significant (P < 0.05).

The results showed that the pillow height had a significant effect on change in subjects' neck pressure, and the neck pressure increased while the chest pressure had decrease trend with the increase in pillow height.

The pillow height had a significant effect on the peak pressure of neck, and the peak pressure of head had a decrease trend with the increase in peak pressure of neck.

'With the increase in pillow height, the neck pressure intensity had an increase trend.

When the pillow was higher than 7 cm, the head peak pressure decreased significantly; relative to absence of pillow, the peak neck pressure intensity with pillow

Table 13. Pressure intensity values under different pillow heights (N/cm^2) (n = 19)

	0 cm	3 cm	7 cm	11 cm	15 cm
CP body	0.22 ± 0.07	0.19 ± 0.07	0.19 ± 0.05	0.20 ± 0.06	0.19 ± 0.06
CP head	0.28 ± 0.14	0.23 ± 0.08	0.24 ± 0.10	0.25 ± 0.10	0.25 ± 0.10
CP neck	0.09 ± 0.05[cde]	0.12 ± 0.5[e]	0.14 ± 0.07[a]	0.14 ± 0.07[a]	0.16 ± 0.07[ab]
CP chest	0.24 ± 0.05[e]	0.22 ± 0.04	0.21 ± 0.05	0.21 ± 0.06	0.21 ± 0.06[a]
CP waist	0.17 ± 0.06	0.16 ± 0.04	0.16 ± 0.04	0.17 ± 0.05	0.17 ± 0.04
CP buttock	0.28 ± 0.07	0.25 ± 0.04	0.26 ± 0.05	0.27 ± 0.06	0.27 ± 0.06
CP thigh	0.12 ± 0.05	0.10 ± 0.03	0.10 ± 0.03	0.10 ± 0.04	0.11 ± 0.05
CP shank-foot	0.19 ± 0.13	0.15 ± 0.05	0.15 ± 0.06	0.16 ± 0.06	0.15 ± 0.07

Notes:
[a]The difference with absence of pillow (0 cm) was significant (P < 0.05);
[b]The difference with Pillow 1 (3 cm) was significant (P < 0.05);
[c]The difference with Pillow 2 (7 cm) was significant (P < 0.05);
[d]The difference with Pillow 3 (11 cm) was significant (P < 0.05);
[e]The difference with Pillow 4 (15 cm) was significant (P < 0.05); the one-way variance analysis of CP chest was not significant.

Table 14. Peak pressure intensity values under different pillow heights (N/cm^2) (n = 19)

	0 cm	3 cm	7 cm	11 cm	15 cm
PCP body	1.12 ± 0.50	0.98 ± 0.31	0.91 ± 0.24	0.95 ± 0.31	0.91 ± 0.27
PCP head	0.90 ± 0.29[e]	0.80 ± 0.29	0.68 ± 0.17	0.70 ± 0.16	0.67 ± 0.12[a]
PCP neck	0.12 ± 0.06[bcde]	0.24 ± 0.12[a]	0.29 ± 0.11[a]	0.32 ± 0.19[a]	0.39 ± 0.20[a]
PCP chest	0.60 ± 0.11	0.61 ± 0.15	0.61 ± 0.15	0.60 ± 0.23	0.61 ± 0.25
PCP waist	0.36 ± 0.18	0.37 ± 0.17	0.36 ± 0.14	0.34 ± 0.13	0.35 ± 0.13
PCP buttock	0.68 ± 0.19	0.67 ± 0.18	0.72 ± 0.22	0.82 ± 0.35	0.75 ± 0.18
PCP thigh	0.22 ± 0.09	0.21 ± 0.62	0.18 ± 0.05	0.20 ± 0.06	0.20 ± 0.07
PCP shank-foot	0.88 ± 0.47	0.78 ± 0.28	0.74 ± 0.20	0.79 ± 0.29	0.78 ± 0.28

[a]The difference with absence of pillow (0 cm) was significant (P < 0.05);
[b]The difference with Pillow 1 (3 cm) was significant (P < 0.05);
[c]The difference with Pillow 2 (7 cm) was significant (P < 0.05);
[d]The difference with Pillow 3 (11 cm) was significant (P < 0.05);
[e]The difference with Pillow 4 (15 cm) was significant (P < 0.05).

increased significantly, and with the increase in pillow height; with pillow height of 11 cm, the peak pressure intensity of buttocks was the highest; the peak pressure intensity of shanks and feet was the highest without pillow.

The head contact area and the chest contact area were highest at the pillow height of 3 cm. Buttock contact area reached the maximum at the pillow height of 7 cm. Neck, waist and thigh contact areas had the trend to increase with increasing pillow height. Relative to the absence of pillow, the use of pillow allows a significant increase in neck contact area.

Table 15. Contact area values under different pillow heights (cm^2) (n = 19)

	0 cm	3 cm	7 cm	11 cm	15 cm
CA body	2814.4 ± 707.5	3010.0 ± 703.4	3054.9 ± 742.8	3136.1 ± 781.9	3116.1 ± 774.8
CA head	167.9 ± 50.6	189.1 ± 49.1	183.3 ± 60.9	186.3 ± 53.0	174.1 ± 61.7
CA neck	50.2 ± 20.4^{bcde}	86.0 ± 42.9^a	111.3 ± 44.6^a	122.4 ± 67.0^a	129.9 ± 63.5^a
CA chest	873.9 ± 237.5	894.3 ± 262.7	846.5 ± 267.5	863.4 ± 256.6	846.8 ± 258.4
CA waist	229.9 ± 79.5	234.2 ± 77.9	246.8 ± 69.8	248.9 ± 77.0	247.7 ± 78.4
CA buttock	643.7 ± 103.0	663.4 ± 120.7	672.8 ± 110.6	668.0 ± 135.0	668.9 ± 135.3
CA thigh	315.9 ± 128.8	339.8 ± 139.7	346.2 ± 151.3	358.3 ± 161.5	360.0 ± 145.9
CA shank-foot	489.8 ± 187.9	519.2 ± 149.2	510.9 ± 146.4	528.3 ± 155.6	519.8 ± 145.2

^{a}The difference with absence of pillow (0 cm) was significant (P < 0.05);
^{b}The difference with Pillow 1 (3 cm) was significant (P < 0.05);
^{c}The difference with Pillow 2 (7 cm) was significant (P < 0.05);
^{d}The difference with Pillow 3 (11 cm) was significant (P < 0.05);
^{e}The difference with Pillow 4 (15 cm) was significant (P < 0.05).

4 Analysis and Discussion

4.1 Analysis on Test Results of Body Pressure Distribution

As shown by the results of body pressure distribution test, the neck pressure intensity, contact area and force increase with the increase in pillow height, indicating that the force neck is obviously increased and allowing more effective support to the neck. Chest force, contact area and pressure intensity have a decrease trend with the increase in waist force, indicating the pillow height has adjusted the posture of spine and reduced the pressure on mattress caused by chest curvature hypnosis, so that the waist fits mattress better, allowing more supports; with the increase in pillow height, the peak pressure intensity gradually transfers from the head to the lower limbs, i.e. buttocks, shanks and feet, indicating that the higher pillow will lift the upper body and chest, while buttocks and feet play a role in preventing the body from sliding down.

4.2 Analysis on Subjective Comfort Evaluation Results

(1) There is a significant negative correlation between subjective comfort score and pillow height, and pillow height has the greatest impact on shoulder and head comforts.
(2) The most comfortable pillow height has a significant correlation with shoulder width.

5 Conclusions and Recommendations

(1) Conclusion of pressure test: with the increase in pillow high, pressure intensity, contact area and force of neck are increased, while the pillow can support the neck and adjust the spine posture.
(2) Correlation conclusion: the pillow height has the greatest impact on the comfort of head and shoulders, the subjective score of comfort has a negative correlation with

the pillow height, and the most comfortable pillow height has a significant correlation with shoulder width. The pillow height of 7 cm shall be the pillow height allowing the most comfortable pressure distribution.

(3) As shown by the results of comprehensive subjective comfort evaluation and body pressure distribution test, the pillow with lying height of 7 cm is the most comfortable one, providing a reference in selection of pillow.

Acknowledgments. This research is supported by China National Institute of Standardization through the "special funds for the basic R&D undertakings by welfare research institutions" (522015Y-3992, 522016Y-4679 and 242016Y-4700) and study on the key technology and standard for the design of product which should meet China's human characteristics (2017NQI).

References

1. Schütz, T.C.B., Andersen, M.L., Tufik, S.: The influence of orofacial pain on sleep pattern: a review of theory, animal models and future directions. Sleep Med. **10**(8), 822–828 (2009)
2. Kyle, S.D., Morgan, K., Espie, C.A.: Insomnia and health-related quality of life. Sleep Med. Rev. **14**(1), 69–82 (2010)
3. Gordon, S.J., Grimmer-Somers, K.A., Trott, P.H.: Pillow use: the behavior of cervical stiffness, headache and scapular/arm pain. Pain Res. **3**, 137–145 (2010)
4. Pan, Z.: Practical Spine Epidemiology. Shandong Science and Technology Press, Jinan (1996). vol. 3, pp. 382
5. Lavin, R.A., Pappagallo, M., Kuhlemeier, K.V.: Cervical pain: a comparison of three pillows. Arch. Phys. Med. Rehabil. **78**(2), 193–198 (1997)
6. Michael, B., Matthias, K., Sonja, M., et al.: Sustained effects of comprehensive inpatient rehabilitative treatment and sleeping neck support in patients with chronic cervicobrachialgia: a prospective and randomized clinical trial. Int. J. Rehabil. Res. **31**(4), 342–346 (2008). Internationale Zeitschrift für Rehabilitationsforschung. Revue internationale de recherches de réadaptation
7. Nancy, A., Joanne, C., Sydney, L., et al.: A comparison of three types of neck support in fibromyalgia patients. Arthritis Care Res. Official J. Arthritis Health Prof. Assoc. **11**(5), 405–410 (1998)
8. Mcdonnell, J.: Sleep posture; its implications. Anal. Bioanal. Chem. (1), 46–52 (1946)
9. Gordon, S.J., Grimmer-Somers, K.: Your pillow may not guarantee a good night's sleep or symptom-free waking. Physiother. Can. **63**(2), 183–190 (2011)
10. Chen, H.L., Cai, D.: Body dimension measurements for pillow design for Taiwanese. Work **41**(6), 1288–1295 (2012)
11. Liu, S.-F., Lee, Y.-L., Liang, J.-C.: Shape design of an optimal comfortable pillow based on the analytic hierarchy process method. J. Chiropr. Med. **10**(4), 229–239 (2011)
12. Minezaki, F., Murakami, S., Shinmura, R., et al.: Ergonomic studies on pillow (Part 1): the height of pillow. J. Home Econ. Jpn. **20**, 187–192 (1969)
13. An, K., Liu, J., Xu, M.: Biomechanical analysis of rest. J. Med. Biomech. (3), 186–191 (1994)
14. Cheng, X.: Clothing Environment. China Textile Press, Beijing (1999). pp. 184–186
15. Yokura, H.: Using the compression properties of pillows to estimate sleeping comfort. Int. J. Cloth. Sci. Technol. **11**(2/3), 160–169 (1999)

16. Park, S.J., Lee, H.J.: Development of selection system of comfort pillow. Hum. Factors Ergon. Soc. Annu. Meet. Proc. **47**(5), 816–820 (2003)
17. He, Y.: Bedding products efficacy studies of the human body—relationship with the human body comfort pillow type structure. Beijing Institute of Clothing Technology (2006)
18. Zheng, X., Qiu, S.: The Human Body Engineering in Life, pp. 103–108. Sichuan Science and Technology Press (1985)

Research on Pressure Comfort of Sofa Based on Body Pressure Distribution and Subjective Experience

Huimin Hu[1(✉)], Yanlong Yao[2], Ling Luo[1], Linghua Ran[1],
Chaoyi Zhao[1], Xin Zhang[1], and Rui Wang[1]

[1] Ergonomics Laboratory, China National Institute of Standardization,
No. 4 Zhi Chun Road, Haidian District, Beijing, China
{huhm,luoling,ranlh,zhaochy,zhangx,wangrui}@cnis.gov.cn
[2] School of Mechanical Engineering,
Zhengzhou University, Zhengzhou, Henan, China
582901493@qq.com

Abstract. With the use of body pressure distribution measurement system, the pressure comfort of sofa was researched by the combination of user's subjective experience evaluation and objective test. Through the different layers of soft sponge placed in sofa seat and backrest surfaces, the experimental conditions of different hardness were simulated. According to the evaluation results of user's subjective experience about sofa comfort and the results of the physical pressure distribution collected objectively under different experimental conditions, the recommended ranges of most comfortable seat and backrest pressures were obtained, which have provided the reference and basis for the improvement and design of sofa.

Keywords: Body pressure distribution · User experience · Comfort evaluation

1 Introduction

With the development of technology and the improvement of social economy, people have increasingly higher demand for humanization of products. It is hoped that the products will not only satisfy the required functions but also be comfortable and easy to use. Seating furniture is a focus of contemporary home furnishings ergonomic research, and sofa is the most comfortable type of seating furniture. At present, people have increasingly higher requirements on comfortable feature of sofa, and the sofa design focuses on providing the greatest comfort and eliminating the body's tension and fatigue [1]. Uncomfortable sofa will affect the rest and work efficiency, resulting in people's sense of fatigue. The main factors affecting the comfort of sofa include structural dimensions and pressure comfort. Studies have shown that local high pressure on the seat interface can lead to deformation of human soft tissue, and thus hinder blood circulation and nutrient supply, so that the human body has the sense of discomfort or fatigue [2]. Reasonable design of pressure has become an important indicator to measure the comfort of sofa. Therefore, we need to research the pressure and comfort of sofa so as to provide reference and basis for improvement and design of sofa.

V.G. Duffy (Ed.): DHM 2017, Part I, LNCS 10286, pp. 26–38, 2017.
DOI: 10.1007/978-3-319-58463-8_3

2 Domestic and Overseas Research Status

With the development of science and technology and the emergence of new testing methods, ergonomic researchers from various countries try to use the advanced testing methods in medical, electrophysiological, psychological and other scientific fields for the experimental research on seat and sitting position comfort. Among them, the major assessment indicators used include intervertebral disc internal pressure, muscle activity point location, body pressure distribution, spinal form and lumbar activity, etc. [3].

In 2003, Looze et al. used a variety of sitting position comfort research methods to research the sitting position comfort. The results showed that the correlation between body pressure distribution and subjective evaluation was the most significant. Therefore, pressure comfort is an important indicator of sitting position comfort [4]. In 2009, Colin Jackson et al. obtained the upper and lower pressure values of the pilot with irritability by measuring the body pressure distribution on the glider seat safety cushion, and the relevant research results have provided the theoretical basis for the design and improvement of the glider seat by [5]. In 2014, Yasuyuki Matsushita et al. measured the body pressure distribution on the buttocks of subjects who had been sitting on the office chair for a long time. Combined with the subjective experience evaluation, it was found that the subjects had obvious discomfort when their hip compression area decreased or the ratio of high compression area increased, and thus it was concluded that the body pressure distribution at sitting posture is an important evaluation indicator of seat comfort [6].

In China, the research on pressure comfort of sofa and other seat has drawn widespread concern. Chen Yuxia, Guo Yong and Zhou Min from Nanjing Forestry University used the body posture pressure distribution to research the comfort of sofa and chair, respectively. The factors influencing the comfort of sofa and chair were analyzed, and the evaluation method of comfort was put forward. In 2009, the research of Chen Yuxia et al. on sofa seat depth showed that the contact area of man and seat surface increased with the increase in seat depth, while the total pressure, average pressure, maximum pressure, average pressure gradient and maximum pressure gradient on seat surface increased first and then decreased with the increase in seat surface depth. When the range difference of seat surface depth was 50 mm, the pressure indicators reached their minimum values.

3 Determination of Evaluation Method

As we all know subjective evaluation methods and objective evaluation methods can complement each other in the comfort evaluation [8]. In this research, the combination of user's subjective experience evaluation and objective evaluation methods was adopted to analyze the relationship between sofa pressure and comfort and research the comfort under different sofa pressures. Subjective experience evaluation is to assess the degree of discomfort under different sofa simulation conditions based on the subjects' subjective state and feelings. The evaluation adopts 5-level rating scale with 0–4 points, under which the higher point represents the stronger discomfort. The rating scale is shown in the figure below.

Objective evaluation is to analyze the impact of sofa on subjects by measuring the body pressure distribution data of subjects under different sofa simulation conditions. Body pressure distribution refers to the pressure distribution of body mass on the sofa seat and backrest surfaces (as shown in Fig. 1). The acting force of sofa on the human body is mainly shown by the pressure stimulation touch on human body. This touch allows human body to get support, while producing a comfortable or uncomfortable feeling. The feeling of comfort or discomfort is closely related to the pressure and its distribution.

Body pressure distribution data was collected with the use of German Novel seat cushion pressure distribution measurement system. In the measurement, the pressure cushion was first laid on the sofa seat surface or backrest surface, and there should be no hard object at the contact position between the subjects and the cushion, which would cause pressure concentration. The data collection was carried out after the pressure distribution was relatively stable. The body pressure distribution measurement system is shown in Fig. 2.

| 无 | 无 | 轻微 | 一般 | 强烈 | 非常强烈 |
| 0 | 1 | 2 | 3 | 4 | |

无	None
轻微	Slight
一般	Moderate
强烈	Intense
非常强烈	Very intense

Fig. 1. Discomfort rating scale

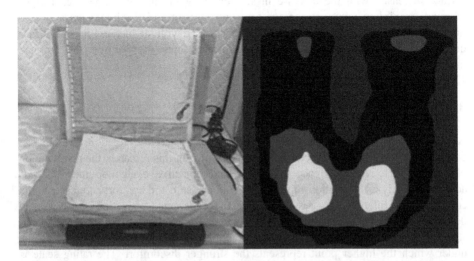

Fig. 2. Novel cushion pressure distribution measurement system

4   Test Preparation and Process

4.1   Test Device

In this research, a sofa simulation test device was first designed to allow adjustment to the inclination of seat and backrest. The test device should meet the following basic requirements:

1. The test device should allow one person to sit, and its seat size should meet the requirements of hip width and seat depth of the fifth percentile adult woman to the 95th percentile adult man; backrest size should meet the shoulder width requirement of the fifth percentile adult woman to 95 percentile adult men.
2. Seat inclination and backrest inclination should achieve angle change, and can be fixed at each angle to meet the different needs of subjects. In this experiment, the sofa simulation test device can change the inclination angles from 0° to 20° with the step size of 2.5°, and the backrest inclination angle can change from 90° to 110°.
3. It should have mechanism stability, safety and no obvious edges and corners or other components that may cause damage.

The test device is shown in Fig. 3:

Fig. 3. Sofa simulation test device

4.2   Selection of Subjects

In this research, the subjects were select by taking into account of age, sex and body size, and they were divided into the young and middle-aged group (20 to 40 years old) and the mid-aged and older group (40–60 years old) by age, the male and female groups by sex, and the lean body group (BMI < 19), the medium body group (19 ≤ BMI ≤ 24) and fat body group (BMI > 24) by the BMI of subjects. The BMI (Body Mass Index) is an important standard commonly used in the world to measure the human's degree of obesity and whether he/she is healthy. The calculation method is as follows: BMI = square of body weight/height (unit: kg/m^2). Subjects were divided into 12 groups, with each group consisting of 2 subjects, and a total of 24 subjects were tested. The detailed grouping of the subjects is shown in Table 1 below.

Table 1. Grouping of subjects

Male			Female		
Young and middle-aged (20–40 years old)	BMI < 19	2 subjects	Young and middle-aged (20–40 years old)	BMI < 19	2 subjects
	$19 \leq BMI \leq 24$	2 subjects		$19 \leq BMI \leq 24$	2 subjects
	BMI > 24	2 subjects		BMI > 24	2 subjects
Mid-aged and older (40–60 years old)	BMI < 19	2 subjects	Mid-aged and older (40–60 years old)	BMI < 19	2 subjects
	$19 \leq BMI \leq 24$	2 subjects		$19 \leq BMI \leq 24$	2 subjects
	BMI > 24	2 subjects		BMI > 24	2 subjects
Total	12 subjects		Total	12 subjects	

4.3   Testing Process

Before the test, the subjects were informed of experiment purpose, experiment contents and way of testing, and assistance was given to them to get familiar with the subjective comfort rating scale. For each subject, the seat and the backrest inclinations of the sofa simulation test device were first adjusted to the most comfortable angle to them, and the subjects received the sofa pressure comfort test with the seat and backrest inclinations that made they feel the most comfortable. Different numbers of sponge cushions were added on the surface to adjust different hardness of the seat, and the subjects were sitting on the sofa simulation test device and naturally leaning on the backrest. With different hardness, the subjects provided their evaluation on comfort of sofa after sitting for 3 to 5 min, respectively. After subjects made the evaluation, the experimenter collected the human body pressure distribution data under the hardness condition. The test scenario is shown in the figure below (Fig. 4).

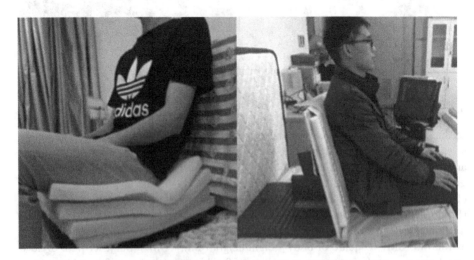

Fig. 4. Test scenario of sofa pressure comfort

The test started from the hard board, with 1–6 soft sponge cushions gradually placed on the seat surface so as to adjust the hardness of seat to simulate the seven experimental conditions. After the completion of tests under 7 work conditions, subjects need to choose the experimental condition under which they felt the most comfortable based on their own comprehensive experience. After the evaluation of seat surface hardness was completed, the softness of backrest was changed gradually in the same way under experimental condition with the most comfortable softness of seat as selected by the subjects. The subjects made subjective experience evaluation of the backrest comfort with different hardness, and the body pressure distribution data was collected. Because the backrest pressure data had no significant change with the increase in sponge cushions at the later stage, the backrest sponge cushion was added to 5 layers at the maximum, namely a total of six experimental conditions of backrest were tested.

5   Results and Analysis

5.1   Pressure Distribution Results of Sofa Seat Surface

The mean value of the peak pressure and the average pressure with the various sponge cushions on the seat surface of the subjects of different body sizes was obtained by processing the collected pressure distribution data on sofa seat surface. The results are shown in Table 2. With the number of sponge cushion as abscissa and the mean value of the peak pressure and average pressure test results as the ordinate, the graph was drawn and the change in seat surface pressure distribution with the change in sponge cushion was obtained as shown in Figs. 5 and 6.

Table 2. Results of pressure distribution on seat surface with different sponge cushion on layers

Number of sponge layers on seat surface	Body pressure distribution on seat surface	Lean body	Medium body	Fat body
0 (hard board)	Peak pressure/$N \cdot cm^{-2}$	3.49	3.08	2.54
	Average pressure/$N \cdot cm^{-2}$	0.65	0.75	0.81
1 layer	Peak pressure/$N \cdot cm^{-2}$	1.90	2.10	2.19
	Average pressure/$N \cdot cm^{-2}$	0.51	0.58	0.65
Number of sponge layers on seat surface	Body pressure distribution on seat surface	Lean body	Medium body	Fat body
2 layers	Peak pressure/$N \cdot cm^{-2}$	1.46	1.83	1.62
	Average pressure/$N \cdot cm^{-2}$	0.46	0.52	0.55
3 layers	Peak pressure/$N \cdot cm^{-2}$	1.25	1.38	1.35
	Average pressure/$N \cdot cm^{-2}$	0.43	0.44	0.51
4 layers	Peak pressure/$N \cdot cm^{-2}$	1.03	1.30	1.19
	Average pressure/$N \cdot cm^{-2}$	0.40	0.44	0.49
5 layers	Peak pressure/$N \cdot cm^{-2}$	0.84	1.10	1.11
	Average pressure/$N \cdot cm^{-2}$	0.38	0.40	0.46
6 layers	Peak pressure/$N \cdot cm^{-2}$	0.83	1.00	1.09
	Average pressure/$N \cdot cm^{-2}$	0.36	0.40	0.44

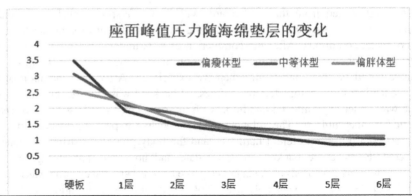

座面峰值压力随海绵垫层的变化	Changes in Peak Pressure on Seat Surface with the Changes in Sponge Cushion
偏瘦体型	Lean Body
中等体型	Medium Body
偏胖体型	Fat Body
硬板	hard board
1层	1 layer
2层	2 layers
3层	3 layers
4层	4 layers
5层	5 layers
6层	6 layers

Fig. 5. Changes in peak pressure on seat surface with the changes in sponge cushion

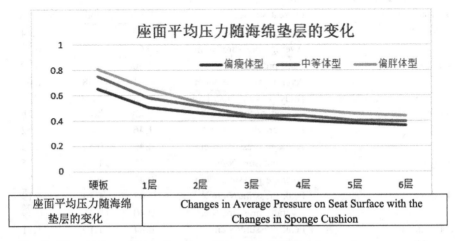

座面平均压力随海绵垫层的变化	Changes in Average Pressure on Seat Surface with the Changes in Sponge Cushion

Fig. 6. Changes in average pressure on seat surface with the changes in sponge cushion

The test results showed that peak pressure and average pressure of seat surface were decreasing with the increase in sponge cushion and stabilized after the cushion reached 5 layers. Compared to the state with hard board, peak pressure and average pressure were significantly reduced when there was sponge cushion.

It can be found by comparison of the data of subjects with different body sizes that the thinner the body is, the smaller the average pressure on seat surface will be. In the state with hard board, however, the thinner the body is, the higher the peak pressure will be, and this is because in the state with hard board, the thinner the body is, the smaller the contact area with the seat surface will be, and it is easy to cause pressure concentration.

5.2 Pressure Distribution Results of Sofa Back Surface

The mean value of the peak pressure and the average pressure with the various sponge cushions on the sofa backrest of the subjects of different body sizes was obtained by processing the collected pressure distribution data on sofa backrest. The results are shown in Table 3. With the number of sponge cushion as abscissa and the mean value of the peak pressure and average pressure test results as the ordinate, the graph was drawn and the change in backrest pressure distribution with the change in sponge cushion was obtained as shown in Figs. 7 and 8.

Table 3. Results of pressure distribution on backrest with different sponge cushion on layers

Number of sponge layers on backrest	Body pressure distribution on backrest	Lean body	Medium body	Fat body
0 (hard board)	Peak pressure/N·cm^{-2}	1.17	0.94	0.87
	Average pressure/N·cm^{-2}	0.33	0.31	0.32
1 layer	Peak pressure/N·cm^{-2}	0.35	0.42	0.48
	Average pressure/N·cm^{-2}	0.12	0.15	0.16
2 layers	Peak pressure/N·cm^{-2}	0.23	0.23	0.29
	Average pressure/N·cm^{-2}	0.10	0.10	0.11
3 layers	Peak pressure/N·cm^{-2}	0.22	0.24	0.21
	Average pressure/N·cm^{-2}	0.09	0.10	0.10
4 layers	Peak pressure/N·cm^{-2}	0.23	0.21	0.22
	Average pressure/N·cm^{-2}	0.09	0.09	0.10
5 layers	Peak pressure/N·cm^{-2}	0.22	0.23	0.20
	Average pressure/N·cm^{-2}	0.08	0.10	0.09

Test results showed that the backrest peak pressure and average pressure were decreasing with the increase in sponge cushion. After the cushion reached 3 layers, the backrest pressure had been very small, and there was basically no change. On the one hand, this is because the backrest became softer and softer with the increase in sponge cushion, and the larger deformation quantity resulted in the increase in contact area between human body and backrest, so the pressure became smaller. On the other hand,

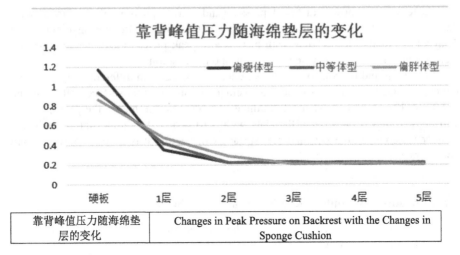

靠背峰值压力随海绵垫层的变化	Changes in Peak Pressure on Backrest with the Changes in Sponge Cushion

Fig. 7. Changes in peak pressure on backrest with the changes in sponge cushion

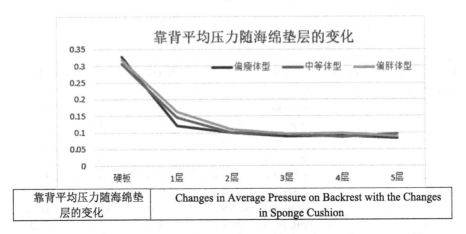

靠背平均压力随海绵垫层的变化	Changes in Average Pressure on Backrest with the Changes in Sponge Cushion

Fig. 8. Changes in average pressure on backrest with the changes in sponge cushion

the seat space was reduced with the increase in cushion sponge. In order to maintain a stable position, the gravity center of human body moved down and thus the seat surface load increased while the backrest surface load reduced. It is another key factor causing reduction of backrest pressure. In addition, the same as the seat surface pressure test results, there was significant reduction in peak pressure and average pressure in the state with sponge cushion when compared to the state with hard board.

It can be found by comparison of the data of subjects with different body sizes that in the state with hard plate, the body size has a significant impact on the peak pressure on backrest, and that the thinner the body is, the higher the peak pressure will be, and this is because the lean body is more likely to cause pressure concentration.

5.3 Subjective Evaluation Results of Seat Surface Comfort

Statistics and analysis was carried out on the subjects' subjective evaluation of seat comfort with different sponge cushions, and all the subjects' evaluation results were obtained as shown in Fig. 9. The statistic results were averaged to obtain the results as shown in Fig. 10. According to the statistical results, it can be found that the subjects' subjective scores of seat comfort generally shows parabolic variation trend. Combined with the measurement results of the pressure distribution on seat surface, it can be found that the seat pressure is decreasing and the comfort of seat surface is getting higher and higher with the continuous increase in sponge cushion. The best comfort

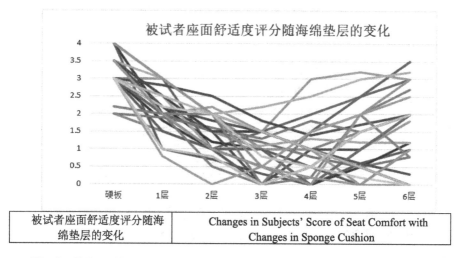

被试者座面舒适度评分随海绵垫层的变化	Changes in Subjects' Score of Seat Comfort with Changes in Sponge Cushion

Fig. 9. Changes in subjects' score of seat comfort with changes in sponge cushion

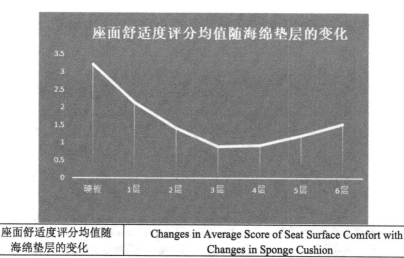

座面舒适度评分均值随海绵垫层的变化	Changes in Average Score of Seat Surface Comfort with Changes in Sponge Cushion

Fig. 10. Changes in average score of seat surface comfort with changes in sponge cushion

evaluation is achieved when there are 3–4 layers. The seat surface pressure changes little after there are 4 layers. When the sponge cushion continues to increase, the seat surface comfort reduces on the contrary.

5.4 Subjective Evaluation Results of Backrest Comfort

Statistics and analysis was carried out on the subjects' subjective evaluation of backrest comfort with different sponge cushions, and all the subjects' evaluation results were obtained as shown in Fig. 11. The statistic results were averaged to obtain the results as

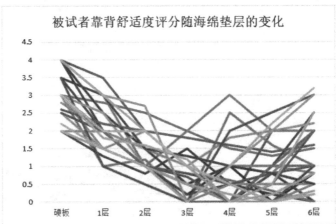

被试者靠背舒适度评分随海绵垫层的变化	Changes in Subjects' Score of Backrest Comfort with Changes in Sponge Cushion

Fig. 11. Changes in subjects' score of backrest comfort with changes in sponge cushion

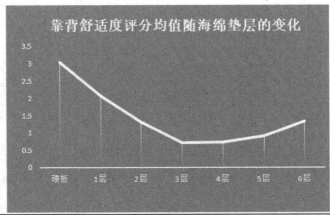

靠背舒适度评分均值随海绵垫层的变化	Changes in Average Score of Backrest Comfort with Changes in Sponge Cushion

Fig. 12. Changes in average score of backrest comfort with changes in sponge cushion

shown in Fig. 12. According to the statistical results, it can be found that the subjects' subjective evaluation results of seat surface comfort are similar with the seat surface evaluation results, and generally show the parabolic variation trend. The best comfort evaluation is achieved when there are 3–4 sponge cushions.

5.5   Most Comfortable Seat Pressure and Backrest Pressure

According to the subjects' subjective experience evaluation and combined with the objective data of seat and backrest pressure distribution, the comfort evaluation of subjects under different seat and backrest pressures can be obtained. This research summarizes the seat pressure and backrest pressure under the most comfortable sponge cushion condition for each subject.

The statistic results showed that the most comfortable seat sponge cushion chosen by subjects was 4.0 ± 1.35 and the most comfortable backrest sponge cushion was 3.25 ± 1.07, consistent with the subjective comfort evaluation results of subjects in the most comfortable conditions.

With the most comfortable seat surface sponge cushion, the peak pressure on the seat surface is 0.89 ± 0.37 N/cm^2 and the average pressure is 0.43 ± 0.06 N/cm^2. We know that the pressure at ischium nodules is at the maximum and gradually reduces to the surrounding in the sitting state. The existing literature stipulates that the pressure at the curvature of joints of human body should not be greater than 3.0 N/cm^2 in sitting position. In this experiment, the subjective evaluation results show that the subjects feel more obvious discomfort when the seat sponge cushion is less than 1 layer and that the peak pressure on seat surface is 2.06 ± 0.61 N/cm^2 and the average pressure thereon is 0.58 ± 0.1 N/cm^2 when there is 1 layer sponge cushion, so the maximum pressure at the human body's ischium nodules with the sitting posture in sofa should not be greater than 2 N/cm^2, and the level about 0.6–1.2 N/cm^2 is the optimal; the seat average pressure should not be greater than 0.6 N/cm^2, and the level of 0.4–0.5 N/cm^2 is the optimal.

With the most comfortable backrest sponge cushion, the backrest has a peak pressure of 0.18 ± 0.09 N/cm^2 and an average pressure of 0.10 ± 0.02 N/cm^2. In this experiment, the subjective evaluation results show that the subjects feel more obvious discomfort when the backrest sponge cushion is less than 1 layer and that the backrest peak pressure is 0.42 ± 0.17 N/cm^2 and the backrest average pressure is 0.14 ± 0.04 N/cm^2 when there is one layer of sponge cushion, so the backrest maximum pressure with the sitting posture in sofa should not be greater than 0.4 N/cm^2, and the level about 0.2 N/cm^2 is the optimal; the backrest average pressure should not be greater than 0.15 N/cm^2, and the level about 0.1 N/cm^2 is the optimal.

6   Conclusions and Prospects

In this research, the pressure comfort of sofa was evaluated by the combination of objective body pressure distribution test and user's subjective experience evaluation. The general law of sofa pressure and comfort was studied, and the recommended range of most suitable seat and backrest pressures was obtained, providing a theoretical basis for the improvement and design of sofa. However, there are many factors that affect the comfort of sofa, and the pressure distribution is only one of the most important factors, so in order to make more scientific evaluation of sofa comfort, it is necessary to carry out research and exploration by taking factors in various aspects into account comprehensively.

Acknowledgments. This research is supported by China National Institute of Standardization through the "special funds for the basic R&D undertakings by welfare research institutions" (522016Y-4679, 522015Y-3992 and 242016Y-4700) and study on the key technology and standard for the design of product which should meet China's human characteristics (2017NQI).

References

1. Weilei, S.: Seat design and evaluation based on human engineering. Mech. Eng. (10), 68–69 (2005)
2. Youli, Z., Shengxiu, J., Shizhong, L.: Biomechanical analysis of human body in sitting position and seat interface. Med. Biomech. **14**(2), 65–73 (1999)
3. Jing, Y.: Research on human body comfort of sofa backrest, Nanjing Forestry University (2008)
4. de Looze, M.P., de KuijtEvers, L.F.M., van Die en, J.: Sitting comfort and discomfort and the relationships with objective measures. Ergonomics **46**(10), 985–997 (2003)
5. Jackson, C., Emck, A.J., Hunston, M.J., Jarvis, P.C.: Pressure measurements and comfort of foam safety cushions for confined seating. Aviation, Space, Environ. Med. **80**(6), 565–569 (2009)
6. Matsushita, Y., Kuwahara, N., Morimoto, K.: Relationship between comfortable feelings and distribution of seat pressure in sustaining a sitting posture for a long time. In: Stephanidis, C. (ed.) HCI 2014. CCIS, vol. 435, pp. 473–478. Springer, Cham (2014). doi:10.1007/978-3-319-07854-0_82
7. Yuxia, C., Liming, S., Yong, G., Shengquan, L.: Research on impact of sofa seat depth on sitting position comfort based on body pressure distribution. J. Northwest For. Univ. **24**(5), 152–156 (2009)
8. Bo, H.: Realization and verification of physiological and ergonomic evaluation method of physical operation in virtual reality. Tsinghua University (2011)

Anthropometric Measurement of the Head of Chinese Children

Linghua Ran, Xin Zhang[✉], and Taijie Liu

Ergonomics Laboratory, China National Institute of Standardization,
Beijing 100191, China
{ranlh,zhangx}@cnis.gov.cn

Abstract. This paper presents the results of a nationwide anthropometric survey conducted on children in China. Seven head dimensions (head length, head breadth, head height, head circumstance, face length, sagittal arc and bitragion arc) were measured from 20,000 children with age ranged from 4 to 17 years old. Mean values, standard deviations for the seven items in five age groups were calculated. The head dimension differences between different age groups and two genders were discussed. It was found that the mean values of the head dimensions showed a gradual increase by age, and there are also differences between the two genders. The two-dimensional distribution of head length and head breadth were established, which could provide data support for relevant products design.

Keywords: Head · Anthropometric measurement · Chinese children · Two-dimensional distribution

1 Introduction

The design of labor and protective equipments are most concerned about the users' head and face shapes. Helmets, protective helmets should fit for the user's head size, the design of gas masks should combine with users' face dimension characteristics, and eye protector design should base on the users' facial width and distance between the eyes. For a good design of protective equipments, it should not only consider their protective functions, but also the users' body characteristics [1]. The human head and face size is an important basis for developing head and face protective equipments. For the minors, the head sizes are also essential for children's personal protective equipments design. For example, the design of headgear, glasses, hats, helmets, dust masks and other safety related products all need children's head and face data. Without such data, the designs cannot fit children properly.

In different countries the anthropometric data are different [2]. It showed that most of the head and face data between the Japanese, Kenyans, South Koreans, The Netherlands, Americans and Chinese have significant difference (p < 0.05). The comparison shows that Asians' head size can be characterized as rounder than Africans', Americans' and European people's heads, and with a flatter back and forehead. So in order to design suitable personal protective equipments for Chinese people, the related body data are necessary.

© Springer International Publishing AG 2017
V.G. Duffy (Ed.): DHM 2017, Part I, LNCS 10286, pp. 39–46, 2017.
DOI: 10.1007/978-3-319-58463-8_4

In order to meet the need of protective products development, China has conducted several head and face size surveys across the whole country. In 1980, the Beijing Labor Protection Institute and the National Academy of Sciences conducted the head size survey which including 9392 samples. Based on these data, the first series of Chinese adults head standard "Head –form of adults" (GB 2428-81) [3] was published in 1981. In this standard, the head features are analyzed and 13 types of head shapes were established based on 29 measurement items. A survey including 22300 adults Chinese was conducted in 1988, which including 7 head face dimensions. The human dimensions database for Chinese adults was established [4]. In 1998, the statistical techniques were used to a small sample (393 samples) survey. Later the "adults head face dimensions" standard (GB/T 2428-1998) [5] was published, and 41 head and face items were covered in that standard. The two national standards are not covered the minors' head and face data.

Some scholars in China also studied the Chinese head data. Li Shuyuan conducted cluster analysis to 30 population groups in China and 5 craniofacial indexes (head length breadth index, head height index, head width and height index, morphological facial index and nasal index) are covered [6]. Zhi did research on the characteristics of pilots' heads and classification, and different classifications of pilots' heads are achieved based on head height, head breadth and head length of Chinese male pilots according to the statistical principle [7]. Ran conducted research on the characteristics of head forms and classification of head forms of Chinese adult [8]. In this paper, the head forms have been classified according to the head height, breadth and length, two-dimensional distributions of head height-length indices and head breadth-length indices have been established. But this research are also not covered the head and face data for minors in China.

In china, a nationwide anthropometric survey project for children from 4 to 17 was completed in 2009. The head data for the children are also included in this survey. The statistical values of head length, head breadth, head height, head circumstance, face length (nasion-menton), sagittal arc and bitragion arc are presented in this paper. Estimates of mean, standard deviation (SD) are included. The differences among age groups, between boys and girls groups are discussed. The two-dimensional distribution of head length and head breadth were established.

2   Methods

2.1   Subjects

To make the anthropometric survey more representatives, a stratified cluster sampling method was used to determine the distribution of the samples. The whole country was divided into six geographical areas according to the ethnographic research result, which was in accordance with the adult anthropometric survey in 1988. The six areas included north and northeast area, central and western area, the lower reaches of the Changjiang River area, the middle reaches of the Changjiang River area, Guangdong-Guangxi-Fujian area, Yunnan-Guizhou-Sichuan area. From the ethnographic point of view, the people in the same area have similar body characteristics. The sample size in each area was determined based on the distribution of children's population reported by China National Bureau of Statistics [9]. One or two cities in each area were selected and some kindergartens, primary schools and high schools were taken from these cities. A number of classes were taken from every selected school, and all the children in the selected classes were measured until the number of children desired in per age group was met. Based on the Report on the Second National Physical Fitness Surveillance (2000) [10], the children were subdivided into five age groups: preschool (4–6 years old), lower primary (7–10 years old), upper primary (11–12 years old), middle school (13–15 years old), high school (16–17 years old). In this survey, for example, 10 years old means ones whose age is from 9.5 to 10.5 years old.

2.2 Dimension Measurements

The 3D Scanner was adopted for head anthropometric survey, and the scan time is less than 10 s one person. The accuracy for the scanner is 3 mm and 2 mm in the horizontal and vertical direction respectively. After each scan, a view to the 3D scan results was required to prevent the scan failure caused by body position shifting. The dimension values obtained were categorized according to gender and age groups and abnormity data examination was conducted.

Before the scanning, the measurement specification and technique requirements were established. The members in the survey team were trained and evaluated to ensure the consistency and reliability of the anthropometric data.

2.3 Data Processing and Statistical Analysis

The head data were taken by Measure Software developed by CNIS. In this paper, head length, head breadth, head height, head circumstance, face length (nasion-menton), sagittal arc and bitragion arc were taken from this software. The definitions for the seven items were consistent with ISO 7250:2004 [11].

This software allows users to calculate head data interactively. The abnormity data examination was conducted. The extreme outliers and unreasonable results were identified and eliminated carefully by using 3σ test, peak value test and logical value test. The head dimensions obtained were categorized according to gender and age groups. The descriptive statistics, including arithmetic means (M), standard deviations (SD), and percentiles (5th and 95th) of the above measurements were calculated for both boys and girls.

3 The Effect of Age and Gender

3.1 The Statistical Values of Head Anthropometric Dimensions

The statistical values of head dimensions in five age groups for boys and girls are presented in Tables 1 and 2. All dimensions are reported in mm.

Table 1. The statistical values of head anthropometric dimensions for boys (mm)

Items	Age 4–6		Age 7–10		Age 11–12		Age 13–15		Age 16–17	
	M	SD	M	SD	M	SD	M	SD	M	SD
Head height	204	12	215	13	221	13	230	13	233	13
Head length	175	7	181	8	185	8	191	9	195	8
Head breadth	152	6	158	6	161	7	165	7	169	7
Head circumstance	513	20	532	22	545	22	561	24	573	21
Face length	95	6	102	7	108	8	116	8	119	7
Sagittal arc	325	17	335	18	337	18	343	18	350	19
Bitragion arc	337	15	349	16	355	16	363	16	367	16

Table 2. The statistical values of head anthropometric dimensions for girls (mm)

Items	Age 4–6		Age 7–10		Age 11–12		Age 13–15		Age 16–17	
	M	SD	M	SD	M	SD	M	SD	M	SD
Head height	203	12	214	11	221	12	226	11	226	11
Head length	171	7	177	8	182	8	186	8	186	7
Head breadth	150	6	156	7	160	7	163	7	164	6
Head circumstance	509	22	531	24	544	22	553	21	554	20
Face length	95	6	102	7	108	8	116	8	119	7
Sagittal arc	318	18	321	18	326	18	329	16	334	17
Bitragion arc	334	14	343	15	352	16	359	15	359	14

3.2   Differences Between Age Groups

From Tables 1 and 2, it can be found that the mean values for the seven head and face dimensions increase gradually by age. Both boys and girls show a trend for significant increase by age, and the age group 4–6 and 7–10 have relatively higher increasing rate. For example, their head circumference increased 6 mm. In the other three age groups, the increasing rates show a slow growth.

Figure 1 shows the increasing rate of head circumference for boys and girls. For boys, the difference of head circumference between age group (4–6) and (7–10) is 19 mm. From (7–10) to (11–12), the data of boys increases by 23 mm, and from (11–12) to (16–17) the increase value is 16 mm and 12 mm respectively. From (7–10) to (11–12), the head circumference of boys have a relatively high increasing speed. For girls, the increase of mean values of head circumference are 22 mm, 13 mm, 9 mm and 1 mm respectively for the age group from (4–6) to (16–17). The high increasing speed of girls' is the age group (4–6) to (7–10). The boy's head circumference increase very fast before 16 years old, and in the (16–17) age groups, the increasing rate also very obvious. But for girls, the increasing for their head circumference is slowing down in the (16–17) age group. It showed that for the boys in (16–17) years old and for girls in their (13–15) years old, their head and face have been basically mature. When the age continues to increase, the head size tends to be stable.

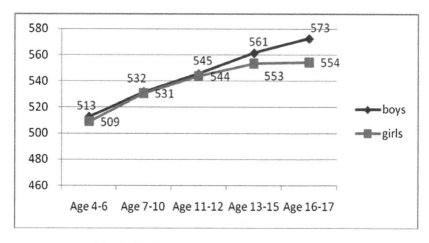

Fig. 1. The increasing rate for head circumference

3.3 Gender Differences

From Tables 1 and 2, it shows that for boys and girls in the five age groups, most of the 7 item data of boys are larger than girls' except for some individual data. Figures 2 and 3 show the difference of four data (head length, head breadth, sagittal arc, bitragion arc) between boys and girls. The differences for the head length and head breadth between boys and girls in the (4–15) years old are 3–5 mm and 1–2 mm, but for the minors in (16–17), the differences for the head length and head breadth are 9 mm and 6 mm. With the increase of age, the difference is also increasing.

The head breadth-length index is used to analyze the difference of head shape for boys and girls. The head breadth-length index = (head breadth/head length) * 100, namely, the proportion of the maximum head breadth against the maximum head length. For the five age groups, these indexes are 86.9, 87.1, 86.9, 86.7, 86.6 for boys and 87.6, 88.2, 87.8, 87.9, 87.9 for girls. For all the age groups, the indexes of girls are larger than boys. It shows that girls have relatively rounder head than the boys.

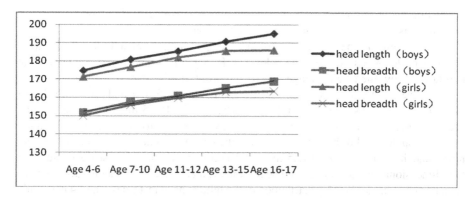

Fig. 2. Head length and head breadth for boys and girls

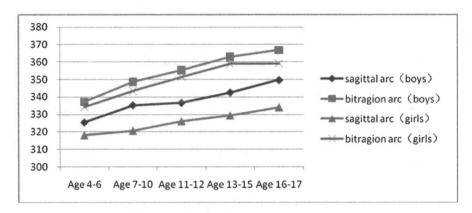

Fig. 3. Sagittal arc and bitragion arc for boys and girls

4 Two-Dimensional Distribution of Head

There are many types of head and face protective products. They need to be reasonably designed by analyzing the size of the various parts of people's head and face. We need to select the main parameters that can represent the main features of the head and face. The main parameters should be easy to measure, to be understood and be accepted by people. Considering the characteristics of each item and the feasibility of the measurement, we choose the head length and head breadth as the main parameters for the product design.

The head type spacing should be determined according to people's "feel domain span" and the actual background of products. For adults, the head length and breadth spacing is 10 mm. for minors, their head size are smaller than adults. If the size spacing is set to 10 mm, maybe the types would be unable to cover a certain populations. Therefore, we set 5 mm as the spacing of head length and head breadth.

After the main parameters are selected and the head size spacing is determined, we can set the head size types according to the distribution frequency of main parameters. How to match head length and head breadth need to calculate the proportion of the population under various conditions (also known as coverage). High coverage shows that products with this size can meet the large population.

The two-dimensional distribution of head length and head breadth for minors were given in Tables 3 and 4 (coverage below 0.5% are not presented). The numbers in the two tables show the size coverage, that is the proportion of the population.

In Table 3, the percentage of the head length in 185 mm and head breadth in 165 mm is 4.95%, it shows that for the head length in the 182.5 mm to 187.5 mm range and head breadth in the 162.5 mm to 167.5 mm range the proportion is 4.95% among the total population. For both boys and girls, the head length in 182.5 mm to 187.5 mm range and head breadth in 157.5 mm to 162.5 mm has the highest coverage. The two-dimensional distribution should be reasonable merge and to set models according to actual production needs. The distribution of the minors head in Tables 3 and 4 can guide

Table 3. Two-dimensional distribution of head length and head breadth for boys (%)

Head length (mm)	Head breadth (mm)							
	145	150	155	160	165	170	175	180
165	/	0.66	0.65	/	/	/	/	/
170	0.76	1.39	1.86	1.17	/	/	/	/
175	0.81	2.21	3.02	2.93	1.43	/	/	/
180	0.65	1.99	3.90	4.20	3.04	1.17	/	/
185	/	1.22	3.65	5.03	4.95	2.59	0.80	/
190	/	0.86	2.02	3.88	4.79	3.50	1.53	/
195	/	/	1.03	2.56	3.69	3.36	1.79	0.74
200	/	/	/	1.16	1.98	2.28	1.54	0.54
205	/	/	/	/	0.95	1.13	0.90	0.57

Table 4. Two-dimensional distribution of head length and head breadth for girls (%)

Head length (mm)	Head breadth (mm)						
	145	150	155	160	165	170	175
165	0.96	1.47	1.07	0.55	/	/	/
170	1.20	2.07	2.85	2.00	0.89	/	/
175	1.10	2.99	4.30	4.57	2.49	1.07	/
180	0.75	2.24	4.57	5.94	4.74	1.84	0.59
185	0.51	1.46	3.51	5.43	5.11	2.80	0.95
190	/	0.59	2.15	3.63	3.71	2.55	0.76
195	/	/	0.81	1.90	1.86	1.55	0.58
200	/	/	/	0.66	0.90	0.64	/

the designers in the production of various types of head and facial products to reduce the blindness of production.

5 Conclusion

This study was conducted to provide foot anthropometric information of Chinese children from 4 to 17 years old, which could be used for the ergonomic design of workspace and products. Seven head and face dimensions extracted from 20,000 children are listed in the forms of mean, standard deviation and percentile values. The differences among five age groups are discussed, the two-dimensional distribution of head length and head breadth were established. The results could provide data support for relevant products design.

Acknowledgment. This work is supported by Quality Inspection Industry Research Special Funds for Public Welfare (201510042) and National Science and Technology Basic Research (2013FY110200).

References

1. Hui, X.: The head and face size of Chinese adult and its application in the design of. China Pers. Protect. Equip. **1**, 16–29 (1994)
2. Ran, L., Zhang, X., Hu, H., Luo, H., Liu, T.: Comparison of head and face anthropometric characteristics between six countries. In: Stephanidis, C. (ed.) HCI 2016. CCIS, vol. 617, pp. 520–524. Springer, Cham (2016). doi:10.1007/978-3-319-40548-3_86
3. GB/T 2428-1981. Head –form of adults
4. GB/T 10000-1988. Human dimensions of Chinese adults
5. GB/T 2428-1998. Adults head face dimensions
6. Su, S., Zheng, L.: Cluster analysis to 30 population groups in China. J. Inn. Mong. Norm. Univ. (Nat. Sci. Ed.) **34**(3), 365–367 (2005)
7. Zhi, H.: Research on the characteristics of pilots heads and classification. Aircr. Des. **34**(4) 2014
8. Ran, L., Luo, H., Zhang, X., Hu, H., Liu, T., Zhao, C.: Research on the characteristics of headforms and classification of headforms of chinese adults. In: Rau, P.-L.P. (ed.) CCD 2016. LNCS, vol. 9741, pp. 679–685. Springer, Cham (2016). doi:10.1007/978-3-319-40093-8_67
9. National Bureau of Statistics: Chinese Demographic Yearbook. China Statistics Press, Beijing (2003)
10. General Administration of Sports of China: Report on the Second National Physical Fitness Surveillance. Sports University Press, Beijing (2000)
11. International Standard, ISO 7250: Basic Human Body Measurements for Technological Design. International standard Organization (2004)

Review on 3D Scanners for Head and Face Modeling

Parth B. Shah and Yan Luximon[(⊠)]

School of Design, The Hong Kong Polytechnic University, Hong Kong, China
parth.shah@connect.polyu.hk, yan.luximon@polyu.edu.hk

Abstract. There is a need of accurate anthropometric data of human head and face for both research and product designing. In past conventional measurements techniques were used to acquire anthropometric measurements for designing of products using scales, calipers, tapes which were less accurate and reliable, but with the advent of 3D scanner it has become very convenient for the researchers to acquire accurate 3D anthropometric head and face measurement. In the last three decades there has been a constant effort in optimizing the 3D scanners for improving its accurate and making it more user-friendly. This study discusses three different types of 3D scanners used for scanning head and face and tries to analyze their performance. The scanners included in the study are: Cyberware 3030 color scanner, Artec Eva 3D scanner and Structure sensor ST01 mode. The study provides an overview of possible advantages and limitations of all the three scanners.

Keywords: 3D scanners · Human head and face · 3D modelling · Ergonomics · Product design

1 Introduction

There is a need of accurate anthropometric data of human head and face for both research and product designing. The products to be used for head and face are designed for one of the following purpose: protective, healthcare, aesthetic. For this they require a good close fit to provide a high level of user comfort. The conventional techniques used in past to acquire anthropometric head data included use of measuring equipments like flexible scales, measuring tapes or calipers to acquire data [1–3]. These techniques were not reliable and did not provide highly accurate anthropometric data [4]. Many researchers have tried to use multiple images taken from different projections to develop 3D models but it is time consuming and cannot provide a highly accurate 3D head and face model due to its complex shape and contour [5, 6]. Medical imaging data like the one from Computerized Tomography (CT) [7] and Magnetic Resonance Imaging (MRI) [8] have been successfully used to develop accurate head and face models but due to its high cost and involvement of use of ionization radiation in CT they are not used that prominently for research and designing.

© Springer International Publishing AG 2017
V.G. Duffy (Ed.): DHM 2017, Part I, LNCS 10286, pp. 47–56, 2017.
DOI: 10.1007/978-3-319-58463-8_5

With the emergence of 3D scanning technique it has been made possible to overcome the limitations of the above techniques and acquire accurate 3D head and face data. 3D scanners have been extensively used from then for wide range of applications from product designing [1, 2, 9], apparel designing [10] to healthcare applications [7, 11]. Also 3D head anthropometric data can be used in research purpose like to study shape variance amongst people belonging to same ethnic group or location [12]. It can also help in understanding the anatomical differences in people belonging to different ethnic groups or locations [13].

There are wide ranges of 3D scanners available today with different specifications. Some are based on the laser scanning techniques where as some use structured light for 3D scanning. The cost of the scanner varies depending on the scanner accuracy and scanner resolution. This study discusses three different types of 3D scanners used for scanning head and face and tries to analyze their performance. The scanners included in the study are: Cyberware 3030 color scanner, Artec Eva 3D scanner and Structure sensor ST01 model. The comparison provides an overview of possible advantages and limitations of all the three scanners.

2 Methods

2.1 Subjects

10 participants (5 males and 5 females) voluntarily participated in the study. They were informed about the scanning procedure and a written consent was obtained from them. Only participants with no facial deformities were considered for the study.

2.2 Equipment

Three different scanners were used for the study: Cyberware 3030 color 3D scanner, Artec Eva 3D scanner, Occipital Structure sensor model ST01. Figure 1 depicts all the three selected scanners.

Cyberware 3030 Color 3D Scanner
Cyberware 300 color 3D scanner is one of the first scanners which were designed to scan human head and face. It creates a lighted profile of head by impounding a low-intensity laser. This profile is captured by a video sensor from two different angles. Multiple such lighted profiles are used to reconstruct a head and face model. Texture is recorder by a second video sensor.

Artec Eva 3D Scanner
Artec Eva 3D scanner uses structured light 3D scanning technique. It is an easy to use hand held 3D scanner which can be used for a wide range of applications. It can be used for partial as well as full body scanning applications. It has high accuracy (0.05 mm) and high resolution. It is a light weight portable and fast scanning device. It can provide good texture details too.

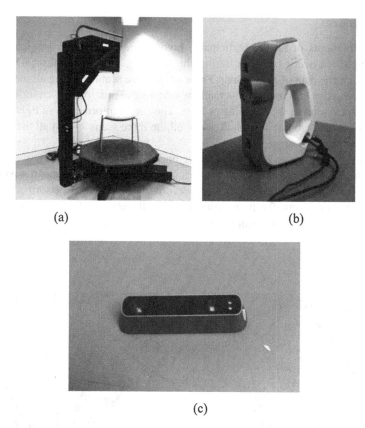

Fig. 1. 3D scanners selected for the study. (a) Cyberware 3030 color 3D scanner, (b) Artec Eva, (c) Occipital Structure sensor model ST01

Occipital Structure sensor Model ST01
Occipital structure sensor is a first 3D scanner for mobile device. It uses a fixed wavelength of safe infra-red light for scanning an object. It is completely software controlled scanner with no buttons and can be used either as a hand held scanner or it can be mounted on an ipad or a tablet on its customized bracket. It has a lower precision (0.5 mm) and works on a rechargeable battery.

Cyberware 3030 color 3D scanner has a designated raised platform where a chair is placed for the participant to sit. The scanner is adjusted such that the scanning field covers the head of the participant. Artec Eva and Structural sensor are both hand-held scanners which were used by an expert technician to acquire scans. All the three scanners have a designated software for data acquisition and processing provided by the supplier.

2.3 Procedure

Head measurements of all the participants involved in the studies were acquired to select a cap to be worn by them during the scanning process because 3D scanners cannot acquire the data of human hair. Participants were scanned using all the three 3D scanners. The order of scanning was randomly decided. Participants were informed not to move or speak during the scanning process. They were informed to sit tight and keep their eyes open and chin at a fixed angle for all the three scans so that all the scans are acquired in uniform posture.

Participant were made to sit on a chair on the platform of the Cyberware 3030 scanner. The scanner was arranged in such a way that the head of the participant to be scanned fits in the scanners field of scan. Before every scan was performed, homing settings were carried out for more reliable scanned output. After which the arm of the scanner moves 360° to acquire a complete 3D scan of the participant's head and face.

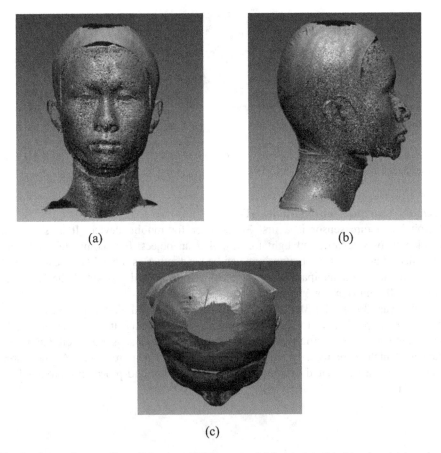

(a)   (b)

(c)

Fig. 2. Scanned output from Cyberware 3030 scanner (a) front view (b) side view (c) top view

While scanning using Artec Eva and Structural sensor the participants were made to sit on a stool and a technician with expertise in using the scanners moved around the participant acquiring the 3D scanning.

The opinion about the scanning comfort during the three scans was also studied. The technicians involved in scanning were interviewed about their comfort and issues during the scan.

3   Results

The raw data acquired from all the 3D scanners was processed using software. A stereolithographic format (STL file format) was developed for the head models developed using the scanners. Figures 2, 3 and 4 depict results of the scanned output for a single participant in three different views i.e. front view, side view and top view.

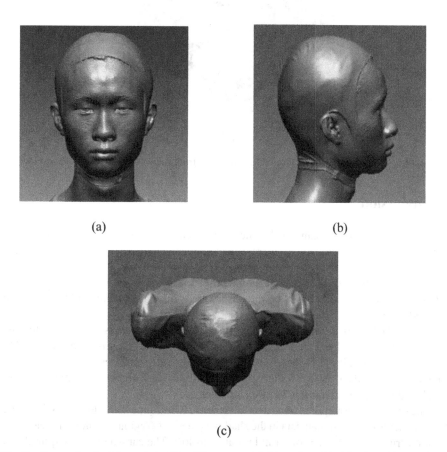

(a)   (b)

(c)

Fig. 3. Scanned output from Artec Eva 3D scanner (a) front view (b) side view (c) top view

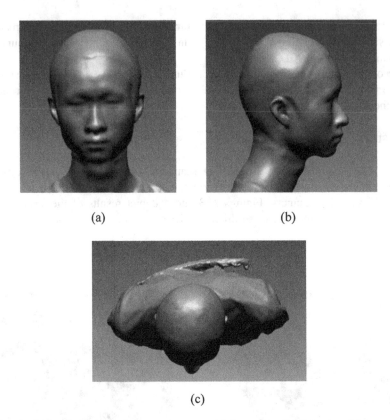

(a)   (b)

(c)

Fig. 4. Scanned output from Structure sensor (a) front view (b) side view (c) top view

4   Discussion

Based on the acquired scan results the three scanners were evaluated. The factors considered for the comparison were scanner accuracy, time and process of data acquisition and processing, the advantages and the limitations of the scanner and possible applications of the scanners and the user friendliness. Table 1. provides a brief detail of all the evaluation based on the observations during the study and based on the scanned output.

Cyberware 3030 is one of the very first generation scanners developed for 3D scanning of human head and face. Many researchers have used Cyberware 3030 scanner in their studies [14–16] to develop 3D head models and design products based on the acquired data. Many initial database and surveys of 3D head models were developed using Cyberware 3030 color scanner.

The scanned data acquired from the Cyberware 3030 scanner had a lot of missing data. The scanner is unable to scan data in the shadowed regions (regions behind ear, below the chin, nostrils). Also in cases of wrinkles data was lost. The ear data is not acquired and hence the scan cannot be helpful in designing any ear based product. The data of head scalp is also lost as the scanner can only scan the areas parallel to its field of view.

Table 1. Over-view of the scanner properties

Properties	Cyberware 3030	Artec Eva	Structure Sensor
Size (cm)	182.5 × 192.5 × 122.5	26.15 × 15.82 × 6.37	11.92 × 2.8 × 2.9
Weight (Kg)	332	0.85	0.095
Frame rate	–	16 frames/second	30–60 frames/second
Cost	High	High	Low
Homing required	Yes	No	No
Time for scanning	High	Low	Low
Time for data processing	Low	High	Low
Point cloud density	High	High	Low
Accuracy of data	High	High	Low
Comfort to person being scanned	More	Less	Less
Comfort to technician	More	Less	Less
Need for technician expertise	No	Yes	Yes
Portability	No	Yes	Yes
Missing data	Yes	No	No
Heating problem	No	Yes	Yes

Another problem with Cyberware scanner is the field of view is very small (30 cm × 34 cm). Hence proper head scan comprising of neck region also cannot be acquired for every individual. Also based on the height of every individual the scanner has to be re-adjusted and aligned parallel to the head of the participant. It is also required to initially perform homing for the scanner every time it is used. Although it has many limitations unlike Artec Eva it does not use any flashing light source making it more comfortable for the person to be scanned.

The data acquired by the Cyberware scanner lacks a lot of information, but various CAD/CAM tools are available in 3D data processing so it is possible to interpolate the data and fill the holes. This affects the accuracy of the scan but can help develop a 3D model which can prove to be helpful in developing customized products for head face.

Even though Artec Eva 3D scanner is accurate, it has a few limitations which need to be discussed. One of the major limitations of Artec Eva is high flashing lights which at times cause some discomfort to the subjects to be scanned. For the same reason it can also not be used to scan a person with epilepsy. It can acquire an accurate scan only if the individual using it has a high level of expertise and experience in using it. If the speed of scanning is too fast or slow the track can be lost leading to a need of second scan. Also the person handling the scanner needs to hold the scanner in one hand and a tablet or a laptop in another hand while scanning, making it difficult to scanning for a long time using it.

The software for data processing for Artec scanner is user friendly and has options for editing the raw scanned data. It has options to perform global registration making sure the minor errors while scanning can be rectified. It also has features like holes filling and smoothening which can help improve the quality of head scanned data. But it takes a high data processing time. The texture data acquired is of a high quality and can help create a precise head and face model.

The scanning time for Artec Eva is less as it does not need any prior homing or calibration. The Artec Eva can be used for developing customized products where high level of accuracy is required. Many researchers have used Artec Eva to achieve a high level of accuracy in 3D head scanning [17–19].

Structure scanner is a smallest sized scanner amongst the three. It can be used as a hand held scanning device or can be mounted on a bracket with an ipad or tablet. It has no buttons on it and hence is totally controlled by the associated software, at times making it difficult for the user while not using a bracket. The scanning process is similar to that of Artec Eva where the person to be scanned sits on a stool and the person acquiring the scan moves around. It can be used for performing a scan of a specific body part or a whole body. Scanning time is less as compared to Cyberware 3030. Like Artec Eva it does not require any calibration or prior homing.

Structure sensor is less accurate as compared to Artec Eva and Cyberware 3030. The data is not very precise but it provides a rough outline of the head and face. It cannot provide accurate facial features or ear data. It can be used for applications which require less accurate data. It is cheaper compared to both Artec Eva and Cyberware 3030 scanner. One of the major limitation of Structure scanner is the amount of heat generated is very high and hence it cannot be used for a long duration of time. But it is easier to use as compared to Artec Eva and does not require a high level of expertise and can be used for a wide range of applications.

Technicians' interview provided an insight about the comfort of use of the three scanners. According to the information provided by the technicians it was realized that Cyberware 3030 color 3D scanner was the most comfortable to use as the technician needs to just operate the device using a software from a console. While considering the other two scanners i.e. Artec Eva 3D scanner and Structure sensor, the technician needs to hold the scanners and move the scanner at a fixed rate. If the technician moves too quickly or slowly, the track of the scan is lost and the scanning process has to be repeated. The technician needs to bend and move to make sure all the regions are scanned, making it uncomfortable while performing scanning for a long time. Heating problem of structure sensor was also inferred to be a reason for the discomfort based on the technician's review.

5   Conclusion

In last few decades the accuracy and precision of the 3D scanners have improved highly. All the three models of 3D scanners examined in this chapter have their own set of advantages and limitations. The older model of 3D head scanners like Cyberware 3030 lacked the ability to scan the shadowed regions. Advanced scanners like Artec Eva and structural scanner are hand held and are user-friendly and portable. Depending on the requirement of accuracy for the application the designer can choose a 3D scanner like Artec Eva or structural scanner for head and face based scanning.

Acknowledgments. The study was financially supported by the RGC/ECS Grant (Ref. No. F-PP2P). The authors would like to thank all the participants involved and the staff at Asian Ergonomics Design Lab for helping in the study.

References

1. Zhuang, Z., Bradtmiller, B.: Head-and-face anthropometric survey of U.S. respirator users. J. Occup. Environ. Hyg. **2**(11), 567–576 (2005)
2. Yokota, M.: Head and facial anthropometry of mixed-race US Army male soldiers for military design and sizing: a pilot study. Appl. Ergon. **36**(3), 379–383 (2005)
3. Quant, J.R., Woo, G.C.: Normal values of eye position and head size in Chinese children from Hong Kong. Optom. Vis. Sci. **70**(8), 668–671 (1993)
4. Kouchi, M., Mochimaru, M.: Errors in landmarking and the evaluation of the accuracy of traditional and 3D anthropometry. Appl. Ergon. **42**(3), 518–527 (2011)
5. Lin, Y.L., Wang, M.J.J.: Constructing 3D human model from front and side images. Expert Syst. Appl. **39**(5), 5012–5018 (2012)
6. Galantucci, L.M., Di Gioia, E., Lavecchia, F., Percoco, G.: Is principal component analysis an effective tool to predict face attractiveness? A contribution based on real 3D faces of highly selected attractive women, scanned with stereophotogrammetry. Med. Biol. Eng. Comput. **52**(5), 475–489 (2014)
7. Xia, J., Ip, H.H., Samman, N., Wang, D., Kot, C.S., Yeung, R.W., Tideman, H.: Computer-assisted three-dimensional surgical planning and simulation: 3D virtual osteotomy. Int. J. Oral Maxillofac. Surg. **29**(1), 11–17 (2000)
8. Lacko, D., Huysmans, T., Parizel, P.M., De Bruyne, G., Verwulgen, S., Van Hulle, M.M., Sijbers, J.: Evaluation of an anthropometric shape model of the human scalp. Appl. Ergon. **48**, 70–85 (2015)
9. Kouchi, M., Mochimaru, M.: Analysis of 3D face forms for proper sizing and CAD of spectacle frames. Ergonomics **47**(14), 1499–1516 (2004)
10. DApuzzo, N.: 3D body scanning technology for fashion and apparel industry. In: Proceeding of SPIE-IS&T Electronic Imaging, vol. 6491. SPIE, San Jose (2007)
11. Lacko, D., Vleugels, J., Fransen, E., Huysmans, T., De Bruyne, G., Van Hulle, M.M., Sijbers, J., Verwulgen, S.: Ergonomic design of an EEG headset using 3D anthropometry. Appl. Ergon. **58**, 128–136 (2017)
12. Zhuang, Z., Shu, C., Xi, P., Bergman, M., Joseph, M.: Head-and-face shape variations of US civilian workers. Appl. Ergon. **44**(5), 775–784 (2013)
13. Ball, R., Shu, C., Xi, P., Rioux, M., Luximon, Y., Molenbroek, J.: A comparison between Chinese and Caucasian head shapes. Appl. Ergon. **41**(6), 832–839 (2010)
14. Luximon, Y., Ball, R., Justice, L.: The 3D Chinese head and face modeling. Comput. Aided Des. **44**(1), 40–47 (2012)
15. Friess, M., Marcus, L.F., Reddy, D.P., Delson, E.: The use of 3D laser scanning techniques for the morphometric analysis of human facial shape variation. BAR Int. Ser. **1049**, 31–35 (2002)
16. Hu, Y., Zhang, Z., Xu, X., Fu, Y., Huang, Thomas S.: Building large scale 3D face database for face analysis. In: Sebe, N., Liu, Y., Zhuang, Y., Huang, Thomas S. (eds.) MCAM 2007. LNCS, vol. 4577, pp. 343–350. Springer, Heidelberg (2007). doi:10.1007/978-3-540-73417-8_42
17. Skals, S., Ellena, T., Subic, A., Mustafa, H., Pang, T.Y.: Improving fit of bicycle helmet liners using 3D anthropometric data. Int. J. Ind. Ergon. **55**, 86–95 (2016)

18. Knoops, P.G.M., Beaumont, C.A.A., Borghi, A., Rodriguez-Florez, N., Breakey, R.W.F., Rodgers, W., Angullia, F., Jeelani, N.U.O., Schievano, S., Dunaway, D.J.: Comparison of three-dimensional scanner systems for craniomaxillofacial imaging. J. Plast. Reconstr. Aesthet. Surg. **70**(4), 441–449 (2017)
19. Lee, W., Jung, H., Bok, I., Kim, C., Kwon, O., Choi, T., You, H.: Measurement and application of 3D ear images for Earphone design. In: Proceedings of the Human Factors and Ergonomics Society Annual Meeting, vol. 60, no. 1, pp. 1053–1057. SAGE Publications, Los Angeles, September 2016

Comparison of Rarefication Techniques for Foot Simulation Using Subject Specific Three-Dimensional Anthropometry Data

Liuxing Tsao, Liang Ma[(⊠)], and Tao Li

Department of Industrial Engineering, Tsinghua University, Beijing 100084,
People's Republic of China
liangma@tsinghua.edu.cn

Abstract. It is believed that one important extrinsic factor that causes foot deformity and pain was the footwear design. A good fit is one of the determinant design characteristics that determine the user's comfort. The fitness is not only geometric match between the shoe last and a static foot but also the fit during walking or running. With the availability of subject-specific three-dimensional foot data, it would be possible to construct a foot surface model for the specific subject and to use the model as a quick and intuitive tool for evaluation of the fitness of a shoe. In this paper, we used subject-specific three-dimensional anthropometry data to build static foot surface model and applied forward kinematics into the foot model to drive it. The static model allows the fitness test of shoe for one time try on, while the dynamic model allows evaluation of the fitness during walking or other activities (with shoe model and gait information given). The anthropometry data were firstly rarefied to ensure the efficiency of data processing. The reduced dataset was further segmented into phalanges using the marker points at the joints of the foot. Finally, the foot surface model was constructed and driven phalanx by phalanx to imitate the movement of human beings. Data rarefication problem was specifically addressed in this paper since it was an art to balancing the data accuracy and the computation efficiency. In total, six rarefication techniques were compared based on three principles: the calculation speed, the visualization effect, and the volume of the specific phalanx. The arch-height technique was selected as the most suitable technique for the reduction of foot anthropometry dataset.

Keywords: Foot simulation · Three-dimensional anthropometry · Footwear design · Data reduction

1 Introduction

It is believed that one important extrinsic factor that causes foot deformity and pain was the footwear design (Hong et al. 2011). The design of footbed, midsole, outsole, the choice of shoe-sole material, and the dimensions of the shoe are all the characteristics to be concerned during footwear design (Cheung and Zhang 2005; Chiu and Wang 2007). Especially, the dimensions of shoe would determine the fit of the shoe to some

© Springer International Publishing AG 2017
V.G. Duffy (Ed.): DHM 2017, Part I, LNCS 10286, pp. 57–68, 2017.
DOI: 10.1007/978-3-319-58463-8_6

extent, then further lead to comfort or discomfort feeling of the users (Krauss et al. 2008; Rout et al. 2010; Ture Savadkoohi 2010).

To ensure the fitness of footwear, foot shape and dimensions are useful parameters to consider during the shoe design. Typical measurements include the length of the foot, the width of the foot, the navicular height, and the arch height etc. (Hong et al. 2011; Rout et al. 2010; Zeybek et al. 2008). These measurements would be classified into different groups and the shoe size system could be set according to the classification. Statistical techniques such as principal component analysis (PCA) and K-means clustering could also be applied when classifying the foot shape (Amstutz et al. 2008; Lee et al. 2012; Lee and Wang 2015).

However, the foot shape could not be accurately described using only two-dimensional measurements. Foot shapes of human beings differ across each other from different aspects. Gender effect is one significant aspect (Krauss et al. 2008; Lee and Wang 2015; Wunderlich and Cavanagh 2001). National differences were detected when comparing the foot shape between Chinese female's feet and Japanese females' feet (Lee et al. 2014). The foot shape of kids and teens was not exactly a scaled down of adults and should also be taken into consideration when design shoes for the developing feet (Mauch et al. 2009). It could be inferred that ignoring the individual differences of foot morphology would lead to improper shoe shape design or shoe fitting. There appeared new techniques to evaluate foot comfort thanks to the development of three-dimensional scanning. It has been proved that three-dimensional scanning offered a precise and accurate approach to extract the foot dimensions (Lee et al. 2014). Other foot shape information such as the foot surface area could also be calculated based on the point clouds (Yu and Tu 2009). Three-dimensional foot models could be built in CAD/CAM environment and the designer could examine the fitness in virtual simulation (Amstutz et al. 2008; Mochimaru et al. 2000). The three-dimensional foot scan provides a novel and practical way for the evaluation of shoe fitness.

Another significant factor that is usually ignored by the designers is the dynamic fit of the shoe, which is, the fit of the shoe during walking, running, or other activities in various environments (Chang et al. 2010). Wearing a shoe or acting with barefoot would lead to various distributions of plantar pressure, which would gradually influence the comfort of users (Burnfield et al. 2004). Schuster (1977) claimed that foot shape of long distance runner would be influenced by foot type and the environment situations. Barisch-Fritz et al. (2014) proved that foot would deform when the participants were bearing weight or walking. It seemed that the evaluation of shoe fitness is not only the geometry match in a static state but also a matter during movements.

With the availability of existing 3-D foot scan database collected from previous studies (Barisch-Fritz et al. 2014; Lee et al. 2012; Lee and Wang 2015; Mauch et al. 2009), together with new technique to measure dynamic gait information of users (Goulermas et al. 2008; Qi et al. 2015), it is possible to improve the shoe fitness evaluation. In this paper, we used subject-specific three-dimensional anthropometry data to build static foot surface model and applied forward kinematics into the foot model to drive it. Since the scanned dataset is usually huge, it would save computing resources if we reduce the dataset first. It was an art to balancing the data accuracy and the computation efficiency, therefore we addressed the problem of data rarefication and compare six data rarefication techniques. The rarefied data could be further driven to imitate the gait of participants. The final static model allows the fitness test of shoe for one time try on, while the dynamic model allows dynamic evaluation of the fitness during walking or other activities (with shoe model and gait information given).

2   Method

2.1   Data Collection

A low cost scanning system named INFOOT was selected to collected the data (Kouchi and Mochimaru 2001). It is a three-dimensional foot scanner using optical laser scanning system. INFOOT scans a foot form and the anatomical landmark points, and measures automatically almost 20 measuring items (marker needed) as maximum. The step was set at 0.5 mm with an accuracy of 1 mm. The scan area covers 400 × 200 × 150 mm. It usually takes 10 s to get one scan.

Seventy-nine male participants (college students) were invited and both their left and right foot were scanned during 2011. To demonstrate the data processing procedure in MatLab, we selected the left foot of No. 70 in the following demonstrations. The full data set of No.70 was shown in Fig. 1. It contained 69,952 data points. The coordinate system of the scanner was also shown in Fig. 1. Besides the scanner coordinate system, we defined an ankle coordinate system to realize the kinematic movements in further sections, which used the midpoint of sphyrion and the most lateral point of lateral malleolus as the origin (O0).

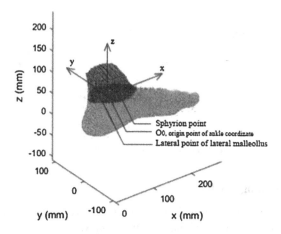

Fig. 1. The full dataset and the coordinate systems.

2.2   Data Rarefication

The original dataset contained a huge volume of points (69,952 points), which would significantly increase the processing time but would not provide more useful information, so we reduced the dataset to around ten percent of the origin volume for further data processing. Six different methods were used and the performance of each method was compared. We named these six methods as: (1) The arch-height method; (2) The body surrounding method; (3) The curvature method; (4) The Euclidean method; (5) The even selection method; and (6) The gridding method. The mechanisms of the six rarefication methods would be briefly explained in the following sections. The first step of all the six rarefication methods was to sort the points according to their coordinates in the order of axis x, axis y, and axis z. The original dataset with all data points would be mentioned as 'Data_Full', the sorted dataset would be mentioned as 'Data_Sort', and the rarefied dataset would be mentioned as 'Data_Rare' hereafter.

The Arch-Height Method (Fig. 2)

1. Set a threshold of arch-height, h_0;
2. Extract the first two points (P_1 and P_2) in 'Data_Sort' and attach the point into 'Data_Rare'. The next point (P_3) in 'Data_Sort' was then picked up and formed an arc with P_1 and P_2. Calculate the arch height h_1:

$$h_1 = ||P_1 P_2|| \sin \theta$$

3. If $h_1 > h_0$, then attach P_3 into 'Data_Rare', else choose the next point in 'Data_Sort' and calculate the arch height;
4. When a new point is selected from 'Data_Sort', calculate the arch heights that formed by this new point and every pair of data points in 'Data_Rare'. Till all the data points in 'Data_Sort' is examined.

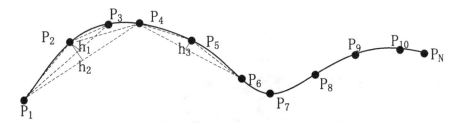

Fig. 2. The arch-height method.

The Body Surrounding Method

1. Calculate the range of the minimum cuboid that covers the scanned data, x coordinates: $\min_x \sim \max_x$, y coordinates: $\min_y \sim \max_y$, z coordinates: $\min_z \sim \max_z$;
2. Divide the cuboid in 1 into several sub-cuboids with the same size (Height = $Size_z$, Width = $Size_y$, Breadth = $Size_x$). The size of the sub-cuboid should be designed according to the data range;
3. In each sub-cuboid, reserve the point that has the minimum distance to the center of sub-cuboid.

The Curvature Method

1. Set a threshold of curvature, e_0;
2. Extract the first two points (P_1 and P_2) in 'Data_Sort' and attach the point into 'Data_Rare'. The next point (P_0) in 'Data_Sort' was then picked up;
3. Calculate the curvature of circumcircle formed by the three points e_1 (it is the reciprocal of the radius of circumcircle). If $e_1 > e_0$, then attach P_0 into 'Data_Rare', else choose the next point in 'Data_Sort' and calculate the curvature;
4. When a new point is selected from 'Data_Sort', calculate the curvatures that formed by this new point and every pair of data points in 'Data_Rare'. The calculation stops when all the data points in 'Data_Sort' are examined;
5. This method relies heavily on the shape of the foot. It is sensitive to any sudden change in curvature, so this method could only be applied in local areas, after segmenting the data into phalanges.

The Euclidean Method

1. Set a threshold of Euclidean distance, d_0;
2. Extract the first point (P_1) in 'Data_Sort' and attach the point into 'Data_Rare'. The next point (P_2) in 'Data_Sort' is then picked up and forms a line segment with P_1. Calculate the Euclidean distance d_1:
3. $d_1 = \sqrt{(x_1 - x_2)^2 + (y_1 - y_2)^2 + (z_1 - z_2)^2}$
4. If $d_1 > d_0$, then attach P_2 into 'Data_Rare', else choose the next point in 'Data_Sort' and calculate the distance between this point with the point in 'Data_Rare'.
5. When a new point is selected from 'Data_Sort', calculate all pairs of distance between this points and every point in 'Data_Rare'. The data could be reserved only if all the distances are greater than d_0. The rarefication ends until all the data points in 'Data_Sort' are examined.

The Even Selection Method

1. Set a data interval N;
2. For every N points in 'Data_Sort', reserve the 1st point and put it into 'Data_Rare'.

The Gridding Method

1. Define a projection plane (XY, YZ or XZ);
2. Divide the plane into grids with the same dimension. The grid size should be designed according to the range of data;
3. Project the three-dimensional points into corresponding grids and calculate the vertical distance to the plane;
4. In each grid, reserve the point that has the median projected distance to the corresponding grid.

2.3 Phalanx Segmentation

The foot data was firstly segmented into five toes and the palm using the line segments between key points (tip of toe, head of metatarsal, midpoint between successive metatarsal heads, etc., see Fig. 3.). Use the joint points on each toe, we could further segment the toes into phalanges (Fig. 4).

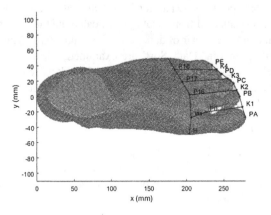

Fig. 3. The key points and line segments used to cut the foot.

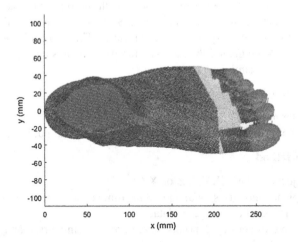

Fig. 4. The phalanges of foot.

2.4 Surface Construction and Model Driven

We used Delaunay Triangulation function to construct the surface model of the foot. Forward kinematics was applied in the surface model so that the model could simulate different postures of the foot. The positions of each phalanx during rotation were calculated according to the transform matrix demonstrated below (Denavit and Hartenberg 1955; Tsao and Ma 2016):

$$
\begin{bmatrix} ^{A}P \\ 1 \end{bmatrix} = \begin{bmatrix} ^{A}_{B}R & ^{A}P_{O_B} \\ 0 \quad 0 \quad 0 \quad 1 \end{bmatrix} \begin{bmatrix} ^{B}P \\ 1 \end{bmatrix} \tag{1}
$$

Where

$^{A}_{B}R(x, \alpha)$, a 3*3 rotation matrix, represented the points in coordinate A rotated around angle x based on plane x-y by an angle α;

^{A}P, a 3*1 vector to describe the coordinate of P in coordinate A;

^{B}P, a 3*1 vector to describe the coordinate of P in coordinate B;

$^{A}P_{O_B}$, a 3*1 translation vector to describe the movement of the origin point of coordinate B into coordinate A.

3   Results and Discussion

3.1   Comparison of Rarefication Methods

Time Consumption. As mentioned in 2.1. Data collection, the full dataset of No. 70's foot contained nearly 70,000 points. We applied all the six techniques to rarefy the full dataset and compared the time consumption of the data processing. To ensure the comparison was meaningful, we restricted the percentage of the rarefied data volume to ten percent or around. The amount of reserved data points and the time consumption were listed in Table 1. The arch-height method, the Euclidean method were the most time consuming since the complexity of these two methods were $O(N^3)$ and $O(N^2)$, respectively. The complexity of other methods was $O(N)$. However, to determine the

Table 1. Number of points reserved and time consumption.

	Parameter used	Number of points	%Original dataset	Time (s)
Arch-height	h = 1.2 mm	6415	9.17%	27.41
Body	60 along x, 40 along y, 30 along z	6956	9.94%	0.19
Curvature	differ across segments	N/A	N/A	N/A
Euclidean	d = 3 mm	7278	10.40%	18.78
Even	N = 10	6995	10.00%	0.07
Gridding	1 mm*1 mm, projected on XZ	6940	9.92%	

Note: The curvature method was applied in local areas, after segmenting the data into phalanges, so the time and number of points were not comparable with other methods.

parameters for arch-height, Euclidean distance, and even selection methods was much easier than other methods.

Visualization Performance. The visualization performance was demonstrated in Figs. 5 and 6. In Fig. 5, we showed how the points in the six rarefied datasets mapped. From the whole foot point cloud, we could figure out a specific trend from the mapping of points in body surrounding method, even selection method, and the gridding method. For the curvature method, the dataset was split out on specific surface regions. The arch-height and the Euclidean method performed well since these methods did not rely on the scanning direction and the local shape of foot surface.

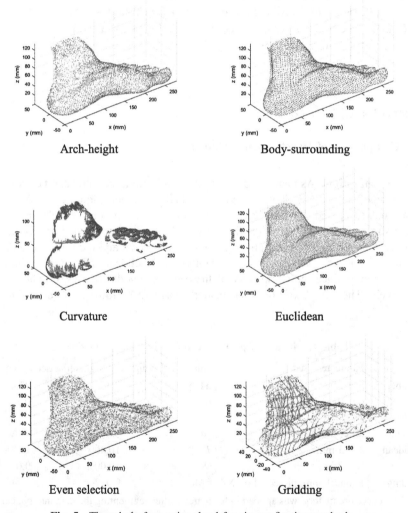

Fig. 5. The whole foot point cloud for six rarefication methods.

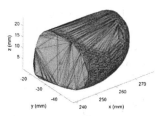

Full dataset, volume=16870.147 mm³

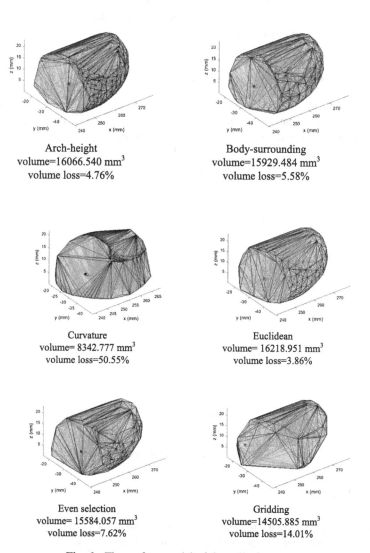

Arch-height
volume=16066.540 mm³
volume loss=4.76%

Body-surrounding
volume=15929.484 mm³
volume loss=5.58%

Curvature
volume= 8342.777 mm³
volume loss=50.55%

Euclidean
volume= 16218.951 mm³
volume loss=3.86%

Even selection
volume= 15584.057 mm³
volume loss=7.62%

Gridding
volume=14505.885 mm³
volume loss=14.01%

Fig. 6. The surface model of the nail of hallux

In Fig. 6, the surface models of the hallux nail were displayed. Comparing with the model constructed with the original dataset, the arch-height, the body-surrounding, and the Euclidean distance method reserved most shape information. Especially, the volume loss of Euclidean distance method was the least among the six methods.

Method Comparison. Considering the balance of computation efficiency and the visualization effects, we suggested that if the time was limited and the scanned data did not follow a specific trend, then the methods with a complexity of O(N) should be selected. However, if time permitted, the arch-height and Euclidean distance methods were suggested due to the acceptable computing speed and the more detailed geo-metrical information offered from the rarefied datasets.

3.2 Forward Kinematics of the Model

With allowable time window, we finally applied the arch-height method to construct the foot surface model and to drive it to perform specific postures. The angle of rotation at the heads of metatarsal and at the ankle were arbitrary defined, 15 degrees and 30 degrees, respectively (Fig. 7). We simplified the deformation of the joint surface by drawing ellipsoids at corresponding joints.

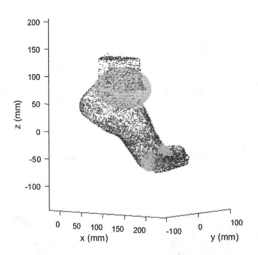

Fig. 7. The foot surface model with defined posture.

4   Conclusion

In this paper, we used subject-specific three-dimensional data points to construct static foot surface model. The foot point cloud was firstly rarefied in six different methods to increase the efficiency for further simulation of kinematic movements. Based on the comparison of time consumption and visualization effects, we selected the arch-height method to rarefy the full dataset. The surface model could simulate defined postures with given parameters at foot joints. Our approach involved the characteristics of the foot for specific subjects and considered the effects of foot movements on shoe fitness. One limitation of this study is that the surface deformation on joints was simplified and the posture of the foot was arbitrary defined. More efforts could be addressed on improving the computation efficiency as well.

Acknowledgements. This work was supported by the national natural Science Foundation of China under Grant Number: 71471095. This study was also supported by Tsinghua University Initiative Scientific Research Program under Grant Number: 20131089234.

References

Amstutz, E., Teshima, T., Kimura, M., Mochimaru, M., Saito, H.: PCA-based 3D shape reconstruction of human foot using multiple viewpoint cameras. Int. J. Autom. Comput. **5**(3), 217–225 (2008)

Barisch-Fritz, B., Schmeltzpfenning, T., Plank, C., Grau, S.: Foot deformation during walking: differences between static and dynamic 3D foot morphology in developing feet. Ergonomics **57**(6), 921–933 (2014)

Burnfield, J.M., Few, C.D., Mohamed, O.S., Perry, J.: The influence of walking speed and footwear on plantar pressures in older adults. Clin. Biomech. **19**(1), 78–84 (2004)

Chang, Y.-W., Hung, W., Wu, H.-W., Chiu, Y.-C., Hsu, H.: Measurements of foot arch in standing, level walking, vertical jump and sprint start. Int. J. Sport Exerc. Sci. **2**(2), 31–38 (2010)

Cheung, J.T.-M., Zhang, M.: A 3-dimensional finite element model of the human foot and ankle for insole design. Arch. Phys. Med. Rehabil. **86**(2), 353–358 (2005)

Chiu, M.-C., Wang, M.-J.J.: Professional footwear evaluation for clinical nurses. Appl. Ergon. **38**(2), 133–141 (2007)

Denavit, J., Hartenberg, R.S.: A kinematic notation for lower-pair mechanisms based on matrices. Trans. ASME J. Appl. Mech. **22**, 215–221 (1955)

Goulermas, J.Y., Findlow, A.H., Nester, C.J., Liatsis, P., Zeng, X.-J., Kenney, L.P.J., Tresadern, P., Thies, S.B., Howard, D.: An instance-based algorithm with auxiliary similarity information for the estimation of gait kinematics from wearable sensors. IEEE Trans. Neural Netw. **19**(9), 1574–1582 (2008)

Hong, Y., Wang, L., Dong Qing, X., Li, J.X.: Gender differences in foot shape: a study of Chinese young adults. Sports Biomech. **10**(2), 85–97 (2011)

Kouchi, M., Mochimaru, M.: Development of a low cost foot-scanner for a custom shoe making system. In: Hennig, E., Stacoff, A. (eds.) Proceedings of the 5th Symposium on Footwear Biomechanics, Zuerich, Switzerland, vol. 2001, pp. 58–59 (2001)

Krauss, I., Grau, S., Mauch, M., Maiwald, C., Horstmann, T.: Sex-related differences in foot shape. Ergonomics **51**(11), 1693–1709 (2008)

Lee, Y.C., Chao, W.Y., Wang, M.J.: Foot shape classification using 3D scanning data. In: Network of Ergonomics Societies Conference (SEANES), 2012 Southeast Asian, pp. 1–6 (2012)

Lee, Y.-C., Lin, G., Wang, M.-J.J.: Comparing 3D foot scanning with conventional measurement methods. J. Foot Ankle Res. **7**, 44 (2014)

Lee, Y.-C., Wang, M.-J.: Taiwanese adult foot shape classification using 3D scanning data. Ergonomics **58**(3), 513–523 (2015)

Mauch, M., Grau, S., Krauss, I., Maiwald, C., Horstmann, T.: A new approach to children's footwear based on foot type classification. Ergonomics **52**(8), 999–1008 (2009)

Mochimaru, M., Kouchi, M., Dohi, M.: Analysis of 3-D human foot forms using the free form deformation method and its application in grading shoe lasts. Ergonomics **43**(9), 1301–1313 (2000)

Qi, Y., Soh, C.B., Gunawan, E., Low, K.-S.: Ambulatory measurement of three-dimensional foot displacement during treadmill walking using wearable wireless ultrasonic sensor network. IEEE J. Biomed. Health Inform. **19**(2), 446–452 (2015)

Rout, N., Zhang, Y.F., Khandual, A., Luximon, A.: 3D foot scan to custom shoe last. Spec. Issue Int. J. Comput. Commun. Technol. **1**(2–4), 14–18 (2010)

Schuster, R.O.: Foot types and the influence of environment on the foot of the long distance runner. Ann. New York Acad. Sci. **301**(1), 881–887 (1977)

Tsao, L., Ma, L.: Using subject-specific three-dimensional (3D) anthropometry data in digital human modelling: case study in hand motion simulation. Ergonomics **59**(11), 1526–1539 (2016)

Ture Savadkoohi, B.: Analysis of 3D scanning data for optimal custom footwear manufacture. University of Trento (2010). http://eprints-phd.biblio.unitn.it/461/

Wunderlich, R.E., Cavanagh, P.R.: Gender differences in adult foot shape: implications for shoe design. Med. Sci. Sports Exerc. **33**, 605–611 (2001)

Yu, C.-Y., Tu, H.-H.: Foot surface area database and estimation formula. Appl. Ergon. **40**(4), 767–774 (2009)

Zeybek, G., Ergur, I., Demiroglu, Z.: Stature and gender estimation using foot measurements. Forensic Science International **181**(1–3), 54.e1–54.e5 (2008)

Construction of Deformable Trunk Atlas of Chinese Human Based on Multiple PET/CT Images: Preliminary Results

Hongkai Wang[1], Xiaobang Sun[1], Li Huo[2], Xin Tang[3],
and Changjian Liu[3(✉)]

[1] Department of Biomedical Engineering, Dalian University of Technology,
Dalian, China
wang.hongkai@dlut.edu.cn
[2] Department of Nuclear Medicine, Peking Union Medical College Hospital,
Beijing, China
[3] Department of Traumatic Orthopaedics, The First Affiliated Hospital of Dalian
Medical University, Dalian, China
dlutbmehomework@163.com

Abstract. Large number of Chinese people have taken PET/CT health screening during the last decade, resulting in thousands of PET/CT images of healthy subjects stored in the hospital databases all over the country. The purpose of this study is to collect PET/CT images of healthy Chinese people and construct digital atlases of trunk region based on a relatively large sample set. Compared to the traditional digital human atlases built from cryosection image of a single subject, the atlases of this study include anatomical and functional information of various living subjects. The technique of statistical shape models is used to model the inter-subject organ shape deformation across the population, therefore the atlas is named "the deformable atlas". This study also aims to measure the anatomical parameters (from CT images) and functional metabolism parameters (from PET images) of Chinese adults with different sexes, ages, and weights. The reconstructed statistical shape models reveal major anatomical variations among the population. We also found significant differences between male and female in different age groups through statistical analysis of organs volumes and CT values in skeleton. The obtained models and parameters will support the applications of education, anatomy-based simulation, knowledge-based medical image analysis and etc.

Keywords: Digital human atlas · Statistical shape models · Anatomy modeling

1 Introduction

In the last decade, digital human atlases of human anatomy have been developed rapidly with the advancement of medical imaging technologies such as CT, MRI, PET and SPECT. Various types of atlases have been constructed focusing on different aspects of human-centered studies. Some atlases aim at providing whole-body scale anatomy, such as the visible human project [1], 3D adult phantoms [2–4], pregnant-female models [5]

© Springer International Publishing AG 2017
V.G. Duffy (Ed.): DHM 2017, Part I, LNCS 10286, pp. 69–77, 2017.
DOI: 10.1007/978-3-319-58463-8_7

and hybrid new born phantoms [6]. Some atlases focus more on specific organs like liver [7], heart [8], pelvis [9], the femur [10], the vertebrae [11]. In recent years, the Human Brain Project motivated the research on brain atlases based on different imaging modalities [12].

The atlases proposed in this paper belongs to the trunk region category. The trunk atlases can be used as anatomical references to be registered with different modalities of target images or as digital phantoms for radiation simulation. However, most of the existing whole-body scale human atlas were constructed based on single or several references subject in a static pose. It is hard to use such atlases to represent a subject with realistic anatomical variations. To compensate the limitation of subject number, the Virtual Population models including ten detailed high-resolution anatomical models created from whole-body MR images [13]. The atlases mentioned above belong to visible human atlas family which models human anatomy in three dimension. Because visible human atlas is a collection of geometric models of human organ structures, no functional or physiological information is incorporated into the atlas.

With the development of digital human modeling, virtual physiological human has been proposed successively. The goal of virtual physiological human is to digitalize physiological information and integrate it into the visible human in order to reflect growth and metabolism of human body. For organ and system level, the European Physiome Project established a functional model of human digestive and musculoskeletal system [14]. However, none of these atlases can incorporate both organ metabolism information and inter-subject anatomical geometry variations into one single model. Overall, the problem of whole-body scale anatomical variance has not been solved completely, leaving a gap in automated medical image analysis to be filled.

To tackle the above problem, a deformable Chinese human trunk atlas is proposed in this paper. This atlas is constructed based on a training set of PET/CT images of healthy Chinese adults. Compared to the existing human atlas, this atlas adapts its organ anatomy using statistical shape models (SSMs) method. Besides, we obtained the metabolism information in major organs through standard uptake values (SUVs) [15] of radioactive tracer from PET images. With this study, we obtained the statistics of anatomical and functional parameters of the sampled population, as well as the inter-subject anatomical variations of major trunk organs. This trunk atlas is also a preliminary result of a whole-body scale atlas which is to be completed in near future.

2   Methods

2.1   Data Acquisition

To construct the deformable Chinese human trunk atlas, 355 PET/CT images of healthy Chinese adults were collected from four large general hospitals located in northeast, southeast, and southwest of china. There are two reasons that we chose PET/CT images rather than MRI images: (1) most of the existing MRI in China focus on partial scanning rather than whole-body scanning (2) the construction of atlas need images of healthy subjects, these images can be acquired from PET/CT health screening.

From the PET/CT images collected, the age of subjects was unevenly distributed, the middle-aged were in the majority. Table 1 lists the number of subjects for each age group.

Table 1. Number of subjects for each age group

Age	21–30	31–40	41–50	51–60	61–70	71–80	All
Total/male/female	8/6/2	54/26/28	129/79/50	92/54/38	60/35/25	12/5/7	355/205/150

2.2 Images Segmentation and Registration

The first step of atlas construction is to segment three-dimensional trunk organs from the CT images. Due to the imperfect image quality of the low-dose CT images of PET/CT scan, we could only segment major organs with millimeter-level accuracy. The segmented organs include skin, muscle, subcutaneous fat, each individual bone, whole heart, lungs, liver, spleen, kidneys, and bladder. Among these organs, most of them were segmented manually except the skeleton and muscle using threshold method. The segmentation result was shown in Fig. 3b.

After the segmentation, all the segmented organs were converted to triangular surfaces meshes. The vertex correspondences between the training subjects were obtained by registering the organ meshes of the reference anatomy model using the point set registration method [16]. The reference anatomy model of whole body male and female anatomy were purchased from the web [17] and were cropped to create the trunk reference meshes. Figures 1 and 2 present the reference anatomy model of whole body and the trunk region. For the organs in trunk region which cannot be segmented properly, we used thin-plate-spline (TPS) transform method [18] to map these organs in the reference anatomy model based on the control points in nearby segmented organs.

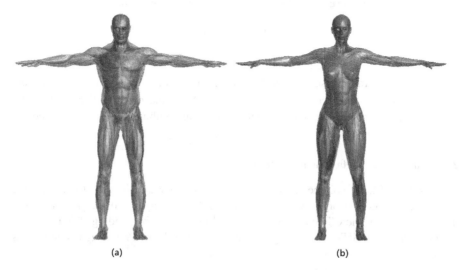

(a)   (b)

Fig. 1. The whole-body anatomy reference model, (a) male, (b) female.

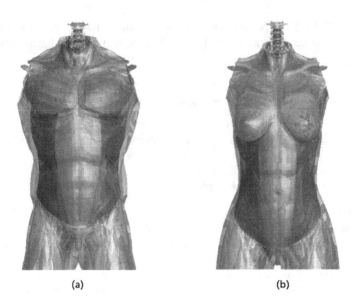

(a)   (b)

Fig. 2. The trunk anatomy reference model, (a) male, (b) female.

2.3 Statistical Shape Modeling

Statistical shape modeling can model the inter-subject deformation of organ shapes. Coordinates for all n points are concatenated to one vector X that describes the shape of the ith subject:

$$X = (x_1^i, y_1^i, z_1^i, x_2^i, y_2^i, z_2^i, \ldots, x_n^i, y_n^i, z_n^i)^T \tag{1}$$

The SSMs were based on a linear point distribution model described as:

$$X = \bar{X} + \Phi b \tag{2}$$

where $X \in R^{3n}$ is a shape instance of the model, $\bar{X} \in R^{3n}$ is the mean value of the shape instances in the training set, $\Phi \in R^{3N \times k}$ is the matrix of k shape modes, which are obtained using principal component analysis (PCA) of the mesh vertices and $b \in R^k$ represents the shape coefficients that control the linear combination of variation modes.

2.4 Functional Metabolism Modeling

Besides the SSM, the volume of each organ was also calculated in order to evaluate the mean and variance of organ volumes of different sexes, ages and weights. The segmented regions of the CT images were mapped into the corresponding PET images to calculate the mean SUV of each organ (Fig. 3c). The SUV of PET image is defined as

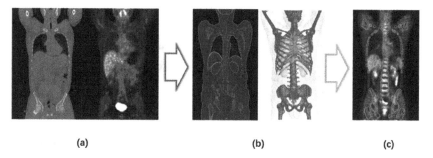

Fig. 3. (a) PET/CT image, (b) CT image segmentation, (c) mapping the bone segmentation result to PET images.

$$SUV_i = \frac{p_i \cdot k/w_i}{C_{inject}/w_{wb}} \qquad (3)$$

where i is the voxel index, p_i is the PET voxel value of voxel i, k is the coefficient to convert voxel value into radiation dose, C_{inject} is the whole body injection dose of radioactive tracer, w_i and w_{wb} are the mass weights of voxel i and the entire body, respectively. SUV represents the ratio of tracer concentration in each voxel to the average concentration of unit body weight, it is commonly used in clinical environment to assess relative PET tracer concentration. In this study, the PET tracer is fluorodeoxyglucose (^{18}F-FDG), which roughly reflects the absorption of glucose in human tissue. By calculating the mean SUV in each organ, we obtain organ-wise measurement of glucose metabolism level of each training subject.

3   Result

So far, we have segmented 138 CT images from the collected dataset, including 77 males and 61 females. Based on the segmented images, SSMs have been constructed for skin and muscles, major trunk organs and spine, respectively. At the current stage, the SSMs are built for all subjects including both sexes. Figures 4, 5 and 6 demonstrates the principal deformation modes of the SSMs.

As revealed by Figs. 4 and 5, the largest inter-subject deformations (i.e. mode 1) are the changes of abdominal volume, which is affected by the amounts of subcutaneous fat and abdominal fat. The accumulation of fat tissue increases the thickness of subcutaneous fat (Fig. 5) and pushes the abdominal organs away from each other (Fig. 4). The second largest the inter-subject deformation is the motion of lungs and thoracic muscles caused by respiration. Such deformation is learned from the different breath holding levels of the training subjects. Figure 6 shows that inter-subject spine deformations mainly occur at upper abdominal vertebrae and lower cervical vertebrae.

Through the statistical analysis of organs volumes, we find that the mean volumes of male thoracic organs are 50–60% larger than females', and the mean volumes of male abdominal organs are 30–40% larger than females' (Fig. 7). Most of the organs

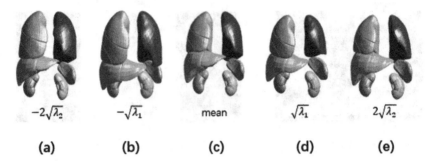

$-2\sqrt{\lambda_2}$ $-\sqrt{\lambda_1}$ mean $\sqrt{\lambda_1}$ $2\sqrt{\lambda_2}$

(a)   **(b)**   **(c)**   **(d)**   **(e)**

Fig. 4. Statistical shape models for major trunk organs, (c) the mean shape of training samples, (b) (d) and (a) (e) shows the variations of the largest and second largest deformation modes, respectively. The magnitudes of shape deformations are marked below each deformation result, where λ_i is the eigenvalue of the ith deformation mode.

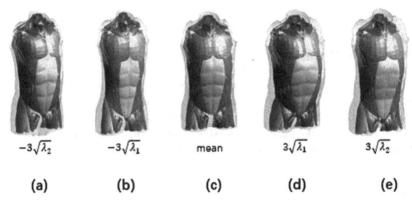

$-3\sqrt{\lambda_2}$ $-3\sqrt{\lambda_1}$ mean $3\sqrt{\lambda_1}$ $3\sqrt{\lambda_2}$

(a)   **(b)**   **(c)**   **(d)**   **(e)**

Fig. 5. Statistical shape models for skin and muscles. The magnitudes of shape deformations are marked below each deformation result, where λ_i is the eigenvalue of the ith deformation mode.

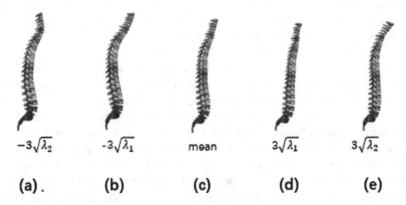

$-3\sqrt{\lambda_2}$ $-3\sqrt{\lambda_1}$ mean $3\sqrt{\lambda_1}$ $3\sqrt{\lambda_2}$

(a) .   **(b)**   **(c)**   **(d)**   **(e)**

Fig. 6. Statistical shape models for spine. The magnitudes of shape deformations are marked below each deformation result, where λ_i is the eigenvalue of the ith deformation mode.

Organ Volume vs. Sex

Fig. 7. Organs volume statistics of different genders

volume increase with weight getting heavy, except for the lungs whose volumes are affected by inconsistent breath holding levels. The CT values (Fig. 8) in skeleton from both genders decrease after the age of 40, this finding coincided well with a previous study based on ultrasonic bone density tests of 8345 Chinese subjects [19]. The result also revealed that females have a significant decline of bone CT values after 40 years old, while the decline of male was not significant. The ^{18}F-FDG SUVs (Fig. 9) of both genders also have a reduction after the age of 40, but the reduction of neither gender is significant.

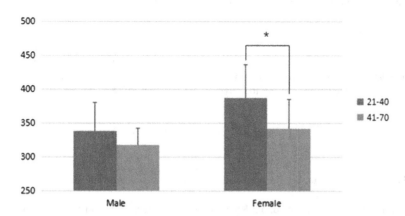

Fig. 8. Average skeleton CT values of male and female in 21–40 and 41–70 age groups. The star means significant difference exists between two age groups ($p < 0.05$) of female subjects.

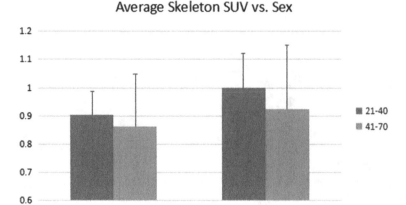

Fig. 9. Average skeleton SUV of male and female in 21–40 and 41–70 age groups. No significant difference was observed between the two age groups of each gender.

4   Discussions and Conclusions

By now, the size of our sample set has reached a preliminary statistical significance, we are still collecting and segmenting more PET/CT images. The outcomes of shape modeling show the change rule of anatomical morphology of Chinese population samples. The statistical analysis of CT value and ^{18}F-FDG SUVs reflects the change of skeleton density and metabolism from the subjects of different ages and sexes. However, this statistical result is still preliminary because our sample size is still limited. As the sample size keeps growing, more statistically meaningful results will be presented and dedicated atlases will be constructed for each gender. A publicly available website is under construction with the scope to share research results within one year.

Acknowledgement. This research was supported by the general program of National Natural Science Fund of China (Grant No. 61571076 and 81401475), the general program of Liaoning Science and Technology Project (Grant No. 2015020040), the cultivating program of Major National Natural Science Fund of China (Grant No. 91546123). The authors sincerely thank all the collaborating doctors for sharing the physical examination PET/CT images.

References

1. Zhang, S., Jie, B., Tan, L.: The application of Chinese visible human dataset. FASEB J. **27**, Ib8 (2013)
2. Sato, K., Noguchi, H., Emoto, Y., Koga, S., Saito, K.: Japanese adult male voxel phantom constructed on the basis of CT images. Radiat. Prot. Dosim **123**, 337–344 (2007)
3. Saito, K., Wittmann, A., Koga, S., Ida, Y., Kamei, T., Funabiki, J., Zankl, M.: Construction of a computed tomographic phantom for a Japanese male adult and dose calculation system. Radiat. Environ. Bioph. **40**, 69–75 (2001)

4. Nagaoka, T., Watanabe, S.: Postured voxel-based human models for electromagnetic dosimetry. Phys. Med. Biol. **53**, 7047–7061 (2008)
5. Shi, C.Y., Xu, X.G., Stabin, M.G.: SAF values for internal photon emitters calculated for the RPI-P pregnant-female models using Monte Carlo methods. Med. Phys. **35**, 3215–3224 (2008)
6. Lee, C., Lodwick, D., Hasenauer, D., Williams, J.L., Lee, C., Bolch, W.E.: Hybrid computational phantoms of the male and female newborn patient: NURBS-based whole-body models. Phys. Med. Biol. **52**, 3309–3333 (2007)
7. Okada, T., Shimada, R., Hori, M., Nakamoto, M., Chen, Y.W., Nakamura, H., Sato, Y.: Automated segmentation of the liver from 3D CT images using probabilistic atlas and multilevel statistical shape model. Acad. Radiol. **15**, 1390–1403 (2008)
8. Frangi, A.F., Rueckert, D., Schnabel, J.A., Niessen, W.J.: Automatic construction of multiple-object three-dimensional statistical shape models: application to cardiac modeling. IEEE Trans. Med. Imag. **21**, 1151–1166 (2002)
9. Ellingsen, L.M., Chintalapani, G., Taylor, R.H., Prince, J.L.: Robust deformable image registration using prior shape information for atlas to patient registration. Comput. Med. Imaging Graph. **34**, 79–90 (2009)
10. Baka, N., Kaptein, B.L., de Bruijne, M., van Walsum, T., Giphart, J.E., Niessen, W.J., Lelieveldt, B.P.: 2D-3D shape reconstruction of the distal femur from stereo X-ray imaging using statistical shape models. Med. Image Anal. **15**, 840–850 (2011)
11. Benameur, S., Mignotte, M., Parent, S., Labelle, H., Skalli, W., de Guise, J.: 3D/2D registration and segmentation of scoliotic vertebrae using statistical models. Comput. Med. Imaging Graph. **27**, 321–337 (2003)
12. Amunts, K., Lepage, C., Borgeat, L., Mohlberg, H., Dickscheid, T., Rousseau, M.É., Bludau, S., Bazin, P.L., Lewis, L.B., Orospeusquens, A.M.: BigBrain: an ultrahigh-resolution 3D human brain model. Science **340**, 1472–1475 (2013)
13. www.itis.ethz.ch/itis-for-health/virtual-population/human-models/
14. Viceconti, M., Clapworthy, G., Taddei, F., Jan, S.V.S.: European virtual physiological human. J. Med. Biomed. **23**, 19–25 (2008)
15. Boellaard, R., Krak, N.C., Hoekstra, O.S., Lammertsma, A.A.: Effects of noise, image resolution, and ROI definition on the accuracy of standard uptake values: a simulation study. J. Nucl. Med. **45**, 1519–1527 (2004)
16. Jian, B., Vemuri, B.C.: A robust algorithm for point set registration using mixture of Gaussians. In: Tenth IEEE ICCV, vol. 1242, pp. 1246–1251 (2005)
17. www.turbosquid.com/3d-models/rigged-complete-male-female-3d-3ds/839850
18. Chui, H.L., Rangarajan, A.: A new point matching algorithm for non-rigid registration. Comput. Vis. Image Underst. **89**, 114–141 (2003)
19. Wang, H.: Investigation of bone mineral density and osteoporosis prevalence in 8345 civil services from Shenzhen. China Mod. Dr. **49**, 11–12 (2011)

Introduction of the Anthropometry in the Early Design of a Nuclear Main Control Room

Shengyuan Yan[1] and Jean Luc Habiyaremye[1,2(✉)]

[1] School of Mechanical and Electrical Engineering,
Harbin Engineering University,
Nantong Street, No. 145-1, P.O. Box 150001, Harbin, China
yanshengyuan@hrbeu.edu.cn, habijealuc@yahoo.fr
[2] School of Science and Technology,
University of Rwanda, P.O. Box 3900, Kigali, Rwanda

Abstract. A nuclear main control room (MCR) is a crucial part of nuclear power plant (NPP) where qualified staffs are monitoring and controlling the function and productivity of the whole plant. In a safely operated NPP, the performance of the MCR personnel is critical. The full height range of the users and the size they exhibit depend primarily on age, gender, body physical characteristics and other data within a population of people. In this case, properly designing MCR and human-system interface (HSI) is central to safe and efficient operations of the plant, since it reduces the occurrence of incidents, accidents and the risks of human related errors.

Therefore, it is essential that the design of the large display panels, control consoles, vertical control panels and machinery rooms must be adequately performed and the application of the anthropometric principles in all design stages of the MCR is a requirement. When human anthropometry is taken into considerations in the design process, the MCR suits better the capabilities and limitations of the operators. During the design process, manufacturers and designers should consider the sizes, shapes, abilities and constraints of the people for whom they are designing. Anthropometric data varies significantly between different communities in various geographical territories.

Keywords: Anthropometric measurement · Human-system interface · Human factors standards · Human capabilities and limitations

1 Introduction

Human lifestyle and the environment are also changing so quickly and consequently affect human anthropometry. Therefore, while designing products, developers are advised to take into considerations two important aspects: First, the data collected over 25 years might not be matching the current population, since measurements such as heights may have changed.

Secondly, there are cases when the target population is not represented by the anthropometric database being used [1]. Besides, the job to carry out more experiments

© Springer International Publishing AG 2017
V.G. Duffy (Ed.): DHM 2017, Part I, LNCS 10286, pp. 78–91, 2017.
DOI: 10.1007/978-3-319-58463-8_8

and constitute new anthropometric databases is tough, too demanding, and extremely expensive and requires a well knowledgeable technical team. And again, there is a very tight market competition and a far-reaching globalization network that push manufacturers and designers to reach various communities from across the world in a very limited time.

Also, some researchers emphasized the importance of taking into account the right high-level requirements in the early design stages to avoid a series of endless modifications that are always necessary to update an incorrect model [2, 3]. To overcome all those challenges, the researchers have developed a UG nx model that complies with the Human-System Interface Design Review Guidelines (NUREG0700). It presents four advantages:

- First, it interconnects all critical parts and equipment of the nuclear control room with the operator's size and keeps them together as one unit.
- Secondly, it presents the capability of allowing the designer to change boundary dimensions when it is necessary.
- Thirdly, it has the high capability of quickly responding to designer's modification, resizing different control room parts and adjusting the remaining parameters automatically.
- Fourthly, it calculates and rebuilds the model using mathematical formula without changing the original design principles.

This paper achieves its goal through the development of the UG nx model that applies human factors standards (HFS) and creates an interconnection between human physical measurements and nuclear MCR parts. Furthermore, a series of mathematical expressions was developed with the pure intention to govern the UG nx MCR model, make it capable of quickly responding to any designer's modification and holding it as one body. This study accomplished its objectives through the following steps:

- First, construction of geometric diagrams that show the relationship between human dimensions, workstation dimensions, console dimensions, large display screen (LDS) dimensions, and control panel dimensions.
- Secondly, developments of mathematical formulas that interlinks human physical measurements with different design characteristics of the structure and hold all the MCR parts together as one unit.
- Thirdly, construction of a UG nx MCR model and insertion of appropriate mathematical expressions that will make it flexible and able to rebuild its parameters whenever there is a designer's modification.
- Fourthly, carrying out experiments and verifying the results to avoid redesign process.
- Lastly, after performing a series of tests, design tables that may serve as designers' guides and system backups were developed for people who may not have access to the model. They contain different measurements of MCR parts and equipment corresponding to the operator's anthropometry.

For the comfort of the users, this report has found that by introducing a new full height range and body size in the early design stages, the MCR model is capable of computing and rebuilding the console and bench-board heights to allow easy reach of controls and keep contact eye on a display area. It was found that this design method will significantly cut down design time, reduce costs and promote the adaptation to rapid changes in the market demand.

1.1 Literature

Human factor engineering at the workplace has attracted researchers' attention for the last few decades. Researchers were concerned about the mismatch between equipment design and anthropometric principles, biomechanics and how they can address complaints reported at the workplace that subsequently reduces accidents and increases productivity. Therefore, an adequate design of the MCR in combination with appropriate HSI is central to the efficient and healthy operation of the plant. They help reduce the occurrence of incidents, accidents and the risks of human error [4]. Previous studies were conducted on Human Factors Engineering (HFE), but HFE alone did not adequately address the issues of human errors since it did not take into account the individuals' variability such as personnel size. Consequently, the operators' performance is affected by unsuitable design features that cause human fatigue and discomfort [5, 6]. Some studies have examined the mismatch between the equipment and operator's dimensions by taking anthropometric measurements of students and the dimensions of their desks and chair and confirmed that most of them could not find a suitable seat [7–9].

While designing a nuclear power plant console panel, the designers must ensure the physical placement of the controls and displays are at a reachable distance and meet operators' visibility requirements [10]. In their studies, Seminara and Parsons [11] identified major and minor deficiencies associated with human factors aspects in nuclear control room such as equipment component located at distant locations or in confined spaces that might reduce operator's performance and cause injuries [11]. Nuclear control room developers have put in many efforts to overcome deficiencies at early design stages, but little is known about combining human factor engineering study with the diversification of human physical characteristics and workplace layout. The objective of this study is to develop an NX model that combines human physical characteristics with MCR equipment and design layout and meets operators' capabilities and limitations.

2 Design of "MCR" Model

In designing interactive systems such as processes, products, and spaces, the designers must explore working conditions, communication and how human beings can interact with the designed system or product. Prototypes are developed to represent any given design before producing a final product and help in the design process and design decisions [12]. The fundamental design principle of this model takes a reference to the international standard guidelines (NUREG0700) (see Table 1). This model is capable of quickly responding to any designer's modification and rebuilding all MCR equipment to match the changes and maintain standard guidelines.

Table 1. Anthropometric data [5]

Standing (without shoes)	Bounding measurements inches (mm)	
	5th %-ile adult female: (mm)	95th %-ile adult male (mm)
Stature	60.0(1524)	73.5(1866.9)
Eye height from floor	55.5(1409.7)	68.6(1742.4)
Shoulder height	48.4(1229.4)	60.8(1544.3)
Elbow height	37.4(949.96)	46.8(1188.7)
Fingertip height	24.2(614.68)	28.8(731.5)
Functional reach	25.2(640.08)	35.0(889)
Extended functional reach	28.9(734.06)	39.0(990.6)
Central axis of body to leading edge of console	5.0(127)	5.3(134.6)
Eye distance forward of central axis to body	3.0(76.2)	3.4(86.4)

2.1 Determination of the Lower Limit (L)

Let's take a random shoulder height (Y_1) (see Fig. 1).

$$Tan(\alpha) = \frac{\Delta y}{\Delta x} = \frac{1544 - 1229}{889 - 640} = \frac{315}{249}$$

$$\Leftrightarrow \Delta x = \frac{\Delta y}{Tan(\alpha)} = \frac{\Delta y}{\frac{315}{249}} \tag{1}$$

$$\Leftrightarrow \Delta x = \frac{249\Delta y}{315}$$

$$Tan(\alpha) = \frac{h}{249 - \Delta x} = \frac{315}{249}$$

$$\Leftrightarrow h = (249 - \Delta x) \times \frac{315}{249} \tag{2}$$

$Y_1 = 1544 - h$, Hence,

$$Y_1 = 1544 - \frac{315}{249} \times z(249 - \Delta x) \tag{3}$$

And

$$Y_1 = 1229 + \Delta y \tag{4}$$

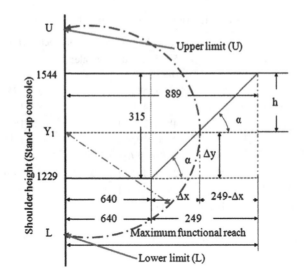

Fig. 1. Shoulder heights and functional reach (Sketch)

By combining Eqs. 3 and 4

$$\Delta y = 1544 - \left(\frac{315}{249} \times (249 - \Delta x)\right) - 1229$$

$$\Leftrightarrow \Delta y = 315 - \frac{315}{249} \times (249 - \Delta x)$$

$$(5)$$

By replacing Δx with its expression in Eq. 3

$$Y_1 = 1544 - \frac{315}{249} \times \left(249 - \frac{249\Delta y}{315}\right)$$

Lower limit (L) according to Fig. 1 becomes:

$$L = Y_1 - (640 + \Delta x)$$

$$\Leftrightarrow L = Y_1 - \left(640 + \frac{249\Delta y}{315}\right)$$

$$(6)$$

2.2   Determination of the Upper Limit

If we consider a random point Y_1 on the vertical axis (see Fig. 1),

$$Y_1 = 1229 + \Delta y$$

$$U = Y_1 + (640 + \Delta x)$$

$$(7)$$

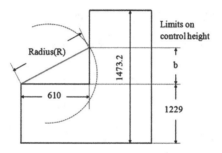

Fig. 2. Functional reach-radius (Sketch)

Replacing Δx by its value the equation becomes:

$$U = Y_1 + \left(640 + \frac{249\Delta y}{315}\right) \tag{8}$$

2.3   Determination of the Limits on Control Height

Control height coincides with the point of intersection between the console and the functional reach radius of the 5th %-ile female (see Fig. 2) (Tables 2 and 3).

$$R^2 = b^2 + 610^2$$
$$\Leftrightarrow b^2 = R^2 - 610^2 \tag{9}$$
$$\Leftrightarrow b = \sqrt{R^2 - 610^2}$$

From Fig. 1 Radius (R)

$$R = \left(640 + \frac{249\Delta y}{315}\right)$$

Replacing R by its value in Eq. 9, we obtain

$$b = \sqrt{\left(640 + \frac{249\Delta y}{315}\right)^2 - 610^2} \tag{10}$$

Control height (C_h) from the floor (see Fig. 2) is equal to:

$$C_h = 1229 + b \Leftrightarrow$$
$$\Leftrightarrow C_h = 1229 + \sqrt{\left(640 + \frac{249\Delta y}{315}\right)^2 - 610^2} \tag{11}$$

Table 2. Random designer's modification on operator's eye and shoulder heights

Design parameters	Operator's eye height	Bottom of the screen (height)	Top of the screen (height)	Screen length	Console height	Benchboard height	Shoulder height	Control height
Min. Eye height (Ehmi)	1410	1308	1542.03	3372.12	2113.21	1188.29	641.78	N/A	N/A
Max.console height (Chmax)	1473	1359	1593.03	3423.12	2113.21	1216.42	669.92	N/A	N/A
Functional area (Fa)	610	1410	1644.03	3474.12	2113.21	1244.55	698.05	1229	1422.65
Console width (Cw)	1016	1461	1695.03	3525.12	2113.21	1272.69	726.18	1249	1469.80
Passageway (Pw)	1250	1512	1746.03	3576.12	2113.21	1300.82	754.32	1309	1578.92
Distance between operator and screen stand (Z)	2266	1563	1797.03	3627.12	2113.21	1328.95	782.45	1381.5	1683.24
Arc of view	60	1613	1847.03	3677.12	2113.21	1356.53	810.03	1432	1747.31
LCD screen rotation	150	1664	1898.03	3728.12	2113.21	1384.67	838.16	1483	1807.63
Min. display height(Dh)	1041	1715	1949.03	3779.12	2113.21	1412.80	866.30	1544	1875.70
Min. benchboard height (Bmin)	686	1743	1977.03	3807.12	2113.21	1428.25	881.74	N/A	N/A
Benchboard thickness (Bth)	12.05	1794	2028.03	3858.12	2113.21	1456.38	909.88	N/A	N/A
		1845	2079.03	3909.12	2113.21	1484.51	938.01	N/A	N/A

Table 3. Random designer's modification on LCD screen rotation angle and arc of view

Design parameters		LCD screen rotation angle	Arc of view	Operator's eye height	Stand height (Sh)	Screen length (D1)	Height on top of screen
Min. eye height	1410	135	69	1715	1949.03	2455.75	3685.51
Console height	1473	150	60			2113.21	3779.12
Functional area	610	155	51			1809.93	3589.38
Console width	406	160	42			1526.41	3383.38
Passageway	1250	163	33			1247.55	3142.07
Length between operator and screen stand	2266	165	24			959.25	2875.60
		171	15			645.40	2586.48
		177	6			283.93	2232.57

2.4 Design of Giant Screen and Its Orientation

Design of the Stand Height. Screens are inclined at an angle greater or equal to 45°
and less than 90° and suspended at a distance of 1250 mm (passageway) for single a
person behind the consoles [5] (see Fig. 3).

$$Tan(\theta) = \frac{1473 - 1410}{610} = \frac{C}{Z}$$
$$\Leftrightarrow C = \frac{63 \times Z}{610} \tag{12}$$

The stand height (S_h):

$$S_h = 1410 + C + \Delta y \tag{13}$$

$$\Leftrightarrow \theta = \arctan\left(\frac{1473 - 1410}{610}\right) = 6°$$

$$Hyp^2 = Z^2 + c^2 \Leftrightarrow Hyp = \sqrt[2]{Z^2 + C^2}$$

Design of the Screen Length. Considering the triangle Hyp, D & E in Fig. 3, the arc
of 75° is reduced by 6° (θ) while the arc of 45° is increased by 6° (θ) (see Fig. 4). "D"
stands for the maximum screen length.

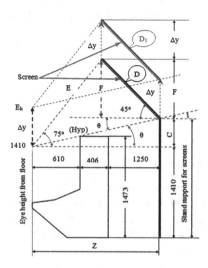

Fig. 3. Large screen position and orientation (Sketch)

$$\frac{D}{Sin(\beta)} = \frac{Hyp}{Sin(\gamma)} = \frac{E}{Sin(\varphi)}$$

$$\Leftrightarrow \frac{D}{Sin(69)} = \frac{Hyp}{Sin(60)} \qquad (14)$$

$$\Leftrightarrow D = \frac{Hyp \times Sin(\beta)}{Sin(\gamma)}$$

Taking into account the economic aspect, material utilization, and owner's requirements, the MCR designer, can reduce the length (D) of the LDS. The length of the screen should vary by decreasing the total arc of view (β), keeping the angle (φ) unchanged and the top angle (γ) continues changing according to the variation of (β) (see Fig. 4).

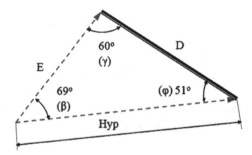

Fig. 4. Determination of screen length (Sketch)

Consequently, when LDS length reduces, the height of the screen also decreases that ultimately helps the designer predict the height of the MCR that can accommodate it (see Fig. 5).

And the Eq. 14 becomes

$$D = \frac{Hyp \times Sin(69 - \Delta^o)}{Sin(180 - 51 - (69 - \Delta^o))}$$

$$\Leftrightarrow D = \frac{Hyp \times Sin(69 - \Delta^o)}{Sin(60 + \Delta^o)} \qquad (15)$$

Where Δ^o is a change in visual field (degrees).

Screen Orientations. The MCR designer has capabilities to reorient the large display screen (LDS) by rotating it either in a forward or backward direction to comfortably suit operator's viewing requirements. In this case, the screen length keeps constant but, the height on the top of the screen varies with a variation of angle (φ) (see Fig. 5).

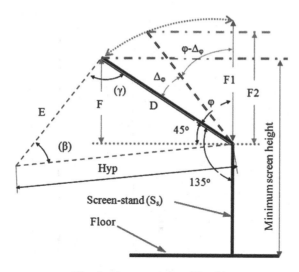

Fig. 5. Screen rotation (Sketch)

The angle between screen stand and the LDS (D) is equal to 135° (see Fig. 5)

$$F_1 = D \times Cos(\varphi)$$

And $F_1 = D \times Cos(180 - 135)$
Let's take any small change in angle $(\Delta\varphi)$ (see Fig. 5)

$$F_2 = D \times Cos(45 - \Delta\varphi))$$

So, vertical projections (F_s) of the screen are given by the following formula:

$$F_s = D \times Cos(45 - \Delta\varphi_s) \tag{16}$$

Height on Top of the Screen (Htop)

$$H_{top} = 1410 + C + \Delta y + D \times Cos(45 - \Delta\varphi_s) \tag{17}$$

2.5   Design of Console Height

The maximum console height is recommended not to exceed 58 in. (1,473.2 mm). The console height must allow the operator a continuous view of the control panel, especially at control panel display height which requires constant monitoring [5].

At initial eye position (Ehmi), the eye cuts through the height of console and makes an angle "Ψ" with the back edge of the console and points to the control panel at the minimum display height (see Fig. 6).

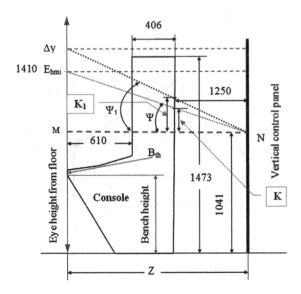

Fig. 6. Console height

$$Tan(\psi) = \frac{E_{hmi} - 1041}{Z} = \frac{K}{1250} \qquad (18)$$

$$\Leftrightarrow K = \frac{1250 \times (E_{hmi} - 1041)}{Z} \qquad (19)$$

The minimum console height (H_{min}) that allows the 5th %-ile female to look over is equal to: $H_{min} = 1041 + K$

Let's consider "Δy" change in eye height

$$Tan(\psi_1) = \frac{E_{hmi} - 1041 + \Delta_y}{Z} = \frac{K_1}{1250} \qquad (20)$$

$$\Leftrightarrow K_1 = \frac{1250 \times (E_{hmi} - 1041 + \Delta_y)}{Z} \qquad (21)$$

Console Height Increment (Δy_c.)

$$\Delta y_c = K_1 - K$$

$$\Delta y_c = \frac{1250 \times (E_{hmi} - 1041 + \Delta_y)}{Z} - \frac{1250 \times (E_{hmi} - 1041)}{Z} \qquad (22)$$

$$\Leftrightarrow \Delta y_c = \frac{1250\Delta y}{Z}$$

3 Results and Discussion

The UG nx MCR model was developed, and all parts, equipment, and layout of the MCR were governed and dimensioned using mathematical expressions. Parameters used to establish formulas interlink personnel measurements with consoles, LDS, passageways, controls and display panels. Mathematical equations hold the model as a single entity and make it capable of responding quickly to any designer's modification.

3.1 MCR Model and How It Works

The process of compiling the data shown in different tables follows five steps:

a. Modify the size of one, two or more parameters at once in the model
b. Click ok
c. The model rebuilds itself
d. Display dimension
e. Take record of new dimensions

Therefore, for design purpose, it is recommended to take records of new dimensions and compile them in a table anytime there is a designer's change. There is the unlimited number of tables that can be developed; it all depends on the part of the model the designer is interested in or the customer requirements. Data compiled in tables will serve as designers' guides for people who may not have access to the NX model.

Eg. When we set the Eye height (Eh) to 1715 mm and functional reach (Fr) to 610 mm in the UG nx MCR model, it resizes and adjusts different parts, then rebuilds to accommodate changes. The NX model resizes the console height and minimum display height to maintain visibility condition (see Fig. 7) and also the bench board height is adjusted to suit the operator's shoulder height, etc. (see Fig. 8).

Fig. 7. visibility condition and console height

Fig. 8. Reach capability

3.2 Experimental Validation

After conducting a series of test and workshop experiments, the researchers have successfully constructed five different prototypes using data resulting from this model. This study confirmed that this NX model is a successful inclusive design tool because it is capable of dealing with data that do not fit in the defined NUREG0700 standard. Also, it presents an advantage to adapt to any other data within a population of people classified according to age, gender or body physical characteristics (see Fig. 9).

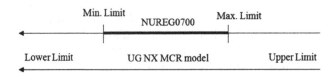

Fig. 9. Comparison between NUREG0700 and NX model

4 Conclusion

The introduction of the anthropometric measurements in the early stage of the MCR design addresses the issue of major and minor deficiencies associated with human factors aspects such as equipment component located at distant locations or in confined spaces. This paper confirmed that the NX model will eliminate design errors that are the root causes of redesign process and a series of endless modifications that are always necessary to update. This design method will significantly cut down design time and substantially reduce costs. It was found that this model is capable of adapting itself to rapid change in market demand.

Acknowledgement. The research team gratefully acknowledges the financial and academic support of the Chinese Scholarship Council in conjunction with Harbin Engineering University and the University of Rwanda.

References

1. Openshaw, S., Taylor, E.: Ergonomics and Design: A Reference Guide. Allsteel Inc., Muscatine (2006)
2. Boy, G.A., Schmitt, K.A.: Design for safety: a cognitive engineering approach to the control and management of nuclear power plants. Ann. Nucl. Energy **52**, 125–136 (2013)
3. Hwang, S.-L., Liang, S.-F.M., Liu, T.-Y.Y., Yang, Y.-J., Chen, P.-Y., Chuang, C.-F.: Evaluation of human factors in interface design in main control rooms. Nucl. Eng. Des. **239**, 3069–3075 (2009)
4. Gouvali, M., Boudolos, K.: Match between school furniture dimensions and children's anthropometry. Appl. Ergon. **37**, 765–773 (2006)
5. U. N. R. Commission, "Human-system interface design review guidelines", NUREG-0700, Rev, vol. 2 (2002)
6. O'Hara, J., Brown, W., Lewis, P., Persensky, J.: Human-System Interface Design Review Guidelines (NUREG-0700, Rev 2), US Nuclear Regulatory Commission, Washington, DC, p. 12 (2002)
7. Nadadur, G., Chiang, J., Parkinson, M.B., Stephens, A.: Anthropometry for a north american manufacturing population, SAE Technical Paper 0148-7191 (2009)
8. Panagiotopoulou, G., Christoulas, K., Papanckolaou, A., Mandroukas, K.: Classroom furniture dimensions and anthropometric measures in primary school. Appl. Ergon. **35**, 121–128 (2004)
9. Ross, J.: Using anthropometrics in designing for enhanced crew performance. Ship Sci. Technol. **5**, 41–56 (2011)
10. Sargent, T.A., Kay, M.G., Sargent, R.G.: A methodology for optimally designing console panels for use by a single operator. Hum. Factors **39**, 389–409 (1997)
11. Seminara, J.L., Parsons, S.O.: Nuclear power plant maintainability. Appl. Ergon. **13**, 177–189 (1982)
12. Buchenau, M., Suri, J.F.: Experience prototyping. In: Proceedings of the 3rd Conference on Designing Interactive Systems: Processes, Practices, Methods, and Techniques, pp. 424–433 (2000)

Human Body and Motion Modelling

Muscle Fatigue Analysis Using OpenSim

Jing Chang[1(✉)], Damien Chablat[1], Fouad Bennis[1], and Liang Ma[2]

[1] Laboratoire des Sciences du Numérique de Nantes (LS2N),
École Centrale de Nantes, 44321 Cedex 3 Nantes, France
{Jing.chang,Damien.Chablat,Fouad.Bennis}@ls2n.fr
[2] Department of Industrial Engineering, Tsinghua University,
Beijing 100084, People's Republic of China
liangma@tsinghua.edu.cn

Abstract. In this research, attempts are made to conduct concrete muscle fatigue analysis of arbitrary motions on OpenSim, a digital human modeling platform. A plug-in is written on the base of a muscle fatigue model, which makes it possible to calculate the decline of force-output capability of each muscle along time. The plug-in is tested on a three-dimensional, 29 degree-of-freedom human model. Motion data is obtained by motion capturing during an arbitrary running at a speed of 3.96 m/s. Ten muscles are selected for concrete analysis. As a result, the force-output capability of these muscles reduced to 60–70% after 10 min running, on a general basis. Erector spinae, which loses 39.2% of its maximal capability, is found to be more fatigue-exposed than the others. The influence of subject attributes (fatigability) is evaluated and discussed.

Keywords: Muscle fatigue analysis · Digital human modeling · Open-Sim · Muscle fatigue model · Muscle fatigability

1 Introduction: Muscle Fatigue and Digital Human Modeling

1.1 Muscle Fatigue

Muscle fatigue is defined as the decrease in maximum force [1]. Work-related muscle fatigue contributes to occupational Musculoskeletal Disorders (MSDs) [2], which makes up the vast proposition of the occupational diseases [3]. As illustrated by Armstrong et al. [4], improper physical work requirements lead to muscle fatigue. It is important to quantify fatigue and to determine the limits of acceptable work requirements [2]. Proper work design would reduce the risk of excessive physical workload.

In the effort to involve muscle fatigue analysis into work design, there are two key problems that bother us. First, in actual working scene, the motion adopted by workers to finish a task would be arbitrary rather than routine and repeated. This makes it difficult to evaluate the exact workload carried by a certain muscle. Fatigue analysis, without the exact information about muscle workload, would

© Springer International Publishing AG 2017
V.G. Duffy (Ed.): DHM 2017, Part I, LNCS 10286, pp. 95–106, 2017.
DOI: 10.1007/978-3-319-58463-8_9

be inaccurate. Second, muscle fatigue process varies a lot among human groups. The utilization of fatigue analysis would be limited without proper consideration about demographical human attribute.

1.2 Digital Human Modeling

Digital human modeling (DHM) technique offers an efficient way to simulate ergonomics issues in the process of work design. The integration of biomechanical models with DHM systems allows us to evaluate musculoskeletal workload in manual work simulations. Related software such as Jack [5], Delmia [6], 3DSSPP [7], Anybody [8], OpenSim [9] are available for work design. All these softwares render realistic mannequins to visualize work tasks. Backward or inverse dynamics methods are used to calculate the muscle-tendon reaction force [10].

Among the mentioned software, the mannequin used by Jack, Delmia and 3DSSPP shall be settled by the gender and the percentile of body height and weight in a given anthropometric database (USA, Canadian, German, Korean, etc.). This makes it easy to apply analysis for a specific group of people. Unfortunately, as a vital parameter of work design, muscle force capacity is not included in the database. It is unreasonable to assume the same muscle capacity among different anthropometric groups while the other measures diverse. Further muscle analysis on the basis of this muscle capability would be low-effective.

In Jack, Delmia and 3DSSPP, a motive task is simulated by the congregation of a set of static tasks with a certain posture. Each working posture is evaluated separately without considering the history of the motion. The external loads, the duration time and the frequency of the posture is identified. By applying strength models or inverse dynamic models, load of several major joints are calculated. In 3DSSPP and Jack, fatigue analysis is available based on the static joint load, task duration and frequency. This method goes well for simple and repetitive tasks. But when it comes to arbitrary task, there would be a great lack of accuracy.

The simulation and analysis by OpenSim and Anybody are more specified. The mannequin is constituted of concrete bones and muscles where musculoskeletal geometry is scaled and adaptive to subjects. The motions obtained by a motion capture system or computed along a simulated task permitted us to have the kinematic information, such as positions, velocities and accelerations of a motion. The inertial properties of body segments are estimated. By applying the Newtonian principles, the prediction of the resultant extrinsic forces and moments are then available.

Although the joint reaction force and muscle load are accessible in OpenSim and Anybody, the accumulation effect has not been taken into account; and no accurate fatigue analysis is available.

1.3 Objectives

In this research, a plug-in to OpenSim is written to involve the muscle fatigue analysis to an arbitrary task. Concrete muscle force capability change is specified and the influence of demographic human attributes is considered. This work is promising to offer a virtual work design platform that helps to predict muscle fatigue.

2 Methodology: OpenSim Human Modeling and Muscle Fatigue Analysis

2.1 Human Modeling and Dynamic Simulation in OpenSim

As mentioned above, OpenSim is a digital human modeling platform. It allows users to build and analyze different musculoskeletal models. A model consists of a set of rigid segments connected by joints. Muscles and ligaments span the joints, develop force, and generate movements of the joints. After the build-up of a musculoskeletal model, OpenSim takes experimentally-measured kinematics, reaction forces and moments as input data. This is usually obtained by motion capture system from a subject. The experimental kinematics (*i.e.*, trajectories of markers, joint centers, and joint angles) are used to adjust and scale the musculoskeletal model to match the dimensions of the subject [9].

For dynamic simulation, an inverse kinematics problem is solved to find the model joint angles that best reproduce the experimental kinematics. Then a residual reduction algorithm is used to adjust the kinematics so that they are more dynamically consistent with the experimental reaction forces and moments. Finally, a computed muscle control (CMC) algorithm is used to find a set of muscle excitations and distribute forces across synergistic muscles to generate a forward dynamic simulation that closely tracks the motion [9]. In this way, the workload of each muscle is accessible along an arbitrary motion, which paves way for the fatigue analysis.

2.2 Muscle Fatigue Analysis

Ma et al. [11] proposed a "Force-load fatigue model based on mechanical parameters. It depicts how muscle force declines with time with consideration of relative workload and intrinsic human attribute. The model was described as a differential function (Eq. 1). According to this model, during a fatiguing process, muscle force capability ($F_{cem}(t)$) changes depending on (a) Maximal (or initial) muscle force capability, F_{max}; (b) External load on the muscle, $F_{Load}(t)$ and (c) Intrinsic muscle fatigability, k. For detailed explanation of this model was introduced in Ma et al. [11,12] and [13] for static and dynamic cases, respectively.

$$\frac{dF_{cem}(t)}{dt} = -k\frac{F_{cem}(t)}{F_{max}}F_{Load}(t) \qquad (1)$$

This model has been mathematical validated in Ma et al. [11] with static MET models and other existing dynamic theoretical models.

In this model, intrinsic human attribute concerning to fatigue rate is taken into consideration, which is referred to fatigability. The definition of fatigability is proposed by Ma and Chang [14] "Muscle fatigability describes a tendency of a muscle from a given subject to get tired or exhausted, and it should only be determined by the physical and psychological properties of the individual subject". According to this model, the decrease rate of muscle capability is in proportion with both work load and current muscle capability. The proportion coefficient k quantifies the tendency of muscle strength descending, and is noted as fatigability.

Fatigability varies significantly among human groups. For example, females are found to be more fatigue-resistant than males [15]; and the older groups shows significantly much less force loss than the younger group after a certain exercises [16]. Fatigability k has been determined by comparing the Force-Load muscle fatigue model with the empirical maximal endurance models [12]. The determined value of k varies from $0.87 \, \text{min}^{-1}$ to $2.15 \, \text{min}^{-1}$ for general muscle groups. Ma et al. [17] also conducted experiments to measure fatigability. In a static drilling task, the fatigability of 40 male workers was identified to be $1.02 \pm 0.49 \, \text{min}^{-1}$ for the upper limbs.

2.3 Muscle Fatigue Analysis in OpenSim

The object of this research is a concrete analysis of muscle fatigue. In another word, how force capability of each muscle declines during an arbitrary motion. According to the Force-load muscle fatigue model, this objective can be achieved on condition of two values: workload on each muscle along the motion and the maximal muscle capability.

Workload on Each Muscle. The muscle force generation dynamics can be divided into activation dynamics and contraction dynamics [18]. Activation dynamics corresponds to the transformation of neural excitation to activation of the muscle fibers. Muscle contraction dynamics corresponds to the transformation of activation to muscle force (Fig. 1).

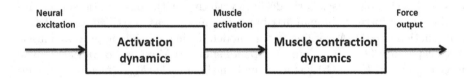

Fig. 1. Muscle force generation dynamics. Adapted from Zajac [18].

Activation dynamics is related to calcium release, diffusion and uptake from the sarcoplasmic reticulum [19]. It is modeled by a first-order differential equation [20]:

$$\frac{da}{dt} = \frac{u - a}{\tau(u, a)} \tag{2}$$

where u is excitation (from 0 to 1), a is activation (from 0 to 1), and τ is a variable time constant.

Muscle contraction dynamics deals with the force-length-velocity relationships and the elastic properties of muscles and tendons. In OpenSim, it is modeled by a lumped-parameter model [9]:

$$\frac{dl_m}{dt} = f_v^{-1}(l_m, l_{mt}, a) \tag{3}$$

where l_m is the muscle length, l_{mt} is the muscle-tendon actuator length, and f_v is the force velocity relation for muscle.

As mentioned in Sect. 2.1, OpenSim develops a CMC algorithm to calculate muscle activation and therefore to distribute joint force among a series of muscles. By applying the CMC algorithm, the workload on each muscle is accessible.

The Maximal Muscle Force Capability of Each Muscle. Muscle activation depends on the neural excitation level. In the case of a certain muscle contraction speed and muscle length, muscle force increases with muscle activation. Full activation (i.e., $a(t) = 1$) happens when a muscle contractile component has been maximally excited (i.e., $u(t) = 1$) for a long time [18]. During an arbitrary motion, muscle kinematics changes from time to time. We calculate the maximal muscle force F_{max} based on the CMC algorithm, in addition that the activation level of each muscle is preset to full level ($a(t) = 1$).

As the final step, a Plug-in is written based on the Force-load muscle fatigue model, with the required inputs obtained by the above methods.

3   Data and Simulation

The plug-in is tested on a three-dimensional, 29 degree-of-freedom human model developed by Stanford [21]. The model, as the other OpenSim musculoskeletal models, is made up of bodies, joints, and muscle-tendon actuators. Specifically, this model consists of 20 body segments, 19 joints and 92 muscle actuators, as shown in Fig. 2. The inertial parameters for the body segments in the model are based on average anthropometric data obtained from five subjects (age 26 ± 3 years, height 177 ± 3 cm, and weight 70.1 ± 7.8 kg).

This model is developed to study the muscles' contribution to the acceleration of the body during running. It covers the muscles that needed for arbitrary running motions. These muscles could be classified into three groups: torso-core muscle group, pelvis-femur muscle group, and lower knee extremities muscle group.

The simulation data is also from the project of Hamner et al. [21]. It is recorded from a healthy male subject (height 1.83 m, mass 65.9 kg) running on a treadmill at 3.96 m/s. A total of 41 reflective markers are placed on the subjects anatomical landmarks during the experiment to scale the model to the subjects anthropometry. Ground reaction forces and markers' trajectories are recorded. The recorded motion lasts for 10 s.

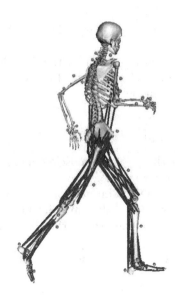

Fig. 2. Full body running digital human modeling. Muscles are represented by red lines. (Color figure online)

In our study, 10 muscles are selected from the three muscle groups to conduct muscle fatigue analysis. The basic characteristics of these muscles are listed in Table 1.

Table 1. Basic characteristics of the analyzed muscles.

Muscle name	Appertained group	Optimal fiber length (m)	Maximal isometric force (N)
Erector spinae	Torso-core	0.120	2500.0
External oblique	Torso-core	0.120	900.0
Internal oblique	Torso-core	0.100	900.0
Adductor magnus	Pelvis-femur	0.131	488.0
Glute maximus	Pelvis-femur	0.142	573.0
Glute medius	Pelvis-femur	0.065	653.0
Tibialis posterior	Lower knee	0.031	1588.0
Lateral gastrocnemius	Lower knee	0.064	683.0
Extensor digitorum	Lower knee	0.102	512.0
Soleus	Lower knee	0.050	3549.0

4   Results of Simulation

During the arbitrary running, workloads on muscles vary from moment to moment. A typical muscle workload change is shown in Fig. 3.

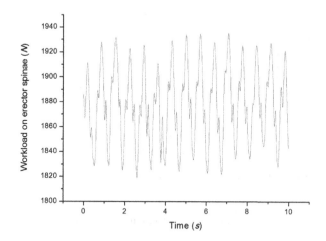

Fig. 3. Workload on erector spinae muscle during 10 s arbitrary running at 3.96 m/s.

4.1   General Muscle Force Decline

In order to investigate the fatigue process, the motion data is duplicated to 10 min. During the running process, muscle force capabilities decline with time. After input the fatigability (k) of the subject, the detail information about force capability changes is accessible. A general view of force capability changes of the selected muscles are shown in Fig. 4. Here the fatigability is set to $1.0 \, min^{-1}$. Generally, the muscles' capabilities reduce to 60% to 70% of their maximum after running for 10 min.

4.2   Comparison Among Different Muscles

The initial and ending force capabilities of the selected muscles are shown in Table 2.

The proportion of force capability reduction is between 30% to 40% for each of the ten muscles. Erector spinae loses the maximal proportion of force. As far as the selected muscles, torso-core muscle group fatigues no less than the pelvis-femur or the lower knee group (average fatigue level: (36.8 ± 2.1)%, (35.1 ± 2.7)%, (36.1 ± 3.2)%, respectively).

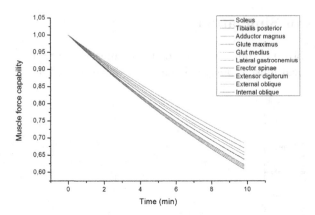

Fig. 4. Force capability lines of ten muscles during 10 min running. $k = 1.0\,\text{min}^{-1}$. Force of each muscle is normalized by its maximum.

Table 2. General information of muscle force capabilities

Muscle name	Appertained group	Initial capabilities (N)	Finial capabilities (N)	Proportion of reduction
Erector spinae	Torso-core	38703.5	23563.3	39.1%
External oblique	Torso-core	19876.2	12926.2	35.0%
Internal oblique	Torso-core	18374.8	11705.9	36.3%
Adductor magnus	Pelvis-femur	10923.7	7322.3	33.0%
Glute maximus	Pelvis-femur	12304.1	8096.3	34.2%
Glute medius	Pelvis-femur	19134.0	11817.8	38.2%
Tibialis posterior	Lower knee	36901.9	22624.1	38.7%
Lateral gastrocnemius	Lower knee	18231.9	12481.3	31.5%
Extensor digitorum	Lower knee	8940.7	5558.1	37.8%
Soleus	Lower knee	95221.7	60708.3	36.3%

4.3   Influence of Fatigability Index k

Fatigability is a subject-specific parameter that might also varies between muscle groups. As mentioned in Sect. 2.2, the determined value of k varies from $0.87\,\text{min}^{-1}$ to $2.15\,\text{min}^{-1}$ for general muscle groups. In the current study, we examine the influence of fatigability by comparing the fatigue level when $k = 1.0\,\text{min}^{-1}$ with that when $k = 2.0\,min^{-1}$. A typical comparison is shown in Fig. 5.

Table 3 manifests the fatigue level comparisons of all the ten muscles. Generally, the muscle reduces to 40% to 50% of its initial maximal capability. The relative sort of muscles' fatigue level remains unchanged.

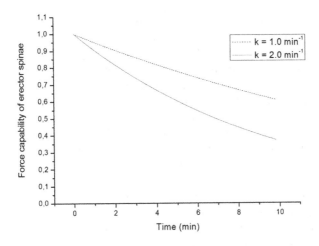

Fig. 5. Force capability lines of erector spinae with different preset k values. Force is normalized by the maximum.

Table 3. Comparison of muscle force capabilities between different fatigabilities

Muscle name	Appertained group	Proportion of capability loss	
		$k = 1.0\,\mathrm{min}^{-1}$	$k = 2.0\,\mathrm{min}^{-1}$
Erector spinae	Torso-core	39.1%	62.9%
External oblique	Torso-core	35.0%	57.7%
Internal oblique	Torso-core	36.3%	59.4%
Adductor magnus	Pelvis-femur	33.0%	55.1%
Glute maximus	Pelvis-femur	34.2%	56.7%
Glute medius	Pelvis-femur	38.2%	61.9%
Tibialis posterior	Lower knee	38.7%	62.4%
Lateral gastrocnemius	Lower knee	31.5%	53.1%
Extensor digitorum	Lower knee	37.8%	61.4%
Soleus	Lower knee	36.3%	59.4%

5   Discussions

According to the simulation data, after 10 min running at the speed of 3.96 m/s, a healthy male subject is likely to lose 30% to 40% of his maximal muscle capability. The requirement of the running task at the current posture is about 5% of his maximal muscle capability. If the task continues, there would be a time in future when the subject's muscle capability reduces to near to the required workload. Muscles will enter into a risk zone [22,23]. Damage will occur to muscles, which increases the risk of MSDs. The subject would change his posture unconsciously [24]. It is important to predict the exhausting time in the early process of work design.

In Hammer's research [21], the quadriceps (pelvis-femur muscle group) and plantar flexors (lower knee muscle group) are the major contributors to acceleration of the body mass center during running, compared with the torso-core muscle group (erector spinae and iliopsoas). While in the current study, erector spinae, who loses 39.2% of its maximal capability, is found to be more fatigue-exposed than the others. Also, torso-core muscle group fatigues no less than the other two muscle groups. This phenomenon indicates that torso-core muscles undertake other supportive functions than contributing to body accelerating, such as counterbalancing the vertical angular momentum of the legs.

A subject with a higher fatigability value ($k = 2.0\,\mathrm{min}^{-1}$) losses about 20% of his maximal capability more than the subject with a lower fatigability value ($k = 1.0\,\mathrm{min}^{-1}$). The influence of fatigability is evident. It is essential to study the fatigability among different human groups.

It should be noticed that the current study considers no effect of fatigue recovery. Future study should integrate the muscle recovery for more accurate calculation.

6   Conclusions and Implications

In this study, a plug-in to OpenSim is written on the base of the Force-load muscle fatigue model and muscle force generation dynamics to obtain the concrete information about how force-output capability of each muscle declines along time.

Simulation on a three-dimensional, 29 degree-of-freedom human model shows that the force-output capability of ten selected muscles reduced to 60–70% after 10 min running at the speed of 3.96 m/s, with a fatigability value of $1.0\,\mathrm{min}^{-1}$. Torso-core muscle group, which has been found to contribute less to the body's acceleration in previous research, shows no less proportion of force loss than the other two groups. The difference in fatigue level caused by the change of fatigability is evident, which emphasizes the necessity of the study and determination of fatigability among different human groups.

This work offers a virtual work design platform that helps to predict muscle fatigue and thereby to control the MSDs risks at the early stage of work design. In future works, the Motion Capture System of the École Centrale de Nantes will be used to acquire data for industrial tasks. A force platform will be used to validate the muscle properties during experiments. The study of the fatigability k as a function of the people will also be addressed in these new experiments.

Acknowledgments. This work was supported by the National Natural Science Foundation of China under Grant numbers 71471095, by Chinese State Scholarship Fund, and by INTERWEAVE Project (Erasmus Mundus Partnership Asia-Europe) under Grants number IW14AC0456 and IW14AC0148.

References

1. Bigland-Ritchie, B., Rice, C.L., Garland, S.J., Walsh, M.L.: Task-dependent factors in fatigue of human voluntary contractions. In: Gandevia, S.C., Enoka, R.M., McComas, A.J., Stuart, D.G., Thomas, C.K., Pierce, P.A. (eds.) Fatigue, pp. 361–380. Springer, New York (1995)
2. Chaffin, D.B., Andersson, G., Martin, B.J., et al.: Occupational Biomechanics. Wiley, New York (1999)
3. Eurogip: Déclaration des maladies professionnelles: problématique et bonnes pratiques dans cinq pays européens Allemagne - Danemark - Espagne - France - Italie. Rapport denquête, 44 p. (2015). www.eurogip.fr/fr/produits-information/publications-d-eurogip/3906-declaration-des-mp-problematique-et-bonnes-pratiques-dans-cinq-pays-europeens
4. Armstrong, T.J., Buckle, P., Fine, L.J., Hagberg, M., Jonsson, B., Kilbom, A., Kuorinka, I.A.A., Silverstein, B.A., Sjogaard, G., Viikari-Juntura, E.R.A.: A conceptual model for work-related neck and upper-limb musculoskeletal disorders. Scand. J. Work Environ. Health 19, 73–84 (1993)
5. Jack: February 2017. http://www.plm.automation.siemens.com/en_us/products/tecnomatix/manufacturing-simulation/human-ergonomics/index.shtml
6. Delmia: February 2017. http://www.3ds.com/products-services/delmia
7. Feyen, R., Liu, Y., Chaffin, D., et al.: New software tools improve workplace design. Ergon. Des.: Q. Hum. Factors Appl. 7(2), 24–30 (1999)
8. Damsgaard, M., Rasmussen, J., Christensen, S.T., Surma, E., De Zee, M.: Analysis of musculoskeletal systems in the anybody modeling system. Simul. Model. Pract. Theory 14(8), 1100–1111 (2006)
9. Delp, S.L., Anderson, F.C., Arnold, A.S., Loan, P., Habib, A., John, C.T., Guendelman, E., Thelen, D.G.: OpenSim: open-source software to create and analyze dynamic simulations of movement. IEEE Trans. Biomed. Eng. 54(11), 1940–1950 (2007)
10. Chaffin, D.B.: Digital human modeling for workspace design. Rev. Hum. Factors Ergon. 4(1), 41–74 (2008)
11. Ma, L., Chablat, D., Bennis, F., Zhang, W.: A new simple dynamic muscle fatigue model and its validation. Int. J. Ind. Ergon. 39(1), 211–220 (2009)
12. Ma, L., Chablat, D., Bennis, F., Zhang, W., Bo, H., Guillaume, F.: A novel approach for determining fatigue resistances of different muscle groups in static cases. Int. J. Ind. Ergon. 41(1), 10–18 (2011)
13. Sakka, S., Chablat, D., Ma, R., Bennis, F.: Predictive model of the human muscle fatigue: application to repetitive push-pull tasks with light external load. Int. J. Hum. Factors Model. Simul. 5(1), 81–97 (2015)
14. Ma, L., Chang, J.: Measurement of subject-specific local muscle fatigability. Adv. Phys. Ergon. Hum. Factors: Part II 15, 215–220 (2014)
15. Yoon, T., Doyel, R., Widule, C., Hunter, S.K.: Sex differences with aging in the fatigability of dynamic contractions. Exp. Gerontol. 70, 1–10 (2015)
16. Kent-Braun, J.A., Ng, A.V., Doyle, J.W., Towse, T.F.: Human skeletal muscle responses vary with age and gender during fatigue due to incremental isometric exercise. J. Appl. Physiol. 93(5), 1813–1823 (2002)
17. Ma, L., Zhang, W., Bo, H., Chablat, D., Bennis, F., Guillaume, F.: Determination of subject-specific muscle fatigue rates under static fatiguing operations. Ergonomics 56(12), 1889–1900 (2013)

18. Zajac, F.E.: Muscle and tendon properties models scaling and application to bio-mechanics and motor. Crit. Rev. Biomed. Eng. **17**(4), 359–411 (1989)
19. Winters, J.M.: An improved muscle-reflex actuator for use in large-scale neuro-musculoskeletal models. Ann. Biomed. Eng. **23**(4), 359–374 (1995)
20. Thelen, D.G., et al.: Adjustment of muscle mechanics model parameters to simulate dynamic contractions in older adults. Trans.-Am. Soc. Mech. Eng. J. Biomech. Eng. **125**(1), 70–77 (2003)
21. Hamner, S.R., Seth, A., Delp, S.L.: Muscle contributions to propulsion and support during running. J. Biomech. **43**(14), 2709–2716 (2010)
22. Ma, L., Zhang, W., Chablat, D., Bennis, F., Guillaume, F.: Multi-objective opti-misation method for posture prediction and analysis with consideration of fatigue effect and its application case. Comput. Ind. Eng. **57**(4), 1235–1246 (2009)
23. Ma, R., Chablat, D., Bennis, F., Ma, L.: Human Muscle fatigue model in dynamic motions. In: Lenarcic, J., Husty, M. (eds.) Latest Advances in Robot Kinematics, pp. 349–356. Springer, Dordrecht (2012)
24. Fuller, J.R., Lomond, K.V., Fung, J., Côté, J.N.: Posture-movement changes follow-ing repetitive motion-induced shoulder muscle fatigue. J. Electromyogr. Kinesiol. **19**(6), 1043–1052 (2009)

Motion Analysis of the Tea Whisk Concerning the Way of Tea

Akihiko Goto[1(✉)], Soutatsu Kanazawa[2], Tomoko Ota[3], Yuka Takai[1],
and Hiroyuki Hamada[4]

[1] Osaka Sangyo University, 3-1-1 Nakagaito, Daito, Osaka 574-8530, Japan
gotoh@ise.osaka-sandai.ac.jp
[2] Urasenke Konnichian, Kyoto, Japan
kanazawa.kuromon.1352.gentatsu@docomo.ne.jp
[3] Chuo Business Group, 1-6-6 Funakoshi-cho, Chuo-ku, Osaka 540-0036, Japan
tomoko_ota_cbg@yahoo.co.jp
[4] Kyoto Institute of Technology, Matsugasaki, Sakyo-ku,
Kyoto 606-8585, Japan
hhamada@kit.ac.jp

Abstract. The way of tea is the Japanese tea ceremony. In this research, one super expert and an expert and beginner were employed as the behavior subject. During the tea-mixing process, the subject's motion and trace were captured by the high-speed camera system from top side of the participants. The coordinates of the right index finger in the x and y direction was captures and analyzed. Base on the data from the high-speed camera system, each key gesture of the subjects were focused, motion feature affected the final teas were extracted and analyzed. The tea-mixing process was divided into three kinds of processes according to the velocity of the tea whisk. In the case of the super expert, the action of the tea whisk was high speed at short time of the first period. And changed gesture and stirred around with uniform speed at second period. At third period, the action was decreased gradually.

Keywords: Tea ceremony · Process analysis · Motion analysis

1 Introduction

"The way of tea" called the "Japanese tea ceremony", is a special ceremonial art preparation and presentation of green tea powder to entertain the guests. The whole process is not only drinking the tea, but also is enjoying the tea ceremony and feeling the tea making guest's heart. Each movement and gesture was always considered as an important part of ceremony. A good tea master can mix the green tea power into the hot water with a period of proper time, which ensures the mixed tea hold the optimal tasting temperature. As same with stirring speed and frequency, the movement skills and stirring track is also one of the most important features influence factors for master. The previous researches of our group were reported about the motion analysis of the way of tea [1–3].

© Springer International Publishing AG 2017
V.G. Duffy (Ed.): DHM 2017, Part I, LNCS 10286, pp. 107–114, 2017.
DOI: 10.1007/978-3-319-58463-8_10

In this research, one super expert, an non-expert and beginner were employed as the subjects. During "the way of tea" performance, the subject's motion and trace were captured by high-speed camera system during the tea-mixing process. Base on the data from the high-speed camera system, each key gesture of the subjects was focused, motion feature effect on final teas were extracted and analyzed.

2   Experimental Procedure

2.1   Subjects and Apparatus

Three persons participated in this experiment. There were one of the grand tea masters in the "Urasenke", a trainee and an inexperienced person. In this paper, there are called super expert, non-expert and beginner respectively. The number of experience years of the super expert was 30 years over. The non-expert has two years of experience. The tea mixing processes of all subjects were measured by a high-speed camera (MEM-RECAM Q1m/Q1v, nac Image Technology Inc.). The camera was set upper the tea bowl and the frame rate of the camera was set for 500 fps.

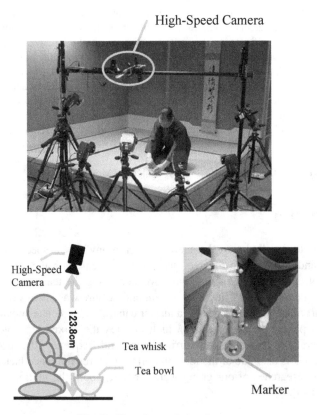

Fig. 1. Experimental situation.

2.2   Analysis Procedure

The track of subject's index finger was measured by the camera during the mixing the tea powder and hot water. The coordinates of a marker on the finger were analyzed by

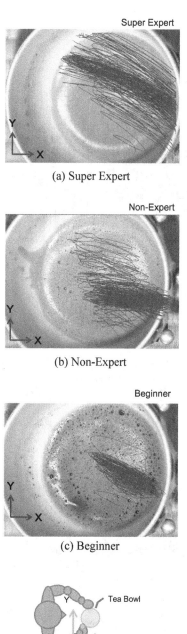

(a) Super Expert

(b) Non-Expert

(c) Beginner

Fig. 2.   Track of the tea whisk in tea bowl.

application software (TEMA, Photron Co., Ltd.). The location and velocity of the marker were calculated during the time. After checking the velocity of the super expert during the time, the working tine was divided into the working types. The experimental situation is shown in Fig. 1.

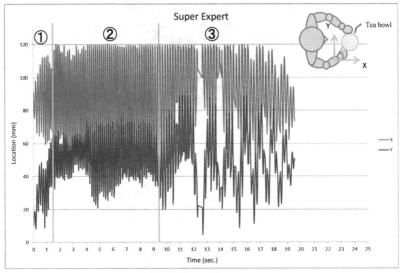

(a) Super Expert

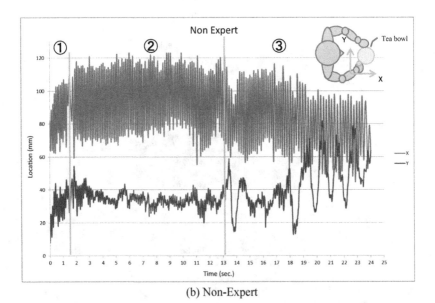

(b) Non-Expert

Fig. 3. Track of the tea whisk about X and Y direction.

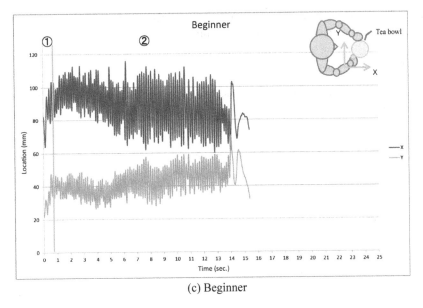

(c) Beginner

Fig. 3. (continued)

3 Result and Discussion

3.1 Track of the Tea Whisk in Tea Bowl

Track of the tea whisk in tea bowl of each subject are shown in Fig. 2. It was clear that each track was different. In the case of the super expert, the track of the tea whisk was widely and intensively in the tea bowl. However, in the case of beginner, the area of the track was very small. Track of the tea whisk about X axis and Y axis direction are shown in Fig. 3. In the case of super expert, the working behavior was divided into three kinds of processes. In the first process, the track of the tea whisk was moved from insertion point to the edge of tea bowl in a short time. In the second process, the track was moved widely from the front side to the depth side. However the track of lateral motion was small. In the third process, the track of lateral motion was widely. In the case of non-expert, the working behavior was able to be divided into three processes with according to the super expert approximately. In the case of beginner, the track was existed in the two processes, so that it was not included the final third process.

3.2 Velocity Variation of Tea Whisk

The velocity variation of the tea whisk is shown in Fig. 4. In the case of the super expert, the velocity of the first process increased rapidly from starting time. The velocity of the second process was almost stable with maximum value. The velocity of the third process decreased gradually to finishing time. In the case of non-expert, the velocity was almost stable during the working time. However, when the process was changed, the velocity decreased and increased rapidly. In the case of beginner, the velocity increased gradually from starting time to finishing time. There was the maximum value of the velocity about finishing time.

3.3   Analysis of Each Process

In the case of the super expert, it was considered that the first process means to mix the tea powder and hot water. During the first process, the tea powder dissolved in hot

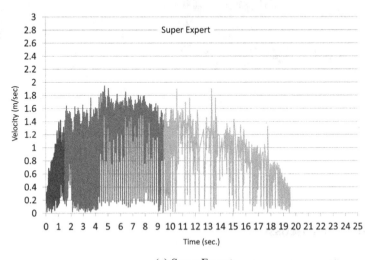

(a) Super Expert

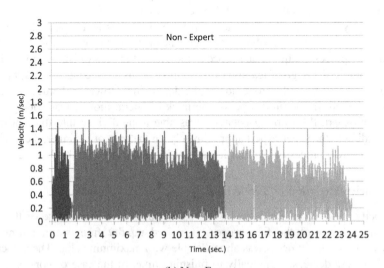

(b) Non-Expert

Fig. 4. Velocity variation of tea whisk.

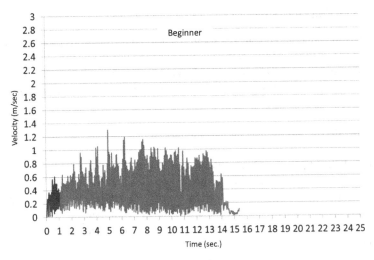

(c) Beginner

Fig. 4. (continued)

water perfectly. The second process means to make the bubble in the green tea probably at stable velocity. The third process means to arrange the babble on the surface of the green tea, so that the tea whisk was moved whole surface of the tea with decreasing the velocity.

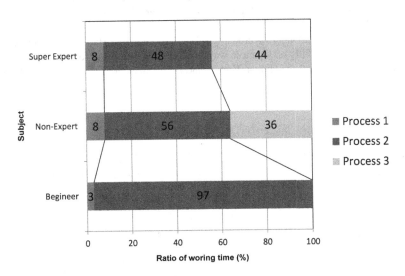

Fig. 5. Ratio of working time on each process.

3.4 Ratio of Working Time

In the case of the super expert, it was spent much time for the third process among the subjects. In the case of non-expert, the tendency of the ratio of working time was similar to the super expert. However, in the case of beginner, it was not included the time for the third process. It was spent almost all time for the second process (Fig. 5).

4 Conclusion

In the case of the super expert, it was cleared that the working time was able to be divided into three processes as follows, the first process was to mix the tea powder and hot water in the tea bowl, the second process was to make the bubble in the green tea and the third process was to arrange the bubble in whole surface of the green tea. Moreover, the third process of the super expert had much time more than non-expert and beginner.

References

1. Kanazawa, S., Ota, T., Wang, Z., Wiranpaht, T., Takai, Y., Goto, A., Hamada, H.: Experience factors influence on motion technique of "the way of tea" by motion analysis. In: Duffy, V.G. (ed.) DHM 2015. LNCS, vol. 9185, pp. 155–163. Springer, Cham (2015). doi:10.1007/978-3-319-21070-4_16
2. Kanazawa, S., Ota, T., Wang, Z., Tada, A., Takai, Y., Goto, A., Hamada, H.: Research on the performance of three tea whisks of "the way of tea" with different experience. In: Duffy, V.G. (ed.) DHM 2015. LNCS, vol. 9184, pp. 95–103. Springer, Cham (2015). doi:10.1007/978-3-319-21073-5_10
3. Aiba, E., Kanazawa, S., Ota, T., Kuroda, K., Takai, Y., Goto, A., Hamada, H.: Developing a system to assess the skills of Japanese way of tea by analyzing the forming sound: a case study. In: Proceedings of the Human Factors and Ergonomics Society 57th Annual Meeting, pp. 2057–2061 (2013)

Visibility Analysis on Swing Motion of the Golf Player Based on Kinect

Zhelin Li[1](✉), Songbin Ye[1], Lijun Jiang[1], Yaqi Wang[1], Deli Zhu[2], and Xiaotong Fu[3]

[1] School of Design, South China University of Technology,
Guangzhou 510006, China
{zhelinli,ljjiang}@scut.edu.cn, gzwoods@qq.com
[2] Department of Sports Management,
Guangdong Vocational Institute of Sports, Guangzhou 510663, China
491014214@qq.com
[3] School of Computer Science and Engineering,
South China University of Technology, Guangzhou 510006, China

Abstract. This article presents an analysis of using the second generation Microsoft Kinect to track user's skeletal joints on golf swing motion. The skeletal joints tracking status data were collected in the experiment based on ten golf players, including four swing postures of eight swing directions. Variance and average value are used to figure out the distribution rule of skeletal joints tracking status information in the eight swing directions. The result shows that the visibility ratio of skeletal joints is between 12.67% and 13.51% in eight swing directions. When swinging directions on −135-degree, −45-degree, 45-degree relative to the Kinect Y-axis plane, it gets the high confidence level. This conclusion can apply to the golf swing motion analytical system based on Kinect sensors.

Keywords: Swing motion · Skeletal joints · Swing direction · Visibility

1 Introduction

People can fully enjoy golf at any age or skill level, for its widespread and increasing popularity. In order to increase Golf-swing playability and make it more suitable for an amateur to practice, the analytical of the golf swing is imperative. Golf professionals aim to educate a golfer on the best approach to utilize the body and club during the swing which will transfer the most amount of energy into the ball and maximize the driving distance [1]. In this paper, Kinect was used to assess the joints' visibility (skeletal joints tracking status information) and extracted joints' coordinate 3D-dimension data.

The capture and analysis of human behaviors such as jumping, running, swing, are common in some domains, including sports science, musculoskeletal injury management and the human-computer interaction [2, 3]. It requires highly accurate motion capture in the analysis of joint angle, position, and angular velocities. It is outside the reach of most users of the highly accurate motion capture systems, whether based on camera or inertia sensor. To popularize motion capture technology, Microsoft

© Springer International Publishing AG 2017
V.G. Duffy (Ed.): DHM 2017, Part I, LNCS 10286, pp. 115–126, 2017.
DOI: 10.1007/978-3-319-58463-8_11

cooperation has rolled out the Kinect which bases on depth camera, as low-cost alternatives. The Kinect uses an infrared based active stereo vision system to get a depth map of the observed scene, and it was designed to recognize human gestures and skeleton joints. There are still challenging problem due to strong noise in-depth data and self-occlusion when using Kinect to analyze the golf swing motion. Yeung et al. [4] evaluated Kinect as a clinical assessment tool for Total body center of mass sway measurement, and their results revealed the Kinect system produced a highly correlated measurement of Total body center of mass and comparable intra-session reliability to Vicon (Motion Capture Systems). Previous studies have indicated a positive relationship between Microsoft Kinect and OptiTrack motion tracking system. Høilund et al. [5] investigated the precision between the Microsoft Kinect and OptiTrack and found that the OptiTrack and the Kinect has been shown to deliver approximately the same results, with some restrictions. Wang et al. [6] examined the first generation Kinect and the second generation Microsoft Kinect and found that the second generation Kinect provides better accuracy in joint estimation while providing skeletal tracking that is more robust to occlusion and body rotation than the first generation Kinect released at 2010. Kinect has limited visible area and could not track the human limbs which behind others limbs. Thus, just one Kinect is not enough for tracking the golf swing motion. However, multiple Kinect sensors have broader visible area even 360 degrees, and users do not need facing the Kinect directly. Williamson et al. [7] using multi-Kinect tracking for dismounted soldier training, and within the Microsoft Kinect Software Development Kit that can be merged using commercially available tools and advanced fusion algorithms to produce better quality representations of users in the real world within a virtual environment. Furthermore, several Kinect coupled with inference algorithms can produce a much better tracked representation as users move around.

In order to figure out accurately joint 3D-dimensional data, Kinect was using to track the joint and figure out each joint visibility ratio during one full golf swing. Tracking a golf swing with only one Kinect sensor could cause tracking all the swing motion to be difficult since swing speed is typically fast, both arms overlap each other, and the self-occlusion in the motions being captured. For obtaining larger visible area, we prepare to use Multiple-Kinect to capture the golf swing.

2   Materials and Methods

2.1   Experimental Equipment

Kinect for Windows 2.0 (Xbox one), Dell M8600 mobile workstation, tripods, iphone7 take photos, Cougar as the hardware. We used the Kinect SDK-v2.0_1409-Setup.exe, skeletal Joint analysis program as the software.

2.2   Experimental Scheme

In this experiment, the subjects are the sophomore professional golf students. The Microsoft Kinect v2 was used to collect four feature golf swing motions which including golf swing setup posture, the top of the swing, impact time and finish swing motions and captured ten students including eight golf swing directions. Golf swing directions take turns every 45-degree from facing directly to the Kinect to −45-degree angle to Kinect coordinate Y-axis, as showed in Fig. 1.

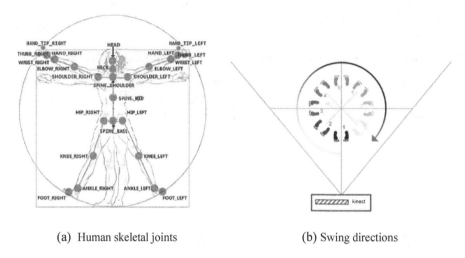

(a) Human skeletal joints   (b) Swing directions

Fig. 1. (a) Human skeletal joints by Kinect. (b) Eight swing directions

2.3   Experimental Procedures

Before the experiment, the eight swing directions position was marked on the ground. Every participant posed the four feature golf swing motion and did the next swing direction. All participants took turns to pose the eight swing directions exactly. Then we collected the skeletal data when giving a sign (Fig. 2).

(a) Setup   (b) Top   (c) Impact   (d) Finish

Fig. 2. Four feature swing postures. (a) Swing setup, prepare to upon the club. (b) Top of swing position. (c) Time of shots the ball. (d) End of golf swing motion

3 Data Analyses

Kinect may perform differently on the same swing posture. In swing directions, the participants were asked to hold on one swing motion posture until we collected 30 frames data. To improve the data reliability, the least joint amount of frames will be extracted as the current swing posture data.

3.1 Joints Moving Distance Analysis of One Full Golf Swing Motion

Each joint has different moving distance on full golf swing. Thus, some joints will be weighted up, and some joints will be weighted down. Figure 3 shows which joint should be weighted up or weighted down using the joints moving distance.

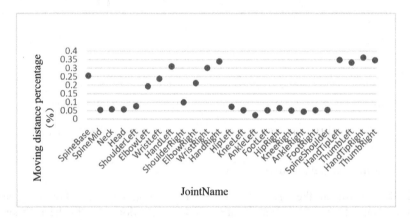

Fig. 3. Joint moving distance on full golf swing motion

Figure 3 describes that joints of SpineMid, Neck, Head, ShoulderLeft, ShoulderRight, HipLeft, KneeLeft, FootLeft, AnkleLeft, HipRight, KneeRight, AnkleRight, FootRight and SpineShoulder's performance are relatively stable. SpineBase, ElbowLeft, WristLeft, HandLeft, ElbowRight, WristRight, HandRight, HandLeft, ThumbLeft, HandRight and ThumbRight joints' performance are unstable. Joints'moving distance averages show how long they go through during full swing motion. The longer distance averages, the more vitality of joint. Combine with joints tracking status of Table 3, some joints will be weighted up or weighted down among these joints.

3.2 Joint Tracking Status Data on Four Swing Postures of Eight Swing Directions

The two following figures demonstrate joint tracking status data which was collected from 10 participants. And the X-axle value means eight swing directions; the Y-axle value means joint accurate tracking status amount. The joints visibility status was presented graphically, as shown in Fig. 4. Total information was shown in Tables 4 and 5. For example, visibility of eight swing directions of ElbowLeft swing_setup posture was presented on scatter diagram. The scatter diagram illustrates that on the swing directions of 3 and 4, the joint tracking status amount of ElbowLeft achieve nine while others are below seven. This statistics data of swing directions 3 and 4 shows high tracking confidence level, while averages the joints data possess highly accurate.

According to the Fig. 4 analytical process, the joints tracking status data was categorized into high tracking confident level and low tracking confident level.

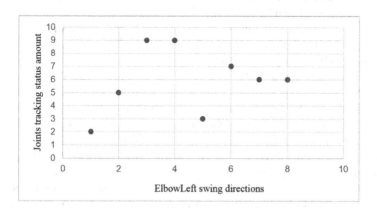

Fig. 4. ElbowLeft Swing_Setup tracking status amount

3.3   Joint Average and Variance

Statistic method of the average value and variance value is used to assess the joints tracking data performance. Joint tracking status data on four swing postures of eight swing directions of ten participants are presented in the two following table.

To assess each joint tracking amount on four swing postures of eight swing directions, the average is used for evaluating that. The average for each joint tracking amount is computed as

$$\bar{x} = \frac{1}{8} \sum_{i=1}^{8} xi \tag{1}$$

xi value means each joint tracking status amount of eight swing directions, $\bar{x}$ value means the joint tracking status amount average value.

The variance for each joint tracking amount is computed as

$$\sigma^2 = \frac{1}{8} \sum_{i=1}^{8} xi - \bar{x} \tag{2}$$

σ^2 value means the variance of each joint tracking status amount of eight swing directions.

Joint tracking status data of four swing postures of eight swing directions' average and variance is presented in Table 3. Table 3 illustrates that joints of SpineBase, SpineMid, Neck, Head, HipLeft, KneeLeft, HipRight, KneeRight, and SpineShoulder maximum average and minimize variance receive high average value and variance. The average of those joints' average is between 8.875 and 10, and the variance is between 0 and 1.6875. Statistic data of average value and variance value represents high tracking confident level. And joints of ShoulderLeft, ElbowLeft, WristLeft, HandLeft, ShoulderRight, ElbowRight, WristRight, HandRight, AnkleLeft, FootLeft, AnkleRight, FootRight, HandTipRight, ThumbLeft, HandTipRight, and ThumbRight are categorized into low tracking confident level since receiving low average value and high variance value.

Combine with the above three tables, joints of SpineBase, SpineMid, Neck, Head, HipLeft, KneeLeft, HipRight, KneeRight and SpineShoulder perform high tracking confident level, while could apply these joints 3D-dimension data to golf swing analytical system. Take ElbowLeft for example. The statistical data shows that the swing posture of swing_setup, ElbowLeft joint obtains nine out of 10 times accurate tracking data on swing directions of 3 and 4. On the swing posture of swing_Top, ElbowLeft joint obtains 10 times accurate tracking data on the swing directions of 1 and 9 out of 10 times on the swing directions of 4. On the swing posture of swing_impact, ElbowLeft joint obtains 10 times accurate tracking data on the swing directions of 1, 2 and 8, 9 out of 10 times on the swing directions of 3 and 4. On the swing posture of swing_Finish, ElbowLeft obtains 10 times accurate tracking data on the swing directions of 4, 5, and 6, and 9 out of 10 times on the swing directions of 3.

Without description all of the joints tracking status information, the two following tables show how to extract to value joint information. These two tables distinguish the joint tracking status data confident level from the different geometric figure. The circle (○) means joint tracking data receive high tracking confident level, the square (□) means joint tracking data receive moderate tracking confident level, triangle (▵) means joint tracking data receive low tracking confident level and the null cells means the data of the joint can't be applied to the application.

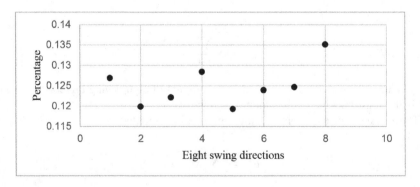

Fig. 5. Total joint tracking data of eight swing directions

3.4 Joints Weight Analysis

From the above discussion results (Fig. 5 and Tables 1, 2, and 3), it shows that joints of WristLeft, WristRight, HandLeft and HandRight have a big contribution to the full swing motion, but have poor performance for the small average value. Joints of WristLeft, WristRight, HandLeft, and HandRight should be weighted down when applying to the golf swing motion analysis system. Joints of SpineBase, SpineMid, Neck, Head, HipLeft, HipRight, SpineShoulder have highly visible and stable performance on the full swing motion. On the basis of golf characteristic, pelvis has important significance on a swing [8]. Thus, HipLeft and HipRight should be weighted up. Joints of ElbowLeft, ElbowRight, KneeLeft, KneeRight, AnkleLeft, AnkleRight, FootLeft, and FootRight receive high average value, also make an important contribution to golf swing should be weighted down. While HandTipLeft, HandTipRight, ThumbLeft, ThumbRight make little contribution to golf swing according to sports biomechanical principles [9].

Table 1. 10 participants joint tracking status data on Swing_Setup and Swing_Top postures of eight swing directions

JointName	Swing_Setup								Swing_Top							
	1	2	3	4	5	6	7	8	1	2	3	4	5	6	7	8
SpineBase	10	10	10	10	10	10	10	10	10	10	10	10	10	10	10	10
SpineMid	10	10	10	10	10	10	10	10	10	10	10	10	10	10	10	10
Neck	10	10	10	10	10	10	10	10	10	10	10	10	10	10	10	10
Head	10	10	10	10	10	10	10	10	10	10	10	8	10	10	10	10
ShoulderLeft	10	9	10	9	8	1	1	10	9	10	10	5	8	1	1	10
ElbowLeft	2	5	9	9	3	7	6	6	10	0	5	9	3	7	6	6
WristLeft	2	5	5	8	1	6	5	5	8	2	6	8	1	6	5	5
HandLeft	1	4	6	4	0	1	3	2	5	1	6	5	0	1	3	2
ShoulderRight	9	9	3	4	8	10	10	10	8	7	8	6	8	10	10	10
ElbowRight	1	4	5	4	4	7	6	6	8	6	3	5	4	7	6	6
WristRight	1	4	6	6	2	2	5	6	6	2	1	8	2	2	5	6
HandRight	0	3	5	3	1	1	4	5	2	0	2	8	1	1	4	5
HipLeft	10	10	10	10	10	10	10	10	10	10	10	10	10	10	10	10
KneeLeft	10	10	8	7	10	9	7	10	10	10	9	9	10	9	7	10
AnkleLeft	10	10	10	6	8	10	6	9	10	10	10	8	8	10	6	9
FootLeft	8	6	7	9	7	9	5	7	7	7	7	9	7	9	5	7
HipRight	10	10	10	10	10	10	10	10	10	10	10	10	10	10	10	10
KneeRight	10	10	5	10	10	10	9	10	10	9	9	8	10	10	9	10
AnkleRight	10	9	4	10	9	8	9	10	10	8	3	10	9	8	9	10
FootRight	9	8	5	8	9	7	7	7	8	7	8	9	9	7	7	7
SpineShoulder	10	10	10	10	10	10	10	10	10	10	10	10	10	10	10	10
HandTipLeft	10	10	10	10	4	7	7	10	8	7	7	9	4	7	7	10
ThumbLeft	10	10	10	10	4	7	6	10	7	6	6	7	4	7	6	10
HandTipRight	10	10	8	9	8	9	10	10	3	6	4	7	8	9	10	10
ThumbRight	10	8	8	9	8	9	10	10	2	6	4	7	8	9	10	10

Table 2. 10 participants' joint visibility status data on Swing_Impact and Swing_Finish postures of eight swing directions

JointName	Swing_Impact								Swing_Finish							
	1	2	3	4	5	6	7	8	1	2	3	4	5	6	7	8
SpineBase	10	10	10	10	10	10	10	10	10	10	10	10	10	10	10	10
SpineMid	10	10	10	10	10	10	10	10	10	10	10	10	10	10	10	10
Neck	10	10	10	10	10	10	10	10	10	10	10	10	10	10	10	10
Head	10	10	10	8	10	9	10	10	10	10	10	10	9	10	10	10
ShoulderLeft	10	10	9	5	9	5	2	10	9	9	7	8	10	9	9	10
ElbowLeft	10	10	9	9	3	7	5	10	4	4	9	10	10	10	8	4
WristLeft	10	10	7	8	1	2	5	10	1	2	6	10	10	10	7	3
HandLeft	9	5	6	5	0	2	4	7	1	0	2	10	9	7	4	4
ShoulderRight	10	8	5	6	6	9	9	10	8	9	9	8	4	0	8	10
ElbowRight	10	8	10	5	3	8	6	10	7	5	9	10	9	8	7	10
WristRight	9	7	6	8	3	6	7	9	5	4	6	9	8	2	8	7
HandRight	1	1	6	8	2	2	5	6	2	1	2	1	2	1	7	8
HipLeft	10	10	10	10	10	10	10	10	10	10	10	10	10	10	10	10
KneeLeft	10	10	10	9	9	9	7	10	8	10	10	9	10	9	9	7
AnkleLeft	10	10	10	8	9	9	5	8	9	9	10	8	7	10	7	9
FootLeft	9	6	8	9	7	8	7	7	10	7	9	7	6	6	9	10
HipRight	10	10	10	10	10	10	10	10	10	10	10	10	10	10	10	10
KneeRight	10	10	10	8	10	8	10	9	9	10	10	7	9	10	10	9
AnkleRight	10	9	6	10	8	7	8	10	10	10	9	8	8	9	9	8
FootRight	9	7	7	9	7	6	8	5	10	9	5	7	2	5	8	9
SpineShoulder	10	10	10	10	10	10	10	10	10	10	10	10	10	10	10	10
HandTipLeft	10	10	10	9	3	7	10	10	7	5	7	10	10	10	8	4
ThumbLeft	10	10	10	7	3	7	10	10	5	5	6	10	10	10	8	4
HandTipRight	10	10	9	7	6	10	9	10	7	4	8	10	10	10	9	10
ThumbRight	10	10	9	7	4	10	9	10	7	3	7	10	10	10	9	10

3.5   Total Joint Tracking Data of Eight Swing Directions

From what has been discussed above, the invalid joint of HandLeft and HandRight are wiped out of the statistical table. And the value joint tracking data is presented in Fig. 5. Figure 5 shows that swing directions 8 receive the highest joint tracking rate of 13.51%, while swing directions 5 receives the lowest joint tracking rate of 11.92%. This result can be applied to Multiple Kinect golf swing analytical system. When using two Kinects, we can locate the Kinect to swing directions 8 and 4, while Kinect should face directly to the user. While using three Kinect, we can locate the Kinect to swing directions 8, 4 and 1, while Kinect should face directly to the user. The more Kinect used, we can locate the Kinect following the law which shows in Fig. 5.

Table 3. Joints tracking status average and variance value

JointName	Average				Variance			
	Setup	Top	Impact	Finish	Setup	Top	Impact	Finish
SpineBase	10.000	10.000	10.000	10.000	0.000	0.000	0.000	0.000
SpineMid	10.000	10.000	10.000	10.000	0.000	0.000	0.000	0.000
Neck	10.000	10.000	10.000	10.000	0.000	0.000	0.000	0.000
Head	10.000	9.750	9.625	9.875	0.000	0.438	0.484	0.109
ShoulderLeft	10.000	6.750	7.500	8.875	13.438	13.438	8.250	0.859
ElbowLeft	5.875	5.750	7.875	7.375	5.609	8.938	6.109	7.234
WristLeft	4.625	5.125	6.625	6.125	4.234	5.609	11.484	12.359
HandLeft	2.625	2.875	4.750	4.625	3.484	4.359	6.938	11.984
ShoulderRight	7.875	8.375	7.875	7.000	6.859	1.984	3.359	9.750
ElbowRight	4.625	5.625	7.500	8.125	2.984	2.234	6.000	2.609
WristRight	4.000	4.000	6.875	6.125	3.750	5.750	3.359	4.859
HandRight	2.750	2.875	3.875	3.000	3.188	6.109	6.359	7.000
HipLeft	10.000	10.000	10.000	10.000	0.000	0.000	0.000	0.000
KneeLeft	8.875	9.250	9.250	9.000	1.609	0.938	0.938	1.000
AnkleLeft	8.625	8.875	8.625	8.625	2.734	1.859	2.484	1.234
FootLeft	7.250	7.250	7.625	8.000	1.688	1.438	0.984	2.500
HipRight	10.000	10.000	10.000	10.000	0.000	0.000	0.000	0.000
KneeRight	9.250	9.375	9.500	9.250	2.688	0.484	0.750	0.938
AnkleRight	8.625	8.375	8.500	8.875	3.484	4.734	2.000	0.609
FootRight	7.500	7.750	7.250	6.875	1.500	0.688	1.688	6.359
SpineShoulder	10.000	10.000	10.000	10.000	0.000	0.000	0.000	0.000
HandTipLeft	8.500	7.375	8.625	7.625	4.500	2.734	5.484	4.734
ThumbLeft	8.375	6.625	8.375	7.250	4.984	2.484	5.734	5.688
HandTipRight	9.250	7.125	8.875	8.500	0.688	6.109	2.109	4.000
ThumbRight	9.000	7.000	8.625	8.250	0.750	7.250	3.984	5.438
Average	**7.905**	**7.605**	**8.310**	**8.135**				

4   Discussion

This study evaluated the human skeletal joint tracking status information with Microsoft Kinect sensor. Low cost, makerless, high tracking accurately makes Kinect be most popular motion captures sensor. Though Kinect does the good performance in the game field, still contains the disadvantage, like low frames, self-occlusion, data jitter.

Destelle et al. [10] proposed to fuse the joint position information obtained from the popular Kinect sensor with more precise estimation of body segment orientations provided by a small number of wearable inertial sensors. The use of inertial sensors can help to address many of the well-known limitations of the Kinect sensor and enhance the joint angle measurement accuracy. We assessed the skeletal joint tracking amount of different swing directions and extract the valuable joint data to form an integral skeleton.

Table 4. Value of joint swing posture on setup and top swing postures

JointName	Swing_Setup								Swing_Top							
	1	2	3	4	5	6	7	8	1	2	3	4	5	6	7	8
SpineBase	O	O	O	O	O	O	O	O	O	O	O	O	O	O	O	O
SpineMid	O	O	O	O	O	O	O	O	O	O	O	O	O	O	O	O
Neck	O	O	O	O	O	O	O	O	O	O	O	O		O	O	O
Head	O	O	O	O	O	O	O	O	O	O	O			O	O	O
ShoulderLeft	O	O	O	O	□			O	O	O	O	△	□			O
ElbowLeft		△	O	O		□	△	△	O		△	O		□	△	△
WristLeft		△	△	□		△	△	△	□		△	□		△	△	△
HandLeft			△						△		△	△				
ShoulderRight	O	O			□	O	O	O	□	□	□	△	□		O	O
ElbowRight			△			□	△	△	□	△		△		□	△	△
WristRight			△	△			△	△	△			□			△	△
HandRight			△					△				□				△
HipLeft	O	O	O	O	O	O	O	O	O	O	O	O	O	O	O	O
KneeLeft	O	O	□	O	□	O	□	O	O	O	O	O	O	O	□	O
AnkleLeft	O	O	O	△	□	O	△	O	O	O	O	□	□	O	△	O
FootLeft	□	△	□	O	□	O	△	□	□	□	□	O	□	O	△	□
HipRight	O	O	O	O	O	O	O	O	O	O	O	O	O	O	O	O
KneeRight	O	O	△	O	O	O	O	O	O	O	O	O	O	O	O	O
AnkleRight	O	O		O	O	□	O	O	O	O	□	O	O	□	O	O
FootRight	O	□	△	□	O	□	□	□	□	□	□	O	□	O	□	□
SpineShoulder	O	O	O	O	O	O	O	O	O	O	O	O	O	O	O	O
HandTipLeft	O	O	O	O		□	□	O	□	□	□	O		□	□	O
ThumbLeft	O	O	O	O		□	△	O	□	△	△	□		□	△	O
HandTipRight	O	O	□	O	□	O	O	O		△		□	□	O	O	O
ThumbRight	O	□	□	O	□	O	O	O		△		□	□	O	O	O

Table 5. Value of joint swing posture on impact and finish swing postures

JointName	Swing_Impact								Swing_Finish							
	1	2	3	4	5	6	7	8	1	2	3	4	5	6	7	8
SpineBase	O	O	O	O	O	O	O	O	O	O	O	O	O	O	O	O
SpineMid	O	O	O	O	O	O	O	O	O	O	O	O	O	O	O	O
Neck	O	O	O	O	O	O	O	O	O	O	O	O	O	O	O	O
Head	O	O	O		O	O	O	O	O	O	O	O	O	O	O	O
ShoulderLeft	O	O	O	△	O	△		O	O		□	□	O	O	O	O
ElbowLeft	O	O	O	O		□	△	O			O	O	O	O	□	
WristLeft	O	O	□	□			△	O			△	O	O	O	□	
HandLeft	O	△	△	△				□			O	O	□			
ShoulderRight	O	□	△	△	△	O	O	O	□	O	O	□			□	O
ElbowRight	O	□	O	△		□	△	O	□	△	O	O	O	□	□	O
WristRight	O	□	△	□		△	□	O	△		△	O	□		□	□
HandRight			△	□			△	△							□	□
HipLeft	O	O	O	O	O	O	O	O	O	O	O	O	O	O	O	O
KneeLeft	O	O	O	O	O	O	□	O	□	O	O	O	O	O	□	O
AnkleLeft	O	O	O	□	O	O	△	□	O	O	O	□	□	O	□	O
FootLeft	O	△	□	O	□	□	□	□	O	□	O	□	△	△	O	O
HipRight	O	O	O	O	O	O	O	O	O	O	O	O	O	O	O	O
KneeRight	O	O	O	□	O	□	O	O	O	O	O	□	O	O	O	O
AnkleRight	O	O	△	O	□	□	□	O	O	O	O	□	□	O	O	□
FootRight	O	□	□	O	□	△	O	△	O	O	△	□		△	O	O
SpineShoulder	O	O	O	O	O	O	O	O	O	O	O	O	O	O	O	O
HandTipLeft	O	O	O	O		□	O	O	□	△	□	O	O	O	O	□
ThumbLeft	O	O	O	□		□	O	O	△	△	△	O	O	O	□	
HandTipRight	O	O	O	□	△	O	O	O	□		□	O	O	O	O	O
ThumbRight	O	O	O	□		O	O	O	□		□	O	O	O	O	O

To ascertain the joint accurate position is common of two studies. Zhang et al. [11] displayed a method of scoring time-sequential postures of the golf swing. Unlike their study, they extracted the time-sequential posture of golf swing features when swing was performed and used HMM-NF models for scoring. They proposed methods can be implemented to identify and score the golf swing effectively with up to 80% accuracy rate.

The results presented here demonstrate the feasibility of using Kinect to analyze golf swing motion. Above analysis and conclusion indicate that human body skeletal joints can be capture most of the joints which extract from Kinect sensor. Tables 1 and 2 show that, different swing directions due to different joint tracking amount. Statistical analyses show Kinect can be placed an ideal location for obtaining high joint tracking confident, while this conclusion can be applied to the golf swing.

5   Conclusions

The overall goal of this study was to investigate visibility of each joint obtained by Kinect on four swing postures of eight swing directions. The results indicate that different swing directions due to different joint tracking amount of swing posture. Our study found that valuable joints can be extracted from various swing directions posture to fill a whole human skeleton. We propose a method of complementary joints which can enhance the valuable joint amount. This research can be applied to Multiple-Kinect golf swing analytical system to enhance the system reliability and robustness.

Acknowledgments. Guangzhou science research special project (201607010308); Guangzhou polytechnic of sport provided the experiment subjects and filed.

References

1. Chu, Y., Sell, T.C., Lephart, S.M.: The relationship between biomechanical variables and driving performance during the golf swing. J. Sports Sci. **28**(11), 1251–1259 (2010)
2. Whyte, E.F., Moran, K., Shortt, C.P., Marshall, B.: The influence of reduced hamstring length on patellofemoral joint stress during squatting in healthy male adults. Gait Posture **31**(1), 47–51 (2010)
3. Van Csamp, C.M., Hayes, L.B.: Assessing and increasing physical activity. J. Appl. Behav. Anal. **45**(4), 871–875 (2012)
4. Yeung, L.F., Cheng, K.C., Fong, C.H., Lee, W.C., Tong, K.Y.: Evaluation of the Microsoft Kinect as a clinical assessment tool of body sway. Gait Posture **40**(4), 532–538 (2014)
5. Høilund, C., Krüger, V., Moeslund, T.B.: Evaluation of human body tracking system for gesture-based programming of industrial robots. In: 2012 7th IEEE Conference on Industrial Electronics and Applications (ICIEA), pp. 477–480. IEEE, July 2012
6. Wang, Q., Kurillo, G., Ofli, F., Bajcsy, R.: Evaluation of pose tracking accuracy in the first and second generations of microsoft Kinect. In: 2015 International Conference on Healthcare Informatics (ICHI), pp. 380–389. IEEE, October 2015

7. Williamson, B., LaViola, J., Roberts, T., Garrity, P.: Multi-Kinect tracking for dismounted soldier training. In: Proceedings of the Interservice/Industry Training, Simulation, and Education Conference (I/ITSEC), pp. 1727–1735, December 2012
8. Lephart, S.M., Smoliga, J.M., Myers, J.B., Sell, T.C., Tsai, Y.S.: An eight-week golf-specific exercise program improves physical characteristics, swing mechanics, and golf performance in recreational golfers. J. Strength Cond. Res. **21**(3), 860–869 (2007)
9. Burden, M.A., Grimshaw, P.N., Wallace, E.S.: Hip and shoulder rotations during the golf swing of sub-10 handicap players. J. Sports Sci. **16**(2), 165–176 (1998)
10. Destelle, F., Ahmadi, A., O'Connor, N.E., Moran, K., Chatzitofis, A., Zarpalas, D., Daras, P.: Low-cost accurate skeleton tracking based on fusion of Kinect and wearable inertial sensors. In: 2014 22nd European Signal Processing Conference (EUSIPCO), pp. 371–375. IEEE, September 2014
11. Zhang, L., Hsieh, J.C., Wang, J.: A Kinect-based golf swing classification system using HMM and Neuro-Fuzzy. In: 2012 International Conference on Computer Science and Information Processing (CSIP), pp. 1163–1166. IEEE, August 2012

Analysis and Modeling of Fatigue During Weight-Bearing Walking

Zhongqi Liu, Ruiming Zhang, and Qianxiang Zhou[✉]

Key Laboratory for Biomechanics and Mechanobiology of the Ministry
of Education, School of Biological Science and Medical Engineering,
Beihang University, Beijing 100191, China
{liuzhongqi, zqxg}@buaa. edu. cn

Abstract. The objective of this study was to discuss the mechanical characteristics and distributed regularity of shoulder, waist and back of the human body through the experiment of weight-bearing walking; to establish the dynamic fatigue model based on stress regularity to provide a reference for the task design of weight-bearing walking and the ergonomics simulation of backpack. Thirteen healthy people participated the experiment that was recruited by internet and they were all men. Every subject made a 21 min weight-bearing walking on the treadmill with the speed of 5 km/h and a 15 kg load. The pressure data of their shoulder, back and waist was collected by pressure measuring system and the feeling of fatigue of the above three body parts of the subjects was asked every 3 min by using Borg scales. The results showed that the force of the subjects' left shoulder and right shoulder was different and the force was higher on one shoulder while it was lower on another shoulder. The stress regularities of waist and back were similar to the shoulders and it was higher on left side of some subjects while it was higher on right side of other subjects. Also the stress on waist and back was different. The stress on shoulder was much higher than it was on waist and back while the stress on back was the lowest. The impulse was calculated based on the stress data of three body parts. The model was established based that the impulse was as dependent variable and the feeling of subjects' fatigue was as independent variables. It showed a strong linear relationship between the pressure impulse of the three body parts and the feeling of subjects' fatigue. The subjects' fatigue could be well predicted during weight-bearing walking by using the linear model of impulse and subjective fatigue. So the conclusion of this study can be made that the stress on shoulder, back and waist is not asymmetric and it was great difference on the body three parts. The shoulder is not only the main bearing pressure part, but also the easiest part of fatigue. The fatigue can be well predicted during weight-bearing walking by the linear model that combine impulse and the feeling of subjects' fatigue.

Keywords: Weight-bearing walking · Fatigue · Mechanical characteristics · Impulse · Modeling

© Springer International Publishing AG 2017
V.G. Duffy (Ed.): DHM 2017, Part I, LNCS 10286, pp. 127–140, 2017.
DOI: 10.1007/978-3-319-58463-8_12

1 Introduction

Weight-bearing Walking is closely related to people's lives, for example, March training for troops, workers' bear-loading, carrying the backpacks to school of students and so on. In the case of weight-bearing walking, the body will make the appropriate adjustments to achieve the body's balance and stability because of the pressure. Research showed that a series of injury problems will incur if people bear load too much or bear the weight for a long time [1–3]. Related medical research also proved that it is easy to cause foot blisters, stress fractures, lower limb joint pain, back muscle strain and the waist dish outstanding disease Under the condition of weight-bearing walking for a long time [4, 5]. Research also found that weight bearing cause many adverse effects to children's growth and development [6, 7]. Therefore, to study on weight-bearing walking is significant to improve the design of backpack and reduce the body's fatigue.

In the relevant research field, studying the effect of weight-bearing walking on the human body took a large part, For example, the effects of weight - bearing walking on human gait and plantar pressure. However, weight-bearing walking is a behavior which caused human fatigue and if we carry out the research from the point of view of the composition and causes of fatigue, the results will be more practical significance, especially it provides a theoretical basis for the ergonomic design of weight-bearing. At present, there are four theories of great impact in this field: Levin's conservation model [8], QquF model [9], theory of Fatigue Motivation [10], and clue competition [11]. Levin's conservation model is a theoretical model of nursing work fatigue, it holds that fatigue is the behavior of the body to protect itself in short supply, but also a clue to the body's ability to imbalance. The QquF model is proposed by Angelique et al. The model is the relationship between external stimuli and fatigue. The theory suggests that when the attractiveness of external stimuli increases, people's feeling of fatigue will be reduced; when the external stimulus load increases, people's feeling of fatigue will be increase. Attractions of external stimuli mean that quality is negatively correlated with fatigue; Load of external stimuli means that quality and fatigue are positively correlated. The theory of fatigue motivation is a kind of theory about the relationship between motivation, fatigue and ability consumption, which was put forward by the American psychologist Maier RF based on previous experiments. And, the theory possesses a certain dialectical, cognitive color and a powerful explanation to phenomenon of life. Pennebaker proposed the clue competition, which is a theory of external stimulus and fatigue and holds that the result of clue competition is a curve relationship between external stimuli and fatigue. Four theories above fundamentally advance a core idea that fatigue is caused by multiple factors together. But at present, the mechanism of human fatigue in motion state has not been well explained, leading the limitations to describe the fatigue state. And it can't reflect the interrelationships between the various mechanisms.

In this paper, subjective and objective way was used together and the weight-bearing walking was as the research object. The Borg scale was used to quantify the fatigue caused by weight-bearing walking of young people. And then we established forecasting model of the fatigue of shoulder, waist and back by analyzing the characteristics of them.

2 Method

2.1 Participants

Sixteen undergraduates participated in the experiment who 3 of them are pre-experimental subjects and they were used to verify the feasibility of the experiment and improve the experimental design. Therefore, there were 13 participants in the formal experiment. All 16 participant were male who their age was 22–25 years, height was 170 ± 4.1 cm, weight was 72.5 ± 4.2 kg, and all of them were in good health. Subjects are required to avoid strenuous exercise before 24 h prior to the experiment and have a fully rest for fear that it would cause fatigue accumulation.

2.2 Apparatus and Task

The subjects were asked to walk on the treadmill carrying a 15 kg weight knapsack. The weight of 15 kg was a appropriate load based on pre-experiment and the load could avoid too light to lead subjects' fatigue and also could avoid too heavy causing body damage. The ground slope was zero degree. The subjects' walking speed 5 km/h and the walking time was 21 min with zero degree of treadmill's slope. The walking speed of 5 km/h referred to the speed requirements of troops March. Experiment time was set of 21 min to allow the subject to achieve a high degree of fatigue during the experiment without losing its physical limit. When the subjects asked to stop walking, in other words, the subjects couldn't continue walking with that walking speed, the experiment was over.

The force values of the shoulder, waist and back during walking were measured by a pressure measuring device. The arrangement of the pressure sensors was shown in Fig. 1. Every 3 min, the Borg scale (see Table 1) was used to inquire the fatigue feeling of the subjects. And the subjects were asked to have an adaptive training before the experiment and wear safety rope during the experiment. When the subjects feel that it's hard to go on the experiment and appear unsteady gait, pale or chest tightness, etc., the experiment should stop immediately. Therefore, two security guards must be on the scene. One was in front of and the other was behind the platform. The experimental scene was shown as Fig. 2.

Fig. 1. The arrangement of force sensors

Table 1. Comfort evaluation forms of shoulders, waist and backs

Body part	Subjective feeling				
	Best	Better	Normal	Ordinary	Poor
Shoulders	Feels a constriction	A little pain	Painful	A strong pain	A strong pain
Waist	Slightly oppressive	Oppressive	Oppressive obvious	A little pain	A strong pain
Backs	Slightly oppressive	Oppressive obvious	A little pain	Painful	A strong pain
Score	0–2	3–4	5–6	7–8	9–10

Note: 0 means no fatigue. 10 means fatigue limit

Fig. 2. Weight-bearing walking experiment

2.3 Procedure

When the subjects arrived at the experiment site, they performed the experiment according to the following process:

(1) The subjects were instructed to know the procedure and the Borg scale;
(2) The pressure sensor was fixed on every subject;
(3) Set the slope of treadmill to 0° and launch it to start the experiment;
(4) Subjects were asked the degree of fatigue feeling with Borg scale every 3 min and the data was recorded by experimenters.
(5) The experiment was stopped After 21 min of walking of subjects.

3   Results

The average pressure on the left side of the shoulder of the 10 subjects was calculated every 3 min, as shown in Table 2.

Table 2. The pressure of subjects' left shoulder (N)

Time (min)	Subject number									
	1	2	3	4	5	6	7	8	9	10
0	0	0	0	0	0	0	0	0	0	0
3	5.22	3.53	3.60	6.51	7.32	5.22	3.53	3.60	6.51	7.32
6	5.10	3.62	4.81	6.63	7.65	5.10	3.62	4.81	6.63	7.65
9	5.31	3.83	4.79	6.81	7.21	5.31	3.83	4.79	6.81	7.21
12	4.98	3.45	3.49	7.68	7.30	4.98	3.45	3.49	7.68	7.30
15	5.22	3.66	3.57	7.71	8.45	5.22	3.66	3.57	7.71	8.45
18	5.33	3.58	4.70	6.64	7.44	5.33	3.58	4.70	6.64	7.44
21	5.40	3.70	3.88	6.80	7.79	5.40	3.70	3.88	6.80	7.79

Similarly, the average pressure of the right shoulder could be calculated and the result was shown in Table 3

Table 3. The pressure of subjects' right shoulder (N)

Time (min)	Subject number									
	1	2	3	4	5	6	7	8	9	10
0	0	0	0	0	0	0	0	0	0	0
3	4.90	7.10	6.33	3.95	4.54	5.23	5.78	3.87	5.44	4.56
6	4.10	5.99	7.10	4.68	3.90	4.67	6.10	4.78	5.89	5.10
9	3.90	6.43	6.65	4.56	4.78	4.98	5.44	4.16	5.99	4.34
12	4.20	5.67	6.22	4.19	3.99	3.67	5.87	4.46	6.21	4.89
15	4.35	6.57	7.21	3.56	4.56	4.78	5.55	4.88	5.87	4.51
18	3.76	5.40	6.65	4.21	3.32	4.57	5.10	4.31	6.22	4.76
21	4.18	5.67	6.36	4.76	4.24	4.10	6.79	5.10	5.19	4.11

Tables 2 and 3 showed that the force on subjects' left shoulder and right shoulder was inconsistent during the weight-bearing walking. But there was a common characteristic of all subjects that the force on one shoulder is smaller and the force of other shoulder is larger. It was also different of the pressure on shoulder of different subjects.

In the same way, the pressure of the waist and back of 10 subjects were calculated as shown in Tables 4, 5, 6, and 7.

Seen from the data of Table 4, 5, 6, and 7, it could be found that the waist and back's force regularities are similar to shoulders'. Furthermore, there was no rule of the force on the same side (left or right) of different people. Specifically, some subjects had a larger stress on left shoulder and a smaller force on right shoulder while others are the opposite. Meanwhile, the pressure on the waist and back of each subject were also different.

Two characteristics could be found from the data of Tables 2, 3, 4, 5, 6, and 7. The first was that the pressure on waist is much smaller than that of shoulder while the force on the back is smaller than waist. The reason for this phenomenon was that the

Table 4. The pressure of left side of subjects' waist (N)

Time (min)	Subject number									
	1	2	3	4	5	6	7	8	9	10
0	0	0	0	0	0	0	0	0	0	0
3	2.31	1.01	0.76	2.10	1.11	1.67	2.57	1.03	2.43	0.89
6	1.78	0.98	0.96	2.05	1.24	1.48	2.35	1.15	1.78	1.01
9	2.65	1.32	0.87	1.98	1.35	1.79	1.98	1.08	2.10	0.91
12	2.43	1.44	1.13	2.22	0.89	1.97	2.13	0.87	2.06	0.98
15	1.67	0.76	0.88	1.76	1.01	1.55	2.11	0.96	1.98	0.96
18	2.19	0.99	1.06	2.37	0.94	1.56	2.47	1.20	1.86	1.13
21	2.57	1.21	1.01	2.08	0.91	1.68	2.15	0.79	2.01	1.02

Table 5. The pressure of right side of subjects' waist (N)

Time (min)	Subject number									
	1	2	3	4	5	6	7	8	9	10
0	0	0	0	0	0	0	0	0	0	0
3	0.87	2.57	2.22	0.97	2.98	2.56	1.22	2.31	1.13	2.42
6	0.79	2.78	2.01	0.85	2.78	2.41	1.26	2.01	1.21	2.57
9	1.01	2.63	2.10	1.01	2.76	2.61	1.16	2.14	1.09	2.64
12	1.11	2.43	1.98	0.97	2.57	2.72	1.07	2.12	1.06	2.31
15	0.96	2.32	2.01	0.92	2.53	2.47	1.36	2.25	0.97	2.58
18	0.89	2.53	2.15	0.88	2.87	2.58	1.18	2.09	1.15	2.68
21	0.93	2.68	2.12	1.03	2.82	2.60	1.25	2.18	1.05	2.41

Table 6. The pressure of left side of subjects' back (N)

Time (min)	Subject number									
	1	2	3	4	5	6	7	8	9	10
0	0	0	0	0	0	0	0	0	0	0
3	0.57	0.89	1.01	0.51	0.78	1.12	0.58	1.13	0.72	1.02
6	0.68	0.78	0.98	0.52	0.84	1.05	0.76	1.21	0.64	0.88
9	0.62	0.84	0.89	0.64	0.73	0.97	0.67	1.07	0.58	0.98
12	0.53	0.83	1.10	0.63	0.72	1.08	0.52	1.05	0.76	0.97
15	0.59	0.75	1.03	0.52	0.81	1.03	0.64	1.01	0.66	1.10
18	0.63	0.78	0.92	0.56	0.83	0.89	0.53	1.14	0.69	1.03
21	0.61	0.87	0.87	0.53	0.76	0.97	0.56	1.05	0.59	1.07

shoulder is the main load-bearing area during weight-bearing walking. The pressure sensor on the shoulder was easier to fix than the waist and back and was always close to the surface of clothing during the experiment. The force on the waist and back was

Table 7. The pressure of right side of subjects' back (N)

Time (min)	Subject number									
	1	2	3	4	5	6	7	8	9	10
0	0	0	0	0	0	0	0	0	0	0
3	0.97	1.03	0.58	1.12	1.21	0.76	0.89	0.78	1.14	0.54
6	1.01	1.06	0.67	1.04	1.16	0.82	0.79	0.86	1.04	0.62
9	0.87	0.96	0.62	1.16	1.17	0.83	0.85	0.63	0.96	0.58
12	0.92	0.91	0.70	1.01	1.08	0.68	0.92	0.84	1.03	0.52
15	0.95	0.85	0.72	1.09	1.14	0.72	0.86	0.75	1.06	0.68
18	1.03	1.12	0.59	0.95	1.01	0.70	0.88	0.82	1.14	0.53
21	1.05	1.04	0.68	1.07	1.04	0.83	0.83	0.77	1.13	0.51

difficult to measure by sensor. On the one hand, during the experiment, limited by sensors' area, subjects' slightly shaking caused that the pressure sensor deviates from its original position or slack and it couldn't be completely contacted with the body. The subject's subjective fatigue score of the shoulder was higher than back and waist. That is to say, the main cause of fatigue was that the shoulders suffer sustained high-intensity pressure, which leading to the whole body fatigue. This proved that the shoulder is the most vulnerable part in the weight-bearing walking, which is consistent with the relevant research results. The second characteristic was that there is no consistency of the stress on the experimenters' shoulder, waist, back. In the other words, when the stress on shoulder of one subject was higher than anther subject, it couldn't make sure that the magnitude of stress on waist of one person is larger than another person. The reason was that each human is an independent individual and there is no exactly same man. Meanwhile, stress-bearing parts were not only the shoulder, waist and back.

4   The Model of Fatigue Evaluation

Impulse of calculus algorithm as follows:

$$I = \int_{t1}^{t2} fdt \qquad (1)$$

Where "I" is the impulse of the force, "t1" and "t2" are the time, and "f" is the force.

When the value of the force f was the average, the impulse of the force I was $I = f \times (t_2 - t_1)$. Taking into account the degree of fatigue would increase with the increase of time, the product of pressure of shoulder, waist, back and time could be calculated every 3 min. The product result could be regarded as a factor in the fatigue evaluation model. The Tables 8, 9, 10, 11, 12, and 13 showed the product which is the result of multiply time by the force of every part on human.

Table 8. The impulse of larger force side of subjects' shoulder (Ns)

Time (min)	Subject number									
	1	2	3	4	5	6	7	8	9	10
0	0	0	0	0	0	0	0	0	0	0
3	939	1278	1139	1171	1317	1242	1040	1062	1497	963
6	1857	2356	2417	2365	2694	2359	2138	2196	2775	2061
9	2813	3513	3614	3591	3992	3675	3117	3241	4120	3180
12	3709	4534	4734	4973	5306	4915	4174	4318	5466	4181
15	4649	5716	6031	6361	6827	6273	5173	5416	6942	5338
18	5608	6688	7228	7556	8166	7470	6091	6568	8262	6397
21	6580	7709	8373	8780	9568	8587	7313	7743	9682	7513

Table 9. The impulse of smaller force side of subjects' shoulder (Ns)

Time (min)	Subject number									
	1	2	3	4	5	6	7	8	9	10
0	0	0	0	0	0	0	0	0	0	0
3	882	1278	648	711	817	941	758	697	979	821
6	1620	2356	1514	1553	1519	1782	1571	1557	2039	1739
9	2322	3514	2376	2374	2380	2678	2349	2306	3118	2520
12	3078	4534	3004	3128	3098	3339	2950	3109	4235	3400
15	3861	5717	3647	3769	3919	4199	3730	3987	5292	4212
18	4538	6689	4493	4527	4516	5022	4433	4763	6412	5069
21	5290	7709	5191	5384	5279	5760	5211	5681	7346	5809

Table 10. The impulse of larger force side of subjects' waist (Ns)

Time (min)	Subject number									
	1	2	3	4	5	6	7	8	9	10
0	0	0	0	0	0	0	0	0	0	0
3	416	463	400	378	536	461	463	416	437	436
6	736	963	761	747	1037	895	963	778	758	898
9	1213	1436	1139	1103	1534	1364	1436	1163	1136	1373
12	1651	1874	1496	1503	1996	1854	1874	1544	1507	1789
15	1951	2291	1858	1820	2452	2299	2291	1949	1863	2254
18	2345	2747	2245	2246	2968	2763	2747	2326	2198	2736
21	2808	3229	2626	2621	3476	3231	3229	2718	2560	3170

Table 11. The impulse of smaller force side of subjects' waist (Ns)

Time (min)	Subject number									
	1	2	3	4	5	6	7	8	9	10
0	0	0	0	0	0	0	0	0	0	0
3	157	182	137	175	200	301	220	185	203	160
6	299	358	310	328	423	567	446	392	421	342
9	481	596	466	509	666	889	655	587	617	682
12	680	855	670	684	826	1244	848	743	808	859
15	853	992	828	850	1008	1523	1093	916	983	1031
18	1013	1170	1019	1008	1177	1804	1305	1132	1190	1235
21	1181	1388	1201	1193	1341	2106	1530	1274	1379	1418

Table 12. The impulse of larger force side of subjects' back (Ns)

Time (min)	Subject number									
	1	2	3	4	5	6	7	8	9	10
0	0	0	0	0	0	0	0	0	0	0
3	175	185	182	202	202	202	160	203	205	184
6	356	376	358	389	410	391	302	421	392	342
9	513	549	518	598	621	565	455	614	565	518
12	679	713	716	779	815	760	621	803	751	693
15	850	866	902	976	1021	945	776	985	941	891
18	1035	1067	1067	1147	1202	1105	934	1190	1147	1076
21	1224	1255	1224	1339	1390	1280	1084	1379	1350	1269

Table 13. The impulse of smaller force side of subjects' back (Ns)

Time (min)	Subject number									
	1	2	3	4	5	6	7	8	9	10
0	0	0	0	0	0	0	0	0	0	0
3	103	160	104	92	140	137	104	140	130	97
6	225	301	225	185	292	284	241	295	245	209
9	337	452	337	301	423	434	362	409	349	313
12	432	601	463	414	553	556	455	560	486	407
15	538	736	592	508	698	686	571	695	605	529
18	652	877	698	608	848	812	666	842	729	625
21	761	1033	821	704	985	961	767	981	835	716

The Borg score and impulses of the bigger force value and the smaller force value on each part of human were plotted. As shown in Figs. 3, 4, 5, 6, 7, and 8.

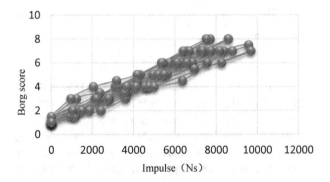

Fig. 3. The scatter diagram of Borg score and impulse of larger force side of shoulder

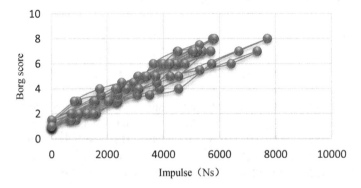

Fig. 4. The scatter diagram of Borg score and impulse of smaller force side of shoulder

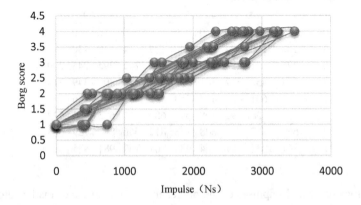

Fig. 5. The scatter diagram of Borg score and impulse of larger force side of waist

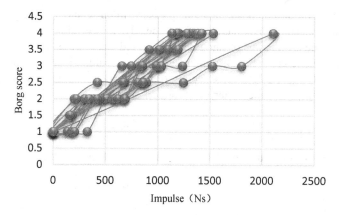

Fig. 6. The scatter diagram of Borg score and impulse of smaller force side of waist

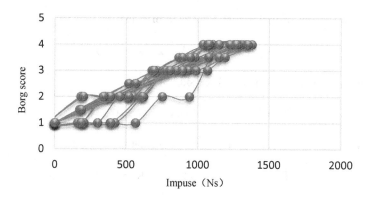

Fig. 7. The scatter diagram of Borg score and impulse of larger force side of waist

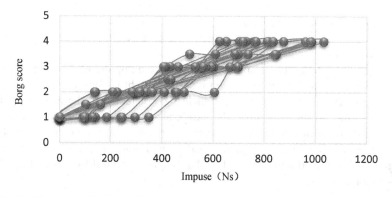

Fig. 8. The scatter diagram of Borg score and impulse of smaller force side of back

The above graphics indicate that the pressure impulse has a strong linear relationship with the subjective feeling of fatigue. Therefore, single linear regression models of fatigue evaluation of shoulder, waist and back were established that the independent variable is the pressure impulse I of the shoulder, waist and back, and the dependent variable is the subjective feeling of fatigue B, as shown in Eqs. 2–7.

The fatigue model of the larger force side of shoulder:

$$B = 1.0 \times 10^{-3}I + 1.223 \quad R = 0.958 \tag{2}$$

The fatigue model of the smaller force side of shoulder:

$$B = 1.0 \times 10^{-3}I + 1.271 \quad R = 0.944 \tag{3}$$

The fatigue model of the larger force side of waist:

$$B = 1.0 \times 10^{-3}I + 1.029 \quad R = 0.947 \tag{4}$$

The fatigue model of the smaller force side of waist:

$$B = 2.0 \times 10^{-3}I + 1.152 \quad R = 0.907 \tag{5}$$

The fatigue model of the larger force side of back:

$$B = 2.0 \times 10^{-3}I + 0.859 \quad R = 0.934 \tag{6}$$

The fatigue model of the smaller force side of back:

$$B = 4.0 \times 10^{-3}I + 0.907 \quad R = 0.925 \tag{7}$$

The fatigue value of shoulder, waist and back of the remaining three persons were calculated with the above model. The value was compared to the subject feeling of fatigue during the experiment of the corresponding body part. The error could be used to verify the model's precision or reliability. The fatigue value of model and the value of experiment were shown in Tables 14, 15, and 16. It could be seen that the error of each model is less than ±1.3, which satisfies the accuracy requirement and prove the model's precision.

Considered the definition of impulse in physics, the impulse of shoulder, waist and back were chose as the fatigue evaluation index of weight-bearing walking. Impulse is the cumulative effect of force on time, which is consistent with the increase in body fatigue over time. At the same time, the independent variable of the model combines the relation of force and time, which fatigue is result from a complex, multi-factor working together. The fatigue evaluation model's high linearity showed that the model is feasible and it proved a theoretical fact that fatigue is caused by a complicated and multi - factor common.

Table 14. The verification result of the first subject

Time (min)	Experiment value			Model value					
	Shoulder	Waist	Back	Shoulder (larger)	Shoulder (smaller)	Waist (larger)	Waist (smaller)	Back (larger)	Back (smaller)
0	1.0	1.0	1.0	1.1	1.1	1.0	1.0	0.8	0.8
3	2.0	1.0	1.0	2.0	2.1	1.4	1.4	1.3	1.3
6	3.0	1.5	1.5	2.8	2.9	1.8	1.8	1.8	1.8
9	3.5	2.0	1.5	3.6	3.7	2.2	2.3	2.2	2.2
12	4.0	2.5	2.0	4.4	4.6	2.7	2.8	2.7	2.5
15	5.0	3.0	2.5	5.3	5.4	3.0	3.4	3.1	3.1
18	7.0	3.5	3.0	6.0	6.3	3.4	3.7	3.6	3.5
21	7.0	4.0	4.0	7.0	7.2	3.9	4.2	4.0	4.0

Table 15. The verification result of the second subject

Time (min)	Experiment value			Model value					
	Shoulder	Waist	Back	Shoulder (larger)	Shoulder (smaller)	Waist (larger)	Waist (smaller)	Back (larger)	Back (smaller)
0	1.0	1.0	1.0	1.1	1.1	1.0	1.0	0.8	0.8
3	2.0	1.5	1.5	2.1	2.0	1.3	1.3	1.3	1.2
6	4.0	2.0	1.5	3.3	3.0	1.7	1.7	1.6	1.7
9	4.5	2.0	2.0	4.1	3.9	2.0	2.1	2.1	2.1
12	5.0	2.5	2.5	5.0	4.7	2.3	2.5	2.6	2.5
15	5.5	3.0	3.0	6.0	5.4	2.6	2.7	3.0	3.0
18	6.0	3.5	3.0	7.3	6.0	2.9	3.1	3.3	3.4
21	7.0	4.0	4.0	8.2	6.9	3.3	3.7	3.9	3.9

Table 16. The verification result of the third subject

Time (min)	Experiment value			Model value					
	Shoulder	Waist	Back	Shoulder (larger)	Shoulder (smaller)	Waist (larger)	Waist (smaller)	Back (larger)	Back (smaller)
0	1.0	1.0	1.0	1.1	1.1	1.0	1.0	0.8	0.8
3	2.0	2.0	2.0	2.0	2.2	1.5	1.3	1.1	1.4
6	3.0	2.0	2.5	3.1	3.0	1.8	1.7	1.5	1.7
9	4.0	2.5	2.5	4.0	4.2	2.3	2.0	1.8	2.3
12	5.0	2.5	3.0	4.9	5.3	2.7	2.3	2.2	2.8
15	6.0	3.0	3.5	5.7	6.1	3.1	2.9	2.5	3.1
18	6.5	4.0	3.5	6.6	7.3	3.5	3.1	2.9	3.6
21	8.0	4.0	4.0	7.6	8.3	4.1	3.5	3.2	4.1

5 Conclusion

It is very important to carry out load-bearing walking fatigue research, to evaluate the damage caused by different load to human body, to scientifically design load task and to improve the design of backpack. So the specific conclusions of this study are as follows:

(1) The shoulder is the main area of bearing pressure and also is the most easily fatigue during the process of weight-bearing walking.
(2) During the weight-bearing walking, the force of the different side of the human's same parts is different and the difference is significant.
(3) The fatigue evaluation model combines the subjective feeling of fatigue and the objective index of the impulse of shoulder, waist and back and it avoid the simplification of fatigue evaluation model of current study, so the model of this study is a improvement.

Acknowledgement. This research was funded by Electronic information equipment system research of Key laboratory of basic research projects of national defense technology (DXZT-JC-ZZ-2015-016).

References

1. Wang, J., Xu, X., Liu, Y.: Dynamic foot pressure measurements and its application to clinical or thopaedics. J. Appl. Biomech. **12**(3), 170–175 (1997)
2. Birrell, S.A., Haslam, R.A.: The effect of load distribution within military load carriage systems on the kinetics of human gait. Appl. Ergon. **41**(4), 585–590 (2010)
3. Rugelj, D., Sevek, F.: The effect of load mass and its placement on postural sway. Appl. Ergon. **42**(6), 860–866 (2011)
4. Wei, J., Song, L.: The development of biomechanics studies on human's load carriage gait. J. Jilin Normal Univ. (Nat. Sci. Edn.) **4**, 122–124 (2010)
5. Yuan, G., Zhang, J., Zhang, M., et al.: The measurement system for dynamic foot pressure and its clinical application **18**(1), 22–25
6. Geng, H.: Foot pressure features of single-shoulder and double-shoulder schoolbag weight walk of children. J. Clin. Rehabil. Tissue Eng. Res. **15**(33), 6267–6270 (2011)
7. Wu, T., Gong, T., Zhou, Y., Zhang, C.: Research on plantar pressure and gait for children aged from 6 to 10 in loading condition. China Leather **44**(13), 24–27 (2015)
8. Gribble, P.A., Hertel, J., Denegar, C.R., Buckley, W.E.: The effects of fatigue and chronic ankle instability on dynamic postural control. J. Athl. Train. **39**, 321–329 (2004)
9. De Rijk, A.E., Schreurs, K.M.G., Bensing, J.M.: What is behind "I'm so tired?" Fatigue experiences and their relations to the quality and quantity of external stimulation. Psychosom. Res. **47**(6), 509–523 (1999)
10. Jing, G., Lang, X., Yao, Z.: The method and countermeasure of fatigue investigate. Jpn. Med. Introd. **24**(12), 566–568 (2003)
11. Xue, X., Wang, T., Zhao, Y., et al.: Connotation of "fatigue" symptom and thought of its quantization evaluation. China J. Tradit. Chin. Med. Pharm. **21**(5), 267–269 (2006)

The Motion Analysis of Transferring from Bed to Wheelchair Conducted in the Nursing Field with Focusing on the Body Pressure Distribution

Hiromi Nakagawa[1](✉), Kazuyuki Mori[1], Koshiro Takahashi[1],
Kazuaki Yamashiro[2], Yoichiro Ogura[2], and Akihiko Goto[3]

[1] Seisen University, Shiga, Japan
nakaga-h@seisen.ac.jp
[2] Kyoto Institute of Technology, Kyoto, Japan
[3] Osaka Sangyo University, Osaka, Japan

Abstract. Occupational low back pain that affects 40–60% of nurses is categorized under non-accidental low back pain caused by the transferring of a wheelchair-bound patient. Prevention is an important issue, since the occurrence of non-accidental low back pain increases the chances for nurses to leave their job. The use of tools is recommended especially with regards to wheelchair transfer assistance since the motion of embracing the patient is the cause of low back pain among nurses. However, an educational program for back pain prevention is yet to be established at the basic level of education at nursing colleges. We were unable to find studies that compared the motions of a skilled nurse versus a nursing student when transferring a patient from wheelchair to bed.

This study attempts to clarify the differences the wheelchair transfer assistance motions of the expert and non-expert through three-dimensional motion analysis, interface pressure measurement, and fatigue study. The purpose of this study is to explicit the tacit nature of the techniques nurses employ when changing body positions. The study observes the motions of an expert and a non-expert by conducting an interface pressure measurement during a wheelchair transfer of a simulated patient. The motions of the transfer are then divided into four aspects and evaluated. As a result, the non-expert displayed flexions in the cervical vertebrae in all four aspects, indicating an instability in posture compared with the expert. Furthermore, the non-expert cited more areas and symptoms of physical fatigue than the expert after the transfer.

Considering the motion analysis results obtained from observing interface pressure, the above-mentioned motions have caused greater contact pressure for the simulated patient when seated, narrowing the surface area of the seat and forcing the patient's position on the seat to become shallow.

Keywords: Motion analysis · Wheelchair transferring · Back pain · Interface pressure · Pressure ulcer

© Springer International Publishing AG 2017
V.G. Duffy (Ed.): DHM 2017, Part I, LNCS 10286, pp. 141–159, 2017.
DOI: 10.1007/978-3-319-58463-8_13

1   Introduction

In the United States, it is reported that 2.5 million people develop pressure ulcer annually, which requires 11 billion US dollars in expense per year, causing an increase in medical care cost [1]. In Japan, the estimated percentage of pressure ulcer incidents is 1.5% in the general ward, and 5.1% in the recuperation ward [2]. It is reported that the medical expense used for the treatment of pressure ulcer and wound dressing material for leg ulcers is 4.4 billion and 43 million JPY. "Never Events" are if the stages III–IV of "hospital-acquired pressure ulcer" occurs after being hospitalized. In Japan where the elderly are more prone to illness, the preventive method for pressure ulcer becomes the important issue from the standpoint of medical safety and the health care economy.

Considering this background, repositioning and early mobilization is recommended in the Clinical Practice Guideline for Prevention and Treatment of Pressure Ulcer provided by National Pressure Ulcer Advisory Panel, European Pressure Ulcer Advisory Panel and Pan Pacific Pressure Injury Alliance [3]. It mentions how to reposition the individual in a way to relieve and disperse the body pressure and use a split leg sling mechanical lift when available to transfer an individual into a wheelchair or bedside chair when the individual needs total assistance to transfer. Remove the sling immediately after transfer. Repositioning and early mobilization is an important nursing technique for the pressure ulcer prevention and management policy. Us Wound, Ostomy Continence Nurses have been providing the education for the people assigned in professional occupations. But, the educational system for this field has not been established in the undergraduate education, nor can many previous study cases be found.

In this study, we conducted the experiment on nursing undergraduate students and Wound, Ostomy Continence Nurses (WOCN). The purpose of this study is examining the nursing technique when repositioning a patient by focusing on the body pressure distribution and explicating the tacit knowledge that underlie the nursing technique of skilled workers. We assigned 2 test subjects consisting of 1 nursing undergraduate students who have finished the clinical practice, and 1 WOCN nurse who has 27 years working experience at the general hospital. We classified nursing student as non-experts, and 1 WOCN as an expert. For an experimental environment, a urethane foam mattress was put on the medical-use bed, and allocated one simulated patient on the bed. The measurement was conducted in the following Transferring from the bed to the wheelchair. The three-dimensional motion analysis was conducted using the MAC 3DSYSTEM (Motion Analysis) with a sampling rate of 100 Hz, and the analysis software was EvaRT, ver 5.0.4.

ERGOCHECK (ABW Co., Ltd.) was used for body pressure measurement. After treating the data of the human pressure measurement by PC, we depicted the pressure distribution between the human body and the mattress for analysis. Moreover, the questionnaire survey regarding fatigue was conducted on the 1 subject before and after the movement measurement experience. We also digitalized the transferring technique used when getting a patient out of bed.

2 Background

2.1 Conditions Around the Occurrence of Low Back Pain Among Nurses

Occupational low back pain can be divided into two categories: accidental, which is caused by injuries sustained at work, and non-accidental, caused by work that involves handling heavy loads or excess strain on the lumbar spine. Low back pain caused by assisting patients during a transfer is classified as the non-accidental category. The rate of low back pain occurrence among nurses is 43% in the U.K. [4], 40–50% in the U.S. [5], 69.7% in Taiwan [6], and 60% in Japan [7]. Japan marked higher occurrence rate comparing other countries. Low back pain occurrence rates in the U.K. are lower than other countries due to initiatives by the National Back Pain Association to raise greater awareness of the issue [8]. Its 1981 publication, the Guide to the Handling of Patients, recommends education, training and the use of assisting devices to combat low back pain among the U.K. nurses. In addition to the Health and Safety Executive, the association established the Manual Handling Operations Regulations [9] that set a load-handling limit of 25 kg per person. This accelerated the installation of mechanical lifts and continues to reduce low back pain for the nurses. In 2003, the Occupational Safety and Health Administration established the Guidelines for Nursing Homes, which recommends the use of nursing care devices and specifies the number of staff that must be present when performing a transfer. According to the National Institute of Occupational Safety and Health, the preventative measures have led to a notable reduction in the occurrence of musculoskeletal injuries that led to reduced working hours, financial compensation and time taken off from work [10].

According to our own Ministry of Health, Labour and Welfare, low back pain that requires rest of more than 4 days at a welfare facility accounts for about 19% of occupational illnesses, and has increased 2.7-fold in 10 years. Within those numbers, 50–70% of nurses reportedly experience low back pain [11]. The conditions in Japan are serious. However, there is no evidence available from randomised controlled trials for the effectiveness of manual material handling (MMH) advice and training or MMH assistive devices for treating back pain [12].

Among the nurses who report low back pain, 47.8% are male, 61.5% are female, with the number of complaints peaking at women in their 30s, then declining from 40s onward, though the reason for this remains unclear [7]. We couldn't find any thesis pertaining to low back pain, gender and age targeting nurses, but according to the ministry [13], the number of complaints rise in accordance with age.

2.2 Motions that Cause Low Back Pain and Its Mechanism

Transfers account for 65.1% of the occurrence of non-accidental low back pain at welfare facilities, especially when transferring from bed to wheelchair, but also during bathing assistance (23.3%), helping with elimination (12.7%). Furthermore, the highest incidence of low back pain (47.8%) came when the caregiver was facing the patient and the burden of supporting the patient is on the back of the care giver [14]. Additionally, when assisting with wheelchair transfer, the embracing motion has been identified as the cause of low back pain [15, 16].

Low back pain is triggered by the loss of lumbar support due to degeneration in the lumbar spinal column. As a result, the nervous system that runs through the spinal column, or the nerve endings present in each structure that makes up the spinal column are mechanically stimulated, which in turn triggers inflammation in the nervous system or areas around it and causes the symptoms of back pain. The intervertebral joints, the paraspinal muscles and the sensory receptors distributed to the posterior elements of the lumbar region are particularly sensitive and contribute to nonspecific acute low back pain caused by movements and posture [17]. Wheelchair transfers by nurses activate the shoulder joints, elbow joints and knee joints. The shoulder joints are innervated from the cervical spine (C4–C8); the elbows, from C4 to Thoracic spine 4; the knee joints, from L5–L7. Psychological stress has been clearly linked to the onset of low back pain, chronic or otherwise [18]. However, we found no studies that demonstrate the effectiveness of early prevention of fatigue and psychological stress on low back pain among nurses.

2.3   Interface Pressure and Pressure Ulcers When Seated in a Wheelchair

A pressure ulcer is localized injury to the skin and/or underlying tissue usually over a bony prominence, as a result of pressure, or pressure in combination with shear. A number of contributing or confounding factors are also associated with pressure ulcers; the significance of these factors is yet to be elucidated. Transferring to a wheelchairs is recommended in Use variable-position seating (tilt-in-space, recline, and standing) in manual or power wheelchairs to redistribute load off of the seat surface. The Clinical Practice Guideline for Prevention and Treatment of Pressure Ulcer provided by National pressure ulcer advisory panel, European pressure ulcer advisory panel and pan pacific pressure injury alliance.

Especially patients who use wheelchairs run a very high risk for developing pressure ulcers, and 27% of the 3,361 with a spinal cord injury reportedly have Stage II (partial thickness skin loss) pressure ulcer [19, 20].

According to Landis [21], arterial capillary pressure is around 26–32 mmHg, and an additional pressure of 70–100 mmHg for more than 2 h has been shown to cause structural damage. Moreover, measuring the pressure distribution in the sacral region of bedridden elderly patients has shown that pressure ulcers develop at 40–50 mmHg [22]. Applying pressure of more than 50 mmHg during a position change constricts the capillaries and cause structural damage. Therefore, this change from a sitting position to a lying position is thought to improve wound healing.

Due to the above, it is believed that adequate amounts of pressure redistribution when seated during a wheelchair transfer can help prevent pressure ulcers. However, we were not able to find any studies of seat pressure distribution comparing nursing students to experts. We believe that measuring the seat surface of the wheelchair will reveal what effect differences in transfer behavior between a nursing student and an expert will have on the body pressure of the simulated patient (SP).

3 Previous Research on Transfer Assistance by Nursing Students

Observing a Japanese nursing student help a patient transition from a supine position in bed to a portable toilet, one study concluded that the most stressful actions on the lumbar spine were standing up, twisting and sitting down. Movements related to upper body elevation places the most stress on the lumbar spine [23].

Most adults flex their lumbar spine to assist people out of bed. The expert, on the other hand, does not and keeps the lumbar region largely extended [24]. Furthermore, the good movements of the expert can be adopted by regular adults. Low back pain contributes significantly to nurses quitting their job and needs to be addressed in order to secure the labor force of nurses [25]. However, with regards to low back pain prevention, there are no lessons on techniques or lectures about position changing in basic nursing education at universities. There are also no educational programs structured around low back pain. We need to raise an awareness about keeping our nurses in good health, and education for preventing low back pain so that we can also stop losing our nurses from back injury.

4 Design Study

The design of this study is research experiment, using a motion capture system to analyze wheelchair transfer motions. The purpose of this research was to study the motions of the non-expert (nursing student) and the expert (WOCN), looking specifically at interface pressure in the nursing techniques they employ in changing body positions, and turning what is tacit knowledge into one that's more explicit. We evaluated the wheelchair transfer motions done by the expert and non-expert, and difference in the interface pressure dispersion of the simulated patient. The research question for this study was what the differences are in the wheelchair transfer motions between the expert and the non-expert, and how those differences would impact low back pain and the patient's interface pressure.

In this study, the expert has been established as a highly proficient nurse who possesses a lot of experience, an intuitive grasp of the clinical situation and can accurately connect an issue with a prescription without second-guessing him or herself. Further more, the non-expert (nursing expert) has been defined as a novice. Novice is defined as beginner with no experience, but who were taught general rules to help perform tasks [26].

5 Motion Analysis of Wheelchair Transfer Techniques that Observe the Interface Pressure of the Nursing Student

5.1 Participants

We assigned two subjects for this study. One subject was a nursing student who had studied basic nursing unit and received basic nursing clinical practice training at a university school of nursing science. And the other was a nurse who worked at a 580-unit hospital specializing in spinal cord injuries and rehabilitation, and with 27 years of experience as a wound ostomy continence nurse (WOCN) educated in the activities covered by this research. The student was the non-expert, and the WOCN was the expert. The SP was a healthy adult (Table 1).

Table 1. Attributions of participants

		Expert (N = 1)	Non-expert (N = 1)	Simulated patient (N = 1)
Age		47	21	24
Gender	Male		1	1
	Female	1		
High (cm)		155.0	176.0	169.0
Body mass index (kg/m^2)		20.8	23.9	20.8

5.2   Procedure and Setting

The movements to be studied were the transfer from bed to wheelchair. We used a height-adjustable bed that allowed the SP to sit in the center of the side frame of the bed with the soles of his feet touching the floor. The scenario was that the patient is unable to stand on his own and requires full nursing care. The participants were briefed on the conditions of the SP and were asked to transfer him from the bed to the wheelchair. As for the positions of the bed and the wheelchair, the latter was placed facing 30° toward the bed, with a slight adjustment to make the transition of the SP a little easier. As for the wheelchair transfer motions and interface pressure, we measured movements of each participant twice per single motion. We had a chair ready for the participants to rest if they got tired.

In measuring the participants' motions and interface pressure, we used a video to record all the movements of the patient's body during the transfer, from the slight shifts to bigger lifting movements. Before and after the wheelchair transfer, we asked the participants to fill out a questionnaire pertaining to fatigued body parts and symptoms they are aware of, using the Assessment tool for fatigue [27].

This research received approval by Osaka Industrial University's Research Ethics Committee (Number 011). We briefed the participants beforehand on the outline of the research on paper and obtained their consent in writing. We informed them that they could stop any time they felt tired to get some rest.

5.3   Classification of the Movements from Bed to Wheelchair

The bed-to-wheelchair motion was categorized into four phases. The first is "assisting from sitting up to standing up," which involved the point at which the assistance began, the point at which the participant's hips were at the lowest position, and the point at which the patient completes standing. The second is "assisting with direction change".

And the third is "assisting to sit in the wheelchair," which covers the movement from the lowest point of the participant's hips while helping with sitting to the end of the seated position of the participant. And finally, "seat readjustment assistance." These motions were analyzed, and each participant's phase was contrasted against the other (Table 2).

Table 2. Motion categories of transfer assistance motion from bed to wheelchair

	Motion categories	Scene
1	Assisting from sitting to standing	(1) The point at which assistance starts
		(2) The lowest point of the participant's hips while assisting standing
		(3) The point at which standing ends
2	Assisting direction change	(1) The point at which direction changes
3	Assisting sitting in the wheelchair	(1) Point at which the participant's hips are at the lowest point while assisting sitting down
		(2) The point at which sitting ends
4	Seat readjustment	(1) Point at which assisting in seat readjustment takes place

5.4   Measurement Methods

Using Motion Capture to Analyze the Wheelchair Transfers of the Expert and Non-expert

The reflector markers were attached to the body surface and movement during transfer assistance were recorded by five cameras to record 3-dimensional footage. Sixteen reflector markers were attached to the subject as shown in Fig. 1: The model had attachments on the head (top, right, left), neck (cervical nerve 7), shoulder, top, bottom (thoracic nerve 12), middle (lumbar nerve 5), trochanter major (TRO), hip, elbow, wrist, thigh, knee, shin, ankle and toe.

For this research, we didn't attach reflective markers to the abdominal area since the patient would block the view. Instead, reflective markers were attached to the back of the participants to achieve a 3-dimensional analysis. The participants' movements that were tracked were assisting the patient from a seated position to the wheelchair. We used a MAC 3D System (motion analysis), sampling rate 100 Hz, creating stick figures to perform a three-dimensional motion analysis. The software was EvaRT Ver. 5.0.4 (motion analysis). We used it to calculate the participant's cervical spine angle, knee joint angle, lumbar flexion angle per motion, as well as the time it took for each movement. We also measured the inter-wrist and inter-ankle distances.

The model had attachments on the head (top, right, left), neck (cervical nerve 7), shoulder, top, bottom (thoracic nerve 12), middle (lumbar nerve 5), trochanter major (TRO), hip, elbow, wrist, thigh, knee, shin, ankle and toe.

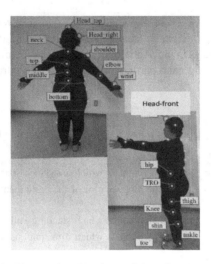

Fig. 1. The attached locations of the reflector markers

Measurement of Interface Pressure of a Simulated Patient at Time of Wheelchair Transfer

One simulated patient lay on a 9 cm-thick polyurethane mattress on a bed used for medical treatment. The interface pressure measurement sheet was set on the wheelchair to measure the interface pressure.

ABW GmbH, ERGOCHECK was used for the interface pressure measurement. ERGOCHECK applies 712 sensors to the sheets. Each sensor detects pressure between human body and mattress per 5–10 cm square. It can serve as a measuring instrument to detect interface pressure. The measurements are classified into two categories: the seated surface after wheelchair transfer, and the seated surface after the seat is readjusted, comparing the expert and non-expert. Once the interface pressure data is processed on a computer, the distribution of pressure on the body and the mattress is drawn out and analyzed, with the expert and non-expert being compared. The mean and standard deviation are calculated by looking at the average pressure and maximum pressure applied by both the expert and the non-expert.

Questionnaire Survey on Fatigue

The assessment tool for fatigue totals scores in five categories – drowsiness, instability, discomfort, weakness, and blurring vision – to benchmark fatigue levels. It also tracks where the fatigue manifests in the body and can obtain the total score of fatigue degree of each body part. It estimates fatigue and pain as well as back pain. Statistics from the fatigue survey were used.

5.5   Results

Time Elapsed in the Four Aspects of the Wheelchair Transfer for Both Expert and Non-expert

The expert spends 68 s in the wheelchair transfer. The breakdown is 18 s for the expert to assist from sitting to standing, 24 s for a direction change, 16 s to assist to a seated position, and 10 s to readjust the seated position. The changing of direction took the most time. The non-expert spends 32 s in the wheelchair transfer. The breakdown is 11 s from sitting to standing, 2 s for the change of direction, 9 s to assist to a seated position, and 10 s to readjust the seated position. Going from sitting to standing took the most time.

The Joint Angles, the Distance Between the Wrists and Between the Ankles in the Motions of the Four Aspects of the Wheelchair Transfer

Please refer to Figs. 2 and 3, for information on the angles of the cervical spine, lumbar, knee joint and elbow joint for the expert and non-expert.

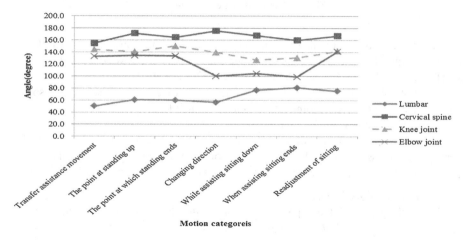

Fig. 2. The joint angle of expert

Assistance From Sitting To Standing

When the expert makes contact with the SP, the body angles of the expert were as follows: cervical spine, 155.2°; lumbar, 50.5°; knee joint, 144.4°; elbow joint, 132.7°. The wrists were 50.0 cm apart, and the ankles were 22.8 cm apart.

When standing, the expert's lower back at its lowest point was: cervical spine, 171.6°; lumbar, 60.9°; knee joint, 140.8°; elbow joint, 134.2°. The wrists were 70.7 cm apart, and the ankles were 41.7 cm apart.

The body angles of the expert after the SP is standing were 164.8° for the cervical spine; 60.3° for the lumbar, 133.6° for the elbow joints. The wrists were 43.3 cm apart, and the ankles were 46.8 cm apart.

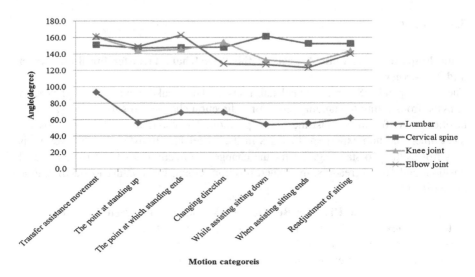

Fig. 3. The joint angle of non-expert

When the non-expert makes contact with the SP, his body angles were as follows: cervical spine, 151.2°; lumbar, 93.0°; knee joint, 160.9°; elbow joint, 161.2°. The wrists were 24.2 cm apart, and the ankles were 52.5 cm apart.

When standing, the non-expert's lower back at its lowest point was: cervical spine, 147.2°; lumbar, 56.1°; knee joint, 144.1°; elbow joint, 149.2°. The wrists were 24.6 cm apart, and the ankles were 52.3 cm apart.

The body angles of the non-expert when the SP is standing were 148.1° for the cervical spine, 68.7° for the lumbar, 145.6° for the knee joint, 163.1° for the elbow joint. The wrists were 22.6 cm apart, and the ankles were 50.3 cm apart.

Direction Change Assistance

The body angles of the expert at the start of the direction change were: cervical spine, 175.7°; lumbar, 56.6°; knee joint, 150.3°; elbow joint, 100.2°. The wrists were 43.0 cm apart, and the ankles were 42.5 cm apart. The body angles of the non-expert at the start of the direction change were: cervical spine, 148.1°; lumbar, 69.0°; knee joint, 154.3°; elbow joint, 128.0°. The wrists were 22.9 cm apart, and the ankles were 49.0 cm apart.

Wheelchair Seating Assistance

While seating the SP, the body angles of the expert were: cervical spine, 167.9°; lumbar, 77.0°; knee joint, 127.1°; elbow joint, 104.3°. The wrists were 50.0 cm apart, and the ankles were 42.5 cm apart. After seating the SP, the cervical spine was 160.1°, the lumbar was 81.1°, the knee joint was 130.6°, and the elbow joint was 99.0°. As far as the distance during the seating, the wrists were 43.0 cm apart, and the ankles were 42.5 cm apart. Afterwards, the wrists were 34.2 cm apart, and the ankles were 34.3 cm apart.

While seating the SP, the body angles of the non-expert were: cervical spine, 161.6°; lumbar, 53.9°; knee joint, 32.5°; elbow joint, 127.1°. The wrists were 33.5 cm apart, and the ankles were 61.6 cm apart. After the seating, the cervical spine was

152.6°, the lumbar was 55.3°, the knee joint was 120.9°, the elbow joint was 123.2°. As for the distance, the wrists were 39.5 cm apart, and the ankles were 62.0 cm apart.

Seat Adjustment Assistance

After completing the seat readjustment, the body angles of the expert were: cervical spine, 167.2°; lumbar, 75.6°; knee joint 141.6°; elbow joint 141.0°. The wrists were 51.1 cm apart, and the ankles were 49.7 cm apart. The expert talked to the patient throughout all the activities, confirming with the patient through each movement.

After completing the seat readjustment, the body angles of the non-expert were: cervical spine, 152.7°; lumbar, 55.3°; knee joint, 143.5°; elbow joint, 140.0°. The wrists were 49.0 cm, and the ankles were 41.9 cm apart. The non-expert did not talk at all during the activities.

The difference in the angle of the cervical spine and Head top between the expert and non-expert when doing wheelchair transfers are show below (Figs. 4 and 5).

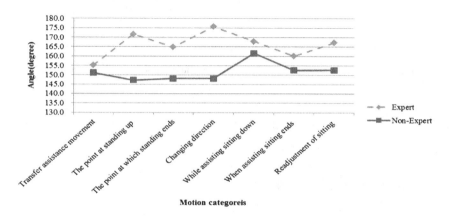

Fig. 4. Comparisons of the angle of expert and non-expert's cervical spine

The Joint Angles, the Distance Between the Wrists and Between the Ankles in the Motions of the Four Aspects of the Wheelchair Transfer

The average angle of the joints during the four phases of activity was researched (Fig. 6). The average angle for the cervical spine was 161.1 ± 6.9 without flexion and some straight extension. In contrast, the non-expert was flexion and carried the burden on his cervical spine. Fatigue was reported in the survey in his trapezius and musculus sternocleidomastoideus. The average anglke of the lumbar was 66.0 ± 11.

The knee joint angle was $139.2 \pm 7.9°$. The elbow joint was $120.7 \pm 18.6°$. The distance of the ankles was 48.9 ± 11.3 cm, whiole the wrists were 40.0 ± 9.0 cm apart.

The angle of the non-expert's cervical spine was $151.6 \pm 4.9°$. The average for the lumbar was $65.4 \pm 13.6°$. The knee joint angle was $144.3 \pm 11.2°$. The elbow joint angle was $141.7 \pm 16.5°$. The wrists were 48.8 ± 12.9 cm apart, while the ankles were 34.9 ± 12.4 cm apart.

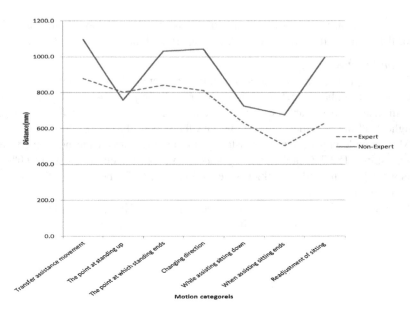

Fig. 5. Comparisons of the head top of expert and non-expert's cervical spine

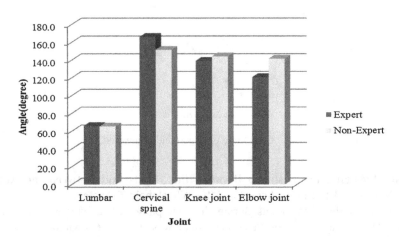

Fig. 6. Average joint angle comparisons for all activities

The Interface Pressure of the Simulated Patient When Seated in a Wheelchair

The area of contact on the seat surface was 1300.0 cm² (Table 3, Fig. 7) after the expert assisted the wheelchair transfer. The maximum contact pressure was 92.8 mmHg, and the average was 27.6 mmHg. After readjusting the seat, the area was 2370 cm². Maximum contact pressure was 70.5 mmHg, and the average was 14.6 mmHg.

Table 3. Area of contact on seat surface after wheelchair transfer

	Seat surface after sitting in wheelchair			Seat surface after seat is readjusted in wheelchair		
	Seat surface (cm²)	Maximum contact pressure (mmHg)	Average contact pressure (mmHg)	Seat surface (cm²)	Maximum contact pressure (mmHg)	Average contact pressure (mmHg)
Expert	1300.0	92.8	27.6	2370.0	70.5	14.6
Non-expert	990.0	95.5	29	285.0	63.9	12.1

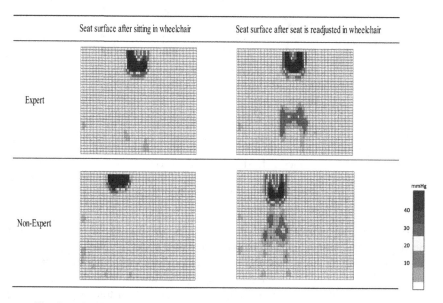

Fig. 7. Distribution of body pressure on seat surface after wheelchair transfer

The area of contact on the seat surface was 990.0 cm² after the non-expert assisted the wheelchair transfer. The maximum contact pressure was 95.0 mmHg, and the average was 29.00 mmHg. After readjusting the seat, the area was 2850 cm². Maximum contact pressure was 63.9 mmHg, and the average was 12.2 mmHg.

The Shifts in the Fatigue Before and After the Wheelchair Transfer as Reported by the Expert and Non-expert

We conducted a survey using the assessment tool for fatigue provided by Working Group for Occupational Fatigue. Before conducting wheelchair transfer activities, the expert reported fatigue and weakness in two places, including her trapezius and left deltoid. After the activity, she reported feeling slight fatigue in her left deltoid and triceps, but the fatigue in her trapezius and stiffness in her shoulders had disappeared (Fig. 8).

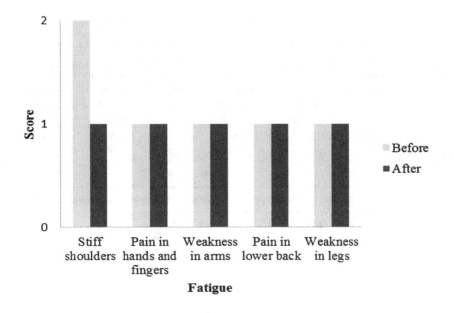

Score: 1. Absence 2. Presence

Fig. 8. Change in the expert's fatigue

Before conducting wheelchair transfer activities, the non-expert reported experiencing slight fatigue in seven places, including the both trapezius, the both psoas major, the right deltoid and the both musculus sternocleidomastoideus. After the activities, he reported feeling quite a bit of fatigue in nine places, including the both trapezius, both psoas major, right deltoid, the both musculus sternocleidomastoideus, and the both orbicularis oculi muscle.

The expert's self-reported symptoms, including drowsiness and discomfort, declined from seven before the activity to five afterwards. Unpleasant feelings dropped from eight to six. Blurriness went from ten incidents to seven, and weakness went from six to five.

The non-expert's self-reported symptoms included drowsiness at twelve points before the activities. That was unchanged after the activities. Discomfort and blurriness both stayed unchanged at six, and pain in the eyes was reported. Unpleasant feelings decreased from nine to five. Weakness rose from five to seven. Stiff shoulders and sore knees were reported (Fig. 9).

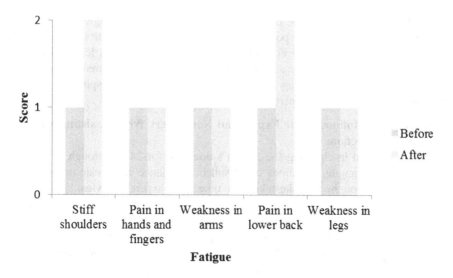

Score: 1. Absence 2. Presence

Fig. 9. Change in non-expert's fatigue

6   Discussion and Conclusions

6.1   Analyzing Aspects of the Expert and Non-expert's Movements During Wheelchair Transfer

Analysis of the four aspects of the wheelchair transfer conducted by experts and non-experts, measuring the expert's timing, angle of the cervical spine, lumbar spine, knee joint, and the distance between wrists and ankles.

Comparing the Motions of the Expert and Non-expert When Assisting a Patient from a Seated to Standing Position

Looking at the time required, the expert took 2.3 times longer than the non-expert. It takes longer because the expert talks with the SP and takes care to note the person's physical abilities while making the transfer. Also, the non-expert put his cervical spine into more anteflexion position than the expert when he touched the SP's body. The non-expert is 11 cm taller than the SP, so he bends into an anteflexion position to make up for the height difference. Also, it is thought that the non-expert doesn't flex his knees and lumbar spine as much as the expert and hasn't learned good body mechanics that suggesting to bend knees to lower the hip position.

The width of the expert's ankles when standing up is 22.8 cm. The width of the non-expert is 24.2 cm, making the width of their feet and support base about the same. The expert angles her back less than the non-expert. The expert flexes her knees more than the non-expert. The expert's position is stable and her center of gravity is low, reducing the stress on her back.

When the lower back of the non-expert is bent the least, the angle of his cervical spine is in a more anteflexion position than when he started, creating fatigue in the trapezius and the musculus sternocleidomastoideus stretching from left to right. The scores rose for stiff shoulders and a feeling of heaviness compared to before the activity. At the end of standing up, the expert kept her lumbar spine in a flexion position more than the non-expert did.

Comparing the Motions of the Expert and Non-expert When Assisting a Patient in Changing Directions

The expert assisted in changing the patient's direction for 24 s. Through experience, she knows that changing directions can result in imbalance and create unease in the patient, so it is thought that she takes her time. The expert's cervical spine is at a 175.7-degree angle when changing directions; the lumbar is at 97.4°. The extension of the cervical spine and the lumbar is clear. The difference in height between the patient and the expert was 9 cm. Since she will be supporting the patient around the chest area, the expert's knees were in a flexion position of 139.6°, lowering the center of gravity.

The knee joint of the non-expert was at a 154.3-degree angle when assisting in the change of direction. Because it was 132.5° and in a flexion position in a sitting posture, it was thought that the pelvis wasn't at a steady height, affecting the stability when making the change in directions. When the non-expert changed directions, his cervical spine and lumbar were in an anteflexion position, and the knees were hardly flexion at all, putting the burden on the L5–L7.

Comparing the Motions of the Expert and Non-expert When Assisting a Patient into a Seated Position on the Wheelchair

When an expert assists a patient into a seated position, the elbow joint is in a 99-degree flexion position, and the wrists are 34.2 cm apart. It is thought that the distance between them is close because the expert will grab the patient's belt and pull his body up.

The non-expert's elbow joint is at a 123.2-degree angle, and the wrists are 39.5 cm apart. The distance is greater when the non-expert puts the patient in a seated position. Also, as when changing directions, the non-expert's cervical spine is in an anteflexion position, and fatigue is thought to appear in the trapezius and musculus sternocleidomastoideus stretching from left to right.

Comparing the Motions of the Expert and Non-expert When Assisting a Patient in Seat Readjustment

The angle of the elbow joint and knee joint of the expert when assisting in seat readjustment are at about the same angles. Also, as when changing directions, the non-expert's cervical spine is in an anteflexion position, and fatigue is thought to appear in the trapezius and musculus sternocleidomastoideus stretching from left to right.

Comparing the Average Joint Angles of the Expert and Non-expert When Performing a Wheelchair Transfer

The expert extends her cervical spine before standing up. Once standing, she tilts slightly forward. This is thought to be because she checks on the stability of the movement by confirming the footing of the SP. Also, she confirms the sitting position and puts the cervical spine in an anteflexion position when sitting.

The non-expert has his cervical spine in an anteflexion position through all the movements. In contrast, the non-expert has a daily appearance of fatigue because he feels it in seven places, including the both trapezius, the both psoas major muscle, the right deltoids, and the both musculus sternocleidomastoideus. After the activity, subjective symptoms include stiff shoulders, a strong feeling of fatigue, and tired eyes. Subjective symptoms and fatigue blend together after the activities. It is thought that keeping the cervical spine in an anteflexion position means the body will bear the brunt of the load.

With wheelchair transfers, the expert keeps her elbow joints more flexion than the non-expert and her wrists farther apart. When the SP is bigger than the nurse, and the nurse can't hold the patient around his lower back, a belt is used to raise him up, which causes the burden on the triceps and the elbow joint. After the activity, feeling fatigue in the left triceps is thought to be because she used her arms for lifting with a belt.

An aid is necessary, but because curriculum concerning the use of aid at nursing schools and medical facilities has not progressed, it's necessary to build this into the educational program to enlighten practitioners.

6.2 The Effect of the Wheelchair Transfer in the Interface Pressure of the Simulated Patient When Seated in the Wheelchair

The interface pressure of the simulated patient when assisted by the expert, the area of contact is wide and the seat is deep. With non-experts, the area of contact is narrow and the seat is shallow. Also, referring to the video recording, the seat remains shallow when assisted by the non-expert and he is unable to steady the patient, having no consciousness of the depth of the seat surface.

The width of the expert's feet during a change of direction and while sitting is 42.5 cm, but the width of the non-expert's feet changes from 49.0 cm during a change of direction to 61.6 cm and 12.6 cm while seating a patient, and flexion is rarely seen, leading to unsteady support. This is thought to increase the risk of the patient falling. By giving feedback to the non-expert using three-dimensional movement analysis and interface pressure when seating, it is possible to actively educate them about wheelchair transfers.

Furthermore, the non-expert applies more body pressure on the seat after transfer, so it is necessary to explain that wider support of the patient's buttocks will help him sit deeply. With this action, readjusting the seat position becomes unnecessary, and the frequency with which the lumbar and cervical spine are in a flexion position can be reduced.

6.3 Challenge Topics for the Non-expert on Wheelchair Transfers

The expert used in this research is a middle-aged woman experiencing typical aging issues such as the decline in estrogen, cardiopulmonary functions and endurance. However, the expert experienced less fatigue and fewer self-described symptoms than the much younger male non-expert when it came to the activities. It's thought that this is because the expert's spine was not anteflexion and the distance between her knees and ankles was uniform, giving her a stable base. The non-expert needs to learn about the techniques for using his cervical spine, knee joints and feet correctly. As there was just one expert and non-expert, we can't make broad conclusions. Our further challenge is to proceed more movement analysis for utilizing the results for basic nursing education.

The purpose of this research was to use an expert and non-expert to focus on interface pressure in posture-changing techniques used in nursing and to explicit the tacit knowledge hidden in the skilled nurses. We estimated the amount of pressure dispersed during wheelchair transfers done by the expert and non-expert. The non-expert had his cervical spine in an anteflexion position during all the activities, and his ankle distance was not consistent when changing directions and sitting. Also, because his knee joint was in a flexion position when changing directions or seating, it became clear that the posture was not stable. Because of this, the non-expert had more aching parts and reported more fatigue than the expert after the activities. By analyzing the interface pressure, the transfer assistance done by the non-expert described above increased the contact pressure when seating the SP, and the area of contact was narrow and the seat was shallow, which suggests that the risk of tissue disorder and falling of the patient from a wheelchair were increased.

References

1. Gibbons, W., Shanks, H.T., Kleinhelter, P., Jones, P.: Eliminating facility-acquired pressure ulcers at ascension health. Jt. Comm. J. Qual. Patient Saf. **32**, 488–496 (2006)
2. The advisory board on Japanese journal of pressure ulcers. Prevalence rate of pressure ulcer, the part and severity of illness of pressure ulcer. JPU **13**(4), 625–632 (2011)
3. National pressure ulcer advisory panel, European pressure ulcer advisory panel and pan pacific pressure injury alliance. Prevention and treatment of pressure ulcers quick reference guideline, vol. 9 (2014)
4. Smedley, J., Egger, P., Cooper, C., Coggon, D.: Manual handling activities and risk of low back pain in nurses. Occup. Environ. Med. **52**, 160–163 (1995). http://dx.doi.org/10.1136/oem.52.3.160
5. Edlich, R.F., Winters, K.L., Hudson, M.A., Britt, L.D., Long, W.B.: Prevention of disabling back injuries in nurses by the use of mechanical patient lift systems. J. Long Term Eff. Med. Implants **14**(6), 521–533 (2004)
6. Chiou, W.K., Wong, M.K., Lee, Y.H.: Epidemiology of low back pain in Chinese nurses. Int. J. Nurs. Stud. **31**, 361–368 (2007). http://dx.doi.org/10.1016/00207489(94)90076-0
7. Fujimura, T., Takeda, M., Asada, F., Kawase, M., Takano, K.: The investigation of low back pain among hospital nurse. JJOMT **60**, 91–96 (2012)
8. National Back Pain Association. The Guide to the Handling of Patients, pp. 1–242 (1997)
9. Health and Safety Executive: Manual Handling Operations Regulations, pp. 1–66 (1992). http://www.hse.gov.uk/pUbns/priced/l23.pdf#search=%27manual+handling+regulations%27. Accessed 5 Feb 2017
10. Collins, J.W., Wolf, L., Bell, J., Evanoff, B.: An evaluation of a "best Practices" muscloskeletal injury prevention program in nursing homes. Inj. Prev. **10**, 206–211 (2004)

11. Ministry of health, labour and welfare, Japan industrial safety and health Association. Prevention of occupational accidents in the health care industry. Low back pain prevention in care workers, pp. 1–15 (2015)
12. Verbeek, J., Martimo, K.P., Karppinen, J., Kuijer, P.P., Takala, E.P., Viikari-Juntura, E.: Manual material handling advice and assistive devices for preventing and treating back pain in workers: a Cochrane Systematic Review. Occup. Environ. Med. **69**(1), 79–80 (2012)
13. Ministry of health, labour and welfare, Comprehensive survey of living conditions (2016). http://www.mhlw.go.jp/toukei/saikin/hw/k-tyosa/k-tyosa13/dl/16.pdf. Accessed 5 Feb 2017
14. Ministry of health, labour and welfare: Revision of low back pain preventive guide-lines in the workplace, and study report of its prevalence (2013). http://www.mhlw.go.jp/stf/houdou/2r98520000034et4-att/2r98520000034mu2_1.pdf. Accessed 5 Feb 2017
15. Owen, B.D.: The magnitude of low-back problem in nursing. West. J. Nurs. Res. **2**, 234–242 (1989)
16. Kelsey, J.L., Githens, P.B., White, A.A., Holford, T.R., Walter, S.D., O'Connor, T.: An epidemiologic study of lifting and twisting on the job and risk for acute prolapsed lumbar intervertebral disc. J. Orthop. Res. **2**(1), 61–66 (1984). doi:10.1002/jor.1100020110
17. Yamashita, T.: Non-specific low back pain. Spine Spinal Cord **25**(4), 244–250 (2012). http://dx.doi.org/10.11477/mf.5002200280
18. Japanese Society of Lumbar Spine Disorders and Japanese Society of Lumbar Spine Disorders: Clinical practice guideline for the management of low back pain 2012, Nankodo, Tokyo (2012)
19. Chen, Y., Devivo, M.J., Jackson, A.B.: Pressure ulcer prevalence in people with spinal cord injury: age-period-duration effects. Arch. Phys. Med. Rehabil. **86**(6), 1208–1213 (2005). doi:10.1016/j.apmr.2004.12.023
20. Moore, Z.E., van Etten, M.T., Dumville, J.C.: Bed rest for pressure ulcer healing in wheelchair users. Cochrane Database Syst. Rev. **17**, Article no. 10: CD011999 (2016). doi:10.1002/14651858.CD011999.pub2
21. Landis, E.M.: Micro-injection studies of capillary blood pressure in human skin. Heart **15**, 209–228 (1930)
22. Sugama, J., Sanada, H., Nakano, N., Masuya, N., Tabata, K.: Reliability and validity of a new multi-pad pressure evaluator for pressure ulcer management. JSPU **2**(3), 310–315 (2000)
23. Shiraishi, Y.: Dynamics of the stress loaded on nurse's back during patient transfer tasks from bed to toilets. JJOMT **57**, 43–49 (2009)
24. Nomura, A.: Development of motion and load analyzing system for nursing care operations. Yokohama National University Repository. Doctoral dissertation, pp. 1–60 (2016)
25. Japanese nursing association: Guidelines on night shift and shift work for nurses (2014). https://www.nurse.or.jp/nursing/shuroanzen/safety/yotu/index.html. Accessed 5 Feb 2017
26. Benner, P.: From Novice to Expert: Excellence and Power in Clinical Nursing Practice, 1st edn. Prentice Hall, Upper Saddle River (2000). Commemorative Edition, pp. 1–310
27. Working Group for Occupational Fatigue (2017). http://square.umin.ac.jp/of/service.html. Accessed 5 Feb 2017

Patella Shape Extraction from 3D Point Cloud Data for Personalized Knee Brace

Hyungan Oh[1,2] and Jinwook Kim[1(✉)]

[1] Imaging Media Research Center, Korea Institute of Science and Technology,
Seoul, Republic of Korea
jwkim@imrc.kist.re.kr
[2] Department of Mechanical and Aerospace Engineering, Seoul National University,
Seoul, Republic of Korea

Abstract. We introduce a novel method to extract the front shape of the patella using 3D point cloud data of the knee obtained with a high resolution scanner or RGB-D camera. The extraction is handled by calculating the angular difference of the normal vector from the center point normal. From the observation of the protrusion of the patella, the outline of the patella can be determined by the starting point at which the deflection of the frontal patella surface increases from the center to the outside. In this paper, we describe the process of patellar shape extraction used for designing a patella protection ring for customized knee braces.

Keywords: Customized knee brace · Patella protection · Patella morphology · Knee cap shape from point cloud

1 Introduction

Along with the expansion of general sports activities, the orthopedic industry has become popular, and the demand for after-surgery management and injury prevention is increasing. In particular, the knee joint is one of the most vulnerable body parts, and patellar instability can cause severe knee injury. Furthermore, the shape of the patella may cause instability of the patella. "Objective patella instability" meaning dislocation of the patella is strongly resistant to the shape of the patella and the inclination of the patella in static and dynamic conditions [1]. Conventional methods of diagnosing a knee joint including a patella are radiographic methods such as X-ray, CT, MRI.

Computed tomography can be used to guide the surgical management of the patella and evaluate the three-dimensional computer modeling of the patellar configuration to design the patella implant [2]. However, three-dimensional modeling and reconstruction by radiography are generally for those who need surgical management and are managed only by clinical institutions. For those who need injury prevention or those who need it after surgery or rehabilitation, it is too expensive and excessive to diagnose the knee. As a result, knee correction is one of those options, and customized knee brace is suitable for prevention and rehabilitation of injuries during exercise and sports.

© Springer International Publishing AG 2017
V.G. Duffy (Ed.): DHM 2017, Part I, LNCS 10286, pp. 160–168, 2017.
DOI: 10.1007/978-3-319-58463-8_14

Many major orthopedic support manufacturers have provided custom functional knee braces. A biomechanical study epidemiologically shows that off-the-shelf braces provide greater resistance in complete extension of the knee and customized knee braces doubling the protective effect [3]. However, existing custom functional braces focus primarily on matching braces around the customer's thighs and calves using standardized patella holes. A patella hole of uniform size and shape may reduce wearing feeling due to the diversity of the shape of the individual patella. Therefore, personalized fittings on the knee cap are needed, and knee joints need to improve proprioception that will optimize the movement and help to reduce the load on joint-related structures such as tendons and ligaments [4].

In this study, we are aiming to extract the outline of patella to design a patella protection ring (patella support) that can be inserted into a customized prosthesis or sleeve.

2 Method

Figure 1 describes the outline of the process. The patella shape extraction process begins with a scan using a high resolution 3D scanner (hereafter referred to as "scanner") or RGB-D cameras. When using the scanner, the output is completely reconstructed, it becomes high precision and high density, so the number of vertices of the output data becomes extremely large. The size of the data should be reduced by down-sampling in pre-process. Unlike the output from the scanner, the capture of the RGB-D camera becomes a little noisy point cloud. Noisy data needs to undergo smoothing processing. After performing shape extraction processing using the preprocessed output from the scanner or RGB-D cameras, the outlier removal processing is performed in order to make the knee support model smoother.

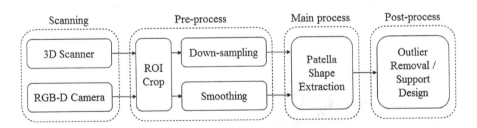

Fig. 1. Patella shape extraction process

2.1 Scanning

The 3D scanning devices used were Artec Spider [5], a blue light technology based high resolution hand-held 3D scanner provided by Artec 3D, and Kinect V2 [6], a time-of-flight sensor based RGB-D camera provided by Microsoft, and RealSense F200 [7], a coded light depth technology based RGB-D camera by Intel. The scanner has the advantage of higher resolution and accuracy for depth cameras. On the other hand, the depth camera is very inexpensive, and it is possible to record motion as a depth image stream.

Using High Resolution 3D Scanner. Since the scanner is a handheld device and scans the object only in steady state, the subject took a slightly deflected posture and formed a knee angle of about 135° at which maximum patella protrusion was observed. Figure 2b shows 3D reconstruction results with 642,012 vertices and 1,284,016 faces.

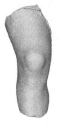
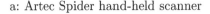

a: Artec Spider hand-held scanner   b: 3D reconstruction

Fig. 2. Scanning by high resolution 3D scanner

Using RGB-D Cameras. The RGB-D camera can capture the depth stream when there is motion. The hardware specifications of Kinect and RealSense cameras indicate the minimum depth range of 40 cm and 20 cm, and maximum frame rates of 30 fps and 60 fps, relatively. Using Kinect, the subject was in a sitting position, repeatedly moved the legs with bending stretching exercises, and placed the camera at about 60 cm from the knee.

Those showing the largest patella protrusion out of the taken depth images were collected and converted into point cloud data. Figure 3b shows the resulting point cloud with 188,638 vertices with no faces. Using the RealSense camera, the

a: RGB image captured   b: Point cloud from depth data

Fig. 3. Scanning by Microsoft Kinect V2

same process as the Kinect capture was executed, but the subject repeatedly performed a single leg squat exercise and placed the camera about 30 cm from the knee.

a: RGB image captured   b: Point cloud from depth data

Fig. 4. Scanning by Intel RealSense F200

2.2   Pre-processing

At the pre-processing stage, we cut out the 3D scanning model and down-sampled it to shorten the calculation time. As a down-sampling method, we created a new point cloud layer using point sampling generated according to the Poisson Disc Distribution using Poisson Disc Sampling described in [8]. Figure 5c shows the down-sampled point cloud with 36,100 vertices.

In the case of RGB-D captured data, it is relatively noisy than the 3D scanning model, so it is necessary to perform smoothing processing. Figure 5e and h show that the point cloud obtained from Kinect has more noisy data than the RealSense data. This is because the knee from Kinect are more distant than Realsense.

As a smoothing method, we smoothed noisy point cloud data using MLS (Moving Least Squares) algorithm implemented in PCL (Point Cloud Library) [9]. MLS approximates the underlying surface using analytic functions such as polynomials based on weighted neighborhoods. The MLS processing is described as:

1. Fit plane to local surface using PCA (Principal Component Analysis)
2. Fit a polynomial function in the set of distances from the points to the surface

$$\sum_{i=1}(p(x_i) - f_i)^2 \theta(\|r_i - r\|)$$

$$\theta(x) = e^{-(\frac{x}{\sigma_r})^2}$$

(1)

3. Project points back to surface

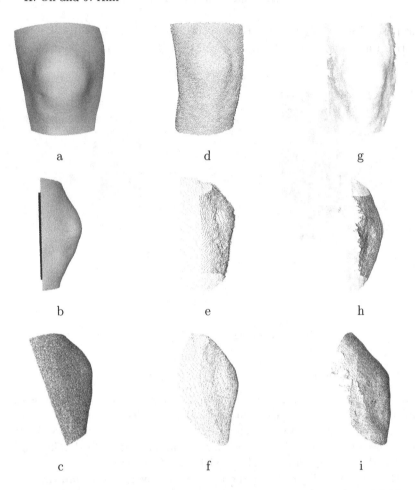

a   d   g

b   e   h

c   f   i

Fig. 5. ROI crops and down-sampled point cloud from Fig. 2b: (a, b, c), and ROI crops and smoothed point cloud from Fig. 3b: (d, e, f) and from Fig. 4b: (g, h, i)

Fifth-order polynomial function was used and the search radius was set to 10 mm for Kinect data and 5 mm for RealSense data to determine the set of distance from point to surface. If setting a search radius greater than 10 mm, the point cloud will be smoother, but the result will be unintentionally flattened. The RealSense data was relatively smooth and a search radius of 5 mm was adequate. Figure 5f and i show the smoothed results from Kinect and RealSense cameras and have vertices of 4646 and vertices of 29,653.

2.3   Patella Shape Extraction

The step of extracting the patella shape begins by selecting the center point of the result point cloud data from the previous process. Once the center point was selected, we collected the vertices in the circular sector defined by the two radius vectors and their included angle. In order to define the circular sector, one radius vector can be determined from the local coordinate at the center point by setting z-axis to the center normal and x-axis to the vector perpendicular to the center normal and parallel to the ground and y-axis to the vector from cross product of two. Either the x- or y-axis can be the starting radius vector.

In this paper, we used the starting circular sector consists of the y-axis as the starting radius vector and 3° of search angle as the included angle, and the other radius vector can be obtained by rotating the start radius vector through the included angle about the z-axis. Using the collected data in the sector, a Two-Term Gaussian Model fitting is adapted to the distance from the center as domain data and the angular difference of vertex normals from the center normal as range data. The equation below is a general expression of a Two-Term Gaussian Model:

$$f(x) = \sum_{i=1}^{2} a_i e^{-(\frac{x-b_i}{c_i})^2} \tag{2}$$

Subsequently, the first derivative of the fitted curve is calculated and the closest peak of the first derivative is set to the data collection distance in the sector. This fitting and peak detection procedure is performed at all around the center of the patella. The first zero-crossing point of the first derivative signifies the side edge of the patella, and the first maximal point of the first derivative indicates the frontal edge of the patella. Figure 6 shows two example sectors when the maximum distance is 70 mm and the searching angle is 3°. The dashed lines in Fig. 6 are multiplied values by 10 from each derivatives for better legibility. In Fig. 6a, the collecting distance was calculated as 19.2 mm between the sector of 63° to 66°. And Fig. 6b shows that the collecting distance was 12.7 mm between the sector of 348° to 351°.

Figure 7 shows that manual selection of the center point exerts insignificant influence on the result of patella shape extraction as long as not picking noticeably outside the patella face. The insignificancy can be verified by Hausdorff distance as shown in Table 1. Hausforff distance in the maximum distance of a set to the nearest point in the other set [10]. Formally, Hausdorff distance from set A to set B is a maximum function, defined as:

$$d_H(A, B) = \max\left\{\sup_{a \in A} \inf_{b \in B} d(a, b)\right\} \tag{3}$$

It is analysed that the extracted patella shape of Fig. 7b and f have less than 0.03 mm of error. And Fig. 7d and f have maximum difference of 0.19 mm, but it is in acceptable range considering the similarity of the shapes extracted.

2.4 Post-processing

In order to design the knee cap protection ring, we can just collect the vertices from the limit described above up to the distance with the suitable width for a person. Next, a ring type point cloud is collected as the basic shape of the

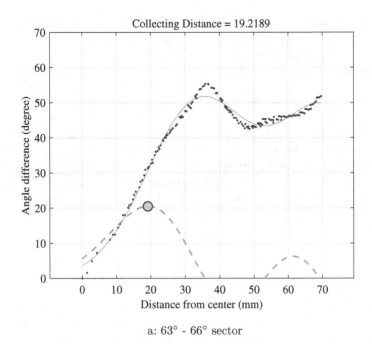

a: 63° - 66° sector

b: 348° - 351° sector

Fig. 6. Collected angle differences of vertex normals (blue dots), fitted curve (red solid line), derivative curve (dashed line), collecting distance indicated by the first peak of the derivative (solid circle) (Color figure online)

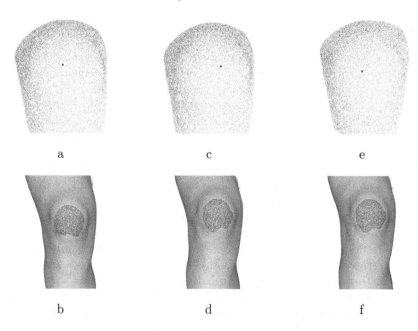

a   c   e

b   d   f

Fig. 7. Extracted patella shape from different center points

Table 1. Mean value of the Hausdorff distance between two point clouds

(unit: mm)		Target point cloud		
		Fig. 7b	Fig. 7d	Fig. 7f
Sample point cloud	Fig. 7b	0	0.1025	0.0231
	Fig. 7d	0.1371	0	0.1404
	Fig. 7f	0.0306	0.1892	0

patella support. As a post-processing, outlier filter can be applied to smooth the ring as shown in Fig. 8. Solidification by the extrusion operation in the normal direction is processed from the smoothed ring shape, and a 3D polygon mesh to be 3D printed is created.

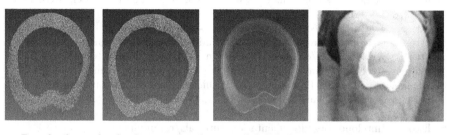

a: Result shape b: Outlier removed   c: Solidified   d: 3D print

Fig. 8. Steps of post-processing

3 Discussion

In this study, we were able to extract the geometric frontal shape of the patella and the protection ring from the 3D scanned point cloud. Using a customized patella protection ring, the knee brace user can release a knee damage due to instability of the patella and proprioception can be increased. In the scanning phase, affordable depth cameras can substitute expensive high resolution scanners and radiography methods. It is also possible to capture depth streams to estimate the path of the patella within the knee joint.

However, captured data from depth cameras are relatively noisy with respect to the 3D scan data. The problem of noise was solved by applying the MLS surface smoothing technique. In addition, extracting the exact shape of the patella is not a complete process for patella protection ring design, as the patella moves around during flexion-extension motion. For customization of the knee brace or sleeve, more design elements are needed to enhance horizontal protection and consider vertical guidance for relaxation. These design elements can be determined by setting different stiffness in both directions. The simplest way to set the difference stiffness is to vary the width and thickness on each side. For example, widening the width in the vertical direction promotes movement of the patella, and when the side is thickened, the patella stabilizes.

Acknowledgements. This research project was supported by the Sports Promotion Fund of Seoul Olympic Sports Promotion Foundation from Ministry of Culture, Sports and Tourism, Korea.

References

1. Panni, A.S., Cerciello, S., Maffulli, N., et al.: Patellar shape can be a predisposing factor in patellar instability. Knee Surg. Sports Traumatol. Arthrosc. **19**, 663–670 (2011)
2. Huang, A.-B., et al.: Comprehensive assessment of patellar morphology using computed tomography-based three-dimensional computer models. Knee **22**, 475–480 (2015)
3. Najibi, S., Albright, J.P.: The use of knee braces, part 1. Am. J. Sports Med. **33**, 602–611 (2005)
4. de Vries, A.J., et al.: The effect of a patellar strap on knee joint proprioception in healthy participants and athletes with patellar tendinopathy. J. Sci. Med. Sport **19**, 278–282 (2016)
5. https://www.artec3d.com/3d-scanner/artec-spider
6. https://developer.microsoft.com/en-us/windows/kinect/hardware
7. http://www.intel.com/content/www/us/en/support/emerging-technologies/intel-realsense-technology/intel-realsense-cameras/intel-realsense-camera-f200.html
8. Corsini, M., Cignoni, P., Scopigno, R.: Efficient and flexible sampling with blue noise properties of triangular meshes. IEEE Trans. Vis. Comput. Graph. **18**, 914–924 (2012)
9. http://pointclouds.org/documentation/tutorials/resampling.php
10. Rote, G.: Computing the minimum Hausdorff distance between two point sets on a line under translation. Inf. Process. Lett. **38**, 123–127 (1991)

Evaluation of Japanese Bowing of Non-experts by Experts

Tomoya Takeda[1($\boxtimes$)], Kazuaki Yamashiro[1], Xiaodan Lu[1],
Shodai Kawakatsu[1], and Tomoko Ota[2]

[1] Kyoto Institute of Technology, Matsugasaki, Sakyo-ku,
Kyoto 606-6585, Japan
t.takeda@taste.jp
[2] Chuo Business Group, 1-6-6 Funakoshi-Cho, Chuo-ku,
Osaka 540-0036, Japan
promot1@gold.ocn.ne.jp

Abstract. Bowing in Japanese greetings is an important move on a daily basis. However, scenes actually receiving guidance are few, and in many cases it is self-taught. In this research, we investigated and analyzed what kind of features are in bowing of non-experts who are done in self-taught, and what kind of motion the experts evaluate. Three experts evaluated the bowing motion of 41 non-experts with 7 full marks, examined the correlation of the three evaluations, clarified the evaluation viewpoint of each evaluator, and as a result, two examiners I was able to find a characteristic evaluation viewpoint. In addition, as a result of performing cluster analysis by the Ward method using the principal component analysis, multiple regression analysis, cluster analysis, the principal component score was used to clarify the evaluation components, it was possible to analyze into 5 clusters, and as a result, we ware possible to classify the bowing of each by feature.

Keywords: Ojigi · Expert · Non-expert

1 Introduction

When saying Japanese greetings ceremony, first of all we have a bow. Greeting ceremonies around the world vary by country, region, time and occasion [1]. In Japan many people bow at the scene of greeting, gratitude or apology. We see bowing in various scenes such as business scene and restaurant, apology press conference, and also public place in train. The characteristics of the Japanese bowing are that scenes and usage are diverse.

Although it is not as daily as in Japan, there are actions of bowing in the world as well. In Christianity bow to represent respect and obedience. In Islam and Judaism it is positioned as being done only to God. Looking at the Western area, the bow of Europe is a movement of "Bow and scrape" which the nobility and the butler see in a movie, etc., draw a right foot, attach a right hand to the body, and move the left hand horizontally horizontally in a motion (On the other hand, a woman pulls one leg diagonally in the back of the back, lightly bends the knee of the other foot, and greets

© Springer International Publishing AG 2017
V.G. Duffy (Ed.): DHM 2017, Part I, LNCS 10286, pp. 169–178, 2017.
DOI: 10.1007/978-3-319-58463-8_15

the spine with the spine stretched, the action called "courtesy") [2]. Howeverit goes without saying that bowing in everyday life is not common in Europe and the Middle Eastern countries because it has a religious background or restricted to aristocracy as described above.

There is a bow in East Asia as well. In China, there was a bow from ancient times, but in modern times it is considerably simplified in everyday life. Korea's "Sitting Bow" (Joru) is a series of actions, such as bending the knees from the standing posture and lightly attaching the forehead to the back of the hand and then standing up again, and it exists as an important manner often used [3]. Also, in Thailand there is a daily greeting action called Wai.

In Japan, bowing is done on a daily basis, but scenes actually receiving guidance are few. In this research, we investigated and analyzed what kind of characteristics the non-experts bowed, what kind of motion the expert would evaluate.

2   Experiment Method

2.1   Recording of Bowing Videos of Unskilled People

For experts to evaluate the bow of non-experts, first of all, non-experts bowed videos were recorded. A marker was added to measure each motion index of a bow of an unskilled person. The marker was attached to the head, shoulders, waist and knees of non-experts. Each bowing motion was recorded with a video camera (Fig. 1).

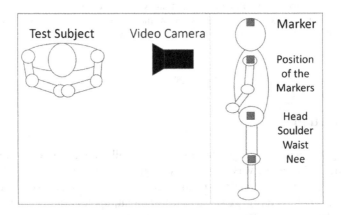

Fig. 1. Measurement graphics

2.2   Motion Analysis and Extraction of Motion Indicators

From the positions of markers of recorded videos, motion analysis was performed by Photoron's two-dimensional motion analysis software TEMA and various motion indices were measured and calculated from the position information of each marker during bowing motion. The various motion indicators are as shown in Table 3.

2.3   Creating an Answer Form

We used a questionnaire form by Google form in order to improve the smooth response environment of experts. We created a form that can be evaluated with 7 full marks by watching 41 bowing videos of non-experts I made 1 for the worst evaluation and 7 for the best evaluation.

2.4   Answers by Experts

Three persons were selected for responding by experts. Both of them are manners lecturers for enterprises, nine years, fourteen years, fourteen years respectively. Experts had a questionnaire form prepared in advance and asked 41 people to evaluate the video by watching one movie and evaluating the impression in seven levels.

3   Result

3.1   Reliability of Evaluation

Intra-Class Correlation (ICC) was calculated using the evaluation value for 41 videos by 3 evaluators (Table 1).

Table 1. ICC

Cronbach's alpha	.642
ICC (2, 1)	.305
ICC (2, 3)	.568

Regarding reproducibility between examiners, ICC (2, 1) was .305. The average value of three evaluators was calculated and the correlation coefficient with the evaluation value of each evaluator was calculated (Table 2).

Table 2. Correlation among evaluators

	Evaluator A	Evaluator B	Evaluator C	Average point of evaluation
Evaluator A	1	.312[*]	.443[**]	.692[**]
Evaluator B	.312[*]	1	.423[**]	.811[**]
Evaluator C	.443[**]	.423[**]	1	.798[**]
Average point of evaluation	.692[**]	.811[**]	.798[**]	1

[*]$p < .05$; [**]$p < .01$

Relationship between impression evaluation of bow and action indicator Table 3 shows the average value of each index of bowing movement.

Table 3. Motion indicator

	M ± SD	Min	Max
Flexion time (sec.)	1.14 ± 0.26	0.60	1.79
Stationary time (sec.)	0.92 ± 0.36	0.31	1.77
Extention time (sec.)	1.01 ± 0.31	0.66	1.80
Total time (sec.)	3.07 ± 0.64	1.88	4.83
Angle at the end of flexion of neck (deg.)	16.7 ± 11.0	−47.9	0.3
Angle at the end of stationary of neck (deg.)	−16.1 ± 10.9	−50.7	2.0
Angle at the end of extension of neck (deg.)	0.69 ± 3.99	−9.86	8.25
Angle at the end of flexion of waist (deg.)	45.3 ± 12.7	−71.5	−16.3
Angle at the end of stationary of waist (deg.)	−43.9 ± 12.6	−70.1	−15.1
Angle at the end of extension of waist (deg.)	0.34 ± 3.92	−8.51	8.85
Angle difference between neck and waist at the end of flexion (deg.)	28.6 ± 14.2	8.3	69.0
Angle difference between neck and waist at the end of stationary (deg.)	27.8 ± 13.5	11.1	62.6
Angle difference between neck and waist at the end of extension (deg.)	1.03 ± 4.59	−8.45	14.42
Synchronization ratio at the time of completion of flexion, at the start of stationary (%)	0.37 ± 0.23	−0.01	0.75
Synchronization ratio at the time of completion of stationary, at the start of extension (%)	0.36 ± 0.23	−0.08	0.81
Synchronization ratio at end of extension (%)	0.89 ± 1.62	−2.80	4.67
Flexion speed of neck (deg./sec.)	15.6 ± 13.1	−69.5	0.3
Extention speed of neck (deg./sec.)	5.82 ± 5.22	−28.4	1.2
Flexion speed of waist (deg./sec.)	42.0 ± 17.5	−92.4	−15.4
Extension speed of waist (deg./sec.)	46.1 ± 17.7	−89.2	−16.2
Center time of bowing movement (sec.)	1.54 ± 0.32	0.94	2.41
Center time of stationary (sec.)	1.61 ± 0.34	0.88	2.49
Center time deviation (sec.)	0.07 ± 0.11	−0.20	0.29
Percentage of flexion time	0.37 ± 0.05	0.27	0.47
Percentage of stationary time	0.30 ± 0.09	0.12	0.46
Percentage of extension time	0.33 ± 0.07	0.22	0.50
Flexion extension balance (sec.)	0.14 ± 0.23	−0.40	0.58
Flexion extension balance ratio	4.50 ± 7.54	−11.76	19.38

Table 4 shows correlation coefficients between the values of impression evaluation of the bow and action index.

In evaluator A, significant positive correlation was found between angle at the end of flexion of neck, angle at the end of stationary of neck, angle at the end of flexion of waist, angle at the end of stationary of waist, flexion speed of neck, and extension speed of neck. And significant negative correlation was found between synchronization ratio at the time of completion of flexion, at the start of stationary and synchronization ratio at the time of completion of stationary, at the start of extension.

Table 4. Correlation between skill evaluations and behavior indicators

	Evaluator A	Evaluator B	Evaluator C	Average point of evaluation
Flexion time (sec.)	.083	−.015	.076	.054
Stationary time (sec.)	.285	.610**	.129	.468**
Extention time (sec.)	.021	.019	.193	.102
Total time (sec.)	.208	.344*	.196	.334*
Angle at the end of flexion of neck (deg.)	.479**	−.103	.085	.147
Angle at the end of stationary of neck (deg.)	.492**	−.150	.073	.122
Angle at the end of extension of neck (deg.)	−.161	−.131	.089	−.083
Angle at the end of flexion of waist (deg.)	.318*	−.369*	−.138	−.143
Angle at the end of stationary of waist (deg.)	.324*	−.350*	−.108	−.118
Angle at the end of extension of waist (deg.)	.164	.225	.237	.275
Angle difference between neck and waist at the end of flexion (deg.)	.087	.251	.190	.24
Angle difference between neck and waist at the end of stationary (deg.)	.094	.207	.160	.20
Angle difference between neck and waist at the end of extension (deg.)	−.280	−.305	−.125	−.307
Synchronization ratio at the time of completion of flexion, at the start of stationary (%)	−.395*	.026	−.076	−.154
Synchronization ratio at the time of completion of stationary, at the start of extension (%)	−.402**	.127	−.035	−.086
Synchronization ratio at end of extension (%)	−.035	−.089	.228	.042
Flexion speed of neck (deg./sec.)	.453**	−.136	.090	.123
Extention speed of neck (deg./sec.)	.502**	−.045	.078	.182
Flexion speed of waist (deg./sec.)	.305	−.295	−.062	−.076
Extension speed of waist (deg./sec.)	.279	−.318*	−.045	−.089
Center time of bowing movement (sec.)	.208	.344*	.196	.334*
Center time of stationary (sec.)	.213	.309*	.126	.287
Center time deviation (sec.)	.052	−.048	−.180	−.086
Percentage of flexion time	−.159	−.590**	−.192	−.442**
Percentage of stationary time	.213	.564**	.052	.386*
Percentage of extension time	−.179	−.323*	.066	−.198

*p < .05; **p < .01

In evaluator B, significant positive correlation was found between stationary time, total time, center time of bowing movement and center time of stationary. And significant negative correlation was found between angle at the end of flexion of waist, angle at the end of stationary of waist, extension speed of waist, percentage of flexion time and percentage of extension time.

Evaluator C did not show any significant correlation with any of the variables.

3.2   Principal Component Analysis to Multiple Regression Analysis, Cluster Analysis

Principal Component Analysis

Principal component analysis was performed using all variables (Table 5). As a result, it was possible to extract from the first principal component to the sixth principal component.

The first principal component is a component related to the flexion angle and flexion extension speed of the site A and was named "neck component". The second principal component is composed of a variable indicating the length of time of operation and is named "motion time component". The third principal component is a component related to the bending angle and flexion extension speed of waist, and is named "waist component". Since the fourth principal component is a component showing the difference between flexion time and extension time, it is named "motion time balance component". Since the fifth principal component is composed of variables concerning flexion time and rest time, it was named "stationary time component". The sixth principal component is composed of variables of the final angle difference and the final angle, so it is named "final posture component".

Multiple Regression Analysis

Multiple regression analysis was performed for each evaluator by the forced input method with six principal component scores as explanatory variables and evaluation points as objective variables (Table 6). Significant regression was obtained for evaluators A, B and average points. Considering the standard regression coefficient, in Evaluator A, the first principal component (neck component) and the third principal component (waist component) were significant positive coefficients. In the evaluator B, the second principal component (motion time component) was a significant positive coefficient, and the fifth principal component (stationary time component) was a significant negative coefficient. On average, the fifth principal component (stationary time component) was a significant negative coefficient.

Cluster Analysis

Cluster analysis (square Euclidean distance) by Ward method was performed using principal component scores. As a result, it was judged from the shape of the dendrogram that it is appropriate to classify into 5 clusters. The values of each variable are shown for each cluster (Table 7). As a result of one-factor analysis of variance, the fifth cluster has the shortest operation time, and the tuning rate at which the cervical flexion angle is the largest is also large, so it is named "fast and big synchronized action type". Next, since the fourth cluster has the longest operation time and the large waist flexion angle, it was named "slowly large motion type". Because Cluster 3 has a short operation time and a small waist flexion angle, it is named "Fast and waist flextion angle small size type".

Since Cluster 2 has a small flexion angle of the neck and deep flexion angle of the lumbar region, it is named "Synchronized no action type". Cluster 1 was named as "asymmetric time type" because the value of the operation time balance component is the largest. For the motion index, significant main effects were observed for all

Table 5. Principal component analysis

	PC1	PC2	PC3	PC4	PC5	PC6
Angle at the end of flexion of neck (deg.)	1.009	-.113	.238	-.040	-.035	.055
Angle at the end of stationary of neck (deg.)	1.007	-.164	.187	-.021	-.080	.049
Synchronization ratio at the time of completion of flexion, at the start of stationary (%)	-1.001	.095	.106	.041	-.025	-.052
Synchronization ratio at the time of completion of stationary, at the start of extension (%)	-.967	.137	.182	.033	.040	-.045
Flexion speed of neck (deg./sec.)	.881	.193	.162	.078	.107	-.043
Extention speed of neck (deg./sec.)	.826	.180	.191	.048	.007	-.243
Center time of bowing movement (sec.)	-.052	1.013	-.037	-.126	-.225	.024
Total time (sec.)	-.052	1.013	-.037	-.126	-.225	.024
Center time of stationary (sec.)	-.054	.972	-.036	.200	-.185	.004
Flexion time (sec.)	-.071	.908	-.060	.187	.355	.001
Extension time (sec.)	-.044	.740	-.057	-.555	.256	.034
Synchronization ratio at end of extension (%)	-.196	-.302	.261	-.208	.086	.022
Angle at the end of flexion of waist (deg.)	.197	-.196	1.012	.007	-.072	.016
Angle at the end of stationary of waist (deg.)	.214	-.229	1.010	-.030	-.079	.025
Extension speed of waist (deg./sec.)	.152	.376	.789	-.164	.127	.071
Angle difference between neck and waist at the end of flexion (deg.)	.605	.048	-.762	-.023	.002	.024
Angle difference between neck and waist at the end of stationary (deg.)	.614	.123	-.754	-.004	.046	.021
Flexion speed of waist (deg./sec.)	.171	.464	.718	.159	.151	-.008
Center time deviation (sec.)	-.014	.048	-.003	.964	.083	-.056
Angle at the end of extension of waist (deg.)	.025	.035	.048	-.899	-.131	-.149
Percentage of extension time	-.001	-.016	-.028	-.703	.549	.036
Percentage of flexion time	-.018	.032	-.006	.545	.951	-.040
Percentage of stationary time	.016	.003	.017	.228	-.921	-.013
Stationary time (sec.)	.001	.527	.019	.108	-.870	.006
Angle difference between neck and waist at the end of extension (deg.)	.002	.023	.018	.491	.053	.912
Angle at the end of extension of neck (deg.)	.027	.061	.068	-.317	-.068	.904

Table 6. Multiple regression analysis

	Evaluator A		Evaluator B		Evaluator C		Average	
	β	p	β	p	β	p	β	p
Neck component	0.450	.003**	−0.196	.129	0.118	.506	0.104	.500
Motion time component	0.091	.517	0.303	.018*	0.141	.412	0.248	.101
Waist component	0.373	.018*	−0.114	.396	−0.074	.688	0.036	.825
Motion time balance component	−0.199	.167	−0.181	.154	−0.292	.100	−0.289	.062
Stationary time component	−0.313	.065	−0.665	.000**	−0.135	.506	−0.508	.006**
Final posture component	−0.108	.471	−0.023	.858	0.024	.894	−0.038	.810
R^2	−.306	.004**	.460	.000**	−.043	.632	.213	.025*

$^{*}p < .05;$ $^{**}p < .01$

Table 7. Cluster comparison

	Cluster1 Asymmetric time type	Cluster2 Synchronized no action type	Cluster3 Fast, waist flexion angle small size type	Cluster4 Slowly large motion type	Cluster5 Fast and big synchronized action type	F	p
n	10	13	8	7	3		
Flexion time (sec.)	1.20±0.12	1.03±0.13	1.13±0.20	1.51±0.18	0.64±0.05	21.37	.000 **
Stationary time (sec.)	0.86±0.16	1.23±0.29	0.64±0.20	0.92±0.45	0.58±0.06	7.42	.000 **
Extention time (sec.)	0.89±0.12	0.85±0.14	0.99±0.14	1.60±0.16	0.75±0.03	42.19	.000 **
Total time (sec.)	2.95±0.19	3.12±0.45	2.75±0.38	4.01±0.53	1.96±0.10	17.69	.000 **
Angle at the end of flexion of neck (deg.)	-22.8±10.0	-9.1±6.1	-11.2±8.9	-21.6±6.8	-32.6±13.2	8.20	.000 **
Angle at the end of stationary of neck (deg.)	-21.6±9.9	-9.6±5.2	-9.3±8.4	-19.9±6.4	-35.1±13.5	9.40	.000 **
Angle at the end of extension of neck (deg.)	-2.78±3.61	-0.17±3.24	4.61±1.88	1.39±3.01	3.89±3.70	7.42	.000 **
Angle at the end of flexion of waist (deg.)	-42.3±10.1	-51.4±12.3	-31.5±9.1	-51.2±8.8	-51.9±10.2	5.56	.001 **
Angle at the end of stationary of waist (deg.)	-41.6±9.9	-49.9±11.7	-29.3±8.7	-50.2±8.8	-49.8±11.1	6.23	.001 **
Angle at the end of extension of waist (deg.)	-2.33±3.37	-1.02±5.05	0.24±3.11	1.96±2.15	2.29±1.43	1.88	.135
Angle diff. between neck and waist at the end of flexion (deg.)	19.5±5.1	42.3±13.1	20.4±10.1	29.5±12.1	19.3±3.0	9.40	.000 **
Angle diff. between neck and waist at the end of stationary (deg.)	20.0±5.2	40.3±12.3	20.0±9.0	30.4±12.5	14.7±2.4	9.28	.000 **
Angle diff. between neck and waist at the end of extention (deg.)	-0.45±3.80	0.84±5.65	4.37±3.45	-0.56±3.99	1.60±3.35	1.64	.185
Sync. ratio at the time of completion of flexion, at the start of stationary (%)	0.52±0.17	0.18±0.12	0.35±0.27	0.44±0.18	0.61±0.12	6.81	.000 **
Sync. ratio at the time of completion of stationary, at the start of extention (%)	0.50±0.17	0.20±0.11	0.30±0.27	0.41±0.18	0.49±0.10	6.98	.000 **
Sync. ratio at end of extension (%)	0.66±1.08	0.35±0.99	2.02±2.30	0.50±2.02	1.89±1.15	1.93	.126
Flexion speed of neck (deg./sec.)	-18.93±7.87	-9.09±6.35	-9.82±8.35	-14.91±6.27	-50.40±16.53	17.77	.000 **
Extention speed of neck (deg./sec.)	-6.35±3.85	-2.96±1.72	-4.91±3.36	-5.52±2.54	-19.62±7.65	15.32	.000 **
Flexion speed of waist (deg./sec.)	-35.3±8.3	-50.9±15.1	-28.3±8.1	-34.1±6.0	-80.9±10.0	16.95	.000 **
Extention speed of waist (deg./sec.)	-44.4±10.3	-58.4±15.8	-30.2±9.0	-33.3±9.1	-70.0±16.6	11.15	.000 **
Center time of bowing movement (sec.)	1.47±0.10	1.56±0.23	1.38±0.19	2.01±0.27	0.98±0.05	17.69	.000 **
Center time of stationary (sec.)	1.63±0.15	1.65±0.23	1.45±0.25	1.97±0.36	0.93±0.07	10.88	.000 **
Center time deviation (sec.)	0.16±0.09	0.09±0.07	0.07±0.09	-0.04±0.12	-0.05±0.03	6.73	.000 **
Percentage of flexion time	0.41±0.03	0.33±0.05	0.41±0.04	0.38±0.03	0.33±0.01	11.53	.000 **
Percentage of stationary time	0.29±0.05	0.39±0.05	0.23±0.06	0.22±0.08	0.30±0.01	14.62	.000 **
Percentage of extension time	0.30±0.04	0.28±0.04	0.36±0.05	0.41±0.07	0.38±0.02	11.46	.000 **
Evaluator A	3.20±1.23	3.69±0.95	3.63±0.74	3.43±0.98	2.33±0.58	1.38	.259
Evaluator B	4.30±1.34	5.46±1.05	3.25±1.91	4.71±1.38	5.00±0.00	3.49	.017 *
Evaluator C	2.60±0.70	3.46±1.56	3.63±1.69	3.86±0.69	2.67±0.58	1.49	.225
Average og evaluation	3.37±0.84	4.21±0.88	3.50±1.36	4.00±0.84	3.33±0.33	1.54	.213
neck component	-0.50±0.75	0.73±0.50	0.28±0.91	-0.16±0.71	-1.89±1.04	10.00	.000 **
operating time component	-0.01±0.30	-0.11±0.61	-0.30±0.59	1.45±0.77	-2.09±0.05	22.95	.000 **
waist component	0.36±0.63	-0.70±0.97	1.05±0.63	-0.12±0.73	-0.72±0.68	7.49	.000 **
operation time balance component	0.74±0.82	0.30±0.84	-0.13±0.84	-1.00±0.74	-1.07±0.24	6.81	.000 **
stationary time component	0.30±0.48	-1.04±0.67	0.83±0.61	0.72±0.95	-0.34±0.18	14.09	.000 **
final posture component	-0.75±0.81	-0.16±0.97	0.89±0.51	-0.01±0.90	0.85±0.93	5.09	.002 **
Operating time factor	-0.15±0.29	-0.10±0.76	-0.28±0.59	1.50±0.73	-1.82±0.08	18.02	.000 **
Neck component factor	-0.26±0.65	0.61±0.45	0.32±0.66	-0.06±0.54	-2.51±1.26	16.11	.000 **
Waist component factor	0.17±0.64	-0.76±0.85	1.12±0.53	0.26±0.67	-0.87±1.05	9.65	.000 **

$^{*}p <.05;$ $^{**}p <.01$

variables except for the final angle B, the final angle difference, and the final synchronization rate.

As a result of one factor analysis analysis with five cluster types as explanatory variables and evaluator's evaluation points as objective variables, a significant main effect was seen in evaluator 2, but other than evaluator 2, significant No main effect was seen.

4 Discussion

Evaluation by three experts resulted in a slight variation. There are features in action indicators that evaluate highly for each evaluator, but when you examine them individually, they are evaluated according to circumstances in which evaluators are placed within the scope of general guidance points.

First, the evaluator A will be described. The evaluator A is evaluated focusing on whether the neck is straight or whether the waist angle is a moderate angle (30 degrees as a salute). The evaluator A is an evaluator who is good at teaching to the person who receives a customer at the dental reception. Since the beauty of the motion of the upper body greatly affects the impression of the customer at the reception, the evaluator A emphasizes the bow that bent from the waist, which made the neck straight, which is consistent with this result. The "bowed bent from the waist with the neck straightened" is a general guidance point in bowing.

Next, the evaluator B will be described. Evaluator B focuses on the length of the bowing rest time and the depth of the bending angle. Evaluator B is an evaluator who is good at teaching in business manners for enterprises. In business etiquette, since respect for partner and confidence influence impression on opponent, emphasis is placed on a clear bow of motion, it seems that bow and long bending angle deep bowing evaluated.

Finally, we will talk about the evaluator C. In the evaluator C, we could not find a significant motion index this time. Evaluator C is an evaluator who provides customer service instruction for employees in the bridal industry. When conducting customer service guidance in the bridal industry, customer service guidance assuming various scenes such as greetings, respect, appreciation, apologies are necessary. The current operation index was a linear analysis by time, angle and speed. We think that it is necessary to find appropriate indicators other than these motion indices or to require further analysis which is not linear analysis in the motion indicator.

In cluster analysis, by classifying into five clusters, it was possible to categorize patterns that are likely to be inexperienced by non-experts. "Asymmetric time type (10 people)" "Synchronized no action type (10 people)" "Fast, waist flexion angle small size (8 people)" "slowly large motion type (7 people)" "Fast and big synchronized action type (3 people)".

In line with these and the significant action indicators, as in Cluster 1, non-expert who has the characteristic of "long flexion time" and unskilled person having characteristics of "long time and large waist angle" as in Cluster 2 Together, it turns out that it accounts for a majority. From these, it is understood that non-experts tend to express "slowly politely and deeply" when fearing to carefully bow the bow, and in presence or absence of synchronization there is noticed that "it is better not to bend the neck". It turns out that there is a difference in bowing behavior depending on whether or not

Cluster 3 has a waist flexion angle of about 30 degrees. Because it is said that 30 degrees is appropriate for expert salute, this cluster can be said to be "done" in terms of the waist flexion angle. However, as for stationary time, further comparison and examination with experts is necessary.

In Cluster 4, the total time is long and in Cluster 5 the total time is short. The waist flexion angle is deep in both Cluster 4 and 5. Both clusters seem to have commonality at first glance, but it is quite different as an expression of actual bow. Cluster 4 has deep flexion with long operation time, so it has a relaxed atmosphere and it is bowing. On the other hand, since the cluster 5 performs a deep bending with a short operation time, it is a very stiff bow. It turned out that there was a very wide variation in the theoretical operating time considered by unskilled persons.

5   Conclusion

In this study, it was found that the viewpoint of the experts was not uniform in one word. Since no significant motion indicator was found for evaluator C, we believe that it is necessary to expand the scope not only for linear analysis but also for quadratic curve analysis and to clarify new behavior indicators in the future. In addition to this, we performed multiple regression analysis and cluster analysis from the principal component analysis, but we would like to expand the range of factor analysis, multiple regression analysis and cluster analysis.

References

1. Tanaka, H.: An analysis of how teaching bowing brings about changes in the bowing movement. s.l.: Shinai-Kiyo (1989)
2. Patrick, B.: Cultural History of Manners and Etiquette, pp. 19–20. Hara-Shobo, Tokyo (2013)
3. Sato, K., et al.: Japan China Korea manner dictionary, pp. 35–37 (2015)

Appropriateness and Impression Evaluation of Japanese Seated Bow

Tomoya Takeda[1](✉), Noriyuki Kida[1], and Tadayuki Hara[2]

[1] Kyoto Institute of Technology, Matsugasaki, Sakyo-ku,
Kyoto 606-6585, Japan
t.takeda@taste.jp
[2] University of Central Florida, 9907 Universal Blvd, Orlando,
FL 32819-8701, USA
Tadayuki.Hara@ucf.edu

Abstract. Japanese bowing has two types, that is, standing bow and seated bow. Though seated bow is used in the scene at tea ceremony or Japanese traditional restaurants, standing bow is the main style in Japanese society at the present. Before Meiji period, sitting bow was often used in the scene of receiving guests in Japanese (*tatami*) room. But after that, service systems have gradually been westernized, and standing bow have become more popular. As a study of researching bowing through experimentation, Gyoba et al. [4] conducted a pair of experiments, one investigating subjective impressions toward the action of bowing, and the other investigating the appropriateness of certain styles in given social contexts. But in this paper we focus on seated bow. This study used video clips of seated bowing actions. The bend angle (30°, 45°, 90°) and duration of the bent posture (0–4 s) were varied. In this experiment, the participants rated their subjective impressions of the bowing actions. It showed the effect that the bend angle and duration of the bent posture impress.

Keywords: Ojigi · Seated position bowing · Japanese bowing · Japanese hospitality

1 Introduction

The number of foreign visitors to Japan is rapidly increasing. Since April 2003, when the "Visit Japan Campaign" promotion to attract tourists from abroad was begun by the Ministry of Land, Infrastructure, Transport, and Tourism [1], over-seas publicity regarding travel to Japan, domestic infrastructure for the sake of foreign visitors, and other such developments have intensified. Despite the Great East Japan Earthquake in 2011, proliferation of the middle class brought on by a weakened yen and economic growth in various neighboring Asian countries led the number of foreign visitors to jump from a mere 5.24 million in 2004 to 13.41 million in 2014, and 19.74 million in 2015. Therefore the government decided to greatly raise the aim of 2020 from 20 million to 30 million.

In terms of Japan's tourism resources which pique the interest of people from other countries, there are factors such as its beautiful scenery of nature as an island nation, its

© Springer International Publishing AG 2017
V.G. Duffy (Ed.): DHM 2017, Part I, LNCS 10286, pp. 179–187, 2017.
DOI: 10.1007/978-3-319-58463-8_16

rich historical and cultural heritage, and other cultural resources. However, after it was decided that the 2020 Summer Olympics and Paralympics would be held in Tokyo, it seemed to become inevitable that the Japanese way of hospitality – known as "omotenashi" – would also rank as an essential tourism resource. This was especially true because of the attention that would be drawn to lodging facilities like hotels, traditional inns, and bed and breakfasts, as well as dining and drinking establishments from casual eateries to high-end restaurants, and other places visitors are certain to see.

The Japan Tourism Agency is supporting regional pre-emptive initiatives as the "Regional 'Omotenashi' Improvement Project Directed at the 2020 Olympics and Paralympics". Concomitant with this movement, there are also efforts to attract customers by strengthening the spirit of "omotenashi" within the service industry, but in order to do so a proper understanding of "omotenashi" is imperative. The Japan Productivity Center has defined "omotenashi" as "work to provide uncompromisingly heartfelt service while valuing the perspective of customers and/or residents" [2]. "Valuing the perspective of customers and/or residents" can be rephrased as "mutualistic service whereby the provider considers the circumstances of the beneficiary and responds with his or her whole heart," as differentiated from service which is unilateral from the side of the provider only. It can be thought that analogous concepts in other countries such as "hospi-tality" (the U.S.), 待客之道 (China), and "hospitalité" (France) vary from "omotenashi" on this point of whether the service is or is not mutualistic [2], and we can say that it safely passes as a peculiarly Japanese tourism resource.

There has been much debate over the question of what kind of service "omotenashi" entails. But even if we start from the basis of the saying that, "'Omotenashi' begins with a greeting and ends with a parting," it seems that we should note the Japanese way of bowing (ojigi) as a first step to studying "omotenashi". The history of bowing being an action of greeting for Japanese people is long, as in the third century Chinese text the Gishi-wajin-den it is recorded that, "When meeting with an important person, Japanese people go to their knees and cast down their heads". Furthermore, the action of casting down one's head, or bowing, has been regarded as showing that one has no enmity toward his or her counterpart, due to the fact that it exposes the back of the head, a point of vulnerability [3].

Bowing is not limited to instances of greeting. It is also performed in various other settings such as to show appreciation or apologize, and is a commonly seen gesture in the course of daily life [4]. Bowing can be done while standing or while sitting. For both there are multiple classifications according to the angle at which the upper portion of the body is bent. Within standing bows, based on the angle of the bow there are the classifications of eshaku ("greeting bow," 15°), keirei ("respect bow," 30°), saikeirei ("highest respect bow," 45°), and hairei ("worship bow," 90°) [5], or the classifications of eshaku (approximately 15°), keirei (approximately 45°), and saikeirei for the gods and buddhas ("highest respect bow used for the gods and buddhas," approximately 90°) [6, 7], among other ways of classifying. However, in most settings calling for conventional business etiquette, eshaku (15°), keirei (30°), and saikeirei (45°) are practically being used as the three classifications of bows [8].

Sitting bows also have classification. Ogasawara way of bow has 9details called "kuhonrei" and the following 3 are popular "eshaku", "futsurei" and "saikeirei". There are Tanaka (1989) and Asada [8] as previous study. Moreover, they are called "Shin", "Gyou" and "Sou" in the order corresponding to "Saikeirei" "Futsurei" and "Eshakurei" in the way of tea.

As a case study of researching bowing through experimentation, Morishita and Iwashita [9] reported that as inexperienced persons lowered their heads when bowing, there was an intensification in the angle of the curvature of their backs; that in comparison to experienced persons the time of remaining still upon bowing was shorter for inexperienced persons; and that despite their being Japanese, the subjects predominantly bowed in a self-taught manner.

Most case study about bow with experiment is targeting standing bow. In other previous study about it, they studied about the aspects such as what kind of bow would prefer or what kind of impression they give.

Henmi and Isayama [10] examined the duration for which pleasure was taken in various types of standing bows, making use of a "standing bow motion stimulus" with the body bent at 45° that was created by three-dimensional computer graphics. Additionally, Gyoba et al. [4] conducted a pair of experiments, one investigating jective impressions toward the action of bowing, and the other investigating the appropriateness of certain styles in given social contexts.

Also they conducted an experiment which consider appropriate movements for movements of bow. Then, they proved 3 tendencies as follows. At greeting moments, the more you impress people with bow in a low politeness and high smooth motion, the more you rate as appropriate. At the moment of appreciation, the more smooth motion give high impression, and at the moment of apology, the more politeness give high impression, the more you rate as appropriate.

As stated at the outset, there is a movement to attract customers by strengthening the spirit of "omotenashi" within the service industry at this time.

Then, we decided to research about what kind of motion judged as appropriate with the sitting bow used in formal scene such as Japanese restaurant and tea ceremony. Using Gyoba et al. [4] as basic instruments, we conducted the experimental tests on researching subjective impression to the motion with real movie which including operated motive information of sitting bow. According to this, motive information operated bend angle and duration of the bent posture.

Gyoba et al. [4] is using the bow movie made by CG. But in contrast to them, we operated bend angle and duration of the bent posture as motive information in the real motion what human do.

Although about the bent angle of sitting bow, there is great variability among literatures, generally, the variabilitiy of eshaku's is from 15° to 30°, futsuurei's is 30° to 90° and saikeirei's is 45° to 90°. We dertermined 30°, 45° and 90° to inspect the clear differences of movements, considering the view of motive repeatability with human. In addition, we provided 5 class (from 0 s to 4 s) with duration of the bent posture. In the experiment, we studied about subjective impression for movement of sitting bow by using SD. And we altered a part of pair of adjectives in SD using example from Gyoba et al. [4] used.

2   Experiment

2.1   Purpose of This Experiment

The purpose was to research the impressions of someone to bow to by operating bend angle and duration of the bent posture.

2.2   The How

Making the Video of Sitting Bow

We placed a video camera in front of the model who bow in sitting. In this case, we conducted 3 sitting bow patterns (30°, 45° and 90°) and he downed his head centering on his waist. To make sure the setup angle, we measured his angle in video taken from lateral by angle gauge after we marked his head and waist. Regarding the duration of bent posture, the model counted accurate time by himself using metronome and made videos at 0 s,1 s,2 s,3 s and 4 s. Recorded over 3times, we selected one of them as the best video for evaluate impression which fall within the acceptable value (approximately 10% both bend angle and duration of the bent posture).

Also as Ogasawara (1975) says "the speed of bending and stretching body should be at a uniform pace", this study followed the concept in regardless of bent angle. We setup other movements in 3 sitting bows as follows by referring Asada 2015. 30° bow is as "Slide down your both hands from knee and touch tatami by only fingertip. Body might have a head forward posture along the movement." 45° bow is as "Move your fingertip a little forward from eshaku form keeping wrist on your knee. And tip your body forward opening both hands." 90° bow is as "Keeping the form of eshaku, put your fingertip under the forehead as rei and make shape of mountain by fingertip. The line from head to back would be flat."

Evaluation of Impression

We had questionnaire on the Internet using Google Form officially by Google. Answers were 21 men and women aged from 23 to 59. On the questionnaire, we gave 15 sitting bow videos (bend angle from 30 to 90°, duration of bend posture from 0 to 4 s) at random and they observed them. Next, they evaluated the each videos by using SD. They started to play each videos whenever they like, evaluated 15 patterns of sitting bow movements and 8 patterns of pair of adjectives with 7 stages. Because adopted the questionnaire which cannot finish with blank, there were no flaws (Fig. 1).

2.3   The Result and Consideration

We decided to study every participant's rating value about all sitting bow videos by every pair of adjectives after calculate the average.

Pair of Adjectives "rude/polite"

We found that on the rating average of this pair of adjectives "rude/polite", the more angle goes to deep, the more rating goes high and the more angle goes to deep, the politer impression would be given. On contrast, in the relation between duration of bend posture, no bend time gave bad impression in regardless of bend angle. Also, we

Fig. 1. Video image

found that while making 1 s duration improved impression, it's not to say over 2 s duration make better impression than (Fig. 2).

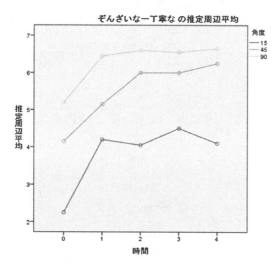

Fig. 2. Pair of adjectives "rude/courteous"

Pair of Adjectives "dishonest/honest"

We also found common element at the pair of adjectives "dishonest/honest" to "rude/polite". The result of this case is almost same as "rude/polite". As the angle gets deeper, it gives a more serious impression, but it is difficult to give a serious impression at any angle for a stationary time of 0 s, the impression improves at 1 s duration, and at 2 s duration, evaluation will not rise further. Add to this, there was an inclination to down the evaluation at 30° and 4 s duration (Fig. 3).

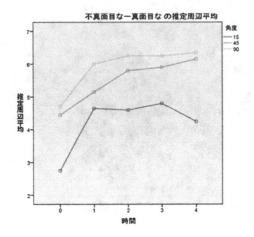

Fig. 3. Pair of adjectives "dishonest/honest"

Pair of Adjectives "polite/impolite"

This pair of adjectives "polite/impolite" has common element to "rude/courteous" though the graph's line shape is opposite because of order. The feature is effectively same but we found the decrease of polite evaluation at 30° bend and 4 duration (Fig. 4).

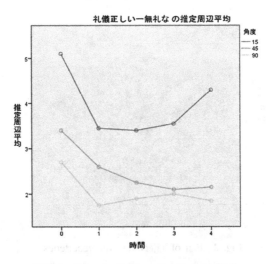

Fig. 4. Pair of adjectives "polite/impolite".

Pair of Adjectives "friendly/unapproachable"

On the rating average of pair of adjectives "friendly/unapproachable, rating of 45° and 90° are close and 30° has different impression. However compared with no duration,

1 s duration express as friendly in regardless of the bend angle, if the more lenghten the duration, the more unapproachable impression you would give (Fig. 5).

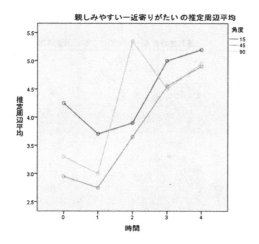

Fig. 5. Pair of adjectives "friendly/unapproachable'

Pair of Adjectives "natural/unnatural"

This pair of adjectives "natural/unnatural" has same rating average as "friendly/ unapproachable". and the impression differs from 30°. Compared with 0 s, 1 s duration make people feel natural, but you would impress unnatural under lenghten duration in regardless of bend angle (Fig. 6).

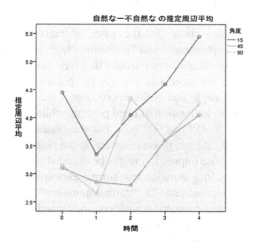

Fig. 6. Pair of adjectives "natural/unnatural"

Pair of Adjectives "uncomfortable/comfortable"

The pair of adjectives "uncomfortable/comfortable" has common element to "friendly/unapproachable", though the graph's line shape is opposite because of order. the feature is effectively same (Fig. 7).

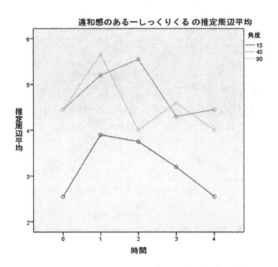

Fig. 7. Pair of adjectives "uncomfortable/comfortable"

3   Consideration

In the standing bow study of Gyoba et al. [4], 45° bend angle got higher score than 15°. The more increase the duration from 0 s, the more score goes up and achieve a peak in 1 s. Then as a result, it was in a gradual decline.

In our study of sitting bow, in the case of pairs of adjectives such as "rude/courteous", "dishonest/honest", and "polite/impolite", the more bend angle goes to deep, the more higher evaluation they would be given. And according to the more bend angle goes to deep, the more you express the politeness, it showed there is a relation between depth of angle and polite impression.

Think about the relation to duration of bend posture, while the duration from1sec to 4 s got stable high score in 45° and 90° bow, but the evaluation downed in case the duration exceeds 3 s in 30°. Although we can impress the politeness with long duration in 45° and 90° bow, the polite impression might be diminished by skewed sense which is given by shallow angle, long duration and formal atmosphere in 30° sitting bow.

About "friendly/unapproachable", "natural/unnatural" and "uncomfortable/comfortable", it is effect that comparing with previous standing bow study of Gyoba et al. [4]. They showed over 1.5 s duration in standing bow make decreasing of smooth score and we proved it is same as sitting bow. Pairs of adjectives "friendly/unapproachable", "natural/unnatural" and "uncomfortable/comfortable" had decrease score, so it is obvious that sitting bow has resemble impression about smoothness as standing bow.

4   Conclusion

In this study, we found that the bend angle and duration of bend posture are very important elements about impression and the impression is different from them. But it is also essential to study about the appropriate judgment on each situation because of sitting bow is used in greeting, appreciating and apologizing scene. Based on this result, we would like to widen a search about how the bend angle and duration of bend posture of sitting bow effect the evaluation which they are appropriate or not to greeting, appreciating and apologizing scene.

References

1. Yoshida, T.: Analysis on the Visitor Arrivals to Japan 2002–2010. Japan Foundation for International Tourism, pp. 123–124 (2013 version)
2. Japan Productivity Center. Investigative Research Project Related to the Promotion of 'The Industrialization of Omotenashi', Directed at Further Development of the Service Industry [Bulletin Report]. Japan as an Information and Economy Society – 2011 Infrastructure Development, pp. 8–13 (2012)
3. Japan Manner and Protocol Association. Lecture Course on Manners that Will Earn Adults Respect (Revised Version). Japan Manner and Protocol Official Examination Standards Textbook. PHP Research Institute, Inc. 63
4. Gyoba, J., Hiroshi, S., Junichi, T., et al.: Subjective impressions of bowing actions and their appropriateness in specific social contexts. Psychol. Res. **85**(6), 571–578 (2015)
5. Koga, H.: A Study of Bowing: Four Types of Bow, Kaetsu University Collected Papers, pp. 57–71 (2012)
6. Dictionary of Manners and Social Etiquette. Jiyukokumin-sha Publishing Co., Ltd., pp. 6–7 (2007)
7. Arai, T., Marina, F., Tatsunori, H., Keitaro, K., Eikou, Y.: Analysis of the Relation between the Bow and Customer Satisfaction in Concierge Service (2010)
8. Asada, M.: The kind of greetings in communication and bows. J. Wakayama Shin-ai Women's Junior Coll. **55**, 81–84 (2015)
9. Iwashita, N., Harumi M.: A consideration of gesticulation and posture: bowing and greetings. Sci. Phys. Educ. **35**(11), 823–826 (1985)
10. Henmi, K., Hinako, I.: Prototype of a System for Adjudicating the Favorability of the Motion of Standing Bows. Inst. Electron., Inf., Commun. Eng.: Tech. Res. Bull. **110**(279), 47–52 (2010)

A Study of Bed-Leaving Prediction by Using a Pressure-Sensitive Sensor

Kengo Wada[✉], Aya Mineharu, Noriaki Kuwahara,
and Kazunari Morimoto

Graduate School of Science and Technology,
Kyoto Institute of Technology, Kyoto, Japan
waw02271@gmail.com

Abstract. Currently in care facilities, a bed-leaving sensor is often used in preventing falls of care receivers during the night. However, these current sensors are usually designed to detect the motion of care receivers getting out of bed and therefore, there are cases in which the care receiver has already fallen from the bed, by the time the sensor had reacted to the movement. It is common knowledge that a person frequently changes position while sleeping. In this research, we focus on the frequency of changes in sleep positions and aim to realize a method for precise prediction of care receivers' attempt in getting out of bed sufficiently before the actual action occurs. We employed the automatic classification method of sleeping positions in the pressure-sensitive sensor, with consideration to privacy of the research subjects, and identified nine types of sleeping positions that are common, with 80.9% accuracy. These results are reported in this paper.

Keywords: Elderly care · Fall prevention · Sleeping position · Pattern recognition

1 Introduction

1.1 Background

Japan is now an extremely aging society. With the growth of the aging population, the number of the people with dementia also increases. In 2012, 15% of the elderly over 65 years old are reported to have dementia which means that about 462 million elderly people in Japan are living with dementia. The elderly with brain disorders such as dementia develop sleep disorders with extremely high frequency. Symptoms of dementia that most frequently appear are sleep-related disorders: irregular sleep-wake patterns such as insomnia, day-night reversal and delirium. Such cases are often accompanied with behavioral disorders, such as violence, wandering, impatience, and excitability. As a consequence of these symptoms, family members and caregivers become exhausted.

In order to support such care of dementia patients during the night, fall preventive movement sensors are often used. Roughly speaking, there are three types of fall preventive movement sensors. The first type of sensor is the mat type in which the sensor is laid next to the bed which detects the pressure on the mat when the care receiver steps onto it. This type of sensor is durable and easy to handle for the nursing staff since it is

V.G. Duffy (Ed.): DHM 2017, Part I, LNCS 10286, pp. 188–197, 2017.
DOI: 10.1007/978-3-319-58463-8_17

less likely to cause false alarms. However, the wiring for the sensor, being also laid next to the bed, can potentially cause care receivers to trip over it resulting in fall accidents. Another problem that may arise with use of the mat type sensor is that the sensor reacts when the nursing staff is closer to the bed in order to aid the care receiver. These things mentioned above, are the problems of the mat type sensors. The second type is the clip type sensor which is the easiest and the most inexpensive option. The clip is attached to the clothing of the care receiver and connected to the sensor switch. When the care receiver gets out of the bed, the sensor is activated, allowing the caregiver to know that the care receiver is in danger of falling. However, because the care receiver often detaches the clip by him/herself it causes a malfunction in the sensor system. The third type of sensor is the type using infrared light. The body movement of the care receiver blocks out the infrared light from the emitter to the light receiving section. This type of sensor is flexible but expensive compared to the other types of sensors. All of the sensors mentioned above, are only designed to detect the moment when the care receiver's action of getting out of bed occurs. Therefore, in principle, they all have the same problem in that, it is often too late to assist the care receiver's action in getting up when the caregiver responds to the sensor call.

We are researching the method for predicting the action of the care receivers getting out of the bed rather than detecting it. In order to implement such a sensor system, we focus on the sleeping position. Due to the fact that, the action of turning over in bed occurs between REM sleep and non-REM sleep [1], we assume that the prediction of waking up can be achieved by monitoring the sleeping positions.

In this paper, we present the results of experimenting with the automatic classification of nine typical sleep positions by using the pressure-sensitive sensor, with consideration to privacy of the experiment subjects.

1.2   Related Work

As a bed leaving prediction method, a method for identifying sleep posture using a pressure sensor has been studied [2]. In this study, sleeping attitude is classified by extracting features from body pressure data obtained from a pressure sensor and using a discriminator such as SVM (Support Vector Machine) [3]. Since the design of the feature quantity greatly affects the discrimination rate, it is regarded as important matter to discover whether or not it is possible to find an effective feature quantity in this machine learning method. As a new approach to this problem, in recent years, Deep learning has attracted attention. As a feature of Deep learning, it is said that it is possible to automatically learn feature quantities designed by humans. It has been reported that the learning model constructed using CNN (Convolution Neural Network), being one of the deep learning techniques has higher accuracy in comparison to the conventional image recognition field method [4].

1.3   Purpose

CNN has few application examples in fields other than image and speech recognition; however, its effectiveness is still unknown. Therefore, in this study, we aim to examine the optimal method for prediction of bed-leaving by comparing the accuracy of classification in sleep positions by adopting two methods, SVM and CNN.

2   Method

2.1   Support Vector Machine

SVM is currently one of the outstanding learning models in terms of recognition performance among many pattern recognition techniques. Support vector machine maps the learning pattern to another higher dimension space using a kernel trick. Based on the learning data, this method identifies a margin hyperplane that maximizes in the distances between individual data points.

2.2   Convolutional Neural Network

Many methods of deep learning have been proposed and various approaches have been studied also in the field of image recognition, but CNN is currently considered to be the most successful. CNN is an extension of the classical multilayered perceptron, but it is characterized by limiting the binding between neurons locally and sparsifying the interlayer bonds based on the findings in the structure of the visual cortex. More specifically, it has a structure in which a convolution layer responsible for local feature extraction of images and a pooling layer (subsampling layer) for summarizing features for each local region are repeated. Since the parameters of the convolution filter are shared at all places in the image, the number of parameters is greatly reduced as compared with a simple total coupled network. Moreover, by interleaving the pooling layer, it is possible to further reduce the number of parameters and at the same time add invariance to the parallel movement of the input, which is indispensable for general object recognition step by step. Intuitively, it can be interpreted that it is a network that co-occurrence of adjacent features on different scales while gradually lowering the input resolution, selectively giving information effective for identification to upper layers. Such an architecture based on repetition of convolution/pooling is from Japan, and Neocognitron [5] developed by Fukushima et al. was the first to appear. After that, based on the propagation method correcting errors, in the 1990's LeCun et al. [6] established a learning method that served as the technical basis of the CNN that is currently used today.

3   Experiment

We classified the sleeping position using the body pressure data obtained from the pressure sensor. Moreover, we compared the recognition rate of SVM and CNN, which are machine learning techniques, and decided the suitable learning model for the bed-leaving prediction.

3.1   Using Data

In this study, we used a pressure sensor system made by Tsuchiya Co., Ltd. to measure body pressure data. The textile type pressure sensor made from conductive fibers was soft and comfortable, even when placed on the bed. The size of the pressure sensitive area is 1840 mm × 800 mm, and there are 80 * 40 sensing points in the sheet. The sensor can output up to 12 frames of data per second. In this experiment, we placed the pressure sensor onto the bed, then placed the mattress cover over it, and fixed the sensor as shown in Fig. 1.

Fig. 1. Pressure-sensitive sensor placed on the bed

Sleeping Posture

It has been reported that there are six typical human sleeping positions [7] as shown in Fig. 2. Among these types of sleeping positions, the first three types are horizontally unsymmetrical, and the left side was distinguished from the right side. Therefore, there were nine types of sleeping positions in total that were subjected to this research.

1. Fetus position: Curling into the fetal position on the bed
2. Log position: Lying on one's side with both arms down by one's side
3. Yearner position: Lying on one's side with both arms out in front
4. Soldier position: Lying on one's back with both arms pinned to one's sides
5. Freefall position: Lying on one's front with one's hands around the pillow, and the head turned to one side
6. Starfish position: Lying on one's back with both arms around the pillow

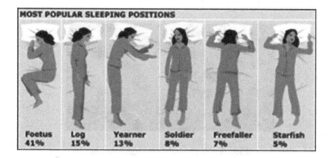

Fig. 2. Typical sleeping positions

Participants

The number of the participants in this experiment was ten people and they ranged from 21 to 27 years of age. Every participant was healthy. Each participant performed the above nine types of sleeping position in their own manners. There were three trials in each position and as a result, we obtained 189 samples (21 samples per position × 9 positions) in total. First, we measured the initial pressure value and then, we instructed the participants to lie on the bed with the nine postures. We then at last, measured the pressure after checking the posture was stable.

3.2   Data Set

Our data set for learning is the pressure data performed the following preprocessing. The pressure sensor used in this study, measures not only the body pressure but also the load of the mattress cover, on the sensor. Moreover, the measurement was unstable due to the influence power supply noise. In an attempt to solve these problems, we obtained plain body pressure data by the subtraction of the initial value from the average measurement. And after, above common processing, in order to convert the preprocessing data into a form suitable for each learning model, an input data set was created by using the method of feature extraction and image transformation.

Subtraction Processing

The measurement values indicate the increment of the pressure from the initial value at the start of measurement. Therefore, the plain body pressure value (as mentioned earlier) can be determined by the subtraction of the initial value from the average measurement value taking into consideration that, when a negative number appears by subtraction, the pressure value was set to zero.

Feature Extraction for SVM

From the preprocessing data, 29 features such as the pressure center and the ratio of the pressure area were extracted, and used as the features.

Image Transformation for CNN

A body pressure data has 3200 (40 × 80) pressure values. We standardized the pressure value from 0 to 255, regarded this pressure value as a pixel value and created an image of 40 × 80 pixels (Fig. 3).

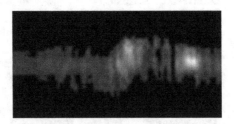

Fig. 3. A pressure image sample

3.3 Performance Evaluation

We classified nine classes of sleeping postures using preprocessed data sets. In this study, we used the "e1071" package of the R statistical software [8] for SVM classifier, and used the "Keras" [9] of CNN framework for CNN classifier. A simple CNN construction is shown in Fig. 4 and hyper parameter setting is shown in Table 1. We used 9-fold cross validation test for evaluating the classification rate of the classifiers.

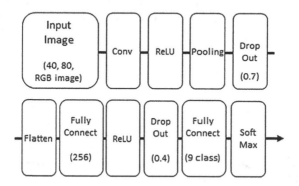

Fig. 4. A simple CNN construction

Table 1. Hyper prameter setting of simple CNN model

OS	Ubuntu 12.04 LTS
GPU	GeForceGTX1080
Backend	TensorFlow
Convolution layer	Kernel size 4 * 4 32 output channels
Pooling layer	MaxPooling Pool size 2 * 2
Epochs	300
Objective	Categorical_crosseentropy
Optimizer	Adam

4 Result and Discussion

In this section, we present the results of the classification rate of the classifiers, moreover tuned of CNN model.

4.1 Plain CNN Model

We classified nine classes of sleeping postures by using SVM and CNN classifier. Table 2 shows the averages of classification rate calculated by a 9-fold-cross-validation.

Table 2. Average of recognition rate

	SVM	CNN
Average	80.9%	71.1%

SVM achieved the best classification rate of 80.9%. As shown in Fig. 5, the difference of $\geq 30\%$ accuracy exists between the training data and the validation data. This indicates that over learning is occurring, and seems that the simple CNN structure is more effective. Therefore, to improve accuracy and to prevent over leaning, we performed the tuning of the CNN model.

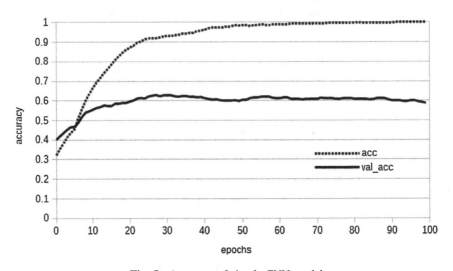

Fig. 5. Accuracy of simple CNN model

4.2   Tuning CNN

In order to find the optimal CNN model in classification of sleep posture, we compared the recognition ratio and training loss of six models as shown in Table 3. The configurations of six CNN models are outlined in Table 3, one per column. In the following, we will refer to these models by their names (A–F). The convolution layer parameters are denoted as "conv (number of channels, number of rows in kernel, number of cols in kernel)". The ReLU activation function is not shown for brevity.

In the six models, the averages of the recognition rates and the learning situations were compared. Among the six models, model C possessed the highest recognition rate of 74.5% (Fig. 6).

Table 3. Configuration of 6 CNN models

A	B	C	D	E	F
(1Conv)	(2Conv)	(1Conv-2)	(2Conv-2)	(1Conv-3)	(2Conv-3)
Input (40 * 80 RGB image)					
Conv(32, 4, 4)	Conv(32, 4, 4) Conv(32, 4, 4)	Conv(32, 4, 4)	Conv(32, 4, 4) Conv(32, 4, 4)	Conv(32, 4, 4)	Conv(32, 4, 4) Conv(32, 4, 4)
MaxPooling					
Dropout (0.7)					
		Conv(32, 4, 4)	Conv(32, 4, 4) Conv(32, 4, 4)	Conv(32, 4, 4)	Conv(32, 4, 4) Conv(32, 4, 4)
		MaxPooling			
		Dropout (0.7)			
				Conv(64, 3, 3)	Conv(64, 3, 3) Conv(64, 3, 3)
				MaxPooling	
				Dropout (0.7)	
Flatten					
Fully-connect (512)					
Dropout (0.3)					
Fully-connect (9)					
Soft-max					

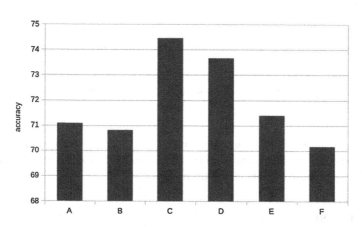

Fig. 6. The recognition rate of 6 models

The layer that had only one Convolution had better accuracy than the one that had two Convolutions, moreover it was thought that better accuracy was achieved by not to having more layers, but to keep it at two layers.

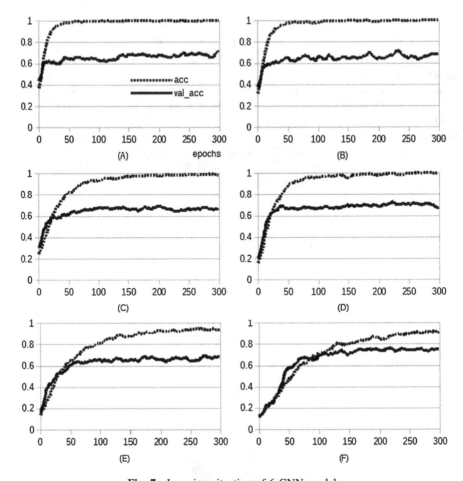

Fig. 7. Learning situation of 6 CNN models

As shown in Fig. 7, it is apparent that adding more layers reduces the process of over learning. Although over learning in model C was greater than in model F, over learning can be improved by increasing the data set in the future. Therefore, as a result, model C was the most suitable classifier model.

5   Conclusion

We classified nine sleeping positions by using the body pressure data obtained from the pressure-sensitive sensor. We compared the versatility of SVM and CNN by using the recognition rate calculated by a nine-fold cross validation test. As a result, the recognition rate of SVM was 80% while the recognition rate of CNN was 70%. Moreover, by tuning CNN, the recognition rate in the best model resulted to be 74%. In conclusion, this study has demonstrated that SVM was a more suitable method in comparison to CNN in classifying sleep posture by using pressure data.

6 Future Work

In this study, we performed an experiment with static pressure data. In order to detect the action of turning over in bed, we will classify sleeping position using dynamic pressure data. In addition, it is also necessary to measure pressure data not only of the young population but of the elderly population as well.

Acknowledgement. We would like to thank Tsuchiya Co., Ltd. for receiving this sensor sheet and system.

References

1. Kogure, T.: Bedclothing and sleep. J. Soc. Biomech. **29**(4), 189–193 (2005). (in Japanese)
2. Mineharu, A.: A study of automatic classification of sleeping position by a pressure-sensitive sensor. In: ICIEV, June 2015 (2015)
3. Burges, C.J.C.: A tutorial on support vector machines for pattern recognition. Data Min. Knowl. Disc. **2**, 121–168 (1998)
4. Krizhevsky, A., Sutskever, I., Hinton, G.E.: Imagenet classification with deep convolutional neural networks. In: Advances in Neural Information Processing Systems, pp. 1097–1105 (2012)
5. Fukushima, K.: Neocognitron: a self-organizing neural network model for a mechanism of pattern recognition unaffected by shift in position. Biol. Cybern. **36**(4), 93–202 (1980)
6. LeCun, Y., et al.: Gradient-based learning applied to document recognition. Proc. IEEE **86** (11), 2278–2324 (1998)
7. Sleep position gives personality clue, BBC News, 16 September 2003. http://news.bbc.co.uk/2/hi/health/3112170.stm. Accessed 2 Feb 2017
8. The R Project for Statistical Computing. http://www.r-project.org. Accessed 2 Feb 2017
9. Keras: Deep Learning Library for Theano and TensorFlow. https://keras.io/. Accessed 2 Feb 2017

Classification of Artery and Vein in Retinal Fundus Images Based on the Context-Dependent Features

Yang Yan[1,2,3], Dunwei Wen[2(✉)], M. Ali Akber Dewan[2], and Wen-Bo Huang[1,2,3]

[1] College of Computer Science and Technology, Changchun Normal University, Changchun 130032, China
yanyang2016@hotmail.com, huangwenbo@sina.com
[2] School of Computing and Information Systems, Athabasca University, Alberta, Canada
{dunweiw,adewan}@athabascau.ca
[3] College of Communication Engineering, Jilin University, Changchun, China

Abstract. In this paper, we present an automatic method based on context-dependent characteristics for the detection and classification of arterial vessels and venous vessels in retinal fundus images. It provides a non-invasive opportunity and effective foundation for the diagnosis of several medical pathologies. In the proposed method, a combination of shifted filter responses is used, which can selectively respond to vessels. It achieves orientation selectivity by computing the weighted geometric mean of the output of a pool of Difference-of-Gaussian filters, whose supports are aligned in a collinear manner. We then configure two combinations of shifted filters, namely symmetric and asymmetric, that are selective for bars and bar-endings, respectively. We achieve vessel detection by summing up the responses of the two filters. Then we extract the morphology and topological characteristics based on the vessel segmentation, and specifically present context-dependent features of blood vessels, including the shape, structure, relative position, context information and other important features. Based on these features, we use JointBoost classifier to construct potential function for conditional random fields (CRFs) model, and train the labeled samples to classify arteriovenous blood vessels in retinal images. The training and testing data sets were prepared according to the results based on DRIVE dataset provided by Estrada et al. The experimental results show that the accuracy of the proposed method for vein and artery detection is 91.1% and 94.5%, respectively, which is superior to that of the state-of-the-art methods. It can be used as a clinical reference for computer-assisted quantitative analysis of fundus images.

Keywords: Retinal image analysis · Vessel segmentation · Classification of artery and vein · Combination of shifted filter responses · Context-dependent features · Conditional random fields

© Springer International Publishing AG 2017
V.G. Duffy (Ed.): DHM 2017, Part I, LNCS 10286, pp. 198–213, 2017.
DOI: 10.1007/978-3-319-58463-8_18

1 Introduction

Fundus retinal structure is the only microcirculation structure that can be directly observed by non-invasive means in the vascular system. Retinal fundus images provide a non-invasive diagnostic approach for pathological diagnosis. Ophthalmologists suggest that cardiovascular diseases, such as hypertension, heart disease, brain atrophy and coronary heart disease, may affect the length of vessels, increase their curvature and tortuosity, or modify the appearance of vessels [1]. Examination and analysis of retinal blood vessels to detect the above changes are helpful for doctors to identify the patients potential to cardiovascular and cerebrovascular diseases and provide timely remedy [2]. The cardiovascular and cerebrovascular diseases and some other systemic diseases, such as atherosclerosis and diabetic retinopathy, affect the retinal vascular structure. For example, arteriovenous vascular morphological changes, such as retinal vein expansion and reduced retinal artery diameter are the early features for diabetes and hypertension retinopathy, respectively [3]. The effects on the retinal arteriovenous caused by various diseases are not the same.

Arteries and veins varies in different stages of retinal disease [4]. These variations have different meaning in the diagnosis and treatment of diseases caused by vascular abnormalities, such as arterial atrophy and venous vessel bleeding [5]. The arteriovenous is also considered separately in the measurement of the amount of oxygen in the blood. Therefore, the high efficiency and accuracy of the classification of arteries and veins would be the basis for computer-aided diagnosis and treatment for various diseases, and also the premise for accurate measurement of many key parameters. Besides, automatic classification of arteriovenous will solve the difficulties of low efficiency and high workload of manual labelling. Thus, our main purpose is to achieve the classification of arteriovenous based on color fundus images to improve the efficiency of diagnosis of eye diseases. This can also be used for the pre-diagnosis of other related ophthalmological diseases, and to use classification results as a clinical reference for computer-assisted quantitative analysis of fundus images.

At present, the methods for retina vascular arteriovenous identification can be divided into two types: semiautomatic and automatic. The semiautomatic method requires the ophthalmologist to select the starting point of the arteriovenous on the main vessel. From the initialized point, the whole blood vessel is marked by the structural information of the vascular frame and the connected information. The automatic method relies on the extraction of vascular characteristics and the use of machine learning techniques, which automatically marks the arteries and veins. Grisan and Ruggeri [6] first proposed a fully automated method for identifying arteriovenous veins. The core idea of this method is to divide the retina image into four quadrants with the optic disc as the center and extract the features for each part of the blood vessels to classify them in each quadrant using fuzzy clustering. Jelinek et al. [7] used different color spaces (RGB, HSL, etc.) to extract different features, and then used different classifiers to improve the recognition rate of arteries and veins. Konderman et al. [8] introduced the contours of blood vessels and the contrast between the blood vessels and the background as features.

Rothaus et al. [9] proposed a semi-automatic method for classifying arteriovenous veins. They use the blood vessel network as a graph model, in which the bifurcation point and cross point of the blood vessel are regarded as graph nodes and the blood vessel segment as the edge connected by nodes. The optimal algorithm is used to obtain the lowest cost result. Niemeijer et al. [10] obtained the brightness and its mean of the vascular edge in the HSL color space, and calculated the feature using the Gaussian function at different angles in the green channel, and used KNN as the classifier. In 2011, Vázquez et al. [11] incorporated several eigenvectors to extract pixel intensity, mean, variance, maximum, and minimum in annular regions with different radii centered on the optic disk. Clustering algorithm is used for the final classification. Vázquez et al. [12] used a multi-scale Retinex image enhancement algorithm in feature extraction before the experiment, which further improved the accuracy of classification.

At present, as there are few studies on the classification of retinal arteries and veins, and some experimental results process on non-public databases, it is difficult to compare the precision on different databases. In the existing methods, some only classify the arteries and veins of the main blood vessels which are parallel to each other. Another is to select the main blood vessel which is sufficiently distinct, and only use the color feature [13, 14]. In practice, however, the recognition rate of the secondary blood vessels near the optic disc is significantly reduced only using features such as color brightness. Thus, although the method has been proposed to reduce the workload of researchers and clinical staff in the current medical research and clinical treatment process, the accuracy and applicability of classification is difficult to achieve clinical requirements, the automatic classification methods of retinal arteriovenous vasculature still need to be improved.

Taking the structure of the retinal arteries and veins into account, we present an automatic method based on context-dependent characteristics for the detection and classification of arterial vessels and venous vessels in retinal fundus images. We configure two combinations of shifted filters, namely symmetric and asymmetric, that are selective for bars and bar-endings, respectively. Specifically, we present context-dependent features of vessels, including the shape, structure, relative position, context information and other important features, and input them into a JointBoost classifier to construct potential function for conditional random fields (CRFs) model. The experimental results based on DRIVE dataset provided by Estrada show that the accuracy of the proposed method (vein 0.911 and artery 0.945) is superior to that of the state-of-the-art methods.

The rest of the paper is organized as follows: in Sect. 2, we explain how the B-COSFIRE filter can be configured to detect blood vessels. In Sect. 3, we propose the method for retinal vessels classification based on context-related features. We provide the experiment results and a discussion in Sect. 4, and finally, we draw conclusions in Sect. 5.

2   Vessel Segmentation Algorithm Based on B-COSFIRE

Retinal vessels segmentation is a preparatory stage for the diagnosis and treatment of retinal-related diseases. Accuracy of vascular extraction directly affects the accuracy of subsequent classification of arteriovenous vessels. In this paper, a segmentation method based on combination of Shifted Filter Responses [15, 16] and Bar Selective (B-COSFIRE [17]) is proposed, it can efficiently detect bar-shaped structures, such as blood vessels. The B-COSFIRE filter is non-linear and direction selective, and is obtained by grouping the outputs of different Gaussian filters (DoG).

The method has good adaptability to the rotation transformation and minor deformation. In addition, unlike other methods based on the manual feature training, COSFIRE does not need a pre-defined filter. But it requires specific template such as a blood vessel, bifurcation point or intersection point for its automatic recognition. Figure 1 shows the basic design of the B-COSFIRE for selecting vertical lines. The DoG response at a given point is the filtered response in a circular region centered on that point. These DoG filters respond to the change in brightness in the input image. In Fig. 1, each gray circle represents the area that supports the central DoG filter. The B-COSFIRE filter computes the relevant DoG responses by weighted geometric averaging to obtain the final response at a given point.

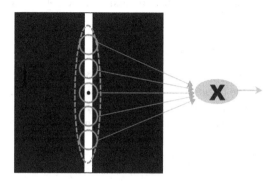

Fig. 1. Sketch of the proposed B-COSFIRE filter. (Source: MIA, 19 p. 48)

B-COSFIRE method is inspired by the related research of lateral geniculate nerve cells. It has been found that lateral geniculate neurons can be divided into two central antagonistic regions. The external inhibitory effect of receptive field is stronger, and the lateral and lateral Stimulation contrast. Rodieck [18] proposed a mathematical model based on Gaussian difference, which uses the difference of two Gaussian functions (DoG) to describe the shape of the receptive field. Their defined DoG function is applied to a Positive center and negative surrounding area, the definition of the $DoG_\sigma(x, y)$ is as follows:

$$DoG(r) = A exp\left(-\frac{r^2}{\sigma_A^2}\right) - B exp\left(-\frac{r^2}{\sigma_B^2}\right) \tag{1}$$

when $A > B$ and $\sigma_A < \sigma_B$, the shape corresponds to the on-center receptive field, and when $A < B$ and $\sigma_A > \sigma_B$, it corresponds to off-center receptive field. We focus on the on-center receptive field, and write the formula specifically:

$$DoG_\sigma^+(x,y) = \frac{1}{2\pi\sigma^2}\exp\left(-\frac{x^2+y^2}{2\sigma^2}\right) - \frac{1}{2\pi(0.5\sigma)^2}\exp(-\frac{x^2+y^2}{2(0.5\sigma)^2}) \qquad (2)$$

where σ is the standard deviation of the external Gaussian function, which determines the range of the circular region of the DoG calculation. The standard deviation of the internal Gaussian function in the formula is defined as $\sigma = 0.5$. Each $DoG_\sigma^+(x,y)$ corresponds to an on-type receptive field, which indicates that the central region is in an active state and the periphery is in a suppressed state.

For a given coordinate (x,y) and the surrounding image intensity distribution $I(x',y')$, the DoG filter (which contains the kernel functions $DoG_\sigma(x-x',y-y')$) responses $c_\sigma(x,y)$ is the convolution of the image and kernel functions:

$$c_\sigma(x,y) \stackrel{\text{def}}{=} |I * DoG_\sigma|^+ \qquad (3)$$

where $|\cdot|^+$ represents half-wave rectification and $*$ is the convolution symbol.

2.1   B-COSFIRE Filter for the Detection of Vascular Trunks

The direction of the B-COSFIRE filter depends on the direction of the bar-like structure. In this paper, the response of $c_\sigma(x,y)$ is analyzed by using a DoG filter with σ as the support domain and N concentric circles locating at the centre. For each point i, this method is used to compute its response. The parameters of the combined shift filter are as follows:

$$S = \{(\sigma_i, \rho_i, \emptyset_i) | i = 1, \cdots, n\} \qquad (4)$$

where σ_i is the standard deviation of the strongest DoG filter, $(\rho_i, \emptyset_i)$ is the polar coordinate representing its position, and n is the number of DoG filters.

Next, we use the response value from DoG to calculate the output of B-COSFIRE. First, the DoG response value is blurred. The fuzzy operation is defined as the maximum value calculated by multiplying the weight of the DoG response, and the threshold is determined according to the maximum value. The weight is a Gaussian function $G_{\sigma'}(x',y')$, σ' is a linear function of the distance ρ_i to the center point, i.e.

$$\sigma' = \sigma_0' + \alpha\rho_i \qquad (5)$$

In order to satisfy the distribution of combined shift filter response -center, the DoG responses after each $\emptyset_i$ in the opposite direction are shifted. According to the distance from the point to the center ρ and the relative angle $\emptyset$, the shift is based on the shift vector $(\Delta x_i, \Delta y_i)$, moving to the center point, where $\Delta x_i = -\rho_i\cos\emptyset_i$, $\Delta y_i = -\rho_i\sin\emptyset_i$, and we define $S_{\sigma_i,\rho_i,\emptyset_i}(x,y)$ as the response of the DoG corresponding S set $(\sigma_i,\rho_i,\emptyset_i)$, and then get the ith tuple fuzzy and shift and obtain the result:

$$s_{\sigma_i, \rho_i, \emptyset_i}(x, y) = \max_{x', y'} \left\{ c_{\sigma_i}(x - \Delta x_i - x', y - \Delta y_i - y') G_{\sigma_i}(x', y') \right\} \tag{6}$$

where $-3\sigma' \leq x', \ y' \leq 3\sigma'$.

Finally, we define the combined shift filter response as the weighted geometric mean of the DoG filtered responses after fuzzy and shift in set S, which is calculated as follows:

$$r_s(x, y) \overset{\text{def}}{=} \left| \left(\prod_{i=1}^{|S|} \left(s_{\sigma_i, \rho_i, \emptyset_i}(x, y) \right)^{\omega_i} \right)^{1 / \sum_{i-1}^{|S|} \omega_i} \right|_t \tag{7}$$

where $\omega_i = exp\left(-\frac{\rho_i^2}{2\hat{\sigma}^2}\right), \hat{\sigma} = \frac{1}{3} \max_{i \in \{1 \cdots |S|\}} \{\rho_i\}$, $|*|_t$ represents that the threshold is $t \in (0, 1)$ times of the maximum response value, and the weighted geometric mean is the AND function. When the fuzzy shift response is greater than 0, the filter will get the response value. The response will smaller as the distance to the center point farther.

In summary, the key to design suitable combination of shift filter is to determine the appropriate bar-like structure direction, so we adjust the parameter set S, adding the direction variable, introducing R_ψ, in order to ensure the rotation invariance and detectable directional bar-like structure:

$$R_\psi(S) = \left\{ (\sigma_i, \rho_i, \emptyset_i + \psi) | \forall (\sigma_i, \rho_i, \emptyset_i) \in S \right\} \tag{8}$$

In this way, the filter obtains the response of each pixel in the direction of $(0°, 15°, 30°, \cdots, 165°)$ to extract the vessel's shape feature in multiple directions, and merge the response, the maximum value obtained is taken as the feature of the pixel:

$$r_s(x, y) = \max_{\psi \in \Psi} \left\{ r_{R_\psi}(x, y) \right\} \tag{9}$$

where $\Psi = \left\{ \frac{\pi}{n_r} i | 0 \leq i \leq n_r \right\}, n_r = 12$. Thus, B-COSFIRE also has rotation invariance.

Although we add different angles in order to increase the rotation invariance, the B-COSFIRE filter is still computationally efficient, it uses an on-center DoG filter plus a maximum value multiplied by the coefficient weighting operation. For a given image (including n pixels), the time complexity of the convolution is $O(n \log n)$, and the time complexity of using the Gaussian function to calculate the weight is $O(kn)$, where k is the number of pixels within a given kernel function. In addition to the linear time complexity of the two fuzzy and translation operations, the calculation of B-COSFIRE is very efficient.

2.2 Vessel Endings Detection

The function defined by B-COSFIRE is logical AND, which responds only when all directions are greater than zero, that is to say, the endings will be ignored. In practice, we find that B-COSFIRE still has a response due to the presence of background noise at the endings, but it is much lower than the response of the middle segment. Therefore, we use an asymmetric B-COSFIRE filter, which calculates a 360° response, which is likely to be the endings in each direction. The filter is set up in the same way as front except that leaving the key points only on one side of the filter center. The asymmetric filter can be well adapted to the vessel endings and double the number of directions when run it to obtain all the direction of the vessel endings, so that the endings could be detected. The retina images were processed using symmetric and asymmetric filters, and the blood vessels were extracted.

3   Vessels Classification Based on Context-Depended Features

3.1   Vessel Feature Selection

Feature selection is the key to the correct classification. This section focuses on the selection of taxonomic features. According to the different function and characteristics of arterial and venous, we summary the differences of retinal arteriovenous in Table 1.

Table 1. Vessels information in color fundus image

Information type	Characteristics
Morphological information	1. In adjacent arterial and venous blood vessels, the vein is wider than the artery 2. Arteries are more curved, veins are straighter
Topology information	1. The same type of blood vessels do not cross, if crossed must be an artery and a vein 2. An artery or vein never crosses a vessel of the same type which means in a cross over point one vessel is artery and the other one is vein. Also, three vessel segments connected to each other through a bifurcation point are of the same type of vessel
Color information	1. The brightness of arterial vessels are higher than veins 2. The central of arteries reflex stronger than the veins

First of all, according to the characteristics of arteriovenous, we extract their morphological and topological characteristics. We use Hessian matrix-based vascular direction calculation method [19] to determine the direction of the characteristics of arteriovenous vessels; we use localized contrast method to detect vessels border and caliber width [20]; and use the chord-to-point distance accumulation method proposed by Han and Poston [21] to obtain the vessels network structural features, such as vessels crossover point, bifurcation point and vessel ending on the vessels segmentation images.

The first rule demonstrates that if three vessel segments are connected to each other through a bifurcation point, then all of the three vessels must be of the same type. The second rule demonstrates that if two vessels cross each other, one is artery and the other one is vein. In addition to the above characteristics, according to structural features of vascular tree, an artery or vein never crosses a vessel of the same type, which means in a cross over point one vessel is artery and the other one is vein. Also, three vessel segments connected to each other through a bifurcation point are of the same type of vessel. These are the priori contents of the contextual spatial relations, which are considered during classification. The distinction of the features are improved by considering the issue that the probability of which class a pixel belongs to is not only related to its own features, but also closely to the information distribution of the surrounding pixels.

Therefore, we propose that when we are modeling each target feature, we model the mutual constraint relationships between them at the same time. We consider the context-dependent feature between the arteriovenous segments. This feature expresses the surrounding information for a given pixel. It does not include only the different structures of the same object, but also the context-dependent information between a pixel and other object structures. Thus, we define the contextual spatial filter to obtain more context-dependent features of blood vessels, such as shape, structure, relative position and context information. These features are then used with the JointBoost classifier to construct the potential function of CRFs model, which is further trained with the labeled samples in order to achieve the retinal image classification of arteriovenous targets.

3.2   Artery and Vein Classification Using Context-Depended Features

A class-based feature is first captured using a rectangular filter suitable for the bar-shaped vessel segmentation. We used a rectangular filter to capture the class-based spatial distribution information [22]. Each rectangular filter generates a seed for each texture distribution, which is defined as $v_{[r,t]}(i)$, the response value of the spatial rectangle filter at pixel i is,

$$v_{[r,t]}(i) = \frac{\sum_{j\in(r+i)}\left[T_j = t\right]}{S(r)} \tag{10}$$

where T_j represents the number of point j, and $S(r)$ is the area of the rectangle. In function $[x]indicator$, if x is true, use 1, and otherwise use 0. The JointBoost [23, 24] algorithm is used to train new weak classifiers on the basis of the weight of the last weak classifier and all training samples. Finally, the strong classifier is obtained by weighted averaging of all weak classifiers. In the initial state, all the training samples are set to the same weight, and each training sample is given a larger weight after each weak classifier obtained. Finally, we get a strong classifier $H(c, i)$, which is the sum of multiple weak classifiers with weighted values [23]:

$$H(c,i) = \sum_{m=1}^{M} h_i^m(c) \tag{11}$$

Each classifier is a weak classifier. The JointBoost classifier borrows the theory of multi-task learning [23, 24]. By setting a set of class C that can share the weak classifiers, the JointBoost classifier implements multi-classification task and get a better generalization effect. Wherein, each weak classifier is a decision-making function:

$$h_i(c) = \begin{cases} a[v_{[r,t]}(i) > \gamma] + b, & c \in \mathbf{C} \\ k^c, & c \notin \mathbf{C} \end{cases} \tag{12}$$

In (12), the weak classifier $h_i(c)$ is composed of an optimizing selected feature $v_{(r,t)}$ and γ, which controls feature values and could be applied to a few classes C. For the weak classifiers that can be shared by class $\mathbf{C}$, the values are determined by the response value $v_{[r,t]}(i)$ and the threshold γ of the spatial filter (r,t) at i, and when $v_{[r,t]}(i) > \gamma$, the value of $h_i(c)$ is $a + b$, otherwise, the value is b. If not shared by the class set C, $h_i(c)$ is always a constant k^c, which can reduce the dissatisfied results caused by the lack of training of the weak classifier, k^c weakens the impact of the uneven distribution of various classes in the samples. Each iteration produces a weak classifier, obtained by optimizing the following objective function [20]:

$$h_i = \arg\min \sum_{c=1}^{C} \sum_{i=1}^{N} w_{i,m-1}^c \left(z_i^c - h(c)\right)^2 \tag{13}$$

where N is the number of all pixels in the training dataset, and z_i^c is the labeled value of pixel i in the training sample. If it belongs to c, it is 1, otherwise the value is -1. The parameter $w_{i,m}^c$ denotes the weight which assigns a larger value to the data of the previous error classification, and gives a smaller value to the previously correctly classified data, thus improving the accuracy of the whole classifier, the formula is expressed as:

$$w_{i,m}^c = \exp\left(-z_i^c H_m(c_i)\right) = w_{i,m-1}^c \exp\left(-z_i^c h_m(c_i)\right) \tag{14}$$

Finally, we get a set of parameters $\left\{ \left\{ r, t, C, a, b, \gamma, \{k^c\}_{c \notin C} \right\}_m \right\}$ after optimizing by using the JointBoosting algorithm.

Thus, the context-depended features of the vessels are combined with the morphological and topological features of the vessels to form a set of eigenvectors. Finally, the CRFs model formed by the above procedure is used to classify the retinal arteries and veins.

4   Experiment Results and Analysis

4.1   Experiment Data

In our experiment, the central processing unit of the computer is Intel Core processor, the core frequency is 3.30 GHz, the system memory is 8 GB, and the software platform is MATLAB R2016a. All the retinal fundus images in the experiment come from the international public database DRIVE (Digital Retinal Images for Vessel Extraction) [25].

The DRIVE database was introduced in 2004 and is publicly available for evaluation of research works on retinal vessel segmentation. This database includes 40 images randomly selected from 400 diabetic patients for the Dutch Diabetic Retinopathy Screening Program. These images were collected by a Canon CR5 3CCD camera with a 45° field of view (FOV) resolution of 768 × 584, 8 bits per RGB channel, and a FOV diameter of approximately 540 pixels. The training and testing data are consisted with 20 images, respectively. The test data is a set of label results which are manually divided by two specialists. The standard segmentation image labeled by the first expert is called gold standard, and we use the segmentation result as the standard reference image.

Estrada et al. [26] provided a sample of arteriovenous labeled samples on the DRIVE database. We then prepared training samples and test samples for the arteriovenous classification experiment. To compare the result of automated vessel classification, our ophthalmologist separated relatively major vessels using blue color for veins and red for arteries. These images are used as gold standard in this paper. Vein is labeled blue, and artery is labeled red.

4.2   Color Fundus Image Preprocessing

For our experiments, we consider the green channel of retinal fundus images as this channel is proven to be more robust for automatic analyses [27–29]. Color retinal images taken with a fundus camera are 24-bit RGB images, where the red, green and blue are 8-bit each. If the image is converted to a grayscale image, it loses many of the original information. Therefore, we extracted the R, G and B components of the retinal fundus images as shown in Fig. 2. Compared with the images of each channel, we find that R channel images were over-saturated, and the B-channel images were blurred and the contrast was low. G-channel images had the most obvious differences between the blood vessels and the background, and the higher contrast ratio, which is the reason why many researchers use this channel for vessel segmentation in their experiments [27–29].

In order to reduce the influence of noise and better detect the blood vessels, we used the contrast limited adaptive histogram equalization (CLAHE) [30] method based on spatial domain enhancement to enhance the retinal fundus G-channel image, so that

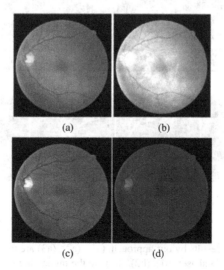

(a)   (b)

(c)   (d)

Fig. 2. The color retinal fundus RGB channel image: (a) The original image; (b) The red channel; (c) The green channel; (d) The blue channel (Color figure online)

retinal fundus G-channel images in each gray-scale distribution is more uniform, the image contrast is higher.

4.3   Fundus Vessel Segmentation in Color Retinal Image

In the experiments, the parameters we used to combine the responses of the two B-COSFIRE filters are listed in Table 2.

Table 2. Parameter settings on DRIVE

Parameter settings	Symmetric	Asymmetric
σ	2.4	1.8
ρ	$\{0, 2, 4, \cdots, 12\}$	$\{0, 2, 4, \cdots, 24\}$
σ_0	3	2
A	0.7	0.1

Figure 3 shows a sample of the results of our approach for segmenting on DRIVE database. In Fig. 3, the first row shows some samples of retinal fundus images, the second row shows the respective expert manual segmentations, and the third row shows

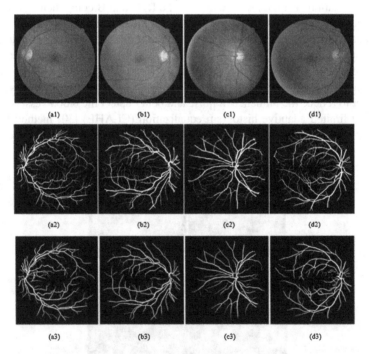

Fig. 3. Examples of final segmentation results on DRIVE database: The first row are the original retinal images of DRIVE database; the second row are the expert hand-labeled image; the third row are the segmentation results by our approach. (a1), (a2), (a3) are the processing examples of 01_test image in DRIVE database; (b1), (b2), (b3) are the processing examples of 02_test image in DRIVE database; (c1), (c2), (c3) are the processing examples of 04_test image in DRIVE database; (d1), (d2), (d3) are the processing examples of 06_test image in DRIVE database.

the segmentation results obtained by our proposed method. From the results, we can see that we got a more complete retinal vessels segmentation with better connectivity of the vessel trunks and endings. It also segmented most of the small blood vessels, which lay a good foundation for the subsequent classification of arteries and veins.

4.4   Arterial and Venous Vessels Classification Results and Analysis

By observing the retinal blood vessel image (see Fig. 4), we can clearly see that the retinal vessels mainly expand from the central optic disc to the surrounding area. In the region near the optic disc, arteries and veins of the vessels are largely distinguished from each other in color and brightness, and as the vessels extend along the optic disc, the diameter of arteries becomes narrower and the degree of arteriovenous distinction becomes smaller. The classification of arteriovenous vasculature was usually done only based on the information of a small area, around 0.5–1 times the diameter of the disc. However, in practical applications, the vessels that are scattered beyond the above range from the optic disc also contain many useful information. Therefore, it is not sufficient to consider only this small area.

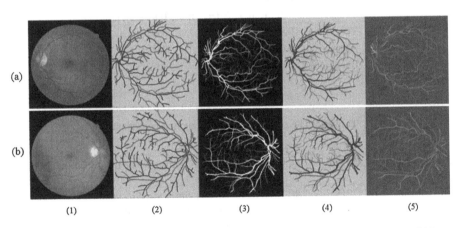

Fig. 4. Row (a) is the processing of 01_test form DRIVE, Row (a) is the processing of 02_test form DRIVE; column (1) is the original images, column (2) is the ground truth labels provided by Estrada, column (3) is the segmented vessel images, column (4) is the A/V Classification results of our approach, column (5) is the segmented vessel images with the labels achieved by our approach superimposed.

In our sample of arteriovenous classification, the distribution of the sample ranges over the global scope of retinal vessels, covering almost all of the retinal arteriovenous information, which can help us make use of all the useful information beyond the small area, though it also increases the difficulty in classification. In this paper, the automatic classification method of retinal arteriovenous arteries and veins does not need to extract the seed points or mark any initial segmentation points for blood vessel segmentation.

This method even does not need to add any artificial factors to influence the selection of sample points, which is obviously advantageous than the many existing semiautomatic methods.

The number of vessel pixels or segments in our approach are more than the other methods as shown in Fig. 4. Our classification range is the global range of vessels in retinal fundus image, rather than limiting it into the disc from 0.5 to 1 times sample points [31]. Even though this consideration increases the difficulties of classification, our accuracy is still high. Table 3 shows the accuracy of our approach on the DRIVE database. The confusion matrix shows the pixel-wise recall accuracy. At present, there is no uniform standard and scale of arteriovenous classification of retinal vessels, and the existing methods are rarely compared with the other methods. So, it is a bit difficult to do a fair comparison of the proposed method with the other existing methods. Nevertheless, we still make a simple comparison as shown in Table 4.

Table 3. Accuracy of our approach on the DRIVE database. The confusion matrix shows the pixel-wise recall accuracy. Row labels indicate the true class, and column labels the predicted class.

Classes	Predicted class		
	Vein (blue)	Artery (red)	Background
Vein (blue)	0.957	0.038	0.004
Artery (red)	0.096	0.885	0.019
Background	0.000	0.000	0.999

Table 4. The comparison of our method and others

Method	Database	Accuracy	Describe
Mirsharif [29]	DRIVE	84.05%	Vessel width greater than 3 for the global range
	DRIVE	90.16%	0.5–1 times the disc radius from the center of the optic disc and vessel width greater than 3
Muramatsu [31]	DRIVE	75%	——
Our approach	DRIVE	Vein 91.1%	Retinal global range
	DRIVE	Artery 94.5%	Retinal global range

5   Conclusion

The research objective of this paper is to classify the arteries and veins in the color fundus images. We have presented an automatic method based on context-dependent characteristics for the detection and classification of arterial vessels and venous vessels in retinal fundus images, and proposed a combination of shifted filter responses approach, which can selectively respond to vessels. It achieves orientation selectivity by computing the weighted geometric mean of the output of a pool of Difference-of-Gaussians filters, whose supports are aligned in a collinear manner. We then configured two combinations of shifted filters, namely symmetric and asymmetric, which are selective for bars and bar-endings, respectively. We achieved vessel detection by summing up the responses of the two filters. Then we extracted the morphology and topological characteristics based on the vessels segmentation, and specifically introduced context-dependent features of blood vessels, including the shape, structure, relative position, context information and other important features, and then used JointBoost classifier to construct potential function for CRFs Model based on these features. The labeled samples were trained to classify arteriovenous blood vessels in retinal images. The training and testing data sets were prepared according to the results based on DRIVE dataset provided by Estrada et al. The experimental results show that the accuracy of the proposed method (vein 91.1% and artery 94.5%) is superior to that of the state-of-the-art methods, it can be used as a clinical reference for computer-assisted quantitative analysis of fundus images.

Acknowledgment. This research is funded by Natural Science Foundation of Changchun Normal University in 2015 (contract number: CCNU Natural Science Co-words [2015] No. 005) and Scientific Research Planning Project of the Education Department of Jilin Province in 2016 (contract number: Ji Edu & Sci Co-words [2016] No. 001). It is also supported by China scholarship Council under the State Scholarship Fund.

References

1. Liew, G., Sim, D.A., Keane, P.A., et al.: Diabetic macular ischaemia is associated with narrower retinal arterioles in patients with type 2 diabetes. Acta Ophthalmol. **93**(1), e45–e51 (2015)
2. Wong, T.Y., Klein, R., Sharrett, A.R., et al.: Retinal arteriolar diameter and risk for hypertension. Ann. Intern. Med. **140**(4), 248–255 (2004)
3. Nguyen, T.T., Wang, J.J., Wong, T.Y.: Retinal vascular changes in pre-diabetes and prehypertension. Diabetes Care **30**(10), 2708–2715 (2007)
4. Macgillivray, T.J., Patton, N., Doubal, F.N., et al.: Fractal analysis of the retinal vascular network in fundus images. In: The IEEE 29th Annual International Conference of Engineering in Medicine and Biology Society, pp. 6455–6458 (2007)
5. Grisan, E., Foracchia, M., Ruggeri, A.: A novel method for the automatic grading of retinal vessel tortuosity. IEEE Trans. Med. Imaging **27**(3), 310–319 (2008)
6. Grisan, E., Ruggeri, A.: A divide et impera strategy for automatic classification of retinal vessels into arteries and veins. In: Proceedings of the IEEE 25th Annual International Conference of Engineering in Medicine and Biology Society, vol. 1, pp. 890–893 (2003)
7. Jelinek, H.F., Depardieu, C., Lucas, C., et al.: Towards vessel characterisation in the vicinity of the optic disc in digital retinal images. In: Image and Vision Computing Conference, pp. 2–7 (2005)
8. Kondermann, C., Kondermann, D., Yan, M.: Blood vessel classification into arteries and veins in retinal images. In: Medical Imaging. International Society for Optics and Photonics, pp. 651247–651247-9 (2007)

Y. Yan et al.

9. Rothaus, K., Rhiem, P., Jiang, X.: Separation of the retinal vascular graph in arteries and veins. In: Escolano, F., Vento, M. (eds.) GbRPR 2007. LNCS, vol. 4538, pp. 251–262. Springer, Heidelberg (2007). doi:10.1007/978-3-540-72903-7_23

10. Niemeijer, M., van Ginneken, B., Abràmoff, M.D.: Automatic classification of retinal vessels into arteries and veins. In: SPIE Medical Imaging, pp. 72601F–72601F-8 (2009)

11. Vázquez, S.G., Barreira, N., Penedo, M.G., et al.: Improvements in retinal vessel clustering techniques: towards the automatic computation of the arterio venous ratio. Computing 90(3–4), 197–217 (2010)

12. Vázquez, S.G., Barreira, N., Penedo, M.G., Saez, M., Pose-Reino, A.: Using retinex image enhancement to improve the artery/vein classification in retinal images. In: Campilho, A., Kamel, M. (eds.) ICIAR 2010. LNCS, vol. 6112, pp. 50–59. Springer, Heidelberg (2010). doi:10.1007/978-3-642-13775-4_6

13. Relan, D., MacGillivray, T., Ballerini, L., et al.: Retinal vessel classification: sorting arteries and veins. In: 35th Annual International Conference of the IEEE Engineering in Medicine and Biology Society (EMBC), pp. 7396–7399. IEEE (2013)

14. Joshi, V.S., Reinhardt, J.M., Garvin, M.K., et al.: Automated method for identification and artery-venous classification of vessel trees in retinal vessel networks. PLoS ONE 9(2), e88061 (2014)

15. Azzopardi, G., Petkov, N.: Automatic detection of vascular bifurcations in segmented retinal images using trainable COSFIRE filters. Pattern Recogn. Lett. 34(8), 922–933 (2013)

16. Azzopardi, G., Azzopardi, N.: Trainable COSFIRE filters for keypoint detection and pattern recognition. IEEE Trans. Pattern Anal. Mach. Intell. 35(2), 490–503 (2013)

17. Azzopardi, G., Strisciuglio, N., Vento, M., et al.: Trainable COSFIRE filters for vessel delineation with application to retinal images. Med. Image Anal. 19(1), 46–57 (2015)

18. Rodieck, R.W.: Quantitative analysis of cat retinal ganglion cell response to visual stimuli. Vis. Res. 5(12), 583–601 (1965)

19. Frangi, A.F., Niessen, W.J., Vincken, K.L., Viergever, M.A.: Multiscale vessel enhancement filtering. In: Wells, William M., Colchester, A., Delp, S. (eds.) MICCAI 1998. LNCS, vol. 1496, pp. 130–137. Springer, Heidelberg (1998). doi:10.1007/BFb0056195

20. Yao, C., Chen, H.: Measurement of retinal vessel widths based on prior knowledge. Sci. Pap. 4(1), 64–68 (2009)

21. Han, J.H., Poston, T.: Chord-to-point distance accumulation and planar curvature: a new approach to discrete curvature. Pattern Recogn. Lett. 22(10), 1133–1144 (2001)

22. Shotton, J., Winn, J., Rother, C., Criminisi, A.: *TextonBoost*: joint appearance, shape and context modeling for multi-class object recognition and segmentation. In: Leonardis, A., Bischof, H., Pinz, A. (eds.) ECCV 2006. LNCS, vol. 3951, pp. 1–15. Springer, Heidelberg (2006). doi:10.1007/11744023_1

23. Torralba, A., Murphy, K.P., Freeman, W.T.: Sharing features: efficient boosting procedures for multiclass object detection. In: IEEE Computer Vision and Pattern Recognition (CVPR), vol. 2, pp. II-762–II-769 (2004)

24. Torralba, A., Murphy, K.P., Freeman, W.T.: Sharing visual features for multiclass and multiview object detection. IEEE Trans. Pattern Anal. Mach. Intell. 29(5), 854–869 (2007)

25. Staal, J., Abramoff, M., Niemeijer, M., Viergever, M., van Ginneken, B.: Ridge-based vessel segmentation in color images of the retina. IEEE Trans. Med. Imaging 23, 501–509 (2004)

26. Estrada, R., Allingham, M.J., Mettu, P.S., et al.: Retinal artery-vein classification via topology estimation. IEEE Trans. Med. Imaging 34(12), 2518–2534 (2015)

27. Mendonca, A.M., Campilho, A.: Segmentation of retinal blood vessels by combining the detection of centerlines and morphological reconstruction. IEEE Trans. Med. Imaging 25, 1200–1213 (2006)

28. Ricci, E., Perfetti, R.: Retinal blood vessel segmentation using line operators and support vector classification. IEEE Trans. Med. Imaging **26**, 1357–1365 (2007)
29. Mirsharif, Q., Tajeripour, F., Pourreza, H.: Automated characterization of blood vessels as arteries and veins in retinal images. Comput. Med. Imaging Graph. **37**(7), 607–617 (2013)
30. Reza, A.M.: Realization of the contrast limited adaptive histogram equalization (CLAHE) for real-time image enhancement. J. VLSI Signal Process. **38**(1), 35–44 (2004)
31. Muramatsu, C., Hatanaka, Y., Iwase, T., et al.: Automated detection and classification of major retinal vessels for determination of diameter ratio of arteries and veins. In: SPIE Medical Imaging. International Society for Optics and Photonics, pp. 76240J–76240J-8 (2010)

A Universal 3D Gait Planning Based on Comprehensive Motion Constraints

Qiang Yi[1(✉)], Renran Tian[1], and Ken Chen[2]

[1] Indiana University-Purdue University, Indianapolis, IN, USA
{yiq, rtian}@iupui.edu
[2] Tsinghua University, Beijing, China
kenchen@tsinghua.edu.cn

Abstract. To realize stable walking and complex motion in the 3D unstructured environment, a parametric universal gait planning is proposed with the consideration of boundary constraints, physical constraints and ZMP stability constraints of locomotion. This approach adopts a spline-based parametric method to simplify the complicated joint trajectory planning problem, and converts it to a constrained optimization problem of the parametric vector. With different gait parameters and boundary constraints, this approach was extended to more complex gait planning. As examples, three different gaits were generated, including start walking, stop walking and kicking a ball.

Keywords: Humanoid robot · Biped walking · Gait planning · Constraints

1 Introduction

Living in human life and coexisting harmoniously with human being is the final goal of humanoid robot research. How to realize stable walking and complex motion in the 3D unstructured living environment is one of the important topics. Because of the essentially unstable characteristic of biped walking, rigorous walking constraints should be considered with 3D gait planning, which requires perfect coordination of joint actuating torques, together with accurate control of ground reaction forces in order to ensure the dynamic balance of the biped walking [1].

ZMP (Zero Moment Point), as the most common dynamic stability criterion, firstly introduced by Vukubratovic [2, 3], was widely used to synthesize and control a stable locomotion [4–7]. In general, ZMP based approach uses one or several high order polynomials to describe the joint motion or ZMP trajectory, along with the optimization of one or several important parameters, for example, energy consumption [8], joint torque [1, 9] and stability margin [10].

In the early 1970s, Chow and Jacobson [11] firstly mentioned the most import factor for a stable biped locomotion was hip motion. The hip motion synthesis should be prior to the synthesis of joint trajectory. Channon et al. [12] accepted this idea and realized a stable walking in seven-link plane robot. It adopts cubic splines to describe the motion of hip and foot, and minimized the energy consumption of biped walking. Park et al. [13] also use a three-order polynomial to describe the trajectory of the hip. With the simplified ZMP, this approach achieved online gait planning on

© Springer International Publishing AG 2017
V.G. Duffy (Ed.): DHM 2017, Part I, LNCS 10286, pp. 214–228, 2017.
DOI: 10.1007/978-3-319-58463-8_19

humanoid robot KHR-3. Chevallereau and Aoustin [14] adopt four-order polynomial to describe joint motions. They hypothesized that the transition between single-support phase and double-support phase was instantaneous, which was modeled as a passive impact. With the constraint of ZMP, several sets of energy optimized walking and running gait were realized in a five DoF (Degrees of freedom) planar biped robot. Huang et al. [10] used two cubic splines to describe hip and ankle motion of swing leg. According to adjustment of the translation distance of body in single-support phase, a biped walking gait with maximum stability region was generated. But this approach didn't include motion constraints in transition. The generated gait was not smooth, and jerk motion may appear when transiting from single-support phase to double-support phase. In [1, 9], Bessonnet and Seguin developed an efficient method with the consideration of four points boundary constrains in gait transition, but their approach didn't count the effect of lateral motion. Based on Bessonnet's method, the stability constrain was introduced in [15], and a biped walking gait of energy optimization was generated. But this research still focuses on the sagittal plane. Tlalolini et al. [16] divided single-support phase to two sub-phases, rotating around the toe and freely swinging in the air. They adopt three-order polynomials to describe joint trajectory. With the analysis of feasible gait constraints, a group of torque-optimized joint trajectory in the 3D environment was synthesized. Furthermore, compared energy consumption with and without rotation motion around toe was studied. But this method only considers the single-support phase, it can not be used for the whole cyclic motion of biped robot.

In this paper, we present a 3D universal parametric gait optimization method, which is firstly introduced by Bessonnet et al. [1]. But we aim at achieving the numerical synthesis of gait steps in the 3D environment [19] and extending it to a universal complicated gait planning. To avoid jerk motion, multi four-order splines were used to describe each joint. In Sect. 2, the comprehensive cyclic gait constraints in the 3D environment were introduced, including six-point boundary constraints, physical constraints, and stability constraints. In Sect. 3, a 13-mass-block constrained dynamic model in the 3D environment was presented. With the spline-based parametric approach, the problem of complex joint trajectory planning in 3D environment became to a constrained optimization problem of the parametric vector in Sect. 4. Section 5 shows the synthetic results of cyclic walking gait. With different gait parameters and boundary constraints, Sect. 6 extended this approach to more complex gait planning, including start gait, stop gait and kicking a ball. The simulated and experimental results demonstrated the effectiveness of this approach. Section 7 shows the conclusions.

2 Comprehensive Gait Constraints in 3D Environment

Biped walking is a periodic phenomenon. A complete cyclic motion can be divided into two phases: a single-support phase (SSP) and a double-support phase (DSP). During the single-support phase, only one foot is in touch with the ground, the other foot swings from the rear to the front. The locomotion system moves as an open tree-like kinematic chain. During the double-support phase, both feet are in contact with the ground. This phase begins with the heel of the forward foot touching the ground, and ends with the toe of the rear foot leaving the ground. The locomotion system is kinematic closed and over-actuated.

Figure 1 shows the basic stick figures of transition between SSP and DSP in both forward and lateral views. Where H_{foot} denotes the distance from the sole to the ankle. L_{foot} denotes the length of foot. L_{calf} and L_{thigh} separately denotes the length of calf and thigh. L_{width} denotes the distance between two hip joints. $[q_1^{\text{si}}, q_2^{\text{si}}, \ldots, q_{13}^{\text{si}}]^{\text{T}}$, $[q_1^{\text{sf}}, q_2^{\text{sf}}, \ldots, q_{13}^{\text{sf}}]^{\text{T}}$, $[q_1^{\text{di}}, q_2^{\text{di}}, \ldots, q_{13}^{\text{di}}]^{\text{T}}$ and $[q_1^{\text{df}}, q_2^{\text{df}}, \ldots, q_{13}^{\text{df}}]^{\text{T}}$ are joint angle vectors, used to describe the start and stop postures of SSP and DSP.

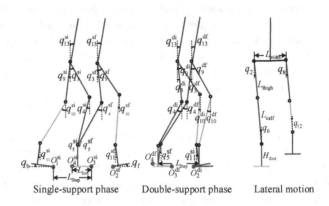

Single-support phase   Double-support phase   Lateral motion

Fig. 1. Stick figures of biped walking

2.1 Boundary Constraints of Cyclic Gait

As stated in above paragraph, a cyclic step is the sequence of two main events, SSP and DSP. In more detail, to crossing over a certain obstacle, the walking step should reach to a specific height. Thus, we divided SSP to two sub-phases. The first phase begins at toeing off, ends at the highest position. The second phase runs from highest position to heel touching. To generate a rolling gait, the DSP was divided to three sub-phases. The first phase describes the rotation around the heel of the front foot. The second phase is the process when both feet fully touching the ground. The third phase describes the rotation around the toe of the rear foot. Thus, to meet the above conditions, a whole cyclic locomotion is described by six-point boundary constraints.

Initial Time of SSP t_{si}. Referring to Fig. 1, the distance between two feet is constant. The swing leg is leaving the ground. To avoid jerk motion, we suppose the toe's speed equals to 0.

$$\begin{cases} \mathbf{p}_{O_2^{\text{si}}}(\mathbf{q}(t_{\text{si}})) - \mathbf{p}_{O_2^{\text{si}}}(\mathbf{q}(t_{\text{si}})) = \begin{bmatrix} L_{\text{step}} - L_{\text{foot}} & L_{\text{width}} & 0 \end{bmatrix}^{\text{T}} \\ v_{O_2^{\text{si}}}(\mathbf{q}(t_{\text{si}}), \dot{\mathbf{q}}(t_{\text{si}})) = \dfrac{\partial \mathbf{p}_{O_2^{\text{si}}}(\mathbf{q}(t_{\text{si}}))}{\partial \mathbf{q}} \dot{\mathbf{q}}(t_{\text{si}}) = \mathbf{0}^{3x1} \\ q_{11}(t_{\text{si}}) = -q_{\text{b}} \end{cases} \quad (1)$$

Where L_{step} the length of step, L_{foot} is the length of the foot, L_{width} is the lateral distance between two feet, $p_{o_1^{si}}, p_{o_4^{si}}$ is the position of point O_1 and point O_4 at t_{si}, q_b is the angle between foot and ground, $\mathbf{0}^{3\times 1}$ is zero vector.

Middle Time of SSP t_{sm}. Swing leg goes to the highest position, the speed of ankle joint is 0.

$$
\begin{cases}
p_{ankle\_sm}^{T}(q(t_{sm})) \cdot e_z = H_{foot} + H_{step} \\
v_{ankle\_sm}^{T}(q(t_{sm}), \dot{q}(t_{sm})) \cdot e_z = [\frac{\partial p_{ankle}(q(t_{sm}))}{\partial q}\dot{q}(t_{sm})]^{T} \cdot e_z = 0
\end{cases}
\tag{2}
$$

Where e_x, e_y, e_z denotes the unit vector of x, y and z-axis. H_{step} is step height. $p_{ankle\_sm}, v_{ankle\_sm}$ is ankle position and speed at t_{sm}.

Transition Time from SSP to DSP t_t. The distance between support foot and heel of swing foot is constant. To avoid jerk motion when transition, we suppose the speed of swing heel equals to 0.

$$
\begin{cases}
p_{o_2^t}(q(t_t)) - p_{o_2^t}(q(t_t)) = [\, L_{step} - L_{foot} \quad L_{width} \quad 0\,]^{T} \\
v_{o_2^t}(q(t_t), \dot{q}(t_t)) = \frac{\partial p_{o_2^t}(q(t_t))}{\partial q}\dot{q}(t_t) = \mathbf{0}^{3x1} \\
q_{11}(t_t) = q_f
\end{cases}
\tag{3}
$$

Where q_f is the angle between the swing foot and the ground.

Finish Time of First Sub-phase in DSP t_{d1}. Swing leg fully touches the ground. The angle speed of ankle joint equals to 0.

$$
\begin{cases}
q_{11}(t_{d1}) = 0 \\
\dot{q}_{11}(t_{d1}) = 0
\end{cases}
\tag{4}
$$

Finish Time of Second Sub-phase in DSP t_{d2}. The rear feet starts to rotate around its toe. To avoid jerk motion, the angle speed of ankle joint is supposed to 0.

$$
\begin{cases}
q_5(t_{d2}) = 0 \\
\dot{q}_5(t_{d2}) = 0
\end{cases}
\tag{5}
$$

Finish Time of DSP t_{df}. The constraints at the finish time of DSP t_{df} are similar to initial time t_{si}, but mirroring joint rotations and velocities with the consideration of cyclic characteristics.

$$
\begin{cases}
q_i(t_{df}) = q_{i+6}(t_{si}), q_{i+6}(t_{df}) = q_i(t_{si}), i = 1, \ldots, 6 \\
\dot{q}_i(t_{df}) = \dot{q}_{i+6}(t_{si}), \dot{q}_{i+6}(t_{df}) = \dot{q}_i(t_{si}), i = 1, \ldots, 6
\end{cases}
\tag{6}
$$

2.2 Physical Constraints

Except the six-point boundary constraints of cyclic motion, to realize stable walking, it must meet the physical constraints, which include singular posture forgiveness, no ground touching of swing leg, coordination of lateral motion, limitation of joint angle and limitation of joint torque.

Singular Posture Forgiveness. Singular posture is defined as the posture when the inverse Jacobian matrix of the robot does not exist. Literature [17] presents three different singular postures in biped walking. To avoid that, the robot should act in a slight squat when walking.

$$p_{13}(q(t)) \cdot e_z + \Delta_z \le H_{\text{foot}} + L_{\text{calf}} + L_{\text{thigh}} \tag{7}$$

Where p_{13} denotes the position of torso, Δ_z is the minimum value of squat.

No Ground Touching in SSP. When walking, the swing leg can not go under the ground. That means the position of bottom surface of swing foot must higher than ground.

$$S_{\text{foot}}^{\text{T}}(q(t)) \cdot e_z > 0^{n_p \times 1}, t \in (t_{\text{si}}, t_{\text{t}}) \tag{8}$$

Where S_{foot} denotes the bottom surface of swing foot, n_p is vertices of the polygon. When the foot shape of the robot is a rectangle, n_p equals to 4.

Coordination of Lateral Motion. The hip joint and ankle joint in lateral motion should have the same value to keep the swing foot be parallel to the support foot.

$$q_2(t) = q_6(t) = -q_8(t) = -q_{12}(t), \ t \in (t_{\text{si}}, t_{\text{t}}) \tag{9}$$

Limitation of Joint Angle. Every joint has a mechanical limitation, the relative rotation angle of each joint should meet the followings constraints.

$$\begin{cases} \theta_{i\_\min} \le \theta_i(q(t)) \le \theta_{i\_\max} \\ \dot{\theta}_{i\_\min} \le \dot{\theta}_i(q(t), \dot{q}(t)) \le \dot{\theta}_{i\_\max} \end{cases} \tag{10}$$

Limitation of Joint Torque. The output torque of each driving motor has a limitation. The constraints are given as followings.

$$|u_i(t)| < u_{i\_\max}, \ i < 13 \tag{11}$$

2.3 ZMP Stability Constraints

The keep the stability of biped walking, the ZMP must be located within the convex hull of all contact points (stable region).

$$\boldsymbol{p}_{\text{zmp}} = [\, x_{\text{zmp}} \quad y_{\text{zmp}} \quad z_{\text{zmp}} \,] \in \boldsymbol{S}^r \tag{12}$$

Where S^r denotes the convex hull of all contact points. Because the foot shape of the real robot in this paper is a rectangle, and the locomotion is only on the flat surface. The constraints of stability can be simply written as the following inequalities.

$$ZMP_{x\text{Lmax}}(t) \leq \boldsymbol{p}_{\text{zmp}}{}^{\text{T}}(\boldsymbol{q}(t), \dot{\boldsymbol{q}}(t), \ddot{\boldsymbol{q}}(t)) \cdot \boldsymbol{e}_x \leq ZMP_{x\text{Rmax}}(t) \tag{13}$$

$$ZMP_{y\text{Lmax}}(t) \leq \boldsymbol{p}_{\text{zmp}}{}^{\text{T}}(\boldsymbol{q}(t), \dot{\boldsymbol{q}}(t), \ddot{\boldsymbol{q}}(t)) \cdot \boldsymbol{e}_y \leq ZMP_{y\text{Rmax}}(t) \tag{14}$$

3   Constrained Dynamic Model in 3D Environment

As stated in Sect. 2, the biped system is assumed to be an open kinematic chain in SSP, but close kinematic and over-actuated in DSP. To realize 3D motion, a 13-mass-block dynamic model was present. Figure 2 shows the configuration and definition of mass blocks in the biped robot, where R1-R13 represent the rotation matrix for each mass block. Setting torso as the base of the robot, the joint motion for both legs can be derived with Denavit-Hartenberg parameters.

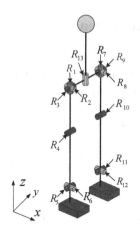

Fig. 2. 13-mass-block robot model

Considering the coupling effect between the forward and lateral movement, a 13-mass-block dynamic model was created. The Lagrange Equation with close-chain constraints shows in the (15).

$$\begin{aligned}
\boldsymbol{M}(\boldsymbol{q}(t))\dot{\boldsymbol{q}}(t) + \boldsymbol{C}(\boldsymbol{q}(t), \dot{\boldsymbol{q}}(t))\dot{q}(t) + \boldsymbol{G}(\boldsymbol{q}(t)) \\
= \boldsymbol{A}_\tau(\boldsymbol{q}(t))\boldsymbol{\tau}(t) + \boldsymbol{\lambda}^{\text{T}}(\boldsymbol{q}(t))\boldsymbol{u}(t)
\end{aligned} \tag{15}$$

Where $M \in R^{13 \times 13}$ denotes the mass matrix, $C \in R^{13 \times 13}$ is the centrifugal and Coriolis inertia matrix. $G \in R^{13}$ is the gravity term. $\tau \in R^{13}$ is the actuating joint torques. u is a six-dimensional vector, which denotes the 3D reacting forces F_r and reacting torques τ_r in DSP, $u(t) \in 0^{6 \times 1}$ in SSP. $A \in R^{13 \times 13}$ is the constant matrix, $\lambda \in R^{6 \times 13}$ the Jacobian matrix of the robot, it is defined as $\lambda(q(t)) = \partial C^d / \partial q$, where C^d is the constraints of the close chain in DSP (shown in Fig. 3). As stated in Sect. 2, the DSP can be divided to three sub-phases. In the first phase, the front foot touches the ground, and rotate around its heel, $C^d \equiv L_s(q(t))$. In the second phase, both feet touch the ground completely, $C^d \equiv L_m(q(t))$. In the third phase, the rear foot starts rotating around its toe, $C^d \equiv L_f(q(t))$.

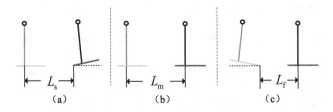

Fig. 3. Constraints of closed chain in DSP

4 Spline-Based Parametrization

Because energy based optimization method easily presents some disadvantages, including discontinuous motion and backlashes on the joints. Thus a performance criterion, defined as the integral quadratic amount of driving torque is adopted. The objective function shows in Eq. (16). Where τ denotes torque vector of joints, u denotes the interacting forces in double-support phase.

$$J(q, \dot{q}) = \int_{t_{si}}^{t_t} \tau^T(t)\tau(t) + \int_{t_t}^{t_{df}} (\tau^T(t)\tau(t) + u^T(t)u(t)) \tag{16}$$

To generate jerk-less motion, several sections of four-order interpolating polynomials are built to describe the joint trajectory. The number of sections is decided by the points of boundary constraints. Suppose the number of sections is N, the k_{th} four-order polynomial is shown in formula (17).

$$\begin{cases} \tau_t = (t - t_k)/(t_{k+1} - t_k) \\ q_i(t) \cong \varphi_{ik}(\tau_t) = \sum_{j=0}^{4} c_{ikj}\tau_t^j \end{cases}, \ t \in [t_k, t_{k+1}] \tag{17}$$

Set $X_i = [x_{i1}^T, x_{i2}^T, \ldots, x_{ik}^T, \ldots, x_{iN}^T]^T$, where $x_{ik} = [c_{ik0}, c_{ik1}, c_{ik2}, c_{ik3}, c_{ik4}]^T$, the trajectory of i_{th} joint can be expressed as formula (18).

$$q_i(t) \cong \phi_i(X_i, t) \qquad (18)$$

Type (18) substitute in (15) and (16), the problem of complicated joint trajectory planning in the 3D environment becomes to a constrained optimization problem of the parametric vector.

$$\min J(X) = \min(\sum_{i=1}^{N} \int_{t_i} [\tau^T(X_i)\tau(X_i) + u^T(X_i)u(X_i)]) \qquad (19)$$

Subjects to the following inequality and equality constraints,

$$\begin{cases} c(c_b(X), c_p(X), c_{zmp}(X)) \leq 0 \\ cep(c_b(X), c_p(X), c_{zmp}(X)) = 0 \end{cases} \qquad (20)$$

Where $c_b(X)$, $c_p(X)$ and $c_{zmp}(X)$ separately denotes boundary constraints of transition between SSP and DSP, physical constraints of feasible gait and ZMP stability constraints.

Typically, constrained and nonlinear minimization problem can be solved by sequential quadratic programming [1, 9]. In this paper, *fimincon* in Matlab Optimization Toolbox was used to obtain the optimal joint trajectory.

5 Cyclic Walking Gait

With different walking parameters, two types of walking gait were generated. The walking speed was 0.15 m/s and 0.4 m/s, representing static and dynamic walking separately. The robot physical model was a kid-size humanoid robot THBIP-II. More details about THBIP-II can be found in the paper [18].

Figure 4 shows the stick figures for both static and dynamic cyclic walking gait. Firstly, we can found that the dynamic walking has a bigger body angle and step size. That means, walking speed can be controlled through the adjustment of body angle.

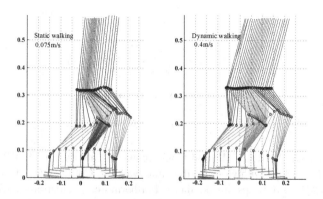

Fig. 4. Stick figures of static and dynamic cyclic walking

Secondly, the body's movement in vertical direction shows the lateral motion takes more effects in static walking than dynamic walking, especially in double support phase. Thirdly, from the foot trajectory, we can found that the swing foot moves to the highest point and holds a while before moving back ground in static walking, but it just sharply moves back ground in dynamic walking. It shows that the static walking gives more benefits for stepping over a certain obstacle.

Figure 5 shows the joint torque. The torque for each joint is successive and smooth. In static walking, the maximum torque happens in the keen joint of the support leg. Different with static walking, it happens in heel lateral joint and heel forward joint of support leg in dynamic walking. That because the dynamic walking need overcomes the inertia force and Coriolis force generated from acceleration. Moreover, the hip rotation joint in both static and dynamic walking is not zero. It even reaches to 12 Nm when transiting from SSP to DSP in dynamic walking. It should be noticed that it can not be obtained from 7-link or 9-link plane robot model. Thus, 13-mass-block model, in a certain condition, can be used for the analysis of coupling problems between lateral motion and front motion.

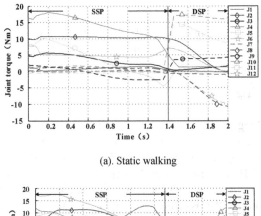

(a). Static walking

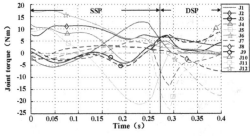

(b) Dynamic walking

Fig. 5. Joint torque of cyclic walking

Figure 6 shows the real ZMP and CoG (center of Gravity) in THBIP-II. In static walking, ZMP overlaps with CoG. In dynamic walking, CoG deviates from the stable region, but ZMP still keeps inside there. Furthermore, fluctuations of ZMP curve occurs when the transition from SSP to DSP because of the lateral motions.

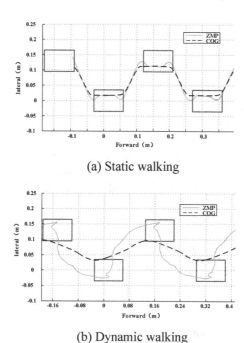

(a) Static walking

(b) Dynamic walking

Fig. 6. ZMP and COG of cyclic walking

6 Complicate Gait Planning

From the analysis of Sect. 2, we can find that the six-point boundary constraints can completely describe the whole 3D cyclic motion, and the synthetic gait is continuous and smooth. When giving different gait parameters and boundary constraints, different gait motion can be obtained. Thus, in this section, we extended this approach to complicated gait planning by using different boundary constraints, but the same physical constraints and stability constraints.

6.1 Start Gait and Stop Gait Planning

In addition to cyclic gait, the robot should start from stationary posture to stable walking and stop from stable walking to stationary posture in the real environment. We defined these two transition process as start gait and stop gait. As shown in Fig. 7, start gait is consists of two single steps, start step and transition step. Stop gait also consists of two single steps, transition step and stop step.

Different with boundary constraints of cyclic gait, there are no constraints of periodicity. The two-point boundary constraints for the start gait and the stop gait are shown in (21), (22) and (23), (24). Where q_0 is stationary posture, q_{cyc} is the initial posture of cyclic gait, which is also described in formula (1) as $q(t_{si})$.

$$q(t) = q_0, \dot{q}(t) = 0^{13\times1}, \quad t = t_{si}^s \tag{21}$$

$$q(t) = q_{cyc}, \dot{q}(t) = \dot{q}_{cyc}, \quad t = t_{tf}^s \tag{22}$$

$$q(t) = q_{cyc}, \dot{q}(t) = \dot{q}_{cyc}, \quad t = t_{ti}^s \tag{23}$$

$$q(t) = q_0, \dot{q}(t) = 0^{13\times1}, \quad t = t_{sf}^s \tag{24}$$

Giving the walking speed as 0.15 m/s, the step in start and stop gait as 0.15 m, the step in transition phase as 0.3 m, the swing height as 4 cm, the percentage of support phase in walking period as 30%, an optimized walking gait which includes start gait, cycle gait and stop gait was generated with the consideration of boundary constraints, physical constraints, and ZMP stable constraints. Figure 7 shows the stick figures of whole biped motion. Figure 8 shows the planned joints curves. Figure 9 is the video frames implemented in THBIP-II biped robot [18]. Figure 10 presents the real ZMP and CoG curves. From these results, we can find the generated gait is smooth and stable.

6.2 Kicking Ball Gait Planning

As an example, a much more complicated gait, kicking a ball was studied in this chapter. The gait of kicking a ball starts from stationary posture, it consists of 6

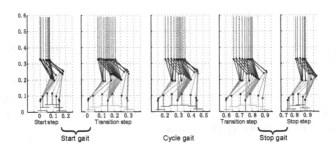

Fig. 7. Stick frame of the whole biped motion including start, cycle and stop gait

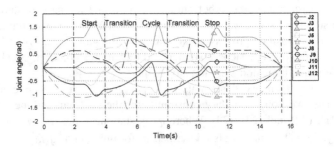

Fig. 8. Joint angles of the whole biped motion including start, cycle and stop gait

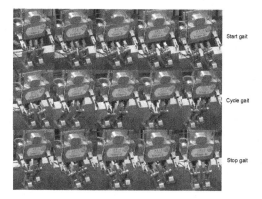

Fig. 9. Video frames of the whole biped motion including start, cycle and stop gait

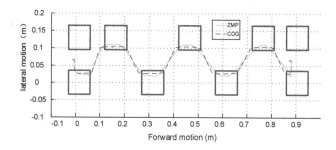

Fig. 10. ZMP and CoG curves of the whole biped motion including start, cycle and stop gait

sub-phases. The first phase is a double-support phase, the main movement in this phase is lateral motion which is used to keep robot stable when kicking the ball. The second sub-phase begins at single leg supporting. During this phase, the swing leg moves to the highest position. In the third phase, a forward motion with acceleration is generated. During this phase, the swing leg moves to the ball's location and touches the ball. After kicking the ball, the speed of swing leg decelerates to zero in the fourth phase. The fifth phase is a recovery process. The swing leg moves from the farthest position to the initial position and goes back to double support phase. The sixth phase is the inverse process of the first phase, the robot goes back to stationary posture. The seven-point boundary constraints for kicking a ball are shown in (25)–(31).

$$q(t) = q_0, \ \dot{q}(t) = 0^{13\times1}, \ t = t_1^k \tag{25}$$

$$q(t) = q_{\text{stable}}, \ \dot{q}(t) = 0^{13\times1}, \ t = t_2^k \tag{26}$$

$$\begin{cases} p_z^{\text{sfoot}}(q(t)) = H_{\max} \\ \dot{q}(t) = 0^{13\times1} \end{cases}, \ t = t_3^k \tag{27}$$

$$\begin{cases} p_x^{\text{sfoot}}(\mathbf{q}(t)) = x_{ball} \\ v_x^{\text{sfoot}}(\mathbf{q}(t)) = v_{\max} \end{cases}, \ t = t_4^k \tag{28}$$

$$\begin{cases} p_x^{\text{sfoot}}(\boldsymbol{q}(t)) = x_{\max} \\ v_x^{\text{sfoot}}(\boldsymbol{q}(t)) = 0 \end{cases}, \ t = t_5^k \tag{29}$$

$$\begin{cases} \boldsymbol{v}^{\text{sfoot}}(\boldsymbol{q}(t)) = \boldsymbol{0}^{3\times 1} \\ \boldsymbol{q}(t) = \boldsymbol{q}_{\text{stable}} \\ \dot{\boldsymbol{q}}(t) = \boldsymbol{0}^{13\times 1} \end{cases}, \ t = t_6^k \tag{30}$$

$$\boldsymbol{q}(t) = \boldsymbol{q}_0, \ \dot{\boldsymbol{q}}(t) = \boldsymbol{0}^{13\times 1}, \ t = t_7^k \tag{31}$$

Setting the position of ball as $[0.02 \quad 0.065 \quad 0]^{\text{T}}$ m, the maximum speed when kicking the ball as 2 m/s, a stable ball kicking gait was generated. Figure 11 shows the joint curve of swing leg, Fig. 12 shows the video frames and real ZMP curve of THBIP-II. From these results, we can find the joint curves are smooth and ZMP always locates in the stable region.

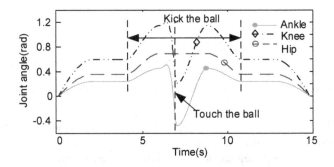

Fig. 11. Joint curve of swing leg

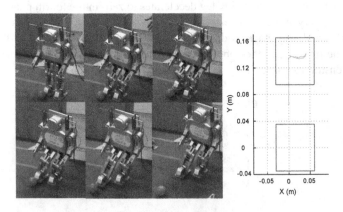

Fig. 12. Video frames and ZMP curve

7 Conclusions

A universal 3D parametric gait planning is proposed with the consideration of comprehensive biped walking constraints. With the analysis of periodic biped walking of robot, six-point boundary constraints of successive and impact-less steps including single-support phase and double-support phase are present. By adopting the parametric gait optimization approach, the complicated joint trajectory planning problem was transformed into the constrained optimization problem of the parametric vector. To solve it, the sequential quadratic programming method was used. With different gait parameters and boundary constraints, this approach was extended to more complex gait planning. As examples, a start gait, a stop gait and a gait of kicking ball were planned and implemented in biped robot THBIP-II. The simulated and experimental results demonstrated the effectiveness of this approach.

References

1. Bessonnet, G., Chessé, S., Sardain, P.: Optimal gait synthesis of a seven-link planar biped. Int. J. Robot. Res. **23**(10–11), 1059–1073 (2004)
2. Vukobratovic, M., Juricic, D.: Contribution to the synthesis of biped gait. IEEE Trans. Biomed. Eng. **16**(1), 1–6 (1969)
3. Vukobratović, M., Borovac, B.: Zero-moment point—thirty five years of its life. Int. J. Hum. Robot. **1**(01), 157–173 (2004)
4. Sun, G., Wang, H., Lu, Z.: A novel biped pattern generator based on extended ZMP and extended cart-table model. Int. J. Adv. Robot. Syst. **12**(7), 94 (2015)
5. Fu, C., Chen, K.: Gait synthesis and sensory control of stair climbing for a humanoid robot. IEEE Trans. Ind. Electron. **55**(5), 2111–2120 (2008)
6. Ha, S., Han, Y., Hahn, H.: Adaptive gait pattern generation of biped robot based on human's gait pattern analysis. Int. J. Mech. Syst. Sci. Eng. **1**(2), 80–85 (2007)
7. Mrozowski, J., Awrejcewicz, J., Bamberski, P.: Analysis of stability of the human gait. J. Theor. Appl. Mech.-Pol. **45**(1), 91–98 (2007)
8. Shin, H., Kim, B.K.: Energy-efficient gait planning and control for biped robots utilizing vertical body motion and allowable ZMP region. IEEE Trans. Ind. Electron. **62**(4), 2277–2286 (2015)
9. Bessonnet, G., Seguin, P., Sardain, P.: A parametric optimization approach to walking pattern synthesis. Int. J. Robot. Res. **24**(7), 523–536 (2005)
10. Huang, Q., Yokoi, K., Kajita, S., Kaneko, K., Arai, H., Koyachi, N., Tanie, K.: Planning walking patterns for a biped robot. IEEE Trans. Robot. Autom. **17**(3), 280–289 (2001)
11. Chow, C.K., Jacobson, D.H.: Studies of human locomotion via optimal programming. Math. Biosci. **10**(3–4), 239–306 (1971)
12. Channon, P.H., Hopkins, S.H., Pham, D.T.: Derivation of optimal walking motions for a bipedal walking robot. Robotica **10**(02), 165–172 (1992)
13. Park, I., Kim, J., Oh, J.: Online walking pattern generation and its application to a biped humanoid robot—KHR-3 (HUBO). Adv. Robot. **22**(2–3), 159–190 (2008)
14. Chevallereau, C., Aoustin, Y.: Optimal reference trajectories for walking and running of a biped robot. Robotica **19**(05), 557–569 (2001)

15. Shi, Z., Xu, W., Zhong, Y., Zhao, M.: Optimal sagittal gait with ZMP stability during complete walking cycle for humanoid robots. J. Control Theory Appl. **5**(2), 133–138 (2007)
16. Tlalolini, D., Chevallereau, C., Aoustin, Y.: Optimal reference walking with rotation of the stance feet in single support for a 3D biped. In: IEEE/RSJ International Conference on Intelligent Robots and Systems, IROS 2008, p 1091–1096. IEEE (2008)
17. Kajita, S., Yisheng, G.: Humanoid Robot. Tsinghua University Press, Beijing (2007)
18. Xia, Z., Liu, L., Xiong, J., Yi, Q., Chen, K.: Design aspects and development of humanoid robot THBIP-2. Robotica **26**(01), 109–116 (2008)
19. Qiang, Y., Ken, C., Li, L., Fu, C.: 3D parametric gait planning of humanoid robot with consideration of comprehensive biped walking constraints. Robot **31**(4), 342–350 (2009)

Development of an Enhanced Musculoskeletal Model for Simulating Lumbar Spine Loading During Manual Lifting Tasks

Xin Yue Zhu[1], Hyun Kyung Kim[2], and Yanxin Zhang[2(✉)]

[1] Department of Mechanical Engineering,
University of Auckland, Auckland, New Zealand
xzhu055@aucklanduni.ac.nz
[2] Biomechanics Laboratory, Department of Exercise Sciences,
University of Auckland, Auckland, New Zealand
hkim319@aucklanduni.ac.nz,
yanxin.zhang@auckland.ac.nz

Abstract. During manual lifting tasks, extreme loads, intervertebral shear forces, repeated loading and improper lifting techniques all contribute to the risks of back pain and injuries. A three-dimensional (3D) multi-segment musculoskeletal model, which includes 49° of freedom (DOFs) and 258 muscle-tendon units, was developed in this study for simulating loading conditions of the lower back during manual lifting tasks. The model was created in OpenSim, an open-source computer simulation platform. The enhanced musculoskeletal model provides a tool for more comprehensive simulations of lifting motions. To evaluate the capacity of the model for estimation of spinal loading, the loading at the L3/L4–L5/S1 under different lifting tasks were examined and compared with published data. The results encourage the feasibility of applying the model to research questions relating to lumbar spine loading.

Keywords: Musculoskeletal model · Biomechanics · Lumbar spine · OpenSim

1 Introduction

As low back injuries remain to be the most frequently occurring injury in occupation-related settings, a comprehensive understanding of spinal loads, muscle forces and the mechanisms behind maintaining trunk stability is essential to mitigate low back injury.

Early biomechanical research for simulating lumbar spine loading in lifting activities resemble basic static models in two dimensions [20, 21]. Recent studies have developed 3D models using dynamic analysis and more detailed musculoskeletal structures of the torso [5, 15]. However, as models became more complex, the number of unknowns significantly exceeds the known parameters. Thus, to resolve the redundancy problem and determine individual muscle forces, different musculoskeletal modelling approaches have been proposed including equivalent muscle models [17], optimization models [7, 15], electromyography (EMG)-assisted models [27], finite element models [26], and multi-body models [22]. However, these models are only

© Springer International Publishing AG 2017
V.G. Duffy (Ed.): DHM 2017, Part I, LNCS 10286, pp. 229–237, 2017.
DOI: 10.1007/978-3-319-58463-8_20

supported by commercially available software or customized programs. Furthermore, most of the models are generic models with limited DOFs, which lack the capability of simulating subject-specific motions performed by individuals.

OpenSim is an open-source musculoskeletal modelling software [10]. A detailed lumbar spine model, including the pelvis, sacrum, lumbar vertebrae, and torso, in OpenSim was firstly developed by Christophy et al. [9]. More recently, a thoracolumbar spine model, including the torso and upper limbs, was developed in OpenSim by Bruno et al. [7]. However, this model was only used to simulate static and isometric conditions.

Therefore, the purpose of the current study was to develop an enhanced OpenSim model with whole-body structures including detailed musculoskeletal representations of the trunk, upper, and lower extremities. The model was evaluated by analysing kinematics and kinetics under dynamic lifting conditions.

2   Methods

2.1   Model Development

A 3D multi-segment, musculoskeletal, whole-body model was developed, including 49 DOFs and 258 muscle-tendon units. The model consists of components for the lower limbs, trunk, and upper limbs.

Lower Limbs. The lower limbs, containing rigid bodies defining the pelvis, thighs, shanks and feet, were sourced from a full-body model (Gait2354) [14] created in OpenSim (Stanford University, Stanford, US). The skeletal portion of the model is modelled as a set of rigid bodies with interconnecting joints. The shank consists of bone geometries for the tibia and fibula, and the foot contains geometries for the calcaneus, navicular, cuboid, cuneiforms and metatarsals. The kinematic relationship between lumbar 5 and the sacrum is based on a study by Anderson and Pandy [2], while the hip joints are represented by a ball and socket joint. The knee joint is based on an earlier model by Delp et al. [11] which formulated transformations for the femur, tibia and patella as functions of the knee angle based on a simple, planar model of the knee in Yamaguchi and Zajac [29]. The pelvic frame of reference is located at the midpoint between the left and right anterior superior iliac spines. In the default position, the pelvic frame of reference aligns with the global coordinate system. It has identified that in the neutral position the pelvis tilts at approximately 13° [6, 19, 28]. This tends to lead to an off-set between the hip flexion angles when comparing experimental data to results found in the literature. In order to simplify this problem, the orientation of the pelvis was modified in the default position such that it exhibits a 13 degree tilt. The lower limbs consist of 48 musculotendon actuators representing 40 muscles. Details of muscles are described in the *muscle model* part.

Lumbar and Torso. The lumbar spine model is modified from a base lumbar model developed by Christophy et al. [9]. The model consists of rigid bodies for the pelvis, sacrum, lumbar vertebrae, and torso consisting of bone geometries for the thoracic spine and ribcage.

The motion of lumbar bodies is represented by six DOFs: flexion-extension, lateral bending, axial rotation, and three translational directions. Each lumbar body consists of an independent coordinate system which contributes to the overall motion of the spine. The net bending of the trunk around three orthogonal directions are distributed throughout the lumbar bodies by describing their individual range of motion as a fraction of the net motion. That is, the rotation of each of the lumbar vertebrae is assumed to be linear functions of the trunk flexion–extension, axial rotation, and lateral bending [9]. The coefficients of the linear functions were obtained through a kinematic study of the lumbar spine during lifting [1].

The dimensions of the base lumbar model were modified to match the dimensions of the torso in the lower limb model. The scale factors were calculated using landmarks in the anterior-posterior, superior-inferior and medial-lateral directions. The distance between the xiphoid process and the spinous process of the 9th thoracic vertebra were calculated for the anterior-posterior direction. The distance between the spinous process of the 1st thoracic vertebra and the spinous process of the 5th lumbar vertebra was used for the superior-inferior direction. Markers were placed on the most lateral points of the 6th rib for the medial-lateral direction.

The scaled lumbar model was incorporated into the lower limb model. The distance between the 5th lumbar vertebra and the sacrum were determined by the ratio of the vertebra height to the height of the intervertebral disc. In Gilad and Nissan [13], the relative height index was found using four measurements, as illustrated in Fig. 1, where b and d measure. The relative height index was calculated by dividing the average of the posterior and anterior measurements as defined in the Eq. 1.

$$Relative\ Height\ Index = \frac{(g+h)}{(b+d)} \tag{1}$$

The vertebral height and g and h measure the intervertebral spacing.

Gilad and Nissan [13] reported a mean height index of 0.402 for the 5th lumbar vertebra. Using the positions of the markers in the OpenSim model, g had a value of 0.020324 and h had a value of 0.021. Thus, by taking the average of intervertebral spacing the distance was estimated to be 0.0083 m. Once the position of the 5th lumbar vertebra was correctly defined, all other bodies in the lumbar model, including the rest of the lumbar vertebrae and the upper torso, were added to the new model.

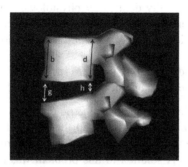

Fig. 1. Measurements for determining the relative height index.

Upper Limbs. Upper limbs were included based on a modified and expanded gait model similar to Gait2354 [14]. In our model, the muscles in the upper limbs were excluded and the components purely consist of skeletal structures because the complexity of these muscles makes it difficult to be modelled reliably.

Muscle Model. The musculature includes the main muscle groups of the lower limb and trunk consisting of 258 muscle fascicles. The main muscle groups included in the model are the erector spinae, rectus abdominis, internal obliques, external obliques, quadratus lumborum, multifidus, psoas major, iliacus, rectus femoris, vastus intermedius, sartorius, gracilis, adductor magnus, pectineus, gluteus medius/maximus, tensor fasciae latae, quadratus femoris, fixme gem, piriformis, biceps femoris, medial gastrocnemius, soleus, and tibialis anterior/posteriors (Fig. 2). The latissimus dorsi was excluded because it has less contribution of trunk stabilisation [9].

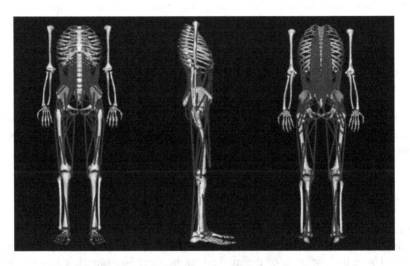

Fig. 2. Anterior, mediolateral, and posterior views of the model.

The muscle models in OpenSim are based on the Hill-type model [16]. An updated Hill-type muscle model was included in the developed model [25]. Thelen's muscle model allows muscles to be fully defined by physiological parameters of the muscle architecture. In order to prevent the model from encountering singularities, it now allows users to define a lower bound for muscle activation as well as maximum pennation angles.

Changes were also made such that the fibre length does not reach a lower bound and that energy is conserved throughout the simulation [25].

Anthropometric Properties. The anthropometric properties of the base models were derived from different sample populations and therefore reflect the characteristics of different subjects. This means that mass and inertial properties are inconsistent throughout the new model. A solution to this problem was to redistribute the overall mass of the generic model to each component in the newly developed model [3].

2.2 Model Evaluation

To evaluate the capacity of the model for estimation of spinal loading, an experiment was performed under lifting tasks. The experiment protocol was approved by University of Auckland's Human Research Ethics committee.

Customized Marker-Set. Amarker-set was formulated, mapping the marker positions during motion-capture. As there are currently no standard marker-sets available for researching lifting mechanics, a marker-set based on the Cleveland Clinic marker-set [24] was designed in the current study.

Experimental Protocol. Eight Vicon MX infrared cameras (Oxford Metric, Oxford, UK) were used to collect the marker positions with a sampling frequency of 100 Hz. Two force platforms (Bertec Corporation, Worthington, Ohio, USA) with a sampling rate of 1,000 Hz were used to measure ground reaction forces. The experiment was conducted on eight healthy, young male adults (age: 21 ± 2.49 years, height: 1.74 ± 0.08 m, weight: 70.76 ± 7.56 kg). Reflective markers of 20 mm in diameter for the clavicle and sternum and 14 mm for all other anatomical landmarks were used. The participants were asked to lift a loaded crate from ground level to a table placed directly in front of them. The crate had dimensions of $40 \times 35 \times 25$ cm (width $\times$ length $\times$ height) and was loaded to make a total weight of either 7 kg or 12 kg. The table had a height of 72 cm and was positioned at a distance of 40 cm from the participants. The participants carried out each task at a self-selected pace, yet all were completed within two seconds. Participants used a squatted lifting technique with some trunk flexion.

Post-Processing. Using the tools available in OpenSim, the biomechanical model was scaled to match the anthropometry of each participant based on measured marker positions. Kinematic analysis was then performed to obtain the positions and orientations of the body segments. Then inverse dynamics and static optimisation analysis were carried out to obtain the muscle forces and joint torques. Subsequently, joint reaction analysis enabled calculation of joint reaction forces at each lumbar vertebra. The compression forces and shear forces of each lumbar joint were examined for the lifting motion trials. The outcomes were presented for peak loads averaged over three repeated trials for each of the eight participants. A paired t-test was performed to compare the difference between the two lifting conditions.

3 Results and Discussion

The L5/S1 and L4/L5 joints exhibited the largest forces with very similar values, whereas the L3/L4 joint showed the smallest forces during lifting motions. The largest of the L5/S1 joint may associate with disc degeneration [8]. Very similar trends were observed for the compressive and anterior shear forces (Fig. 3); the first peak occurring immediately after lifting off and the second peak occurring when the crate was lowering on the table. Shear forces change directions, from posterior to anterior, at the L3/L4 joint. This is a result of the spine's lordosis – the natural curve of the spine. Shear forces act in the anterior direction in lower vertebrae and in the posterior direction for upper vertebrae.

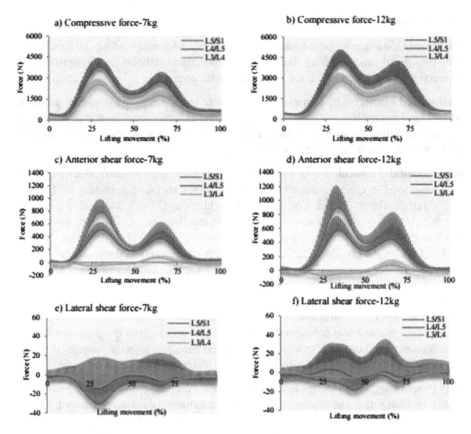

Fig. 3. 3D *lumbar spinal force patterns after time-normalised for each lumbar level throughout* lifting motion with two lifting weights. Positive values indicate anterior and right lateral direction.

These results have shown trends similar to what is expected from basic knowledge of lumbar spine loading. Thus, it encourages the feasibility of applying the developed model to research in lumbar spine loading and future opportunities to investigate low back pain and injuries. When lifting a heavier weight, the peak compressive and anterior and lateral shear forces showed higher lumbar spinal loading than with a 7 kg weight for most joints (Fig. 4).

The current results were generally in accordance with previous literature [3–5, 12]. Recently this model has been adopted other experimental study and showed good agreement with previous reported lumbar loading and trunk muscle forces [18]. We also compared the simulation results with reported measured intradiscal compressive forces [23] and showed a good match.

One of the major assumptions involved in the developed model is the approximation of human structures into rigid segments. For example, the kinematics of the thoracic and cervical spine was not considered and was, instead, modelled as a single rigid structure. Adding kinematics to these structures can provide more accurate representations of vertebral movement. Another one is the assumption of simple pivotal

a) Peak compressive forces

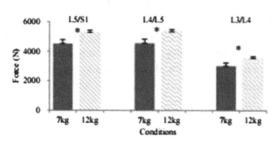

b) Peak anterior shear forces

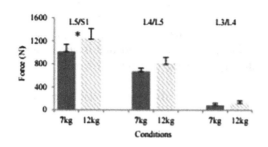

c) Peak lateral shear forces

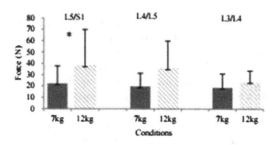

Fig. 4. Peak 3D lumbar spinal forces for each lumbar level throughout lifting motion. A paired t-test was performed. * indicates a significant ($p < 0.05$) difference between the two lifting conditions.

joints. Although translational motions of the spine were included, there are still mechanisms of the joint that have not been modelled. In addition, passive structures provide friction and tension during extreme flexion and extension motions. Future work could be done to improve the model by incorporating the passive structures. In addition, we assume that the rotation of each of the lumbar vertebrae is linear functions of the lumbar flexion–extension, axial rotation, and lateral bending. Although this approach may introduce some uncertainties of the kinematic data, it's more uncertain to place small reflective markers on processes of each lumbar processes as the skin movement artefacts will make the measurement unreliable during dynamic movement.

Although the model presented in this study has been designed for the purpose of investigating low back loading, the generality of the model means that it can also be applied to other research questions. Motions that involve whole-body dynamic movement can be simulated and analysed using this model. An example would be gait analysis for patients with cerebral palsy, which includes much more trunk movement than gait for those not affected by cerebral palsy. Due to the accessibility of the model, the opportunities for its application and development are endless.

4 Conclusion

This study provides an advanced and accessible tool for investigating lumbar spine loading. The developed model will support research involved in predicting risk levels for a variety of manual handling tasks. The developed model includes detailed musculoskeletal structures. Methods for performing experiments for occupational lifting tasks have been presented. The results from the lifting experiment are similar to the results from some of the literature. Further validation is needed to verify the accuracy of the model when applied to a specific research question.

Acknowledgements. The authors would like to thank John Yang for the assistance in this project.

References

1. Aiyangar, A.K., Zheng, L., Tashman, S., Anderst, W.J., Zhang, X.: Capturing three-dimensional in vivo lumbar intervertebral joint kinematics using dynamic stereo-X-ray imaging. J. Biomech. Eng. **136**(1), 011004 (2014)
2. Anderson, F.C., Pandy, M.G.: A dynamic optimization solution for vertical jumping in three dimensions. Comput. Methods Biomech. Biomed. Eng. **2**(3), 201–231 (1999)
3. Andersson, G.B., Chaffin, D.B., Pope, M.H.: Occupational biomechanics of the lumbar spine. In: Occupational Low Back Pain, pp. 20–43. Mosby, St. Louis (1991)
4. Arjmand, N., Shirazi-Adl, A.: Model and in vivo studies on human trunk load partitioning and stability in isometric forward flexions. J. Biomech. **39**(3), 510–521 (2006)
5. Bazrgari, B., Shirazi-Adl, A.: Spinal stability and role of passive stiffness in dynamic squat and stoop lifts. Comput. Methods Biomech. Biomed. Eng. **10**(5), 351–360 (2007)
6. Boulay, C., Tardieu, C., Hecquet, J., et al.: Sagittal alignment of spine and pelvis regulated by pelvic incidence: standard values and prediction of lordosis. Eur. Spine J. **15**(4), 415–422 (2006)
7. Bruno, A.G., Bouxsein, M.L., Anderson, D.E.: Development and validation of a musculoskeletal model of the fully articulated thoracolumbar spine and rib cage. J. Biomech. Eng. **137**(8), 081003 (2015)
8. Chaffin, D.B.: A computerized biomechanical model-development of and use in studying gross body actions. J. Biomech. **2**(4), 429–441 (1969)
9. Christophy, M., Senan, N.A.F., Lotz, J.C., O'Reilly, O.M.: A musculoskeletal model for the lumbar spine. Biomech. Model. Mechanobiol. **11**(1–2), 19–34 (2012)

10. Delp, S.L., Anderson, F.C., Arnold, A.S., et al.: OpenSim: open-source software to create and analyze dynamic simulations of movement. IEEE Trans. Biomed. Eng. **54**(11), 1940–1950 (2007)

11. Delp, S.L., Loan, J.P., Hoy, M.G., Zajac, F.E., Topp, E.L., Rosen, J.M.: An interactive graphics-based model of the lower extremity to study orthopaedic surgical procedures. IEEE Trans. Biomed. Eng. **37**(8), 757–767 (1990)

12. Ferguson, S., Gaudes-MacLaren, L., Marras, W., Waters, T., Davis, K.: Spinal loading when lifting from industrial storage bins. Ergonomics **45**(6), 399–414 (2002)

13. Gilad, I., Nissan, M.: A study of vertebra and disc geometric relations of the human cervical and lumbar spine. Spine **11**(2), 154–157 (1986)

14. Hamner, S.R., Seth, A., Delp, S.L.: Muscle contributions to propulsion and support during running. J. Biomech. **43**(14), 2709–2716 (2010)

15. Han, K., Zander, T., Taylor, W.R., Rohlmann, A.: An enhanced and validated generic thoraco-lumbar spine model for prediction of muscle forces. Med. Eng. Phys. **34**(6), 709–716 (2012)

16. Hill, A.: The heat of shortening and the dynamic constants of muscle. Proc. Roy. Soc. Lond. Ser. B: Biol. Sci. **126**(843), 136–195 (1938)

17. Hughes, R.E., Chaffin, D.B.: The effect of strict muscle stress limits on abdominal muscle force predictions for combined torsion and extension loadings. J. Biomech. **28**(5), 527–533 (1995)

18. Kim, H., Zhang, Y.: Estimation of lumbar spinal loading and trunk muscle forces during asymmetric lifting tasks: application of whole-body musculoskeletal modelling in OpenSim. Ergonomics 1–24 (2016, just-accepted)

19. Kuntz IV, C., Levin, L.S., Ondra, S.L., Shaffrey, C.I., Morgan, C.J.: Neutral upright sagittal spinal alignment from the occiput to the pelvis in asymptomatic adults: a review and resynthesis of the literature. J. Neurosurg.: Spine **6**(2), 104–112 (2007)

20. Lee, K.S.: Biomechanical modelling of cart pushing and pulling. Diss. Abs. Int. Part B: Sci. Eng. [DISS. ABST. INT. PT. B- SCI. ENG.] **43**(2), 1982 (1982)

21. McGill, S., Norman, R.W.: Reassessment of the role of intra-abdominal pressure in spinal compression. Ergonomics **30**(11), 1565–1588 (1987)

22. Rupp, T., Ehlers, W., Karajan, N., Günther, M., Schmitt, S.: A forward dynamics simulation of human lumbar spine flexion predicting the load sharing of intervertebral discs, ligaments, and muscles. Biomech. Model. Mechanobiol. **14**(5), 1081–1105 (2015)

23. Schultz, A., Andersson, G., Ortengren, R., Haderspeck, K., Nachemson, A.: Loads on the lumbar spine. validation of a biomechanical analysis by measurements of intradiscal pressures and myoelectric signals. J. Bone Joint Surg. **64**(5), 713–720 (1982)

24. Sutherland, D.H.: The evolution of clinical gait analysis: part II kinematics. Gait Posture **16**(2), 159–179 (2002)

25. Thelen, D.G.: Adjustment of muscle mechanics model parameters to simulate dynamic contractions in older adults. J. Biomech. Eng. **125**(1), 70–77 (2003)

26. Toumanidou, T., Noailly, J.: Musculoskeletal modeling of the lumbar spine to explore functional interactions between back muscle loads and intervertebral disk multiphysics. Front. Bioeng. Biotechnol. **3** (2015)

27. van Dieën, J.H., Kingma, I., Van der Bug, J.: Evidence for a role of antagonistic cocontraction in controlling trunk stiffness during lifting. J. Biomech. **36**(12), 1829–1836 (2003)

28. Vialle, R., Levassor, N., Rillardon, L., Templier, A., Skalli, W., Guigui, P.: Radiographic analysis of the sagittal alignment and balance of the spine in asymptomatic subjects. J. Bone Joint Surg. Am. **87**(2), 260–267 (2005)

29. Yamaguchi, G.T., Zajac, F.E.: A planar model of the knee joint to characterize the knee extensor mechanism. J. Biomech. **22**(1), 1–10 (1989)

Smart Human-Centered Service System Design

Usability Evaluation Plan for Online Annotation and Student Clustering System – A Tunisian University Case

Miao-Han Chang[1(✉)], Rita Kuo[2], Fathi Essalmi[3], Maiga Chang[1],
Vive Kumar[1], and Hsu-Yang Kung[4]

[1] Athabasca University, Athabasca, Canada
chang.miaohan@gmail.com, maiga.chang@gmail.com
[2] New Mexico Institute of Mining and Technology, Socorro, USA
[3] University of Kairouan, Kairouan, Tunisia
[4] National Pingtung University of Science and Technology, Neipu, Taiwan

Abstract. When students learn in schools, they usually annotate words and concepts that they think important in the text. Sometimes students might overlook some important information while studying and they might not be able to answer questions of quizzes or exams properly. If they can be reminded about the potentially important words and concepts, they may achieve better academic performance. The research team develops an online annotation and student clustering system which not only allows teachers can create online reading activities for students and review students' annotations on the e-text but also clusters students into different groups based on their annotations via bio-inspired clustering approach. This paper talks about the experience and process that the research team had in a Tunisian university to execute an evaluation study.

Keywords: Annotation · Bio-inspired approach · Clustering · Usability · Diffusion of innovation

1 Introduction

About ten years ago, students still prefer to print out the materials than the digital version, especially in academic reading because they prefer to make highlights, underlines, and write some notes on the materials [6]. However, with the development of technology, students are used to read digitalized materials on digital devices, such as computers and tablets, instead of read the printed papers [5]. In 2014, Chen and Chen's [3] study shows that no matter students prefer to read printed version or digital version, their reading attitudes have no difference.

Even students using digital devices to read learning materials, their behaviors on digital devices might still be similar to what they did on the printed papers. When students read materials assigned by teachers, they usually take notes and highlight important words/sentences [3]. Students have their prefer ways to take annotations while reading; they may annotate words in different ways (e.g., highlighting, underlining, or double-underlining). For example, when John, Andrew, and Mary read a text – "Every

© Springer International Publishing AG 2017
V.G. Duffy (Ed.): DHM 2017, Part I, LNCS 10286, pp. 241–254, 2017.
DOI: 10.1007/978-3-319-58463-8_21

year in the U.S. factories release over 3 million tons of toxic chemicals into the land, air and water" – in the "Pollution" article[1], they will use different annotations ways and have different focus. John only circles the word "air"; Andrew underlines the whole sentence; and, Mary highlights the three words – "air", "water", and "land".

While reading an article, students might not want to annotate some important keywords intentionally or simply overlook those words accidentally. When they preparing exams and doing homework with the annotated article, they may skip those un-annotated words because they believe that all important words or concepts already have been annotated by them earlier. For example, while answering a question of "Environment Pollution" in the mid-term exam, John may only mention the toxic chemicals released to air because he didn't annotated "land" and "water" earlier. The incomplete answer for the mid-term question may make him lose marks.

To avoid themselves missing important thing, students always try to borrow friends' textbooks and notes before the exam comes. While preparing the forthcoming written exam and quiz, they take their friends' annotations as reference. In the previous example, John may borrow Mary's annotated text before the final exam comes. If he does so for the final exam preparation, he might probably notice the "land" and "water" highlighted by Mary are missed in his text copy. He might also circles the words on his copy so it has more complete annotations and he would probably have better answer for the question when he writes the exam.

2 Literature Review

2.1 Reading Activities in Digital Materials

Some studies show that people are getting used to read on the screen. In 2005, Liu has asked participants to think about their reading habits in the past ten years [6]. 83% of participants report that their electronically reading is increased. In Chrzastowski and Wiley's research [2], students can choose to use digital books or get the printed books for their reading activities. When they choose the printed books, the research team sends the hard copies to students; on the other hand, when they prefer using digital books, they can read the materials online. The result shows that students prefer the digital books more than the printed ones.

Bounie et al. [1] have discovered that Amazon sells more digital books than printed books. Especially in higher education, digital materials are popular in undergraduate and graduate students [11]. Lopatovska and colleagues' research [5] shows the reasons that people choose digital books include (1) digital books are convenient (58%); (2) study for school's need (55%); (3) there is no printed version available (49%); (4) it is easy to use (48%); (5) digital books costs less (46%); (6) the feature of searching in the text (43%); (7) the interactive features (36%); and (8) they just want to use digital books (80%).

---

[1] http://webpage.pace.edu/jb44525n/page5.html.

Because people's reading preference has changed to digital devices, Tashman and Edwards' research [11] focuses on analyzing people's reading behaviour son digital materials. The participants in their study write reading diaries when they do Active Reading activities. There are approximately 25% of the diaries shows that participants use both papers and computers for finishing their Active Reading tasks. They also find that 63% of diaries in doing their reading activities are performed on computers only.

Above studies show that people's reading hobbits are changed to digital reading materials and they feel comfortable to read on the screen. If people get used to annotate on the paper-based reading materials, they might also have the same habit and need when they read on the digital devices. The next section discusses the research related to annotations on digital devices.

2.2   Annotations on Digital Material

In traditional learning, teachers always give students reading assignments that ask students to read pieces of articles on papers or in a text. Reading and annotating articles are students' routine jobs of study. Chen and Chen's research [3] discovers that when students use paper-based way to study, students are frequently highlighting or underlining words, phrases, or passages, writing short comments in blank space, between lines, or near figures. Before an exam, students can find some annotations that may important to themselves by reviewing other students' annotated text.

Nowadays, digitalized materials are common to be used and students may use digital devices like computers and tablets for their studying. Hoff et al. [4] classify functions provided by existing annotation systems into four categories: media formats support (e.g., support web document, office documents, PDF, or multimedia.), annotation functions (e.g., user can annotate on articles), interactions management (e.g., is this annotation private, group, or public shared? Do I want to get notifications when others make new annotations), and repository implementation (e.g., the repository is local, global, or client-server). The four categories help researchers understand the gaps between the annotation features that students need and current widely accepted annotation systems have.

Some other research provide annotation service to help users read and annotate articles on their computers. Yang et al. [12] have developed a web-based annotation platform – Personal Annotation Management System (PAMS) – where users can highlight, underline, attach notes and do voice recordings to the text in an article. Su and colleagues [9] and Yang and colleagues [13] improve the PAMS system, i.e., PAMS 2.0, to know students' perceptions toward the collaborative annotation system and how the collaborative annotation system helps students improve their reading competence.

Another research provides a system which combines annotation service and collaborative learning together. Pearson et al. [8] aim to provide students an annotation system to help students learn better. They provide a collaborative system, BuddyBooks, to students and ask students to read article as teams. While students read articles, members in the same group have to stay at the same place and discuss. When students read and annotate on the article, the actions will be sent to other group member's pad. Every members can see others' annotations in different highlighted colors. If one student wants others to look at a particular paragraph in the article, he or she can just point it out on his or her pad and others will receive notification at the side bar and can easily follow. The result shows that students believe sharing members' annotations is useful and enjoy the feature while doing reading activity.

In Pearson, Buchanan and Thimbleby's research [8], they allow students to review other students' annotations only in small group. The research team aims to provide students not only an online annotation system but also an annotation recommender so they can receive annotation suggestions to find useful ones instead of reviewing a small group of classmates' annotations on their own. To find useful annotation suggestions for students, the relations between students' annotations and their annotation behaviours are needed to be analyzed.

Above mentioned research allow students to use different ways to annotate their reading materials. The common annotation ways are underline, highlight, and note-taking. Other functions provided by annotation systems include, for example, students can attach multimedia resources (such as audio and video) to a word or sentence and students can collaborate with others in a group (such as point out an annotation). Melenhorst [7] records students' annotation behaviors in the annotation tool to identify the relationship between reading phases and annotation ways (e.g. highlighting words and sentences, taking notes, copying passages to notepad, etc.). With showing the relations between reading phases and annotation ways on two-dimensional plane, Melenhorst has found that students use different annotation ways in different reading phases.

3 Evaluation Plan

The perceived usability toward the proposed system from both students and teachers are necessary to be known. This section talks about the experience and process that the research team had in a Tunisian university to execute an evaluation study. We start from introducing how to recruit participants include teacher(s) and students to explaining the stages that both teacher(s) and students would be done.

First of all, the teachers and students who are teaching and studying in Higher Institute of Computer Science and Management of Kairouan (ISIGK), Kairouan, Tunisia, are the potential participants of the evaluation study. The courses that teachers teach include educational games or languages in first and second year master degree's students. The research team first approaches to the teachers and ask for their willingness of adopting the proposed system in their courses so students need to use the online annotation system for reading activities and the student clustering results would be provided for them.

As soon as a teacher agrees to adopt the system in his or her course, he or she is required to prepare few reading activities for students. As Fig. 1 shows below, six reading activities are created for students in the 3-month study and each of them has its

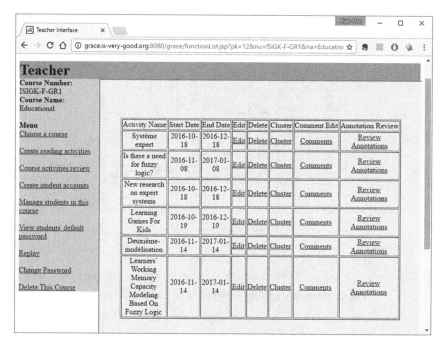

Fig. 1. List of reading activities

own starting and end date so students can only do the particular reading activities within the predefined periods. The reading activities can be created in any language. In the case, the teacher has reading activities in both of English and French. He or she can also edit the reading activities, check out the cluster results, and review students' annotations.

Before students can start using the system for doing the reading activities, they need to first fill out a questionnaire about their experience of using any kind of e-readers. Further details and descriptions of the questionnaire can be found at Table 4 in Sect. 4.2 below. For accessing the reading activities, they also need to have accounts to sign in the system. The teacher can import a student list to create accounts for his or her students in batch.

With the account created by their teacher, students can see all the reading activities the course(s) they enrolled has, the reading time periods, and the forthcoming reading activities. When they want to do particular reading activity, they can simply click the correspondent "Reading" link to start as Fig. 2 shows. However, they cannot enter to do a reading activity prior its start date. Although they can no longer do any further annotation on the reading material after the end date of a reading activity, they can still review the reading activity and the annotations they made earlier.

When students start a reading activity, as Fig. 3 shows, on the top of the window is the annotation function panel, students can choose their preferred annotation ways for their annotations; on the left-hand side of the window is the reading material; and, on the right-hand side of the window is student's sidebar notes. Even students they

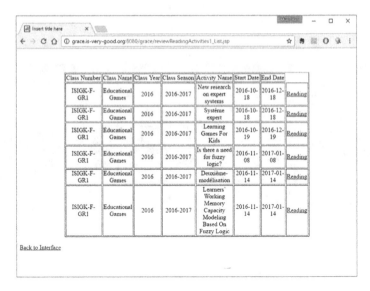

Fig. 2. Student's reading activities in all enrolled course(s)

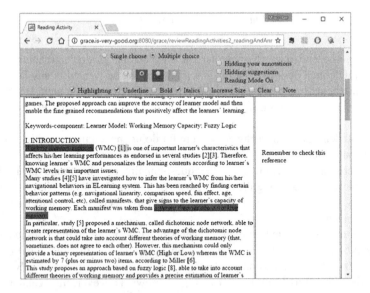

Fig. 3. Reading and note taking in the proposed system

accidently close the window, the system will still recover their annotations because the system is implemented in AJAX technique – the system sends and retrieved data to and from backend services asynchronously.

At the end of the 3-month study, students are asked to fill out another questionnaire which asks for their experience of using the Online Annotation System. The details and explanation of the questionnaire can be found at Table 5 in Sect. 4.2. At the same time, the research team also asks the teacher to review the clustering results. If the teacher doesn't agree with the results, he or she can edit the results. After that, the research team interviews the teacher and asks him or her the questions to get idea of whether or not the system can help him or her to teach better, whether or not the clustering results meet his or her expectation, and how he or she thinks about the system. The detailed interview questions are listed in Table 1.

Table 1. Interview questions for teacher

Questions
1. Do you like the Online Annotation System? Why? Can you give us some examples or reasons?
2. How do you feel about the system? Could you please elaborate it further?
3. Is the Online Annotation System easy to use?
4. What do you think about the management functions of reading activities?
5. What do you think about the management functions of clustering results?
6. What do you think about the clustering results of students?
7. Can you find student's learning problems when you review students' annotations? How? Can you share couple of examples with us?
8. Could you identify any behaviour feature that connects to potential learning problems? Do you see any features that can be used to distinguish students' learning problems?
9. Does finding students' learning problems is more quickly by reviewing the clustering results? Why? Could you please explain the reasons?
10. Do you think the use of the Online Annotation System improve your teaching performance? Please elaborate it further or give examples?
11. Would you want to use the Online Annotation System in the future? Why? Can you share with us your reasons?
12. Would you recommend others to use the Online Annotation System? Why? Can you share with us your reasons?
13. Does the Online Annotation System meet your needs? How? Could you please elaborate it further, perhaps with real cases?
14. Any feature that you think the Online Annotation System needs to have? Or is anything currently missing in the Online Annotation System?

4 Research Model and Questionnaire

4.1 Research Model and Hypothesis

Providing a system for students to use, the research team wants to know the students' perceptions toward it. We assume that there are three factors may affect the perceived usability of the system: (1) student's experience of using e-readers, (2) student's demographic information, and (3) student's experience of using the system. The research model shown in Fig. 4 is built based on the seven research questions (listed in Table 2) we have.

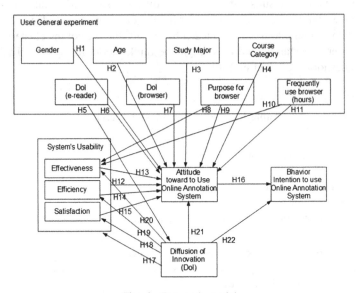

Fig. 4. Research model

Table 2. Research questions

Questions
1. Will student's major affect his or her attitude toward the use of the online annotation system?
2. Will the age the student started to use e-reader application have correlation with his or her perceived experience of using e-reader application?
3. Will student's purpose of using browsers affect his or her attitude toward the use of the online annotation system?
4. Will the perceived system usability affect student's attitude toward the use of online annotation system?
5. Will perceived efficiency of the online annotation system affect student's attitude toward the use of the system?
6. Will the perceived satisfaction of the online annotation system affect student's attitude toward the use of the system?
7. Will student's experience of using e-reader applications affect his or her perceived usability of the online annotation system?

According to the research model, we have the following seven hypotheses made and would like to test them via the analysis of data collected with two questionnaires (Table 3).

Table 3. Hypotheses

Hypotheses
1. Students who are major in technology will be more positive toward the use of the online annotation system than other students
2. The age that student started to use e-reader applications have positive correlation with his or her perceived experience of using the applications
3. Student's purpose of using browsers will affect his or her attitude toward the use of the online annotation system
4. The perceived system usability will positive affect their attitude toward the use of the online annotation system
5. The perceived efficiency of the system's usability will positive affect their attitude toward the use of the online annotation system
6. The perceived satisfaction of the system's usability will positive affect their attitude toward the use of the online annotation system
7. Student's experiences of using e-reader applications will positive affect system's usability

4.2   The Questionnaire

This evaluation plan includes two five-point Likert-scale questionnaires. The first questionnaire is Diffusion of Innovation questionnaire (DoI) and this questionnaire has 24 items. The purpose of DoI questionnaire is to get idea of students' experiences and thoughts of using any kind of e-reader applications so the connection between their perceptions toward the system and their attitudes toward e-reader applications can be found. For instance, will students who think the use of e-reader application can help them learn better make them perceived more positive toward the Online Annotation System? The factors and correspondent items that DoI questionnaire has can be found in Table 4.

Table 4. Diffusion of Innovation questionnaire

Factor	Items
Relative advantage	1. Using an e-reader application with annotation functions enables me to understand the key concepts of the reading activities more quickly
	2. Using an e-reader application with annotation functions improves the quality of annotations I make
	3. Using an e-reader application with annotation functions makes easier to do reading activities
	4. Using an e-reader application with annotation functions improves my learning performance
	5. Using an e-reader application with annotation functions gives me greater control over my study schedule
Compatibility	6. Using an e-reader application with annotation functions is compatible with all aspects of my study in school

(*continued*)

Table 4. (*continued*)

Factor	Items
	7. Using an e-reader application with annotation functions is completely compatible with my current study in the class
	8. I think that using an e-reader application with annotation functions fits well with the way I like to study
	9. Using an e-reader application with annotation functions fits well with the device I prefer to use
Complexity	10. My interaction with e-reader application with annotation functions is clear
	11. My interaction with e-reader application with annotation functions is understandable
	12. Learning to use an e-reader application with annotation functions is easy for me
	13. Overall, I believe that an e-reader application with annotation functions is easy to adopt into my study
Trialability	14. I've had a great deal of opportunities to try an e-reader application with annotation functions for studying
	15. I know where I can go to satisfactorily try out various uses of an e-reader application with annotation functions for studying
	16. Before deciding whether or not to adopt an e-reader application with annotation functions, I would need to use it on a trail basis
	17. Before deciding whether or not to adopt an e-reader application with annotation functions, I would need to properly try it out
	18. I would like to be permitted to use an e-reader application with annotation functions on a trial basis long enough to see what it can do
Observability	19. It is easy for me to see people using e-reader application with annotation functions in the school
	20. I have had a lot of opportunities to see people using e-reader application with annotation functions to study
	21. It is easy for me to see others' annotations when we all use e-reader application with annotation functions
	22. I can see how others annotate the content of an article or book when we use e-reader application with annotation functions
	23. I see people searching and finding the desired content quickly in an e-reader application
	24. I can tell how different that I annotate an article or book from others when we use e-reader application with annotation functions

After students use the Online Annotation System doing their reading activities and before the semester is end, the research team asks students to fill out the usability questionnaire. This questionnaire asks students whether or not they think the system is useful for them as well as their willingness of using the system later. The questionnaire has forty-one five-point Likert point items for four higher level factors: Like, Effectiveness, Efficiency, and Satisfaction. Each higher level factor has sub-factors.

There are 5 items for Like factor; 16 items for the three sub-factors of Effectiveness factor; 10 items for the two sub-factors of Efficiency factor; and 10 items for the two sub-factors of Satisfaction factor.

Table 5. Usability questionnaire

Factor (HL)	Sub-factor	Items
Like		1. I believe it is a good idea to use an Online Annotation System
		2. Once I started using the Online Annotation System I found it is hard to stop
		3. I like to use the Online Annotation System
		4. As a student I like to use Online Annotation System to study
		5. The Online Annotation System is pleasant to use
Effectiveness	Ease of learning	6. I could imagine that most people could learn how to use the Online Annotation System very quickly
		7. I needed to learn a lot of things before I could get going with the Online Annotation System
		8. Learning to use the Online Annotation System is easy for me
		9. It is easy for me to remember how to do the reading activities in the Online Annotation System
		10. I find it takes a lot of efforts to become skillful at using the Online Annotation System
		11. I quickly became skillful with the Online Annotation System
	Ease of use	12. I think the Online Annotation System is easy to use
		13. I think that I would need the support of a technical person to be able to use the Online Annotation System
		14. I find the various functions in the Online Annotation System were well integrated
		15. I think there is too much inconsistency in the Online Annotation System
		16. I find the Online Annotation System very cumbersome to use
	User interface design	17. The interface of the Online Annotation System is pleasant
		18. The user interface of the Online Annotation System is confusing
		19. The Online Annotation System requires minimal steps for doing my reading activity
		20. The logical design of this Online Annotation System is good, I have no difficulty in using it
		21. The Online Annotation System is user friendly

(continued)

Table 5. (*continued*)

Factor (HL)	Sub-factor	Items
Efficiency	Information	22. Whenever I make a mistake while using the Online Annotation System I recover easily and quickly
		23. The information (such as couurese list, reading activity list, activity starting date, and activity ending date) provided by the Online Annotation System is clear
		24. It is easy to find the information I needed
		25. The information provided by the Online Annotation System is easy to understand
		26. I find the Online Annotation System unnecessarily complex
		27. I can use the Online Annotation System without written instructions
	Usefulness	28. I believe I understand the reading materials more in-depth by using the Online Annotation System
		29. Using the Online Annotation System gives me greater control over my time to finish my reading activities
		30. The Online Annotation System enables me to accomplish the reading activity more quickly
		31. Using the Online Annotation System improves my learning performance
Satisfaction	Behavioural intention to use	32. I think that I would like to use the Online Annotation System frequently
		33. I feel very confident using the Online Annotation System
		34. I plan to use an Online Annotation System in the future
		35. Assuming that I have access to an Online Annotation System, I intend to use it
		36. I intend to continue to use the Online Annotation System in the future
		37. I will recommend others to use the Online Annotation System
	Expectation	38. This Online Annotation System has all the functions and capabilities I expect it to have
		39. I expect that I would use the Online Annotation System in the future
		40. The Online Annotation System meets my needs
		41. The Online Annotation System works the way I want it to work

5   Conclusion

This paper explains the details of the evaluation plan and procedure, research questions and hypotheses and the two questionnaires used for data collection. The evaluation plan wants to know whether or not the proposed system can help teacher to know students learning problems as well as the students' perceptions toward the usability of the system. The study also collects students' experiences and thoughts about the use of e-reader application before they start using the Online Annotation System. The research team chooses to use both of Diffusion of Innovation and Usability questionnaire. With the analysis of the collected responses of the two questionnaire, we are not only can verify the effectiveness of the system and students' willingness of the system, but also can find whether or not students' pre-experiences and attitudes toward e-reader applications will affect their perceived usability of the system and intention of keeping to use the system in the future.

This evaluation plan has already got approval from Athabasca University's Research Ethic Board. The research team plans to do the 3-month study from April to June, 2017, in Tunisia. We have already found a teacher who is interested in adopting the system in his class in computer science in ISIGK, Tunisia. We also would like to find another teacher who teaches English or French course so we could know whether or not students in different disciplines perceived the usability of the Online Annotation System differently.

References

1. Bounie, D., Eang, B., Sirbu, M., Waelbroeck, P.: Superstars and outsiders in online markets: an empirical analysis of electronic books. Electron. Commer. Res. Appl. **12**(1), 52–59 (2013)
2. Chrzastowski, T.E., Wiley, L.N.: E-book use and value in the humanities: scholars' practices and expectations. Libr. Res. Tech. Serv. **59**(4), 172–186 (2015)
3. Chen, C.M., Chen, F.Y.: Enhancing digital reading performance with a collaborative reading annotation system. Comput. Educ. **77**, 67–81 (2014)
4. Hoff, C., Wehling, U., Rothkugel, S.: From paper-and-pen annotations to artefact-based mobile learning. J. Comput. Assist. Learn. **25**(3), 219–237 (2009)
5. Lopatovska, I., Slater, A., Bronner, C., El Mimouni, H., Lange, L., Ludas Orlofsky, V.: In transition: academic e-book reading in an institution without e-books. Libr. Rev. **63**(4/5), 261–275 (2014)
6. Liu, Z.: Reading behavior in the digital environment: changes in reading behavior over the past ten years. J. Doc. **61**(6), 700–712 (2005)
7. Melenhorst, M.: Observing professionals taking notes on screen. In: International Professional Communication Conference, pp. 540–545. IEEE (2005)
8. Pearson, J., Buchanan, G., Thimbleby, H.: Investigating collaborative annotation on slate PCs. In: 14th International Conference on Human-Computer Interaction with Mobile Devices and Services, pp. 413–416. ACM (2012)
9. Su, A.Y., Yang, S.J., Hwang, W.Y., Zhang, J.: A web 2.0-based collaborative annotation system for enhancing knowledge sharing in collaborative learning environments. Comput. Educ. **55**(2), 752–766 (2010)

10. Su, A.Y.S., Yang, S.J.H.: Improving annotation categorization performance through integrated social annotation computation. Expert Syst. Appl. **37**(12), 8736–8744 (2010)
11. Tashman, C.S., Edwards, W.K.: Active reading and its discontents: the situations, problems and ideas of readers. In: SIGCHI Conference on Human Factors in Computing Systems, pp. 2927–2936. ACM (2011)
12. Yang, S.J., Chen, I.Y.L., Shao, N.W.: Ontology enabled annotation and knowledge management for collaborative learning in virtual learning community. Educ. Technol. Soc. **7** (4), 70–81 (2004)
13. Yang, S.J., Zhang, J., Su, A.Y., Tsai, J.J.: A collaborative multimedia annotation tool for enhancing knowledge sharing in CSCL. Interact. Learn. Environ. **19**(1), 45–62 (2011)

Research on Multi Human-Computer Interface Design of Household Electrical Appliances

Jiali Dong[1(✉)], Rui Li[1], Zhangyu Ji[2], and Canqun He[2]

[1] Jiangsu University, Zhenjiang, China
996626018@qq.com
[2] College of Mechanical and Electrical Engineering of Hohai University,
Changzhou, China

Abstract. With the development of information technology, human-computer interaction interface instead of the traditional buttons, knobs and other control components bring a powerful, concise appearance of modern household appliances to the users. However, this kind of human-computer interaction software interface makes many old people and children who use electric appliances confused when facing the products because of the variety of functions and the high level of information. To solve this problem, the aim of this study is to meet the needs of different users in the home appliance for the different needs of the user interface, by using the theory of universal design, user needs, user experience and so on. The design model of multi human-computer interface household appliances is constructed, which can be used as reference for the design and development of household appliances and make household appliances have a more excellent user experience.

Keywords: Multi human computer interface household appliances · User needs · User experience · Home appliance product design and construction model

1 Introduction

The 50th CES (Consumer Electronics Show) was held in Las Vegas from January 4, 2017 to January 8, 2017. Every year CES brings many unexpected new technologies, which are applied to products and make people have many new experiences. These products have more excellent function, increasingly intelligent operation and simpler appearance. However, with these new experience, people need learn to use intelligent operation interfaces and master and manipulate these products. Only through the complex steps can excellent performance be shown. It is not difficult for young people to grasp the operation of these products, but it is not easy for the elderly and children. Some scholars such as John Clarkson and Simeon Keates put forward the concept of inclusive design, similar universal design and available design that product should meet the needs of all users [1], but these design concepts give no explicit solutions to specific problems. Therefore, this paper proposes that the multi interface design of household electrical appliances can solve the complicated operation interface of high-performance household electrical appliances.

© Springer International Publishing AG 2017
V.G. Duffy (Ed.): DHM 2017, Part I, LNCS 10286, pp. 255–270, 2017.
DOI: 10.1007/978-3-319-58463-8_22

2   Analysis of Design Demand for Existing Household Electrical Appliances

2.1   Existing Household Electrical Appliances Categories and Sample Selection

Electrical appliances which entered ordinary families in the twentieth century become increasingly rich after more than 100 years of development and have been an indispensable part of people's lives. Up to now, there is no uniform standard for household appliances internationally. By convention, household electrical appliances are divided into large and small ones according to the size and white and black ones according to the performance and the color of traditional electrical appliances. The classification of household appliances are shown in Table 1.

Table 1.   Classification of household appliances

Classification basis	Classification of household appliances	Appliances categories
According to the size of household appliances	Large household appliances	Refrigerator, TV set, air conditioner, etc.
	Small household appliances	Cooker, oven, juicer, etc.
According to the performance and the color of traditional electrical appliances	White household appliances	Washer, refrigerator, air conditioners, etc.
	Black household appliances	TV set, home theater, etc.

In order to more clearly understand the needs of home users for household appliances, we made a classified questionnaire survey on household appliances owned by the user's home. Eight kinds of common household electrical appliances were surveyed, covering large and small household appliances and white and black ones. A total of 119 valid questionnaires were collected and the results are shown in Fig. 1.

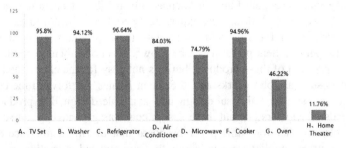

Fig. 1.   The survey data of household electrical appliance ownership

According to the results of 119 valid questionnaires, it can be seen that the amount of household appliances family ownership is large currently and the ownership proportion from high to low is followed by refrigerator, TV set, cooker and washer. The human-computer interface of refrigerator is relatively simple and human-computer interaction is mainly to pick and place ingredients, hence TV set, washer and cooker were selected as the typical household electrical appliance categories for human-computer interface analysis in this study.

2.2 Analysis of Design Demand for Existing Household Electrical Appliances

There are two main design directions about the current household appliances. One direction is household electrical appliances, mainly for young people, which pursuit excellent performance and high-tech [2] and the operation interface is highly intelligent and complicated to operate and users need learn how to use. Samsung TV set and remote control are shown in in Fig. 2. The other direction is household electrical appliances for the elderly to use [3]. Skyworth TV set and remote control are shown in Fig. 3. Such appliances usually have low prices and are concerned about the physiological and psychological needs of the elderly. They have simple operation and simple functions and little attention is paid to their appliance performance and quality. These two mainstream design directions are the design based on a single population as the target user.

Fig. 2. Samsung QLED TV set and remote control (Source: Samsung Electronics Official Website)

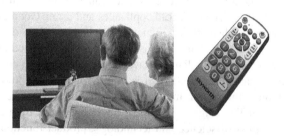

Fig. 3. Skyworth TV set and remote control (Source: Pacific Computer Network)

According to the current mainstream design directions of household appliances, the demographic structure of Chinese family was investigated which is shown in Fig. 4.

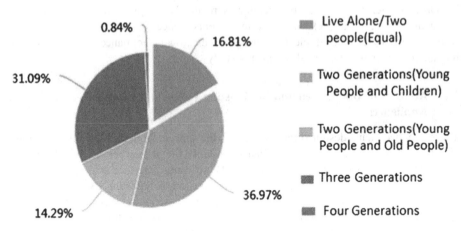

Fig. 4. Survey data of Chinese family demographic structure

According to the survey data of questionnaire, it can be seen that single age structure of the family accounts for only 16.81% of the total, which also includes the single age structure of young and middle-aged and the single age structure of the elderly. Nearly 100% of the market's products are designed for less than 20% of households and it almost can not find household appliances specifically designed to meet the needs of families with multiple age groups. Therefore, the design of household appliances to meet the needs of families with multiple age groups will have a huge market space.

3   Analysis of Existing Household Electrical Appliances Interface

Human-computer interface, also known as the user interface or user interface, refers to the surface of the interaction when users interact with the product and the medium of interaction between user and product. Users input instruction to the machine through the interface and the machine receives the information, gives user feedback, and then runs according to the instructions to achieve product functionality. Household appliance interface is the bridge between household appliances and users. Good product interface design will give users a pleasant experience while bad interface design is a barrier between users and products, isolating the user's product use demand and desires.

Early household electrical appliances have single function, the control interface is based on mechanical hard interface, which is usually buttons and knobs, and product feedback information is the sound, indicator, pressure and key stroke, etc. Household electrical appliances of this stage have simple operation and a high degree of availability. With the progress of science and technology, product function becomes more and more powerful and household appliances can achieve more subdivision function.

At the same time, information technology is also applied to the design of household appliances and display screen and touch screen as important soft interfaces have become an indispensable part of modern household appliances. At this point, the difficulty of operation of household electrical appliances increases and the degree of usability decreases. Young and middle-aged users who are skilled at operating computers and smart phones in work and life can quickly grasp the control of soft interface. However, it is very difficult for the elderly and children in the family to master the operation of soft interface.

The comparative analysis of the usability of household appliance interface is shown in the Table 2.

Table 2. The comparative analysis of the usability of household appliance interface

House-hold appli-ance interface classifi-cation	Application and devel-opment of interface in household appliances	Imple-mentation of house-hold ap-pliance function	Manipu-lation and feed-back	Manipulation difficulty & Usability evaluation	Examples of product images
Hard interface	Early household appliances	Simple function	Buttons, knobs, indica-tor, sound, etc.	Low difficulty, easy to operate, no need or only simple learning High availability, suita-ble for multiple age groups	
Soft interface	Modern household appliances	Rich function	Display screen, buttons, knobs, sound, etc.	Moderate difficulty, some complex opera-tion, through learning and repeated operations can be mastered Relatively high availa-bility, suitable for mul-tiple age groups with learning ability	
Soft interface as a focus, hard interface as a supple-ment	Intelligent household appliances	Powerful and re-fined function	Large display, touch screen, buttons, sensors, etc.	High difficulty, the high level of soft interface operation, operations need to learn High uncertainty, af-fected by the interface level, suitable for young and middle-aged with strong learning ability	

4 The Model of Multi Human-Computer Interface Household Appliances

It can be seen from Table 2 that when the function of household appliances becomes increasingly rich and powerful, the operation becomes more complex and adaptive user groups are getting less. In order to make household appliances better meet the needs of families with multiple age groups, solving the contradiction between high performance and complicated operation of household electrical appliance becomes a research topic urgently needed to solve the current design of household electrical appliances. In the premise of meeting the high performance, multi-interface design can be a good solution to this problem.

Processes of household appliance interface design and product design are similar and user-centric, relying on the needs of users to develop. Figure 5 is the household appliance interface design process.

Fig. 5. The household appliance interface design process

4.1 Classification of User Groups

Design psychology expert Norman divided users into four categories "novice user, average user, expert user and casual user" [4]. Novice users cannot complete the use process of product relying on past experience when facing products and need to learn to achieve the average user level to complete the smooth operation of the product. Expert users are more familiar with the product and can skillfully operate the product, or even develop new use functions. Casual users do not often use the product for a variety of reasons, are not familiar with the product and can not successfully operate the product.

The Fig. 6 are the results of investigation on the TV set, washer and cooker family operators. According to the survey, it can be seen that the main use of groups of household electrical appliances are the young and middle-aged crowd, followed by the elderly, and children use less household appliances. Among them, the use of children in TV sets is similar to that of the elderly.

According to the survey, home users can be classified into young people, some elderly people and children which together constitute the average user base, as shown in Fig. 7.

Each user group for the interface learning ability is shown in Fig. 8. Expert user who is the electric operation master in home users accepts the existing high-performance household appliance interface without any barrier. Average user can master the operation mode through learning and be skilled at operating usual electric appliances while novice user has difficulty in completely grasping the full operation of high-performance products even through learning, so novice user needs a more

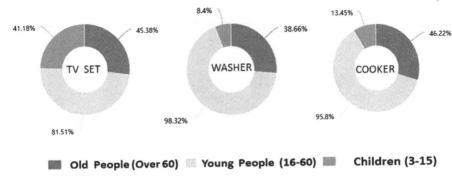

8.4%

41.18%   45.38%   38.66%   13.45%   46.22%

TV SET   WASHER   COOKER

98.32%   95.8%

81.51%

■ Old People (Over 60) ░ Young People (16-60) ▨ Children (3-15)

Fig. 6. The results of investigation on TV set, washer and cooker family operators

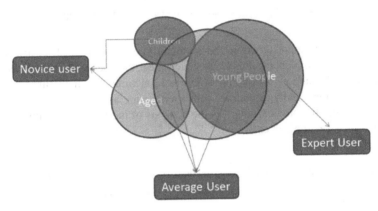

Fig. 7. The diagram of home user classification

intuitive and simple operation interface. Casual user with weak operation ability in home users may be home visitors or users with poor learning ability in the family needs the most intuitive and clear interface. When the product interface does not constitute an obstacle for casual user and novice user, average user and expert user can quickly grasp the operational flow.

4.2 Function Analysis of Household Appliance

Researchers also divide users into ordinary user and quality user according to the user's demand for product functionality. Ordinary users have no more requirements for the product, and as long as the product can reliably complete the basic use of functions and they can easily operate on it while quality users pursue more complete product experience and more abundant product functions [5]. Traditional household electrical appliances have no basic operational problems due to the single function and simple operation. Modern product interface problems result from function enhancements and performance improvements, and the analysis of functions can help us determine the selection of function interface.

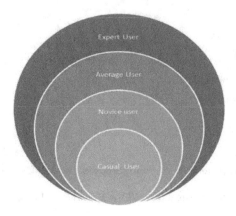

Fig. 8. The comparison diagram of home user operating capacities

Here, we call the main function and commonly used function of electrical appliances as basic functions, some functions which meet the user's individual needs and occasionally used functions as quality functions, functions which are integrated with intelligent technology and can interact with users or are achieved relying on the network as intelligent functions. Table 3 is the analysis of the functions of three types of household electrical appliances.

Table 3. Comparative analysis of functions of household electrical appliances

Product category	Basic function	Quality function	Intelligent function
TV set	On/off, program live, volume, etc.	Screen adjustment, program source, sound effects, etc.	On-demand, games, education, interaction, household appliances multimedia centers, etc.
Washer	Standard washing, single rinse, single dehydration, etc.	Disinfection, sterilization, self-cleaning, drying, etc.	Intelligent delivery of detergent, washing data identification, remote control of the washing progress, etc.
Cooker	Cooking, porridge, heating etc.	Clay pot, steamed fish, cake, appointment, timing, etc.	Intelligent APP, remote control operation, etc.

4.3 Multi-interface Design Solutions

Through the comparative analysis of existing products, it can be seen that the difficulty of the interface operation of high performance household appliances is mainly due to increased quality functions and intelligent operation, and complex hierarchical structure increases the difficulty of interface operation.

The soft interface of intelligent household appliances is difficult to operate and user experience is enhanced by hard interface design.

The intelligent degree of modern household appliances is getting higher and higher. According to the data from AVC, it can be seen that the penetration rate of smart TV, smart air-conditioning, refrigerator's intelligence and washer's intelligence has reached 79%, 21%, 10% and 16% respectively in the first half of 2016 [6]. Intelligence of household appliances becomes increasingly apparent and complex operating problems are also highlighted, in which the problem of TV control is particularly prominent.

With the development of intelligence, the traditional operation hard interface gradually disappears. The simple product design that enterprise pursues hides hard interface to the back of the product. Samsung TV set is shown in Fig. 9. Users do not know how to open the machine when facing such a high-tech product because no operation interface could be found in the front and side of the product. Casual user and novice user have to read a thick specification and learn to operate the product in order to know the location of hidden open key, which brings much discomfort to them. In view of this problem, setting up operation interface in the front of product should be taken into consideration, such as power key, volume adjustment keys, etc.

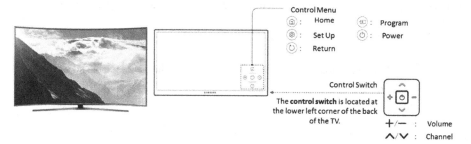

Fig. 9. The diagram of Samsung TV set and operation interface (Source: Samsung Electronics Official Website)

The increase of quality function leads to complex interface and the hidden quality function interface makes the product easy to operate.

From the multifunctional washer interface shown in Fig. 10, it can be seen that novice user does not know what to do and how to operate the product smoothly when confronted with such a complex interface, resulting in poor user experience. Functions can be classified for this problem. One is commonly used and basic functions which are intuitively arranged in the product surface through traditional hard interface and the other is less commonly used quality functions which are hidden through soft interface, so that the product interface not only is simple and clear, but also meets the demand of quality users for function.

Through the study, it can be found that the most commonly used functions are basic function which is suitable for hard interface to realize product operation. The application of quality function is less and the combination of soft and hard interface can be used to control the product. Intelligent function is mainly for average

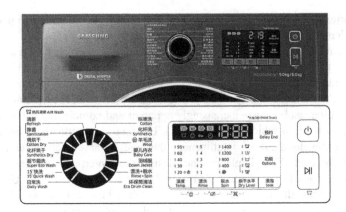

Fig. 10. Samsung washer and interface instruction (Source: Samsung Electronics Official Website)

user and expert user to choose the operation and there is no difficulty in the operation basically, so the design of soft interface as a focus and hard interface as a supplement can be adopted. Table 4 shows function and interface selection table for household appliances.

Table 4. Function and interface selection table for household appliances

Functional classification of household appliances	TV set	Washer	Cooker	Interface selection
Basic function	On/off, program selection, volume adjustment, etc.	Standard laundry procedures, single washing, single dehydration, etc.	Rice, porridge, heating, etc.	Hard interface
Quality function	Screen adjustment, program source, sound effect selection, etc.	Disinfection, sterilization, self cleaning, drying, etc.	Claypot, steamed fish, cake, appointment, timing, etc.	Hard interface and soft interface
Intelligent function	On-demand, games, education, interaction, household appliances multimedia centers, etc.	Intelligent delivery of detergent, washing data identification, remote control of the washing progress, etc.	Intelligent APP, remote control operation, etc.	Soft interface as a focus and hard interface as a supplement

Feedback effect of touch screen product operation is not clear, user experience is poor and the host operation to select the traditional hard interface can enhance user experience.

Japanese designer Abe Ase proposed tactile experience design [7] and emphasized that user experience can be enhanced through the design of touch. Figure 11 is the application of intelligent touch screen to cooker and the product looks simple and beautiful. However, the interactive experience of cold and hard touch screen is not ideal because the user cannot experience tactile press feedback when pressing the screen during operation, and no touch-screen button border makes user fear of misoperation, which leads to poor user experience. In the tactile experience, traditional button or knob interfaces allow users a more intuitive understanding of machine feedback to instructions through the key stroke and rotation, at the same time, the traditional hard interface with clear edge reduces the probability of misoperation, which results in good user experience.

Fig. 11. Intelligent cooker operation interface (Source: Taobao)

Construction of multi interface design process for household appliances.

Through the above analysis, in the household appliance interface design, the first step is to distinguish among home users, and then product functions are divided into basic functional demand, quality functional demand and intelligent functional demand according to the needs of users. Basic functional demand is suitable for design of intuitive hard interface, so that product meets the operational needs of all users, and quality function and intelligent function adopt a combination of hard and soft interface design according to the specific situation. Figure 12 shows the flow chart of multi interface design of household appliances constructed through the study.

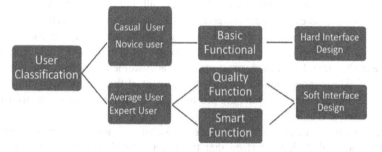

Fig. 12. The flow chart of multi interface design of household appliances

5 Design Principle of Hard Interface for Multi Interface Household Electrical Appliances

Multi interface design of household electrical appliances includes hard interface design and soft interface design. Soft interface design which is mainly aimed at average·user and expert user has been analyzed in more detail in a lot of research for quality users, and is not discussed here. In the construction of hard interface in multiple interfaces, casual user and novice user including the elderly and children need be taken into account. Therefore, the following principles should be paid attention to in the hard interface design.

5.1 Hard Interface Arranged in the Location that User Can Intuitively Perceive

We can simplify any product into a positive cube as shown in Fig. 13. The front of the product faces users and four sides around the front can also intuitively perceived by users, so master operation of hard interface should be arranged in the five side, allowing users perceiving operating position. The main control interface should be avoided arranging in the back of the product, which brings use disorder to novice user and casual user for the first time. Even average user and expert user may feel inconvenient in the operation because the manipulation position is not visible.

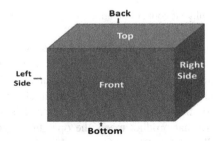

Fig. 13. Six surface chart of household appliances

The front, top, bottom, left and right sides are all intuitively perceived by the user, and the hard interfaces can be arranged in these areas. In the selection of interface arrangement area, considering that the top and bottom areas may be constrained by user, product, or spatial dimensions, sometimes it is not suitable for arranging the interface in this area. In addition, most users are accustomed to right-handed operation, so the right side is more suitable for the arrangement of the user interface than the left side. Based on the above analysis, the product hard interface arrangement priority area table is shown in Table 5.

Figure 14 is the main control interface of Samsung household TV and picture A shows the original design interface that the main control buttons are located in the

Table 5. The selection table of household appliance interface

Household appliance category	Priority of hard interface arrangement from good to bad
Smart TV set	Front > Right side > Left side > Top side > Bottom side > Back
Multifunctional washer Multifunctional cooker	Front/Top side > Left side/Right side > Bottom side/Back

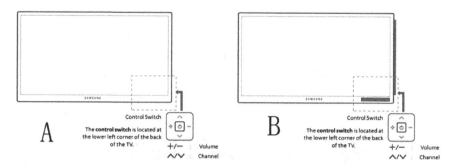

Fig. 14. The location of Samsung TV main control button and the proposed location map (Color figure online)

lower left corner of the TV. Users can not find the location of hard interface intuitively in the operation, which brings use of obstacles. In order to avoid operational obstacles, it is recommended that the main control interface is set on the front or right side of the TV set, such as the red area of picture B, so that the user interface is easy to find and convenient to operate.

5.2 Simplification Principle of Hard Interface Function

The function of modern household electrical appliances is becoming increasingly abundant, and there are a lot of subdivision quality functions. For example, laundry procedure of washer includes standard washing, quick washing, strong washing, wool washing and so on. If all of these functions are displayed on the operating panel, too many choices can interfere with the user, hence basic functions, quality functions and intelligent functions of electrical appliances should be distinguished in the design of product hard interface. The basic function is realized through the hard interface design. When choosing the hard interface to control the product, the basic function quantity must be strictly controlled in order to effectively achieve the interface simplification and enhance user experience. At the same time, quality function and intelligent function are hidden in the soft interface, and the segmentation function of product can be realized effectively through the reasonable design of soft interface. The basic functions of three research products which can complete the control of product through hard interface design are summarized in Table 6.

Table 6. The selection table of household appliance interface

Household appliance category	Basic function	Interface selection
Smart TV set	On/off, program switching, volume adjustment, etc.	Buttons, knobs, slide buttons, etc.
Multifunctional washer	Standard washing, single washing, single dehydration, etc.	
Multifunctional cooker	Rice, porridge, heating, starting, etc.	

Figure 15 is the comparison diagram of a simplified interface design and the original design. Figure A is the original design of Samsung washer interface and Figure B is the simplified hard interface of the washer operation panel.

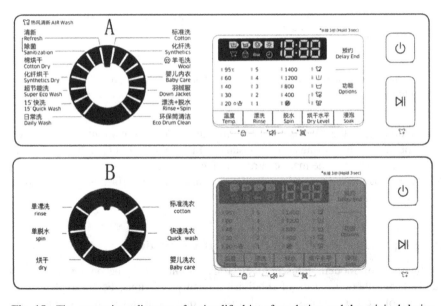

Fig. 15. The comparison diagram of a simplified interface design and the original design

5.3 Interface Feedback Principle of Human-Computer Interaction

After the user issues instructions to the product through interface, clear interactive feedback can allow users to determine that the machine has received instructions. The feedback of current household appliances on the market is good, but some household appliances use touch-screen or membrane keys to achieve human-computer interaction. Interfaces without pressure and stroke usually can not give a good tactile feedback to users, hence this feedback needs to be achieved and enhanced through design. Taking the physical and psychological characteristics of the elderly in the family into account, the feedback can be enhanced appropriately based on the original design, such as increasing the size of the screen and the key, adding the indicator light, expanding and extending the sound prompt and so on [8].

5.4   The Operating Instructions Can Be Added According to the Principle of Inclusive Design

The design goal of multi interface of household appliance products is aimed at meeting the needs of families with multiple age groups. Considering that novice user and casual user are not familiar with the operation process, increasing the operating instructions in the user interface can help users quickly grasp the operation process and thereby achieve convenient operation. The reference of product design method of Japanese household appliance manufacturers for the elderly, the operation process marked by number 1, 2, 3 allows users, even novice users or casual users, to see operating steps of the product at a glance, and complete the basic operation of the product quickly through instructions [9].

The diagram of washer interface marked by operating instruction numbers is shown in Fig. 16.

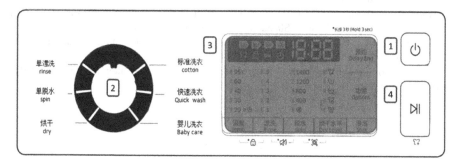

Fig. 16. The improvement plan of washer interface design

6   Conclusion

With the development of science and technology, the quality of household appliances has been greatly improved and a single product can meet different user's demand for personalized products. However, with the increase in segmentation function of electrical appliances, product operation becomes complicated. It is easy for average user and expert user in the family to grasp the complex operation through learning, while it is difficult for novice user and casual user in the family to grasp it through learning. In this case, designers should take full account of the differences in home users and give different interface solutions for different needs of users, so that the product can better meet the needs of families with multiple age groups.

Multi interface design not only improves the availability of products, but also can reduce user's feeling of inferiority caused by difficult operation, so that all family members feel the joy of science and technology. Multi interface design of household appliances will also become an important direction of the future development of household appliances.

Acknowledgment. This study is financially supported by Basic Study Funding of Central University (2013B34214).

References

1. He, C.Q.: Discussion on the theory and method of universal design. Hunan: Packag. Eng. **28** (2), 119–121 (2007)
2. Li, W.Z., Yin, X.C.: Research on human-machine interface of intelligent home appliances. China Appl. Technol. **1**, 52–54 (2016)
3. Yao, J., Feng, B.: Interface interactive design of information products for the elderly from the perspective of experience. Packag. Eng. 26(2), 67–71 (2015)
4. Donald, A.N.: The Design of Everyday Things. CITIC Publish House, Beijing (2010)
5. H, J.X.: Research on the Interface Design of Modern Home Appliance Products. Nanjing University of Aeronautics, Nanjing (2013)
6. Summary and Prospect of 2016 H1 color TV market (2016). http://www.199it.com
7. Kenya, H.: Dialogue in Design. Shandong People Press, Jinan (2010)
8. Dai, J.F., Lu, J.T.: Research of old-age product interface design based on product semantic. Dev. Innov. Mach. Electr. Prod. **21**(5), 71–78 (2008)
9. Jiao, J.: Vision Design Research of Smart Rice Cooker Operation Interface for the Elderly. Beijing Institute of Technology, Beijing (2015)

Research on Image Design of Historical and Cultural Blocks from the Perspective of User Experience

Rong Han[✉], Yang Hu[✉], and Rui Li[✉]

Jiangsu University, Zhenjiang, China
33315935@qq.com

Abstract. In this research, users' values of perception and experience of historical and cultural blocks are measured and evaluated; case study of Xijin Ferry in Zhenjiang is made, and general comments of various users on the image of the street are collected, which is developed into a part of block information visualization research mode by giving certain values. Meanwhile, through the research, the optimization ideas and innovation measures for new interactive form of image design of historical and cultural blocks are put forward, and it is proposed to accurately grasp the forward-looking appeal points of user experience, actively develop information channels and interactive content, and address users' needs of virtual experience and situational communication with the help of various information expression ways.

Keywords: User experience · Historical and cultural blocks · Image design

1 Research Background

1.1 The Necessity of Methodology and Demonstration

With the advent of the era of experience economy, people's voice and requirements in the tourism experience are more and more prominent, the previous scholars always began to study historical and cultural districts from the perspectives of geography, informatics, tourism and so on. In this paper, the image design of Xijin ferry, Zhenjiang City historical and cultural blocks was measured of bidirectional perception. At the same time, the interdisciplinary integration of design disciplines will also give the tourism discipline a unique experience. The most important feature of user experience is to highlight the needs of the user experience as the center, so this article measured the user perception of such image design by field survey, and then come up with optimization strategies, condensate out a suitable standards and programs for the image design. This requires to center on the audience, to create a specific environment and atmosphere, to create a series of personalized, participatory activities, so that the audience to get an unforgettable experience.

© Springer International Publishing AG 2017
V.G. Duffy (Ed.): DHM 2017, Part I, LNCS 10286, pp. 271–280, 2017.
DOI: 10.1007/978-3-319-58463-8_23

1.2   The Necessity of Warping and Improved Properties

As the regional context of the carrier, historical and cultural blocks emphasizes the user behavior in the street space and cognitive state. In order to achieve the cultural value of historical and cultural blocks, on of cultural tourism, and the optimization of the image design of the block is one of the recessive demand factors to stimulate the vitality of the historical and cultural blocks, the purpose is to carry out effective information transmission. From the consumer's point of view, the sense of experience, layered image design will play a driving role, but the lack of design may inspire the user's negative emotions; from the district managers point of view, scientific and effective image design can bring economic benefits and reduce operating costs.

2   The Core Structure of the System

2.1   Defining Analysis

The user experience is an individualized feeling of individual stimulation, which consists of five modules: sense, feel, think, act and relate (Fig. 1). Historical and cultural blocks is a city (town) area, which has a certain space limit, because of the social and cultural factors. It reflects the historical and cultural value of the whole environment, showing the typical features of the city in a historical period, reflecting the historical development of the city. The word "image" is defined as an abstract concept in the study of tourism in the West. It contains the impressions of the past, the reputation and the evaluation among colleagues. In the unabridged dictionary, the definition of "image" is defined as: literary art is a special means of reflecting reality, That is, according to real-life phenomenon to choose, Thus to create a synthesis of the ideological content and aesthetic significance of a specific vivid picture. People's perception of the image is a bottom-up information processing. The tourism image factor drives the user and will have a key incentive effect. The image design of the historical and cultural blocks around the block tour space and the inherent cultural information. It has many functions such as orientation, cultural communication, visual

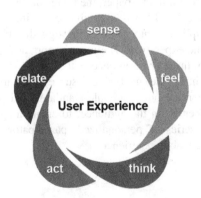

Fig. 1. Five modules of user experience

communication and so on, It is not only to meet the physiological needs of users and security needs exist, it is to achieve people's sense of belonging and identity and other emotional needs of the inevitable way.

2.2 System Processing

Contemporary cognitive psychology regards man as an information processor, it believed that the essence of human cognitive process is the process of information processing. Contemporary cognitive psychology as the information processor, that the human cognitive process is the nature of information processing. According to the information processing model of cognitive psychology, the image of historical and cultural blocks is a kind of mental model produced by the public through the process of receiving, selecting, sensing and memorizing the destination information. The occurrence of perception needs to rely on the user's own knowledge and experience and cognitive model, and subject to the constraints of individual characteristics. Therefore, the user's values, personality and motivation and other psychological factors and by age, gender, education, occupation, income and other demographic factors constitute the historical and cultural blocks of the image of the endogenous variables. Gunn (1972) describes the process of the formation of a tourist destination image in the human brain as Original Image and an Induced Image. Fakeye and Crompton (1991) further summarized the formation of tourists and potential tourists image as Original Image, Induced Image and Composite image (Fig. 2). The original image is the image formed before the potential tourist arrives at the destination, which is obtained through television, network, newspapers and magazines, radio, books and word of mouth. The induced image is that the potential tourists have a certain motive of travel, and the subject spontaneously search for information to process, compare and select the acquired knowledge. Potential tourists, through the cognition of native image and image, produce tourism desire and transform into tourists. After arriving at destination, potential tourists can make a composite image through personal experience and past cognition. The original image of historical and cultural blocks and the promotion of the image has a certain foundation, but the composite image feedback and re-design of the interaction is slightly scarce.

3 Sample and Data

3.1 Model Building

This paper selects Xijin ferry historical and cultural blocks (Figs. 3, 4, 5, 6, 7 and 8) in Zhenjiang as the sample, which is located in the west of Zhenjiang City Pan foothills, in the history of the long-term as the only ferry to the north of the Yangtze river, bear the naval port, passenger ferry, ferry wharf righteousness and other functions, has an important strategic position. Since the Six Dynasties, the Yangtze River shipping owners and merchants in to this, gradually formed xijindu ancient title area. The internal block shops, economic prosperity, has important historical value and the value of tourism, Xijin ferry image elements are divided into tourism resources, tourism facilities, tourism services, industry management, community participation, tourism

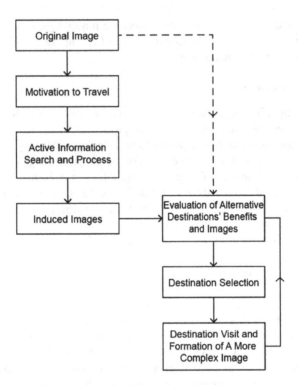

Fig. 2. A model of a tourist's image formation process

Fig. 3. The zhaoguan stone tower

environment, tourism and culture etc. The design scale of this paper will consider the above factors into consideration, referring of the whole image and the uniqueness of the purpose of image in Echtner and Ritchie (1993), in Xijin ferry within a specific marker location and specific factors, according to the different attributes of the object to be designed.

Fig. 4. The ancient street

Fig. 5. A millennium at a glance

Fig. 6. The daidu pavilion

Fig. 7. The guanyin cave

Fig. 8. The general map of xijin ferry historical and cultural blocks

Firstly, the author has conducted several research to provide a guide for the following design of volume survey. In order to ensure the information source of comprehensive and objective, investigation object selection using multi azimuth sampling method, the object will be divided by age into 18–30, 31–50, 51–70 three age groups, then they will confirm his category and according to the situation by the investigators and respondents on issues related to the answer to fill in the questionnaire. Through the reliability test data of the questionnaire, the Cronbach coefficient is 0.76, which show that the reliability of it is good, and the further statistical analysis will be conduct. The questionnaire includes 4 parts: the first part is about the sociology characteristics; the second part and the third part adopts 5 point scale method of Likert, respectively evaluate the user oriented information system for visual image perception and image perception degree of the historic district consists of parts. 1–5 point value assessment indicates the perception of the user from negative to positive; the forth part assessment the user access to the information. In this investigation, 100 questionnaires were issued for each age group, with a total of 300 copies. The effective recovery 298 and the recovery rate was 96%. After the screening of the original questionnaire, we have got 271 effective questionnaires, the effective rate was 94%.

3.2   Statistical Verification and Results Discussion

Sociological Structure of Sample. Form the point of view of the effective sample composition, overall sex ratio female (Table 1); the overall structure in high educational background, college degree or above accounted for 51.3% (Table 2), from the tourist market or potential market point of view, relatively reasonable structure. Among them, 49.4% of users said they had a tour of other historical and cultural blocks.

Table 1. Gender structure of respondents

	Frequency	Percent	Valid percent	Cumulative percent
Valid female	160	55.36	55.72	55.72
Male	129	44.65	44.28	100
Total	289	100	100	

Table 2. Education structure of respondents

	Frequency	Percent	Valid percent	Cumulative percent
Valid primary school and below	29	10.03	7.75	7.75
Junior middle school to senior high school	117	40.48	40.96	40.96
University or above	143	49.48	51.29	100
Total	289	100	100	

The Analysis and Discussion of the User Oriented System Identification. This part from the logo design, system facilities planning in two aspects, after the investigation of the age of the user to do the research found that the data presented with a certain difference (Table 3), indicating that the different ages of the user oriented system multiple demands.

Statistics show that the three age of the user perception of the design of the guidance system overall positive bias, but from the individual influence factors show the numerical point of view, there are still some differences. The standard deviation among 3-a-M, 3-b-M, 3-g-M, 3-f-M is bigger, it can to a certain extent on the label carrier design and system planning guidance are to be improved. According to the general survey, about 33.5% of users said they are "looking for a position" through "access to information according to the sign guidelines"; more than 54.8% of users said that they visit by map and casual way, "according to the sign one by one to watch" users only 12.1%; about "do you think Xijin ferry is oriented system to guide the of your help?", the mean in statistics was 1.959, the SD value is smaller, which show that the user has a lag of Xijin ferry oriented system design of perception and attitude. For the above problems, when use the information as the first dressing to adjust the layout, we should ensure that users in the space "at the brand orientation, distribution of all clues can be effective to play the expected role". First of all, to ensure clear system design, namely the dominant indicators to create a clear composite image, the participants have system the perception of the specific cultural transition of the specific cultural transition zone, consciously grasp the whole scenic tourist information context, will guide the information context according to the level classification, corresponding to different nodes arrangement of different types of indicators, it is visual information channel between the blocks, the culture landscape connecting channel. Secondly, pay attention to the course of system design the length of time when "from feel to reaction and then to memory", to ensure that all elements are found in time, the user can understand immediately take cation. Context is a comprehensive, nature geographical basis of regional history and culture. The three-dimensional combination of tradition and social psychology, from the design of layout should be refined to the image information, available elements selected and cultural block space-time resonance, which is the Xijin ferry Cultural District architectural style, cultural history, culture connotation and culture combined with the strategy of mining, combined with the culture of the street signs image elements phase beauty to create to achieve as ideographic, or give the subtraction of image design is figurative, high values of common elements in assisted extraction optimization design.

Table 3. The perception of audience's influence on the composition of historical and cultural blocks

Influence factor		Design of guiding sign				Guidance system facility planning				Experience factors				Scenic factors						
		a. Size	b. Graphs	c. color	d. Style	e. Continuity	f. Richness	g. Accuracy of location targeting	h. The amount of information	i. Catering	j. Entertainment	k. Shopping	l. Accommodation	m. Ancient Street	n. Zhao guan Stone Tower	o. Dai du Pavilion	p. Guanyin Cave	q. A millennium at a glance	r. Fifty-three slope	s. Life Club
The First age level	M	3.63	3.61	2.81	2.85	3.05	2.55	3.21	2.58	3.82	3.64	3.53	3.31	4.25	4.11	3.25	3.03	4.04	2.32	2.02
	SD	0.80	0.65	1.17	0.61	1.14	0.82	1.08	0.88	0.83	0.94	0.69	0.83	0.74	0.66	0.91	0.73	0.74	1.15	0.94
The Second age level	M	3.83	2.97	3.08	3.42	2.75	2.97	3.87	3.02	4.01	3.22	3.67	2.71	3.96	4.08	3.61	3.18	3.82	2.71	2.02
	SD	0.71	1.04	1.37	0.68	1.09	1.02	1.22	0.94	0.53	0.64	0.95	0.85	0.68	0.45	1.21	0.94	0.65	0.91	1.46
The third age level	M	3.66	3.11	2.54	3.56	2.89	3.54	3.02	2.44	4.13	3.68	4.09	2.38	4.07	4.15	3.45	3.52	3.49	2.02	2.74
	SD	0.70	1.43	1.27	0.94	1.26	0.63	1.37	0.60	0.78	0.95	0.52	1.26	0.62	1.02	0.88	1.65	0.82	0.67	0.96

Statistics shows that three ages of user oriented system design the overall perception of positive bias, but from the individual factors influence the numerical point of view, there are still some differences. The difference of 3-a-m, 3-b-m, 3-g-m, 3-f-m numerical is large, This can be explained to a certain extent, the design of the identification system and the system planning of the guidance system need to be improved.

Analysis and Discussion on the Way of User's Perception of Historical and Cultural Blocks Image. For the consideration of user's information pathways, with "impressive degree" and "degree of representativeness of tourist attractions" for the measurement basis (Table 3), relatively high degree of recognition of the block spots visible to users, with the overall style attractions coordination. According to the value in 3-f-M and interpretation system on users, access information blocks way of research results, the three age layers of the user demand for information media are significantly different. The young users said that access to information blocks in the way is limited, design and configuration of modern interactive equipment urgently overall planning. The first age users use the network and media advertising to obtain image caused by the proportion of 67%. Compared with ages of third about 47% users said to Xijin ferry information about channel mouth, then through travel agencies and other professional bodies to tour blocks. Composite technology allows the transfer of information. Type of historical and cultural landscape changing, information technique increasing emphasized beyond time and space. To ensure the information conveyed clearly, with the development of new media when the trend of application. The Ministry of industry and information technology data show that the number of 2015–2016, 3G/4G network users is growing rapidly, as of September 2016, mobile phone penetration rate has reached 95.8/100; 3G/4G network users increased to 885 million, accounting for the proportion of mobile phone users reached 67.3%. The popularity of smart mobile phone and based on network technology, nowadays people have been used to obtain information on the APP in the phone platform. Based on this, the message may not be materialized form of restrictions. The users can be realized when the Ferries not block caused by image through the implantation of mobile phone APP, the elements will represent a higher degree of the virtual exhibition the development and change of historical and cultural blocks. APP provides real-time downloadable short video, the participants practice lead to self display and slow the internal driving force, users can access their own location and orientation information, the use of mobile terminal blocks overview in a more complex environment in the district.

4   Conclusion

To sum up, this study is based on interdisciplinary research and collaborative innovation, Based on the historical and cultural blocks of Xijin ferry, Zhenjiang City, this paper measures the perceived value of the three types of users from the quantitative and qualitative aspects, and concretely ranks the merits and demerits of the cultural elements, It makes the later maintenance and improvement, the development of the design through the statistical analysis of the atlas for academic support, to achieve a more complete, systematic, scientific image design. First of all, to establish information display mode by user categories. There are differences in the demand of different age groups, Young users are the main users of information technology equipment, whose needs of the block information are stronger than the older users, relatively speaking, older users need to be more intuitive visual display of information; secondly, a sound guide system should be planed. The improvement of the design of the guidance system, in the neighborhoods, from the information cue points to the contents of the hierarchical classification and block-oriented design style improvement, is urgent. The integrated design of the system can not be ensured at present, but the sites with high perceived value in this survey can be set as the key node of the image sensing system, which can be highlighted in the system. It is suggested that the hierarchical relationship of the guidance system should be fully considered to ensure the continuity and perfection of user-oriented process. Finally, a human-computer interaction system should be established. Designers should accurately grasp the forward-looking demands of user, and actively carry out the development of information channels and content, to meet with the needs of the users' virtual experience, communication and other needs with a variety of information presentation, enhance the interactive experience from the physical space to virtual space of users, to ensure Users to get more experience and satisfaction the process of viewing.

Acknowledgments. Jiangsu Province ordinary university graduate student training innovation project (Grant No. SJZZ15-0135).

References

Xie, Y.: Research on Tourism Experience: for Positivist Science, China Tourism Press, Beijing (2010). (in Chinese)

Song, Y.: The characteristics and designing principles of experience tourism, Special Zone Economy, Shumchun (2007). (in Chinese)

Schmitt, B.H.: Experiential Marketing: How to Get Customers to Sense, Feel, Think, Act, and Relate to Your Company and Brands, The Free Press, New York (1999)

The concept of historical and cultural blocks which is a legal term since July 1, 2008, to which the implementation of "historical and cultural city towns and villages Protection Ordinance (Decree No. twenty-fourth of the State Council) has a clear definition

Huang, Z., Li, X.: On the Image Perception and Promotion Pattern of Tourist Destination, Tourism Tribune, Beijing (2002). (in Chinese)

Gitelson, R.J., Crompton, J.L.: The planning horizons and sources of information used by pleasure vacationers. J. Travel Res., Denver (1983)

Fakeye, P.C., Crompton, J.L.: Image differences between prospective, first-time, and repeat visitors to the lower Rio Grande Valley. J. Travel Res., Denver (1991)

Xie, C., Huang, Y.: A Research on the Organizational Model of Planning Destination Image Based on Social Participation, Tourism Tribune, Beijing (2002). (in Chinese)

Gao, L.: Discussion and Practice of the Navigation Design for Tourist Area, Zhuang shi, Beijing (2009). (in Chinese)

Li, L.: Discussion on the design of urban tourism image, Tourism Tribune, Beijing (1998). (in Chinese)

Qiu, Q.: 2016 China Mobile consumer analysis, China Business and Market, Beijing (2017). (in Chinese)

Comparative Analysis of Wheelchair Transfer Movements Between Nurse and Care Worker

Yasuko Kitajima[1]([⊠]), Yuka Takai[2], Kazuaki Yamashiro[3],
Yoichiro Ogura[3], and Akihiko Goto[2]

[1] Faculty of Nursing, Tokyo Ariake University of Medical and Health Sciences,
2-9-1 Ariake, Koto-ku, Tokyo 135-0063, Japan
kitajima@tau.ac.jp
[2] Faculty of Design Technology, Osaka Sangyo University, 3-1-1 Nakagaito,
Daito, Osaka 574-8530, Japan
{Takai,gotoh}@ise.osaka-sandai.ac.jp
[3] Department of Advanced Fibro-Science, Kyoto Institute of Technology,
Matsugasaki, Sakyo-Ku, Kyoto 606-8585, Japan
{k.yamashiro546,ujikintoki7}@gmail.com

Abstract. It is considered that, even though it is for the same purpose, there is a difference in the methods of body position changing or wheelchair transfer between nurses and care workers. The authors had attempted in the previous study to develop a self-learning support tool for nursing students. As a part of the previous experiment, wheelchair transfer method discussed in the nursing technique textbook commonly used among nursing students was extracted. Then, this movement was filmed in order to produce an "example video". We showed this "example video" to our test subjects consisting of care workers, and asked them to imitate the wheelchair transfer movement shown in the video. During this experiment, we received feedbacks from the test subjects that claimed; "We do not take this approach when transferring an elderly to and from a wheelchair in care work". Even though care worker are all categorized as "care profession", there are positions, such as Certified Care Worker and Certified Social Worker, that require national qualifications. There are also positions, commonly referred to care worker, that does not require any qualification. An unqualified care worker is required to receive the initial training seminar, and one of the professions that are qualified to become the instructor of this seminar is nurse. If there is a difference in the methodology between nurses and care workers, it means that the techniques taught by nurses were transformed through time in order to adapt to the environment of frontline care work. As movements involved in body position changing or wheelchair transfer are type of technique that is physically demanding and could potentially cause backache for both nurses and care workers, it is highly significant that the current technique is improved and becomes an easier technique for the practitioners. Therefore, in this study, we engaged veterans of both nursing and care work, measured their movement during body position changing and wheelchair transfer, and examined the characteristics of movements of each subject. In general, the location where a nurse conducts the movement in discussion is a hospital ward. On the other hand, it would normally be a facility such as a nursing home for a care

© Springer International Publishing AG 2017
V.G. Duffy (Ed.): DHM 2017, Part I, LNCS 10286, pp. 281–294, 2017.
DOI: 10.1007/978-3-319-58463-8_24

worker. Between a hospital ward and a care facility, there are many differences such as the legally required size of a room or the fact that one place is for medical treatment and the other is for living, resulting in dissimilarities such as the positioning of beds. By exploring the difference in the movement of nurses and care workers, while taking these factors into consideration, it is possible that improved methods for body position changing and wheelchair transfer that are better adapted to the environment could be devised.

Keywords: Wheelchair transfer · Nurse · Care worker · Nursing and nursing care

1   Introduction

In Japan, the population aged 65 or older reached a record high with 33.9 million as of October 1, 2015. The population aging rate—a rate of population aged 65 or older out of the entire population—reached 26.7% and this also set a record high [1]. Everyone hopes that elderly people live a long, healthy and autonomous life. However, it is not rare to find people who unfortunately cannot live life on their own terms due to illness or injury. World Health Organization (WHO) developed the concept of "healthy life expectancy" in 2000. The healthy life expectancy denotes a period in which a person can live a healthy, everyday life without receiving care or becoming bedridden, and the Ministry of Health, Labour and Welfare estimated it for the first time in 2010. In 2010 in Japan, the average life expectancy was 79.55 for men and 86.30 for women, and the average healthy life expectancy was 70.42 for men and 73.62 for women [2]. This means that males continue to live approximately 9 years and women approximately 12 years after they come to require care or become bedridden. Given the present circumstance in which the population that requires care increases while the population that provides care declines, nursing care issues for elderly people have gone well beyond individual or household problems; they have become social problems.

It is misleading to simply call elderly people who need care as such, since the degree of necessity differs from one individual to another; some people require simple assistance for their everyday lives while others require aid that falls under the category of medical treatment in addition to assistance for everyday lives. We may call the former as someone who requires simple nursing care and the latter as someone who requires both nursing and nursing care. Is it the nursing specialist or nursing care specialist who takes care of everyday lives of elderly people? The reason why this kind of question emerges is because difference in specialty between nursing and nursing care has not become clear, and their specialties are confused or are not properly understood in our society. If you are able to do nursing, you would be expected to be able to do nursing care, and you may say that it is hard to draw a clear boundary between their duties at a nursing home. What then is the difference between the nursing and nursing care?

Both roles have been carried out by specialists referred to by the name of the certified care worker (kaigo fukushishi) and the nurse (kangoshi) respectively. According to Ministry of Health, Labour and Welfare, the certified care worker is a nationally licensed practitioner who uses the appellation "certified care worker" to engage in the business of providing care for a person with physical disabilities or mental disorder and intellectual disabilities that make it difficult to lead a normal life, and to provide instructions on caregiving to the person and the person's caregiver based on Certified Social Worker and Certified Care Worker Act (Act No. 30 of 1987) [3]. On the other hand, the nurse refers to a person under licensure from the Minister of Health, Labour and Welfare to provide medical treatment or assist in medical care for injured and ill persons or puerperal women, as a profession, according to the Article 5 of Act on Public Health Nurses, Midwives, and Nurses (Act No. 203 on July 30, 1948) [4]. Thus the difference is clearly stated in the legal language. Furthermore, their difference can also be understood from the perspective of criteria for building training facilities. According to "Items concerning Campus and School Facilities and Facility Equipment"—which is building criteria for training facilities of certified care workers, "regarding educationally necessary equipment and instruments or models, prepare the following items and seek to enrich mechanical instruments for education according to new nursing care needs" [5]. To be more specific, items that must be prepared for education are: model dolls for practice, human skeletons, adult beds, transfer lifts, sliding boards or sliding mats, wheelchairs, simple bathtubs, stretchers, excretion tools, walking aid sticks, safety sticks for the blind, audiovisual equipment, cooking utensils for people with disabilities, dishes for people with disabilities, a set of Japanese futons, suction kits, feeding tube kits, medical tables or medical wagons, suction training model, tube feeding training model, cardiopulmonary resuscitation kits for practice, manikins. Compared with the criteria for building nurse training facilities [6], what certified care worker training facilities are obliged to be furnished with that nurse training facilities are not are: transfer lifts, sliding boards or sliding mats, simple bathtubs, walking aid sticks, safety stick for the blind, cooking utensils for people with disabilities, dishes for people with disabilities. It was found that the characteristic of those that are required for certified care worker training facilities and are not required for nurse training facilities is that they are mechanical instruments necessary for assisting a target subject for everyday move, everyday lives of having a meal or taking a bath. They are considered necessary tools for practicing skills that must be acquired in order "to perform nursing care for a person with disabilities according to his or her mental and physical conditions", which gives a general idea about certified care workers as prescribed by the Certified Social Worker and Certified Care Worker Act. Basic education for nurses does not require learning how to use tilted equipment for nursing care. We can say that differing criteria for building training facilities also reveals difference in content of education between the nursing and nursing care. If you take a close look at the specific educational contents, you will find that there too is a clear difference. To take education of wheelchair transfer movement, which is mandatory as technical education for both nursing and nursing care trainees as an example, there is no section for a technique of transferring a patient using nursing equipment in 4 textbooks for basic nursing care techniques published by 4 major publishing companies and used generally by nursing training schools. It is sometimes included in a reference used as a supplementary reader, but the so-called "textbooks" generally include only the method of transferring a patient to a wheelchair using body mechanics. On the other hand, the transfer method taught to certified care workers differ from the method taught to nurses. Although this depends on the textbook, one example is a certified care worker transferring a person in need of care to the wheelchair by kneeling down on the floor. Nurses have never been taught such a method.

Secondly, if you look at the criteria for allocating personnel for building nursing-care insurance facilities, the number ascends in the order of doctors, nurses, and certified care worker. To put it in an extreme way, even if there were 40 doctors, they would not be able to take care of everyday lives of persons in need of care due to an increase in labor costs. Although nurses can take care of everyday lives of them just as do certified care workers, this too is not a realistic option seen from the perspective of labor costs. According to the 2015 Basic Survey on Wage Structure released by Ministry of Health, Labour and Welfare, the average age of nurses is 38.2 years old and their average salary is 329,200 yen, while the average age of certified care workers is 39.7 years old and their average salary is 223,500 yen [7].

There is a preceding study that attempted to reveal through an interview how nurses and certified care workers who were working in the same facility perceived specialty of each other, in order to delineate confusions of specialty for nursing and nursing care. There, it was found that they raised as specialty for nursing "health management", "health assessment", "medical care", and as the specialty for nursing care. "accepting resident's life at home as such regardless of clinical condition", "appreciating what the resident believes", etc., and it centered on helping a resident to live a well-organized everyday life in line with resident's thoughts and feelings [8]. This study was an attempt to mutually understand their professions and clarify their roles within a facility to provide better living to people in need of care. This study is considered to involve an objective to positively clarify specialty of the nursing care and the nursing.

As seen above, the difference in specialty between nursing and nursing care has been revealed from the difference in educational curriculum, criteria for building facilities, etc. Nevertheless, similarity in skills demonstrated by them leads to confusion of their specialties. However, few studies have mentioned detailed difference in skills between them as a matter of fact. Therefore, this study takes "wheelchair transfer"—which is an univocal expression expressed by both nursing and nursing care—as an example, in the aim of revealing whether true difference is manifested in behavior between them. Study participants in this experiment are a skilled nurse who had experience of using sliding boards at hospitals, but never had hands-on experience at nursing homes, and a skilled certified care worker who was working at a nursing home as a care worker. They were asked to transfer a participant from a wheelchair to a bed using a slide board, which was typically developed to help a single caregiver with transferring a subject. Their movements were recorded using motion capture, and their difference was examined using three dimensional data. Furthermore, a series of movements was filmed using a video camera, and the difference in movements and duration of transferring was visually checked. Movements were classified into movements common to them, movements differing between them, and characteristic movements for discussion to reveal the difference between the nursing and nursing care.

2   Methods

2.1   Participants

The skilled certified care worker had 8.5 years of experience, was 165 cm tall, weighed 68 kg, was aged 35, with 8.5 years of experience of using the slide board. The skilled nurse had more than 20 years of experience (never had experience of working at a nursing home), was 164 cm tall, weighed 52.5 kg, was aged 48, with several times of using the slide board.

2.2   Procedures

The study certified care worker was asked to transfer a model that mimicked a person in need of care, and the study nurse was asked to transfer a model that mimicked a patient, from a wheelchair to a bed. The person in need of care and the patient were asked to sit in a wheelchair, and the certified care worker and the nurse were asked to transfer respectively the person in need of care and the patient who were both seated in a wheelchair to a bed using a sliding board.

A sliding board is a welfare device used to transfer a person in need of care or a patient from their wheelchair to a bed, car, portable toilet, etc. Sliding boards are either made of woods or plastic, and they are generally slippery on the top side and non-slip treatment is done on the back side. A sliding board can be used for transfer assistance for even those who have difficulty standing up, maintaining a standing position, or changing the direction, as long as they can adopt a sitting posture. Because it is a welfare device that allows a caregiver to achieve the purpose by shifting the subject's center of gravity without the caregiver lifting a person in need of care or a patient who cannot stand up, it is said to reduce strain put on the caregiver [9]. Both caregivers were asked to repeat the above movement several times.

2.3   Recording Procedures

The assisting movement was filmed using a digital video camera. Simultaneously, an optical motion capture system—MAC3D SYSTEM (a Motion Analysis product) was used to measure coordinates of each marker. Sampling frequency was set to 120 Hz. Infrared reflective markers were attached in 25 sites of the entire body of the certified care worker, 26 sites of the entire body of the nurse, 7 sites on head and shoulders of the person in need of care who was assisted by the certified care worker, 21 sites on the entire body of the patient who were assisted by the nurse, 8 locations of the wheelchair. As for the coordinate system, the horizontal direction from the study participant was plotted on x-axis, the front-back direction was plotted on y-axis, and the vertical direction was plotted on z-axis.

3 Results

3.1 Movements of Certified Care Worker

The standing position at the beginning of the movements was in front of the wheelchair in which the person in need of care is seated (Fig. 1). The certified care worker removed armrests on both sides of the wheelchair before he started transferring the person in need of care (Fig. 2).

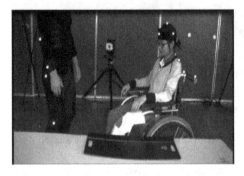

Fig. 1. Standing position of the certified certified care worker before beginning the movement.

Fig. 2. The position of armrests.

The certified care worker had the person in need of care shift to the front half of the seat by having him vertically shift his weight on the wheelchair seat. On this occasion, the certified care worker adopted a posture as if he placed himself over the top of the person in need of care, first supporting the buttocks of the person in need of care, and having him transfer to the front half of the seat while vertically shifting the weight of the person in need of care (Fig. 3).

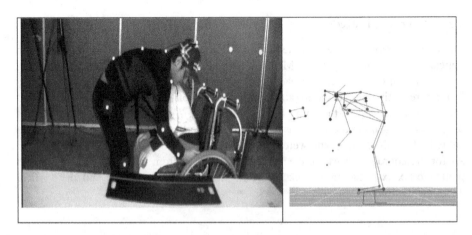

Fig. 3. The certified care worker transferring the person in need of care to the whole area of the seat-1.

Afterwards, the certified care worker located his finger tip in the direction of the floor side, inserting the arms to the direction of armpit from the backside of the person in need of care, and moving the person in need of care to the assumed position (Fig. 4).

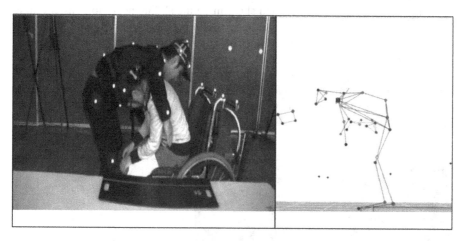

Fig. 4. The certified care worker transferring the person in need of care to the whole area of the seat-2.

The certified care worker kneeled down on side of the knee opposite to the side of the transferring bed, stretched arms from the chest side to the side of the armpit to which the person in need of care would be tilted, supported and tilted the person in need of care, and inserted the sliding board underneath the lifted buttock on the side opposite to the tilted side (Fig. 5). The tilted angle of the person in need of care was X-Z plane 45.2° X-Y plane 40.5°. On this occasion, the brake lever of the wheelchair which would get in the way was removed.

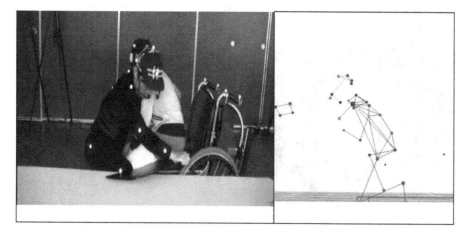

Fig. 5. The certified care worker insert the sliding board.

The certified care worker released the arm inserted in the tilted-side of the armpit of the person in need of care, and inserted the other arm in the opposite side of the armpit —which is a moving direction of the person in need of care—in the similar manner, and placed the released arm on the iliac region of the person in need of care, pushed him using the arm, tilted his body, and slid him on the sliding board to transfer him to the bed. (Fig. 6) On this occasion, the body of the person in need of care was rolled largely toward the moving direction. Furthermore, the face of the person in need of care was positioned in the moving direction, and the face of the certified care worker was positioned in the opposite direction from the forward direction. The certified care worker slid the person in need of care on the sliding board as if rotating him around an axis. After having finished sliding, the sliding board was pulled off in a series of movements (Fig. 7).

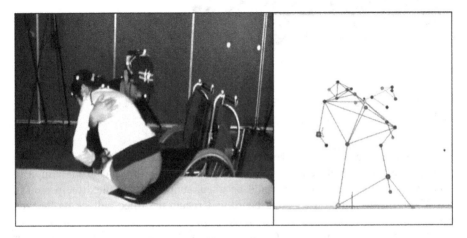

Fig. 6. The certified care worker sliding the person in need of care on a sliding board.

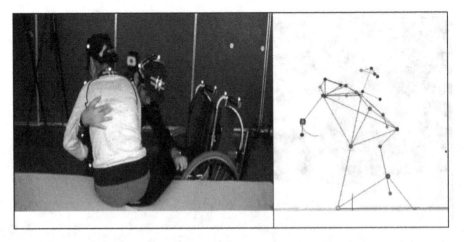

Fig. 7. The certified care worker pulling off the sliding board.

3.2   Movement of the Nurse

The standing position before beginning the movement was in front of the wheelchair in which the patient sat. Before beginning the transfer of the patient, only the armrest on the moving side of the patient was removed (Figs. 8 and 9).

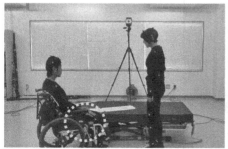

Fig. 8. Standing position of the nurse and the position of armrests 1.

Fig. 9. Standing position of the nurse and the position of armrests 2.

The nurse had the buttocks of the patient keep in the same position as when he sat on the wheelchair for the first time, rolled the patient on the seat while the nurse himself remained standing, slid a sliding board underneath the lifted buttock (Fig. 10). The nurse rolled the patient by pushing up the side of the buttock he wanted to lift. The patient tilted 19.2° to the X-Z plane and 37.1° to the X-Y plane. The brake lever of the wheelchair remained attached.

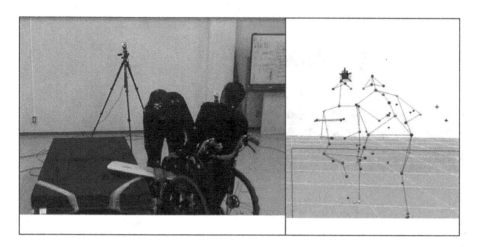

Fig. 10. The nurse insert the sliding board.

The patient put his arms around the neck of the nurse, and the nurse supported the back of the patient and moved his body upward to let his body stand up once, and then slid him on the sliding board. The upper body of the patient was hardly leant. At this time, the face of the nurse was oriented toward the moving direction of the patient (Fig. 11). After having finished sliding, the sliding board was pulled off in a series of movements (Fig. 12).

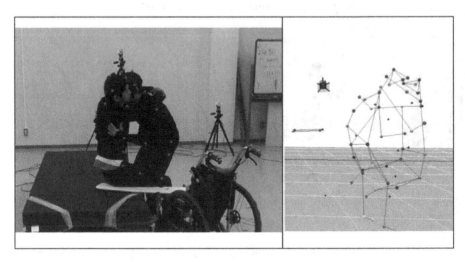

Fig. 11. The nurse sliding the patient on a sliding board.

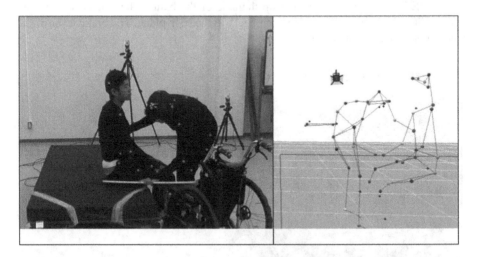

Fig. 12. The nurse pulling off the sliding board.

4 Discussion

Both certified care worker and the nurse have tried to begin movement by standing in front of the subject seated in a wheelchair. As a preparation before beginning transfer assisting movement, the certified care worker removed armrests on both sides of the wheelchair, while the nurse removed only the armrest in the moving direction of the patient. This seems to be because the certified care worker thought armrests would get in the way as he moved the person in need of care to the front half of the seat in the subsequent movement. This can also be explained by the fact that basic nursing education teaches students not to remove safety devices to secure the maximum patients' safety, so he might thought that if, unlike the certified care worker, it is not necessary to change the sitting position of the patient on the wheelchair seat, it is not necessary to remove armrests—safety devices. Furthermore, because basic nursing education teaches students to maximally use remaining functions of patients to prevent disuse syndrome, if the upper limb movements can be performed well, the transfer method of the patient herself holding armrests to support her own body while transferring from the wheelchair will be selected in line with, even if the lower limbs are weakened to the point of requiring a wheelchair. Thus, we can conclude that the nurse did not have to remove the armrest because he thought not doing it would not interrupt the assisting movement.

Secondly, the certified care worker moved the sitting position of the person in need of care in order to make it easy to insert the sliding board below the buttocks of the person in need of care. This is a transfer method in which the caregiver rolls the person in need of care to the left and to the right several times to reduce the area on which the buttocks of the person in need of care rest and to transfer her while minimizing friction. This method is considered reasonable and has also been incorporated for nursing care as it makes it easy to transfer a heavy subject. However, if you look at Figs. 3 and 4, the certified care worker bent his back considerably to adopt a forward head posture, and inserted arms from the back of the person in need of care to perform the movement. Thus, from the principles of body mechanics, this movement can be said to strain the body of the caregiver. The principles of the body mechanics require that they apply mechanics to human beings to perform safe, efficient or effective tasks. They involve techniques of human motions, movements with regard to postures and its sustenance, by applying mechanical principles to physical sites such as arms and legs, elbows and knees, backbone, etc. In the nursing or nursing care field, they involve a technique of reducing strain of the caregiver, and of preventing back pain, etc. [10]. One of the important elements of body mechanics is to allow wider room for the base of support and to lower the center of mass in such a way that the center of mass is positioned within the base of support in order to stabilize the body of the caregiver. Moreover, it is important to efficiently use force. The posture and movements of the caregiver when transferring a subject require lumbar discs to have greater load bearing capability. If, however, force is used efficiently, the object of the same weight can be moved and carried with lesser effort, and the strains on the body will be reduced [11]. The certified care worker adopted a forward head posture by bending his spine at the lower back. This is a posture that increases load on the spine in the musculoskeletal system. The erector spinae that surrounds the vertebral column cannot bear bigger load imposed when transferring the body of a person, and adoption of an inappropriate working posture to lift a weighty object tends to lead to unequal distribution of mechanical loads to the intervertebral disc, which increases the risk of back problems. No such posture was observed in the movements of the nurse. It is often said that care workers are suffering low back pain, and it is necessary to review the posture they adopt when providing care.

Before performing the movement of inserting a slide board beneath the buttocks of the person in need of care, the certified care worker kneeled on the floor (Fig. 5). To explain this from the principles of body mechanics, kneeling on the floor broadens the area of the base of support and stabilizes the center of mass of the certified care worker. This enables both the certified care worker and the person in need of care to perform safer and easier transfer movement. Transferring a person in need of care by kneeling on the floor is mentioned in a textbook of nursing care techniques [12]. On the other hand, the nurse performed all transfer movements from the beginning to the end of the movements while standing. This is due to the fact that basic nursing education or hospital rule mandates treating a space within 20 cm from the floor as a dirty space [13]. For this reason as well as from the perspective of prevention of hospital infection, the nurse did not have the idea of kneeling on the floor, and he will not adopt the method, however broader the base of support can become.

When the certified care worker inserted a sliding board beneath the buttocks of the person in need of care, the tilted angle of the person in need of care was 45.2° to the X-Z plane and 40.5° to the X-Y plane. The nurse tilted angle of the patient was 19.2° to the X-Z plane and 37.1° to the X-Y plane. The certified care worker tilted the body of the subject greater than did the nurse. Although tilting the subject to a greater degree will increase the risk of falling, it reduces the area that the buttocks touch on the seat of the chair, allowing a caregiver to insert the slide board more deeply. The larger the area of the sliding board inserted, the lesser the strain that the sliding movement puts on the body of the caregiver. Even though both the certified care worker and the nurse performed movement to roll the subject, there was a large difference in their tilted angles. We suspect that this difference arose from the difference in ADL (Activities of Daily Living) of subjects that they are normally taking care of. It is assumed that the smaller the level of autonomy in ADL of a subject, the greater the caregiver suffers from strains. Moreover, if it is necessary to assist a subject by a caregiver alone, it is necessary to obtain a method that would not strain the body of the caregiver. In case of a nurse who works at a hospital, it is easy to assemble human resources when transferring a patient from a wheelchair. By contrast, in case of a certified care worker who often does it alone in a nursing home or in a nursing care situation, it is considered that the best method they came up with from their circumstances was to tilt the person in need of care as much as possible and to insert the sliding board. The same goes for the method they acquired of assisting a subject by means of kneeling on the floor as mentioned above.

In the movement of sliding the subject on the sliding board, the face of the person in need of care was oriented toward the moving direction, and the face of the certified care worker was positioned more distant from the moving direction than that of the person in need of care. On the other hand, the face of the nurse was positioned to see moving direction of the patient. The nurse confirmed safety of the transfer position, by visually checking the moving direction of the patient. In the movement of the certified care worker sliding the person in need of care on a sliding board, the certified care worker looked like transferring the person in need of care by utilizing the momentum created when the person in need of care fell to the moving direction after the certified care worker inserted and tilted a board to the same or even a greater degree than the degree by which the person in need of care was tilted, in contrast to the nurse sliding the upper body of the patient without tilting it. If this method is employed, it is necessary to orient the face of the person in need of care toward the backward direction. Moreover, tilting the person in need of care reduces the area that hips of the person in need of care touches on the sliding board, thus reducing friction and making it more slippery. Furthermore, the person in need of care who was about to be transferred on a sliding board would feel safe if he were able to see the moving direction. We assume that this difference between them has arisen out of difference in facilities where their specialties have been exercised. At a hospital, it is necessary to transfer a patient who is put on a drip or is inserted a catheter in a safe manner. If the patient has reduced ADL, it is necessary to ensure safety by transferring the patient through the hands of multiple nurses. By contrast, the second priority of the certified care worker—provided that he is able to confirm the safety of the moving destination of the person in need of care in advance to beginning the movement—is how the certified care worker can transfer the person in need of care by himself without straining his body. Because it is impossible for certified care workers to request assistance of others in nursing care like situations and nursing facilities require transferring many persons in need of care, the industry suffer a persistent lack of human resources and certified care workers often need to assist transferring a subject alone. Thus, protection of health of the certified care workers is prioritized.

Finally, no big difference was found between the certified care worker and the nurse concerning the movement of pulling off the sliding board.

5   Conclusion

This study was premised on the fact that due to similarity of skills exercised between the certified care worker and the nurse, their specialties were confused and thus it attempted to reveal the difference in skills between the certified care worker and the nurse. The movements of transferring from a wheelchair performed by both the certified care worker and the nurse were taken as examples to examine if there is a genuine difference in their movements. It was found that there was a clear difference in their movements. The fact that the difference emerges in educational curriculums that train personnel in each specialized field, and the difference in circumstances in which the wheelchair transfer skills are primarily exercised, and the difference in subjects of being transferred from the wheelchair are considered factors that gave rise to this difference. They are the same in that they developed a method that would not strain body of the caregiver themselves and that they performed movement while ensuring safety of their subject. In hospitals, however, there are regulations to prevent hospital infection, and treatment will be prioritized for a patient, there are cases where a nurse assisting transfer of a patient alone is deemed inappropriate. In case of certified care workers, a certified care worker will often encounter situations of transferring a person in need of care from a wheelchair alone, so as to make up for the lack of human resources. This is true even if the person in need of care has reduced ADL. In such a case, the priority is to select movement of transferring the subject without straining the body of the certified care worker. One useful method for a certified care worker is to kneel on the floor to transfer the person in need of care. From these considerations, we think we have successfully revealed the difference in specialty between certified care workers and nurses.

References

1. Cabinet Office, Government of Japan: White paper on aging society 2015, pp. 2–6 (2016). (in Japanese)
2. A website of the Ministry of Health, Labour and Welfare: The average life expectancy and healthy life expectancy. (in Japanese). http://www.mhlw.go.jp/bunya/kenkou/dl/chiiki-gyousei_03_02.pdf. Accessed 4 Feb 2017
3. A website of the Ministry of Health, Labour and Welfare: Outline of Certified Care Worker. (in Japanese). http://www.mhlw.go.jp/kouseiroudoushou/shikaku_shiken/kaigohukushishi/. Accessed 4 Feb 2017
4. Act on Public Health Nurses, Midwives and Nurses: Article 5 (Act No. 203 on 30 July 1948) final revision, Act No. 83 on 25 June 2014. (in Japanese)
5. Ministry of Health, Labour and Welfare: On policies concerning building and managing training facilities of certified social workers and training facilities of certified care workers, pp. 47–48, 28 March 2008. (in Japanese)
6. Ministry of Health, Labour and Welfare: On Instruction Guideline for Managing Training Facilities of Nurses, etc., pp. 41–43, 31 March 2015. (in Japanese)
7. Ministry of Health, Labour and Welfare: The 2015 Basic Survey on Wage Structure "Contractual cash earnings and scheduled cash earnings and annual special cash earnings by profession" released, 18 February (2016). (in Japanese)
8. Yasuda, M., Yamamura, E., Kobayashi, T., Terashima, H., Yabe, H., Itakura, I.: Study on the specialties as well as the cooperation of nursing and care work: from interview with nurses and care workers working at the nursing home. Bull. Dep. Nurs. Seirei Christopher Coll. **12**, 89–97 (2004). (in Japanese)
9. Kubota, S.: The Way to Improve the Living Environment Using Assistive Devices, pp. 50–55. Japanese Nursing Association Publishing Company, Tokyo (2017). (in Japanese)
10. Ogawa, K.: Assisting Nursing and Care: Work Posture and Movement, Learning Body Mechanics Through Illustration, pp. 53–54. Tokyo Denki University Press, Tokyo (2010). (in Japanese)
11. Shijiki, Y., Matsuo, M., Syuuda, A.: Basic Nursing Skills and Techniques, pp. 141–143. Medicus Shuppan Publishers, Suita (2017). (in Japanese)
12. Kubota, S.: op.cit., pp. 53–55
13. Okaniwa, Y.: Visual guide to nursing practice. In: Clinical Nursing Practice, vol. 2. Medic Media, pp. 5–6 (2015). (in Japanese)

Capacity Allocation in a Service System: Parametric and Data-Driven Approaches

Liping Liang[1], Guanlian Xiao[1], and Hengqing Ye[2]([✉])

[1] School of Business, Lingnan University, Tuen Mun, Hong Kong, China
lipingliang@ln.edu.hk, xglian@gmail.com
[2] Faculty of Business, Hong Kong Polytechnic University, Hung Hom,
Hong Kong, China
hq.ye@polyu.edu.hk

Abstract. We study the capacity allocation problem for a service system that serves its customers with a deterministic service time under a service level requirement. The service level is measured by the probability of customers waiting longer than a pre-specified duration. We model the system as an $M/D/1$ or a $G/D/1$ queue and examine two approaches to determining the capacity: a parametric approach based on the effective bandwidth theory and a data-driven approach based on the sample average approximation. We conduct a numerical study to investigate the effectiveness of these two approaches, and find that the data-driven approach is more streamlined, accurate, and widely applicable.

Keywords: Queueing · Effective bandwidth · Sample average approximation

1 Introduction

Our study is motivated by a problem in the operations of the specialist outpatient clinics (SOPCs) in Hong Kong public hospitals. The SOPCs need to reserve capacity for urgent appointment request while maintaining high utilization of the expensive specialists' time [2]. When new cases are referred to the SOPCs in public hospitals, they are triaged, and the patients' first consultation appointments are made based on their clinical conditions. Patients are classified as categories of urgent, semi-urgent, and routine, and according to a service level requirement, the urgent and semi-urgent (regarded as high-priority class) patients need to be arranged to have their first medical consultations within 2 weeks and 8 weeks respectively as far as possible. In an SOPC, a quota of service capacity is generally reserved for high priority patients, and the remaining capacity for the routine patients. Since a health care system involving many resources is too complicated to be adjusted on a daily basis, a quota is used to control the workload. In practice, it is observed that routine patients often suffer from prolonged waiting time while the quota for high priority patients are not fully utilized. Therefore, an important operational problem is to determine

© Springer International Publishing AG 2017
V.G. Duffy (Ed.): DHM 2017, Part I, LNCS 10286, pp. 295–307, 2017.
DOI: 10.1007/978-3-319-58463-8_25

the minimum capacity (i.e., quota) reserved for the high priority class so that the service level requirement is met and at the same time the waiting time for routine patients can be reduced.

To address the problem, we study a G/D/1 queueing system that models the service operations for high priority class. We assume that the service time is deterministic. (In the SOPC problem, the daily quota is fixed though the consultation times for patients may slightly vary; refer to [11] for similar practices.) The service level is measured by the probability of customers waiting longer than a pre-specified duration. The problem in question is to find the capacity allocation to meet a required service level. It should be noted that this model applies not only to the SOPC operations, but also to problems in other health care services and other service systems in similar situations.

We propose two solutions: a parametric approach based on the effective bandwidth theory (e.g., [3]), and a data-driven approach based on the sample average approximation (e.g., [1]). The former approach builds on the vast amount of classical studies on the G/D/1 (or M/D/1) queue and its waiting time distribution; refer to, e.g., [3,9]. The other approach relates to more recent researches in developing the so-called date-driven approach for operations management problems, e.g., [5,8].

The effective bandwidth theory provides an explicit approximation for the tail probability of the waiting time distribution under suitable assumptions on the arrival and service processes. Hence, the performance measures under study can be estimated via estimating the key parameters such as the arrival rate of the system. It can also be used for theoretical analysis. In contrast, using our data-driven approach, specifically the sample average approximation, we are able to construct the performance measures such as the waiting time and its tail probability directly from the primitive data such as the interarrival times. It is simple and easy to implement, and can incorporate bootstrapping to improve the accuracy. Moreover, it can be applied to more general scenarios, for example, to a system with time varying arrivals or general interarrival time distribution. The numerical study also demonstrates that it provides a accurate result than the parametric approach.

The rest of the paper is organized as follows. We describe the model in Sect. 2. The two solution methods, a parametric approach and a data-driven approach, are introduced and analyzed in Sects. 3 and 4, respectively. We then conduct a numerical study in Sect. 5. All the proofs are relegated to the appendix.

2   Model Description

We consider a classical G/G/1 queueing system. Customers arrive at the system following a renewal process with arrival rate λ, and receive service following the order of arrival. Denote the interarrival time between consecutive arrivals by A_m, $m = 1, 2, \cdots$. Denote the service time of the m-th customer by X_m, $m = 1, 2, \cdots$, and the service rate by c, where $c > 0$. Assume that the interarrival time sequence and service time sequence are mutually independent i.i.d. random sequences, and they all have finite moments.

Let w_m be the waiting time of the m-th arrival, $m = 1, 2, \cdots$. Following the well-known Lindley equation (e.g., [7]), the waiting time for the m-th arrival can be written as,

$$w_m = (w_{m-1} + X_{m-1} - A_{m-1})^+. \tag{1}$$

Under the normal traffic condition, i.e., $\lambda < c$, the system will enter into the steady-state and the waiting time distributions will approach a stationary distribution as $m \to \infty$.

The maximum customer waiting time specified in the service level requirement is denoted by $b > 0$, and the probability of waiting no more than b denoted by $1 - \alpha$. Therefore, we will find the minimum service capacity c that satisfies

$$Pr(w > b) \le \alpha, \tag{2}$$

where the random variable w represents the stationary waiting time and its distribution depends on c.

We introduce two useful tools for our analysis below, namely, the effective bandwidth approach and the sample average approximation.

Lemma 1 (Effective bandwidth, see Kelly [3]). Let A and X be random variables representing the inter-arrival time and service time distributions, and κ a positive constant satisfying $E(e^{\kappa X})E(e^{-\kappa A}) = 1$. Then, there exist constants $a_1, a_2 \le 1$ such that

$$a_1 e^{-\kappa b} \le Pr(w > b) \le a_2 e^{-\kappa b}.$$

For the result in Lemma 1, Kingman [4] first specified the constants as

$$a_1 = \inf_{x>0} \frac{\int_x^{+\infty} dF(y)}{\int_x^{+\infty} e^{\kappa(y-x)} dF(y)}, \quad \text{and} \quad a_2 = 1;$$

and later Ross [6] improved the bounds as

$$a_1 = \frac{e^{-\kappa b}}{\sup_{r \ge 0} E[e^{\kappa(U-r)} | U > r]} \quad \text{and} \quad a_2 = \frac{e^{-\kappa b}}{\inf_{r \ge 0} E[e^{\kappa(U-r)} | U > r]}. \tag{3}$$

In the above, we let $U = X - A$ and its cumulative distribution function be $F(x)$.

The second tool is the sample average approximation of the tail distribution of the stationary waiting time w. We have the following result.

Lemma 2 (Chang [1]). The tail probability of the stationary waiting time can be estimated as:

$$Pr(w > b) = \lim_{m \to \infty} Pr(w_m > b) = \lim_{m \to \infty} E[I_{(w_m > b)}] = \lim_{n \to \infty} \frac{\sum_{k=1}^n I_{(w_k > b)}}{n} \tag{4}$$

where $I_{(x)}$ is an indicator function, which is equal to 1 if the condition x is true and equal to 0 otherwise.

3 Parametric Approach via Effective Bandwidth

Consider the M/D/1 system, where the arrival is Poisson and the service time for each customer is equal to the constant $1/c$. Applying Lemma 1 to the M/D/1 system, we can bound the tail distribution of the stationary waiting time w as,

$$\frac{1 - e^{-\lambda/c}}{1 - e^{-(\kappa+\lambda)/c}} e^{-\kappa b} \leq Pr(w > b) \leq e^{-\kappa b}. \tag{5}$$

The proof of the above bounds is relegated to the appendix.

Observe that as $b \to \infty$, both bounds approach 0. In addition, it is interesting to note that the gap between the coefficients in the above upper and lower bounds diminishes when the traffic intensity λ/c approach 1; that is,

$$1 - \frac{1 - e^{-\lambda/c}}{1 - e^{-(\kappa+\lambda)/c}} \to 0, \quad \text{as } \frac{\lambda}{c} \to 1. \tag{6}$$

(Refer to the appendix for detailed justification of the above result as well.) Given these observations, we will choose the upper bound as an estimation of the tail probability of the stationary waiting time w. Hence, enforcing the service requirement in (2) is reduced to requiring the above upper bound being equal to α, that is,

$$e^{-\kappa b} = \alpha, \quad \text{or } \kappa = -\frac{\log(\alpha)}{b}. \tag{7}$$

We solve the equation, $e^{\kappa/c} E(e^{-\kappa A}) = 1$ in Lemma 1 and obtain the required capacity c as,

$$c = \frac{\kappa}{\log(1 + \kappa/\lambda)}. \tag{8}$$

Using (7) and (8), we propose the following procedure to estimate the required capacity, at each time when new data becomes available.

Repeat for each time $t = 1, \ldots, T$:

1. Let n_t be the number of arrivals by time t; collect data of inter-arrival times $A_i, i = 1, \cdots, n_t$;
2. Calculate the sample mean as $\lambda_t = 1/\sum_{i=1}^{n_t} A_i$, and then the required service capacity as $c_t = \kappa/\log(1 + \kappa/\lambda_t)$.

An observation from the above procedure is that the estimate c_t converges to the target given in (8) as time $t \to \infty$. However, it should be noted that c_t does not give an unbiased estimate of c at any finite time t. Specifically, denote $f(\lambda) \equiv \kappa/\log(1 + \kappa/\lambda)$. Clearly, it is concave in λ. Therefore, we have

$$E(c_t) = Ef(\lambda_t) \leq f(E(\lambda_t)) = c.$$

The data-driven approach introduced in the next section avoids this pitfall and gives a more direct approximation.

4   Data-Driven Approach via Sample Average Approximation

The data-driven approach applies to the more general G/D/1 system, compared to the parametric approach in Sect. 3. As the service time is deterministic, the Lindley equation in (1) can be used to estimate a customer's waiting time w_m upon her arrival (i.e., whenever A_m is observed). Therefore, Lemma 2 suggests an estimate of the probability $Pr(w > b)$ by $Pr_t := \sum_{m=1}^{n_t} I_{(w_m > b)}/n_t$ at any time t, where n_t denote the number of arrivals by time t. Recall, given the (primitive) arrival data by time t, the performance measures, i.e., $w_1, \cdots, w_{n_t}$ and Pr_t, are functions of the suppressed parameter c. Thus, we propose the following procedure to estimate the required service capacity.

Repeat for each time $t = 1, \ldots, T$:

1. Collect data of inter-arrival times A_i, $i = 1, \cdots, n_t$;
2. Search the minimum c, denoted by c_t, that ensures $Pr_t \leq \alpha$.

The procedure can be improved by applying bootstrapping to generate a sufficiently long sample path, $\{\tilde{A}_i, i = 1, \cdots, N\}$. Here, N is a sufficiently large integer, and each interarrival time, $\tilde{A}_i$, is drawn with equal probability from the set of interarrival times, $\{A_i, i = 1, \cdots, n_t\}$, that is available by time t. Then, in the above procedure, calculate the probability (estimate) Pr_t as:

$$Pr_t = \frac{\sum_{i=1}^{N} I_{(w_i > b)}}{N},$$

where the waiting time w_m is now determined by (1) with A_i replaced by $\tilde{A}_i$.

5   Numerical Studies

We conduct a numerical experiment to compare the parametric approach with the data-driven approach using combinations of parameters in Table 1. The numerical experiment will run $4 \times 4 \times 4$ times, covering all combinations of the parameters.

Table 1. Parameters

λ	b	α
5	2	2%
10	5	5%
15	7	8%
20	13	10%

5.1   Convergence Analysis

First we investigate the rate of convergence of each approach. Since both parametric and data-driven approaches can be applied to $M/D/1$ system, we compare their numerical results for this case.

Given an arrival rate λ and a capacity c, we can use effective bandwidth theory, i.e., Lemma 1 along with (3), to calculate the upper bound and lower bound of the tail probability. Hence, we can determine the capacity c by binary search so that the tail probability meets the service level requirement with the specified values of b and α. Table 2 shows the (relative) error between the upper bound and lower bound for different arrival rates and capacities (λ and c) for $\alpha = 0.05$. The error, or ratio, is given as $(UB - LB)/LB$. Consider the case that the average arrival rate is $\lambda = 20$ and it is required that customers be served within 7 days ($b = 7$). When the service capacity ranges from 20.05 to 20.4 (or, the traffic intensity varies from 99.75% to 98.03%), the error is always kept under 3%, which is consistent with the observation given in (6). A similar observation can be found for the case of $\lambda = 10$ and $b = 7$. Hence, these observations indicate that both bounds as given in Lemma 1 can be used as an effective approximation for the tail probability of the stationary waiting time of customers.

Next we use the bounds given in (3) as the benchmark for evaluating the data-driven approach and parametric estimation described in Sects. 3 and 4.

Table 2. Errors of bounds using effective bandwidth for Poisson arrival process

λ	c	κ	UB	LB	Ratio	λ	c	κ	UB	LB	Ratio
10	10.05	0.10	0.4937	0.4966	0.58%	20	20.05	0.10	0.4951	0.4966	0.30%
10	10.1	0.2000	0.2438	0.2466	1.14%	20	20.1	0.2000	0.2452	0.2466	0.57%
10	10.2	0.4000	0.0594	0.0608	2.30%	20	20.2	0.4000	0.0601	0.0608	1.15%
10	10.3	0.6000	0.0145	0.015	3.33%	20	20.3	0.6000	0.0147	0.015	2%
10	10.4	0.8000	0.0035	0.0037	5.41%	20	20.4	0.8000	0.0036	0.0037	2.70%

Define the relative gap, $|c_d - c|/|c_e - c|$, where c_d and c_e are the capacity estimated using the data-driven and parametric approaches, and c is the optimal service capacity computed using the given parameters (λ, b and α). In other words, it is the ratio of the gap between the data-driven estimated capacity and the optimal capacity to the gap between the effective bandwidth estimation and the optimal capacity. Below, as we do not have the exact optimal capacity c, we will use its two bounds and the average of both.

We use the values of the three parameters λ, b and α in Table 1, fixing one of them at a time and varying the other two. For each combination of the parameter values, we calculate the relative gap.

The Impact of λ. Figure 1 plots the average of relative gaps for all combinations of parameter values given a fixed value of λ. We can see that for any $\lambda > 0$, the relative gap (ratio) is less than 100%, which indicates that the data-driven approach outperforms the parametric approach. In addition, as the arrival rate λ increases the performance difference of the two approaches diminishes.

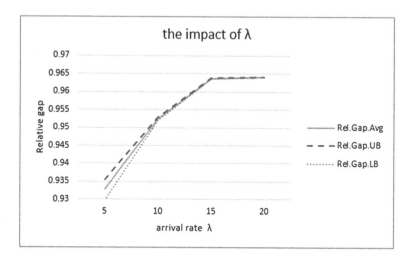

Fig. 1. The impact of λ

The Impact of b and α. Figures 2 and 3 plot the average of relative gaps for all combinations of parameter values given a fixed value of b and a fixed value of α, respectively. Figure 2 shows that as the waiting time target b decreases, the relative gap is greatly reduced; that is, the data-driven approach performs much better than the parametric approach for a shorter waiting time target b. As the relative gap is below 100% for a large range of values of b, the data-driven approach outperforms the parametric approach. Figure 3 shows a similar pattern as Fig. 2 except that the relative gap decreases at large values of α.

Extreme Cases. Figures 1, 2 and 3 demonstrate that the data-driven approach performs much better than the parametric approach at small values of the parameters λ, b and α. Figure 4 shows the estimated capacities by the two approaches for small values of λ, b and α.

In the figure, 'PE' represents 'parametric estimation', 'BUB' and 'BLB' are the estimated upper bound and lower bound by effective bandwidth for a given (actual) arrival rate. From the figure, the gap between the upper bound and lower bound with actual arrival rate as benchmark is very small, hence they provide a reliable estimate when all parameters are known. We also observe that both parametric and data-driven estimations converge to the theoretical optimal capacity as time becomes longer, and that the data-driven approach converges slightly faster.

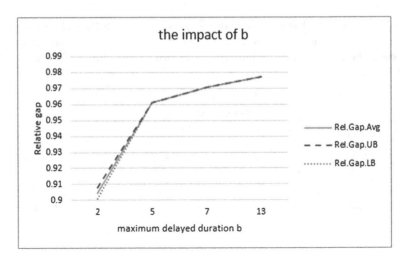

Fig. 2. The impact of b

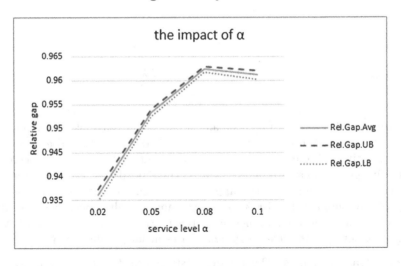

Fig. 3. The impact of α

5.2 Advantages of Data-Driven Approach over Parametric Approach for G/D/1 Queue

The numerical result in Sect. 5.1 for the M/D/1 system has shown that the data-driven approach performs better than the parametric approach in all combinations of our parameter values. We examine if the finding still holds for a more general queueing system, for example, $G/D/1$. We investigate the performance of parametric estimation in this case by using Lemma 1.

Stability and Accuracy of Estimating the Parameter κ**.** For the parametric estimation, in order to estimate the tail probability of waiting time, we

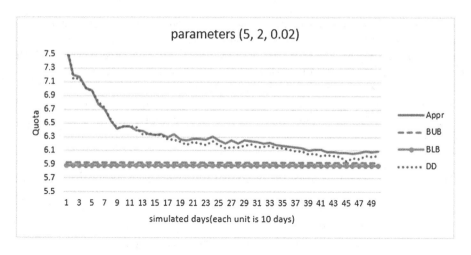

Fig. 4. Extreme case analysis

need to first estimate the parameter κ in the upper bound and lower bound as given in (5). For a general arrival process, by Lemma 1 the upper bound and lower bound for the tail probability of waiting time depend on the (empirical) cumulative density function of the number of daily arrivals. We use exponential distribution for the inter-arrival time, and the numerical results are listed in Table 3. The computation is conducted as follows: Generate a large number of exponentially distributed samples and use empirical cumulative distribution function to approximate its distribution, and then use (3) to derive the estimated parameter κ_e. κ is calculated by (3) based on the assumption of exponential inter-arrival time. Theoretically the two numbers should be the same because they are based on the same distribution and parameter values. As shown in Table 3, however, κ_e (by parametric estimation) does not converge to the real optimal κ, which indicates that the estimation formulated by effective bandwidth does not work any more when the interarrival time is fitted by the empirical distribution.

Table 3. Gaps of bounds when the inter-arrival time has a general distribution

λ	b	ϵ	c	κ_e	κ	c	κ_e	κ	c	κ_e	κ
20	7	10^{-1}	23	0.5	6.0822	21	0.5	2.0822	20	0.5	0.0822
20	7	10^{-2}	23	0.5	6.0822	21	0.5	2.0822	20	0.5	0.0822
20	7	10^{-3}	23	0.159	6.2343	21	0.5	2.0822	20	0.5	0.0822
20	7	10^{-4}	23	0.0154	6.3621	21	1.9105	2.0822	20	0.2788	0.0822
20	7	10^{-5}	23	0.0015	6.3745	21	1.9521	2.1139	20	0.0878	0.0822
20	7	10^{-6}	23	0.0001	6.3758	21	1.9562	2.1139	20	0.0277	0.0822

Parametric Estimation for the Case of Log-Normal Distribution. Consider the case with log-normal interarrival time that has parameters (μ_1, σ_1). For comparison, also scale its mean to be $1/\lambda$. We apply the effective bandwidth theory explained in Lemma 1 to show the gap between two bounds.

As we can see from Table 4, the gaps of two bounds are all greater than 10%, and in some cases (e.g., the 1st and the 4th cases) the upper bound can not be found in reasonable time. Therefore, the parametric approach based on effective bandwidth does not give a reliable estimate here.

Table 4. Gaps of bounds when the inter-arrival time has a lognormal distribution

λ	μ_1	σ_1	c	κ_e	UB	LB	Gap
20	0.1	0.1	20.5	0.0738	∞	0.7356	-
20	0.1	0.1	20.6	0.0618	0.7078	0.6318	12.03%
20	0.1	0.1	20.7	0.0532	0.6891	0.3759	83.32%
20	0.1	0.1	20.8	0.0468	∞	0.8731	-
20	0.1	0.1	20.9	0.0418	0.8142	0.743	9.58%
20	0.1	0.1	21	0.0378	0.7675	0.5117	50.00%

According to the above two numerical experiments, when the arrival process is more general (i.e., not necessarily Poisson), the parametric approach does not give an accurate approximation for the tail probability of waiting time while the data-driven approach works well.

Acknowledgement. This study is supported in part by Hong Kong RGC under grant TBRS T32-102/14N.

Appendix

5.3   Proof of (5)

We analyse $e^{-\kappa b}/E[e^{\kappa(U-r)}|U > r]$ with respect to $1/c \geq r > 0$, in order to obtain its upper bound and lower bound:

$$\frac{e^{-\kappa b}}{E[e^{\kappa(U-r)}|U > r]} = \frac{e^{-\kappa b}}{E[e^{\kappa(\frac{1}{c}-r-A)}|A < \frac{1}{c} - r]}$$

$$= \frac{e^{-\kappa b}\int_0^{\frac{1}{c}-r}\lambda e^{-\lambda x}dx}{\int_0^{\frac{1}{c}-r}e^{\kappa(\frac{1}{c}-r-x)}\lambda e^{-\lambda x}dx} = \frac{e^{-\kappa b}(1 - e^{-\lambda(\frac{1}{c}-r)})}{\frac{\lambda e^{\frac{\kappa}{c}-\kappa r}}{\kappa+\lambda}(1 - e^{-(\kappa+\lambda)(\frac{1}{c}-r)})}$$

$$= \frac{e^{-\kappa b}(1 - e^{-\lambda(\frac{1}{c}-r)})}{e^{-\kappa r}(1 - e^{-(\kappa+\lambda)(\frac{1}{c}-r)})} = \frac{e^{-\kappa b}(e^{-\lambda r} - e^{\frac{-\lambda}{c}})}{(e^{-(\kappa+\lambda)r} - e^{\frac{-(\kappa+\lambda)}{c}})}.$$

Let

$$g(r) = \frac{e^{-\lambda r} - e^{\frac{-\lambda}{c}}}{e^{-(\kappa+\lambda)r} - e^{\frac{-(\kappa+\lambda)}{c}}},$$

and take the first-order derivative,

$$g'(r) = \frac{dg(r)}{dr} = \frac{(\lambda+\kappa)(e^{-(\lambda+\kappa)r} - e^{-\frac{\lambda}{c}-\kappa r}) - \lambda(e^{-(\lambda+\kappa)r} - e^{-\frac{\lambda+\kappa}{c}})}{e^{\lambda r}(e^{-(\kappa+\lambda)r} - e^{\frac{-(\kappa+\lambda)}{c}})^2}.$$

Let the numerator of $g'(r)$ be $\tilde{g}(r)$, i.e., $\tilde{g}(r) = \kappa e^{-(\lambda+\kappa)r} - (\lambda+\kappa)e^{-\frac{\lambda}{c}-\kappa r} + \lambda e^{-\frac{\lambda+\kappa}{c}}$, we will investigate the sign of $\tilde{g}(r)$:

$$\tilde{g}'(r) = \frac{d\tilde{g}(r)}{dr} = -\kappa(\lambda+\kappa)e^{-(\lambda+\kappa)r} + \kappa(\lambda+\kappa)e^{-\frac{\lambda}{c}-\kappa r},$$

then:

$$\tilde{g}'(r) \begin{cases} < 0, r < \frac{1}{c}, \\ = 0, r = \frac{1}{c}, \\ > 0, r > \frac{1}{c}. \end{cases}$$

Thus, $\tilde{g}(r)$ attains its minimum at $r = 1/c$, its minimum value is 0. Therefore $g(r)$ is increasing in r, and

$$\inf_{r>0} g(r) = \lim_{r\to 0} g(r) = \frac{1 - e^{\frac{-\lambda}{c}}}{1 - e^{\frac{-(\kappa+\lambda)}{c}}},$$

$$\sup_{r>0} g(r) = \lim_{r\to\frac{1}{c}} g(r) = \frac{\lambda}{\kappa+\lambda}e^{\frac{\kappa}{c}} = 1.$$

The tail distribution of the queue length is:

$$\frac{1 - e^{\frac{-\lambda}{c}}}{1 - e^{\frac{-(\kappa+\lambda)}{c}}} e^{-\kappa b} \le Pr(w > b) \le e^{-\kappa b}.$$

Justification of (6)

We will prove a stronger conclusion: For any $\epsilon \in (0,1)$, there exists a $\hat{\rho} \in (0,1)$ such that

$$\frac{1 - e^{-\hat{\rho}}}{1 - e^{-\hat{\rho}+\frac{3-\sqrt{\frac{24}{\hat{\rho}}-15}}{2}}} = 1 - \epsilon.$$

Meanwhile, for any $\lambda/c \ge \hat{\rho}$, we have

$$0 \le 1 - \frac{1 - e^{\frac{-\lambda}{c}}}{1 - e^{\frac{-(\kappa+\lambda)}{c}}} \le \epsilon.$$

Let

$$f(\rho) = \frac{1 - e^{-\rho}}{1 - e^{-\rho+\frac{3-\sqrt{\frac{24}{\rho}-15}}{2}}}.$$

The proof will be divided into two steps:

Firstly, we prove

$$\kappa < \frac{-3c}{2} + \frac{\sqrt{24\frac{c}{\lambda} - 15c}}{2}.$$

Let

$$h(x) = e^{\frac{x}{c}} - 1 - \frac{x}{\lambda}, \quad h'(x) = \frac{1}{c}e^{\frac{x}{c}} - \frac{1}{\lambda},$$

then $h(x)$ attains its minimum value at $c\ln(c/\lambda)$, with the minimum value being $\frac{c}{\lambda} - 1 - \frac{c}{\lambda}\ln(\frac{c}{\lambda})$. Since the function $g_1(x) = x - 1 - x\ln x$ is decreasing in x and $g_1(1) = 0$, we have $g_1(\frac{c}{\lambda}) = \frac{c}{\lambda} - 1 - \frac{c}{\lambda}\ln(\frac{c}{\lambda}) < 0$. Thus, $h(x)$ is decreasing in $(-\infty, c\ln(\frac{c}{\lambda})]$, and increasing in $[c\ln(\frac{c}{\lambda}), +\infty)$. Moreover, $h(0) = 0$ and $h(c\ln(\frac{c}{\lambda})) < 0$. It has one and only one $\kappa > 0$, satisfying $h(\kappa) = 0$. Therefore, if there is a y_0 such that $h(y_0) > 0$, then we have $y_0 \geq \kappa$.

Let y_0 satisfy $g_3(y_0) = \frac{y_0}{c} + \frac{y_0^2}{2c^2} + \frac{y_0^3}{6c^3} - \frac{y_0}{\lambda} = 0$. Then, we have $h(y_0) > 0$. Meanwhile, y_0 can be derived as $\frac{-3c}{2} + \sqrt{24\frac{c}{\lambda} - 15c}/2$, and furthermore we have $\frac{-3c}{2} + \sqrt{24\frac{c}{\lambda} - 15c}/2 > \kappa$.

Next, we prove

$$0 \leq 1 - \frac{1 - e^{\frac{-\lambda}{c}}}{1 - e^{\frac{-(\kappa+\lambda)}{c}}} \leq \epsilon.$$

By taking the first-order derivative toward to ρ, it can be shown that $f'(\rho) \geq 0$. Moreover, $\lim_{\rho \to 0} f(\rho) = 0$, $\lim_{\rho \to 1} f(\rho) = 1$, thus $1 - (1 - e^{\frac{-\lambda}{c}})/(1 - e^{\frac{-(\kappa+\lambda)}{c}}) \geq 0$ and for any $\epsilon \in (0, 1)$, $\exists \hat{\rho}$ satisfying:

$$\frac{1 - e^{-\hat{\rho}}}{1 - e^{-\hat{\rho} + \frac{3 - \sqrt{\frac{24}{\hat{\rho}} - 15}}{2}}} = 1 - \epsilon.$$

According to the result in the first step, the following inequality holds:

$$\frac{1 - e^{\frac{-\lambda}{c}}}{1 - e^{\frac{-(\kappa+\lambda)}{c}}} \geq f(\frac{\lambda}{c}).$$

Since $f(\rho)$ is increasing in ρ, we have for any $\lambda/c \geq \hat{\rho}$,

$$\frac{1 - e^{\frac{-\lambda}{c}}}{1 - e^{\frac{-(\kappa+\lambda)}{c}}} \geq f(\frac{\lambda}{c}) \geq f(\hat{\rho}) = 1 - \epsilon,$$

and therefore,

$$1 - \frac{1 - e^{\frac{-\lambda}{c}}}{1 - e^{\frac{-(\kappa+\lambda)}{c}}} \leq \epsilon.$$

References

1. Chang, C.-S.: Stability, queue length, and delay of deterministic and stochastic queueing networks. IEEE Trans. Autom. Control **39**(5), 913–931 (1994)

2. Gupta, D., Denton, B.: Appointment scheduling in health care: challenges and opportunities. IIE Trans. **40**(9), 800–819 (2008)
3. Kelly, F.P.: Effective bandwidths at multi-class queues. Queueing Syst. **9**(1–2), 5–15 (1991)
4. Kingman, J.: Inequalities in the theory of queues. J. Roy. Stat. Soc. Ser. B (Methodol.) **32**(1), 102–110 (1970)
5. Liyanage, L.H., George Shanthikumar, J.: A practical inventory control policy using operational statistics. Oper. Res. Lett. **33**(4), 341–348 (2005)
6. Ross, S.M.: Bounds on the delay distribution in GI/G/1 queues. J. Appl. Probab. **11**(2), 417–421 (1974)
7. Ross, S.M.: Stochastic Processes, vol. 2. Wiley, Princeton (1996)
8. Rudin, C., Vahn, G.-Y.: The big data newsvendor: practical insights from machine learning. Available at SSRN 2559116 (2014)
9. Wolff, R.W.: Stochastic Modeling and the Theory of Queues. Prentice Hall, Englewood Cliffs (1989)
10. Talluri, K.T.: The Theory and Practice of Revenue Management. Kluwer Academic Publisher, Boston (2004)
11. Patrick, J.: A Markov decision model for determining optimal outpatient scheduling. Health Care Manag. Sci. **15**(2), 91–102 (2012)
12. Tan, H.H.: Another martingale bound on the waiting-time distribution in GI/G/1 queues. J. Appl. Probab. **16**, 454–457 (1979)

User Groups and Different Levels of Control in Recommender Systems

Christine Mendez[1], Vlatko Lukarov[1], Christoph Greven[1],
André Calero Valdez[2(✉)], Felix Dietze[2], Ulrik Schroeder[1],
and Martina Ziefle[2]

[1] Learning Technologies Research Group, RWTH Aachen University,
Ahornstraße 55, 52074 Aachen, Germany
christine.mendez@rwth-aachen.de,
lukarov@cil.rwth-aachen.de,
{greven, schroeder}@cs.rwth-aachen.de
[2] Human-Computer Interaction Center, RWTH Aachen University,
Campus-Boulevard 57, 52074 Aachen, Germany
{calero-valdez, dietze, ziefle}@comm.rwth-aachen.de

Abstract. The aspect of control in recommender systems has already been extensively researched in the past. Quite a number of studies performed by various researchers reported that an increase in control had a positive effect for example on user satisfaction with a system, or recommendation accuracy. Recent studies investigated whether this positive effect of control applies to all users, or finer distinctions have to be made between different user groups, which in turn require different levels of control. Those studies identified several characteristics, along which users could be divided into groups: expertise in recommender systems, domain knowledge, trusting propensity, persistence. They reported different needs of control for different user groups. However, the effect of those characteristics has not been systematically examined with regard to all three recommendation phases introduced earlier by Pu and Zhang, namely *initial preference elicitation, preference refinement, result display*. This paper suggests, that for different levels of expertise and trust, different levels of control are necessary during preference elicitation, whereas persistence does not play a prevalent role in this phase. Further assumptions are made for preference refinement and result display. In addition to the three phases, *context, type of information required* and *visualization of control methods* are identified as factors influencing the request of users for control.

Keywords: Recommender systems · User groups · Controllability · User satisfaction

1 Introduction

The research focus in the area of recommender systems has shifted from recommendation algorithms, to the users and their needs [16]. Various studies covering the aspect of control in recommender systems reported a positive effect of control on user satisfaction on various systems (e.g. [1, 2, 10, 11]). In general, user involvement and

© Springer International Publishing AG 2017
V.G. Duffy (Ed.): DHM 2017, Part I, LNCS 10286, pp. 308–323, 2017.
DOI: 10.1007/978-3-319-58463-8_26

interactive interfaces do have immediate impact and effect on the user experience. So far, to our knowledge, only a few studies examined the general assumption that more control automatically leads to better user experience. A more fine-grained distinction between user-groups revealed, that different levels of control are requested by different users [7–9, 12]. In those studies, researchers distinguished users by varying levels of the following characteristics: expertise in recommender systems, domain knowledge, trusting propensity, and persistence. In fact, they found that different user groups responded differently to an increase in control. This paper provides an overview over past results by classifying them according to the phases of the recommendation process. For each phase we will discuss suggestions for further empirical research and formulate hypotheses based on previous research.

2 Controllability in Recommender Systems

One way to introduce controllability in recommender systems is to actively involve the user in the recommendation process (workflow). The user can shape and improve his profile within the system; change and adapt the way recommendations are presented to him; provide additional context information which the system cannot implicitly collect in order to receive more suitable suggestions. These are just a small set of user activities in different stages/phases of the recommendation process which increase controllability. In the following section we will provide detailed overview of different interaction techniques and activities, and how were they used in different phases of the recommendation process.

2.1 Ways to Control the Recommendation Process

Looking at existing work that deals with controllability and user interaction with recommender systems, it is clear that there are different ways to allow the user to influence the recommendation process. Some notable examples are creating a user profile by "giving binary or multi-scale scores" to items, tagging items, weighting of item attributes, critiquing recommendations, The list of intervention possibilities throughout the recommendation process goes on and on [13].

In order to facilitate the comparison of different controlling capabilities, we will classify them with respect to key activities in the recommendation process or phases identified by Pu and Zhang: (i) (Initial) Preference Elicitation. In the initial phase the system gains initial knowledge about the user and establishes accurate interest profile in order to recommend items that match the user's taste. [13] (ii) Preference Refinement. In this phase, the system refines the user's preferences after the initial phase of recommendation. In this phase, the user has the opportunity to alter (update) his preferences in order to receive more appropriate recommendations from the system. Activities like adding supplementary ratings to sample items, or evaluating the recommendations themselves via critiquing can help the recommender system from going in the wrong direction with the recommendations. (iii) Result Display Strategies. In this phase, the generated recommendations are presented to the user [13]. In the following sections we will present exemplary studies, which implemented control mechanisms for each of the three phases. Figure 1 provides an overview of these exemplary studies. It illustrates how those examples support the different recommendation phases and summarizes their findings on how those control mechanisms affect the user.

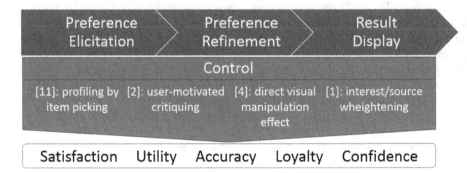

Fig. 1. Three recommendation phases with examples of control mechanisms and correlations to several positive aspects.

During Initial Preference Elicitation

In their study, McNee et al. [11] compare varying amounts of user control in the sign up process for the online movie recommender platform "MovieLens". New users are asked to rate 10–15 movies they have seen, in order to create a user model and receive better recommendations. They found that the users may not only be involved by rating movies suggested by the system (system-controlled approach), but also the users themselves can suggest and rate movies they had seen in the past (user-controlled approach).

They discovered that the user models created with the user-controlled interface were more accurate than the others and that the users were more satisfied with their recommendations than those in the other focus group. Furthermore, participants in the user-controlled group tended to return to the system and showed a more active use after the sign-up process [11]. McNee et al. call them more "loyal" to the system and attribute this to their personal involvement in the initial preference elicitation. Although the sign-up process in this condition took the users almost twice as long, they did not perceive it as being lengthy. This, McNee et al. argue is also due to their involvement with the system [11].

Loepp et al. [10] present another way to exploit user interaction in the initial preference elicitation process. They specifically stress that their approach helps in overcoming the cold-start problem and can be applied for a user who does not have or want a permanent profile [10]. In this particular case, the user picks different sets of items, instead of rating individual items. The increase of user-provided information leads to positive user feedback w.r.t. fit, novelty of the results, control, effort and adaption [10] in the recommendation process, when compared to the manual search or automated recommendations with no user interaction. Lastly, they derived from their observations that their approach is especially well suited for users who do not have formed a concrete search goal yet [10].

During Preference Refinement

One example for an increase in control during preference refinement is discussed by Chen and Pu [2]. They examine different kinds of critiquing-based recommender systems. Generally speaking, these systems allow the user to improve or narrow down their results by critiquing the recommendations they received earlier. Chen and Pu compare dynamic critiquing (as a form of system-proposed critiquing) with user-motivated critiquing. In this comparison they analyze both objective (decision accuracy, task completion time, interaction effort) and subjective (perceived cognitive effort, decision confidence, trusting intentions) criteria [2]. They observe that user-motivated critiquing required less effort and resulted in a higher decision accuracy. Also this system was perceived as less demanding in terms of critiquing effort by their participants. The perceived critiquing effort was also correlated with the users' confidence in the results. The higher the user's confidence, the lower their perceived effort [2].

Gretarsson et al. [4] developed an interactive visualization that allows the user to explore their Facebook friends' interests and thus pick recommendations or results of interest: SmallWorlds. In their design, they graphically depict the user surrounded by alternating layers containing both their friends and their friends' items of interest, which are unknown to the user so far. Initially, the distance between a user and a friend is defined by the amount of common interests. The more items they have in common so far, the closer a friend (and their respective interests). Dragging a friend or an item nearer to the user increases their weight and highlights related items that might match the user's taste.

Gretarsson et al. [4] found that this mapping for the process of weighting or selection is very intuitive and easy to handle. Furthermore, their results indicate that people could easily find common tastes. The same holds for popular and interesting items which were easy to identify. Their participants also stated that using SmallWorlds was easier than browsing a text-based interface for common interests and new recommendations. The parallel comparison of their friends was perceived as an exceptional advantage.

Upon Result Display

Bostandjiev et al. [1] developed a system called TasteWeights. Although they also rely on Facebook data to create recommendations, their interface and interaction possibilities differ from the SmallWorld concept. Their surface is divided up into three columns. The first column contains a user profile with their (Facebook) items listed. The second column consists of three parts, representing three different recommendation engines which use the profile data to come up with recommendations. The recommendations are displayed in the third column. Each column allows the user to control the weight of an item or a recommendation technique. The impact on the other columns are immediately displayed on the graphical interface. For their study, Bostandjiev et al. compared the user satisfaction and recommendation accuracy when they were allowed to manipulate a set of various interaction possibilities in the system.

They found that the possibility of interacting with all three columns (which also includes an immediate (or direct) observation of the impact on the recommendations) lead to the most accurate recommendations and was perceived useful in the recommendation process. The full interaction condition also outperformed hybrid recommendation approaches using the same engines but offering no interaction to the user [1].

Ekstrand et al. [3] also let users control the algorithm with which their recommendations are created. While TasteWeights allowed the user to weight the contribution of a recommender engine to the result set, Ekstrand et al. let the user choose one algorithm which creates the whole result set.

They found, that not even a third of the users they recorded, used the opportunity to switch between different recommendation algorithms to get different result sets. Those who did, tended to use the system rather actively in general [3]. One can argue that such behavior indicates (but does not prove) that there might be a correlation between active users and the need of control. Examining only the users who switched between recommenders, it became clear that they tend to experiment with the obtained results early during a session, but settle for one algorithm rather quickly (no further changes in later sessions/during that session). For those users, user satisfaction and recommendation accuracy is high [3].

2.2   User Reactions to Levels of Control

As the examples show, there are several ways of giving more control to the user during all phases of the recommendation process. The general results show that an increased level of control is well-appreciated by the users. An increase in control lead for example to increased recommendation accuracy [1, 2, 11], fit, novelty [10], and thus user satisfaction [1] and a better feeling of control and adaption [10, 11] in various studies. Moreover, Chen and Pu could report that more control in critiquing-based recommenders cost their users less effort [2]. A similar result was obtained by Parra and Brusilovski [12]: The majority of their participants stated that using their visual control mechanisms facilitated their task compared to a baseline interface with no control options.

Harper et al. [5] also reported positive feedback to increased control levels in their experiment. Users report that their "adjusted lists better represent their preferences" and "subjects responded positively to a survey question if they would use a [control] feature" like the one used in the study [5]. This feedback is particularly interesting since users also reported usability issues with the given system. This suggests that the benefit of the control options outweighed inconveniences during the use of the tools.

Such positive results lead Hijikata et al. [6] to examine whether the mere feeling of being in control is enough to obtain higher user satisfaction during the use of a recommender system, without actually intervening in the process. In their study they compared two user groups: The first group using actual control mechanisms, while the other users were presented with 'placebo controls' which had no effect on the recommendations. They found that actual control correlated positively with user satisfaction, whereas the fake controls showed no such effect [6]. This is an important result in so far as it supports the claim, that the user's participation in the recommendation process is a valid contribution to its results. This underlines the importance of using tools for including the user in the recommendation process.

Starting from those general results, a few attempts were made to distinguish between several user groups and their individual needs of control. Researchers started posing the question whether control is actually desirable for all kinds of users, or if there are certain characteristics which lead to different user reactions. Table 1 gives an overview of user categorizations from past research work. Different user groups are distinguished from the uniform crowd according to certain user characteristics. Those groups are then separately confronted with different levels of control. By doing so, the results reflect a more diverse population with users who have different prerequisites and needs. Concrete results of past work will be presented in the next section.

Table 1. Influence of control increase on different user groups, based on [4, 8].

user category	user type	cause
expertise (with RS)	novice	☺
	professional	☺
domain knowledge	beginner	☹
	expert	☺
trustfulness	sceptics	☺
	trustful	☺
satisficer/maximizer	satisficer	☹
	maximizer	☺

3   Distinguishing User Groups and Their Specific Needs

When developing an interactive system in general, the two most important questions one needs to answer are: Who are the users, and how are they going to use the system? In the following sections we try to categorize the different user groups and identify their specific needs within the context of controllability of recommender systems. We considered different factors, such as, information type, context, goal, interface or results visualization, and others, when distinguishing the different user groups and addressing their specific needs.

3.1   Previous Work

Jameson and Schwarzkopf [7] question the assumption that more control leads to more user satisfaction. In their study they found that both automatic and manual updating of recommendations on a hotlist had supporters amongst their participants. They identify the following factors that must be taken into account when giving control to users [7]:

1. The nature of the application and of the adaptation involved
2. Individual differences among users in terms of preferences, experience and ways of approaching the tasks in question
3. Contextual factors like speed of internet connection
4. Random situational factors like the nature of the information retrieved during the process.

Parra and Brusilovski [12] introduced a hybrid recommender system called Set-Fusion, which gives control to the user during both preference refinement and result visualization. It allows to adjust the weight of each of the different recommendation approaches that contribute to generating results. Furthermore, the results are visualized in an interactive Venn diagram which allows further inspection of an item and filtering the results according to certain criteria (for further details, see [12]).

They examined the effect of those control opportunities on user engagement and user experience with the system. In addition to the work of Jameson and Schwarzkopf, they considered concrete user characteristics: (i) User expertise (domain), (ii) User experience with the underlying system, (iii) trusting propensity, (iv) user experience with recommender systems in general [12].

They found that "past expertise of different kinds appears to be an important factor", influencing the user experience [12]. Their users showed more engaged use of the recommender system in the examined use case. Moreover, they perceived a higher diversity in the results [12]. This can be seen as contributing to a positive user experience. Parra and Brusilovski also found that a higher trusting propensity leads to increased trust in the visualization tools provided. What is interesting is that they found further characteristics like gender and native language to correlate with certain behavior [12], which is to be analyzed further in the next section.

In their online study, Knijnenburg et al. [9] rely on the TasteWeight system for social recommendations. They allow for different levels of control (none, item-control, friend-control) and inspectability (display the whole graph or just a list of results during the inspection phase). Their results show that both control conditions lead to higher system understandability with a notably lower inspection time. This ultimately leads to a higher perceived quality of the recommendations. Furthermore, they discovered a positive effect of trusting propensity on user satisfaction and a negative effect of expertise on user control. But although experts tend to feel less in control, they had higher ratings for perceived recommendation quality and satisfaction with the system [9]. In [8] they compare user satisfaction with different interaction methods: (i) no interaction: list of items by popularity, (ii) sort: sorting a given list by an attribute (from a list of possibilities), (iii) explicit: weighting attributes, (iv) implicit: having weights assigned according to their browsing behavior, (v) hybrid: combination of (iii) and (iv). Each of those interaction techniques corresponds to a concept of decision making [8]. They then tested which interaction method was preferred by users with different levels of certain characteristics: domain knowledge, trusting propensity and persistence.

Indeed, Knijnenburg et al. could confirm their prediction that there was no overall best system, but that users preferred different systems according to their user group. For example, novice users had higher results for perceived control with the first system (where actually they did not have any opportunity of manipulation), whereas experts experienced the least control in this condition. A surprising finding was that the level of perceived control between the other three systems did not differ significantly for experts. Furthermore, as Knijnenburg et al. expected, experts showed the highest user interface satisfaction with the hybrid system, which was the least satisfying for novices [8].

The results for trusting propensity were different from what had been expected beforehand. Different controlling conditions provoked no significant difference for the measured understandability of the system. There was however a positive correlation between trusting propensity and perceived system effectiveness for method (i) no interaction, (iii) explicit, (iv) implicit. Regarding the user interface satisfaction, trusting propensity correlated positively with the explicit and implicit interface. Persistence, i.e. the span between maximizers who strive for the optimal result w.r.t all aspects of their research and satisficers who are content with the first result which matches an acceptance criterion, showed no effect on understandability, perceived effectiveness, control, or user interface satisfaction for any of the conditions [8].

4   Further Possible Factors to Distinguish Appropriate Amount of Control

After reviewing previous work on different user-groups and their control preferences, we would like to point out further possible areas of research which were not covered by previous studies. Also further factors were identified which, in certain circumstances, might have an influence on the amount of control desired by the user.

Recommendation Phase: In the second chapter, different recommendation methods were introduced and assigned to the three key activities - initial preference elicitation, preference refinement, and result displaying - defined by Pu et al. [13]. In order to make a more fine-grained distinction between user needs, we propose that those phases in the recommendation process themselves function as factors which influence the adequate amount of control for a certain user group. We already presented that different recommendation methods offer different opportunities for the user to intervene in the recommendation process and thus control its results. We propose that those ways of interaction are not equally well suited for different user groups, as will be examined further in this chapter. Finally, we will take a closer look at previous findings from different papers and compare and relate their outcomes. Based on this theoretical analysis, further guidelines are proposed for the implementation of control in recommender systems which still might need further confirmation by evaluations.

During Initial Preference Elicitation
In the studies presented in this section, no further differentiation between users was made in order to better understand their needs of control in the first phase of preference elicitation. We took the user characteristics that were examined in the other recommendation phases (preference refinement and result display) and reflected upon their possible interaction with control methods and other relevant factors in the first phase. This reflection leads to the following outcomes.

In preference elicitation the type and nature of the required information has a significant impact on creating the user profile, or creating the item's characteristics within the recommender system. This information can be classified in three categories: personal information, domain-specific information, and context information.

Personal Information: If the initial preference elicitation does not require any prerequisite knowledge, novices, as well as, experts are capable of intervening in the recommendation process by creating a profile and providing personal information. This activity requires low level of cognitive effort. Hence, one could argue that both user groups would appreciate a high level of control. This could be achieved by similar methods to those used by McNee et al. [11] who allowed participants to come up with their own items (in terms of interests, characteristics, etc.) instead of having them rate given options during creation of their profile. This would be an easy and understandable way for users with different levels of domain knowledge to exert control and refine their results. In order to facilitate the task, one could also provide optional suggestions, as in the hybrid interface of [11].

Users who are rather skeptical might also appreciate elaborate control methods that allow them to specify what information to share and what to keep to themselves, as opposed to more trusting users.

Domain-Specific Information: This type of information also elicits and contains personal preferences, but at the same time this kind of information is more specific to their domain of knowledge and operation. In their study, McNee et al. [11] required domain-specific information, when they asked to either rate given films, or to come up with films one has already seen and then rate those. As their results show, users who were given more control in their study tended to be more loyal to the system in a later stage of use. Nevertheless, this focus group had the most participants that gave up on the sign up process. Further examinations of this correlation could provide new knowledge. A possible finding could be (a) that users who were given more control yielded better results and invested more energy in the recommendation process. Both factors that could explain their observed loyalty. One could also argue that (b) given the high rate of people who gave up in the sign up process, only those users who are highly interested in the domain (in this case 'music') were willing to invest more effort into initial preference elicitation. Their loyalty could thus be attributed to their interest in the domain and not to the sign up- and recommendation process.

Based on (b) we would argue that during preference elicitation if domain-specific information is required, experts value an increase in control more than novices.. This suggests that during preference elicitation, it would make sense to confront the user with a "slimmed down interface" which requires a minimal level of interaction, but gives the user the freedom to provide more information, putting in extra effort. The user should always have the opportunity to give up some personalization for more comfort and ease of use. The user thus could cut right to the chase, or take time to configure their profile. If the system in use is designed for a user to come back, it could hint that a later refinement is always possible and/or ask the user if they wanted to make more configurations when they sign in the next time. During the next phase, novices should be given the opportunity to make more elaborate adjustments as their expertise in the domain and the system itself increases (see also next section).

With such two-fold interface, the user may choose their preferred way of preference elicitation. Instead of letting users control content, they are able to control how an entire step in the recommendation process is designed. We are thus proposing a different kind of control method which focuses less on results, but more on the user and their satisfaction with the system. Again, this solution might also be appealing to persons who are less trustful, since they do not have to fill in information, they consider inappropriate.

In this context, we would like to recall the following guideline: The effort a user must invest in the system must be lower than the necessary effort to solve the task manually by himself [11, 12]. In the light of the previous argumentation it is important to differentiate between user groups when it comes to the term effort or "cognitive effort". Cognitive effort is composed differently depending on the user's domain knowledge. A novice already has to put effort in order to cope with the information and causalities inherent to a problem, also referred to as its cognitive load, e.g. by Sweller [15]. Experts, on the other hand, know their way in the domain and have more capacities to invest into system specific control structures. This is why a novice can only be expected to handle a lower amount of control than an expert to achieve their respective goal. This is why, especially on their first encounter with the system, they should be in the position to decide on the complexity they think they can handle. Users could also differ in the goal they want to achieve. To use again the example of a music recommender, the goal to "find new music that I like" could mean different things to different user groups. The criteria (domain specific) that have to be met in order to yield a satisfying result are probably more complex and diverse for an expert than for a novice. This aligns with Pu et al. [13] who suggest in their design guidelines to optimize preference elicitation "to favor a small effort in the initial sign-up process" [13]. Their idea to implement an "incremental preference elicitation method" (see preference refinement phase) is picked up and expanded further by not only allowing them to apply the same intervention methods over and over, but also by providing them with an increasing set of tools for refinement. In our opinion this supports the idea of letting users control part of the recommendation process and their (item specific) control opportunities in order to achieve their respective goals.

Regarding persistence, we would argue that the amount of control available for the user does not play such an important role in the initial recommendation phase. As maximizers and satisficers mainly differ in their interaction with a given set of results, one can conclude that their preferences of control might differ more in a later phase.

Context: Apart from the user preferences, Ekstrand et al. [3] mention "context" as a factor influencing the choice of an appropriate recommendation algorithm. In their study they determine the user's context by relating to their behavior. This means that they exploit indirect user information in order to improve their choice of algorithm. We would consider context more generally as an important factor in the recommendation process. Since during one "recommendation session", the context does not change, or if it does the change is gradual and in most cases user-inspired, we consider it appropriate to define context during preference elicitation. All subsequent iterations of refinement and filtering can be based on the initial definition.

The definition of a context of use is another opportunity for a user to be in control. Contrary to [3], we would suggest allowing users to characterize their context the same way as they are allowed to characterize themselves e.g. in their profile for user modelling. As the user knows best in what context they use the recommender, it seems natural to involve them in the definition of the context created by the recommender system. Especially for distrusting users, it might be a more agreeable option to control the amount of information they share about their context of use (e.g. on a mobile device, for private use, at a certain location, etc.) instead of feeling supervised, or tracked by a system. As with personalization, one could consider offering the user to contribute information or to explicitly allow services like GPS (as seen with mobile apps), tracking user behavior or not to use context information at all. Again, the amount of control could be variable and should be adjustable at any time.

During Preference Refinement

The second phase is the one that was investigated the most with respect to user groups in previous studies. Characteristics like expertise (in both domain and recommender systems), persistence or trusting propensity and their relation with control in recommender systems were already analyzed by Parra and Brusilovski [12] for example. As described earlier, they analyzed those characteristics using SetFusion, which implements several control methods using visual representation and feedback. Knijnenburg et al. [9] investigated in a similar direction: They also examined the level of users' trust, persistence, and expertise using the TasteWeights recommender system. This system also allows the user to interact on a graphical interface and gives visual feedback.

Interface: Although those studies already gave insight into the relation between user characteristics and control, there are several possibilities where further research can be done. First of all, as hinted above, the recommender systems examined in [9, 12] both give control to the user in the form of graphical tools like sliders and diagrams. Critiquing-based recommenders, as described by Chen and Pu [2] follow a different approach which is more based on textual representation of information. It might be worth investigating how given user characteristics like trusting propensity, expertise (recommenders/domain), and persistence influence the amount of control desired in such a system where control is implemented in a different form.

We suggest that, overall, users feel less in control in a more text-based interface, than in a graphical interface like [9, 12]. We base this statement on the fact that in the graphical approach not only the controls are represented graphically, but also their impact is mostly immediately visible on screen (see levels of inspectability in [9]). This parallel display of controls and effect differs notably from critiquing-based recommenders. Those use a rather iterative approach: A list of results can be filtered (more or less flexible) by critiquing single elements and a new list is generated which is then displayed. The relation between a concrete critique of an attribute is harder to track in the newly generated list because it puts cognitive load on the user, and on the other hand, changes cannot be reverted as easily as in [9, 12].

Nevertheless, we would predict that more control, as exemplified by Chen and Pu in their "example critiquing interface" [2] would be appreciated by both novices and experts. Their example critiquing interface allows freely combining critiquing units to customized compound critiques. As they explain themselves, similarity-based critiquing ("give me similar items"), quality-based critiquing ("items like this but cheaper") and quantity-based critiquing ("items like this but $100 cheaper") can all be modelled through their interface [2]. This allows a user to be vague and unspecific in their critiques, depending on their goals and previous knowledge. In this situation, novices have the choice of starting with critiquing units or they can freely combine them. Compared to predefined compound critiques, this avoids the fear of changing undesired values, by picking a compound critique that does not fit well. For experts the freedom of choice w.r.t attributes and values gives them the opportunity to leverage their domain knowledge in order to find the most fitting result in few steps.

The process of filtering on the basis of a more personally tailored set of results, which is possible with increased control in critiquing-based recommender systems should be highly appreciated by maximizers, who have a high level of persistence. With the opportunity to fine-tune given results in any possible way, their striving for "the best" possible outcome should be best supported with a high amount of control as in the example critiquing interface [2]. User with a lower level of persistence might appreciate this opportunity as well, but will probably be equally satisfied when presented only with less control like in the dynamic- (system-proposed-) critiquing interface.

Goal/Context of Use: As during the process of preference elicitation, it could also be beneficial to give a sort of "meta control" to the user in the phase of preference refinement: instead of letting the user control attributes of the recommended items, it might be helpful to give the user a choice on how preference refinement is implemented. The reason for this proposition can be illustrated by the case of critiquing-based recommender systems: Critiquing-based recommender engines implement preference refinement as a process of further and further refining queries and narrowing down results. In order to do so, the values of an items attribute can be refined in each iteration of critiquing. This approach can be a strength and a weakness at the same time. It depends on the goal or context of use of the recommender system. If a user is searching for a specific item (e.g. something to purchase on an e-commerce platform) as in [2], the critiquing approach is promising. It helps the user in getting more and more specific results by narrowing down the result set w.r.t certain attributes. This can be accomplished, even if the user is not that familiar with the domain or start his search with a vague idea of how exactly the item will be. If, on the other hand, the user hopes for a variety of different, surprising items (e.g. in a music recommender), critiquing might be unsuitable to achieve this goal. Depending on the context of use, the concept of controlling-based recommenders can be more or less suited. In general, we would identify a user's goal in the recommendation process as a factor that could influence the appropriate type of control or recommendation concept to present to the user. Since this goal can change from session to session, it might be reasonable to allow user to change the default control method to a more convenient one during preference refinement.

Upon Result Display

During result display, one must keep in mind that any form of control that can be given to the user does not influence given recommendations as such. In the result display phase, the user gets to interact with the results of his query. We therefore divide the interaction into the following processes: (i) *getting an overview* of the result set,

(ii) *inspecting the features* of a specific result, (iii) *comparing items* (e.g. common/different attributes and values) (iv) finding out *reasons for the recommendation* (v) *choosing a result*. They have been identified based on processes in the related work:

  (i) *Overview*: The first one is obvious, since there must be a way to inspect all results produced during the process. It is further supported by Knijnenburg et al. [9] who accentuate the advantages of displaying the relationships between recommendation results and the users' configurations of the system [9] in an overview

 (ii) *Feature inspection*: The second is based on Pu et al. [13]: They explain that supplementary information displayed with an item "may have significant impact on user satisfaction and confidence" [13]. This indicates that (ii) is a recurring activity upon result display.

(iii) *Result Comparison*: This phase must precede the choice of a result (v)

 (iv) *Reasons for Recommendation*: Pu et al. [13] also name *finding out the reasons for recommendation* (iv) as a criterion for good interfaces. Also, the interfaces of SetFusion [12], SmallWorlds [4] or TasteWeights [1] explicitly put focus on visualizing how a recommendation was created, which also supports (iv) as an important activity. Another indicator for the importance of reviewing this process upon result display.

  (v) *Choosing a result*: This directly follows from the recommender systems nature of being a "decision support tool" [13].

Any control method in the result display activity should be designed to support the user in at least one of the processes (i)–(v). We suppose that specifically for distrusting people, transparency of the recommendation process is an important issue. For users with a low level of trusting propensity it is more important to inspect how a result was created, than for other users. Consequently, more control w.r.t (iv) is requested by distrusting users. One can also argue that users with high persistence would benefit from more control in finding out about the reasons for a recommendation. Generally, since maximizers are more likely to inspect and compare a great variety of results, it would make sense that they would request an increased level of control supporting all processes (i)–(v).

Design of Control Mechanisms: Regarding different levels of (domain) expertise, one should take into account the representation of controls as a factor which influences the amount of control requested by a user. We expect a carefully designed, explorable graphical representation of the recommendations to help the user in understanding how results were created. Furthermore, interacting with the results on a graphical interface could help users get better insight into the referred domain. This could reveal factors in the recommendation process which the user did not consider as relevant before. Such a learning process could result in an increase in domain expertise, and thus a further improvement of the configurations and of the recommendations. For novices, we specifically see the potential for such a process in a graphical user interface, which is why they could benefit from more control, under the precondition that the tools they use are easy to handle. The same holds for the graphical representation of the result set as such: Visual indicators such as links, colors and proximity for example are easier to read than text. They can convey meaning which the users may be unable to discover themselves without further support of the system. Especially novices in a domain might lack previous knowledge which is necessary to put given results into context. Verbert et al. [14] made an observation which supports this idea: TalkExplorer uses colors, connections and proximity in its result display, as explained above. Their results show that users gain more insight than when using a ranked list [14]. Parra and Brusilovski made another observation, which leads to a more general interpretation: they observed that native speakers tended to use less interactions than non-natives [12]. On a more general level, one could say that the graphical tools were easier to understand and use, than to accomplish the task on their own for people being at some kind of disadvantage. This disadvantage can be a language-barrier, lack of prerequisite knowledge, or other factors. Therefore, one could argue that users with disadvantages tend to rely more on controlling mechanisms in order to explore the domain and facilitate the task they are working on. Yet this is only the case if those control mechanisms are easy to understand and can be handled intuitively, thus reducing cognitive load. This idea is supported by the observations of Parra and Brusilovski [12]: they found that more items were selected from the results, when control methods (sliders and Venn diagram) were used on the result display. But they also found that the sliders were used more frequently than the diagram to narrow down the results. This supports the hypothesis that less ordinary mechanisms are used less often, at least upon the first encounter. We would attribute this to the fact that unknown graphical representations require cognitive effort, which is a sparse resource and needs to be spent on the resolution of the task itself. Experts, according to this reasoning, might not be so fond of many graphical tuning methods. As they understand the domain, they do not need as much support in interpreting the results they are presented with.

5 Conclusion

Throughout the previous sections we tried to explain, the claim that an increase in control is always appreciated by users of recommender systems cannot be accepted in its universality. Results from previous research showed that for specific user groups, more control does not necessarily result in higher user satisfaction. So far, recurring attributes that are used to differentiate between user groups are domain or system expertise, trusting propensity and persistence. By putting given results in the context of the three key activities of the recommendation process, preference elicitation, preference refinement and result display, it became clear that there are many cases in which the relationship between those user characteristics and the need for control remains unexamined. For those cases we offered suggestions and predictions based on more general research on control in recommender systems. Furthermore, for the three phases, additional factors could be identified that potentially distinguish further user groups: The nature of information required by the user and the context of use during preference elicitation, the interface in use and again the context or goal of use during preference refinement, and finally the design of control mechanisms upon result display. Those may also influence user satisfaction.

The guidelines formulated in this paper are merely of theoretical nature. However, they are based on an extensive review of existing work in the field. To empirically examine their validity could pose a starting point for new research to improve users' control in recommender systems.

Acknowledgements. The authors thank the German Research Council DFG for the friendly support of the research in the excellence cluster "Integrative Production Technology in High Wage Countries".

References

1. Bostandjiev, S., O'Donovan, J., Höllerer, T.: TasteWeights: a visual interactive hybrid recommender system. In: Proceedings of the Sixth ACM Conference on Recommender Systems, Dublin, Ireland, 09–13 September 2012, RecSys 2012, pp. 35–42. ACM, New York. https://doi.org/10.1145/2365952.2365964
2. Chen, L., Pu, P.: Evaluating critiquing-based recommender agents. In: Proceedings of the 21st National Conference on Artificial Intelligence, vol. 1, p. 157. AAAI Press/MIT Press, London/Cambridge (1999, 2006)
3. Ekstrand, M.D., Kluver, D., Harper, F.M., Konstan, J.A.: Letting users choose recommender algorithms: an experimental study. In: Proceedings of the 9th ACM Conference on Recommender Systems, Vienna, Austria, 16–20 September 2015, RecSys 2015, pp. 11–18. ACM, New York (2015). https://doi.org/10.1145/2792838.2800195
4. Gretarsson, B., O'Donovan, J., Bostandjiev, S., Hall, C., Höllerer, T.: Smallworlds: visualizing social recommendations. Comput. Graph. Forum **29**(3), 833–842 (2010). Blackwell. http://dx.doi.org/10.1111/j.1467-8659.2009.01679.x
5. Harper, F.M, Xu, F., Kaur, H., Condiff, K., Chang, S., Terveen, L.: Putting users in control of their recommendations. In: Proceedings of the 9th ACM Conference on Recommender Systems, Vienna, Austria, 16–20 September 2015, RecSys 2015, pp. 3–10. ACM, New York (2015). https://doi.org/10.1145/2792838.2800179
6. Hijikata, Y., Kai, Y., Nishida, S.: The relation between user intervention and user satisfaction for information recommendation. In: Proceedings of the 27th Annual ACM Symposium on Applied Computing, Trento, Italy, 26–30 March 2012, SAC 2012, pp. 2002–2007. ACM, New York (2012). https://doi.org/10.1145/2245276.2232109
7. Jameson, A., Schwarzkopf, E.: Pros and cons of controllability: an empirical study. In: Bra, P., Brusilovsky, P., Conejo, R. (eds.) AH 2002. LNCS, vol. 2347, pp. 193–202. Springer, Heidelberg (2002). doi:10.1007/3-540-47952-X_21
8. Knijnenburg, B.P., Reijmer, N.J., Willemsen, M.C.: Each to his own: how different users call for different interaction methods in recommender systems. In: Proceedings of the Fifth ACM Conference on Recommender Systems, Chicago, Illinois, USA, 23–27 October 2011, RecSys 2011, pp. 141–148. ACM, New York (2011). https://doi.org/10.1145/2043932.2043960
9. Knijnenburg, B.P., Bostandjiev, S., O'Donovan, J., Kobsa, A.: Inspectability and control in social recommenders. In: Proceedings of the Sixth ACM Conference on Recommender Systems, Dublin, Ireland, 09–13 September 2012, RecSys 2012, pp. 43–50. ACM, New York (2012). https://doi.org/10.1145/2365952.2365966

10. Loepp, B., Hussein, T., Ziegler, J.: Choice-based preference elicitation for collaborative filtering recommender systems. In: Proceedings of the SIGCHI Conference on Human Factors in Computing Systems, Toronto, Ontario, Canada, 26 April–01 May 2014, CHI 2014, pp. 3085–3094. ACM, New York (2014). https://doi.org/10.1145/2556288.2557069

11. McNee, S.M., Lam, S.K., Konstan, J.A., Riedl, J.: Interfaces for eliciting new user preferences in recommender systems. In: Brusilovsky, P., Corbett, A., Rosis, F. (eds.) UM 2003. LNCS (LNAI), vol. 2702, pp. 178–187. Springer, Heidelberg (2003). doi:10.1007/3-540-44963-9_24

12. Parra, D., Brusilovsky, P.: User-controllable personalization. A case study with SetFusion. Int. J. Hum.-Comput. Stud. **78**, 43–67 (2015). doi:10.1016/j.ijhcs.2015.01.007. Elsevier

13. Pu, P., Chen, L., Hu, R.: Evaluating recommender systems from the user's perspective. Survey of the state of the art. User Model. User-Adapt. Interact. **22**(4–5), 317–355 (2012). doi:10.1007/s11257-011-9115-7. Springer

14. Verbert, K., Parra, D., Brusilovsky, P., Duval, E.: Visualizing recommendations to support exploration, transparency and controllability. In: Proceedings of the 2013 International Conference on Intelligent User Interfaces, Santa Monica, California, USA, 19–22 March 2013, IUI 2013, pp. 351–362. ACM, New York (2013). https://doi.org/10.1145/2449396.2449442

15. Sweller, J.: Element interactivity and intrinsic, extraneous, and germane cognitive load. Educ. Psychol. Rev. **22**(2), 123–138 (2010). doi:10.1007/s10648-010-9128-5. Springer US

16. Valdez, A.C., Ziefle, M., Verbert, K.: HCI for recommender systems: the past, the present and the future. In: Proceedings of the 10th ACM Conference on Recommender Systems, Boston, Massachusetts, USA, 15–19 September 2016, RecSys 2016, pp. 123–126. ACM, New York (2016). https://doi.org/10.1145/2959100.2959158

A Study on the Odor in "Omotenashi", Japanese Hospitality

Harumi Nakagawa[1] and Noriaki Kuwahara[2(✉)]

[1] Salon de Harufun KYOTO, Kyoto, Japan
yhsnaka@sirius.ocn.ne.jp
[2] Kyoto Institute of Technology, Kyoto, Japan
nkuwahar@kit.ac.jp

Abstract. In Japan, there are many songs and stories about fragrances in classical literature. In addition to burning incense in Buddhism rituals, Japanese created a unique world so called "Kodo." This also shows that the Japanese have been in history with scents. Regarding the aroma of hospitality, it is necessary to consider the preference of the scent when greeting people. In order to know the preference to the scent of hospitality and Japanese traditional culture, we conducted the questionnaire survey to Japanese males and females using different fragrances of different types and examined the results.

Keywords: Odor · Perfume · Japanese hospitality · Japanese tradition

1 Introduction

The history of fragrance is as old as time. There are a vast number of scents in the world. It is often said that humans can feel and differentiate between about 40,000 kinds of scents [1]. The variety of reactions that scents can bring to living things are immeasurable. Also, scents can sometimes be harmful. However, it is essential for human beings to have their own signature fragrance. A vast amount of scientific information is naturally coded into many perfumes [2]. The etymology of "perfume" stems from Latin "per-" and "fumum."

People feel happy when they experience a pleasant scent. On the other hand, people feel uncomfortable when they sniff an unpleasant stench. We Japanese value our own unique sense of hospitality: "Omotenashi," very much. And we often enjoy using a variety of scents in our daily lives. We enjoy scents by ourselves and our family. Sometimes we use fragrances as part of our unique sense of hospitality.

We make original perfumes based off of other people's preferences, and depending on the season, and depending on the unique atmosphere of our house, we make our selection and transfuse fragrances into a piece of test paper in order to produce the scent. In addition, we burn incense, sprinkle room fragrance, and even use aroma diffusers, aroma pots, and aroma oil etc.

By creating a custom scent, we create a specifically relaxed atmosphere, glamor and personality. We always gauge our guests' reaction at that time, and we try to make a mental note for the next time we will create a unique scent.

© Springer International Publishing AG 2017
V.G. Duffy (Ed.): DHM 2017, Part I, LNCS 10286, pp. 324–335, 2017.
DOI: 10.1007/978-3-319-58463-8_27

In Japan, there are many songs and stories about fragrances in classical literature. In addition to the incense burned in the Buddhist ceremony, we Japanese also have created a unique imaginary world called "Koudo." That allows us to enjoy fragrances in their original form. The fragrance creates a special atmosphere and takes people to a comfortable and dreamy world [3]. This also shows that the Japanese have been with experimenting with fragrances for a long, long time. At every stage of life, each scent represents our state of mind. The heart of our hospitality and fragrances are deeply connected.

In hospitality-inspired scents, while entertaining people, it is necessary to consider the preference of the scent to the nose of the beholder. In order to properly identify their taste, we used different types of perfume and conducted a questionnaire survey on Japanese men and women. Afterwards, we analyzed the results and verified the tendency towards people's hospitality and Japanese aroma.

2 Method

2.1 Incense Tones Used in the Experiment

A note is a word used to express the category to which a scent may belong. Each note has its own style, but because the classification of incense tone has its own categorization for perfume companies and organizations, it is not necessarily scientifically correct. First of all, we will introduce 11 representative notes as shown below. Each of notes appears frequently in every perfume recipe. By grasping the characteristics of the scent, it becomes possible to catch the image of the perfume more specifically [4]. This time, we used five kinds of fragrance, 'green' notes, 'citrus' notes, 'floral' notes, 'woody' notes, and 'chypre' notes. Attached is a list of commonly used notes.

1. Green note: fresh, clean, natural, gentle, intellectual
2. Citrus notes: fresh, cool feeling, refreshing, cheerful, youthful
3. Floral notes: elegant, romantic, soft, gorgeous
4. Fruity note: cute, juicy, cheerful, youthful
5. Woody note: serene, delicate, mysterious, quiet, calm
6. Chypre note: sophisticated, elegant, chic, grown up
7. Fougere note: dandyish, typical scent for men, elegant, deep
8. Marine note: fresh, light, reminiscent of the ocean, sky and the universe, transparent, open-minded
9. Gourmand note: pretty, unique, youthful, sweet
10. Spicy note: originality, powerful, impact, warm
11. Oriental note: smooth, sexy, passionate

2.2 Scents Used for a Questionnaire Survey

In this experiment, we used five different notes (A to E) below and conducted a questionnaire survey.

(A) SAMSARA Guerlain 1989 (Woody Note) Eau De Toilette
Samsara is a Sanskrit word, meaning 'a never-ending cycle of life and death;' that is, a journey to the state of Nirvana. The secret ingredient of Samsara is the usage of Jean Paul's 'Sandalwood.' Since sandalwood overpowers our olfactory organs, it is notorious as a fragrance that is hard to handle. It disappears almost immediately after sniffing. Although it may seem contradictory, there is a tenacious strength and scent retention, so it keeps down the fragrance used together. The composition opens with a spread of bergamot which is typical of Guerlain, and abundant jasmine of middle note spreads with accents of rose, narcissus, and ylang ylang. The fragrance moves on to a strong finish with sandalwood, vanilla, coumarin [5].

(B) DIORISSIMO Dior 1956 (Floral notes) Eau De Toilette
Diorissimo smells extremely refreshing. With a freshness reminiscent of fresh greens, it gives the patient the sense that the fragrance came directly from the ground. The fragrance lingers for a long while, reminding the beholder of the flowering of delicate flowers. Then, just as that same splendid fragrance that melts your heart appeared, it disappears like waking from a dream. Roudnitska blended lilac, jasmine, and rose to express this scent, and made faint a deep forest with civet and sandalwood. Diorissimo is a magical perfume [6].

(C) No. 19 Chanel 1970 (Green note) Eau De Toilette
No. 19 uses sandalwood and oak moss accents, but weakens the usual sweetness of 'Lily of the Valley,' 'Rose de Mai' and 'Jasmine of the Middle' in a slight leather and musk. In addition hyacinth exudes freshness [7].

(D) MITSUKO Guerlain 1919 (Chypre note) Eau De Toilette
'Mitsuko' begins with the crystal clear aroma of bergamot, and a harmonius mix of synthetic peach, rose, and a jasmine spread. The Fragrance settles on notes of oakmoss, vetiver, cedar wood, black pepper, cinnamon, and ambergris. There are many other famous perfumes inspired by Mitsuko. Mitsukois a common Japanese woman's name; specifically, it is a heroine of Farrell's "La Bataille." Mitsuko was the wife of Japanese navy general but was also in love with a young British naval officer. Since Mitsuko couldn't express her feeling to him, it was kept secret in the heart [8].

(E) CARON PARIS (Citrus note) Eau De Toilette
Caron was introduced in 1904 by Ernesto Daltrov, at a perfume shop in Paris. It is a Maison Fragrance brand that always draws from the traditional fragrances and maintains it's position as an innovative producer in the field. We have proposed a unique and fragile fragrance that cannot be imitated by outsiders using only the highest quality essences. This signature fragrance will frequently remind the beholder of dreams or something unforgettable. Caron understands the perfume as a work of art deeply and continues to fascinate women [9]. It is a citric fragrance and because it is a unisex fragrance, it is characterized by a light gentle fragrance that can be used by both men and women.

2.3   Participants of a Questionnaire Survey

A total of 59 participants took part in the questionnaire survey (23 males and 36 females). The average age of males and females are 45.4 and 32.2, respectively.

2.4   Method of a Questionnaire Survey

We distributed a set of 6 sheets of questionnaires with a pencil and eraser to the participants. The first piece of the questionnaire is a description formula for the purpose of investigating participant's awareness of scent (Appendix A). The second to sixth questionnaires are for evaluating the impression of five types of scents A, B, C, D, and E. For that reason, we selected 22 different sensuously stimulating words for the fragrance images used in evaluating five kinds of scents A to E. I also prepared two questions asking whether participants felt nostalgic about Japanese hospitality or Japanese tradition from the scents. Regarding each scent, participants gave scores between +3 and −3 points for each sentiment word and were evaluated. Finally, with free description, we asked participants the impression of scent (Appendix B).

We installed five types of scented bottles on the mount written as A, B, C, D, and E as shown in Fig. 1.

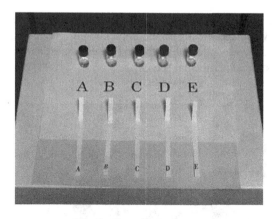

Fig. 1. Experimental setup

We asked one of the participants to decide the order in which to distribute the 5 scents; afterwards, half of the participants evaluated the scents in that order and the other half did in the opposite order.

As soon as prep was completed, the participants started questionnaires. We took the participants and administered the first scent around the end of the first description questionnaire. The fragrance was attached to the tip of the test paper. Participants brought the fragrance-attached parts of the test paper close to their noses and sniffed the fragrance slowly. After the smelling portion had finished, we ask the participants to answer the questionnaire.

As for the way of testing scents, we demonstrated how to smell using the test paper as shown in Fig. 2. When the participants finished describing the evaluation questionnaire of their impression of one scent, we administered the next scent.

Fig. 2. Method of testing a scent

Since the questionnaire consists of one question for one scent, we asked participants to answer singularly and specifically on the impression of the fragrance in and of itself, not comparing. Finally, we collected all the test papers, questionnaires and fragrances. Figure 3 shows the experimental scene.

Fig. 3. Experiments being performed

2.5   Data Analysis Method

In this paper, we focus on the questionnaire items of No. 23: "Do you feel as if these scents are traditionally Japanese?", and No. 24: "Do you feel as if these scents are reminiscent of Japanese hospitality fragrances?" We investigated the impressions of Japanese tradition and hospitality that were felt per each scent that was smelled. We also examined whether those impressions were different for males and females.

3 Results of a Questionnaire Survey

3.1 Correlation Between Feelings of Japanese Tradition and Hospitality

We show the three-dimensional histogram of Japanese traditional and hospitality evaluation values in Fig. 4. We calculated Pearson's product-to-moment correlation using the results of Japanese tradition and hospitality by using R system. As a result, we obtained a correlation coefficient of 0.57 with p < 0.01. From the feedback, we discovered a moderate correlation between the sense of Japanese tradition and the hospitality assessment of the scents.

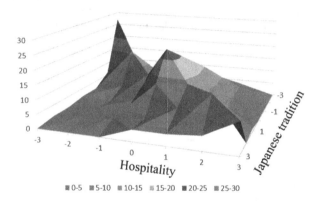

Fig. 4. Three-dimensional histogram of Japanese traditional and hospitality evaluation values

3.2 Result of Hospitality Feeling

We examined the results of the hospitality nostalgia survey against the 5 scents, and whether there is a difference in the evaluation scores between the scents. First, we performed a Bartlett test to investigate the size of the variance between each level of the scent factors, and we discovered that the variances correlated statistically ($p > 0.05$). Next, by a one-way analysis of the variances, we tested whether there was any significant difference in the average value of each level of scent factor. As a result, a statistically significant difference was recognized ($p < 0.05$). Finally, multiple comparisons were carried out by the Bonferroni method. There was a significant difference only between D and B as shown Fig. 5 ($p < 0.05$). We conducted a two-way analysis of variances by scent factors and gender factors. As a result, it was recognized that there was a statistically significant difference in both the scent factor and gender factor ($p < 0.05$). There was no interaction between scent factor and gender factor ($p > 0.05$).

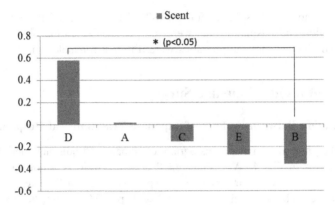

Fig. 5. Result of hospitality feeling

In order to observe the difference in gender factor, we compared the results of the male group and female group as shown in Figs. 6 and 7, respectively. We performed a one-way analysis of the variances in order to test whether there was a significant

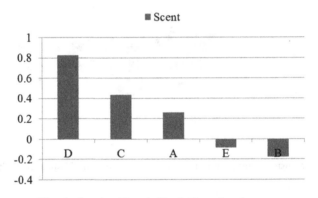

Fig. 6. Result of hospitality feeling of male group

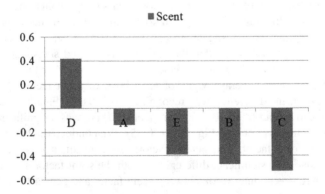

Fig. 7. Result of hospitality feeling of female group

difference in the average value of each level of scent factor. As a result, no statistically significant difference was recognized in either group (p > 0.05).

Result of Japanese Traditional Feeling

We examined the evaluation results of Japanese traditional feelings per the 5 scents, and gauge whether there is a difference in the evaluation scores between the scents. Firstly, we performed Bartlett test to investigate the equality of the variance between each level of the scent factor, and showed that each level of the scent factor had the equality of the variance statistically (p > 0.05). Next, by one-way analysis of variance, we tested whether there was a significant difference in the average value of each level of scent factor. As a result, a statistically significant difference was recognized (p < 0.01). Finally, multiple comparisons were carried out per the Bonferroni method (p < 0.01). There was a significant difference only between D and other scents as shown Fig. 8. We conducted a two-way analysis of variance by scent factor and gender factor. As a result, it was recognized that there was a statistically significant difference in the scent factor (p < 0.01), but no significant difference in gender factor (p > 0.05). There was no interaction between scent factor and gender factor (p > 0.05).

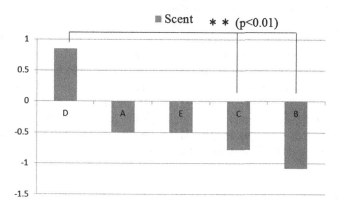

Fig. 8. Result of Japanese tradition feeling

4 Discussion

A correlation was found in the evaluation of the feedback regarding hospitality and Japanese tradition feelings. The reason for this is presumed to be that Japanese people have a nostalgic feeling of hospitality, ingrained as a part Japanese tradition. In addition, D: MITSUKO has gained high scores in both hospitality and Japanese tradition feelings. As for Japanese tradition feeling, the score of B: DIORISSIMO was low for both male and female groups. There was no significant difference in hospitality feeling, but it is interesting that the score of C: No. 19 was different for both males and females; males' average score of C was higher than females' average score of C.

No. 19 was reviewed favorably by both men and women because of the refreshing fragrance of Galvanum (parsley family of plants), but notably men prefer the Galvanum scent most of all. Galvanum is sometimes made as an image of that green tea. Green tea is preferred all over the world. There are also many perfumes using the smell of green tea. It can be said that No. 19 has the fragrance of the image of green tea that the Japanese prefers to drink. By thinking about green tea, it seems that men felt a stronger sense of hospitality than the females. There is also a masculine note in the green fragrance, which is also considered to be a reason why the men chose No. 19 as hospitable scent.

In this questionnaire survey, we chose scents which used such as sandalwood and cedar wood (Pinaceae/Japanese cypress) in consideration of the scent of Japan and the scent of hospitality. Sandalwood is said to be of high quality, especially incense from Mysore, India, which is most frequently used as a material indispensable for incense and odor even at present.

According to the result of the questionnaire survey of this time, the reason why D got a positive impression as a scent that makes one feel a sense of hospitality and Japanese tradition is because a woody scent was felt; which is a characteristic often associated with Japanese tradition and hospitality. And such a scent is featured in Chypre note. In other words, any fragrance that gives off the impression of Japanese tradition and hospitality is deeply connected.

Japanese people seem to be seen amongst images of tree and forest scents. For Europeans who live in houses made of stone, it might be immensely charming to live in houses made of wood. The scent of the Hinoki (Japanese cypress) bath calms down for the Japanese people. The history of the Japanese use of fragrance began with the arrival of Buddhism in 538 A.D. "Kunkou," which burned fragrant wood, resin or balsam and so on would have been the beginning. Of course, in Japan as in other countries, the incense of the religious ceremony was indispensable as an important instrument that creates a mysterious atmosphere [10]. Knowing this, it can be understood that the existence of tree scents are inherent in the Japanese tradition.

5 Conclusion

A questionnaire survey was conducted on 60 male and female scents perceived and their effect on the recalling of nostalgia, specifically Japanese tradition and hospitality. D: Mitsuko got a significantly higher score for Japanese tradition and hospitality feelings out of five scents as to be tested. D: Mitsuko is a Chypre note, a smell of wood, a smell of forest. It is suggested that Japanese tradition and hospitality are deeply linked to the scent of wood and the scent of forest for Japanese.

Appendix A

(Questionnaire 1)

☆ Date   year   month   day   hour   min

☆ Gender   (male ·female)   ☆ Age (years old)

1 · Are you sensitive to scents?   (Yes · No)

2 · Are you interested in scents?   (Yes · No)

3 · Is your physical condition good today?   (Yes · No)

4 · Do you feel good today?   (Yes · No)

5 · Do scents make you better?   (Yes · No)

6 · Do scents make you brighter?   (Yes · No)

7 · Did you have enough sleep?   (Yes · No)

8 · Are you hungry?   (Yes · No)

9 · What kind of scents do you like? (   )

10 · Why do you like these scents? (   )

11 · Is perfume necessary for everyday life?   (Yes · No)

12 · Do you like a perfume?   (Yes · No)

13 · Are you wearing perfume every day?   (Yes · No)

14 · Have you ever worn perfume?   (Yes · No)

15 · When do you put perfume? (   )

16 · What do you feel about the difference between when you add perfume and when you do not have it?
(   )

17 · For what do you put perfume? (   )

18 · What do you imagine of the scent of Japan? (   )

19 · What do you imagine of the scent of hospitality? (   )

20 · Where do you think the scent is most necessary? (   )

Thank you for your cooperation.   Perfumer · Harumi Nakagawa

Appendix B

(Questionnaire 1)   ★for scents of A~E

1	Like	+3	2	1	0	1	2	−3	Dislike
2	Pleasant	+3	2	1	0	1	2	−3	Unpleasant
3	Comfortable	+3	2	1	0	1	2	−3	Uncomfortable
4	Strong	+3	2	1	0	1	2	−3	Weak
5	Light	+3	2	1	0	1	2	−3	Heavy
6	Masculine	+3	2	1	0	1	2	−3	Feminine
7	Powdery	+3	2	1	0	1	2	−3	Oily
8	Sweet	+3	2	1	0	1	2	−3	Bitter
9	Clear	+3	2	1	0	1	2	−3	Fuzzy
10	Dry	+3	2	1	0	1	2	−3	Moist
11	Refreshing	+3	2	1	0	1	2	−3	Annoying
12	Gentle	+3	2	1	0	1	2	−3	Sharp
13	Clean	+3	2	1	0	1	2	−3	Messy
14	Elegant	+3	2	1	0	1	2	−3	Wild
15	Graceful	+3	2	1	0	1	2	−3	Cheap
16	Adult-like	+3	2	1	0	1	2	−3	Childish
17	Mature	+3	2	1	0	1	2	−3	Immature
18	Young	+3	2	1	0	1	2	−3	Old
19	Calm	+3	2	1	0	1	2	−3	Violent
20	Sensual	+3	2	1	0	1	2	−3	Neat
21	Oriental	+3	2	1	0	1	2	−3	Western
22	Positive	+3	2	1	0	1	2	−3	Negative
23	Japanese tradition feeling	+3	2	1	0	1	2	−3	No Japanese tradition feeling
24	Hospitality feeling	+3	2	1	0	1	2	−3	No Hospitality feeling
25	What do you feel this scent?	(							)

Thank you for your cooperation.   Perfumer・Harumi Nakagawa

References

1. Tonosaki, K.: The Identity of the Smell and Flavor, p. 32. Seishun Publishing Company, Tokyo (2004)
2. Dove, R.: The Essence of Perfume, p. 2. Hara Publishing Company, Bothell (2010)
3. Shoyeido: Book of Smell, p. 2. Kodansha Ltd. Publishers, Tokyo (1990)
4. Shinma, M.: The Golden Rules of Perfume, pp. 30–31. Hara Publishing Company, Bothell (2010)
5. Dove, R.: The Essence of Perfume, pp. 190–191. Hara Publishing Company, Bothell (2010)
6. Dove, R.: The Essence of Perfume, pp. 150–151. Hara Publishing Company, Bothell (2010)
7. Dove, R.: The Essence of Perfume, p. 167. Hara Publishing Company, Bothell (2010)
8. Dove, R.: The Essence of Perfume, pp. 105–106. Hara Publishing Company, Bothell (2010)
9. http://www.concent.co.jp/category/caron/?utm_source=overture&utm_medium=cpc. Accessed 28 Feb 2017
10. Arai, S., Kobayashi, A., Kawasaki, M., Yajima, I.: Encyclopedia of Perfume and Flavor Materials, p. 73. Asakura Publishing Company, Tokyo (2000)

Delivering Personalized Information to Individuals in Super Smart Society

Kentaro Noda[1]([✉]), Yoshihiro Wada[1], Sachio Saiki[1], Masahide Nakamura[1], and Kiyoshi Yasuda[2]

[1] Graduate School of System Informatics, Kobe University, 1-1 Rokkodai, Nada, Kobe, Japan
{noda,wada}@ws.cs.kobe-u.ac.jp, sachio@carp.kobe-u.ac.jp, masa-n@cs.kobe-u.ac.jp
[2] Chiba Rosai Hospital, 2-16 Tatsumidai-higashi, Ichihara, Japan
fwkk5911@mb.infoweb.ne.jp

Abstract. In the emerging super smart society, the flood of large-scale and heterogeneous information makes the digital divide in information reception a more serious problem. In this paper, we present a service, called Tales of Familiar (ToF), which autonomously delivers personalized information to individual end users in the super smart society. In ToF, every user is associated with a *familiar*, which is an agent working as an exclusive partner of the user. ToF first generates tales, which are narratives delivered by the familiar, from various information sources, such as direct messages, Web information, sensors, and SNS. The generated tales are sifted for individual users based on personal preferences of the users. Finally, the familiar delivers the selected tales using voice, text or images in an appropriate timing. In this paper, we particularly study the concept, the overall architecture, and data schema of ToF.

1 Introduction

With the rapid advancement of IoT (Internet of Things) [6,7] and cloud computing [2] technologies, the Japanese government has announced the *realization of a super smart society* [4] in 2020 as a part of the 5th Science and Technology Basic Plan. The super smart society is the next-generation society, where heterogeneous systems are inter-connected over cyber and physical spaces, to provide advance and sophisticated services for individual citizens. In the announcement of the Japanese government, the super smart society is expected as a future society, which uses ever more emerging technologies such as robots, AI, bigdata, IoT and novel network devices. Thus, the plan creates the greatest impact on past economy and society.

It can be imagined easily, in the super smart society, that there would be a great flood of large-scale and heterogeneous information, which is incomparable with the current society. Without proper treatment, *digital divide* would be more serious between people who can use the information well and ones who cannot.

© Springer International Publishing AG 2017
V.G. Duffy (Ed.): DHM 2017, Part I, LNCS 10286, pp. 336–347, 2017.
DOI: 10.1007/978-3-319-58463-8_28

Thus, to survive the super smart society, technologies with which one can appropriately collect, analyze and utilize the information become more important.

Towards the oncoming super smart society where large-scale and heterogeneous information are produced, we especially focus on the following three problems with respect to the *information reception by human users*.

Problem P1 (Barrier of Active Access to Information)
Currently, when a user wants to get information, the user has to access the data source *actively by himself*. To find desired information, the user must perform information search with a PC or a smartphone. However, it is difficult for an elderly person or a physically challenged person to search the information, and even to use such high-tech devices with complicated operations.

Problem P2 (Complexity of Identifying Relevant Information)
The super smart society produces and delivers a massive amount of information. However, the actually useful information varies among users, time, contexts, and locations. With the increase of irrelevant information, it becomes more difficult for every user to identify relevant information.

Problem P3 (Discomfort for Mass-Oriented Expression)
Generally, information is expressed in a popularized style, so that all information receivers (including human users and machines) can recognize it easily. For this, the information sender does not consider how *individual* receivers feel with respect to the way of writing. Thus, there is a possibility that a receiver feels uncomfortable by its expression, even if the receiver reaches desired information.

To cope with Problems P1, P2, and P3, this paper proposes a new service, called *Tales of Familiar* (hereinafter, called *ToF* for short), which autonomously provides information exclusively relevant to a given user. Intuitively, a *tale* refers to a narrative (or story) generated from an information source, so that the original information is easily received by the user. A *familiar* originally means a fairy that belongs exclusively to a human master, or a very close friend. Thus, ToF is a service where an agent (as a familiar) always stays by a user and provides exclusively relevant information (as tales) for the user.

The proposed service ToF mainly consists of three parts. First, as a solution to Problem P3, we propose the *tale generation service*. This service produces tales automatically or manually from various information sources in the super smart society. The information sources include direct messages, Web pages, sensors, smart systems, and SNS. A tale is a narrative derived from an information source and is expressed in familiar's spoken language. The tale generation service translates the original information in the mass-oriented expression into the one with more friendly and personalized expression.

Second, to cope with Problem P2, we propose the *tale sifting service*. From massively generated tales, the tale sifting service sifts (i.e., selects) only relevant tales appropriate for the user at that time. The criteria of the sift is based on the preference and context of the user.

Finally, we develop the *familiar* to address Problem P1. A familiar is an agent that autonomously speaks selected tales to the user. It is implemented in a form of a robot, a virtual agent, or an IoT-embedded stuffed doll. A familiar tells a selected tale to a user in an appropriate timing. Thus, relevant information is automatically delivered in a preferred expression. So the user does not have to search desired information actively any more.

In this paper, we especially present the concept of ToF, the architecture with essential components, and features of each component. More specifically, we first discuss definitions of the tale, the tale generation service, the tale sifting service, and the familiar. Then, we design the system architecture of ToF, and the data schema to realize the service. Finally, based on the data schema and a use case scenario, we explain the workflow of the proposed service.

2   Preliminaries

2.1   Super Smart Society

The super smart society [4] is defined by a society that is capable of providing the necessary goods and services to the people who need them at the required time and in just the right amount; a society that is able to respond precisely to a wide variety of social needs; a society in which all kinds of people can readily obtain high-quality services, can overcome differences of age, gender, region, and language, and can live vigorous and comfortable lives. The Japanese government aims for its realization by 2020. Emerging technologies such as IoT, AI, bigdata and Robot are key components to achieve the society.

We have been using various information in a cyber world, such as e-mail, Web pages, and SNS. In addition to that, with the emerging IoT and cloud computing technologies, now we can accumulate a massive amount of information in a real world, such as health information, car running data and operational status of devices. It is expected that collecting such heterogeneous data over cyber/physical worlds and using the data horizontally across various application fields will create new values. Such continuous activities build the foundation of the super smart society.

2.2   Expansion and Diversification of Information Sources

Due to the spread of the Internet, a massive amount of data are published by human beings every day, from various information sources, including e-mail, Web sites, and SNS. In the super smart society, more data are generated by machines including IoT, sensors and smart systems. Thus, information sources become much more diverse and heterogeneous. Such machine-generated data include activity measures obtained by a smart watch, operation logs of a smart appliance, and environment sensor readings [9] within a smart city [5]. These new information sources yield much more realistic and timely information. On the other hand, we must understand characteristics of each information source, and deal appropriately with larger amount of information more than ever.

As an effective means to handle a huge and wide variety of the information, *curation service* [8] (e.g. Digg [1]) has received a lot of attention in recent years.

The curation is an intellectual activity that collects information on the Internet from a certain viewpoint of a curator, combines these information to create a value, and shares the value within the community. Since the curation service provides well-organized information from an interesting perspective, consumers can obtain relevant information easily. However, the current curation service mainly deals with the Web information only. Also, the curation is conducted subjectively based on the service operator. In this regard, the curation service just summarizes information for the mass but does not personalize for the individuals.

2.3   Challenges in Receiving Massive and Diverse Information

Considering how an end user receives information within the super smart society, we have identified the following three challenges.

First, assuming that the super smart society is developed as an extension of the existing ICT [3] over the Internet, a user has to access the information source *proactively by themselves* to obtain necessary information. The way to accessing the information relies on digital devices, including PCs and smartphones. The use of the digital devices becomes too complex especially for information illiterates. Thus, the digital divide becomes more serious. This challenge corresponds to Problem P1 in Sect. 1.

Second, when a massive amount of diverse information are delivered, the amount of information that are irrelevant or inaccurate for the user increases accordingly. The more information a user can see, the more time the user spends for treating the information. Thus, it would be more difficult for the user to reach relevant information. This challenge corresponds to Problem P2 in Sect. 1.

Finally, the information on the Internet is generally described in a popularized expression, so that the information can be recognized by the mass receivers. The information producer does not necessarily consider how individual receivers feel for the expression. Hence, the receiver might feel uncomfortable by the mass-oriented expression. Assuming that the super smart society is the society for individuals, every user should be able to feel comfortable when he/she receives the information. This challenge corresponds to Problem P3 in Sect. 1.

Some people are able to obtain necessary data rapidly and accurately from a massive amount of information. However, the situation is not easy for information illiterates such as elderly people, physically challenged people, people who are not good at machines, and people who are very busy for work. Without proper treatment, the digital divide with respect to receiving information would be more further serious in the super smart society.

3   Proposed Service

In this study, we propose a new information delivery service, *Tales of Familiar* (ToF, for short) to cope with Problems P1, P2 and P3 indicated in Sect. 1.

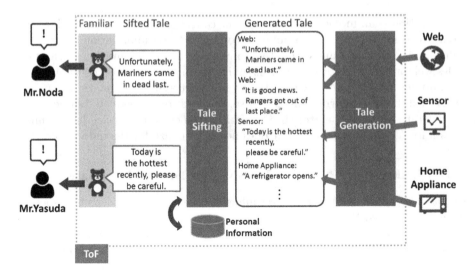

Fig. 1. Use case scenario

3.1 Concept

ToF is an information delivery service that collects information from the heterogeneous sources in the super smart society, and delivers the relevant information to individual users. The information is automatically delivered to a user in such a way that an agent called *familiar* speaks *tales* to the user. Intuitively, a tale refers to a narrative (or story) generated from an information source, so that the original information is easily received by the user. A familiar originally means a fairy that belongs exclusively to a human master, or a very close friend. Thus, the concept of ToF is that an agent (as a familiar) always stays by a user, and provides exclusively relevant information (as tales) for the user.

We explain a use case scenario of ToF using Fig. 1. First, ToF produces tales in the *tale generation* service. Each tale is created from information which collected from an information source such as a Web page, a sensor, or a smart appliance. ToF then sifts the tales in the *tale sifting* service. From massively generated tales, ToF selects only relevant tales appropriate for the user based on personal preference and actions of the user. Finally, a familiar associate to each user speaks the selected tales to the user.

ToF comprises the following key components: (C1) Tale, (C2) Tale Generation, (C3) Tale Sifting, (C4) Familiar. We describe these components in the following sections.

3.2 Tale

A tale refers to information expressed as a narrative (or a story) in familiar's spoken language. The original information source in a popularized style is converted into a tale in a more friendly and personalized style, so that a user can easily receive and understand the information. We suppose that every tale is created automatically or manually using some appropriate methods, from various information sources in super smart society. For example, let us consider a tale that "Mariners came in dead last!" We suppose that this tale has been created from a sports news Web site for baseball fans of Seattle Mariners.

Each tale has meta-information including an information source, a provider, a category, and a delivery method. In the above example, the source is "the sports news Web site", the provider is the author of the article (or application), the category is "sport/baseball", and the delivery method is "voice" or "text". The meta-information attached to each tale will be used in the tale sifting and the tale provision by the familiar.

We can see in Fig. 1 that there are two pools of tales, where one is a pool for generated tales, and another is a pool for sifted tales. The former pool contains a lot of tales that do not assume specific receivers, and the latter contains tales exclusively selected for individual users.

3.3 Tale Generation

In the tale generation, ToF translates the information into tales in familiar's spoken language. The original information is collected from various information sources in the super smart society. In Fig. 1, tales are generated from three information sources of Web, a sensor and, a home appliance. Moreover, two tales "Unfortunately, Mariners came in dead last!" and "It is good news! Rangers got out of last place!" are produced from the Web.

The tale "Today is the hottest recently, please be careful!" is generated using a temperature sensor of the smart home. This tale is generated from the current room temperature value and the average value of the past several days. On the other hand, the tale "A refrigerator opens" is generated from the status of a smart refrigerator, which alerts the user to save the energy.

Multiple tales can be generated from the same information source, since there are many ways to express the information as a tale. For example, let us consider a sports Web news that Seattle Mariners and Texas Rangers have switched positions. For this news, we can generate two tales "Unfortunately, Mariners came in dead last!" for Mariner's fans, and "It is good news. Rangers got out of last place!" for Ranger's fans. In this way, we can choose more personalized expressions for individual users with different preferences.

In the tale generation, the original information expressed in the popularized style is translated into a tale expressed in a more friendly and personalized style. Thus, we aim to solve Problem P3 in Sect. 1.

3.4 Tale Sifting

In the tale sifting, ToF sifts all the generated tales, and selects only tales relevant for a user at that time. The tale sifting is performed for every user based on *personal information* of the user. In this paper, the personal information involves user's profile, age, sex, hobby, preference, taste, dislike, and so on. As mentioned before, every generated tale has a set of meta-data. For every tale, ToF evaluates whether or not the user is interested in the tale, by collating the meta-information and the personal information. Thus, all generated tales are sifted for each user.

In Fig. 1, we can see that the tales are sifted for Mr. Noda and Mr. Yasuda, according to their personal information. In this example, we assume that Mr. Noda is a Mariners fan. Thus, the tale related to Mariners is picked up, as the tale is characterized by the "sports/baseball" category by the meta-data. Also, we assume that Mr. Yasuda lives in a smart home. Thus, the tale generated from his smart home is selected. Note that this tale is relevant to Mr. Yasuda only, since the tale is generated from Yasuda's home. So, the tale is not selected for Mr. Noda.

In the tale sifting, a lot of generated tales are sifted so that individual users can focus on only valuable and interesting tales. Thus, we aim to solve Problem P2 in Sect. 1.

3.5 Familiar

The familiar delivers selected tales to the user. We suppose that a familiar is implemented in a form of a robot, a virtual agent, or an IoT-embedded stuffed doll. According to the concept, every familiar belongs exclusively to a user. There are various types of familiars, and different familiars have different capabilities for delivering the tales. For example, the stuffed doll as a familiar provides tales by voice, while the virtual agent as a familiar delivers tales by an avatar, text and images. Also, a familiar is deployed in various places within a house, such as entrance, living room and others.

A familiar monitors the sifted tales, and delivers them to the user by an appropriate trigger. The trigger of the tale delivery can be user's request, user's proximity detected by a sensor, arrival of the emergency tale, fixed time and so on. When there are multiple tales in a familiar, the familiar delivers a tale with higher priority first. We suppose that the priority value is determined by the urgency, the elapsed time from the tale generation, the degree of matching to user's interest.

If the user wants to know more details of the tale, the user can access to information sources, as long as the familiar has a capability. For example, if a tale was generated from a Web site, and the familiar type is a virtual agent, then the user can access to the Web page displayed on a screen of the virtual agent. Also, a familiar can receive a feedback of the tale from the user. The user's feedback is used to update the user personal information, to grasp user's preference more accurately. In Fig. 1, there are two familiars whose types are both stuffed doll. Each of the two familiars is respectively assigned to Mr. Noda and Mr. Yasuda. They deliver sifted tales relevant to them.

The familiar delivers sifted tales to the user autonomously, considering appropriate time, place, and situation. Therefore, the user can obtain relevant information passively, without operating PC or smartphone by themselves. Thus, we aim to solve Problem P1 in Sect. 1.

4   Service Design

4.1   System Architecture

Figure 2 shows the system architecture of ToF. In this architecture, first, *Writer* collects information from information sources, and generates tales. The generated tales are stored once in a global repository of tales, called *GTale*. Then, *Picker* picks up tales relevant for every user from tales stored in GTale. The sifted tales are stored in a local repository of tales, called *LTale*. There is also a case that the tale which Writer generates for a particular person is directly stored in LTale. Finally, *Familiar* delivers the tales stored in LTale to the user. In proposed architecture, ToF is composed of the following five components.

S1:GTale. Gtale is a repository that stores global tales. It is a data pool deployed in the cloud. Tales in Gtale are generated by the original information with mass-oriented expression, extracted from Web, API, sensors and so on. GTale stores tales just after the tale generation by Writer and before the tale sifting by Picker.

S2:LTale. LTale is a repository that stores local tale. It is a data pool independently associated with every user. LTales stores tales just after the tale sifting by Picker. The tales here are the ones sifted from GTale, or the ones directly imported from Writer.

S3:Writer. Writer is a module that generates tales from various information sources. Writer also puts the generated tales in GTale or LTale. There are various types of Writer for different information sources, such as Web, sensor, direct mail, and others. Tales dedicated for a particular user can be forwarded to LTale directly. Such tales are generated typically from private services such as direct message and smart home. Writer is responsible for (C2) *Tale Generation* in Sect. 3.

S4:Picker. Picker is a module that picks up tales relevant to a user from GTale, and stores the selected tales in LTale. For each tale, Picker considers in which context the tale should be delivered, and determines an appropriate familiar to deliver the tale. Picker is responsible for (C3) *Tale Sifting* in Sect. 3.

S5:Familiar. Familiar is an agent that delivers the tales in LTale to the user. It also receives feedback from the user. Familiar is responsible for (C4) *Familiar* in Sect. 3.

4.2   Data Schema

We here design data schema of ToF, in order to achieve efficient management of tales. Figure 3(1) shows the whole data schema represented by an ER diagram. This diagram follows a notation proposed in [10], where a square shows an entity, $(+\!\!-\!\!\in)$ shows a parent-child relationship, $(+\!\!-\!\!\cdots)$ shows a reference relationship, and $(+\!\!-\!\!\circ+)$ shows a sub-type relationship. Figure 3(2) shows the data schema around GTale including such as GTale and GTag. Figure 3(3) shows

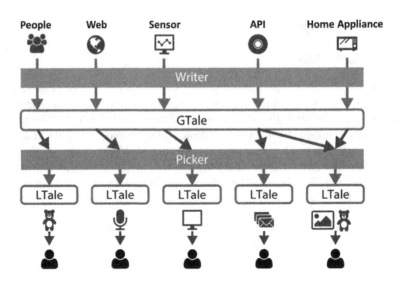

Fig. 2. Whole architecture

the data schema of master information including Provider, User, Content Type, Category, Favorite and Interest. Figure 3(4) shows the data schema around LTale including LTale, LTag, Delivery, Familiar and Capability. We describe the details of each table (i.e., entity) as follows:

GTale: This table stores tales in Gtale. GlobalID is a primary key to identify each tale. Body represents a body text of the tale. Source describes the information source of the tale. CreatedAt denotes date when the tale is created. ExpiredAt denotes an expiry date when the tale is nullified. For example, if the expired date is 2016-11-23 21:11:11, Picker does not pick up that tale after expired date. CategoryID is a reference to the category of the tale. Content-typeID is a reference to the content-type of the tale. When Writer generates a tale, Writer has to generate meta-data to insert the tale into the GTale table.

GTag: This table stores tags of the global tale. Each tag is one of meta-information of global tale. GroballID and sequence are composite primary key. Tag describes an element of the tale. When Picker picks up tales, Picker will use GTag table.

Familiar: This table stores familiar information. FamiliarID is a primary key to identify each familiar. ProviderID means the owner of the familiar. Also, providerID refers to User table and assigns the user that familiar should provide tale for. Place describes the place of the familiar.

Capability: This table stores familiar's capability for delivering the tales. FamiliarID and sequence are composite primary key. Content-typeID is a reference to the content-type of the tale.

LTale: This table stores tales in LTale. FamiliarID and localID are composite primary key to identify each tale. FamiliarID is a reference to the familiar which provide the tale. Therefore, we manage local tale for each familiar.

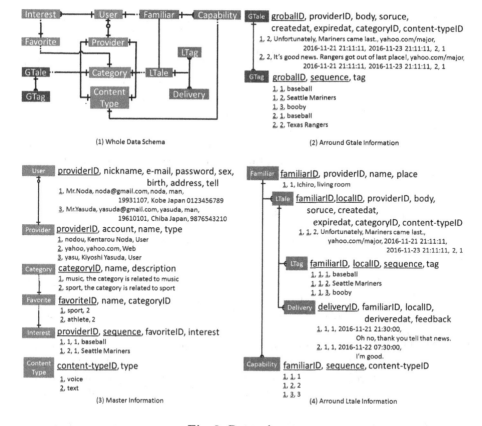

Fig. 3. Data schema

Body, source, categoryID and content-typeID are duplicated from GTale table. Familiar provides tales for the user using this table.

LTag: This table stores tags of the local tale. FamiliarID, localID and sequence are composite primary key. FamiliarID is a reference to the familiar which provide the tale. Tag is duplicated from GTag table.

Delivery: This table stores the log of tale provision. DeliveryID is a primary key. FamiliarID is a reference to tale provider. LocalID is a reference to provided local tale. DeliveredAt represents provided date Feedback describes the user reaction. The user's feedback is used to provide tale again, study the user response and update the user personal information. Familiar stores feedback of provided tale in this table.

Provider: This table stores provider information. ProviderID is a primary key to identify each provider.

User: This table stores user personal information. That include nickname which familiar calls, e-mail, password. For example, the user, providerID is 3 in Fig. 3(3), is called "Mr.Yasuda" from familiar. The user is one of the information provider. The instance which type is User in Provider table refers to User table also.

Category: This table stores tale category. Picker picks up tales using this table.

Content Type: This table stores method of delivering tale. Picker decides familiar which provide tale using this table.

Favorite: This table stores favorite thing. This table is used to register what user is interested in. For example, the phrase "sports" in "What your favorite sport?" is stored in this table. FavoriteID a primary key to identify each favorite thing. Also, a FavoriteID corresponds to a CategoryID and connects user interest thing with tale category.

Interest: This table stores the user interest thing. ProvideID and sequence are composite primary key. Also, this table has reference relationship for Favorite table. Picker picks up tales using this table.

4.3 The Entire Flow of the Service

We describe how to execute the use case scenario in Fig. 1, based on proposed data schema.

Assumption: Tale provider is "yahoo.com" on Web site. We assume the tale which Mr.Noda is interested in is produced (refer to Provider and User in Fig. 3(3)). Mr.Noda have the familiar called Ichiro (refer to Familiar in Fig. 3(4)).

STEP1: The information about the rank of American League in Major League Baseball is posted in "yahoo.com". Writer produces tales from that information and stores these tales in GTale. Each tale spotlights each baseball team. When a tale is produced, Writer produces tags of that tale also (refer to GTale and GTag in Fig. 3(2)).

STEP2: Picker gets personal information of Mr.Noda from personal information database. Picker compares user interest in personal information to tag and category of each tale in GTale and evaluates whether each tale is appropriate for the user. Thus, picker picks up the tale such as "Unfortunately, Mariners came last." which is appropriate for Mr.Noda.

STEP3: This tale should be provided by voice, because of the content type of tale (refer to ContentType in Fig. 3(3)). Picker checks Ichiro can manage that content type and stores the tale in LTale. At the same time, sequences and tags in GTale about stored tale are duplicated and stores in LTag (refer to LTale and LTag in Fig. 3(4)).

STEP4: Ichiro is placed on the living room (refer to Familiar in Fig. 3(4)). Ichiro finds Mr.Noda in the living room by the motion sensor and provides tale by voice. "Mr.Noda, unfortunately, Mariners came last". Mr.Noda replies "Oh no, thank you tell that news". Familiar stores that feedback and the log of tale provision in Delivery (refer to Delivery in Fig. 3(4)).

5 Conclusions

In this paper, toward Super Smart Society, we proposed the autonomous information delivery service for information illiterate. In the proposed service, a massive amount of tales are produced from various sources of information. Produced tale is sifted and only the tale which is appropriate for the user is picked up. Sifted tale is provided for the user autonomously by familiar. Familiar is the IoT device that has sensor and microphone. As the future challenges, we have to develop a prototype of proposed service and test that service.

Acknowledgments. This research was partially supported by the Japan Ministry of Education, Science, Sports, and Culture [Grant-in-Aid for Scientific Research (B) (No. 16H02908, No. 15H02701, No. 26280115), Young Scientists (B) (No. 26730155), and Challenging Exploratory Research (15K12020)].

References

1. Digg. http://digg.com/
2. Armbrust, M., Fox, A., Griffith, R., Joseph, A.D., Katz, R., Konwinski, A., Lee, G., Patterson, D., Rabkin, A., Stoica, I., Zaharia, M.: A view of cloud computing. Commun. ACM **53**(4), 50–58 (2010)
3. Dutton, W.H.: Information and Communication Technologies: Visions and Realities. Oxford University Press, Inc., Oxford (1996)
4. The Japanese Ministry of Education, Culture, S.S., Technology: The 5th science and technology basic plan (2016)
5. Hollands, R.G.: Will the real smart city please stand up? City: Anal. Urban Trends Cult. Theory Policy Action **12**(3), 303–320 (2008)
6. Gubbi, J., Buyya, R., Marusic, S., Palaniswami, M.: Internet of Things (IoT): a vision, architectural elements, and future directions. Future Gener. Comput. Syst. **29**(7), 1645–1660 (2013)
7. Atzori, L., Iera, A., Morabito, G.: The internet of things: a survey. Comput. Netw. **54**(15), 2787–2805 (2010)
8. Rosenbaum, S.: Curation Nation: How to Win in a World Where Consumers are Creators. McGraw-Hill Education, New York (2011)
9. Sakakibara, S., Saiki, S., Nakamura, M., Matsumoto, S.: Indoor environment sensing service in smart city using autonomous sensor box. In: 15th IEEE/ACIS International Conference on Computer and Information Science (ICIS 2016), Okayama, Japan, pp. 885–890, June 2016
10. Watanabe, K.: Hanbai Kanri System de Manabu Modeling Koza. Shoeisha, Tokyo (2008). (in Japanese)

Study of the Effects of Japanese Tea Ceremony Will Give the Peace of Mind of Guests

Tomoko Ota[1]([✉]), Tomoya Takeda[2], Xiaodan Lu[2], Noriyuki Kida[2], Tadayuki Hara[3], and Akihiko Goto[4]

[1] Chuo Business Group, 1-6-6 Funakoshi-cho, Chuo-ku, Osaka 540-0036, Japan
tomoko_ota_cbg@yahoo.co.jp
[2] Kyoto Institute of Technology, Matsugasaki, Sakyo-ku,
Kyoto 606-6585, Japan
t.takeda@taste.jp, luxiaodan0223@gmail.com,
kida@kit.ac.jp
[3] University of Central Florida, 4000 Central Florida Blvd., Orlando,
FL 32816, USA
tadayuki.hara@ucf.edu
[4] Osaka Sangyo University, 3-1-1 Nakagaito, Daito, Osaka 574-8530, Japan
gotoh@ise.osaka-sandai.ac.jp

Abstract. Tea ceremony, which is considered to be the representative of Japanese traditional culture, is used as one of methods to learn the spirit of "Omotenashi" that is a particularly Japanese form of hospitality. That is because when conducting a tea ceremony, care and sympathy shown toward one's guest is considered to be the most important. In tea ceremony, there are attitudes, such as "Treasure Every Meeting, For It will Never Recur" that are crucial when hosting guests. Especially, attitudes that "the host must prepare thoroughly for the guests, stage a pleasant experience" and "the guests enjoy the preparation of the host" are important. In "Omotenashi", the side that is providing the service and the side that is receiving the service are equal, and the guest and the host (the one who invites guest) are also equal in tea ceremony. Moreover, there are many types of utensils (tea things) that are used for tea ceremony. Many of them are specific to tea ceremony, and the ways they are used are also unique Originally, tea ceremony (Sado) was called "Chato" or "Cha no Yu". The name "Sado" was adopted in early Edo period, and it is used until today. The ultimate aim of tea ceremony is the sense of harmony between the host and the guest. Therefore, elements such as tea things, chiefly among them the tea bowl, or hanging scroll with Zen wisdom hang in the alcove of tea room are more than just individual artworks. Rather, they are parts that constitute the whole, and the passing time of tea ceremony itself is regarded as a total work of art. The traditional Japanese act of boiling water, prepare tea and serve it, and the style and art based on this act, is considered to be a particularly Japanese "Omotenashi". In tea ceremony, the host that is holding the ceremony invites guests after careful preparation, and the guests are expected to understand the intention of the host, behave appropriately to the situation and show gratitude. In other words, they create pleasant space by the host and the guests becoming one. This "reciprocity of the host and the guests" is also called "unity of the hosts and the guests". In our series of research, we study that the Japanese tea ceremony will

© Springer International Publishing AG 2017
V.G. Duffy (Ed.): DHM 2017, Part I, LNCS 10286, pp. 348–357, 2017.
DOI: 10.1007/978-3-319-58463-8_29

give the peace of mind of guests or not. We made several groups as customer of tea ceremony. Each customer set heart rate mater and measured the R-R interval. After the experiment we analyze the peace of mind on each step (called Otemae) of the tea ceremony. We found that peace of mind is different for each group. By analyzing peace of mind in the tea ceremony, we will be able to enjoy Omotenashi, based on the spirit of tea that aims to "Treasure Every Meeting, For It will Never Recur".

Keywords: Tea ceremony · Heart rate · Process analysis · The peace of mind of the guest

1 Introduction

In Japanese culture there are many items in which name includes Chinese character of Dou, Do or Michi (道). For example; international sport of Jyudo, Japanese fence of Kendo, Japanese archery of Kyuudo, next new olympic game event of Karatedo, Japanese flower arrangement of Kado, enjoying smell of Koudo, Charigrapy of Syodo, and enjoying powder tea of Sado are good item. Dou is Japanese people's sense of values and the meaning of Dou is training of person's mentality through activity in one item.

Among them Sado was established by Rikyu Sen during Azuchi-Momoyama period (1573–1603). The main concept is OMOTENASHI mind which is Japanese hospitality. In Sado each action involves the meaning and it can be said that all of action is supported by OMOTENASHI mind. A once-in-a-lifetime chance concept which we cherish our encounter is good example.

Recently Sado has been of particular interest among business persons for training mentality. In tea ceremony room person's mental becomes steady and such environments create new findings of business. However, there very few researches which discuss about people's physiological response in tea ceremony room. In this paper participant heart periods were measured. The participants were selected as 5 categories; Japanese persons who knows Sado well, Japanese person who did not know Sado, Japanese students, foreign students who attended tea ceremony explanation lecture or not. Value of tone and entropy was calculated and generation of peaceful mind c in the tea room was discussed.

2 Tea Ceremony

Tea ceremony supported by Urasennke can be divided into 7 processes. Those are 1, Enter the room and sit down 2, Sweets are served 3, Tea-serving manners begin 4, Eat sweets 5, Tea is served 6, Drink tea 7, Head towards the end.

As shown in Fig. 1.

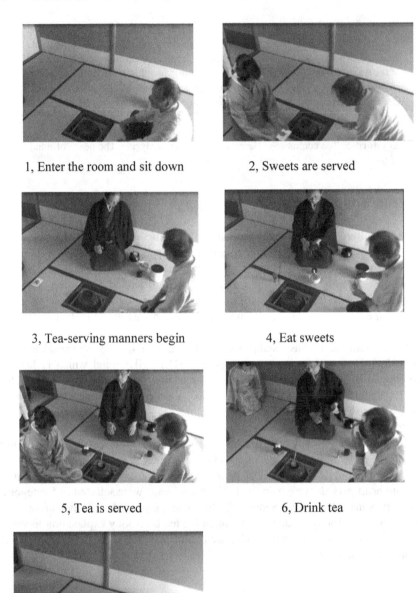

1, Enter the room and sit down

2, Sweets are served

3, Tea-serving manners begin

4, Eat sweets

5, Tea is served

6, Drink tea

7, Head towards the end

Fig. 1. Process of tea ceremony.

3   Experimental Procedure

Tea ceremony room is shown in Fig. 2 The area is 7.3 m^2 which is composed by 4.5 sheet of Tatami. One Tatami is 90 cm × 180 cm. Shape is square. On Friday, November 4th, Inside Umekoji Park Green mansions.

Fig. 2. Tea ceremony room

Experiment plan
Experiment subject waiting room Laboratory A. Heart rate experiment Laboratory B.
   Subject group 8 mats

   10:00 Start of experiment 10:00 ③Japanese students
   11:10 ①Kyoto's peoples 12:20 Break time
   13:10 ④Tea ceremony explanation lectured foreign students
   14:20 ⑤Tea ceremony explanation not lectured foreign students
   15:30 ②Osaka's peoples
   16:40 The experiment end

   Autonomic nervous activity is evaluated by measuring the heart beat interval (RRI) with your feeling of tension and relaxation when tea-serving manners.

1. Subject wearing heart rate meter in separate room. After wearing, confirm that the sensor and the monitor are connected.
2. Everyone presses the video camera's shooting start and heart rate meter switch at the same time. Then rest for about 10 min. Camera charge hold the video camera with your hand and shoot.
3. After that, move to tea room. In the meantime, video camera keeps shooting. Heart rate meter remains measured.
4. Set the camera in the tea room. And, everyone starts about position.
5. After finishing, the shooting of the video camera is ended. The heart rate meter is also ended.

4 Result and Discussion

4.1 Behavior of Participants in Tea Ceremony Room and Process Analysis

According previous analysis tea ceremony can be divided into 7 process. Table 1 shows participants behavior in tea ceremony room.

Table 1.

Time (Minute)	Time (Seconds)	Subject A (Umemura)
0	0	Heart rate monitor is started
1	16	Enter the room
1	28	Sit
1	50	Instruct students to prepare a seat chair
2	5	Make subject A' legs comfortable
2	23	Chat with subject B
2	37	Watch the students bring the seat chair
2	47	Chat about how to use the chair
3	20	Watching sweets being brought in, reseat straight sitting (sit up straight)
3	30	Watch sweets which Ms. Ota bring
3	35	Take a bow
3	37	Talk with Ms. Ota
3	39	Bow to Ms. Ota
3	45	Watch Ms. Ota leaves the room
3	49	Watch his/her sweets
3	55	Watch Ms. Ota bringing sweets
3	59	Watch sweets
4	2	Subject A bows and brings his/her sweets in front
4	9	Watch his/her sweets
4	15	Change the position of his/her sweets and watch it
4	20	Watch sweets which Ms. Ota bring
4	23	Watch sweets of Subject C
4	30	Take a bow
4	32	Watch his/her sweets
4	48	Watch sweets of Subject D
4	59	Watch Ms. Ota going away
5	4	Watch his/her sweets
5	6	Watch sweets which Ms. Ota bring
5	11	Watch sweets of Subject E
5	15	Take a bow
5	18	Watch sweets of Subject E

(*continued*)

Table 1. (*continued*)

Time (Minute)	Time (Seconds)	Subject A (Umemura)
5	20	Watch Mizuya that it is a chest of drawers in a tea-ceremony room
5	31	look around for
5	35	Watch the kettle
5	41	Talking to subject B to eat sweets, everyone tries to eat sweets
5	47	When they tried to eat sweets, the tea master came and they bowed
5	51	Observe the movement of the tea master
5	55	Watch the tea ceremony equipment the tea master placed
6	18	Observe the tea master movement and tea ceremony equipment
6	44	It is suggested to eat sweets and he/her bows
6	51	Cut the sweets
7	3	Eat the sweets
7	24	Put the paper in a tatami mat and observe the movement of the tea master
7	52	Change the position of the paper and look at the paper
7	59	Talking about sweets with the tea master
8	3	Observe the movement of the tea master
9	23	Scratch the face
9	25	Observe the movement of the tea master
10	15	See Ms. Ota coming into the room
10	17	Observe the movement of the tea master
10	31	Watch the finished tea (Watch a made tea)
10	36	Change posture (because the tea master told that it is okay to make my legs comfortable)
10	43	Watch Ms. Ota bringing tea
10	46	reseat straight sitting. (sit up straight) 正座: straight sitting
10	47	Watch Ms. Ota's movement
11	1	Take a bow
11	4	Move the tea in front
11	8	Take a bow
11	10	Pick up the tea bowl (hold the tea bowl)
11	13	Turn the tea bowl clockwise
11	17	Drink tea
11	31	Finishing drinking tea and wiping the tea bowl with his/her fingers
11	38	Turn the tea bowl and put it
11	39	Take a bow
11	42	Put a cup in front
11	45	Talk with Ms. Ota
11	48	Observe the movement of tea master
11	53	Watch his/her tea bowl and chat
12	0	Observe the movement of the tea master

(*continued*)

Table 1. (*continued*)

Time (Minute)	Time (Seconds)	Subject A (Umemura)
12	7	Watch the finished tea (Watch a made tea)
12	13	Move the tea bowl
12	15	Watch the tea of subject B
12	20	Observe the movement of the tea master
12	22	Watch the tea of subject B
12	23	Observe the movement of the tea master
12	40	Pass the tea bowl to Nakatsugi (the mediator)
12	44	Observe the movement of the tea master
13	2	Watch subject B
13	4	Watch the tea of subject C
13	36	Observe the movement of the tea master
13	48	Watch the tea of subject C
13	49	Chat with the tea master
13	55	Observe the movement of the tea master
14	10	Listen to the tea master's speech and chat with each other (everyone)
14	36	Observe the movement of the tea master
14	40	Watch the tea of subject D
14	41	Observe the movement of the tea master
15	2	Listen to the voice of subject D, and watch his/her
15	3	Observe the movement of the tea master
15	5	Watch the tea of subject E
15	7	Observe the movement of the tea master
15	12	Watch the finished tea (Watch a made tea)
15	33	Watch the kettle
15	40	Watch the tea of subject E
15	43	Observe the movement of the tea master
16	9	Take a bow
16	14	Observe the movement of the tea master
16	32	Chat with the tea master
18	25	Observe the movement of the tea master
18	40	The tea master told that it is okay to make his legs comfortable, then Subject A bowed and started a chat
19	4	Observe the movement of the tea master
19	19	Take a bow
19	28	Make his/her legs comfortable, and chat about heartbeat by all the members
20	31	Stand up and leave the room

This is useful data for investigate serenity by using RR interval of heart rate meter. Therefore, precious observation was needed. In this table process 1 is from 0:00 to 03:20, 2 is from 03:20 to 05:47, 3 is from 05:47 to 06:44, 4 is from 06:44 to 08:03, 5 is from 08:03 to 11:17, 6 is from 11:17 to 11:42 and 7 is from 11:42 to 20:31. Figure 3 shows example photos just before and after drinking tea. Right side white shirt man was focused. Before drinking tea, his face was very nervous, on the other hand after drinking we can found smile on his face. This simple result suggests us that tea ceremony brought some change in feelings.

Fig. 3. Example photos just before and after drinking tea.

4.2   RR Interval Measurements

Tone-entropy method

The methodology of analysis has been described in detail previously. [1–3] In brief, acquired heart periods (R-R intervals) are transformed into percentage index (PI) time series:

$$PI(n) = \frac{H(n) - H(n+1)}{H(n)} \times 100$$

where [H(n)] is a heart period time series, and n a serial number of heart beats. The tone is defined as an arithmetic average (first-order moment) of this PI time series as:

$$\sum_n \frac{PI(n)}{N}$$

where N is a total number of PI terms. The entropy is defined on PI probability distribution by using Shannon's formula [4]:

$$-\sum_i p(i) \log_2 p(i)$$

where p(i) is a probability distribution that PI(n) has value in the range, $i \leq PI(n) < i + 1$, i an integer.

In this experiments Data 3 min before and after of drinking tea was selected. Value of tone and entropy was calculated and mean value was obtained.

The tone, balance between acceleration (PI > 0; decrease of heart period) and inhibitions (PI < 0; increase of heart period) of the heart, because positive PI reflects instantaneous accelerations and negative. PI instantaneous inhibition of heart, respectively. At first sight, one might consider that the tone is tobe zero for stable heart rate process. However, the actual tone is not zero, rather reflects the sympathy-vagal balance faithfully as appreciated in all the previous studies [1–3]. The entropy evaluates total acceleration-inhibition activities, or total heart period variations, in a familiar unit of bit. As the results of Wilcoxon signed-rank test, tone decreased significantly (p < .05), whereas entropy didn't change.

Figure 4 shows the entropy and tone charge before and after drinking tea. Both values shows decreasement that means total acceleration-inhibition activities are decreased by the entropy data, and also the tone tends decreasement, which indicate relaxation of feeling. The tone data is significant at 5% level.

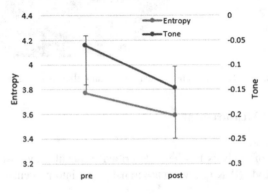

Fig. 4. Tone-average and Entropy-average

5   Conclusion

In this paper the peace of mind of the guest during Japanese tea ceremony can be obtained or not was discussed. The systematic experiments were performed and the number of participants were 25 totally including 5 different groups. First the process analysis was made during tea ceremony and 3 min before and after drinking tea was focused. By using heart rate meter value of tone and entropy was calculated. Consequently, peaceful mind can be generated by drinking tea was clarified.

References

1. Amano, M., Oida, E., Moritani, T.: Age-associated alteration of sympatho-vagal balance in a female population assessed through the ton-entropy analysis. Eur. J. Appl. Physiol. **94**, 602–610 (2005)
2. Oida, E., Moritani, T., Yamori, Y.: Tone-entropy analysis on cardiac recovery after dynamic exercise. J. Appl. Physiol. **82**, 1794–1801 (1997)
3. Oida, E., Kannagi, T., Moritani, T., Yamori, Y.: Aging alteration of cardiac va-gosympathetic balance assessed through the tone-entropy analysis. J. Gerontol. **54A**, M219–M224 (1999)
4. Shannon, C.E.: Amathematical theory of communication. Bell Syst. Tech. **J27**, 379–423 (1948)
5. Amano, M., Oida, E., Moritani, T.: A comparative scale of autonomic function with age through the tone-entropy analysis on heart period variation. Eur. J. Appl. Physiol. **98**, 276–283 (2006)

An Overview of Open Source Software Systems for Smart Development of Virtual Environments

Daniele Regazzoni, Caterina Rizzi, and Andrea Vitali[✉]

University of Bergamo, Dalmine (Bergamo), Italy
{daniele.regazzoni, caterina.rizzi,
andrea.vitalil}@unibg.it

Abstract. This paper presents an overview of main open source software, low-cost devices and related SDKs (Software Development Kits) that can be used to develop custom applications based on virtual and augmented reality. At present, the high modularity of the open source software for computer graphics allows developing custom applications with high quality for several research and industrial fields. To this end, we introduce a general-purpose software framework, which permits to manage the synchronization among the SDKs of different low-cost devices. Mentioned devices and software modules have been exploited to develop three applications in different fields.

Keywords: Open-source software · Low-cost devices · Virtual reality

1 Introduction

Open source software systems are becoming very interesting to develop commercial and industrial solutions in several fields. Usually, they are provided from communities that continuously update the software architecture with new modules. The high frequency of updates forces the community to follow a rigid versioning of own code repositories and, thus, each new released version is always totally tested and improved through bug fixing. High control quality of open source code becomes a good starting point to develop commercial applications. This is true for the development of virtual environments in several research and industrial contexts in which the basic features are common, such as the interaction with 3D environment using head mounted displays (HMDs), hand-tracking devices, motion capture (Mocap) systems, and so on.

HMDs allow the visualization of 3D environments by emulating the depth sense using stereo cameras. At present, there are several HMDs that make available a software development kit (SDK) to interface the device with a custom application, such as Oculus Rift [1], HTC Vive [2] and Google Cardboard [3].

Hand-tracking devices permit the detection of hands and fingers with high precision. Among many solutions, the most interesting ones are the Leap Motion device [4] and the Duo3D [5].

© Springer International Publishing AG 2017
V.G. Duffy (Ed.): DHM 2017, Part I, LNCS 10286, pp. 358–368, 2017.
DOI: 10.1007/978-3-319-58463-8_30

A Mocap system is able to record movements of objects and people. Recorded actions of the human body are used to animate the virtual avatar of a person and can be used to study the cinematic behavior (e.g., gait analysis). Among the different Mocap systems, the optical ones are attracting more and more interest. They can be subdivided in two main categories: marker-based and marker-less. The marker-less systems can be based on low-cost devices such as, Microsoft Kinect v1 and v2 and Sony PS Camera.

The aim of this paper is to introduce an overview of main low-costs systems (both software and hardware), which are used to create virtual and mixed reality applications for research and industrial contexts. The paper shows how it is possible create several software interfaces between different open-source SDK in order to create application for custom-fit products. According to this approach, three applications have been developed and briefly described.

2 Overview of Main Open Source Systems and Low-Cost Devices

Open source systems have been selected on the base of the experience matured in the development of innovative virtual and mixed reality applications. Selected systems have been classified and subdivided according to the final purpose of the application.

2.1 Basic 3D Environments

The software development of a basic 3D environment needs a module to develop the graphical user interface (GUI) and a module to manage the 3D environment. Among many possible solutions, two important open source systems allow developing a complete 3D basic environment in a simple and fast way:

- Qt, used for developing multi-platform applications and GUIs [6]. It is a cross-platform application framework to develop software application that can be run on various software and hardware platforms with little or no change in the underlying codebase. Qt is widely used by many organizations, including but not limited to European Space Agency, Panasonic, Philips, Samsung, Siemens and Volvo.
- VTK (Visualization Tool Kit), used to manage the 3D rendering. It supports a wide variety of visualization algorithms and advanced modeling techniques [7]. At present, VTK is used worldwide in commercial applications, research and development and represents the basis of many advanced visualization applications such as: Molekel, ParaView, VisIt, VisTrails, MOOSE, 3DSlicer, MayaVi, and OsiriX.

2.2 Low-Cost Devices for Virtual/Mixed Reality Environments

To interact with mixed environments, the developer has to create a set of software interfaces among the devices and the 3D environment. In our approach a virtual/mixed reality environment application comprises:

- Hand-tracking using Leap Motion SDK [4, 8]. It makes available a set of modules to easily detect a broad type of gestures. To make the interaction simple and comfortable, a Natural User Interface (NUI) has been studied and designed [9–11]. An ad-hoc module has been developed that extends the class of VTK to interact with the virtual environment of the final application [12].
- Immersive vision in a 3D virtual world using Oculus Rift SDK 2.0 [1, 13, 14]. The mixed reality environment is automatically visualized in the user's field of view of the Oculus Rift when the 3D object is detected and, thus, the user can start to execute his/her work using hands/fingers detected by the Leap Motion [15, 16], which is mounted on the front of the Oculus Rift as shown in Fig. 1.

Fig. 1. Leap motion device mounted on oculus rift.

2.3 Motion Capture System

A motion capture system allows tracking human motion in space and analyzing acquired data for detecting key-features useful inside the developed application. We consider a marker-less Mocap solution, which uses multiple low-cost depth cameras [17–19] (Fig. 2(a)) such as Microsoft Kinect v2 (Fig. 2(b)) [20].

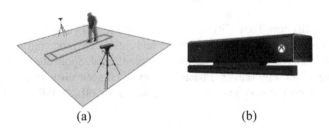

(a)   (b)

Fig. 2. (a) Layout of Mocap system based on multiple Kinect v2; (b) A Microsoft Kinect v2.

The solution uses a commercial application, named iPisoft suite [21], to manage acquired data. It is composed by two applications: iPiRecorder and iPiStudio. IpiRecorder allows data recording acquired by two Kinect v2. IpiStudio imports acquired data in a virtual environment and allows the data elaboration and the creation of the avatar virtual skeleton, which can be exported in several file formats, among which BVH and FBX.

Once the file has been exported, an application to analyze the acquired animation can be developed by using several modules of the open source platform named Blender [22]. Blender is an application for 3D modeling and animation and it can be adopted as a module inside a custom application for specific purposes. In our context, it is used to manage body shape animations and automatic association of an animation to the 3D human avatar to define different body postures. Blender makes available several features very useful to simplify the use of a motion animation acquired by a Mocap system.

3   Software Interfaces

Several software interfaces are required in order to create a proper data exchange among the devices used in a mixed reality application. Depending on the type of applications, at least two software interfaces have to be developed: (i) the synchronization of different coordinate systems related to the 3D environment and the chosen devices (e.g., the head mounted display and/or the hand-tracking device); (ii) the interface between new software modules and Blender for body mesh animation.

In the following sections we introduce the solutions we adopted for the aforementioned interfaces.

3.1   FrameworkVR

FrameworkVR is a general-purpose software library, fully independent of the application the developer wants to implement. It allows using HMD and hand tracking devices inside an application where the 3D environment has been implemented by using VTK and Qt. It automatically manages the synchronization among the orientation systems of VTK, and the interaction devices SDK. Furthermore, it makes available a set of software modules to create a Natural User Interface by following the finite state machine (FSM) approach. A set of virtual widgets has been developed in order to simplify the design of the NUI [23].

Figure 3 shows the UML diagram, which describes the interface of FrameworkVR with the Oculus Rift HMD and Leap Motion for hand tracking.

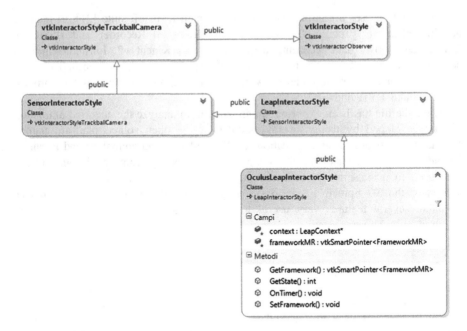

Fig. 3. UML diagram: interface with the oculus rift and the leap motion.

3.2 Blender in a Custom Application

In addition to the augmented interaction, some applications require also the possibility to work with the model of human body (acquired with a 3D scanner) assuming different postures according to the goal of the application. Therefore, the system should be able to associate data coming from a Mocap system with the human body model (usually a polygonal mesh). Blender makes available a set of automatic and semiautomatic features in order to perform mentioned tasks. These operators are named rigging and animation retargeting. The 3D rigging relates group of vertexes of the body mesh to the nearest bone composing the skeleton acquired with the Mocap solution. When running the animation, the body mesh accurately follows it. Retargeting permits the translation of an animation from a skeleton to another one, which can be composed by either the same or different set of bones. This is necessary when the skeleton of the acquired human avatar is different from the skeleton used for animation. This is mandatory when the animation is acquired with a marker-based motion capture system.

The functionalities of Blender are available through software development in Python. Furthermore, C++ embeds Python in a very simple way and, thus, the developed application exploits the functionality of Blender efficiently interfacing C++ classes and the other SDKs and Python modules.

4 Developed Applications

FrameworkVR as well as mentioned devices, SDKs and open sources tools have been exploited to develop three applications in different contexts. The applications concern highly customized products that are designed around the human body: lower limb prosthesis and made-to-measure garments. Figure 4 portrays the aforementioned tools and devices that have been exploited for each application.

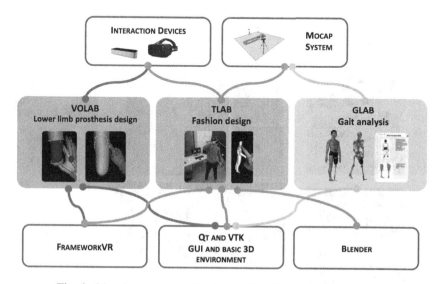

Fig. 4. Mapping among applications and devices and software tools.

4.1 Tailor LABoratory - TLAB

Taylor LABoratory (TLAB) permits to emulate tailor's tasks [24]; in particular, we focus the attention on the first step of the design process during which the tailor gets the measures of the customer's body, also in specific postures [9]. As shown in Fig. 4, TLAB exploits FrameworkVR to synchronize VTK, OculusRift and Leap Motion SDKs, and uses a Mocap system and Blender to define the different body postures necessary to get right customer's measures. A NUI has been designed in order to take measures using hands along the 3D human body model. For this aim, a virtual tape measure has been developed specializing a VTK widget to emulate the real one used by the tailor.

Blender has been used to manage body animations and automatic association of an animation to the 3D human avatar. The human being is acquired using a 3D body scanner (e.g., Kinect v1 and Skanect) and his/her human motion with a Mocap solution composed of two Kinect v2 and IpiSoft.

Then, the acquired skeleton is linked to the 3D human avatar in the correct position and the vertex groups are generated and populated according to the position of each vertex to the nearest bone of the skeleton. When the automatic 3D association is completed, the skeleton can be moved and the 3D human avatar is animated accordingly, and needed postures generated.

In addition, Blender is also used to export/import 3D models in several animation format, such as BVH, DAE so that the 3D human body can be used within a 3D clothing system to design a made-to measure garment for the specific customers.

A set of body postures (composed by BVH files) can be easily generated and the user/tailor can get the measures by hands interacting with the 3D human model by interacting with the Leap motion. Figure 5 portrays the described workflow.

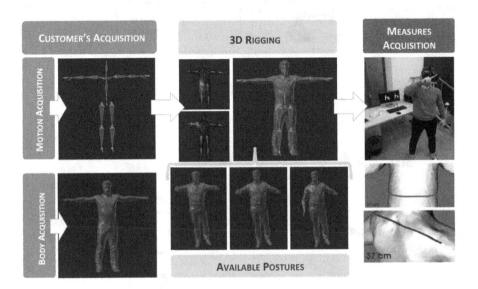

Fig. 5. TLAB workflow. Measures refer to a men shirt

4.2 Virtual Orthopedic LABoratory - VoLAB

VoLab is a mixed reality environment to design lower limb prosthesis based on a knowledge based CAD system known as SMA, i.e., Socket Modelling Assistant [25]. The architecture of VoLAB (Fig. 6) consists of: three Kinect v2, Oculus Rift v2.0, Leap Motion device placed on the front side of Oculus Rift and a Personal Computer that runs SMA and manages the synchronization of devices through the middleware.

SMA has been developed to design the 3D socket model of lower limb prosthesis according to operations made by technicians during traditional hand-made manufacturing process. It provides a set of virtual modelling tools starting from the 3D model of the residual limb and anthropometric data of the patient. Among the several operations to model a socket, the load/off-load zones definition and the trim-line sketching (i.e., the upper part of the socket) are the most important ones.

The SMA 3D environment, which have been developed using VTK, and the interaction paradigm have been totally re-designed according to the use of Oculus Rift

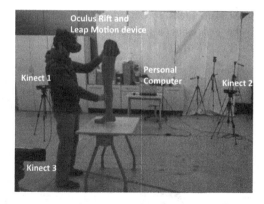

Fig. 6. VoLAB hardware architecture.

and Leap Motion device and synchronized thanks to FrameworkVR. Also in this case, a NUI has been defined as well as a set of gestures and 3D virtual widgets with which the user can design the final socket for a lower limb prosthesis. Figure 7 shows the VoLAB virtual tools with which the user can interact using his/her hands and, thus, emulates operations traditionally done during the manufacturing process.

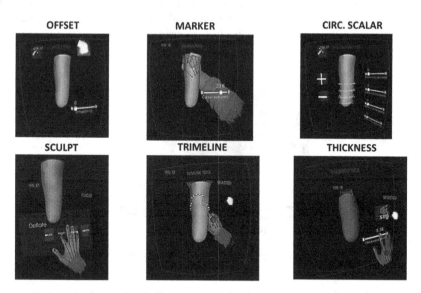

Fig. 7. VoLab virtual tools

4.3 Gait Laboratory – GLab

GLab is a virtual gait analysis tool that merges the 3D model of the residual limb acquired by means of 3D scanners (e.g. a laser scanner) or diagnostic device (e.g., Magnetic Resonance Imaging and Computed Tomography) with pressure data acquired during amputee gait. Pressure data are acquired by using Tekscan system (Fig. 8(a)) [26] while the gait using a marker-less Mocap system composed of two Kinects v2 and iPiSoft (Fig. 8(b)) [27].

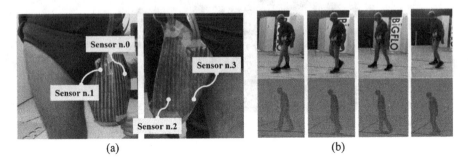

(a)   (b)

Fig. 8. Tekscan sensors applied on the residual limb (a). Gait acquisition with Mocap system while the patient wears pressure sensors (b).

The application has been developed using Qt and VTK. It permits the automatic mapping of pressure data on the residual model and detection of gait abnormalities. First, each pressure sensor on the residual limb model is marked with a color. This operation allows defining the sensors stripe area and mapping them over the virtual 3D model. The user assigns a different color to each stripe to exclusively distinguish each one from the other ones (Fig. 9(a)).

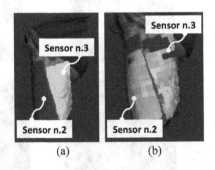

(a)   (b)

Fig. 9. Mapping of the pressure values gathered with Tekscan sensors.

Then, each single sensel (i.e., a single sensor cell along the stripe) is mapped with a 3D surface on the virtual residual limb model. Once the data have been mapped, values measured by each sensel of each sensor stripe can be quickly visualized during the animation of the gait. Figure 9 shows an example of resulting pressure color map (Fig. 9(b)).

On the other side, the application imports the animation relative to the acquired gait. This permits to synchronize pressure data and animation of gait analysis in order to study possible correlation between pressure and different phases of gait cycle.

When pressure mapping has been done and the gait data animation has been imported the user can easily analyze the gait phases in order to detect eventual criticalities. Finally, the application proposes modifications to the prosthesis settings according to detected abnormalities.

5 Conclusions

Smart and low-cost devices coming from the gaming industry are able to provide interesting performances in research and industrial 3D applications. By the way, they are not intended to ease data exchange and to be used together; moreover, there are 3D modelling and animation libraries and tools that can be fruitful exploited. The paper describes a set of low-cost and open source solutions that can be used for developing virtual environments. Three applications have been developed exploiting open-source software and low-cost devices. Two applications use Oculus Rift and Leap Motion devices in order to create a virtual environment in which the user can interact by using his/her hands to design the custom-fit product. The third one uses a low-cost makerless Mocap system.

The developed applications are under evaluation by experts of each related sector and preliminary feedback have been very promising. The use of open source systems has permitted to dramatically decrease the development time of the applications and increase the quality of the final software architecture due to a smaller number of software bug during the software test before the final deployment of the application.

References

1. Oculus Rift. https://www.oculus.com/
2. HTC Vive. https://www.vive.com/eu/
3. Google Cardboard. https://vr.google.com/cardboard/
4. Leap Motion. https://www.leapmotion.com/
5. Duo3D. https://duo3d.com/
6. Qt. https://www.qt.io/
7. VTK. http://www.vtk.org/
8. Jung, S., Hughes, C.E.: Pilot study for telepresence with 3D-model in mixed reality. In: Shumaker, R., Lackey, S. (eds.) VAMR 2015. LNCS, vol. 9179, pp. 22–29. Springer, Cham (2015). doi:10.1007/978-3-319-21067-4_3
9. Kaushik, M., Jain, R., et al.: Natural user interfaces: trend in virtual interaction. arXiv:1405. 0101 (2014)
10. NuiGroup. http://nuigroup.com/go/lite
11. Thakur, A., Rahul, R.: User study of hand gestures for gesture based 3D CAD modeling. In: ASME 2015 International Design Engineering Technical Conferences and Computers and Information in Engineering Conference. American Society of Mechanical Engineers (2015)

12. Colombo, G., Rizzi, C., Facoetti, G., Vitali, A.: A preliminary study of new interaction devices to enhance virtual socket design. In: ASME 2014 International Design Engineering Technical Conferences and Computers and Information in Engineering Conference. American Society of Mechanical Engineers (2014)

13. Martins, V.F., Sampaio, P.N.M., Mendes, F.D.S., Lima, A.S., De Paiva Guimarães, M.: Usability and functionality assessment of an oculus rift in immersive and interactive systems using voice commands. In: Lackey, S., Shumaker, R. (eds.) VAMR 2016. LNCS, vol. 9740, pp. 222–232. Springer, Cham (2016). doi:10.1007/978-3-319-39907-2_21

14. Dias, P., Pinto, J., Eliseu, S., Santos, B.S.: Gesture interactions for virtual immersive environments: navigation, selection and manipulation. In: Lackey, S., Shumaker, R. (eds.) VAMR 2016. LNCS, vol. 9740, pp. 211–221. Springer, Cham (2016). doi:10.1007/978-3-319-39907-2_20

15. Hodson, H.: Leap motion hacks show potential of new gesture tech. New Sci. **218**(2911), 21 (2013)

16. Juanes, J.A., et al.: Analysis of the oculus rift device as a technological resource in medical training through clinical practice. In: Proceedings of the 3rd International Conference on Technological Ecosystems for Enhancing Multiculturality. ACM (2015)

17. Gris, I., Rivera, D.A., Novick, D.: Animation guidelines for believable embodied conversational agent gestures. In: Shumaker, R., Lackey, S. (eds.) VAMR 2015. LNCS, vol. 9179, pp. 197–205. Springer, Cham (2015). doi:10.1007/978-3-319-21067-4_21

18. Jie, M.: Research on motion model for technique movements of competitive swimming in virtual interactive environment. In: Lackey, S., Shumaker, R. (eds.) VAMR 2016. LNCS, vol. 9740, pp. 233–242. Springer, Cham (2016). doi:10.1007/978-3-319-39907-2_22

19. McNamara, C., Proetsch, M., Lerma, N.: Investigating low-cost virtual reality technologies in the context of an immersive maintenance training application. In: Lackey, S., Shumaker, R. (eds.) VAMR 2016. LNCS, vol. 9740, pp. 621–632. Springer, Cham (2016). doi:10.1007/978-3-319-39907-2_59

20. Regazzoni, D., Rizzi, C., Comotti, C., Massa, F.: Towards automatic gait assessment by means of RGB-D Mocap. In: ASME 2016 International Design Engineering Technical Conferences and Computers and Information in Engineering Conference. American Society of Mechanical Engineers (2016)

21. iPi Soft. http://ipisoft.com/

22. Blender. https://www.blender.org/

23. Colombo, G., Rizzi, C., Facoetti, G., Vitali, A.: Automatic generation of software interfaces for hand-tracking devices. In: ASME 2015 International Design Engineering Technical Conferences and Computers and Information in Engineering Conference. American Society of Mechanical Engineers (2015)

24. Vitali, A., Rizzi, C.: A virtual environment to emulate tailor's work. Comput.-Aided Des. Appl. 1–9 (2017, in press)

25. Colombo, G., Rizzi, C., Facoetti, G., Vitali, A.: Mixed reality to design lower limb prosthesis. Comput.-Aided Des. Appl. **13**(6), 799–807 (2016)

26. Tekscan, Inc. https://www.tekscan.com

27. Regazzoni, D., Rizzi, C.: Patients' evaluation based on digital motion acquisition. Comput.-Aided Des. Appl. **13**(6), 808–815 (2016)

Bowing Style in Japanese Famous TV Program

Asuka Takenaka[1(✉)], Xiaodan Lu[2], Yasuyo Takenaka[3],
Yuki Miyamoto[4], and Tomoko Ota[4]

[1] Doshisha University, Karasuma-higashi-iru, Imadegawa-dori, Kamigyo-ku,
Kyoto 602-8580, Japan
Asuka.1204.1997@gmail.com
[2] Kyoto Institute of Technology, Matsugasaki, Sakyo-ku,
Kyoto 606-6585, Japan
luxiaodan0223@gmail.com
[3] Kyoto, Japan
luxiaodan02230519@gmail.com
[4] Chuo Business Group, 1-6-6 Funakoshi-cho, Chuo-ku, Osaka 540-0036, Japan
miyamoto.yuki12@gmail.com, tomoko_ota_cbg@yahoo.co.jp

Abstract. Japanese national broadcasting NHK provides 15 min TV drama program every morning. That is called as national TV program and many people enjoy it. Every half year contents of drama is changed. Recently "ASA GA KITA" was televised. This drama described one lady life who established the first insurance company almost 100 year ago. In the program bowing style was different from that at present, and viewers felt that it was very cute bowing and loved it very much, so that viewing rate was very high. In this paper classification of bowing style appeared in this program and comparison between those styles and present bowing. Also relation between bowing style and viewing rate was discussed.

Keywords: TV program · Viewer rating · Standing bowing · Sitting bowing

1 Introduction

TV program greatly affects Japanese daily life. People can communicate each other by talking about contents of TV program and often guide people to one direction of political movement. In this paper we examine Japanese people hospitality so called OMOTENASHI in famous TV program; "Asa-Dora". In OMOTENASHI bowing is very important, so that bowing style and scene were investigated. Through bowing style Japanese people attitude was discussed. First the meaning of "Asa-Dora" was explained and high viewer rating dram "Asa ga kita" was presented. In this drama all of bowing seens scene were picked up and the style was divided into 6 type and relation between the style and scene was discussed.

2 The Meaning of "Asa-Dora"

<"Dora" is short for "Drama"> It is the drama broadcast in the morning slot every day. Especially, it refers to "Television novel" it had been broadcasted from 1961 by *NIPPON HOSO KYOKAI* (NHK). It is general term the drama broadcast by NHK. Broadcasting form is changing gradually, but the basic form is one story is 15 min are

© Springer International Publishing AG 2017
V.G. Duffy (Ed.): DHM 2017, Part I, LNCS 10286, pp. 369–375, 2017.
DOI: 10.1007/978-3-319-58463-8_31

broadcasted 6 days a week for a half year (26 weeks, about 156 times). It is picked up on media as Japanese representative drama with "epic drama". This is only the drama program audience rating of every time and every week is released. Most of the stories are home drama based on the heroine's life and their family, and the main character is basically woman.

3   The Story of "*Asa ga kita*"

In end of Edo period, she was born as the second daughter into wealthy merchant family in Kyoto. Her name is *Asa* (Haru) who is the tomboy likes Sumo very much. She has a sister *Hatsu* (Miyazaki Aoi) who is eager to lessons of Koto and sewing. They married into their fiancés in Osaka, and they lived through a turbulent Era in Osaka.

Asa got married to *Shinjiro* (Tamaki Hiroshi) who is the second son at a famous exchange company *Kanoya* in Osaka, but after began Meiji Era, their business had been critical because it couldn't meet the new era. Shinjiro said "Making money isn't my nature." and he began amusing with shamisen. When Kanoya will go bankrupt, Shinjiro took the new job to Asa "the management of a coal mine". He said "It is the age of coal now." His words made Asa became absorbed in "business" she has be interested from she was a child.

Asa went to Kyushu there are a lot of coal by oneself, and she met coal miners who didn't work while drinking. On the one hand, Hatsu married into the oldest exchange company *Sannojiya*, but it went bankrupt due to the Meiji Restoration. After that Hatsu disappeared like skipped town at night. Asa could find her at last, and she offered supporting money to Hatsu. However, she and her husband *Soube* (Tsukamoto Yu) declined it, and they went to Wakayama to restart their lives.

The time has passed, Asa was working as businesswoman, but there were a lot of trouble in male-oriented society. One day, she met *Godai Tomoatsu* (Dean Fujioka) who makes an effort for development of Osaka. He said "Support people who are going to start new business!" Asa accepted the bank business, and supported a lot of people. Then, she also trained the first women bank clerk.

Kanoya begin life insurance business, and their business expansion was progressive. Asa accepted the final job was founding the first girls' school. She could collect donation by her vitality and virtue. The day of foundation, Asa talked to students about her thought of education for girls.

After that, she back out of all business, and decided to live the rest of her life with Shinjiro. At last, she talked to students about her thought from her experience.

4   Audience Rating and Reputation of "Asa ga kita"

4.1   "Asa ga kita" Average Audience Rating is the Highest in the World 23.5

"Asa" of the title means morning in English. This title has a meaning "This drama will make the world brightly such as the morning coming lead opening the new world."

It is the effective to make the highest rating that an era setting is the period of great change from end of Edo to Meiji. Today this society was enveloped in sense of hopelessness, and we can't see the future well. We can be absorbed in this drama because there is how the woman lived through this turbulent era with great paradigm shift.

In addition, this is important Kansai was the theater of this drama because if it was in same era, we can see it from different viewpoint depend on each position. It makes new discovery. Almost Bakumatsu restoration drama was mainly samurai story when Edo was the theater of drama. In this case, it wasn't interesting because there was a custom in samurai family. However, on "Asa ga kita", there are a lot of Osaka merchant with vitality.

Haru who performed Asa went well with the character. Her fresh performance as amateur actress matched the young hostess in exchange company and person in charge of coal mine. She could become the heroine who we want to cheer her.

Older sister Hatsu also worked actively in the first half of this drama. She gave large depth because of her life and character different from Asa. This is one of "double heroine" structure, amateur actress Haru and versatile actress Miyazaki Aoi, so viewer saw this drama while comparing the two lives.

"Asa ga kita" has three factors of Asa-Dora's royal road "woman's biography", "working drama", and "grown up story".

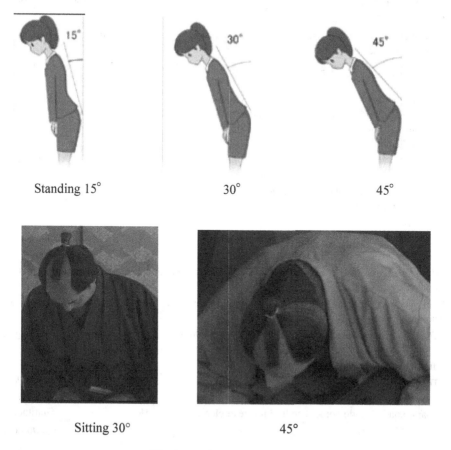

Standing 15°   30°   45°

Sitting 30°   45°

Fig. 1. Various bowing style

5 Observation

"Asa ga kita" was watched carefully and bowing scene was picked up. The bowing style was classified into 6 kinds; sitting bowing and standing bowing, and inclination angle was 15°, 30° and 45°. Examples are shown in Fig. 1. Scene was categorized into 5 kinds: Greeting, Apologizing, Acknowledgment, Requesting and Thanks. Total observation time was 360 min 24 times broadcasting.

6 Results

Total 70 scene was observed. These data was summarized in Table 1. The type of bowing, scene, person name who did bowing, person name whom was received bowing were appeared in this table.

Table 1. Bowing scenes

Expression and action when they are bowing	Person who bow	Situation
Sitting Bow 15°		
"May I come in?" When Asa's mother go into a room and open the fusuma	Asa's mother	Greeting
"I'm sorry." Asa's father get angry because Asa play with an abacus	Asa	Apologize
"I'm sorry." Asa's father tell Asa to learn etiquette	Asa	Apologize
"You are absolutely right." Shinjiro's father said to Asa's father to wedding won't be done because Shinjiro's older brother died	Asa's father	Approve
"Certainly." Mother-in-low tell Asa to wear beautiful kimono when she go out, but it doesn't her intention	Asa	Approve
"I'm sorry, you are right." Asa learned about trust of the company from father-in-law	Asa	Apologize
Sitting Bow 30°		
"Please have a nice stay." Shinjiro leave the room	Shinjiro	Greeting
"I'm sorry." run in the corridor and open the fusuma	Asa	Apologize
"Huyu, please be sure to take care of Asa." Mother ask Fuyu to take care of Asa	Huyu	Request
"I'm very sorry." Asa's father don't tell about the death of Shinjiro's brother	Asa's father	Apologize
"Thank you for wating." Shinjiro was lating for wedding	Shinjiro	Greeting
"I'll leave it to you." When Shinjiro's mother leave the room. After that she bowed keeping silent	Shinjiro's mother	Request
"Thanks a lot." Father-in-law appreciates Asa that she wants to maintain family business as daughter-in-law	Shinjiro's father	Gratitude
"Thank you." Asa do some mending for head clerk.	Head	Gratitude

(continued)

Table 1. (*continued*)

Expression and action when they are bowing	Person who bow	Situation
"I'm very sorry." Ume apologize because Asa say about the management of the company	Ume	Apologize
"Thank you for your thoughtfulness." Asa worrys about the company.	Shinjiro's father	Gratitude
"Please take care." Huyu give the letter written on cloth to Asa when they met by coincidence	Huyu	Greeting
"I'm sorry. I said only strange things though you listen to me."	Asa	Apologize
Sitting Bow 45°		
"We showed disgraceful attitude." Asa's father found shinjiro was seeing Asa when she danced with abacus. Mother 45°/Father 30°	Asa's father and mother	Apologize
Asa's parents apologize because Asa run out of room. Mother 45°/Father 30°	Asa's father and mother	Apologize
"I hope your next visit." to guest who came to the company	Staff who is sitting	Request
"Welcome."	Shinjiro's father/ Asa/ Hatsu	Greeting
"I'm the older son, Shotaro." self-introduce	Shotaro	Greeting
"I'm the older daughter, Hatsu."	Hatsu	Greeting
"I'm the second daughter, Asa."	Asa	Greeting
"Please take care of my brother." Shinjiro's brother greets them	Eizaburo	Greeting
"I'm very sorry." Shinjiro leave the room	Shotaro	Apologize
"I'm Hastu." Hatsu greet the family-in-low	Hatsu	Greeting
"Yes." Sobe's mother said to Hatsu that you should be mature as son's wife, and Hatsu responded to her	Hatsu	Approval
"I'm sorry." Asa fell down because she was distracted by an insect on tatami, and her leg was about to hit Sobe's face	Asa	Apologize
"Thank you for your help you show to me." Godai come to the company	Sobe	Greeting
"I'm sorry." Staff apologized	staff	Apologize
"Please." Sobe's father request that fiancée change Asa to Hatsu	Sobe's father	頼む
"Certainly." Ume asked to take care of Hatsu	Ume	Approval
"OK." Fuyu asked to take care of Asa by mother	Fuyu	Approval
"I'm sorry." Shinjiro's father offer to postpone we marriage	Shinjiro's father	Apologize
"Please don't mention it." Shinjiro's father said it when Asa's parents apologized	Shinjiro's father	Apologize
"I'm very sorry." Asa apologized she sent letter brazenly when Shinjiro's brother wasn't good	Asa	Apologize
"Nice to meet you." At wedding ceremony	All present	Greeting

(*continued*)

Table 1. (*continued*)

Expression and action when they are bowing	Person who bow	Situation
"I'm sorry that I went out without permission. Asa went out to meet Hatsu without permission	Asa	Apologize
"I'm sorry." Asa ask her father-in-low to help his business, but it was declined	Asa	Apologize
"I really apologize." Hatsu's mother-in-low got angry because she heard that Hatsu's mother ask Hatsu about her business	Hatsu's mother	Apologize
"Don't meddle in other people's business." Asa interfered in business, and be worned her father-in-low	Asa	Apologize
"OK. Thank you father." Asa's father-in-low left a business case to Asa	Asa	Gratitude
"Please work hard together." Recoganized that Asa is a member of his business	Father-in-low	Request
"Yes,sir." father-in-low left a business case to Asa	Asa	Request
"Yes, I correct it immediately." Father-in-low asked Asa to count all money	Asa	Gratitude
"Good morning." Asa saw Shinjiro going out	Asa	Greeting
"I'm very sorry. It was my foult." Asa returned money for almost guest	Asa	Apologize
"Please, I'd like to lend us money." Sobe and Hatsu went to Hatsu's house to lend money	Sobe Hatsu	Request
"Thank you to see me." Asa saw Tamatoshi who is wealthy merchant in Nara	Asa	Gratitude
"Thanks." Tamatoshi rend Asa money.	Asa	Gratitude
Standing Bow 15°		
"Good bye." Sobe's mother left the house	Sobe's mother	Greeting
"Thank you." Hatsu ask her mother to appoint Ume who is Asa's assistant, and her mother was convinced	Hatsu	Request
"Thanks." Sobe gave Hatsu a textile when she open the door	Hatsu	Gratitude
"Good morning." Shinjiro greeted the shop staff	Shinjiro	Greeting
"Work hard together." After morning assembly, Shinjiro and staffs greeted each other	Shinjiro's father/staff	Greeting
"I'll go right away." When Hatsu go out with Sobe, Asa visited them and talked. He has gone	Hatsu	Apologize
"Sorry, sorry." Head clerk apologize men at the room where Asa stay	head clerk	Apologize
"I am Saisuke Godai." Godai greeted Shinjiro	Godai	Greeting
"I'm in a hurry. Good bye." Hatsu greeted Asa and head clerk	Hatsu	Greeting
Standing Bow 30°		
"Sorry." A handgun got into Asa's kimono and she has run after, so she talked big for Godai. But after that she apologized	Asa	Apologize
"I looked forward your coming." When going Shiraoka house	Head clerk	Greeting

(*continued*)

Table 1. (*continued*)

Expression and action when they are bowing	Person who bow	Situation
"I'm very sorry." Hatsu apologize Shinjiro because Asa hid in a closet	Hatsu	Apologize
"Please do me a favor." Asa asked Sobe to smile for Hatsu	Asa	Request
"I'd like to grant my request." Hatsu asked her mother to choose Ume, not Fuyu as Asa's assistant	Hatsu	Request
"Very sorry, Shinjiro." Staff was about to hit Shinjiro	Staff	Apologize
"Hello." Asa greet to master of syamisen Miwa	Asa	Greeting

Standing Bow 45°

"I hope your next visit." to guest who came to the company	Asa's father	Request
"I'm sorry." Shinjiro forget to wedding and go to see autumn leaves	Clerk	Apologize

Table 2. Classification of bowing style and scene

	Sitting bow			Standing bow			
	15°	30°	45°	15°	30°	45°	
Greeting	1 16%	3 25%	9 27%	5 56%	2 28%		
Apologizing	3 50%	4 33%	13 38%	2 22%	3 43%		
Acknowledgment	2 33%		3 9%				
Requesting		2 16%	5 15%	1 11%	2 28%		
Thanks		3 25%	4 12%	1 11%			
Total	6 9%	12 17%	34 49%	9 13%	7 10%		70 100%

7 Discussion and Conclusion

Table 2 shows statistic of bowing style. The sitting 45° bowing is almost a half of total number. And then the order is sitting 30°, standing 15° and standing 30°. The standing 45° is very rare case.

Japanese people life style is Tatami culture, so that sitting bow is majority. The meaning of 45° is, that is deep bowing, apologize. It can be said that bowing style contains the expression of person's feeling. Apologize feeling brings deep bowing, so that from bowing style we can estimate person's feeling.

Combinatorial Auction Based Mechanism Design for Course Offering Determination

Anton Vassiliev, Fuhua Lin[(⊠)], and M. Ali Akber Dewan

School of Computing and Information Systems,
Athabasca University, Edmonton, Canada
anton.a.vassiliev@gmail.com,
{oscarl,adewan}@athabascau.ca

Abstract. Course Offering Determination (COD) is a strategy of an educational institution to maximize the satisfaction of the students and the enrollment of the courses within budget and other resource constraint. COD is a resource allocation problem which is difficult to solve due to the complexity in students' preferences and resource constraints. In this paper, a mechanism for interactive and dynamic decision making is proposed to solve the problem. In this mechanism, the agents negotiate using a protocol which is based on a multi-unit Combinatorial Auctions (CA). To solve the Winner Determination Problem (WDP) in CA, we modified the Branch On Bids (BOB) algorithm to account for multi-unit nature of courses as well as the other constraints from students and administrators. A case study demonstrates the ability and effectiveness of the proposed mechanism in COD for the graduate and undergraduate level studies.

Keywords: Course Offering Determination · Combinatorial auctions · Winner Determination Problem · Branch On Bids · Multi-agent systems

1 Introduction

Every semester or every year administrators of academic programs in colleges and universities must determine the courses that their institution will be offering for the upcoming semester or year. We refer to the task of determining the set of courses to be offered as Course Offering Determination (COD). The main question COD attempts to answer is: *What course offering determination strategy for a program in an institution maximizes the satisfaction of the students and maximizes the enrollment of the courses within the budget and the other resource constraints* [1]*?*

The importance of COD cannot be overestimated. For students, the courses offered drive their ability to graduate, timelines for achieving selected majors, prospects regarding the continuation of academic career and overall success in the job market. For institutions and program administrators, student's satisfaction with the courses offered leads to higher the enrollment. Career and academic achievements upon graduation of the students shape the reputations of the institutions. The courses offered also affect the institutions' budget and consume other resources such as the availability of instructors,

© Springer International Publishing AG 2017
V.G. Duffy (Ed.): DHM 2017, Part I, LNCS 10286, pp. 376–392, 2017.
DOI: 10.1007/978-3-319-58463-8_32

lecture halls, experiment laboratories etc. Today in practice, to determine the course offerings, a program administrator uses the history of offered courses and resource availability. The best judgment and experience of the program administrator plays the vital role among the various deciding factors. This process does not directly consider students' preferences and lacks precision in budget and resource allocation.

In this paper, we model the COD problem as a multiagent dynamic constraint resource allocation problem and design a mechanism for interactive and dynamic decision-making to solve the problem. In the proposed mechanism, the agents negotiate using a protocol based on a multi-unit combinatorial auctions (CA) [2]. To solve the Winner Determination Problem (WDP) in CA, we extend the Branch On Bids (BOB) algorithm to account for multi-unit nature of courses as well as other constraints from students and administrators. The application of CA to COD aims to improve process transparency, lower transaction costs, and introduce a robust method to account for the complementary nature of values for the offered courses.

The rest of the paper is organized as follows: Sect. 2 reviews the related work. Section 3 presents the proposed multiagent system for COD. Section 4 discusses the modified BOD algorithm for COD. Section 5 discusses the performance of the algorithm. Section 6 concludes the paper and discusses the future work.

2 Literature Review

There have been considerable researches in multiagent course scheduling [3], collaborative learning environment [4], student advising application [5], time-table scheduling system for educational institutions [6] and collaborative personal study planning system [7]. Recently, some researches have also been done on multiagent-based solutions for COD that addresses the issues of balancing student preferences with institution's limited resources [1]. The Single Transferable Vote (STV) protocol [8] is used to aggregate student preferences, and the COD negotiation protocol is modeled via Petri Nets [9]. The COD system and the negotiation protocol are modeled via Contract-Net Protocol (CNP) [10] and Monotonic Concession Protocol (MCP) [11].

The COD system proposed in this paper is inspired by the system in [1] and expands upon it with the use of CAs. It introduces bids on course bundles and offers simplicity and transparency to the end users while retaining all the efficiency associated with the previous approach of [1]. CAs allows several functional flexibilities and advantages over conventional auction design [2]. It allows bidders to bid on bundle of items instead of limiting to the bid on a single item at a time. Bidding on bundles allows accounting for the complimentary values of the items composing the bundles, which may result in increased economic efficiency and higher utility for both buyers and sellers.

CAs have been used in many large-scale real-life applications with a great success. To name a few, Sears used CAs to design the auction of eight hundred and fifty-four delivery routes and reducing its logistic costs by thirteen percent [12]; the Federal Communications Commission (FCC) used CAs for selling spectrum licenses for wireless services [13, 14]; the London Transport used CAs to distribute city bus routes between bidding contractor companies [15]; and Bell Laboratories proposed a CA based system for allocating airport time slots in USA [16].

An imperative topic for CAs is the bidding language. A bidding language assigns semantic meaning to syntactic constructs that are used for definition and representation of combinatorial bids. Certainly, the way we represent bids has a great influence on the CA protocol design and we must approach it with caution, keeping the specifics and the goals of our COD application in mind. Moreover, the cardinality of the bidding space in CAs is quite large (2^m) with m number of auctioned items, so a succinct language that does not require excessive bidding is of the great importance. Logical languages and generalized logical languages provide very powerful syntax with flexible semantics [17]. They offer the ability to express complex preferences to a considerable depth with ease. Bidding languages for mixed multi-unit CAs expand that ability to include bids with quantity ranges [18].

While this expressive power injects the possibility for a wide range of bidding combinations, they introduce increased complexity to winner determination. In the proposed mechanism, we rely on a simpler version of a bidding language to streamline the initial design of the CA-based COD protocol, with little or no loss to COD functionality. To determine the most efficient assignment of the bundles to the winning bidders, the CA auctioneer must solve the Winner Determination Problem (WDP) [19]. The main challenge of WDP is that it is an intractable NP-complete problem and it presents significant difficulties for time-efficient and space-efficient solutions. There exist many algorithms that offer both exact and approximate solutions for WDP [2]. The most obvious solution is the explicit, full enumeration of all possible combinations. However, this approach is impractical and the computational effort quickly grows intractable.

The more sophisticated solutions to this problem are the Integer Programming [20] that searches the extreme of the objective function that represents the CA, the Dynamic Programming [21] that splits the CA into smaller problems using the bottom-up principle and the Branch On Bids (BOB) [2] that minimizes the search spaces by pruning branches that would not provide a satisfactory solution. The BOB stands outstanding than the others because it offers an efficient method to model multi-unit auctions [22] and a way to utilize problem-specific heuristics to prune search branches and improve efficiency [23]. For this research, the multi-unit auctions and problem-specific heuristics serve as compelling reasons for selecting the BOB as the way to solve the WDP.

3   Multi-agent System for COD

The proposed multi-agent system consists of three types of agents: Auctioneer Agent (AA), Student Agent (SA) and Administrator Agent (AD). The Auctioneer Agent (AA) plays the role of mediation between AA and SAs by using a protocol based on CA. It enables a negotiation between multiple SAs and the AD, which results in a set of courses.

A graphical outline of a COD process is shown in Fig. 1, where AA, SAs and AD are involved in negotiation for an optimal course offering using CA. In this architecture, SA, AD, and AA represent a student, a program administrator and a CA auctioneer, respectively. The SA and AD work in the best interest of the human actors they represent and the AA agent coordinates their effort via a CA-based protocol to achieve a mutually agreeable and efficient solution. The COD negotiation is triggered by the AD agent which prepares a set of must offer courses and a set of negotiable courses and forwards them to the AA and SA agents. The SA agent generates bids for the CA protocol and the AA agent manages the auction.

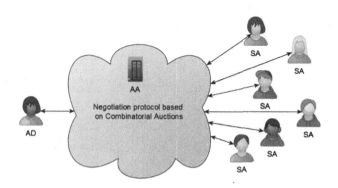

Fig. 1. Multi-agent system for COD.

3.1   Combinatorial Auction (CA) Based Negotiation Protocol

Two important concepts that are needed to be clarified first to explain the CA-based negotiation protocol: *negotiable courses* and *course bidding points*. The CA-based negotiations for COD begins before course registration for a school year. Program administrators notify their respective AD to begin building a set of must-offer courses, a set of must-not-offer courses, and a set of *negotiable courses*. The list of must-offer courses and must-not-offer courses depends on previous faculty commitments and does not depend on student preferences. Program courses that are not included in the must-offer and must-not-offer sets comprise the set of *negotiable courses. Course bidding points* are used for bidding that are allotted to each SA at the beginning of a program and are never refilled. A winning bid will withdraw the spent points from the student's account, thus emulating the use of money in conventional auctions.

CA-based negotiation protocol works in the following steps. The set of negotiable courses and the set of must-offer courses are forwarded to AA. The AA agent forwards these courses to all SAs and initiates a CA-based negotiation. The SAs begin to negotiate by working with the students to update the study plan based on the students' preferences, must-offer courses, and negotiable courses, and thus determine the set of available courses for bidding. The students select the bundles of available courses that she/he will prefer to take over the school year and places their bids on these bundles. Each student can place multiple bids at each round, and once the set of bids is determined, it is forwarded to AA. The AA aggregates the bids from all students and uses BOB algorithm to solve the WDP for the current bidding round. A complete flow diagram for CA-based negotiation protocol is shown in Fig. 2.

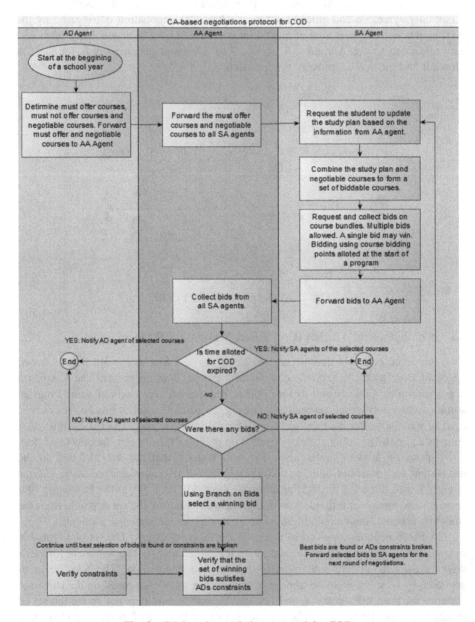

Fig. 2. CA-based negotiation protocol for COD.

3.2 Branch on Bids (BOB) Algorithm

A modified version of BOB algorithm is used in the proposed architecture considering the multi-unit nature of courses and the other constraints from SA and AD. In each round, the winning set of bids is verified with AD to ensure that the winning solution complies with the AD's constraints. The BOB algorithm is executed until registration is completed or until the AD's constraints are satisfied. At this point, the winning bids are forwarded to SAs and the next cycle of the protocol begins. The protocol terminates when the time allotted for the auction is expired or if no more bids were placed. The last selected set of winning bids combined with must offer courses form the course offering for the year. As the proposed mechanism of COD relies on the BOB algorithm to find the best bids, we reviewed a generic BOB algorithm [22, 23] to solve WDP in CA below this section. The modified version of BOB algorithm used for the proposed mechanism is explained in Sect. 4.

Combinatorial Auction (CA) can be defined by a set of items $M = \{i_1, \ldots, i_m\}$ available for bidding, where $|M| = m$; and a set of bids $B = \{b_1, \ldots, b_n\}$ generated by the bidders, where $|B| = n$. A bid b_j is defined as a two-tuple, $b_j = <S_j, p_j>$, where S_j is the set of bidding items and p_j is the bidding price such that $S_j \subseteq M$, $p_j \geq 0$. To identify the winner in CA, the WDP is solved with the following function:

$$\max \sum_{j=1}^{n} p_j x_j \tag{1}$$

where $\sum_{j|i \in S_j} x_j \leq 1$, $i = 1, \ldots, m$, and $x_j \in \{0, 1\}$. Here, $x_j = 1$ signifies a winning bid b_j and $x_j = 0$ signifies a losing bid b_j. Here, we must maximize the sum of winning bids, while ensuring that the sets of items in winning bids do not intersect. The last condition is imposed by the assumption that each offered item is unique. The unique item requirement must be relaxed for solving COD. The BOB algorithm to solve a

Table 1. Terms and symbols used in BOB (see Algorithm 1)

Terms and symbols	Description
IN	Set of bids that are labeled winning on the path to the current search node
IN*	Set of bids that are winning in the best allocation found so far
g	Revenue from the bids in *IN*
f^*	Revenue from the bids in *IN**
e_j	Exclusion count for bid b_j
M'	Set of unallocated item in the current search path
h	Upper bound on the revenue from the unallocated items, M'
$c(i)$	This is the admissible heuristic for estimating revenue for item $i \in M'$. The $c(i)$ is calculated using the formula $max_{j|i \in S_j, e_j = 0} p_j / |S_j|$. This can be interpreted as the maximum per-item bidding price among all bids containing the item i and that are not part of IN or IN*
ChooseBranch	Selecting a bid b_k to branch on. Let B_0 be a set of bids, where $B_0 \subseteq B$ and $\forall b_j \in B_0$, $e_j = 0$, then $b_k \in B_0$ and $\forall b_j \in B_0 \frac{p_k}{\sqrt[2]{|S_k|}} \geq \frac{p_j}{\sqrt[2]{|S_j|}}$

typical WDP in CA is presented in Algorithm 1, where all the terms and symbols used in the algorithm is listed in Table 1.

Algorithm 1. Branch On Bids (BOB) Pseudo code.

```
1:   begin
2:       if g>f* then          //if current search is better, remember it as all-time best
3:           IN→IN*
4:           g→f*
5:       end if
6:       h = Σᵢ∈ₘ· c(i)         //Calculate the upper bound
7:       if g+h≤f* then         // Check if this branch can produce better results than
                                    we already have. // If not – bound
8:           return
9:       end if
10:      Select a bid bₖ using ChooseBranch algorithm
11:      if bₖ = NULL then
12:          return
13:      end if
14:      IN U {bₖ} → IN    // Prepare to branch on bₖ
15:      eₖ=1
16:      ∀ bⱼ∈B| bⱼ ≠ bₖ and Sⱼ ∩ Sₖ ≠ ∅   // Update the exclusion count for all
                                                  the bids that share items with bₖ
17:      eⱼ = eⱼ + 1
18:      BOB (M`- Sₖ, g + pₖ)          // Branch in
19:      IN - {bₖ} → IN                // Prepare to branch out
20:      ∀ bⱼ∈B| bⱼ ≠ bₖ and Sⱼ ∩ Sₖ ≠ ∅   // Update the exclusion count for all
                                                  the bids that share items with bₖ
21:      eⱼ = eⱼ − 1
22:      BOB(M`,g)                     //Branch bₖ out
23:      eₖ = 0                        // Done with this branch
24:      return
25:  end
```

In *ChooseBranch* function, the square root of cardinality of item subsets has been shown to be effective at selecting bids with balance between high price bids, but with large number of items, verses bids with low item count, but also with low bidding value [22, 24]. This is an important feature that under proper circumstances may result in faster convergence to the winning bid allocation. The BOB (see Algorithm 1) takes M' and g as its input. Upon completion of BOB execution, $IN*$ contains the set of winning bids. The first call is BOB(M, 0).

3.3   Interaction Model and Bidding Language

The visual interactions model is presented in Fig. 3. All COD interactions that happen during CA negotiations are listed in Table 2 with their descriptions.

Bidding language used for auction is introduced below, where we assign semantic meaning to syntactic constructs that are later used to define student's course bids.

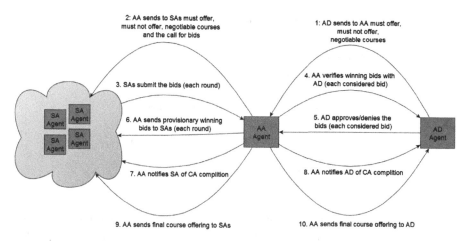

Fig. 3. COD interaction model

Table 2. COD interaction model

Step	From	To	Description
1	AD	AA	AD sends to AA the sets of must offer, must not offer and negotiable courses
2	AA	SA	AA sends to SAs the sets of must offer, must not offer, negotiable courses and the call for bids
3	SA	AA	SAs submit the bids (each CA round)
4	AA	AD	Each time a new bid is considered as a provisional winning bid, AA sends the set of provisional winning bids to AD for verification against resource constraints
5	AD	AA	AD approves or denies the provisional winning bids proposed in step 4. The decision is based upon available school resources
6	AA	SA	Upon completion of each round, AA sends all provisionary winning bids to SAs. New round begins by cycling to step 3. Students place new bids against provisionary winning bids in step 6
7	AA	SA	AA notifies SA of CA completion
8	AA	AD	AA notifies AD of CA completion
9	AA	SA	AA sends the final course offering to SA
10	AA	AD	AA sends the final course offering to AD

Definition 1: A *submission* is consisted of three-tuple $<B, sa, po, co>$, where $B = \{b_1, \ldots, b_n\}$ is a set of bids with $|B| = n$, sa is the name of the SA agent submitting the bid, po is the total amount of course bidding points available for the SA agent, and co is the maximum number of courses the student can take. An example for a submission is given in Table 3.

Table 3. An example for a submission

Variable	Value for example 1
Submission	<B, "sa1", 10, 6>
B	$\{b_1, b_2, b_3\}$
b_1	$<S_1, 6>$
S_1	{"comp501", "comp503", "comp504"}
b_2	$<S_2, 6>$
S_2	{"comp504", "comp505", "comp506"}
b_3	$<S_3, 2>$
S_3	{"comp601"}

Definition 2: A *bid* b_j is a two-tuple $<S_j, p_j>$, where $S_j = \{s_1, \ldots, s_k\}$ with $S_j \subseteq M$, $|S_j| = k_j$, $k_j \leq co \leq m + l + t$, and p_j is the amount of course bidding points assigned to this bid by the student.

A set of courses available for bidding is defined as $M = \{i_1, \ldots, i_m\}$ with $|M| = m$. This is a set of courses the students can bid on. A set of must-offer and negotiable courses are defined as $O = \{o_1, \ldots, o_n\}$ with $|O| = l$ and $N = \{n_1, \ldots, n_t\}$ with $|N| = t$, respectively.

A set of rules are while selecting the winning bid using the CA protocol. The set of bids B is interpreted by the CA protocol as a non-exclusive OR concatenation of the bids, baring the rules follows:

- Winning bids from the same student may not contain intersecting sets of courses.
- Winning bids may not add up to a total exceeding the amount of course bidding point available to the student
- The number of courses comprising winning bids may not exceed maximum number of courses the student can take
- The courses comprising winning bids may not contradict course interrelationships (for example there may not be any anti-requisites)

4   Modified Branch on Bids (BOB) Algorithm for COD

In contrast to the traditional bidding strategy, a notable change is needed in the proposed COD to adjust the fact that multiple students can bid on the same course or on the same combination of courses and can win. This is allowed because multiple students can take the same course or the same combination of courses at the same time in educational institutions. The only restriction is that the total number students is not allowed to exceed a pre-specified limit which is the maximum enrollment for that course. The above constrained are enforced by the AD agent. We address this challenge through using the notion of multi-unit auctions [22], with the number of available course units equal to the enrollment limit for the course. Using this approach, we can apply the Branch-on-Bids algorithm with only minor modifications.

Algorithm 2. Modified Branch On Bids (BOB) for COD

1:     If $g>f^*$, then $IN{\rightarrow}IN^*$, $g{\rightarrow}f^*$ //if current search is better, remember it as the all-time best

2:     h=$\sum_{i\in M} c(i)$ //Calculate the upper bound

3:     // Check if this branch can produce better results than we already have.
      If $g+h\leq f^*$, return () // If not – bound

4:     Use the *ChooseBranch* algorithm to select a bid b_k to branch on
      If no such bid exists, return

5:     IN U $\{b_k\}$ $\rightarrow$ IN // *Prepare to branch on b_k*
      e_k=1

6:     Verify that IN set satisfies the SA_Constraints and the AD_Constraints
      If not then IN - $\{b_k\}$ $\rightarrow$ IN; e_k=0; EX U $\{< d,b_k >\}$ $\rightarrow$ EX;
      Return to step 4

7:     // Update the set of available course units U`.
      For each course in S_k subtract 1 from the matching course unit in U`

8:     // Update the set of available courses M`.
      If an item $i_j \in$ M` and $u_j = 0$ then M`=M`-$\{i_j\}$

9:     // Update the exclusion count for all the bids that share courses with b_k
      // and have no enrollment places available
      $\forall$ $b_j{\in}B|$ $b_j \neq b_k$ and $S_j \cap S_k \neq \emptyset$ and $\exists$ an item $i_e \in S_j \cap S_k$ s.t. $u_e = 0$
      then $e_j = e_j + 1$

10:    BOB(M`, U`, $g + p_k$, d+1) //Branch in

11:    IN - $\{b_k\}$ $\rightarrow$ IN //Prepare to branch out

12:    / Update the exclusion count for all the bids that share courses with b_k
      // and have no enrollment places available
      $\forall$ $b_j{\in}B|$ $b_j \neq b_k$ and $S_j \cap S_k \neq \emptyset$ and $\exists$ an item $i_e \in S_j \cap S_k$ s.t. $u_e = 0$
      then $e_j = e_j - 1$

13:    // Update the set of available course units U`.
      For each course in S_k add 1 to the matching course unit in U`

14:    // Update the set of available courses M`.
      If an item $i_j \notin$ M` and $u_j \geq 0$ then
      M`=M`+$\{i_j\}$

15:    //Update the exclusions set EX
      Remove all exclusions for branch d
      $\forall$ $ex_j{\in}EX$ s.t. $d_j = d$
      EX = EX – $\{ex_j\}$

16:    //Branch b_k out
      BOB(M`, U`, g, d)

17:    //Done with this branch
      e_k=0;
      return

Reusing and adjusting the formal definition of CAs from Sect. 3, we define CA in the context of COD as a three-tuple $<M, U, B>$, where $M = \{i_1,\ldots,i_m\}$ with $|M| = m$ is a set of courses available for bidding; $U = \{u_1,\ldots,u_m\}$ with $|U| = m$ specifying the maximum enrollment for the matching course; and $B = \{b_1,\ldots,b_n\}$ is a set of bids by students. Finally, the WDP can be defined same as Eq. (1). It is to be mentioned that, in the context of COD an item (a course or a course package) within a bid will always have quantity of exactly one because a student can only enroll in a course once per semester. Therefore, we use a modified version of multiunit WDP [22]. We also add to the set of constraints all limits induced by the limitations of SA agents (see submission interpretations in subsection 3.3) and the resource limitations enforced by the AD agent.

The modified BOB for WDP in the proposed COD relies on the adjusted variables outlined in Table 4 and the proposed BOB algorithm is presented in Algorithm 2. BOB takes on input the set of available courses, their associated available enrollment limits, current search revenue and branch depth. The first call of this algorithm is BOB (M, U, 0, 1). Upon the completion of the algorithm execution the IN^* set will contain the set of winning bids.

Table 4. Branch on Bids for Course Offering Determination variables

Variable	Definition
M'	The set of available courses (courses that have available enrollment places). Can be thought of as a set of auction items that still have available inventory
U'	The set of course units matching M'. When branching in on a bid, the course units for the courses in the bids get subtracted a unit. When branching out on a bid, the course units for the courses in the bid get an extra unit. In other words, this variable tracks available enrollment places in a course
$c(i)$	The admissible heuristic for estimating revenue for item $i \in M'$ $c(i) = max_{j\|i\in S_j, e_j=0} u_i * p_j / \|S_j\|$ (this formula can be interpreted as the number of available course units multiplied by the maximum per-item bidding price among all bids containing the item i and that are not part of IN or IN^*)
d	The depth of the current branch
EX	A set of "exclusion" two-tuples $<d, b>$ A tuple represents a bid b excluded at branch depth d due to violation of Administrator or Student constraints
$ChooseBranch$	The heuristic algorithm for selecting a bid b_k to branch on Let B_0 be a set of bids s.t. $b_j \in B_0$ iff $b_j \in B$ and $e_j = 0$ and $<d, b_j> \notin EX$ for any integer d Then $b_k \in B_0$ and $\forall\, b_j \in B_0\, \frac{p_k}{\sqrt[2]{\|S_k\|}} \geq \frac{p_j}{\sqrt[2]{\|S_j\|}}$
$SA\_Constraints$	Winning bids from the same student may not contain intersecting sets of courses Winning bids may not add up to a total exceeding the amount of course bidding point available to the student The number of courses comprising winning bids may not exceed maximum number of courses the student is allowed to take The courses comprising winning bids may not contradict course interrelationships (for example there may not be any antirequisites)
$AD\_Constraints$	For the purpose of this paper, the AD agent will enforce the maximum number of courses that the school can offer

5 Result and Discussion

5.1 Solution Quality

Distributed multi-agent system based solution quality is a complex, multifaceted topic that involves, amongst others, those of social welfare of agent societies, individual rationality, stability and efficiency [25]. The practical side of COD solution quality should be measured through a pilot project that would follow a group of participating students through their academic progress for a period of one or more semesters. The student's subjective utility with the program and academic performance may be compared to those of non-participating students, drawing the conclusions on the quality of proposed solution. Because of technical complexity of the solution quality measurement and time constrained involved with a pilot program, we followed up with a discussion on a case study based on the quality analysis principles as outlined in [25].

The CA-based COD algorithm is a form of a negotiation mechanism that uses CAs to provide a transparent and economical solution for COD. The mechanism aims to benefit the crucial players of the system: the students and the administrators, increasing social welfare through the mutually satisfactory solution. We measure social benefit of the students through the value they assign to the courses in their bids, and the administrator's benefit through student enrollment (subject to the resource constraints). It follows that since CAs maximize the economical payoff through increasing the course bidding points revenue, the CA-based COD algorithm should lead to the course selection most beneficial within the constructed environment.

Moreover, the proposed solution encourages student's participation in the bidding process through the potential to improve the course offerings for the bidding student. Participation in the bidding process will always lead to the results that are at least as good as for non-participating students thus providing the individual rationality. The bidding process and the limited course bidding points inject stability into the protocol, promoting truthful bidding for the courses the students are interested in.

5.2 Performance

An unsatisfactory performance may render even the best designs unusable in practice. In the case of CA-based COD algorithm, the WDP is solved off-line and therefore the expectation is that the problem is solved in a reasonable time and the solution process does not consume much computational resources in a manner that significantly detrimental to the rest of the services in an academic institution. The looseness of this performance requirement is possible because the COD needs to be addressed only once a semester or once a year, and the bidding rounds are executed once a day (or possibly on some other prolonged schedule) during the COD process and do not require immediate response.

The version of BOB utilized in this paper is a search algorithm that builds and traverses a binary bid-search tree by branching on bids [22]. The performance of BOB is proportional to the number of leaves in our search tree which is not greater than $(nk/m + 1)^{\lfloor m/k \rfloor}$, where n is the number of bids, m is the number of items, and k is the smallest number of items among all bids.

The number of leaves is exponential on the number of items (courses available for bids), but polynomial on the number of bids. This is an important and positive observation because program administrators can control the number of biddable items (courses) in case of unsatisfactory algorithm performance. The number of bids, however, depends on the number of students and their personal preferences and involvement, and therefore is harder to control.

The performance of original BOB algorithm is analyzed in [23]. Bid sets containing from five hundred to two thousand bids for sets of ten items were solved in less than six seconds. While bid sets containing four hundred and fifty bids for sets of forty five items were solved in less than twenty seconds. In the context of COD these results appear to be very promising. We can estimate that the number of items (courses) in most COD auctions is unlikely to exceed a few dozen. The number of bids will vary between programs and schools and will greatly depend on student enrollment, however

Table 5. Partial flow of BOB for COD example

Execution Step	BOB Step	Comments
1:	n/a:	BOB ($\{c1, c2, c3, c4, c5\}$, $\{u1 = 1, u2 = 2, u3 = 2, u4 = 1, u5 = 1\}$, 0, 1)
2:	1:	n/a
3:	2:	$h = c(c1) + c(c2) + c(c3) + c(c4) + c(c5) = 2 + 4 + 3 + 2 + 2 = 13$
4:	3:	$13 > 0$ – proceed
5:	4:	Following the ChooseBranch algorithm we select bid $<\{c1, c2\}, 4>$
6:	5:	IN = $\{<\{c1, c2\}, 4>\}$ $e_1 = 1$
7:	6:	No constraint violations – proceed
8:	7:	$U' = \{u1 = 0, u2 = 1, u3 = 2, u4 = 1, u5 = 1\}$
9:	8:	$M' = \{c2, c3, c4, c5\}$
10:	9:	No bids intersect with b_1 – proceed
11:	10:	BOB($\{c2, c3, c4, c5\}$, $\{u1 = 0, u2 = 1, u3 = 2, u4 = 1, u5 = 1\}$, 4, 2)
12:	1:	IN* = $\{<\{c1, c2\}, 4 >\}$, f* = 4
13:	2:	$h = c(c2) + c(c3) + c(c4) + c(c5) = 0 + 3 + 2 + 2 = 7$
14:	3:	$4 + 7 = 11 > 4$ – proceed
15:	4:	Following ChooseBranch algorithm we select bid $<\{c4, c5\}, 4>$
16:	5:	IN = $\{<\{c1, c2\}, 4>, <\{c4, c5\}, 4>\}$ $e_3 = 1$
17:	6:	No constraint violations – proceed
18:	7:	$U' = \{u1 = 0, u2 = 1, u3 = 2, u4 = 0, u5 = 0\}$
19:	8:	$M' = \{c2, c3\}$
20:	9:	$e_2 = 1$
21:	10:	BOB($\{c2, c3\}$, $\{u1 = 0, u2 = 1, u3 = 2, u4 = 0, u5 = 0\}$, 8, 3)
22:	1:	IN* = $\{<\{c1, c2\}, 4>, <\{c4, c5\}, 4>\}$, f* = 8
23:	2:	$h = c(c2) + c(c3) = 0 + 3 = 3$
24:	3:	$8 + 3 = 11 > 8$ – proceed
25:	4:	At this point there are not more bids available – return

for most the programs it will remain under a few thousand. It appears likely that WDP for COD may be solved within a reasonable time-frame, measuring seconds or minutes.

5.3 A Case Study

In this section, we provide a simple case study that illustrates the partial listing of the BOB for COD algorithm flow that terminates the listing at the first leaf. Please note the simple form of the student preference submissions, which represents a clear improvement over precedence, grouping and progression model used in [1, 26]. Rationality for the winning bids is also easy to understand, which should lead to students expressing their preferences through bidding rounds with higher precision.

In the case study, we assume that due to resource constraints (*AD_Constraints*) we can offer at most five courses, where

M = {c1, c2, c3, c4, c5}
U = {u1 = 1, u2 = 2, u3 = 2, u4 = 1, u5 = 1}
Submission1: <{<{c1, c2}, 4>, <{c3, c4}, 3>}, sa1, 10, 4>
Submission2: <{<{c4, c5}, 4>}, sa3, 10, 4>

The execution flow is provided in Table 5.

We terminated our example at step 25, however the algorithm will continue to explore remaining branches, determining {<{c1,_c2}, 4>, <{c4,_c5}, 4>} as the winning bids. Figure 4 shows the complete progress of the algorithm in a graphical form. The bright orange rectangles represent bids in the IN set, the grey rectangles represent the excluded bids.

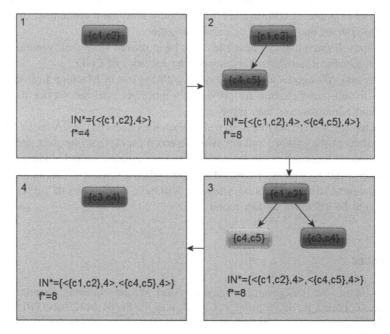

Fig. 4. BOB for COD example.

6 Conclusions

The main contribution of this research is the introduction of CAs to the process of the COD negotiations. CAs bring a few benefits to distributed negotiation protocols, for instance: accounting for the complimentary values of the course bundles, increased economic efficiency, expressive negotiations format that lowers transaction costs and high level of transparency that ensures fairness.

The challenge of efficient negotiation was met with introduction of multi-unit auctions, and the ability for multiple students to win bids on the same courses was handled through multi-unit auctions. The intractable WDP was tackled using the BOB algorithm that offers polynomial performance on bids and generalization that includes the multi-unit solutions.

The expected performance of the CA-based COD solution promises to be within reasonable and practical limits. The most computation-costly part of the algorithm, the WDP, is solved off-line and is expected to complete execution within seconds or minutes for the most extreme cases.

A potential area of interest for CA-based COD research may be the application of it to the Massive Open Online Courses (MOOC). The scale and popularity of online programs serve as a powerful argument in favor of application of CA-based COD, which aspires to improve economic efficiencies. Further experiment and elaboration of the CA-based COD solution will be done to improve its efficiency and flexibility:

- The bidding language may be extended to include complex logical combinations of bids, such as "AND" and "EXCLUSIVE OR";
- Student and Administrator constraints may be improved to provide more realistic rules. For example, Administrators may not only limit the total number of courses, but also courses that may not be offered together;
- The *ChooseBranch* and c(i) heuristics may be improved from their general form to more applicable algorithms that consider the specifics of COD;
- The SA and AD agents may be extended with the use of Machine Learning techniques to self-customization for providing a more personalized service to the students and administrators they represent.
- A data mining system may be designed to learn the effects of the CA-based COD on the welfare of the system, and empower research for further improvements.
- The proposed mechanism can be extended to have multiple-round bidding that may promotes a fair allocation of coveted courses. When a student is unable to obtain a desired course in an early round, she or he will have more points to bid for courses that might be offered in a later round.

References

1. Lin, F., Chen, W.: Designing a multiagent system for course-offering determination. In: Boella, G., Elkind, E., Savarimuthu, B.T.R., Dignum, F., Purvis, M.K. (eds.) PRIMA 2013. LNCS (LNAI), vol. 8291, pp. 165–180. Springer, Heidelberg (2013). doi:10.1007/978-3-642-44927-7_12

2. Schwind, M.: Combinatorial auctions for resource allocation. In: Schwind, M. (ed.) Dynamic Pricing and Automated Resource Allocation for Complex Information Services. LNEMS, vol. 589, pp. 137–190. Springer, Heidelberg (2007). doi:10.1007/978-3-540-68003-1_5

3. Oprea, M.: MAS-UP-UCT: a multi-agent system for university course timetable scheduling. Int. J. Comput. Commun. Control 2(1), 94–102 (2007)

4. Vassileva, J., McCalla, G., Greer, J.: Multi-agent multi-user modeling in I-Help. User Model. User-Adap. Inter. 13(1), 179–210 (2003)

5. Hamdi, M.S.: MASACAD: a multiagent-based approach to information customization. IEEE Intell. Syst. 21(1), 60–67 (2006)

6. Tariq, M., Mirza, M., Akbar, R.: Multi-agent based university time table scheduling system. Int. J. Multidiscip. Sci. Eng. 1(1), 33–39 (2010)

7. Vainio, A., Salmenjoki, K.: Improving study planning with an agent-based system. Informatica 29, 453–459 (2005)

8. Bartholdi, J.J., Orlin, J.B.: Single transferable vote resists strategic voting. Soc. Choice Welfare 8(4), 341–354 (1991)

9. Fehling, R.: A concept of hierarchical Petri nets with building blocks. In: Rozenberg, G. (ed.) ICATPN 1991. LNCS, vol. 674, pp. 148–168. Springer, Heidelberg (1993). doi:10. 1007/3-540-56689-9_43

10. Smith, R.G.: The contract net protocol: high-level communication and control in a distributed problem solver. IEEE Trans. Comput. C-29(12), 1104–1113 (1980)

11. Rosenschein, J.S., Zlotkin, G.: Rules of Encounter: Designing Conventions for Automated Negotiation Among Computers. MIT Press, Cambridge (1994)

12. Ledyard, J., Olson, M., Porter, D., Swanson, J., Torma, D.: The first use of a combined-value auction for transportation services. Interfaces 32(5), 4–12 (2002)

13. Crampton, P., Kwerel, E., Rosston, G., Skrzypacz, A.: Using spectrum auctions to enhance competition in wireless services. J. Law Econ. 54(4), 167–188 (2011)

14. Porter, D., Rassenti, S., Roopnarine, A., Smith, V.: Combinatorial auction design. Natl. Acad. Sci. 100(19), 11153–11157 (2003)

15. Vries, S., Vohra, R.: Combinatorial auctions: a survey. Informs J. Comput. 15(3), 284–309 (2003)

16. Rassenti, S., Smith, V., Bulfin, R.: A combinatorial auction mechanism for airport time slot allocation. Bell J. Econ. 13(2), 402–417 (1982)

17. Boutilier, C., Hoos, H.: Bidding languages for combinatorial auctions. In: International Joint Conference on Artificial Intelligence, Seattle, USA, August 2001

18. Cerquides, J., Endriss, U., Giovannucci, A., Rodriguez-Aguilar, J.: Bidding languages and winner determination for mixed multi-unit combinatorial auctions. In: International Joint Conference on Artificial Intelligence, Hyderabad, India, January 2007

19. Lehmann, D., Müller, R., Sandholm, T.: The winner determination problem. In: Cramton, P., Shoham, Y., Steinberg, R. (eds.) Combinatorial Auctions, pp. 297–318. MIT Press, Cambridge (2006)

20. Anderson, A., Tenhunen, M., Ygge, F.: Integer programming for combinatorial auction winner determination. In: International Conference on Multiagent Systems, Boston, MA, July 2000

21. Rothkopf, M., Pekec, A., Harstad, R.: Computationally manageable combinatorial auctions. Manag. Sci. 44(8), 1131–1147 (1998)

22. Sandholm, T., Suri, S.: BOB: improved winner determination in combinatorial auctions and generalizations. Artif. Intell. 145, 33–58 (2003)

23. Sandholm, T., Subhash, S., Gilpin, A., Levine, D.: CABOB: a fast optimal algorithm for combinatorial auctions. In: International Joint Conference on Artificial Intelligence, Seattle, USA, August 2001

24. Lehmann, D., O'Callagham, L., Shoham, Y.: Truth revelation in rapid, approximately efficient combinatorial auctions. J. ACM **49**(5), 96–102 (2002)
25. Sandholm, W.: Distributed rational decision making. In: Multi-agent Systems, pp. 201–258. MIT Press, Cambridge (1999)
26. Armstrong, A.J.: Optimizing course-offerings with MAS. Master's Essay, Athabasca University, Athabasca, Alberta, March 2012
27. Weiss, G.: Multiagent Systems - A Modern Approach to Distributed Artificial Intelligence. MIT Press, London (1999)
28. Conitzer, V.: Making decisions based on the preferences of multiple agents. Commun. ACM **53**(3), 84–94 (2010)
29. Stone, P., Veloso, M.: Multiagent systems: a survey from a machine learning perspective. Auton. Robot. **8**(3), 345–383 (2000)
30. Wooldridge, M., Jennings, N.R., Kinny, D.: The gaia methodology for agent-oriented analysis and design. J. Auton. Agents Multi-agent Syst. **3**(3), 285–312 (2000)
31. Winikoff, M., Padgham, L.: Agent-oriented software engineering. In: Multiagent Systems, pp. 695–758. MIT Press, Heidelberg (2014)
32. Dorca, F.A., Lopes, C.R., Fernandes, M.A.: A multiagent architecture for distance education systems. In: IEEE International Conference on Advanced Learning Technologies, Athens, Greece, July 2003
33. Graesser, A., Chipman, P., Haynes, B., Olney, A.: AutoTutor: an intelligent tutoring system with mixed-initiative dialogue. IEEE Trans. Educ. **48**(4), 612–618 (2005)
34. Mitrovic, A., Ohlsson, S.: Evaluation of a constraint-based tutor for a database language. Int. J. Artif. Intell. **10**, 238–256 (1999)
35. Wilson, D.C., Leland, S., Godwin, K., Baxter, A., Levy, A., Smart, J., Najjar, N., Andaparambil, J.: SmartChoice: an online recommender system to support low-income families in public school choice. AI Mag. **30**(2), 46–58 (2009)
36. Lin, F., Leung, S., Wen, D., Zhang, F., Kinshuk, McGreal, R.: E-advisor: a multi-agent system for academic advising. Int. Trans. Syst. Sci. Appl. **4**(2), 89–98 (2008)
37. Cernuzzi, L., Molensini, A., Omicini, A., Zambonelli, F.: Adaptable multi-agent systems: the case of the gaia methodology. Int. J. Softw. Eng. Knowl. Eng. **21**(4), 491–521 (2011)
38. Moraïtis, P., Petraki, E., Spanoudakis, N.I.: Engineering JADE agents with the gaia methodology. In: Carbonell, Jaime G., Siekmann, J., Kowalczyk, R., Müller, Jörg P., Tianfield, H., Unland, R. (eds.) NODe 2002. LNCS (LNAI), vol. 2592, pp. 77–91. Springer, Heidelberg (2003). doi:10.1007/3-540-36559-1_8
39. Wooldridge, M.: A modern approach to distributed artificial intelligence. In: Multiagent Systems, pp. 27–77. MIT Press, Cambridge (1999)
40. Symeonidis, A., Mikas, P.: Agent Intelligence Through Data Mining. Springer, Heidelberg (2005)
41. Russel, S., Norvig, P.: Artificial Intelligence: A Modern Approach. Prentice Hall, Upper Saddle River (2010)
42. Sturm, A., Shehory, O.: Agent-oriented software engineering: revisiting the state of the art. In: Shehory, O., Sturm, A. (eds.) Agent-Oriented Software Engineering, pp. 13–26. Springer, Heidelberg (2014). doi:10.1007/978-3-642-54432-3_2
43. JASON. http://jason.sourceforge.net/wp/. Accessed Nov 2015

Design and Evaluation of a Human-Like Puppet as an Input Device for Ergonomic Simulation

David Wiegmann[1(✉)], Holger Brüggemann[1], and Andreas Rausch[2]

[1] Institute for Production Technology, Ostfalia University of Applied Sciences,
Wolfenbüttel, Germany
{david.wiegmann,holger.brueggemann}@ostfalia.de
[2] Department of Informatics, TU Clausthal, Clausthal-Zellerfeld, Germany
andreas.rausch@tu-clausthal.de

Abstract. Although ergonomic simulation offers great potential, it is still rarely used in production planning processes compared to other simulation tools. The main reason for this is the immense effort in time needed for creating movements and controlling the digital human model. We will present here a special input device for controlling the posture of a digital human model. Thus, we have developed a small physical puppet. The posture of the puppet can be manipulated and is mapped to the controlled digital human model. To evaluate the usability, we conducted a study in which we compared it to the mouse based user interface along the learning curve. The results show that the users postured the digital human model significantly faster with our input device than with the mouse.

Keywords: Ergonomic simulation · Graspable user interface · Usability

1 Introduction

Ergonomic simulation enables a lot of possibilities to improve the ergonomics and productivity of manual production processes. Despite its potential, ergonomic simulation is used quite rarely in production planning processes compared to other simulation methods e.g. robotic simulation. The main reason for this is the great amount of time required to control a digital human, which, in turn, is often needed to create human movements in the simulation [1]. Basically, it is possible to set a posture of a digital human model by forward or by inverse kinematics. Using forward kinematics, the user has to set every single joint; this requires experience and time. On the other hand, inverse kinematics based on posturing is a fast method. It, however, frequently leads to unsatisfactory postures. Apart from these methods, it is possible to use motion capture systems for controlling the digital human, often requiring preparation time and effort as well as physical prototypes of product and equipment.

© Springer International Publishing AG 2017
V.G. Duffy (Ed.): DHM 2017, Part I, LNCS 10286, pp. 393–403, 2017.
DOI: 10.1007/978-3-319-58463-8_33

To reduce the time needed for posturing in human simulation, we have been following a new approach. Consequently, we have developed a special input device. A small physical puppet is used to control the posture of a digital human model. We already introduced the prototype of our input device, named *Human Input Device (HID)* elsewhere [2]. In this paper, we want to present our sophisticated version and the evaluation of our input device.

2   Related Work

There have been several other projects where graspable input devices controlled the posture of virtual rigged characters [3–14]. Most of them focus on computer animation e.g. the *Dinosaur Input Device* [3], which was one of the first entities of its kind in input devices. It was made to control virtual dinosaurs playing in the movie Jurassic Park. *Monkey* [4] was the first humanlike input device for controlling a digital human. It was used for ergonomic simulation in product design and controlled a very rudimentary digital human. A more modern input device for ergonomic simulation in product design was presented by Yoshikazi et al. [5]. Their actuated puppet also controlled a very simple digital human with only a few degrees of freedom compared to modern human models used in ergonomic simulation.

Moreover, an evaluation has not yet been made whether if it is useful to control a digital human for ergonomic simulation of production processes with such a graspable user interface. Yoshikazi et al. [5] conducted a study to evaluate their input device for posturing processes in general. But they used their input device to control a simple virtual artist's doll. Today's digital human models used in ergonomic simulation are more complex. Furthermore, the posturing process did not represent manual production processes.

3   Design

The dimensions of the puppet correspond with the 50th percentile of the German population and is scaled by the factor 1:4.25. The puppet is an input device with 22 degrees of freedom and is designed to control the digital human model *Jack* by *Siemens PLM*. Thus, we have developed a plugin to use in the simulation tool *process simulate*. In comparison to related input devices, our input device is able to control a posture of a digital human model with 77 degrees of freedom. Hence, we have now designed a suitable skeleton for the puppet derived from the Jack model. As a result the postures of Jack and the puppet nearly match, although the input device has only 22 degrees of freedom (see Fig. 1).

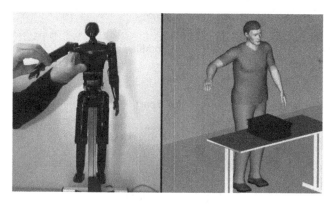

Fig. 1. Setting a posture with the human input device to the digital human model *Jack*

3.1 Mechanics

Using the *Jack* model, we determined the skeleton of the puppet. Figure 2 shows which joints can be manipulated, where a schematic (left) and the final version (right) of the skeleton is shown.

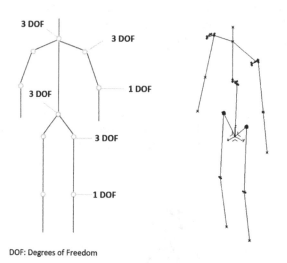

Fig. 2. Schematic (left) and final (right) version of the skeleton

We tried to separate the mechanical structure into functional parts and shaping parts. For the functional parts, we designed a special bearing, which encapsulates an encoder and represents the center of each joint of the puppet (see Fig. 3). The bearing is designed for conventional manufacturing processes and it is equal for every joint. With two adjusting screws, it is possible to set the friction of the joint for compensating gravity.

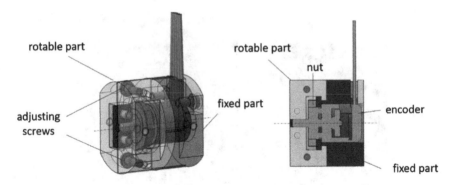

Fig. 3. Joint structure

The individual shaping parts are connected to the bearings and ensure that the puppet looks as similar as possible to Jack. These parts are designed for modern additive manufacturing processes. Due to the encoder, it is only possible to measure a single degree of freedom per each joint. Hence, we had to substitute three dimensional joints e.g. the hip by three serial connected joints. In addition, we simplified the spine and the clavicle-shoulder group by three serial connected joints each. The values of the joints are used for controlling the whole group including e.g. each vertebra of the spine. Consequently, the posture of the digital human model still looks natural. Figure 4 (left) shows the shape of *HID* compared to *Jack*.

3.2 Interface

We developed a small customized board, including a microcontroller to decode the signals of the encoder (see Fig. 4, right). These boards are integrated inside the shaping parts of the puppet. Each Microcontroller monitors the signals of one encoder and converts them to an angle. Furthermore, they are slave participants to an I^2C bus.

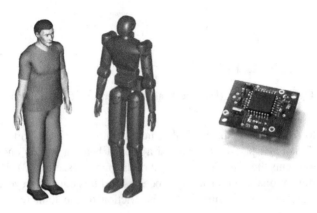

Fig. 4. Shape of the *HID* compared to *Jack* (left) and customized board (right)

We subsequently developed a controller box, which contains a main board. Through an additional microcontroller on it, representing the master participant to the bus, the joint values are provided to our plugin in *process simulate*. Finally, our plugin, based on the API of *process simulate*, maps the posture of the puppet to *Jack* with no noticeable latency. Furthermore, the user can use the plugin for saving characteristic poses to generate keyframe based movements of the digital human model.

4 Evaluation

We conducted a study to see if our input device is suitable for ergonomic simulation of production processes. The study is designed to see if our input device has higher usability along the learning curve for controlling the posture of a digital human model for ergonomic simulation compared to the mouse. The following research questions thus needed to be answered:

RQ1: Are users along the learning curve more effective if they use the *HID* instead of the mouse for posturing a digital human model.

RQ2: Are users along the learning curve more efficient if they use the *HID* instead of the mouse for posturing a digital human model.

RQ3: Are users along the learning curve more satisfied if they use the *HID* instead of the mouse for posturing a digital human model.

4.1 Design of the Study

Task

In our study users should perform a core task in ergonomic simulation. They should manipulate the posture of the digital human model *Jack* to different target postures. We defined in total six different target postures, which all considered manual production processes (see Fig. 5). Thus, the digital human model interacts with equipment and products. One half of the postures represents final postures of a movement e.g. reaching a part in a container and the other half represents intermediate postures of movements. One part was defined with the *HID* and the other part with the mouse. The six scenes consisting of digital human model, equipment and product are duplicated and ordered next to the original scene. But the posture of *Jack* is set to a neutral default posture. The users now had to manipulate the default postures to the target postures repeatedly with mouse and *HID*. The users should terminate the posturing process if they are satisfied with the approximation of the manipulated and target posture or, if they notice that they are not making any progress in accuracy. Manipulating the posture with the mouse, users used the normal graphical user interface in *process simulate*. They could decide whether to use direct or inverse kinematics. Taking a learning curve into consideration, each participant repeated the run seven times. The first six runs with a maximal distance of two days and the last run with a distance of two weeks to the sixth run to consider the reusability.

Fig. 5. Target postures

Participants

We conducted the study with 14 participants. Eleven of them were male and three female. They were between 18 and 34 years old. All of them were students of mechanical engineering and had no experience in ergonomic simulation.

Order Balancing

To minimize the effect on the posturing process of which input device is used first for manipulating the posture, we divided the participants into two different groups. We consequently altered the type of input device which was used first. The order of group A is the inversion of group B (see Fig. 6).

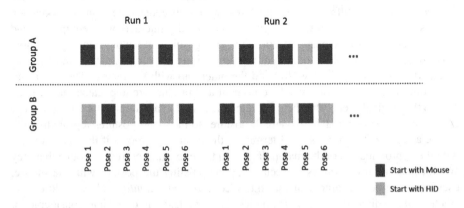

Fig. 6. Alter of the first input device for each posturing process of both groups

Variables

The independent variables, which we changed in this study, are the type of input device, the different runs and the participants. The dependent variables are the three components of usability: effectiveness, efficiency and satisfaction. The controlled variables are the target postures and the order in which an input device is used for posturing.

Operationalization of the Dependent Variables

For measuring the dependent variables, we had to derive values which represent them and which can be measured. To measure the accuracy, we determined each deviation of the target posture and the manipulated pose. Thus, we summed up the absolute value of the difference for every joint between the target posture and the manipulated posture. With each run we noted the average accuracy out of all six postures made with the mouse and *HID*. We also measured the execution time of the posturing processes to consider the efficiency. For every run, we determined the average execution time out of all six postures achieved with the mouse and *HID*. We then asked the participants after each run how satisfied they were while using the two types of input devices. They had to rate their satisfaction on a scale from one to ten, where ten being high and one is low.

Hypotheses

For each run we formulated the following three hypotheses:
RQ1:
  H_0: The achieved accuracy with the mouse is higher or the same
  H_1: The achieved accuracy with the mouse is less

RQ2:
  H_0: The achieved execution time with the mouse is shorter or the same
  H_1: The achieved execution time with the mouse is longer

RQ2:
  H_0: The achieved user satisfaction with the mouse is higher or the same
  H_1: The achieved user satisfaction with the mouse is lower

4.2   Procedure of the Study

Before the first run, the users where introduced to both input devices, which took ca. 30 min. First they were shown how to use the input devices and then they could try them out. The procedure was carried in a normal office at a work station equipped with two monitors. On the first monitor they had a 3d-view and on the second the graphical dialogs of the input devices. The *HID* were initially positioned next to the monitor, but the user were given explicit permission to relocate them as they wished. Moreover, they could choose whether to stand or sit while using the *HID*.

4.3   Results

Figures 7, 8 and 9 show the average values and confidence intervals (95%) of the average execution time, accuracy and the rating of the user satisfaction per each run and input device.

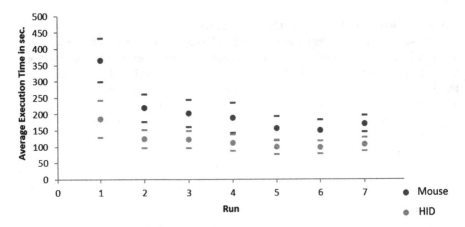

Fig. 7. Average values and confidence intervals (95%) of the average task execution times per run

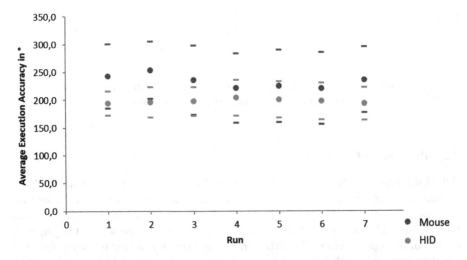

Fig. 8. Average values and confidence intervals (95%) of the average accuracy per run

A Shapiro-Wilk-Test showed that we can assume that one part of the variables is distributed normally and another part is not. We verified the hypotheses with paired sample t-tests or Wilcoxon signed-rank tests depending on whether normally distributed variables are considered or not. Table 1 shows the results of the multiple

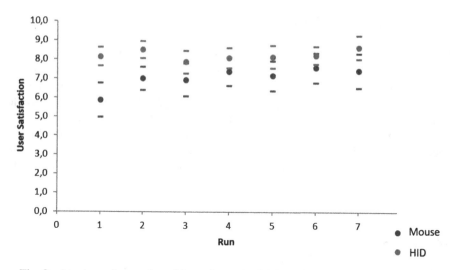

Fig. 9. Average values and confidence intervals (95%) of the user satisfactions per run

testing. We used the Bonferroni-Correction to compensate the increase in type 1 error, due to multiple testing. Hence, we divided our total $\alpha = 0.05$ by the number of hypotheses (21), which leads to a partial type 1 error $\alpha_p = 0.00239$ for each hypothesis.

Table 1. Test results

Run	Variable	Test	p-value	Test desicion
1	Accuracy	Wilcoxon signed-rank test	0.032	Accept null hypothesis
2	Accuracy	Wilcoxon signed-rank test	0.003	Accept null hypothesis
3	Accuracy	Wilcoxon signed-rank test	0.15	Accept null hypothesis
4	Accuracy	Wilcoxon signed-rank test	0.3415	Accept null hypothesis
5	Accuracy	Wilcoxon signed-rank test	0.2165	Accept null hypothesis
6	Accuracy	Wilcoxon signed-rank test	0.2755	Accept null hypothesis
7	Accuracy	Wilcoxon signed-rank test	0.024	Accept null hypothesis
1	Execution time	Paired sample t-test	0.0000...	Reject null hypothesis
2	Execution time	Paired sample t-test	0.0000...	Reject null hypothesis
3	Execution time	Paired sample t-test	0.0000...	Reject null hypothesis
4	Execution time	Paired sample t-test	0.0000...	Reject null hypothesis
5	Execution time	Paired sample t-test	0.0000...	Reject null hypothesis
6	Execution time	Paired sample t-test	0.0005	Reject null hypothesis
7	Execution time	Paired sample t-test	0.0000...	Reject null hypothesis
1	User satisfaction	Wilcoxon signed-rank test	0.006	Accept null hypothesis
2	User satisfaction	Wilcoxon signed-rank test	0.002	Reject null hypothesis
3	User satisfaction	Wilcoxon signed-rank test	0.0225	Accept null hypothesis
4	User satisfaction	Wilcoxon signed-rank test	0.022	Accept null hypothesis
5	User satisfaction	Wilcoxon signed-rank test	0.04	Accept null hypothesis
6	User satisfaction	Wilcoxon signed-rank test	0.0455	Accept null hypothesis
7	User satisfaction	Wilcoxon signed-rank test	0.0615	Accept null hypothesis

5 Conclusion and Future Work

The test results show that the participants where significantly faster in posturing when using the *HID* instead of the mouse. This result was shown along the whole monitored learning curve. Although all average values of accuracy or user satisfaction achieved with the *HID* where higher than the average values achieved with the mouse, it could not be shown that these values where significantly higher. Nevertheless, what was clear was that using the *HID* minimizes the effort required for posturing a digital human model in ergonomic simulation for inexperienced users in the learning process. To verify that it is useful to use the *HID* for ergonomic simulation, we are now planning to conduct an additional study with domain experts.

References

1. Wiegmann, D., Brüggemann, H.: Entwicklung einer menschenähnlichen Puppe als Eingabegerät für die Menschsimulation. In: Rabe, M., Clausen, U. (eds.) Simulation in Produktion und Logistik 2015. Fraunhofer, Stuttgart (2015)
2. Mun, J.H., Rim, Y.H.: Human Body Modeling. In: Canetta, L., Redaelli, C., Flores, M. (eds.) Digital Factory for Human-oriented Production Systems, pp. 165–186. Springer, London (2011). doi:10.1007/978-1-84996-172-1_10
3. Knep, B., et al.: Dinosaur input device. In: Katz, I., et al. (eds.) Conference on Human Computing Systems (CHI 1995), pp. 304–309. ACM Press/Addision-Wesley Publishing Co., New York (1995). doi:10.1145/223904.223943
4. Esposito, C., et al.: Of mice and monkeys: a specialized input device for virtual body animation. In: Symposium on Interactive 3D Graphics (I3D 1995), ACM, New York (1995). doi:10.1145/199404.199424
5. Yoshikazi W., et al.: An actuated physical puppet as an input device for controlling a digital manikin. In: Conference on Human Factors in Computing Systems (CHI 2011), pp. 637–646. ACM, New York (2011). doi:10.1145/1978942.1979034
6. Bradford Paley, W.: Designing special-purpose input devices. Comput. Graph. **9**(4), 55–59 (1995). doi:10.1145/307710.307729
7. Arai, K.: Cyber bunraku. In: Lynn, P., et al. (eds.) The 24th International Conference on Computer Graphics and Interactive Techniques (SIGGRAPH 1997), p. 87. ACM, New York (1997). doi:10.1145/259081.259184
8. Barakonyi, I., Schmalstieg, D.: Augmented reality in the character animation pipeline. In: Special Interest Group on Computer Graphics and Interactive Techniques Conference (SIGGRAPH 2006), ACM, New York (2006), Article No. 75. doi:10.1145/1179849.1179943
9. Barakonyi, I., Schmalstieg, D.: Augmented reality agents in the development pipeline of computer entertainment. In: Kishino, F., Kitamura, Y., Kato, H., Nagata, N. (eds.) ICEC 2005. LNCS, vol. 3711, pp. 345–356. Springer, Heidelberg (2005). doi:10.1007/11558651_34
10. Weller, M.P., et al.: Posey: instrumenting a poseable hub and strut construction toy. In: 2nd International Conference on Tangible and Embedded Interaction (TEI 2008), pp. 39–46. ACM, New York (2008). doi:10.1145/1347390.1347402

11. Feng, T.-C.; Jiang, B.: Motion capture data retrieval using an artist's doll. In: 19th International Conference on Pattern Recognition (ICPR 2008), pp. 1–4. IEEE, Piscataway (2008). doi:10.1109/ICPR.2008.4761301
12. Hayes, C.: Starship troopers. In: The 25th International Conference on Computer Graphics and Interactive Techniques (SIGGRAPH 1998), p. 311. ACM Press/Addision-Wesley Publishing Co., New York (1998). doi:10.1145/280953.282447
13. CELSYS, Inc.: Humanoid Input Device – Qumarion. http://www.clip-studio.com/quma/en/products/qumarion (June 2014)
14. Jacobson, A., et al.: Tangible and modular input device for character articulation. In: ACM Transactions on Graphics (TOG), vol. 33(4). ACM, New York (2014). doi:10.1145/2601097.2601112

Object-Oriented User Interface Customization: Reduce Complexity and Improve Usability and Adaptation

Le Zhang[1(✉)], Qing-Xing Qu[1,3], Wen-Yu Chao[1],
and Vincent G. Duffy[1,2]

[1] School of Industrial Engineering, Purdue University, West Lafayette, USA
zhan1255@purdue.edu
[2] School of Agriculture and Biological Engineering,
Purdue University, West Lafayette, USA
[3] Department of Industrial Engineering, Northeastern University, Shenyang,
People's Republic of China

Abstract. The purpose of this research is to improve the usability and adaptation of complex information system (CIS) by reducing the complexity. The paper introduces CIS, the complexity of CIS, usability and adaptation issues of CIS, and potential solutions for these issues. Research suggests User Interface (UI) customization can address usability and adaptation issues in CIS. This research proposes the Object-Oriented User Interface Customization (OOUIC) framework to reduce the complexity of CIS, in order to improve the usability and adaptation. The OOUIC approach suggests that classifying users by user roles, e.g., job roles, can reduce the complexity. Use Case Analysis (UCA) can identify actors (job roles) and use cases (goals, tasks, and functions) to develop use case diagrams, tasks diagrams, and function models. Based on model-driven modeling, the mapping between use case diagrams, task diagrams, and function models enables automatic selection of abstract UI and development of concrete UI for each job role. Building connections between vendor UI (V-UI) and concrete UI to generate the adaptable vendor-free UI (MyUI) can ensure the reuse of UI customization on whichever V-UI. The efficiency, robustness, and maintainability of the method had been justified in previous studies. This research proposes a two-phase study by using the product lifecycle management (PLM) system as an example to illustrate that the framework can reduce complexity and improve usability and adaptation.

Keywords: Adaptation · Complex information system · Product lifecycle management · Usability · Use case analysis · User interface customization

1 Introduction

With the growth of computer technology, the information system (IS) becomes a computer-based system which can collect, manage, store, and share information among various users [1]. With current IS technology, multiple users can handle many sets of information in a short time, simultaneously. As the human's demand of managing complex information growing, the IS becomes multifunctional and consists of heterogeneous

© Springer International Publishing AG 2017
V.G. Duffy (Ed.): DHM 2017, Part I, LNCS 10286, pp. 404–417, 2017.
DOI: 10.1007/978-3-319-58463-8_34

components. A complex system is defined as any system composed of a great number of heterogeneous entities which may interact with each other to create multiple levels of structure and organization [2]. The heterogeneous entities can be systems, humans, information, and environments elements. Thus, when a IS requires interaction between many heterogeneous systems and users from multiple expertise to manage different sets of information, it can become a Complex Information system (CIS) [2].

As the concept of CIS emerges from recent years, there is not a standard definition of this term. Albers and Still [3] specified four characteristics of CIS: complex work environments, complex information contexts, complex technologies, and complex topics. A complex work environment includes collaborations between multiple users to achieve different goals and often is accompanied by distractions, interruptions, and pauses [4]. This characteristic consists of three aspects: complex users, goals, and environments. The complexity of information presents not only by the variety of information but also by its dynamic feature. The information diversity requires users from different expertise (complex topics) and different technologies or applications to conduct the analysis. Also, the analysis methods, information presentations, and expertise can be varied (complex technologies) due to the dynamic nature of complex information [5]. The complex information overlaps with complex technologies and complex topics. The complex topic is highly associated with users' background and the information [6]. Adapting Albers and Still's definition, this research proposes five complex aspects: user, goal, information, technology, and environment (Fig. 1). This

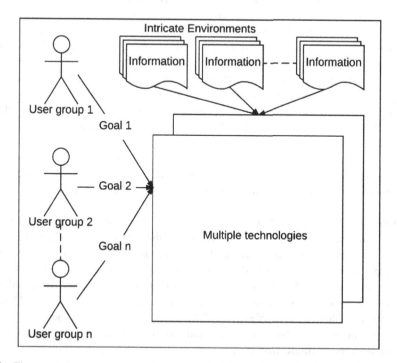

Fig. 1. Five complex aspects of CIS: user, goal, information, technology, and environment (based on Albers and Still's four characteristics of CIS [3])

research defines CIS as any information system which requires collaborations among different users in an intricate environment to use multiple technologies dealing with numerous sets of dynamic information to achieve various goals.

Previous CIS research hasbeen conducted on product lifecycle management systems, software configuration management systems, resource management systems, healthcare systems, and financial systems [5, 7–11]. These systems are enterprise systems implemented in organizations to manage complex information, such as product data, software configuration, customers' information, and financial data. An organization can involve multiple job roles, various business goals, and intricate environments. Thus it can be seen that enterprise systems follow the CIS's definition and five complex aspects. This research focuses on enterprise systems and uses PLM system as an example to illustrate the usability and adaptability of CIS.

CIS brings not only benefits to progressing large sets of information but also a series of usability and adaptation issues to users using its User Interface (UI). As UI is the software unit that can directly interact with users [12], this research focuses on CIS's UI design. Usability is to ensure effectiveness, efficiency, and satisfaction for a specified set of users to achieve a particular set of tasks in a specific environment [13]. The usability issues caused by complexity include redundancy, unorganized layout, and poor learnability. The purpose of developing multifunctional UI is to enable multiple user roles to achieve various goals and manage different types of information within one single UI. However, the low usage of other functions and information by a particular user role results in redundancy [14]. Redundancy can cause misused functions, inefficiency of locating functions and information, and hard to memorize UI features [15]. Even though designers put efforts in organizing many functions and information in a single UI, users still have trouble to understand the multifunctional UI and blame it for causing unsatisfied experience [9]. Moreover, the difficult nature of CIS applications and multifunctionality result in poor learnability. For instance, converting an engineer from using one PLM system to another PLM system (new vendor or upgraded system) can require six months and $20,000 investment [16]. Adaptation refers to the properties of a system that can automatically adapt its behavior and interaction to suit the user's needs, expertise, and requirements [17]. CIS tends to sacrifice the adaptation and use one single UI to integrate multiple functions and information to satisfy various users' needs [18]. Even though there is research proposes using adaptive UI can improve the adaptation of CIS, the complexity results in difficulties to develop self-adjust UI for various users [19].

These usability and adaptation issues all have connections of the complexity of CIS. The purpose of this research is to investigate the complexity of CIS and improve usability and adaptation. The structure of this paper is as follows. This section introduces CIS and its usability and adaptation issues. The next section reviews relevant works in improving usability and adaptation of CIS. After analyzing potential solutions, the third section proposes the Object-Oriented UI Customization (OOUIC) framework to reduce the complexity of CIS, in order to improve the usability and adaptation. The fourth section provides a study to evaluate the OOUIC approach. The last section suggests future works.

2 Relevant Research

The ultimate goal of this research is to improve usability and adaptation of CIS. However, adaptive UI and common User-Centered Design (UCD) methods might not be sufficient to address issues in the CIS's unique atmosphere. In order to identify appropriate methods for CIS, this section reviews UI adaptation, UCD methods, and UI customization approach.

2.1 User Interface Adaptation, Customization, and Personalization

Adaptation is associated with personalization and customization [20]. Similar to adaptive UI, personalization relies on the artificial intelligence and machine learning to predict user preference and tailor the UI to increase its personal relevance to an individual or a category of individuals [21]. Not to mention the faultiness of machine learning technology, identifying complex user requirements in CIS is a great challenge. Relying on UI to do self-adaptive to fit complex customers' needs is impractical.

In contrast, UI customization, which refers to the capability of enabling users to adapt the UI to meet their requirements on specific tasks [22], can be a potential solution to improve both usability and adaptation of CIS. Against static and adaptive UI, UI customization builds an adaptable UI which enables users to control UI design to provide higher perceived efficiency levels, thus greater satisfaction [23]. The research found that UI customization can improve users' perceived ease of use, satisfaction, user experience, willingness to use, and performance [24]. Thus, UI customization is a potential solution to improve both adaptation and usability. The challenge to implement UI customization is to ensure robustness, efficiency, and maintainability in a complex setting [25].

2.2 User-Centered Design

User-Centered Design suggests placing users at the center of the design to allow them to influence the design shape and giving extensive attention to their needs in each stage of design processes [26]. UCD emphasizes user involvement and provides many methods to evaluate and develop usability design, such as questionnaire, interview, focus group, use case, scenario analysis, cognitive walkthrough, and heuristic evaluation [27]. However, research indicates that UCD approach might not be sufficient to identify user requirements in CIS [3].

As potential users of CIS can come from different backgrounds, simply applying questionnaire, interview, and focus group can collect very diverse user requirements. Satisfying different expert requirements in a single UI is hard. Forcing a single UI to include all the needs can cause functional conflicts and redundancy [7]. Another limitation of UCD methods is the development of CIS requires domain expertise. It limits the application of user-free formative methods, e.g., cognitive walkthrough and heuristic evaluation, since designers are not familiar with terminologies and functionalities of the CIS [28]. Applying UCD method in CIS requires reducing the complexity, e.g., separating users into groups to collect requirements and designing for particular user roles. The Use Case Analysis (UCA), which can identify user goals and group requirements by goals, is one UCD method that can handle complexity [29]. Thus, this research suggests using UCA to reduce the complexity of CIS.

2.3   Object-Oriented Design Method

Based on UCA, Lin and Lee [30] proposed the Object-Oriented Analysis (OOA) method to investigate the complex relationship between users' objects and UI elements for the development of CIS. The approach suggests end-users' objects are associated with their requirements and desired system behaviors.

As shown in Fig. 2, the approach classifies user roles (in a PLM system, user role can be an engineer, manager, and customer) and execution platforms (a PLM system can be smart device application, desktop application, web application) and groups them into client units, e.g., customers using an iPhone application. When customizing UI for a specific user in a user role, the user and a platform can be a unit, e.g., a specific engineer called Jack using a desktop application. For each client unit, identify which trigger event enacts users to accomplish a specific use case. A trigger event can be a message or another use case. The use case is a set of scenarios that narratively describe interactions between the user and the system to achieve a specific goal. One client unit can have multiple trigger events and use cases. Based on the use case and the user role's characteristics, designers can build user role profile and functions for this user role, e.g., engineers' profile and engineers' functions. For a specific user in a user role who wants to customize functions, the user's characteristics will be used to generate customization profile, e.g., an engineer called Jack has Jack's profile and Jack's customized functions. All information will be stored in a use case bank for the system to determine which UI should be provided to the user.

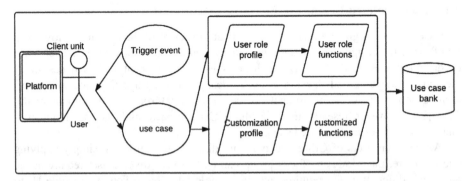

Fig. 2. The framework of object-oriented analysis in UI customization (modified based on Lin and Lee's diagrams [30])

With the use case bank, a system can judge which platform the user is using. Since the widget and size in different platforms are different, the UI should be designed for each individualplatform. Based on user role profile and customization profile, the system judges: what is the user' role, which user role functions should be provided, whether this user has customized functions, and which customized functions should be provided. When a trigger event occurs, the system judges which use case will happen. Based on user role profile and customization profile, the system provides UI for the user to accomplish the use case.

The OOA method can customize UI for each user role, platform, use case, and aspecificuser. The advantage of this approach is that it classifies user requirements into detail groups. For this reason, 'it can ensure the robustness of identifying complex requirements in CIS. However, customize UI for every individual user is time-consuming and not economical. A more efficient approach is required.

2.4 Model-Driven Design

Model-Driven Development (MDD) proposed automatic UI customization to increase efficiency and consistency when developing variants of an UI [31]. However, purely automatic UI customization relies on unstable machine learning technology and can cause usability issues as adaptive UI does. To avoid this dilemma, Pleuss [32] proposed Semi-Automatic UI Customization (SAUIC) on the basis of Model-Based User Interface Development (MBUID) and Software Product Line (SPL) [33, 34]. The MBUID suggests derivation of an UI from a set of UI models by considering users, platforms, and environments. The SPL's idea is to build a series of templates of an UI to achieve mass production by using templates. Merging two methods, SAUIC inherits efficiency and usability.

The SAUIC process (Fig. 3) has a family of abstract UI templates for one kind of software. Abstract UI is the unit that includes the most basic elements of an UI to achieve a task, e.g., abstract UI of a normal searching function includes an input box, a search button, and a list of search results. One UI can have different abstract UI templates, e.g., search by name, search by ID, advanced search. Then designers define UI configuration of which elements are required for the software, e.g., the UI only needs search by name. After having the specific abstract UI for the software, designers can manually adjust the UI layout for a user role, a platform, and an environment. All

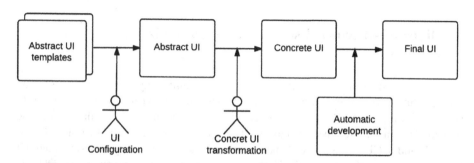

Fig. 3. The framework of semi-automatic UI customization (modified based on Pleuss's Model-Driven Development model [25])

manual adjustments can automatically convert to a concrete UI, which is a preview of the adjusted UI. Last, the concrete UI will automatically transfer to the final UI, which is the UI for users.

Research justified that the SAUIC approach ensures not only the efficiency but also the usability of UI customization [25]. However, the model did not specify a robust method for manual customization. Thus, OOA should be integrated into the SAUIC approach.

2.5   User-Centered User Interface Customization

Implementing OOA in SAUIC can ensure the efficiency and robustness in UI customization of one software. However, switching software and upgrading software are common in an organization. Maintainability is essential for UI customization. The maintainability is to ensure the UI customization can be implemented in a dynamic environment, including changing the software vendor, upgrading software, and switching to another type of software. Wu [35] and his colleagues propose a User-Center UI Customization (UCUIC) to enable the extension of a customized UI to other vendor UIs.

The UCUIC method (Fig. 4) allows users to select desired functions from a vendor UI (V-UI) to customize a MyUI for a specific user. The MyUI also allows the user to adjust the UI configuration. All customized behaviors are stored in a database so that the tool can regenerate the MyUI when the software switches to a new V-UI.

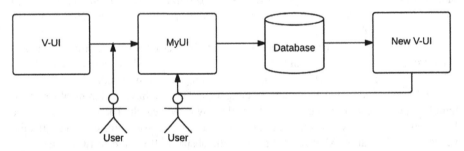

Fig. 4. The framework of user-centered UI customization (modified based on Wu's user interface customization model [35])

3   Objective-Oriented User Interface Customization Framework

This research suggests that UCA can reduce the complexity by grouping users by specific characteristics, e.g., job roles. Also, UI customization can improve the usability and adaptation of CIS. Robustness, efficiency, and maintainability are the keys to the implementation of UI customization in CIS. Thus, this research integrates OOA, SAUIC, and UCUIC into a systematic approach to achieve Objective-Oriented UI Customization (OOUIC) in CIS. This section describes the framework of OOUIC (Fig. 5).

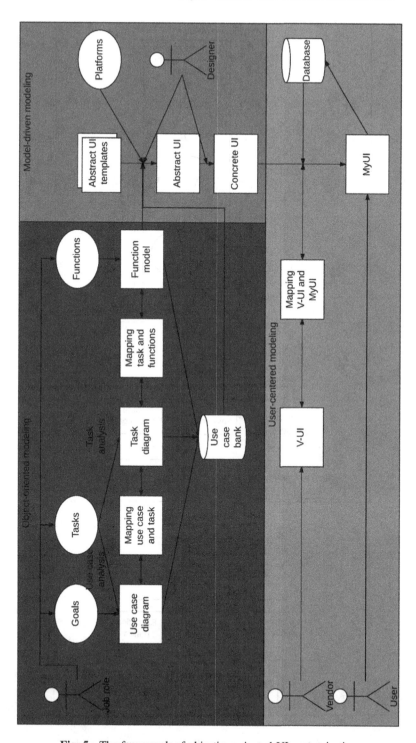

Fig. 5. The framework of objective-oriented UI customization

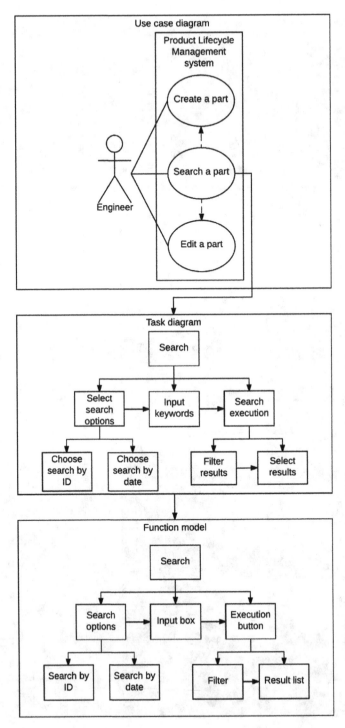

Fig. 6. Use case diagram, task diagram, and function model

3.1   Object-Oriented Modeling

The OOUIC framework includes three phases: Object-Oriented Modeling (OOM), Model-Driven Modeling (MDM), and User-Centered Modeling (UCM). The first phase is OOM. The OOUIC framework can classify users by their job role, e.g., engineers, managers, customers. A job role is a description of what a person does in an organization [36]. Most companies use a job title to name a job role.

UCA will be applied to collect each job role's goals, tasks, and required functions to develop use case diagram, task diagram, and function model (Fig. 6). Developing a use case diagram can identify a job role's goals and the required tasks to achieve these goals. For example, an engineer's goal is to design a part in a PLM system. The engineer needs to create a part, edit the part, and search the part.

A task diagram illustrates all detailed steps to achieve a task. In Fig. 6, the task diagram shows steps to achieve a search task. Vertical arrows connect sub-steps, e.g. to select a search option, a user can choose search by ID or search by name. Horizontal arrows show the sequence of a series of steps, e.g., filter results first, then select the desired result. The reason to have a task diagram is to help designers eliminate unintended steps. For example, a job role does not require search options, the select search options and its sub-steps can be removed from the diagram.

A function model is to map task diagram to a software's functions. Each step in task diagram has a corresponding function in the function model, and the function is described in a way that system can understand. Thus, the system can eliminate the unintended functions from the UI.

There are mappings between use case diagram, task diagram, and function model so that other diagrams can make a corresponding change to the adjustment in one diagram. These diagrams and mappings are stored in the use case bank for designers to create abstract UI.

3.2   Model-Driven Modeling

The next phase is MDM. A group of abstract UI templates is designed for achieving each function in different platforms. Based on the platform and the user's job role, the system will automatically develop abstract UI for the user role. To ensure the usability, designers can manually adjust the UI configuration during the process of creating abstract UI. With the abstract UI, designers can manually adjust UI layout to develop a concrete UI.

Based on SPL, the system can leverage abstract UI templates and use case bank to build concrete UI automatically. All manual designs are not necessary. However, when a new job role or specific requirements come in, manual design can satisfy special needs and improve the usability.

3.3   User-Center Modeling

The UCM phase is to ensure the maintainability of the model. A CIS can have multiple applications, and these applications can change dynamically. For example, in a PLM system, product development engineers need CAD software to design 3D model; managers need ERP software to manage resources; sales need CRM software to communicate with customers. In addition, companies can change software vendors or upgrade software to another version. It is inefficient to redo customization when there is a change in the software.

User-center modeling suggests developing MyUI for each user. A MyUI is converted from the concrete UI. Users can manually customize MyUI. The MyUI's information (concrete UI and user's customization behaviors) is stored in a database. Based on the database, the system can automatically build a mapping between V-UI and MyUI. Thus, the user only needs to use one MyUI; the system can take care of the dynamic changes in V-UIs.

4   Application in PLM System UI Customization

The purpose of building the OOUIC framework is to emerge with an efficient, robust, and maintainable approach to improve the usability and adaptation of CIS. Previous studies had validated the efficiency, robustness, and maintainability of the methods implemented in OOUIC [25, 30, 35]. This research proposes using an observation of PLM system UI customization to investigate whether the approach can improve usability and adaptation. As complexity is a major factor that can influence the usability and adaptation, this research also will assist in determining the relationship between complexity, usability, and adaptation.

4.1   Hypotheses

Hypothesis 1: Comparing to V-UI, the MyUI can significantly reduce the UI complexity.
Hypothesis 2: Comparing to V-UI, the MyUI can significantly improve user performance and perceived usability. They can highlight the relationship with usability and adaptation.

4.2   Methods

The observation includes two phases. The first phase will apply OOUIC method to develop MyUI for the PLM system. As previous research indicates that "fifteen to twenty participants are required to elicit user requirements in Use Case Analysis [37] ", this study will conduct the UCA with 20 participants to develop case diagrams, task diagrams, and function models. Abstract UI templates will be developed based on Siemens Teamcenter and PTC Windchill. Prototypes of MyUI for multiple job roles will be developed by using UCA results and Abstract UI templates.

The second phase is to conduct a scenario analysis to measure and compare the complexity, usability, and adaptation between MyUI and two V-UIs (Siemens

Teamcenter and PTC Windchill). According to UCA, one task will be chosen as the scenario. Previous research suggests having 30 participants can receive statistically significant results [38]. Thus, this study will recruit 30 to 40 PLM users from the manufacturing company to conduct the task on MyUI and two V-UIs. Alemerien's [39] UI complexity metrics (alignment, grouping, size, density, and balance) will be used to measure complexity. The metrics include both objective measures of UI structure and participants' subjective rating. Previous studies indicate that adaptation is associated with user performance and user experience measures, such as task time, errors, and perceived usability [23, 40]. According to Albert's book [38], this study defines task success, task time, and errors as performance measures, and usefulness, ease of use, satisfaction, and ease of learning as self-reported measures (perceived usability). The measures can highlight the relationship with usability and adaptation. ANOVA will compare the complexity, user performance, and perceived usability between MyUI and two V-UIs. The expected result is there is a significant difference between MyUI and V-UIs.

5 Conclusion

In conclusion, UI customization can be an effective way to improve usability and adaptation of CIS. This research proposes the OOUIC framework by combining OOA, SAUIC, and UCUIC as an efficient, robust, and maintainable approach to customize UI for CIS. However, further study is required to investigate the improvement of complexity, usability, and adaptation of MyUI, in the comparison of V-UI.

The complexity of user, goal, information, and technology can be reduced by applying the OOUIC framework for UI customization. However, a complex environment can still cause serious usability issues, such as interruptions, distractions, and unintended pauses. Among these complex environment issues, the interruption can easily cause harmful effects on users' cognitive and physical work process and result in barriers to system adoption [41]. In the future work, the effect of interruptions on MyUI and V-UI should be studied.

Acknowledgement. Authors are grateful to the support of Professor Nathan Hartman (Purdue Polytechnic Institute) and Product Lifecycle Management Center of Excellence at the Purdue Polytechnic Institute. Authors also want to thank master students Shefali Rana and Apoorva Sulakhe (Purdue Industrial Engineering) for providing valuable advice.

References

1. Davis, G.B., Olson, M.H.: Management Information Systems: Conceptual Foundations, Structure, and Development. McGraw-Hill Inc., New York City (1984)
2. Bihanic, D., Polacsek, T.: Models for visualisation of complex information systems. In: Proceedings of the International Conference on Information Visualisation, pp. 130–135. IEEE (2012)

3. Albers, M., Still, B.: Usability of Complex Information Systems: Evaluation of User Interaction. CRC Press, Boca Raton (2010)

4. Spaulding, C.R., Gibson, W.S., Schreurs, S.F., et al.: Systems engineering for complex information systems in a federated, rapid development environment. Johns Hopkins APL Tech. Dig. **29**, 310–326 (2011)

5. Wang, W., Hsieh, P.: Beyond routine: symbolic adoption, extended use, and emergent use of complex information systems in the mandatory organizational context. In: ICIS 2006 Proceedings, vol. 48, pp. 733-750 (2006). http://aisel.aisnet.org/icis2006/48

6. Tiwari, S., Gupta, A.: A systematic literature review of use case specifications research. Inf. Softw. Technol. **67**, 128–158 (2015). doi:10.1016/j.infsof.2015.06.004

7. Mirel, B.: Interaction Design for Complex Problem Solving: Developing Useful and Usable Software. Morgan Kaufmann, Burlington (2004)

8. Levary, R.R.: Computer integrated manufacturing: a complex information system. Prod. Plan. Control **7**, 184–189 (1996). doi:10.1080/09537289608930340

9. Lu, X., Wan, J.: Model Driven Development of Complex User Interface, MDDAUI (2007)

10. Song, X., Li, B.H., Chai, X.: Research on key technologies of complex product virtual prototype lifecycle management (CPVPLM). Simul. Model. Pract. Theory **16**, 387–398 (2008). doi:10.1016/j.simpat.2007.11.008

11. Warman, A.R.: Developing complex information systems: the use of a geometric data structure to aid the specification of a multi-media information environment. London School of Economics and Political Science (United Kingdom). Doctorate dissertation (1990)

12. Laurel, B., Mountford, S.J.: The Art of Human-Computer Interface Design. Addison-Wesley Longman Publishing Co., Inc., Boston (1990)

13. ISO FDIs: ISO 9241-210: 2009. Ergonomics of human system interaction-Part 210: human-centered design for interactive systems. Int. Organ. Stand. (ISO) Switz. (2009)

14. Veneziano, V., Mahmud, I., Khatun, A., Peng, W.W.: Usability analysis of ERP software: education and experience of users' as moderators. In: SKI 2014 - 8th International Conference on Software, Knowledge, Information Management and Applications (SKIMA) (2014). doi:10.1109/SKIMA.2014.7083560

15. Allanic, M., Durupt, A., Joliot, M., et al.: Towards a data model for PLM application in bio-medical imaging. In: 10th International Symposium on Tools Methods Competitive Engineering TMCE, pp. 365–376 (2014)

16. Bartholomew, D.: PLM: Boeing's dream, airbus' nightmare. Baseline (2007)

17. Schneider-Hufschmidt, M., Malinowski, U., Kuhme, T.: Adaptive User Interfaces: Principles and Practice. Elsevier Science Inc., Amsterdam (1993)

18. DeLone, W.H., McLean, E.R.: Information systems success: the quest for the dependent variable. Inf. Syst. Res. **3**, 60–95 (1992)

19. Akiki, P.A., Bandara, A.K., Yu, Y.: Adaptive model-driven user interface development systems. ACM Comput. Surv. **47**, 1–33 (2014). doi:10.1145/2597999

20. Blom, J.: Personalization - a taxonomy. Conf. Hum. Factors Comput. Syst. ACM 313–314 (2000). doi:10.1145/633292.633483

21. Fan, H., Poole, M.S.: What is personalization? Perspectives on the design and implementation of personalization in information systems. J. Organ. Comput. Electron. Commer. **16**, 179–202 (2006). doi:10.1207/s15327744joce1603&4_2

22. Rivera, D.: The effect of content customization on learnability and perceived workload. In: CHI 2005 Extended Abstracts on Human Factors in Computing Systems, pp. 1749–1752 (2005). doi:10.1145/1056808.1057013

23. Findlater, L., McGrenere, J.: A comparison of static, adaptive, and adaptable menus. In: Proceedings ACM CHI 2004, vol. 6, pp. 89–96 (2004). doi:10.1145/985692.985704

24. Hui, S.L.T., See, S.L.: Enhancing user experience through customisation of UI design. Procedia Manuf. **3**, 1932–1937 (2015). doi:10.1016/j.promfg.2015.07.237
25. Pleuss, A., Wollny, S., Botterweck, G.: Model-driven development and evolution of customized user interfaces. In: EICS 2013 – Proceedings of the ACM SIGCHI Symposium on Engineering Interactive Computing Systems, pp. 13–22 (2013). doi:10.1145/2480296.2480298
26. Abras, C., Maloney-Krichmar, D., Preece, J.: User-centered design. Bainbridge, W. Encycl. Hum.-Comput. Interact. Thousand Oaks Sage Publ. **37**, 445–456 (2004). doi:10.3233/WOR-2010-1109
27. Williams, A.: User-centered design, activity-centered design, and goal-directed design: a review of three methods for designing web applications. In: Proceedings of the 27th ACM International Conference on Design of Communication, pp. 1–8. ACM (2009)
28. Albers, M.J.: Communication of Complex Information: User Goals and Information Needs for Dynamic Web Information. Routledge, Abingdon (2004)
29. Lee, J., Xue, N.: Analyzing user requirements by use cases: a goal-driven approach. IEEE Softw. **16**, 92–101 (1999)
30. Lin, J., Lee, M.-C.: An object-oriented analysis method for customer relationship management information systems. Inf. Softw. Technol. **46**, 433–443 (2004). doi:10.1016/j.infsof.2003.09.001
31. Voelter, M., Groher, I.: Product line implementation using aspect-oriented and model-driven software development. In: Software Product Line Conference 2007, SPLC 2007, 11th International, pp. 233–242 (2007). doi:10.1109/SPLINE.2007.23
32. Pleuss, A., Botterweck, G., Dhungana, D.: Integrating automated product derivation and individual user interface design. In: Proceedings of the 4th International Workshop on Variability Modelling of Software-Intensive Systems, Linz, Austria, 27–29 January 2010, pp. 69–76 (2010)
33. Szekely, P.: Retrospective and challenges for model-based interface development. In: Bodart, F., Vanderdonckt, J. (eds.) Design, Specification and Verification of Interactive Systems 1996. (EUROGRAPH), pp. 1–27. Springer, Vienna (1996). doi:10.1007/978-3-7091-7491-3_1
34. Clements, P., Northrop, L.: Software Product Lines: Practices and Patterns. Addison-Wesley, Boston (2002)
35. Wu, L., Yu, P., Wei, J., et al.: A method for user-centered interface customization and development of a prototype system. In: Proceedings of the 2010 2nd WRI World Congress on Software Engineering (WCSE), vol. 1, pp. 197–200 (2010). doi:10.1109/WCSE.2010.46
36. Sandhu, R.S.: Role-based access control. Adv. Comput. **46**, 237–286 (1998)
37. Adolph, S., Cockburn, A., Bramble, P.: Patterns for Effective Use Cases. Addison-Wesley Longman Publishing Co., Inc., Boston (2002)
38. Albert, W., Tullis, T.: Measuring the User Experience: Collecting, Analyzing, and Presenting Usability Metrics. Newnes, Burlington (2013)
39. Alemerien, K., Magel, K.: GUIEvaluator: a metric-tool for evaluating the complexity of Graphical User Interfaces. In: Proceedings of the International Conference on Software Engineering and Knowledge Engineering SEKE, pp. 13–18 (2014)
40. Van Velsen, L., Van Der Geest, T., Klaassen, R., Steehouder, M.: User-centered evaluation of adaptive and adaptable systems: a literature review. Knowl. Eng. Rev. **23**, 261–281 (2008). doi:10.1017/S0269888908001379
41. Lee, B.C.: Human cognitive performance in healthcare information system environment and its application on nursing tasks. Purdue University. Doctorate dissertation (2013)

Human-Robot Interaction

A Study of Utilizing Communication Robots for Teaching Preschoolers a Good Manner

Hiroyoshi Fukuta$^{(\boxtimes)}$, Noriaki Kuwahara, and Kazunari Morimoto

Kyoto Institute of Technology, Kyoto, Japan
21.fukuta@gmail.com

Abstract. In recent years, opportunities for communication between preschool children and others are decreasing. The reason is that the birth rate in Japan is declining and in many families, both parents have jobs. Therefore, the parents spend less time with their children at home. In order to raise a child as an independent person, it is important to educate children adequately while the child's ego is germinating. However, in recent years, the burden of kindergarten teachers has increased, and there is concern that the environment for educating preschool children becomes worse. The purpose of this research is to investigate the possibility for reducing the burden on kindergarten teachers by training young children with robots that they are interested in.

Keywords: Communication robot · Preschooler · Education · A bow after saying words and kindergarten

1 Introduction

Families who cannot make time for domestic activities because the husband and wife both work have increased in Japan. Therefore, education in kindergarten for preschool children is more important than education in the home. In addition, in this globally competitive, modern society, more parents make their children take lessons from a young age to try to raise the odds that their child will grow up in excellent conditions. The important thing in children's growth is not only to increase their academic ability but also to nurture their personality and humanity. In order to make our children grow up as independent people, it is important for us to provide sufficient education to children in the period when their egos are developing.

However, kindergarten teachers are decreasing in Japan because they're working long hours for low wages. Therefore, securing kindergarten teachers becomes difficult, and it isn't possible to add more kindergarten classes. The number of children waiting to find space in a kindergarten class increases.

Robots are beginning to be used in kindergarten children's attendance management, but the possibility of the utilization in education is unknown. However, the performance of current robots is progressing and robots can communicate nearly as well as man. Robots are expected to resolve the human labor shortage and improve educational effects [1]. Study has been conducted on robots for kindergarten education [2–4]. When utilization of robots in kindergarten education can give a kindergarten student an

© Springer International Publishing AG 2017
V.G. Duffy (Ed.): DHM 2017, Part I, LNCS 10286, pp. 421–434, 2017.
DOI: 10.1007/978-3-319-58463-8_35

education with fewer teachers, we can expect a shorter waiting time for children going to kindergarten.

As a preliminary study, we investigated the kindergarten child's reactions and the thoughts of a kindergarten teacher when we installed a robot in the classroom.

2 Methods

We investigated the kindergarten child's reaction and the thoughts of a kindergarten teacher when we installed a robot in the classroom. A robot did the greeting which is oneway to investigate the possibility of using a robot in kindergarten education. We also investigated whether a kindergarten child greeted a robot, when a robot greeted a kindergarten child.

2.1 Experimental Equipment

We used MEEBO, which is a communication robot (UNIFA Corporation). MEEBO has been developed as the robot that watches a kindergarten child. We used MEEBO because we'll be able to utilize MEEBO in an educational setting. MEEBO has sound and facial recognition functions (Fig. 1).

Fig. 1. Communication robot - MEEBO

Moreover, a smart-phone-type remote control is attached to MEEBO. This remote control is freetel priori2 of the SIM free smart phone. When MEEBO and a remote control are under the same Wifi environment, it's possible to operate MEEBO by remote control. As for the operating method, first of all, we connect the remote control to optional Wifi. Next, a QR code is generated on the remote control when connected to Wifi. Finally, MEEBO can read the QR code using its QR reading function, and we can connect it to the same Wifi network as the remote control. It's possible to operate

MEEBO by remote control in this way. The operations that can be performed by remote control are greetings, recreational activities and taking pictures. When we press a button, MEEBO moves (Fig. 2).

Fig. 2. Remote controller of MEEBO

2.2 Experiment Conditions

We investigated at the Harumidai kindergarten in Sakai City, Osaka. We experimented with 79 kindergarten children from 2 to 6 years old. Moreover, we put MEEBO at the position that was slightly lower than the height of children so that MEEBO could easily recognize the faces of the children. A kindergarten teacher stayed by the children during the experiment. We performed experiments for each child.

2.3 Program Creation

Teachers of Harumidai kindergarten are teaching "GOSENGOREI" as a greeting. The students are supposed to bow after the greeting (Fig. 3).

We created a program that has MEEBO bow after saying certain words. We created the program using "VstoneMagic", the programming software of MEEBO. We can create the program to work like a flow chart. It's possible to create the program by adding order blocks of face recognition, facial flattery and sound (Fig. 4).

We visited Harumidai kindergarten before creating the program. We wanted to see how teachers taught greetings followed by bows. The program was created based on that. The flow of the program for MEEBO performing a bow after saying certain words is indicated on Fig. 5.

Fig. 3. Bow after the greeting

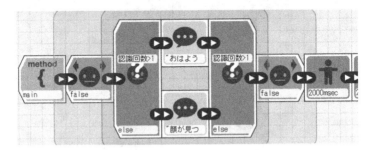

Fig. 4. VstoneMagic

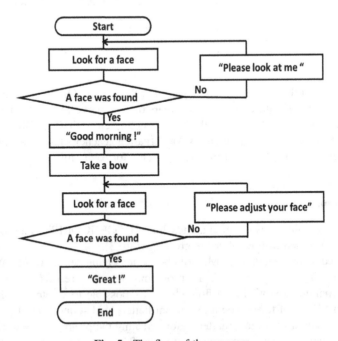

Fig. 5. The flow of the program

The program is preserved with java programming language inside. It's possible to program the program created by VstoneMagic with java programming language. We corrected the program a little on eclipse. Moreover, we set it so that MEEBO could perform the program by remote control.

2.4 Beginning Questionnaire

We gave a questionnaire to 15 kindergarten teachers of Harumidai kindergarten (male 1, female 14) before doing this investigation. The questions of the beginning questionnaire are indicated below (Table 1).

Table 1. Beginning questionnaire

1. How many years are you a kindergarten teacher ?		
A. Less than 5 years	B. More than 5 years, less than 10 years	C. More than 10 years
2. How do you think to using a robot for kindergarten education ?		
A. I think it's good.	B. I don't think it's good.	C. Neither A nor B
3. Please tell me the reason that you answered in question 2.		

2.5 Kindergarten Children's Reaction and Concluding Questionnaire

We took a video during the experiment to see whether kindergarten children would greet a robot when a robot greeted them. We gave a questionnaire to 15 kindergarten teachers of Harumidai kindergarten (male 1, female 14) after conducting this investigation. The questions of the concluding questionnaire are indicated below (Table 2).

Table 2. Concluding questionnaire

1. How many years are you a kindergarten teacher ?		
A. Less than 5 years	B. More than 5 years, less than 10 years	C. More than 10 years
2. How did you think to using a robot for kindergarten education ?		
A. I thought it's good.	B. I didn't think it's good.	C. Neither A nor B
3. Please tell me the reason that you answered in question 2.		
4. If you have any other opinions, please tell me.		

3   Results

3.1   Beginning Questionnaire

The results of question 1 and question 2 of the beginning questionnaire are indicated in Figs. 6 and 7.

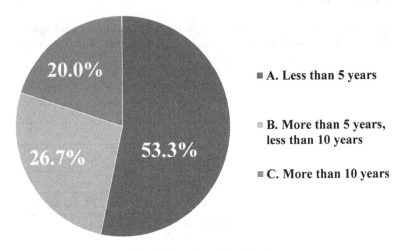

Fig. 6. Results of question 1

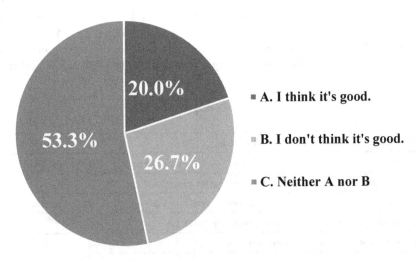

Fig. 7. Results of question 2

Kindergarten teachers with less than 5 years of experience accounted for 53.3% of all teachers at Harumidai kindergarten. Teachers with less than 10 years of experience but more than 5 accounted for 26.7% of all teachers. Teachers with more than 10 years of experience accounted for 20.0% of all teachers.

Moreover, teachers who answered "C. Neither A nor B" to question 2 accounted for 53.3% of the whole. Teachers who answered "B. I don't think it's good" to question 2 accounted for 26.7% of the whole. Teachers who answered "A. I think it's good" to question 2 accounted for 53.3% of the whole.

Figure 8, shows the percentage of respondents in question 2 based on length of service.

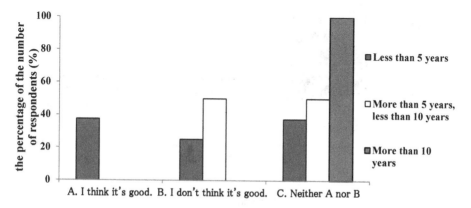

Fig. 8. Results of question 2 based on length of service

Teachers who answered "A. I think it's good" to question 2 had less than 5 years of experience. Teachers who answered "C. Neither A nor B" to question 2 were teachers with more than 10 years of experience. Teachers who answered "C. Neither A nor B" to question 2 accounted for 50.0% of teachers who had less than 10 years but more than 5 years of experience. Moreover, teachers who answered "B. I don't think it's good" to question 2 accounted for 50.0% of teachers who had less than 10 years of experience but more than 5 years.

As for the reasons that teachers answered "A. I think it's good" to question 2, answers included "Because I think personal use of robots is increasing," and "kindergarten children seemed to have an interest in learning from a robot." As for the reason that teachers answered "B. I don't think it's good" to question 2, 25% of those teachers said, "The position of the teacher is diminished." The other 75% answered, "It's better to have human contact because there is no feeling in a robot." As for the reason that teachers answered "C. Neither A nor B" to question 2, 25.0% of teachers answered "I can't tell unless I try to see it," while 62.5% answered "I think it's good, but I think it's difficult for the robot."

3.2   Kindergarten Children's Reaction

Kindergarten children were very interested in MEEBO. There were a lot of kindergarten children who aggressively tried to speak to MEEBO. On the other hand, there were some kindergarten children suffering a little in the presence of MEEBO. The chart about the kindergarten children's reaction when MEEBO performed a greeting followed by a bow is indicated in Fig. 9. Kindergarten children were classified into three groups: (1) The kindergarten child who didn't greet, (2) The kindergarten child who greeted without bowing(the kindergarten child who did the greeting with words but didn't bow), (3) The kindergarten child who did a greeting in words and a bow.

■ (1) The kindergarten child who didn't greet

▧ (2) The kindergarten child who greeted without bowing (the kindergarten child who did the greeting which isn't a bow after saying words)

■ (3) The kindergarten child who did a greeting of a bow after saying words.

Fig. 9.   Children's reactions

Kindergarten children in (1) accounted for 27.9% of the whole of Harumidai kindergarten students. Kindergarten children of (2) accounted for 43.0% of the whole. Kindergarten children of (3) accounted for 29.1% of the whole.

3.3   Concluding Questionnaire

The results of question 2 of the concluding questionnaire are indicated in Fig. 10.

Teachers who answered "C. Neither A nor B" to question 2 accounted for 46.7% of the whole. Teachers who answered "B. I didn't think it was good" to question 2 accounted for 20.0% of the whole. Teachers who answered "A. I thought it was good" to question 2 accounted for 33.3% of the whole.

The percentage of respondents in question 2 based on length of service is shown in Fig. 11.

Teachers who answered "A. I thought it was good" accounted for 50.0% of teachers with less than 5 years of experience and 33.3% of teachers with more than 10 years of experience. Teachers who answered "B. I didn't think it was good" accounted for 33.3% of teachers with more than 10 years of experience, 12.5% of teachers with less than 5 years and 25.0% of teachers with less than 10 years but more than 5 years of experience. Teachers who answered "C. Neither A nor B" accounted

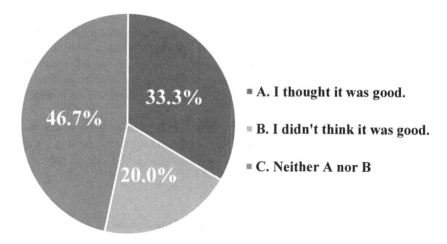

Fig. 10. Results of question 2

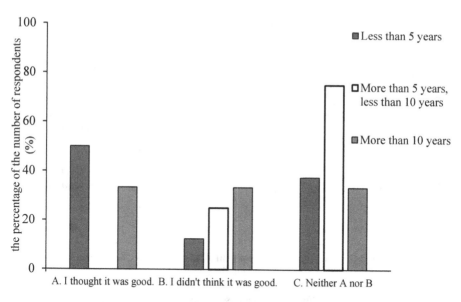

Fig. 11. Results of question 2 based on length of service

for 37.5% of teachers with less than 5 years of experience, 75.0% of teachers with less than 10 years but more than 5 years, and 33.3% of teachers with more than 10 years.

As for the reason that teachers answered "A. I thought it was good" to question 2, teachers who answered, "Children can learn a greeting happily because children were very interested in the robot" accounted for 60.0%, and teachers who answered, "I think that it will be a good stimulus for children because there are few opportunities to interact with a robot" accounted for 40.0%. As for the reason that teachers answered "B. I didn't think it was good", teachers who answered, "There is no feeling in a robot" accounted for 33.3%, and teachers who answered, "There are few variations of conversation with a robot" accounted for 66.7%. As for the reason that teachers answered "C. Neither A nor B", teachers who answered, "It's effective to use a robot, but I think child's concentration doesn't last because the conversation of the robot was slow" accounted for 85.7%, and teachers who answered, "I think it's good that a child plays with a robot, but I think it's better for education to be about human interaction" accounted for 14.3%.

There were two opinions in question 4. The first opinion is that teachers want a robot to recognize the face and the name of each child and to call the name of the child. The second opinion is that they think it's better to change the size of the robot to something a little bigger.

3.4   Comparison of Beginning and Concluding Questionnaires

We compared the beginning and concluding questionnaires. First, the chart that shows comparisons of question 2 is indicated in Fig. 12.

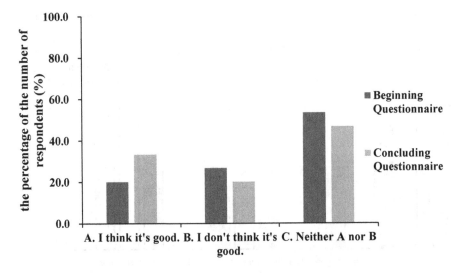

Fig. 12. Comparison of question 2

Figure 12 shows the percentage of respondents who answered "A. I think it's good" to question 2 increased by 13.3%. The percentage of respondents who answered "B. I don't think it's good" to question 2 decreased by 6.7%. Moreover, the percentage of respondents who answered "C. Neither A nor B" to question 2 decreased by 6.6%.

Figures 13, 14 and 15 show comparisons of question 2 based on length of service.

Figure 13 shows the percentage of respondents who answered "A. I think it's good" to question 2 increased by 12.5%. The percentage of respondents who answered "B. I don't think it's good" to question 2 decreased by 12.5%.

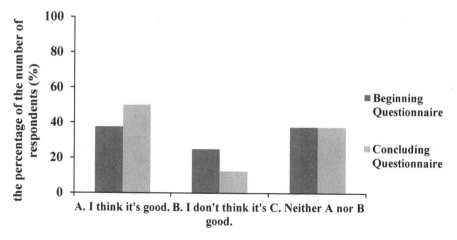

Fig. 13. Kindergarten teachers with less than 5 years of experience

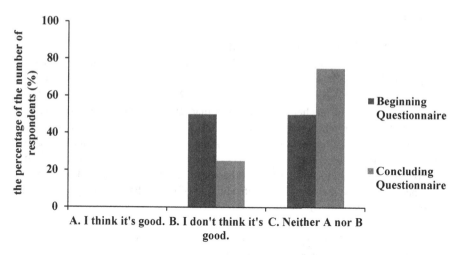

Fig. 14. Kindergarten teachers with more than 5 years of experience but less than 10 years

Figure 14 shows the percentage of respondents who answered "B. I don't think it's good" to question 2 decreased by 25.0%. Moreover, the percentage of respondents who answered "C. Neither A nor B" to question 2 increased by 25.0%.

Figure 15 shows the percentage of respondents who answered "C. Neither A nor B" to question 2 decreased by 66.7%. Moreover, the number of respondents of C is equal to the number of respondents of A and also equal to the number of respondents of B.

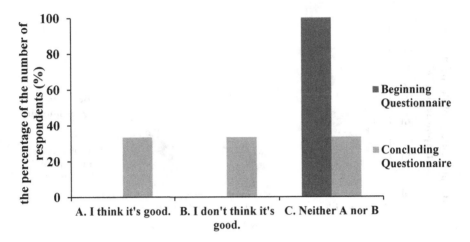

Fig. 15. Kindergarten teachers with more than 10 years of experience

4   Discussion

As shown in Fig. 8, teachers who answered "A. I think it's good" to question 2 of the beginning questionnaire were teachers with less than 5 years of experience. Teachers who answered "C. Neither A nor B" to question 2 were teachers with more than 10 years of experience. Teachers who answered "C. Neither A nor B" to question 2 accounted for 50.0% of teachers who had less than 10 years but more than 5 years of experience. Moreover, teachers who answered "B. I don't think it's good" to question 2 accounted for 50.0% of teachers who had less than 10 years but more than 5 years of experience. Teachers with less than 5 years of experience are interested in utilizing a robot for kindergarten education. On the other hand, teachers with more than 5 years of experience seem to be resistant to the introduction of robots because they are proud of the work they have done for many years.

Looking at the results comparing the beginning and concluding questionnaires, the percentage of respondents who answered "A. I think it's good" to question 2 of the concluding questionnaire increased by 13.3%, and the percentage of respondents who answered "B. I don't think it's good" decreased by 6.7%. Moreover, Fig. 13 shows the percentage of respondents who answered "A. I think it's good" to question 2 increased by 12.5%, and the percentage of respondents who answered "B. I don't think it's good" to question 2 decreased by 12.5%. Figure 14 shows the percentage of respondents who answered "B. I don't think it's good" to question 2 decreased by 25.0%. Therefore, the number of teachers who think it's good to use a robot for kindergarten education increased. Moreover, the number of teachers who don't think it's good to use a robot for kindergarten education decreased. This result was obtained because children were interested in the robot and were enjoying time with the robot. On the other hand, conversation of was slow because facial recognitive functions didn't operate well for kindergarten children with differences in height. There was also the problem that MEEBO has few variations of conversation. We're planning to conquer the problems we identified in this investigation and improve the robot. That way, there is a possibility that teachers who think it's good to use a robot for kindergarten education will increase.

Some kindergarten children were very interested in MEEBO and there were a lot of kindergarten children who aggressively try to speak to MEEBO. On the other hand, some kindergarten children were scared of MEEBO. There were many older children and year - round children in the former group. There was many young children in the latter. We found four reasons that some kindergarten children were suffering. The first reason is because they are not familiar with kindergarten yet. The second reason is because they felt tension and fear in conversing with a strange object. The third reason is because they were tense in the different circumstances. The fourth reason is because they have felt uneasy because the conversation of the robot was slow. Facial recognitive functions didn't function well for kindergarten children with different heights, and execution of the program where MEEBO performs a bow after saying certain words was behind schedule. Therefore, MEEBO's conversation slowed down. It's necessary to improve and wide the scope of facial recognition.

As shown in Fig. 9, kindergarten children of (2) accounted for 43.0% of the whole. MEEBO can only move its neck when it bows because its lower back doesn't bend. Therefore, MEEBO didn't seem to be doing a bow and the kindergarten children didn't do the verbal greeting and bow. It's necessary to get the robot to bend.

5 Summary

- The percentage of teachers who answered "C. Neither A nor B" in question 2 was the largest in both the beginning and concluding questionnaires.
- We found out that most children are very interested in the robot.
- When MEEBO performed a verbal greeting followed by a bow, the number of the kindergarten children who could perform a verbal greeting and a bow was small. However, 72.1% of Harumidai kindergarten children returned a greeting to MEEBO.
- Children could learn happily by using a robot. On the other hand, conversation was slow because facial recognition functions didn't operate well for kindergarten children with different heights. Moreover, there was also a problem that MEEBO has few variations of conversation.
- There were two opinions in question 4. The first opinion is that teachers want a robot to recognize the face and name of each child and to call out the name of the child. The second opinion is that the teachers think it's better to increase the size of the robot.

6 Conclusion

We found out that kindergarten children tended to have an interest in the robot, and that kindergarten teachers are expecting to utilize robots but also have a feeling of uneasiness.

When the problems of the speed of the conversation, facial recognition and the individual recognition of names and faces by MEEBO are solved, there will be a possibility for kindergarten education using MEEBO.

Acknowledgements. We received generous support from UNIFA Corporation and the Corporation Education System Research Center. We are grateful for their support. We would like to offer our special thanks to everybody at Harumidai kindergarten who cooperated pleasantly.

References

1. Fumihide, T.: Social robotics research and its application at the child education environment. J. Robot. Soc. Jpn. **29**(1), 19–22 (2011)
2. Robins, B., Dautenhahn, K., Te Boekhorst, R., et al.: Robotic assistants in therapy and education of children with autism: can a small humanoid robot help encourage social interaction skills? Univ. Access Inf. Soc. **4**(2), 105–120 (2005)
3. Fumihide, T., Takeshi, K.: The use of robots in early education: a scenario based on ethical consideration. In: Robot and Human Interactive Communication, pp. 558–560 (2009)
4. Javier, R.M., Fumihide, T., et al.: The RUBI project: a progress report. In: Human-Robot Interaction, pp. 333–339 (2007)

Quantification of Elegant Motions for Receptionist Android Robot

Makoto Ikawa[2], Etsuko Ueda[1]([✉]), Akishige Yuguchi[2],
Gustavo Alfonso Garcia Ricardez[2], Ming Ding[2], Jun Takamatsu[2],
and Tsukasa Ogasawara[2]

[1] Osaka Institute of Technology, Osaka, Japan
etsuko.ueda@oit.ac.jp
[2] Nara Institute of Science and Technology, Nara, Japan

Abstract. To improve the general image of robots, in this study we describe a method of achieving "elegant motions based on women's sense" in an android robot. There have been many books published in Japan containing advice for women on how to have elegant manners. Our approach was to quantify the elegant motions that are qualitatively expressed in these etiquette books, using an android robot. In this research, we focused on arm- and face-based motions, such as giving directions, with an emphasis on "reception" tasks. We programmed the robot to perform desirable motions, such as "show the palm to a guest and do not raise the hand higher than the shoulder," which are commonly expressed in the manners books. For each implemented motions, many patterns could be generated by changing certain parameters, such as the movement speed, the angle of the arm and the hand, and the distance and angle to the indicated location. We verified these motions using a subjective evaluation and discussed the elegant and quantified motions based on the result.

Keywords: Elegant motion · Android robot · Human-robot interaction

1 Introduction

With the ever-expanding market for service robots in Japan, the level of interaction between robots and human is also increasing. Robots employed in this field are required to establish a good relationship with humans in various situations of daily life. To achieve this, the robots need to be accepted by people from all walks of life and both genders. To assist in yielding this outcome, the androids must learn how to display elegant behavior, which is one of the main criteria by which people accept others in human society.

There is a great deal of activity in the research field on movement and human psychology. For example, there has been a paper on human-friendly speed patterns and delivery positions in hand-over actions [1], a study on the generation of robotic movements in humans [2], and a proposal for a robotic system that

© Springer International Publishing AG 2017
V.G. Duffy (Ed.): DHM 2017, Part I, LNCS 10286, pp. 435–446, 2017.
DOI: 10.1007/978-3-319-58463-8_36

can perform movements to effectively cooperate with humans [3]. In addition, we have seen studies in which android robots that are capable of facial expressions have been employed in face-to-face selling [4], as receptionists, and in school education [5].

However, there are only few cases that have examined the "beauty" or "elegance" of robot motion. To address this, we herein attempt to improve the general impression of robots by implementing "elegant robot motions that based women's perception." More specifically, we will describe how we quantified the elegant motions of an android robot when performing "pointing actions" in its role as a receptionist.

2   Elegant Behavior

Many etiquette books for women have been published in Japan, with their contents being widely accepted as indicating desirable behavior. In this research, we therefore treated the descriptions in these texts as denoting the gold standard of elegant motions. We collated the common features of elegant motions that were frequently described in different books, implemented motions in android robots, performed subjective evaluations, and quantified the qualitative features of elegant motions based on the results.

We studied descriptions of elegant motions contained in nine etiquette books [6–14] published in Japan. Table 1 shows examples of the qualitative definition of elegant motions extracted from these publications.

Table 1. Examples of elegant behavior

Motion	Description	Ratio[%]
Pointing	Extend fingertips neatly	100
	Show the palm to the guest	28.6
	Point the palm diagonally upward	14.3
	Arm should not be raised above the shoulder	14.3
	Point the front of the body toward the guest	14.3
Passing and receiving objects	Pass objects with both hands	87.5
	Face the guest side in front	62.5
	Pass objects with arc trajectory	12.5
	Close the fingers	12.5
	Tighten both side so as not to open up too much	12.5
Turning around when being called	Turn the whole or upper body	100
	Turn around slowly	75
	Turn shoulder before turning face	50

Fig. 1. Actroid SIT

Table 2. Movable parts (for pointing action)

Movable parts	Motions
Left arm	Hand twisting
	Elbow bending
	Open-close movement of shoulder
	Arm twisting
	Open-close movement of side
	"Fall in" pose
Right arm ˙	Open-close movement of shoulder
	Rotation of upper arm
Waist	Rotation
Neck and Head	Neck bending
	Head turning

3 Implementation of Elegant Motions to an Android Robot

In this research, we used the Actroid SIT, which is an android robot manufactured by KOKORO Co., Ltd. Figure 1 gives an overview of Actroid SIT. This robot's body is coated with silicon, making it closely resemble a human. Actroid SIT has 42 degrees of freedom and is driven by pneumatic actuators. Table 2 shows the movable parts used in the "pointing task", which is the focus of this research.

The robot's task was to point to a sign printed on a sheet of A4 paper with the legend "Venue entrance" written on it in Japanese, as shown in Fig. 2. The sign was situated higher than the robot's waist and set so that its top would be pointed at when the hand position was at its highest. Figure 3 indicates the details of the relative location between the sign and the robot. The sign was 101 cm from the floor to the bottom edge of the sign and 11.5 cm from the edge of the partition to the sign. The bottom left corner of the sign was located 45 cm from the android's left wrist, while the top left corner was located 40 cm from the left shoulder and the bottom edge was 12.5 cm from a line extending horizontally from the robot's waist.

We selected the following two features from the definition in Table 1 for quantification:

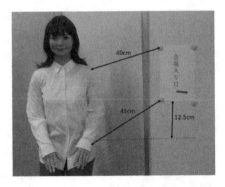

Fig. 2. Pointing action   **Fig. 3.** Location of robot and sign

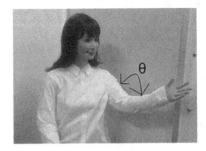

(a) Rotation of forearm   (b) Angle between forearm and upper arm

Fig. 4. Controlled angle

1. For the feature that "the palm faces the guest and the palm direction is diagonally upward," the forearm rotation angle (shown in Fig. 4(a)) was quantified.
2. For the feature that "the arm should not rise above the shoulder," the angle formed by the upper arm and forearm (shown in Fig. 4(b)) was quantified.

By controlling these angles, a plurality in the pointing motion was generated. The implementation procedure for the robot motion is described below.

Step 1. Start pose, target pose, and intermediate pose were generated using a motion creation software (Fig. 5).
Step 2. Cubic spline interpolation was performed between these three poses and each joint angle at each time was obtained.
Step 3. The speed of motion between each posture generated in Step 2 was determined. It had been observed in a previous study that the arm velocity of the reaching movement described a "bell" shape [15]. This was reflected in the present experiment after manually adjusting the movement speed.

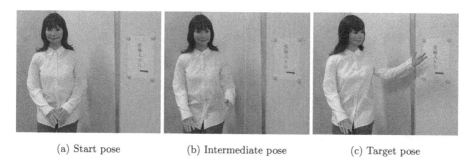

(a) Start pose	(b) Intermediate pose	(c) Target pose

Fig. 5. Keyframe posture

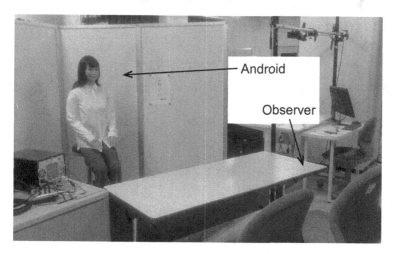

Fig. 6. Experimental environment

4 Subjective Evaluation

4.1 Evaluation Method

The observer was sitting facing the android, as shown in Fig. 6, and observed the robot's generated motion. The observed motion was evaluated using Thurston's pairwise comparison method and the SD method. The observers comprised five men and five women aged from their 20 s to 40 s.

In this experiment, robot behaviors originated from five patterns of different (1) angles of rotation of the forearm and (2) angles of the upper arm and forearm were presented, with the observers performing the following evaluations:

1. Pairwise comparison: All combination pairs were compared and participants selected the motion that they considered the most "elegant" in each trial.
2. SD method: The observers evaluated each motion on a 5-point scale using adjective pairs of "elegant - vulgar," "smooth - awkward," "polite - rude," "beautiful - ugly," and "fast - slow."

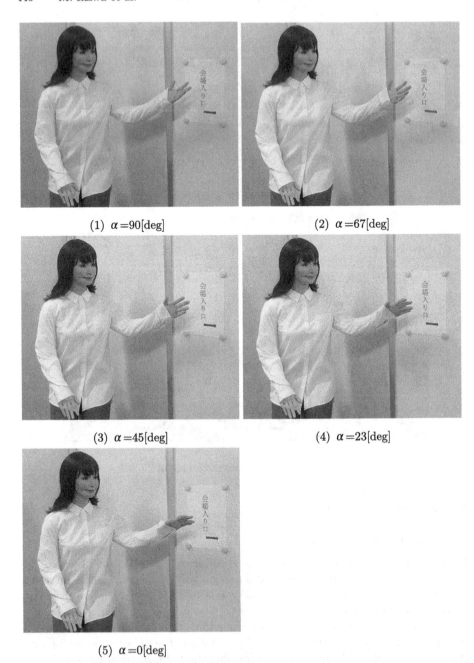

(1) $\alpha = 90[\deg]$ (2) $\alpha = 67[\deg]$

(3) $\alpha = 45[\deg]$ (4) $\alpha = 23[\deg]$

(5) $\alpha = 0[\deg]$

Fig. 7. Five pointing motions with various palm directions

4.2 Subjective Difference with Variation of Palm Direction

By changing the rotation angle of the forearm to 90 [deg], 67 [deg], 45 [deg], 23 [deg], and 0 [deg], the robot presented five motions with different palm directions. The target poses in each motion are shown in Fig. 7. In these motions, the angle between the upper arm and forearm was fixed at $\theta = 150$ [deg].

Table 3 shows the results of the pairwise comparison. Numerical values are given horizontally, denotes the "9" (row = 90, column = 67) the number of people who evaluated that 90 [deg] was more elegant when comparing 90 [deg] and 67 [deg]. Figure 8 shows the scale value of the elegance calculated from the comparison result using Thurston's method. This value indicates that elegance became greater as it increased in the positive direction. Based on Fig. 8, the movement was most elegant when the rotation angle of the forearm was 90 [deg], with the quality decreasing as the angle decreased from that position.

Table 3. Result of pairwise comparison (palm direction)

		B				(deg)
		90	67	45	23	0
A	90	-	9	10	10	10
	67	1	-	8	10	10
	45	0	2	-	9	10
	23	0	0	1	-	9
	0	0	0	0	1	-

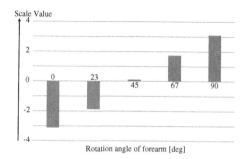

Fig. 8. Scale value of "elegance" (palm direction)

Figure 9 shows the results of subjective evaluation using the SD method. Factor analysis was performed using the evaluation results from the ten observers. Those with an eigen value of 1 or more were extracted as a common factor and the factor loadings were obtained by Promax rotation. Table 4 shows the calculated factor loadings. From Table 4, in the first factor, the factor loadings of the adjective pairs of "beautiful vs. ugly," "elegant vs. vulgar," and "polite vs. rude" were high. It could be said that the first factor represents "gracefulness"; likewise, it can be said that the second factor is a factor concerning "smoothness." Figure 10 shows the factor score of the first factor at each angle, while Fig. 11 shows the factor score of the second factor at each angle. From Fig. 10, the highest level of "elegance" was seen at 90 [deg], while according to Fig. 11, the smoothest angle was 67 [deg].

4.3 Subjective Difference with Variation of Hand Height

By changing the angle between the upper arm and the forearm to 180 [deg], 165 [deg], 150 [deg], 135 [deg], and 120 [deg], the robot presented five motions with

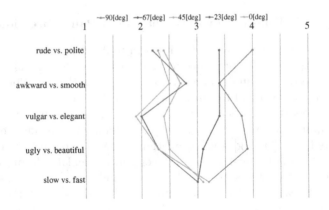

Fig. 9. SD profile (palm direction)

Table 4. Factor loading (palm direction)

	1st factor	2nd factor
Beautiful vs. ugly	0.888	−0.101
Elegant vs. vulgar	0.879	0.004
Polite vs. rude	0.829	0.256
Smooth vs. awkward	0.298	0.505
Fast vs. slow	0.163	−0.403

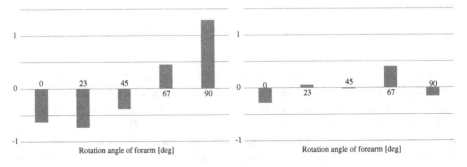

Fig. 10. Factor score of 1st factor (palm direction)

Fig. 11. Factor score of 2nd factor (palm direction)

different hand heights. The target poses in each motion are shown in Fig. 12. In these motions, the rotation angle of the forearm was fixed at $\alpha = 90$ [deg].

Table 5 shows the results of the pairwise comparison and Fig. 13 shows the scale value of elegance. Based on the pairwise comparison, the robot was most elegant when the angle between the upper arm and forearm was 135 [deg]; it transpired that the angle between 135 [deg] and 150 [deg] appeared elegant.

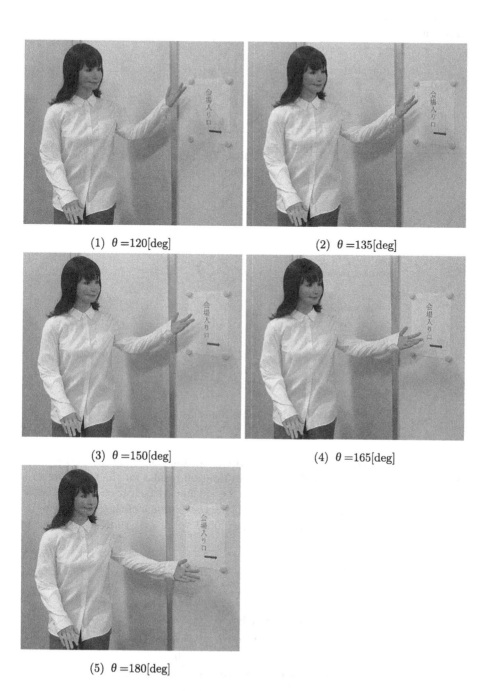

(1) $\theta = 120[\deg]$ (2) $\theta = 135[\deg]$

(3) $\theta = 150[\deg]$ (4) $\theta = 165[\deg]$

(5) $\theta = 180[\deg]$

Fig. 12. Five pointing motions with various hand heights

Table 5. Results of pairwise comparison (palm direction)

		B				(deg)
		180	165	150	135	120
A	180	-	4	2	4	5
	165	6	-	6	4	5
	150	8	4	-	7	9
	135	6	6	3	-	10
	120	5	5	1	0	-

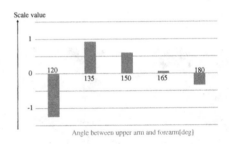

Fig. 13. Scale value of "elegance" (hand height)

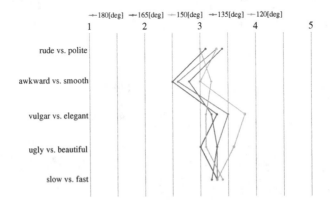

Fig. 14. SD profile (hand height)

Figure 14 shows the results of the impression evaluation using the SD method. Factor analysis was performed using the evaluation results for the ten observers, as in the previous section. Table 6 shows the calculated factor loadings.

Based on Table 6, in the first factor, the factor loadings of the adjective pairs of "beautiful vs. ugly," "elegant vs. vulgar," and "polite vs. rude" were high. It

Table 6. Factor loading (hand height)

	1st factor
Beautiful vs. ugly	0.882
Elegant vs. vulgar	0.769
Polite vs. rude	0.559
Smooth vs. awkward	0.335
Fast vs. slow	−0.351

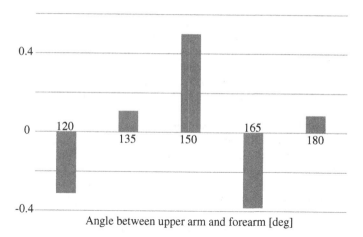

Fig. 15. Factor score (hand height)

could be stated that the first factor represents "gracefulness." Figure 15 shows the factor score of the first factor at each angle.

From Fig. 15, it can be established that the robot was most "elegant" when the angle between the forearm and upper arm was 150 [deg].

5   Conclusion

By changing the rotation angle of the forearm, and the angle between the upper arm and forearm, we made the android robot to perform various motions. From the results of the ten observers' impression evaluations of these motions, we quantified the features of elegant motions. The results of the evaluation showed that the most elegant pointing motion of the Actroid SIT was achieved when the rotation angle of the forearm was 90 [deg] and the angle of the upper arm and forearm was between 135 [deg] and 150 [deg].

In the future, we will further analyze differences in impression due to the gender gap and the appearance of the robot. We will also compare the motions of humans and androids in terms of beauty.

References

1. Shibata, S., Sahbi, B.M., Tanaka, K., Shimizu, A.: Research on human-friendly robot motions: motion of a robot holding out an object to a human. Trans. JSME **64**(617), 279–287 (1998). (in Japanese)
2. Shibata, S., Inooka, H.: Emotional evaluations on robot motions by using rating scale method. J. Ergon. **31**(2), 151–159 (1995)
3. Kankubo, K., Shibata, S., Jindai, M., Yamamoto, T., Shimizu, A.: Psychological evaluation of a personal-robot cooperating with instructions of the fingers. Trans. JSME **68**(676), 239–246 (2002). (in Japanese)

4. Watanabe, M., Ogawa, K., Ishiguro, H.: Can androids be salespeople in the real world? In: Proceedings of the 33rd Annual ACM Conference Extended Abstracts on Human Factors in Computing Systems, pp. 781–788 (2015)
5. Hashimoto, T.: Human-robot communication mediated by facial expressions. Jpn. J. Psychon. Sci. **34**(1), 134–138 (2015). (in Japanese)
6. Iwashita, N.: Knowledge of Beautiful Lady. Artists House Publishers Co. Ltd., Los Angeles (2006). (in Japanese)
7. Igaki, R., Suwa, E., Tanaka, M.: Beautiful Lady's Behavior Manner Course. Nikkei Home Magazine (2013). (in Japanese)
8. Shimohira, K.: Beautiful Manners for A Lovely Woman. Nagaoka Shoten (2005). (in Japanese)
9. Iwashita, N.: Elegant manners and attentiveness remaining in the manners impression of a woman showing beautiful well understood by illustration. Nagaoka Shoten (2006). (in Japanese)
10. Nishida, H.: Beautiful Behavior to Change You. Wanibooks Corporation (2009). (in Japanese)
11. Igaki, R.: Manners and Tricks of Behavior. Gakushu-kenkyuusho Inc., Tokoyo (2006)
12. Sakura, M.: Cinderella Manners. Shufunotomo infos Inc., Tokyo (2015). (in Japanese)
13. Igaki, R.: Good Manners for a Elegant Lady. Yamato shobo, Tokyo (2014). (in Japanese)
14. Ogura, Y.: Graceful Woman Manners Book. Seiunsya, Tokyo (2007). (in Japanese)
15. Kawato, M.: Brain's Theory of Computation. Sangyo Tosho, Tokyo (1996). (in Japanese)

Design of a Robotic Workmate

Sarah Luisa Müller[✉], Stefan Schröder, Sabina Jeschke,
and Anja Richert

IMA/ZLW & IfU, RWTH Aachen University, Aachen, Germany
{sarah.mueller,stefan.schroeder,sabina.jeschke,anja.
richert}@ima-zlw-ifu.rwth-aachen.de

Abstract. In the near future, robots and people will work hand in hand. Through technical development, robots will be able to follow social rules, interact and communicate with people and move freely in the environment. The number of these so-called social robots will increase significantly especially in production spaces forming hybrid human-robot-teams. This expected increasing integration of robots in production environments raises questions on how to design an ideal robot for hybrid collaboration. While most of the research focuses on the technical aspects of human-machine interactions, there is still a strong need for research on the psychological and social aspects that influence the cooperation within hybrid teams.

In addition to existing research work, the present research project investigates how the appearance and accuracy of a robot influences the outcomes of a collaborative task (i.e. performance, perceived team functionality and trust) within a Wizard-of-Oz experiment, which was set in a virtual reality setting.

One major finding was that the accuracy of the robot influenced the level of trust, faulty robots were perceived as less trustworthy. Furthermore, the appearance of the robots influenced the perceived team functionality and the collaborative performance. Industrial robots led to a higher task reflexivity and performance.

The results will help to improve the future designs of robots, focusing on psychological needs of the human partners.

Keywords: Industry 4.0 · Social robotics · Hybrid human-robot-teams · Human-robotic interactions · Anthropomorphism · Reactions · Cooperation

1 Introduction

So far, robots are still largely separated from human workers in production spaces. There are only a few examples where robots and humans work together such as in a new fulfillment center of Amazon in New Jersey [1]. Through technological development and adapting standards especially in the field of safety [2], the number of shared workspaces and closer human-robot collaborations will increment. Increasing numbers of robots can reduce production costs in the long term, compensate physical limitations of human workers, and countervail production peaks and staffing bottlenecks. Whereas most of the research on human-robot collaboration focuses on technical

© Springer International Publishing AG 2017
V.G. Duffy (Ed.): DHM 2017, Part I, LNCS 10286, pp. 447–456, 2017.
DOI: 10.1007/978-3-319-58463-8_37

aspects, there is still a strong need to investigate the psychological and social pre-requisites for effective collaboration as pointed out by Charles et al. [3].

Human-robot interaction can vary in many ways, e.g. in the type of task, the ratio of humans and robots, or the understanding of roles [4, 5]. Instead of just coexisting, human and robot might be able to cooperate in the future, which means to share a common goal and interact in a coordinated way [6]. It might even be possible to speak of hybrid human-robot teams. Although, the term team is usually used for human teams, recent research has transferred the concept repeatedly on robots. Classically, a team is defined as two or more individuals, who have specific roles, perform inter-dependent tasks, are adaptable, and share a common goal [7]. The closer and more equitable the interaction becomes, the more important are human factors [8]. Char-alambous and collegeagues [9] gave a first framework of human factors which influ-ence effective implementation and execution of hybrid human-robot collaboration. Among others, the factors trust in the robots and the robot's reliability play a crucial role.

People often take for granted that machines and robots work perfectly and act unaware of actual dangers. This automation-induced complacency effect is caused particularly through automation reliability [10]. Hancock and colleagues [11] examined critical factors for trust development in hybrid teams in a meta-analysis. They also pointed out that the robot's performance has the strongest association with trust. Even if the robot's performance influenced the level of trust, Salem and colleagues [12] found out that manipulating the robot's behavior did not influence people's decision to work with them. This leads to two hypotheses:

H_1: The accuracy of a robot's behavior influences the level of trust. A faulty robot will be perceived as less trustworthy.

H_2: The accuracy of a robots' behavior does not influence the perception of the team functionality.

Experiments have shown that a robot's appearance systematically influences the humans' affect towards them. This effect, originally proposed by Jentsch [13] and Freud [14], is called "Uncanny Valley" [15] after the form of the diagram which illustrates the conjecture to describe the effect. Correspondingly, humanoid robots are more popular than industrial robots (until they are too anthropomorphic and the response becomes revulsion). Humanlike appearance is also associated with human attributes, people tend for example to delegate responsibility better to humanlike then to machinelike robots [16]. This finding is supported also by Hancock and colleagues [11], who saw the characteristics of the robot (like anthropomorphism) also as an influential factor on trust. The robot's look rises expectations of the robot's role and behavior in the situation, wherefore hybrid collaboration can be improved trough a matching of the robot's appearance and the given task. A robot that confirmed the expectations increases peoples' sense of the robot's compatibility with its job, and hence their compliance with the robot [17]. In a production environment, an industrial robot will match the situation better than a humanoid, which leads to the following hypotheses:

H₃: The robot's appearance influences the level of trust. A humanoid robot will be perceived as more trustworthy.

H₄: The robot's appearance influences the perception of the team functionality. An industrial robot will create a higher perceived team functionality.

H₅: The robot's appearance influences the performance of the collaborative task. An industrial robot will lead to a higher performance.

To test these hypotheses, a virtual reality experiment with four experimental groups was conducted which is described in the next section. Then a description of the sample follows and the results are reported. In the last section, the results and limitations are discussed and an outlook is given.

2 Method

To analyze hybrid collaboration in a controlled experiment, a Wizard-of-Oz[1] experiment was designed within a virtual reality setting using a Virtual Theater[2] and an Oculus Rift Development Kit 2 (DK2) Head-Mounted Display (after the concept described in [18, 19]).

In a virtual production hall (see Fig. 1), the participants needed to fulfil a task that could only be successfully achieved via a cooperation with the mobile, voice-controlled

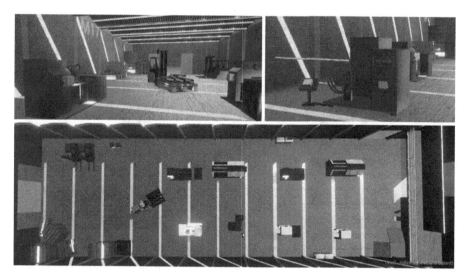

Fig. 1. Impressions of (a) the production hall, (b) the chain host and (c) the floorplan.

---

[1] The participants interact with the system that they believe to be autonomous, but which is actually being operated by an unseen human being.

[2] The Virtual Theater (by MSE Weibull) is an immersive simulator that combines the natural user interfaces of a Head Mounted Display and an omnidirectional conveyor belt. Through a tracking system, the user's position and orientation in virtual space could be determined. It was combined with a wireless presenter (Logitech Wireless Presenter R400), which served as an input device.

robot Charles[3]. To get used to the virtual environment, exploration time was provided where participants could walk freely through the production hall and get information about the different machines (e.g. lathes, bending machine) by pressing the corresponding buttons. The robot stood in the production hall and offered help operating the machines through a textual interface, which was also read aloud. Participants were told that they could give the robot instructions by saying "Go to machine..." ("Gehe zu...") or "Press the button" ("Benutze..."). The robot could only operate machines with a red button; the human could only operate machines with a green button, which the participant had to figure out by try and error. The names of the machines were visible as numbers over the machines. The actual task instructions were given when they operated a specific machine: The task was to operate an electric chain hoist by alternately pressing a green and a red button. To ensure the power supply, human or robot needed to stand on a platform. They had to pull as much of the rope as possible within five minutes starting from the moment when the instruction was activated. The total time within the Virtual Theatre was 15 min in average.

In a 2 × 2 design, the robot's characteristics were manipulated. The robot appeared either as an industrial or humanoid robot (see Fig. 2) and operated either reliably or imperfect in response to the human operator. Participants were randomly assigned to the conditions. The behavior of the robot in both conditions was standardized by the specifications of an activity (see Fig. 3).

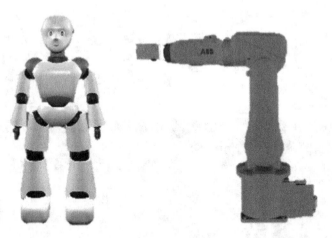

Fig. 2. Design of the humanoid and industrial robot.

[3] The production hall and the robots were designed using Cinema 4D and implemented with Unreal Engine (game engine) and C++.

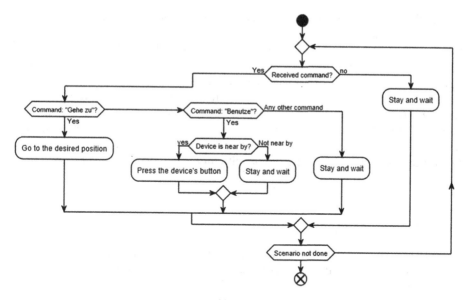

Fig. 3. Activity diagram for the reliable condition

The experiment was framed with an online pre- and a post-survey using SoSci Survey[4]. The pre-survey was designed to get insights into the personal characteristics of the participants and the post-survey to gain information of the individual, subjective assessment of the hybrid teamwork. An overview of the complete questionnaires is reported in Table 1.

Table 1. Questionnaires of the pre- and post-survey. Questionnaires used for the analysis in this paper are starred (*).

Pre-survey		Post-survey	
Public Attitudes Towards Robots	[20]	NASA-Task Load Index (NASA-TLX)	[21]
Negative Attitude toward Robots Scale (NARS)	[22]	Questionnaire on teamwork (FAT)*	[23]
Locus of control in dealing with technology (KUT)	[24]	Trust scale*	[25]
10 Item Big Five Inventory (BFI-10)	[26]	Short Stress State Questionnaire (SSSQ)	[27]
Short Stress State Questionnaire (SSSQ)	[27]	Simulator Sickness Questionnaire (SSQ)	[28]
Godspeed*	[29]	MEC Spatial Presence Questionnaire (MEC-SPQ)	[30]

---

[4] www.soscisurvey.de.

For the analysis in this paper, we analysed the level of trust towards the robot with an adaption of the questionnaire of Schaefer [25] as well as the team functionality with the Questionnaire of Teamwork (FAT) by Kauffeld and Frieling [23] in dependence of the robot's characteristics. Trust was evaluated by entering a percentage value. Exemplary questions are "How much percent of the time did the robot work properly?" or "How much percent of the time did the robot work well in the team?". Team functionality was assessed using a six-point Likert-scale with verbalized endpoints. Examples are "Our goals are realistic and achievable. – Our goals are unrealistic and unachievable." or "We reach all goals with ease. – Sometimes we get the impression that we cannot achieve our goals.". Reliability for the individual FAT subscales varied between $\alpha = .64$ and $\alpha = 89$ [23].

3   Results

In order to test the hypotheses described above, factorial analyses of variance (ANOVA) with the fixed factors appearance and behaviour of the robot were conducted using SPSS 24.

Robots which performed reliable were trusted more ($\bar{x} = 61.70, SD = 14.37$) than robots which performed faulty ($\bar{x} = 55.27, SD = 16.66$). This main effect of the robot's accuracy on the level of trust was significant, F (1, 108) = 4.65, $p = .033$, $\omega^2 = .04$. Hence, hypothesis H_1 is confirmed. The main effect of appearance and the interaction effect were not significant, thus hypothesis H_3 cannot be confirmed.

Robot's appearance[5] influenced some FAT dimensions. There was a significant main effect of the robot's appearance on orientation, F (1, 108) = 6.16, $p = .014$, $\omega^2 = .05$, and task management, F (1, 108) = 4.23, $p = .039$, $\omega^2 = .04$. The humanoid condition had higher values in both dimensions ($\bar{x} = 2.85, SD = 1.01$ vs. $\bar{x} = 2.39, SD = .97$ for goal orientation and $\bar{x} = 3.12, SD = 1.10$ vs. $\bar{x} = 2.75, SD = .85$ for task management) indicating less goal orientation and task management. The dimensions can also be summarized as task reflexivity [31]. The other dimensions of the FAT, which can be summarized as social reflexivity, did not reveal significant main effects, so hypothesis H_4 can be partially confirmed. The teams with both the industrial and the humanoid robot can be classified as fully functioning teams (see Fig. 4). The main effects of behaviour and the interaction effects were not significant, too, which goes along with hypothesis H_2.

---

[5] Considering the Godspeed Test to measure the users' perception of the robot, the humanoid robot was rated as more humanlike ($\bar{x} = 2.06, SD = .53$ vs. $\bar{x} = 2.38, SD = .77$), t (114.54) = −2.94, $p = .004$. Humanoids were also perceived as more animated ($\bar{x} = 2.54, SD = .57$ vs. $\bar{x} = 2.75, SD = .71$), t (151) = −2.09, $p = .038$, likeable ($\bar{x} = 3.19, SD = .48$ vs. $\bar{x} = 3.78, SD = .53$ $\bar{x} = 3.78, SD = .53$), t (151) = −7.15, $p < .001$, and intelligent ($\bar{x} = 3.09, SD = .67$ vs. $\bar{x} = 3.39, SD = .58$), t (151) = −2.84, $p = .005$. No influence was found in the level of perceived safety ($\bar{x} = 2.69, SD = .52$ vs. $\bar{x} = 2.54, SD = .58$), t (151) = 1.69, $p = .093$.

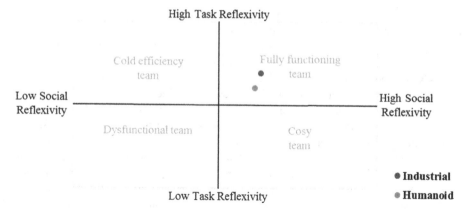

High Task Reflexivity

Cold efficiency
team

Fully functioning
team

Low Social
Reflexivity

High Social
Reflexivity

Dysfunctional team

Cosy
team

● **Industrial**

● **Humanoid**

Low Task Reflexivity

Fig. 4. Team functionality of the hybrid teams after West [31].

There was a significant main effect of the robot's appearance on the performance, $F (1, 104) = 5.06$, $p = .027$, $\omega^2 = .05$). In collaboration with the humanoid robot, the performance ($\bar{x} = 3.26, SD = 2.25$) was not as good as with the industrial robot ($\bar{x} = 4.26, SD = 2.31$), which goes along with hypothesis H_5. The main effect of the robot's behaviour as well as the interaction effect between appearance and behaviour on performance were not significant.

4   Discussion

This study examined the impact of the design of a robotic workmate (appearance and behaviour) on the trust placed in the robot, the perceived team functionality, and the objective team performance (which might be an effect of time – with more time provided for task fulfilment, an impact is assumed). It was found that a faulty robot was perceived as less trustworthy, but that its accuracy did not affect the team functionality and team performance. An industrial appearing lead to a higher task reflexivity and a better collaborative performance, but no influence of the appearance on the level of trust was found.

The lacking influence of appearance on trust and social reflexivity might be a result of the currently still predominant mental model of robots which considers robots – independently of their look – more as a tool than an actual teammate [32]. This might be also enhanced by the design of the study, which assigned the participants as an operator of the robot who commands it. Although a natural bidirectional language interface was chosen and the robot listened to a human name, which should emphasize the equality of the team members, the robots did not seem to introduce a high sense of unity.

Further work will continue to explore how the participants' characteristics (e.g. personality, attitude towards robots) influence the performance of hybrid collaboration and the subjective perception of it. Through analyzing the interactions between human and robot during the experiment (via video analysis), it will also be considered whether human-robot teams experience team development and whether the stages of human team development can be transferred to hybrid teams.

The study gives first implications of how a robotic workmate should be designed, taking into account the interactions with a human partner. Nevertheless, the limitations of this study should be considered. First, due to technical issues and simulation sickness of some participants, comparatively few test subjects were included in each condition of the experiments; hence, the statistical power was limited. Second, the sample consisted mainly of students and it is possible that construction workers, who will be the actual end-users, will perceive hybrid collaboration in a different way. Third, habituation effects might occur, so that the described patterns might not remain over time. Fourth, a virtual environment setting was used to guarantee a safe interaction with a robot and to manipulate the robot's characteristics easily. However, it must be explored whether the findings are transferable to real production environments.

Acknowledgments. The authors would like to thank the German Federal Ministry of Education and Research (BMBF) for the kind support within the joint project ARIZ (Arbeit in der Industrie der Zukunft) and acknowledge the RWTH Start-Up for the kind support within the project SowiRo (Socializing with Robots).

References

1. Knight, W.: Inside Amazon. At a new fulfillment center in New Jersey, humans and robots work together in a highly efficient system. MIT Technol. Rev. (2015)
2. Lazarte, M.: Robots and humans can work together with new ISO guidance. http://www.iso.org/iso/home/news_index/news_archive/news.htm?refid=Ref2057 (2016). Accessed 13 Jan 2017
3. Charles, R.L., Charalambous, G., Fletcher, S.: Your new colleague is a robot. Is that ok? In: Proceedings of the International Conference on Ergonomics & Human Factors, pp. 307–311 (2015)
4. Scholtz, J.: Theory and evaluation of human robot interactions. In: Proceedings of the 36th Hawaii International Conference on System Sciences (2002). doi:10.1109/HICSS.2003. 1174284
5. Yanco, H.A., Drury, J.: Classifying human-robot interaction: an updated taxonomy. In: IEEE International Conference on Systems, Man and Cybernetics (2004). doi:10.1075/z.124.02int
6. Han, Y.: Software Infrastructure for Configurable Workflow Systems. A Model-Driven Approach Based on Higher Order Object Nets and CORBA, 1st edn. Wissenschaft und Technik, Berlin (1997)
7. Salas, E., Dickinson, T.L., Converse, S.A., Tanndenbaum, S.I.: Toward an understanding of team performance and training. In: Swezey, R.W., Salas, E. (eds.) Teams: Their Training and Performance, pp. 3–29. Ablex Publishing Corporation, Norwood (1992)
8. Haeussling, R.: Die zwei Naturen sozialer Aktivitaet. Relationalistische Betrachtung aktueller Mensch-Roboter-Kooperationen. In: Rehberg, K.-S. (ed.) Die Natur der Gesellschaft: Verhandlungen des 33. Kongresses der Deutschen Gesellschaft für Soziologie in Kassel 2006, pp. 720–735. Campus Verlag, Frankfurt am Main (2008)

9. Charalambous, G., Fletcher, S., Webb, P.: Human-automation collaboration in manufacturing: identifying key implementation factors. In: Proceedings of the 11th International Conference on Manufacturing Research (2013). doi:10.1201/b13826-16

10. Wickens, C.D., Sebok, A., Li, H., Sarter, N., Gacy, A.M.: Using modeling and simulation to predict operator performance and automation-induced complacency with robotic automation: a case study and empirical validation. Hum. Factors (2015). doi:10.1177/0018720814566454

11. Hancock, P.A., Billings, D.R., Schaefer, K.E., Chen, J.Y.C., de Visser, E.J., Parasuraman, R.: A meta-analysis of factors affecting trust in human-robot interaction. Hum. Factors (2011). doi:10.1177/0018720811417254

12. Salem, M., Lakatos, G., Amirabdollahian, F., Dautenhahn, K.: Would you trust a (faulty) robot? Effects of error, task type and personality on human-robot cooperation and trust. In: Proceedings of the Tenth Annual ACM/IEEE International Conference on Human-Robot Interaction (2015). doi:10.1145/2696454.2696497

13. Jentsch, E.: On the psychology of the uncanny (1906) 1. Angelaki: J. Theor. Hum. (1997). doi:10.1080/09697259708571910

14. Freud, S.: The 'Uncanny'. The Standard Edition of the Complete Psychological Works of Sigmund Freud, vol. XVII, pp. 217–256 (1919)

15. Mori, M., MacDorman, K., Kageki, N.: The uncanny valley [from the field]. IEEE Robot. Automat. Mag. (2012). doi:10.1109/MRA.2012.2192811

16. Hinds, P.J., Roberts, T.L., Jones, H.: Whose job is it anyway? A study of human–robot interaction in a collaborative task. Hum.-Comput. Interact. (2004). doi:10.1207/s15327051hci1901&2_7

17. Goetz, J., Kiesler, S., Powers, A.: Matching robot appearance and behavior to tasks to improve human-robot cooperation. In: Proceedings of the 12th IEEE International Workshop on Robot and Human Interactive Communication ROMAN (2003). doi:10.1109/ROMAN.2003.1251796

18. Richert, A., Shehadeh, M.A., Muller, S.L., Schroder, S., Jeschke, S.: Socializing with robots: human-robot interactions within a virtual environment. In: The 2016 IEEE Workshop on Advanced Robotics and Its Social Impacts, IEEE ARSO 2016, 7–10 July 2016, Shanghai, China, pp. 49–54. IEEE, Piscataway (2016). doi:10.1109/ARSO.2016.7736255

19. Richert, A., Shehadeh, M.A., Müller, S.L., Schröder, S., Jeschke, S.: Robotic workmates—hybrid human-robot-teams in the industry 4.0. In: Proceedings of the 11th International Conference on e-Learning, pp. 127–131 (2016)

20. Special Eurobarometer 382: Public Attitudes towards Robots. European Commission (2012). http://ec.europa.eu/public_opinion/archives/ebs/ebs_382_en.pdf. Accessed 30 Mar 2016

21. Hart, S.G.: NASA-Task Load Index (NASA-TLX): 20 years later. In: Proceedings of the Human Factors and Ergonomics Society Annual Meeting (2006). doi:10.1177/154193120605000909

22. Nomura, T., Kanda, T., Suzuki, T., Kato, K.: Psychology in human-robot communication: an attempt through investigation of negative attitudes and anxiety toward robots. In: Proceedings of the 13th IEEE International Workshop on Robot and Human Interactive Communication (2004). doi:10.1109/ROMAN.2004.1374726

23. Kauffeld, S., Frieling, E.: Der Fragebogen zur Arbeit im Team (F-A-T). Zeitschrift für Arbeits- und Organisationspsychologie A&O (2001). doi:10.1026//0932-4089.45.1.26

24. Beier, G.: Kontrollüberzeugungen im Umgang mit Technik. Rep. Psychol. **9**, 684–693 (1999)

25. Schaefer, K.E.: The perception and measurement of human-robot trust. Dissertation, University of Central Florida Orlando, Florida (2013). http://etd.fcla.edu/CF/CFE0004931/Schaefer_Kristin_E_201308_PhD.pdf. Accessed 17 June 2016

26. Rammstedt, B., Kemper, C.J., Klein, M.C., Beierlein, C., Kovaleva, A.: Eine kurze Skala zur Messung der fünf Dimensionen der Persönlichkeit. 10 Item Big Five Inventory (BFI-10). methoden, daten, analyse (2013). doi:10.12758/mda.2013.013

27. Helton, W.S., Näswall, K.: Short stress state questionnaire. Eur. J. Psychol. Assess. (2015). doi:10.1027/1015-5759/a000200

28. Kennedy, R.S., Lane, N.E., Berbaum, K.S., Lilienthal, M.G.: Simulator sickness questionnaire. an enhanced method for quantifying simulator sickness. Int. J. Aviat. Psychol. (1993). doi:10.1207/s15327108ijap0303_3

29. Bartneck, C., Kulić, D., Croft, E., Zoghbi, S.: Measurement instruments for the anthropomorphism, animacy, likeability, perceived intelligence, and perceived safety of robots. Int. J. Soc. Robot. (2009). doi:10.1007/s12369-008-0001-3

30. Wirth, W., Schramm, H., Böcking, S., Gysbers, A., Hartmann, T., Klimmt, C., Vorderer, P.: Entwicklung und Validierung eines Fragebogens zur Entstehung von räumlichem Präsenzerleben. Die Brücke zwischen Theorie und Empirie: Operationalisierung, Messung und Validierung in der Kommunikationswissenschaft. Köln: von Halem, pp. 70–95 (2008)

31. West, M.A.: Effective Teamwork. Personal and Professional Development. British Psychological Society, Leicester (1994)

32. Phillips, E., Ososky, S., Grove, J., Jentsch, F.: From tools to teammates. toward the development of appropriate mental models for intelligent robots. In: Proceedings of the Human Factors and Ergonomics Society Annual Meeting (2011). doi:10.1177/1071181311551310

The Effects of the Robot Patient's Patient-Likeness on Nursing Students

Mitsuhiro Nakamura[1](✉), Yasuko Kitajima[1], Jun Ota[2], Taiki Ogata[2],
Zhifeng Huang[3], Chingszu Lin[2], Noriaki Kuwahara[4], Jukai Maeda[1],
and Masako Kanai-Pak[5]

[1] Faculty of Nursing, Tokyo Ariake University of Medical and Health Sciences,
2-9-1 Ariake, Koto-ku, Tokyo 135-0063, Japan
{m-nakamura,kitajima,jukai}@tau.ac.jp
[2] Research into Artifacts Center for Engineering (RACE),
The University of Tokyo, 5-1-5 Kashiwanoha, Kashiwa-shi,
Chiba 277-8568, Japan
{ota,ogata,lin}@race.u-tokyo.ac.jp
[3] Faculty of Automation, Guangdong University of Technology,
No. 100 Waihuan Xi Road, Guangzhou Higher Education Mega Center, Panyu,
District Guangzhou, People's Republic of China
lnyahzf@126.com
[4] Department of Advanced Fibro-Science, Kyoto Institute of Technology,
Matsugasaki, Sakyo-ku, Kyoto 606-8585, Japan
nkuwahar@kit.ac.jp
[5] College of Nursing, Kanto Gakuin University, 1-50-1 Mutsuura Higashi,
Kanazawa-ku, Yokohama-shi, Kanagawa 236-8501, Japan
kanaipak@kanto-gakuin.ac.jp

Abstract. In this research we conducted experiments for the purpose of clarifying the learning effectiveness of self-study by nursing students using the robot patient and the effect of more "patient-like" robot on the self-study of nursing students. The robot patient are 160 cm height, 40 kg weight. A motor is installed into the shoulder and elbow joints of both upper limbs, and a thermo-brake is installed in both knee joints. Triggered by the vocal greeting of the nurse, the motor and thermo-brake can be respectively controlled and can reproduce the paralysis of the upper and lower limbs and express pain via audio. We conducted an experiment targeting 12 nursing students at a nursing university. We conduct self-study of wheelchair transfer 6 times using the robot patient and we graded the students' skills using a wheelchair transfer scoring checklist drafted in advance by nursing teachers. Because the score clearly rises, showing that the robot patient is effective for self-studying wheelchair transfer. Also, by conducting self-study using robots which reproduce the entire human body of patients, students who had never interacted with patients were able to be cognizant of patients closer to reality. It was clarified in our questionnaire survey that the students felt the weight of patients, the difficulty of assisting the limbs of patients with paralysis and pain, the difficulty of keeping the patients safe, etc.

Keywords: Patient robot · Simulated patients · Nursing student · Nursing skill · Nursing education

© Springer International Publishing AG 2017
V.G. Duffy (Ed.): DHM 2017, Part I, LNCS 10286, pp. 457–465, 2017.
DOI: 10.1007/978-3-319-58463-8_38

1 Background

Nursing practice at hospitals by nursing students is the most important opportunity to connect nursing theories and skills implementation for nursing students in nursing education [1]. However, as nursing work diversifies and becomes more complicated due to the highly developed modern medical care, changes in disease structure, increased age of patients, and reduction in average number of days of hospitalization, nursing students are experiencing the problem of being able to experience fewer nursing skills in nursing practice. According to a survey by the Japanese Nursing Association in 2002 [2], more than 70% of new nurses only identify the 4 items "bed making", "linen changing", "vital sign measurement", and "height and weight measurement" out of 103 items as "skills they recognize they can perform alone when starting employment", creating a situation where nurses are working who have not acquired sufficient nursing skills while studying at educational institutions. Due to the gap between the skills required by new nurses at the time of hiring and the skills learned at the time of graduation, unfortunately 9.7% of new nurses lose or leave their jobs within 1 year of starting employment [4]. For this reason, it can be said that the creation of a structure which allows nurses to acquire a certain level of nursing skills by graduation is a social need demanded to the field of nursing education.

In addition to nursing practice, nursing students also spend time engaging in in-school training to acquire the skills required as nurses. Normally, after acquiring knowledge in classes on nursing skills, nursing students undergo in-school training under the instruction of teachers to acquire nursing skills. One-on-one practice between students and teachers is the most effective learning method for nursing skills [5], but for example of the our university, instruction is conducted by 4 teachers for 60 students, making it difficult for all students to receive sufficient instruction due to a lack of teacher personnel resources. Furthermore, there is also a study showing that the amount of time a teacher spends directly instructing a student in in-school training is 9.4 min [6], resulting in difficulty for nursing students to acquire skills due to limited time resources as well.

In order to solve these various problems, our research team is continuously conducting research into the automation of nursing skill acquisition.

Nursing students aim to acquire nursing skills which they cannot sufficiently acquire in classes and training by repeating self-study outside of class hours, but there are many cases where repeated self-study only results in them acquiring skills incorrectly. This is because the nursing students execute actions based on their own judgment in self-study, and although they need to notice what is wrong with their actions and correct the problems, their ability to objectively perceive their own actions is insufficient, causing them to not notice what is wrong with their actions and believe they are correct [7]. In other words, in order to acquire nursing skills it is essential for there to be a third party who can objectively evaluate the actions of nursing students and provide feedback. However, the lack of human and time resources makes it impossible for teachers to evaluate the self-study of students. And so our research team, believing that an automated system which can appropriately evaluate and provide feedback on the nursing skills conducted by students could solve these problems, has been conducting research necessary for the construction of such a system.

First of all, we examined whether nursing students can acquire nursing skills not through teaching methods which provide feedback depending on the problem points and learning characteristics of students which are normally used by teachers to teach students to acquire nursing skills, but rather through simple feedback which does not indicate specific methods for improvement but simply whether or not the actions are correct. The results showed that nursing students can acquire nursing skills only with simple feedback indicated whether "correct" or "incorrect" and without indicated specific methods for improvement, and furthermore that simple feedback has even more effective learning results than self-study via audio-visual teaching materials and textbooks which have been traditionally utilized [8, 9]. This experiment suggested the possibility that the presence of teachers, which had previously been thought essential for acquiring nursing skills, can be replaced by an automated simple feedback system.

Next we developed a nursing skill evaluation system utilizing the KINECT sensor by Microsoft [10] (Fig. 1).

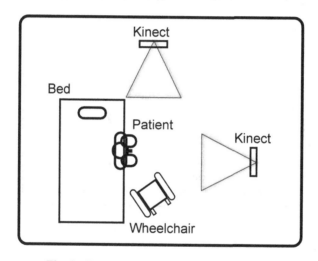

Fig. 1. Room used in experiment by KINECT.

This system automatically evaluates the wheelchair transfer skill wherein a patient is transferred from a bed to a wheelchair by digitizing the movements of the nursing students using the KINECT sensor and provides feedback (Fig. 2) for each check item to the nursing students. This system is designed to enable students to use it alone without involvement by teachers or system engineers.

We conducted an experiment on 5 nursing students to evaluate the effectiveness of this system. In the experiment we had the students use the system for self-study after taking a test on wheelchair transfer skills before using the system. Lastly, we conducted a wheelchair transfer skill test again and had a teacher score the test. The results confirmed a statistically significant improvement in score after using the system compared to before using the system [11, 12] (Fig. 3).

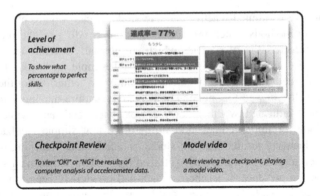

Fig. 2. Feedback screen of nursing skill evaluation system by KINECT.

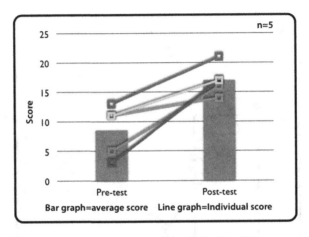

Fig. 3. Score by self-learning system.

This experiment proved that the automated self-study system was effective in acquiring nursing skills compared to traditional self-study conducted by nursing students alone. In other words, nursing students can learn correct nursing skills even without a teacher by conducting self-study of nursing skills using this system.

The care-recipients in the series of experiments were healthy persons with nursing qualifications and work experience. If the person playing the role of patient knows what actual patients are like they can behave "like patients", but it is difficult for nursing students to behave "like patients", because nursing students don't know patient due to do not have experience of nursing practice at hospitals. Using the example of the wheelchair transfer, not only do the legs of patients with paralysis feel heavier than the legs of a healthy person, it is difficult for nurses to move them. Furthermore, when moving the arms of patients with joint pain in their arms, patients will intentionally restrict their arm movement to avoid the pain, so nurses must be more cautious when passively moving their arms. It is difficult for nursing students who have had little opportunity to actual interact with patients to reproduce these patient behaviors. It is difficult to say that nursing students playing the role of patients in training are reproducing the paralysis and pain of actual patients, and furthermore they may move the same as healthy persons due to feeling bad for the students playing the role of nurse and wanting to make it as easy as possible for them. The result is that training proceeds without students being able to truly learn the important points to know when assisting patients with pain and paralysis. It is difficult for nursing students to acquire nursing skills under these circumstances. In order to solve this issue it is necessary for nursing students to understand how paralysis and pain manifest in patients by actually interacting with them, but the nursing practice time, which is the only time when nursing students can interact with patients, is limited and it is difficult to increase the nursing practice time in the curriculum. In recent years there are vigorous efforts being made to train members of the public to be simulated patients (Simulated or Standardized Patients; hereinafter "SP") able to realistically play the roles of patients considering their physical, mental, and social conditions not only for nursing education but also medical education. However, SP training is said to require about 4 months of time, and furthermore continuous training and support is essential for mastering SP, resulting in a situation where the number of SPs cannot be said to be keeping with the demand for SPs [13]. Therefore, this research team concluded that a robot patient which can reproduce the restricted movements of limbs caused by paralysis and pain caused by load on joints would be a solution for a variety of problems and developed a robot patient [14, 15]. We equipped the robot with functions to reproduce paralysis and express pain due to excessive load on joints.

In this research we conducted experiments for the purpose of clarifying the learning effectiveness of self-study by nursing students using the robot patient and the effect of more "patient-like" robot on the self-study of nursing students.

2 Purpose

The purpose of this research is to clarify the following 2 points.

(1) Clarify the effectiveness of self-study by nursing students by using our robot patient.
(2) Clarify the effect of more "patient-like" robot patient on the self-study of nursing students.

3 Methods

We conducted an experiment according to the following procedures targeting 12 nursing students (9 3rd-year students and 3 4th-year students) at a nursing university.

(1) View a wheelchair transfer instructional video created by nursing teachers.
(2) Conduct self-study of wheelchair transfer 6 times using the robot patient.
(3) Conduct questionnaire survey regarding self-study using the robot patient. The questionnaire asked the students' impressions regarding the robot, points of improvement, etc., in a free description format.

In (2) above we graded the students' skills using a wheelchair transfer scoring checklist drafted in advance by nursing teachers.

Below is a summary of the specifications of the robot patient developed in this research.

160 cm height, 40 kg weight. A motor is installed into the shoulder and elbow joints of both upper limbs, and a thermo-brake is installed in both knee joints. Triggered by the vocal greeting of the nurse, the motor and thermo-brake can be respectively controlled and can reproduce the paralysis of the upper and lower limbs and express pain via audio (Fig. 4).

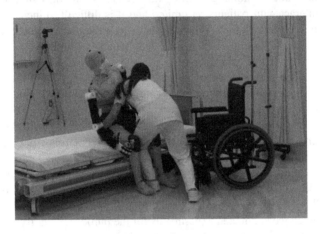

Fig. 4. Scene of experiment

This research was conducted after an ethical review by the Tokyo Ariake University of Medical and Health Sciences (No. 138-2, approved July 26, 2016).

4   Results

The score transition of self-study using the robot patient is shown in the following table (Table 1). The highest score was 23, the lowest score was 7. The most difference between the highest score and the lowest score was 14.

In the free description of the questionnaire survey, the following kinds of answers were received.

"When students are playing the role of patients they provide unnecessary assistance to avoid burdening the person playing the role of nurse with their body weight, but the robot does not, making it feel likely an actual patient."

"I think the robot was good because the body weight was heavy."

"The robot was too heavy for me to lift. Are actual patients this heavy?"

"With other students it feels like practicing with friends, but a robot doesn't feel like a friend so I was nervous."

Table 1. Scores of the subjects

#	Grade	The number of self-learning						Difference*
		1	2	3	4	5	6	
1	3	14	17	19	16	20	**22**	8
2	3	9	15	18	20	20	**23**	14
3	3	9	14	13	13	15	**18**	9
4	3	14	17	19	16	20	**22**	8
5	3	9	11	16	18	19	**20**	11
6	3	11	16	20	18	20	**21**	10
7	4	11	15	16	15	18	**20**	9
8	3	10	18	18	**19**	18	18	9
9	4	8	16	**18**	10	15	**18**	10
10	4	8	15	18	20	**21**	17	13
11	3	7	12	**16**	14	**16**	13	9
12	3	9	16	15	13	14	**19**	10

*Difference between the highest and lowest points.
Bold is the highest score.

"The robot seemed heavy, which made me worried about whether I can transfer actual patients who are heavier than the robot when I start nursing practice."

"It is hard to practice again and again when a friend is playing the role of patient, but with a robot I can."

"I was rude, because the robot felt strongly like "a thing" rather than a human."

"It felt like I was practicing with an actual patient."

"The robot is paralyzed and can't move, so it felt more like a patient."

5 Discussion

Because the score clearly rises, showing that the robot patient is effective for self-studying wheelchair transfer. These results are the same as the results of the other experiments regarding nursing skills conducted by this research team in the past, and further support the usefulness of automated nursing skill acquisition systems for self-study. However, in our previous experiments we used systems which partially reproduced the symptoms and conditions of patients, but did not reproduce the entire body of a patient. Therefore, it was useful to focus on only a certain nursing skill and master it. However, nursing students do not care part of the patient's body in nursing practice at hospitals. Nursing students care for the whole-patient approach. So, It is important that the robot patient must reproduce the whole, not a part. Nursing education simulators currently on sale in Japan are also simulators which reproduce only parts of patients to specialize in subjects of study, while in this research we were able to confirm the effectiveness of robot patient which reproduce the entire body of a patient.

Also, by conducting self-study using robots which reproduce the entire human body of patients, students who had never interacted with patients were able to be cognizant of patients closer to reality. It was clarified in our questionnaire survey that the students felt the weight of patients, the difficulty of assisting the limbs of patients with paralysis and pain, the difficulty of keeping the patients safe, etc. Until then, nursing students were practicing between students, but nursing students were making new discoveries about patients. It shows the difficulty of nursing students playing the role of patients.

Furthermore, it was suggested that it is impossible to acquire nursing skills provided to actual patients with patients played by nursing students.

This research confirms that students can acquire wheelchair transfer skills via self-study using the robot patient and suggests that several problems inherent to self-study for acquiring nursing skills conducted with fellow students can be solved by using the robot patient.

6 Conclusion

It was clarified that nursing students can acquire wheelchair transfer skills through self-study using the robot patient. By studying with the robot patient that reproduces the entire body of a patient, students felt the difficulty of providing care caused by patients' body weight, paralysis, and pain.

References

1. Wong, J., Wong, S.: Towards effective clinical teaching in nursing. J. Adv. Nurs. **12**(4), 505–513 (1987)
2. Japanese Nursing Association.: Survey of Basic Nursing Skills of Freshman Nurses (2002). (in Japanese)
3. Japanese Nursing Association.: Survey of Early Departure of New Graduate Nurse (2004). (in Japanese)
4. Fukui, T.: A survey on the status of basic nursing skill acquired by new graduate nurses. Jpn. J. Nurs. Adm. **19**(4), 254–261 (2009). (in Japanese)
5. Kanai-Pak, M., Kitajima, Y., Hirata, M., Takabatake, Y., Nakamura, M., Maeda, J.: Effect and problem of ideal nursing skill education. In: Abstracts of the 30th Academic Conference of Japan Academy of Nursing Science, p. 243 (2010). (in Japanese)
6. Nakamura, M.: Building the foundation for a new nursing skill education system based on patient moving. Special Interest Group of Nonverbal Interface, Human Interface Society, Handout (2011). (in Japanese)
7. Kanai-Pak, M.: Innovation in collaborative research between nursing and engineering: a new approach for skill acquisition. Jpn. J. Nurs. Res. **44**(6), 554–558 (2011). (in Japanese)
8. Maeda, J., Kitajima, Y., Nakamura, M., Hirata, M., Aida, K., Takabatake, Y., Kanai-Pak, M., Kuwahara, N., Ota, J.: Does simple feedback improve nursing skills in self-learning? Jpn. J. Med. Inform., 222–223 (2011) (in Japanese)

9. Nakamura, M., Maeda, J., Kitajima, Y., Aida, K., Kanai-Pak, M.: Possibility of acquiring nursing skills by self-study effect of machine evaluation. In: Abstracts of the 31th Academic Conference of Japan Academy of Nursing Science, vol. 31 (2011) (in Japanese)

10. Huang, Z., et al.: Feedback-based self-training system of patient transfer. In: Duffy, Vincent G. (ed.) DHM 2013. LNCS, vol. 8025, pp. 197–203. Springer, Heidelberg (2013). doi:10.1007/978-3-642-39173-6_24

11. Nakamura, M., et al.: The Relationship between Nursing Students' Attitudes towards Learning and Effects of Self-learning System Using Kinect. In: Duffy, Vincent G. (ed.) DHM 2013. LNCS, vol. 8026, pp. 111–116. Springer, Heidelberg (2013). doi:10.1007/978-3-642-39182-8_13

12. Huang, Z., Nagata, A., Kanai-Pak, M., Maeda, J., Kitajima, Y., Nakamura, M., Aida, K., Kuwahara, N., Ogata, T., Ota, J.: Automatic evaluation of trainee nurses' patient transfer skills using multiple kinect sensors. IEICE Trans. Inform. Syst. 97(1), 107–118 (2014)

13. Shinozaki, E., Sakata, S., Watanabe, Y., Abe, K., Ban, N., Fujii, T.: The process of standardized patient from novice to expert. Bull. Dept. Nurs. Seirei Christopher Univ. 22, 3–44 (2014). (in Japanese)

14. Lin, C., Huang, Z., Kanai-Pak, M., Kitajima, Y., Nakamura, M., Kuwahara, N., Ogata, T., Ota, J.: Robot patient imitating paralysis patients for nursing students to learn patient transfer skill. In: Chen, W., Hosoda, K., Menegatti, E., Shimizu, M., Wang, H. (eds.) Proceedings of the International Conference on Intelligent Autonomous Systems (IAS-14), pp. 384–395. Springer, Cham (2016)

15. Huang, Z., Katayama, T., Kanai-Pak, M., Maeda, J., Kitajima, Y., Nakamura, M., Aida, K., Kuwahara, N., Ogata, T., Ota, J.: Design and evaluation of robot patient for nursing skill training in patient transfer. Adv. Robot. 29(19), 1269–1285 (2015)

A Tactile Expression Mechanism Using Pneumatic Actuator Array for Notification from Wearable Robots

Hirotake Yamazoe[1(✉)] and Tomoko Yonezawa[2]

[1] College of Information Science and Engineering, Ritsumeikan University,
1-1-1 Nojihigashi, Kusatsu, Shiga 525-8577, Japan
`yamazoe@fc.ritsumei.ac.jp`
[2] Faculty of Infomatics, Kansai University, 2-1-1 Ryozenji, Takatsuki,
Osaka 569-1095, Japan
`yone@kansai-u.ac.jp`

Abstract. We propose a tactile expression mechanism that can make physical contact and provide direction indications. We previously proposed a wearable robot that can provide physical contact for elderly support in outdoor situations. In our current scheme, wearable message robots, which we mounted on the user's upper arm, give such messages to users as navigational information, for example. Using physical contact can improve relationships between users and robots. However, our previous prototypes have a problem because the types of tactile expressions (that the robots can make) are limited. Thus, we propose a tactile expression mechanism using a pneumatic actuator array for wearable robots. Our proposed system consists of four pneumatic actuators and creates such haptic stimuli as direction indications as well as stroking a user's arm. Our wearable robots were originally designed as appropriate support and communication for two types of physical contact: *notification* and *affection*. Our proposed mechanism for physical contact and direction indications naturally extends not only notification but also the affection abilities of the robot. Our robots and our proposed mechanism are expected to support the mobility of senior citizens by reducing their anxiety on outings.

1 Introduction

The world's aging societies continue to face a variety of serious problems related to lifestyle changes, such as an increase in nuclear families. In these societies, the elderly and the disabled who are living alone sometimes need the support of caregivers to overcome their anxiety even when they just want to leave their homes for a walk or go shopping. However, due to a shortage of caregivers and volunteers and the emotional burden of seeking help, such people often withdraw from society. Such withdrawal from society causes even greater problems, including advanced dementia.

© Springer International Publishing AG 2017
V.G. Duffy (Ed.): DHM 2017, Part I, LNCS 10286, pp. 466–475, 2017.
DOI: 10.1007/978-3-319-58463-8_39

During outings, the elderly and the disabled face two main problems: *physical problems*, especially for seniors, caused from impaired body functions, and *cognitive problems*, which can exacerbate memory loss and attention deficit issues. Such problems can result in serious accidents. The use of power suits [14] solves some of these physical problems by compensating for partial power loss. On the other hand, cognitive problems can cause memory loss and attention deficit issues. For people with dementia, the instructions or the purpose of their outings might be forgotten, which can be risky [11] during outings.

We focus on cognitive problems and solve them with robots. We are researching wearable message robots that can care for and support such people during their outings [18, 21]. Since our robots are wearable, they can provide support to users anytime and anywhere. In addition, since *physical contact* is intuitive and critical for communication, our robots have a mechanism for making two types of physical contact: *notification* and *affection*. Notifications are robot behaviors made when the robot wants to tell the user something, such as patting the user's arm before saying something. Affections are behaviors that show the robot's internal states, such as embracing the user's arm. We believe that both behaviors are important for achieving natural communication and good relationships between users and robots [23].

Considering support in outside situations, indicating directions is also essential, for example, when the robot wants to convey the idea of "Please look over there." Even though pointing by the robot's arm is a natural way to indicate directions, the DoFs of our wearable robot arms are insufficient for such behaviors. Unfortunately, increasing the number of DoFs in the robot arm also increases its weight. Vocal notifications are another natural way for directional indications by robots. However, vocal information is sometimes difficult to hear and understand outside, especially in crowded situations. In addition, although louder voices simplify notification, personal messages might be embarrassing: "It's time for a toilet break." Thus, in this paper, we propose wearable robots that can make not only physical contact but also give direction indications.

2   Related Research

Various researches exist on haptic stimuli as displays for mobile situations. Research has investigated vibration stimuli as feedback on the touchscreens of mobile devices [5]. Directional indicators have also been discussed using vibro-tactile devices [4, 6], gyro moments [1, 20], and a combination of skin stretches and vibro-tactile stimuli [2, 8]. These researches physically notify users of information.

Considerable researches have also been conducted on anthropomorphic behaviors, such as affection, the attention of robots and agents [9], and wearable haptic interfaces [3, 16]. The effectiveness of anthropomorphic expressions using pointing, facing, and the gazing of the robots and agents has been confirmed in various experiments [9, 24, 25]. Their multimodal behaviors are effective; however, the behaviors have been discussed without including physical contact by robots.

Communication robots or agents as media have also been developed based on the premise of ongoing communication between people [12,13]. Other schemes feature a wearable avatar robot on the shoulder [7]. A mobile-phone type robot was also proposed [10].

We have been researching support for elderly outings, especially toilet problems, such as a toilet map acquisition system [19] and a toilet timing suggestion system [15]. To achieve such an elderly support system based on such researches, appropriate mechanisms for transmitting the support information are also important. For such purposes, we proposed a wearable message robot that combines haptic stimuli and a robot's anthropomorphic behaviors to enable feeling actual physical contact from the robot [21,23] and a simplified system [18].

In this paper, we propose a mechanism that can make not only physical contact but also provide direction indications for effective elderly support in outdoor situations.

3   Previous Prototypes of Our Wearable Robots with Physical Contact

First, we introduce the previous prototypes of our wearable robots [18,21].

3.1   First Prototype

Figure 1 shows the first prototypes of our wearable message robot [21]. As described above, both *notification* and *affection* are important for human-robot communication. This prototype system performs both behaviors.

Figure 2 shows the system configuration of the first prototype. The system consists of a stuffed-toy robot that includes sensors, actuators, and a fixing textile. It has two degrees of freedom (DoFs) in its head and one in its left hand. A 3D-accelerometer with a 3D-compass detects the activities of both the user and robot, and there is a speaker inside the robot. In the fixing textile, a vibration motor is attached for haptic stimuli. We placed an antenna of capacitance (as used in a theremin) on the lower part of the fixing strap to measure the thickness of the user's clothing and to adjust the strength of the haptic actuations.

The system's fixed parts weigh about 350 g, including the stuffed-toy robot, the actuators, and the battery. But since this prototype requires a small PC (400 g), its total weight is about 800 g.

By simultaneously combining the motions of the robot and the haptic stimuli, our proposed system provides users with a feeling of physical contact from the robot. To express a notification, the robot repeatedly pats the user's arm, while a short-term vibration simultaneously creates haptic stimuli to express the physical contact of the robot's touch. This behavior is seen during a caregiver's initial contact with a patient. To express affection, the robot turns its face toward the user, and a simultaneous pressure stimulus relays the physical contact of the robot's hugging behavior.

Fig. 1. System view of first prototype [21]

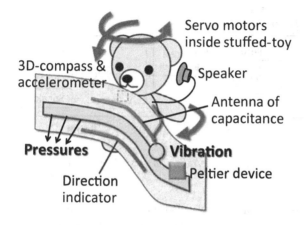

Fig. 2. System configuration of wearable message robot [21]

3.2   Second Prototype

Next, we introduce the second prototype of our wearable message robot [18]. This simplified version of our first prototype solved the previous weight and robustness problems. The first prototype included several sensors and actuators and can realize various behaviors and tactile expressions. On the other hand, considering the actual use cases for seniors or patients with dementia, the detailed system's robustness is insufficient. Furthermore, since it is too heavy to wear for everyday use, we designed a simplified configuration of our message robot to achieve greater robustness and lighter weight.

Figures 3 and 4 show the appearance and configuration of the second prototype. In the simplified system, we employ smartphones proactively. Since the latest smartphones are generally equipped with a triaxial accelerometer and a compass, we employed these sensors to estimate the user's situation and

Fig. 3. System view of second prototype [18]

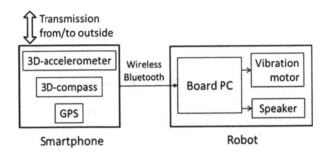

Fig. 4. Configuration of second prototype [18]

activities. Since smartphones are also equipped with a global positioning system (GPS), we are investigating whether the location and velocity information obtained from the GPS can be exploited to estimate the user's context. The robot includes a vibration motor for tactile presentation and a speaker for auditory presentation. These actuators are controlled by a small board PC (Raspberry PI). The board PC and smartphone are connected through Wifi or Bluetooth. A pocket is included on the fixation strap for storing the smartphone. The robot's weight (including a battery) is about 250 g and it is about 18 cm tall. Thus, the entire system's weight including the robot and the smartphone is about 350–400 g (most smartphones weigh less than 150 g).

3.3   Problems of Previous Prototypes

As described in this section, we proposed two prototypes of wearable robots that can make physical contact. However, our previous prototypes have a problem because the types of physical contact that the robots can make are limited. Table 1 shows the tactile expressions of the previous prototypes. The first can make two expressions (one in notification and another in affection), and the

Table 1. Tactile expressions of previous prototypes

	Types	Expressions
1st	Notification	Drawing attention
	Affection	Embracing
2nd	Notification	Drawing attention

second can only make one expression. Thus, in this paper, we propose a tactile expression mechanism that can make various physical contact expressions for wearable robots.

4 Tactile Expression Mechanism Using Pneumatic Actuator Array

Next, we propose and describe our proposed tactile expression mechanism using a pneumatic actuator array for wearable robots.

Figure 5 shows its appearance with the proposed mechanism. Figure 6 is the proposed mechanism's configuration for tactile expressions. The proposed mechanism is used as a fixed part of the robot. In the following description, we use the actuator numbers shown in Fig. 6.

Four actuators are arranged around the user's arm. By shortening a portion of the actuators, various directions can be indicated. We employ pneumatic actuators (SQUSE PM-10RF) that are shortened by increasing their internal pressure. The overall system configuration for direction indications is shown in Fig. 7. The pneumatic actuators require a compressor (SQUSE ACP-100) and a pressure control unit (PCM-200).

Fig. 5. System view of proposed system

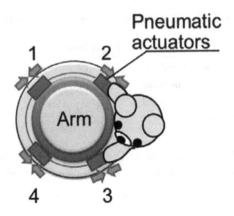

Fig. 6. System design of direction indication

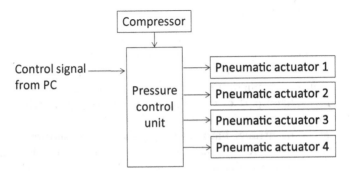

Fig. 7. System configuration

Table 2. Tactile expressions of proposed mechanism

Types	Expressions
Notification	Indicating directions
	Drawing attention
Affection	Embracing
	Stroking
	Clinging

Our proposed mechanism is designed for making both a *notification* and showing *affection*. We designed two types of notification and three types of affection, as shown in Table 2.

Notification Expressions: As with the notification expressions, we design expressions for indicating directions and drawing the attention of users. Although indicating directions is not a physical contact, direction indications are essential during such outdoor support situations as navigation. Thus, the main purpose

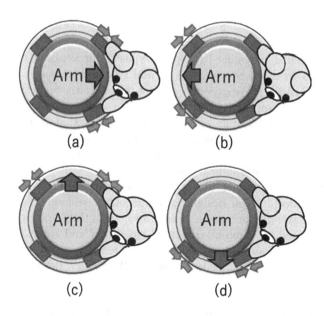

Fig. 8. Motion design of direction indication

of the proposed mechanism is realizing direction indications. The basic idea for indicating directions was proposed in the literature [17].

Figure 8 shows examples of motion designs for indicating four directions. In these designs, two adjacent actuators are shortened simultaneously, and pulling sensations are generated in the same direction of the shortened actuators. For example, in Fig. 8(a), the system indicates the left direction (toward the robot) by shortening actuators 2 and 3. In addition, we can make diagonal directions by activating just one actuator.

Unfortunately, we have not experimentally evaluated the effectiveness of our motion designs for our proposed mechanism yet. Instead, several people have used it from whom we obtained comments and feedback. Some recognized the direction indications, but others could not. These results suggest the need for further improvements of such actuation ways as strength or timing. On the other hand, although the current implement remains relatively unsophisticated, some did recognize the indications. Thus, our system's basic mechanism for indicating directions can achieve directional indications.

In addition, as physical contacts for notification expressions, we design expressions for drawing the attention of users. These robot behaviors grab the user's arm by its left/right hand and are implemented by shortening the actuator (2 or 3) located at the robot's hand. We aim to realize similar expressions for the patting behaviors of the first prototype.

Affection Expressions: As with the affection expressions, we designed embracing, stroking, and clinging expressions as shown in Table 2. The details of the affection expressions are described in the literature [22].

5 Conclusion

In this paper, we first introduced two prototypes of our wearable message robots that snuggle up to the user's upper arm and transmit messages to users after making physical contact. We expect our robot to reduce the anxiety of the elderly during outings and support their participation in such events.

We also proposed a tactile expression mechanism that can make physical contact and provide direction indications for our wearable robots. Our proposed system consists of four pneumatic actuators and creates not only physical contact but also provides direction indications.

Future work will experimentally evaluate our system's effectiveness and investigate such detailed motion designs of actuators as different combinations of shortened actuators and actuation timing and strength. Appropriate behaviors will be investigated to combine direction indication and robot behaviors. We are also investigating an integrated support system for seniors that consists of our method, a toilet map acquisition system [19], and a toilet timing suggestion system [15].

Acknowledgements. This research was supported in part by JSPS KAKENHI 15H01698 and 25730114.

References

1. Amemiya, T., Sugiyama, H.: Haptic handheld wayfinder with pseudo-attraction force for pedestrians with visual impairments. ASSETS **2009**, 107–114 (2009)
2. Bark, K., Wheeler, J., Premakumar, S., Cutkosky, M.: Comparison of skin stretch and vibrotactile stimulation for feedback of proprioceptive information. In: Symposium on Haptic Interfaces for Virtual Environment and Teleoperator Systems, pp. 71–78 (2008)
3. Bonanni, L., Vaucelle, C., Lieberman, J., Zuckerman, O.: TapTap: a haptic wearable for asynchronous distributed touch therapy. In: CHI 2006 Extended Abstracts, pp. 580–585 (2006)
4. Cassinelli, A., Reynolds, C., Ishikawa, M.: Augmenting spatial awareness with haptic radar. In: International Symposium on Wearable Computers (ISWC 2006), pp. 61–64 (2006)
5. Fukumoto, M., Sugimura, T.: Active click: tactile feedback for touch panels. In: CHI 2001 Extended Abstracts, pp. 121–122 (2001)
6. Kajimoto, H.: Electrotactile display with real-time impedance feedback using pulse width modulation. IEEE Trans. Haptics **5**(2), 184–188 (2012)
7. Kashiwabara, T., Osawa, H., Shinozawa, K., Imai, M.: TEROOS: a wearable avatar to enhance joint activities. In: CHI 2012, pp. 2001–2004 (2012)
8. Kojima, Y., Hashimoto, Y., Fukushima, S., Kajimoto, H.: Pull-navi: a novel tactile navigation interface by pulling the ears. In: ACM SIGGRAPH 2009 Emerging Technologies (2009)
9. Kozima, H.: Infanoid: a babybot that explores the social environment. In: Socially Intelligent Agents: Creating Relationships with Computers and Robots, pp. 157–164 (2002)

10. Minato, T., Sumioka, H., Nishio, S., Ishiguro, H.: Studying the influence of hand-held robotic media on social communications. In: Social Robotic Telepresence in ROMAN 2012 Workshop, pp. 15–16 (2012)
11. Rowe, M.A., Feinglass, N.G., Wiss, M.E.: Persons with dementia who become lost in the community: a case study, current research, and recommendations. Mayo Clin. Proc. **79**(11), 1417–1422 (2004)
12. Saadatian, E., Samani, H., Toudeshki, A., Nakatsu, R.: Technologically mediated intimate communication: an overview and future directions. In: Anacleto, J.C., Clua, E.W.G., Silva, F.S.C., Fels, S., Yang, H.S. (eds.) ICEC 2013. LNCS, vol. 8215, pp. 93–104. Springer, Heidelberg (2013). doi:10.1007/978-3-642-41106-9_11
13. Sekiguchi, D., Inami, M., Tachi, S.: RobotPHONE: RUI for interpersonal communication. In: CHI 2001 Extended Abstracts, pp. 277–278 (2001)
14. Tanaka, T., Satoh, Y., Kaneko, S., Suzuki, Y., Sakamoto, N., Seki, S.: Smart suit: soft power suit with semi-active assist mechanism-prototype for supporting waist and knee joint. ICCAS **2008**, 2002–2005 (2008)
15. Tsuji, A., Yonezawa, T., Yamazoe, H., Abe, S., Kuwahara, N., Morimoto, K.: Proposal and evaluation of the toilet timing suggestion method for the elderly. Int. J. Adv. Comput. Sci. Appl. **5**(10), 140–145 (2014)
16. Wang, R., Quek, F., Tatar, D., Teh, J., Cheok, A.: Keep in touch: channel, expectation and experience. In: CHI 2012, pp. 139–148 (2012)
17. Yamazoe, H., Yonezawa, T.: Direction indication mechanism by tugging on user's clothing for a wearable message robot. In: ICAT-EGVE 2015 (2015)
18. Yamazoe, H., Yonezawa, T.: Simplification of wearable message robot with physical contact for elderly's outing support. In: Proceedings of the 2nd International Conference on Human-Agent Interaction (HAI 2014), pp. 35–38 (2014)
19. Yamazoe, H., Yonezawa, T., Abe, S.: Automatic acquisition of a toilet map using a wearable camera. In: Joint 7th International Conference on Soft Computing and Intelligent Systems and 15th International Symposium on Advanced Intelligent Systems (2014)
20. Yano, H., Yoshie, M., Iwata, H.: Development of a non-grounded haptic interface using the gyro effect. In: HAPTICS 2003, pp. 32–39 (2003)
21. Yonezawa, T., Yamazoe, H.: Wearable partner agent with anthropomorphic physical contact with awareness of clothing and posture. In: The 18th International Symposium on Wearable Computers (ISWC 2013), pp. 77–80 (2013)
22. Yonezawa, T., Yamazoe, H.: Haptic interaction design for physical contact between a wearable robot and the user. In: HCII 2017 (2017 to appear)
23. Yonezawa, T., Yamazoe, H., Abe, S.: Physical contact using haptic and gestural expressions for ubiquitous partner robot. In: IEEE/RSJ International Conference on Intelligent Robots and Systems (IROS 2013), pp. 5680–5685 (2013)
24. Yonezawa, T., Yamazoe, H., Utsumi, A., Abe, S.: Gaze-communicative behavior of stuffed-toy robot with joint attention and eye contact based on ambient gaze-tracking. In: Proceedings of the ICMI 2007, pp. 140–145 (2007)
25. Yoshikawa, Y., Shinozawa, K., Ishiguro, H., Hagita, N., Miyamoto, T.: The effects of responsive eye movement and blinking behavior in a communication robot. In: Proceedings of the IROS 2006, pp. 4564–4569 (2006)

Haptic Interaction Design for Physical Contact Between a Wearable Robot and the User

Tomoko Yonezawa[1]($\boxtimes$) and Hirotake Yamazoe[2]

[1] Faculty of Infomatics, Kansai University, 2-1-1 Ryozenji, Takatsuki,
Osaka 569-1095, Japan
yone@kansai-u.ac.jp
[2] College of Information Science and Engineering, Ritsumeikan University,
1-1-1 Nojihigashi, Kusatsu, Shiga 525-8577, Japan
yamazoe@fc.ritsumei.ac.jp

Abstract. In this paper, we propose a framework for a bidirectional haptic interaction system for a wearable robot as an anthropomorphic communication method. Humans have various ways to communicate with others. One of them is physical contact. To build intimate or familiar engagement between the robot and our focused users such as elderly people, children, and care receivers, we focused on bidirectional physical contact with emotional expression. The system adopts our prototype for a wearable robot that creates haptic stimuli with kinetic motions, as though it pats, seizes, or pulls the user's clothes on her/his arm. Our discussion focuses on the interaction design of the robot with a stepwise change inthe habituation that affects the internal state of the user and the user's interpretation of the physical contact and then we tentatively establish patterns for the robot's physical contact.

1 Introduction

According to recent tendencies toward aging societies and nuclear families, there are a large number of elderly people and children who act alone in their daily lives. They sometimes experience social withdrawal because of various difficulties such as anxiety regarding outings without any attendant or the psychological burden of appealing to others for assistance. Their isolated lives make them lack communication.

On the other hand, there are caregivers to help elderly adults and children. The caregivers talk and touch their clients. Even though the main purpose of caregivers is to support their care receivers' lives, the communication with caregivers also provides social stimuli for the care receivers. However, few care receivers can experience such communication throughout their whole lives because of the lack of caregivers. Thus, we proposed that anthropomorphic robots [1] could help such people if the robots are designed like a caregiver for each user.

Accordingly, we have developed multiple prototypes of a stuffed-toy robot that cuddles up to the user's upper arm [2–6]. Among various modalities for communication, our system focuses on haptic stimuli. The system especially targets

© Springer International Publishing AG 2017
V.G. Duffy (Ed.): DHM 2017, Part I, LNCS 10286, pp. 476–490, 2017.
DOI: 10.1007/978-3-319-58463-8_40

outing scenes, and we have proposed direction indication [5] as one application. However, the features of anthropomorphic media are not just intelligibility in such indications or notification but also include empathetic and emotional communication.

Here, we focused on empathetic and emotional touches in care. A concept proposed by Gineste called "humanitude [7]" is a breakthrough method for caregivers, especially for people with dementia, using communication steps: (1) looking at the patient in the patient's field of view to create eye contact, (2) touching the patient's body, (3) talking to the patient, and (4) letting him/her walk. The effectiveness of the humanitude method has been verified [8]. Similarly, "validation [9]" by Feil is another approach. The definition and techniques of validation are a little more complicated than those of humanitude; however, the concepts of both humanitude and validation are similar, that is, *empathy and respect* for the patients.

With these communication methods in care, not only for people with dementia but also for children or other people who need support, empathetic attitude is considered the most important characteristic in order to actualize warm support like human or living beings. However, while physical contact in humanitude or validation is expected to create such a positive effect, some people do not like to be touched by others. It is assumed that there is not a sufficient relationship of trust between the caregiver and the care receiver in such cases.

In this paper we propose a framework for bidirectional haptic communication with a wearable robot based on anthropomorphism for familiar engagement. From the viewpoint of the relationship development, we consider the first or earliest contacts should be a weak stimulus. Accordingly, in order to design a wearable robot not only as a temporary partner for an outing but also for much more familiar relationships with trust, we discuss the design of the bidirectional physical contact by considering the user's situation and habituation to the robot.

2   Related Research

2.1   Interaction Design for a Communication Robot

Giannopulu proposed *enrobotment* [10] as a method for the development of children, especially those with autism, who cannot mirror the relationship of object-self-other. Here, a robot has the potential to be interpreted as an artificial object or communicative presence as the other. We have previously discussed the proposed robot system with haptic interaction from the viewpoint of enrobotment [11]. The acceptability of the robot system should meet some requirements, stepwise levels of communication, though not just for autism children. Before basic communication, the robot should show the potential for communication. To maintain the anthropomorphism for sustainability, the robot should behave as though it has a human-like internal state that is changed by the interaction. In this paper we discuss a framework for the internal states of both the robot and the user to be suitable for the stepwise habituation in human-robot interactions.

There are researches on multimodal expressions of robots, such as gaze [12,13], gesture [14], personal space [15], and facial expression [16]. Among various modalities, the appropriate use of physical contact helps with warm and intelligible communication, as the concept of humanitude has shown [7]. In order to show an empathetic attitude to the user using our proposed robot, we especially focused on both the haptic modality and the stepwise change in the habituation. In various communication modalities, haptic communication with physical contact is recognized as an intimate or familiar expression. Therefore, the proposed robot system presupposes the user's attention to the robot while establishing a better relationship.

2.2 Social Touches

Social touches [17] have been discussed as a human-human communication channel in psychology for decades. In recent years, research has been conducted on tactile human-robot interaction [18,19]. Recognition of the user's touch [20] as well as expression of the robot's social touch [21,22, etc.] have been discussed from the viewpoint of both the mechanical structure and the design for haptic stimuli.

We have developed a haptic-sensible stuffed-toy device [23] as an outlet target for the user's mental suffering. In order to support indirect communication with the user and other people, the stuffed toy contains touch sensors to detect the user's input, recognize the type of touch, and then post a comment on an SNS corresponding to the user's touch. This would be effective for the people who do not have the chance to express their personal emotions. In addition to the input from the user, the artificial physical contact is also expected to become an emotional vent for people who have difficulty in their minds. In this paper we propose a framework for emotional and bidirectional physical contact between the robot and the user that is applicable for our wearable robot prototypes [2–6].

3 Hardware of Previously Developed Robots

Before considering the interactional design of bidirectional physical contact, we introduce three hardware configurations for the robots [2–6], as shown in Figs. 2, 3, 4, 5 and 6. The purpose of the proposed robots is to support elderly people during outings, so the robots are designed to be wearable.

3.1 Prototype Robot with Vibration Motor and Pressure Actuator

The first prototype has three servomotors; one motor is attached to the one-degree-of-freedom (DOF) left arm, and two motors are attached to the two-DOF head of the robot. The cuff of the blood-pressure monitor is used not only for loading the robot but also for creating a haptic pressure and for attaching to the user's upper arm. A small vibration motor is attached on the inner side.

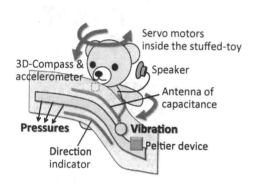

Fig. 1. Structures of the first prototpe robot [2,3]

Fig. 2. View of the first prototpe robot [2,3]

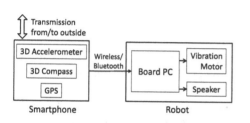

Fig. 3. Configuration of the second prototpe robot [4,29]

Fig. 4. View of the second prototpe robot [4,29]

The robot also contains Peltier devices to create temperature stimuli. Figure 1 shows the hardware equipment in the robot.

The robot makes anthropomorphic physical contact by (1) the motion of the robot and (2) the haptic stimuli from the actuators. Figure 2 shows a view of the first robot prototype. Subjective evaluation demonstrated the effectiveness of both the haptic stimuli and the anthropomorphic motion using this robot [2,3]. The robot can not only notify the user various signals corresponding to the alert or message but also express affection as an emotional element. For example, the robot expresses warm hugs by a pressure stimulus on the arm from the cuff and the Peltier device at 40 °C. The robot also expresses its fear by a strong vibration with a cold temperature at 5 °C.

3.2   Prototype Robot in Simplified Structures

As a simplified robot system, we have also developed a smartphone-based system as a second prototype [4,5]. The system was developed as a wearable messaging

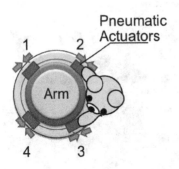

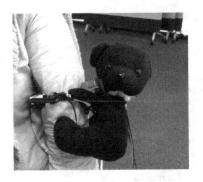

Fig. 5. Structures of the third prototpe robot [5]

Fig. 6. View of the third prototpe robot [5]

robot but without any servomotors. The versatility of the system should be improved to be light weight and easy to adopt for common devices. We tried to maintain the anthropomorphism as well as to simplify the system by removing kinetic motion mechanisms.

Figure 3 shows the simplified configuration of the wearable message system. The internal smartphone in the stuffed toy provides multiple-sensors' signals, such as those of an accelerometer, a geomagnetic sensor, and GPS. The sensors in the smartphone can be used as an ambient device to estimate the user's activities. A small board PC communicating with the smartphone in the robot is also connected to a board PC (Raspberry PI) via Wi-Fi to generate both a vibration through a vibration motor and the robot's voice through a small speaker. The total weight of the second prototype is 150 g, which succeeded at reducing the first testbed by 100 g.

Figure 4 shows a view of the wearable stuffed toy. While the purpose of the simplification in this prototype system was focused on the daily support of information acquisition when the user is out of the house, multiple applications adopting the system should be investigated. For instance, the service application on mobile devices, the smartphone's GPS could be used to provide a walking navigation system [24]. The system could also be applied for our developed notification system regarding the user's toilet timings, as suggested from the user's activities [25]. Thus, the second prototype is assumed to be practical but limited.

The notifications from the stuffed toy are also considered to be softer compared to the first prototype; however, the trusting relationship is not engaged in this structure. From the viewpoint of the trusting relationship, affective expression should also be investigated.

3.3 Prototype Robot with Pneumatic Actuators

Based on the previous prototype robot, we developed a wearable robot with multiple pneumatic actuators and touch-pressure sensors (piezo). The system produces haptic stimuli as though it pats, seizes, or pulls the user's clothes on her/his arm. The robot includes servomotors to generate kinetic motions of the robot, and multiple pulling devices with multiple vibration motors to create the illusion of physical contact from the robot. In order to enable two-way haptic communication, the robot also includes multiple touch sensors in its head and back.

The robot was mainly developed to indicate directions. The multiple pneumatic actuators work in predetermined orders to create directional sensations on the user's upper arm [28], where the array of pneumatic actuators is lined up on the periphery. For example, when it is necessary to notify the user of directions, the robot gazes in the direction and simulates directional touch by generating a motion of its head with pneumatic stimuli from the opposite direction to the indicatied direction with a time lag. Figure 5 shows the structure of the third prototype robot, and Fig. 6 shows a view of the robot. Different from these approaches to signal notification, we developed anthropomorphic touch from the viewpoint of affective and emotional expression from the robot.

4   System Design

In order to develop the interaction design for bidirectional physical contact, we investigated the basic parameters and expressions for each robot.

4.1   Interaction Types in Physical Contact

First, we describe interaction types of physical contact between humans from the viewpoint of active/passive states.

Active and Passive Physical Contact: There are several modalities for communication. Humans display nonverbal expressions such as gaze, gesture, and intonation. Touches are used for transmitting information to another person, such as beginning communication and expressing emotions. From the viewpoint of spontaneous motivation, the touch from a person is considered to be an *active* touch. On the other hand, passive touch is considered to be categorized into a reaction to another person. A touch can send a signal to another person without making a sound and can also be a push-type communication. The way of touching another person is affected by one's internal state.

Thus, the internal state of the robot should reflect human-like social touch. In fact, there are robots related to the intrinsic motivation [26,27]; however, they are not currently related to emotional activities. In this paper our bidirectional physical contact design includes the internal state of the robot itself.

Types of Interaction Directions: Next we consider one-way and bidirectional touches. In various communications we sometimes use touch while another person talks or displays facial expressions. One-way touches are often used in personal communication to draw another person's attention and interest. Reactions to another's active touch appear especially in gestures, gazes, or verbal expressions. Compositive communication using one-way physical contact will enable (a) the intelligible expression as seen in the engagement of the personal message from the robot even in low volume voice, and (b) the sensitive expression such that the robot can stop saying something as though the robot were taken its breath when the user emotionally touches on the robot.

On the other hand, there are few cases of bidirectional touch without any other modality. These cases are limited to familiar, intimate, or emotional communications. Of course, they include animal-like, instinctive interactions. Here, we focused on bidirectional physical contact to design a flow for trusting relationship and support affection for a familiar relationship. Although there are multiple combinations of modalities with touches in real-life communications, we restricted other modalities in order to focus solely on the touch.

4.2   The First Demonstration System: Mimic Interaction

Mimicry is one of the basic, elementary methods in human communication, and several researches have designed the interaction with virtual agents using paralinguistic intonation [30], facial expression [31], subconscious self-touching gesture [32], and so on. ELIZA is one of the oldest interactive systems, using text chat repeating the user's word [33].

Based upon these simple but effective systems for virtual communication, the first prototype of our interaction design using the third hardware prototype adopted mimicry in haptic interaction. The robot contains two touch sensors on the top-forward and back sides of its head, which are allocated to each pair of pneumatic actuators 1–2 and 3–4 in Fig. 5. The strength and length of the user's touch to the robot's head are converted into actions by the pairs of pneumatic actuators with a two-second delay.

In accordance with the hardware configuration of the third prototype, the robot mimics a haptic expression. For instance, the robot shortly fastens its arms around the user's upper arm in a short-term stimulus when the user slaps the head of the robot. When the user strokes the robot's head, the robot reacts to the user's input by the operations of the two pairs of pneumatic actuators in turns as though it is stroking the user's arm. When the user tightly cuddles up to the robot's head, the robot gives the user's arm a hug at a strength corresponding to the user's input.

4.3   Human-Robot Interaction Design Policy for Physical Contact

Here, we discuss the policy for human-robot interaction design with anthropomorphic physical contact from the viewpoint of human-like communication.

Unsurprisingly, the system requires both the recognition of the user's expressive touch and the robot's expression of touch for the interaction. A short-term, simple interaction is easily established by the recognition of touch input and the expression of touch output; however, long-term, verisimilar communication is based on the internal state of one's mind.

In order to consider long-term communication with physical contact, the robot should (1) realize stepwise communication from the viewpoint of habituation, (2) contain intrinsic motivation for communication with an aspect of satisfaction, and (3) be affected by the trusting relationship with the user. The configuration aims to become the comprehensive design for interactive physical contact, including active or passive touch and one-way or bidirectional touch, with heterogeneous robots.

Figure 7 shows the basic flow of the interaction design with physical contact. The system has a mechanism for detecting physical contact from the user, internal-state data of the robot, and a physical contact expression mechanism. The user's emotional estimation is based on the data analysis of haptic inputs. We classified the types of touch from the data for emotional estimation. Figure 8 shows our simple expected categories of physical contact corresponding to the emotional state by strengths and lengths of touch.

When it is necessary to notify the user of something without the robot's internal desire, the robot does so through a simple touch that is in short term with a relatively strong intensity in order to be intelligible. In the case of urgent notifications, the touch should be repeated according to the degree of the urgency. On the other hand, when the robot has an internal desire to touch the user, the robot makes affective and emotional physical contact, such as embracing the user's arm. The enfolding expression should be a long-lasting touch with a soft intensity. The user's simple reaction to the robot as notification would become simple as described in the above example, for the robot's expression. On the other hand, when the user has an internal desire for communication, he or she is expected to use a relatively long-lasting touch with soft intensity, such as a stroke or embrace.

In order to satisfy the internal desire of the robot, the user's reactions are ranked by the level of satisfaction: (1) the positive reactions in the physical contact to the robot's emotional touch, (2) the simple reactions to the robot's emotional touch as the user's confirmation, or (3) no reaction.

From the basic configuration of the bidirectional physical contact system, it is expected to create a robot that cultivates its warm mind corresponding to the haptic interaction with the user and touches the user actively, corresponding to the current internal state, such as the emotional state or satisfaction. The reactive expressions of physical contact can be changed by each-time interaction with the user.

Stepwise Communication Design: We have proposed a stepwise interaction model for enrobotment [11], a procedure to make robots familiar to children [10]. In the early interaction between the robot and the user, the system should consider the level of the user's nervousness regarding the robot. Our previous investigation contained four levels of tactile interactions between a robot and a child in accordance with the acquisition of the trusting relationship, as shown in Table 1: the user's interest without touch (level 0), the short touch interaction started by the user as confirmation of safety and interactivity (level 1), long-lasting physical contact such as strokes given by both the robot and the user

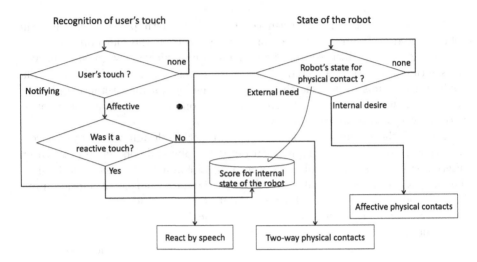

Fig. 7. Basic flow of communication including physical contact

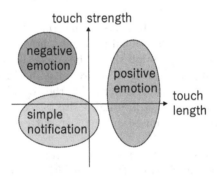

Fig. 8. Expected categories of physical contact corresponding to emotional state

as emotional or expressive communication (level 2), and continuous physical contact, such as a hug when the robot is accepted as a reliable and persistent presence with a trusting relationship for affective interaction (level 3).

The table should also describe each direction of the communication. For example, level 1 currently involves simple touch. It is better to adopt mimicry or shortened mimicry of the user's touch for the simplest engagement when the robot uses passive touch.

Here, we should consider a parameterization of the habituation to calculate the internal state and to design the expressions and reactions with physical contact. Habituation is considered to reduce nervousness [34]. In the situation with the user's high nervousness, the robot should provide a weak stimulus to the user, while the given stimulus should be perceived as strongly corresponding to the nervousness. In order to realize the appropriate social touch from the robot corresponding to the user's internal state, the robot should have internal models of both the robot and the user.

Table 1. Pre-designed stepwise communication in physical contact for enrobotment

Step	Level of communication	Content	Example
Level 0	Just interested	Without touch	–
Level 1	Confirmation of safety and interactivity	Short-term and simple touch	Tap or clapping the user's body
Level 2	Emotional, and/or expressive communication	Long-term physical contact	Strokes or short-time hug
Level 3	Trusting relationship	Continuous physical contacts	Long-time hugs or holding hands

Internal Models for Bidirectional Physical Contact: As with human-human communication, the robot should assume not only its internal state but also the user's internal state as a "mental model of others [35]." In addition to the internal states, we consider that the strength of the robot's motivation for the communication needs to be prepared.

The preliminary prototype for the tactile interaction model used the robot's internal satisfaction value corresponding to the robot's desire for the physical contact and the reaction from the user. On the other hand, the emotional circumplex model [36] has two axes: valence and arousal. The PAD model [37] has three: pleasure (which is similar to valence), arousal, and dominance. These models do not merely demonstrate momentary emotions but also everything from long-term emotion to temperament and personality [38]. The satisfaction is regarded to be related to the arousal and pleasure. Accordingly, our robots with physical contact adopt these segmentalized parameters as the internal state model, which reflect the results of the interaction instead of the simple satisfaction value.

The motivation for communication is to be relieved of nervousness about the relationship. The first state of the relationship, level 0 in the previously explained stepwise interaction, is in a highly nervous state, as shown in Fig. 9-I. When there is a positive interaction with the user, the internal state of the robot changes to Fig. 9-II in Fig. 9. The goal of the motivation is to reach Fig. 9-III. If there is some negative interaction, the state moves to Fig. 9-IV. When there is no reaction from the user, the robot's state gradually moves to Fig. 9-V. θ in Fig. 9 is the change of the emotional state with a basic route from Fig. 9-I to Fig. 9-III.

Next, we discuss the conversion of the touch input corresponding to the receiver's internal state. For example, when the user is in the internal state at Fig. 9-I, a strong stimulus would be converted into a negative impression in the sensitive situation. On the other hand, the variation of the interaction would enable the growth of a trusting relationship in a favorable situation. Therefore, it is important to convert the external stimulus into the interpreted emotion of the receiver based on the receiver's internal state, not only to create action and reaction by a simple mechanism. Figure 10 shows the proposed conversion into the emotion for both the robot and the user. There should also be a relation

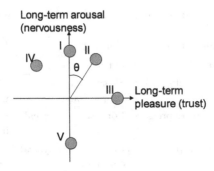

Fig. 9. Internal states and motivation for communication

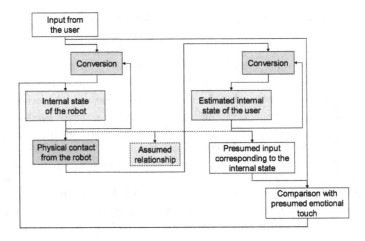

Fig. 10. The conversion of the external touch input into the internal state

between the internal states of both the robot and user via physical contact. Both internal state models allow the robot to have aspects of (a) honest expressions corresponding to its internal state and (b) the robot's concern for the user corresponding to her/his internal state. The long-term internal state as emotion toward each other should be considered based on the assumed relationship between them in the future.

Common Expressions of Physical Contact for Different Robots: Finally, the common expressions of physical contact from the robot should be investigated for heterogeneous robots. The expressive design of the physical contact involves the problem of the acquisition of the sensor data for automatic emotional estimation. In our preliminary test using a stuffed toy containing a touch sensor, the patterns of physical contact and the user's emotional expression observed by the sensor were classified by the length and the strength of the touch as we expected. The robot's physical contact corresponding to the robot's internal state should be based on the patterns of the user's expressive touches.

Table 2. Patterns of physical contact for the third prototype

Expressions	Types	Patterns
Notification	Indicating directions	Activate one or two actuators located in the direction to indicate
	Drawing attention	Activate actuators located at robot's hand
Affection	Embracing	Activate all actuators
	Stroking	Activate actuators (1, 2) and (3, 4) alternatively
	Clinging	Activate actuators in sequence (Ex. (1, 4)-(1, 2, 3, 4)-(2, 3))

From the viewpoint of the compatibility of the design, we assigned the strength of physical contact to the actuators in each robot we developed corresponding to the power of the haptic stimuli. The vibration motors in the first and second prototype are considered to provide narrow and weak stimuli. On the other hand, the pneumatic actuators in the third prototype are considered to generate large and strong stimuli, even when only one actuator is used.

According to the characteristics of stimuli from each actuator, the patterns of physical contact are converted. In Table 2, there are different types of physical contact for the four pneumatic actuators in the third prototype. The notifying touch without an emotional element is generated through simple conversion of the strength and width. The affective touch varies among several patterns. The embracing expression, which is a robot behavior where the robot embraces the user's arm, is implemented by shortening all of the actuators. The stroking expression, which is a robot behavior where the robot strokes the user's arm, is implemented by alternatively activating actuators 1 and 2 and actuators 3 and 4. Clinging, which is a robot behavior where the robot pulls the user's arm or clothing while hanging on to the user, is implemented by sequentially activating actuators (1, 4)-(1, 2, 3, 4)-(2, 3). The strength, width, and length of the touch are interpreted through (1) the internal states of both the robot and the user and (2) characteristics of the actuators.

For the other prototypes, the placement and the characteristics of the actuators, such as vibration motors, should be used for the conversion of the stimuli. If there is no substitute actuator for the robot, the strength and timing of the stimuli should be designed in order to complement the missing actuator.

5   Conclusion

In this paper, we discussed the framework for a bidirectional haptic interaction system for our wearable robots. In order to involve various interactions, we classified types of physical contact (active or passive touch and one-way or bidirectional touch) and designed policies for the haptic communication. Based on the configurations of the wearable robots, we proposed an interactive physical contact mechanism and the flow of the communication with the internal states of both the robot and the user. There are three methods for communication with bidirectional physical touch: the stepwise change of the levels, the emotional effect on the interpretation of the touch, and the generation of the physical touch that transforms from the commonly designed expression into the appropriate physical contact by changing the strength and width corresponding to each actuator in each robot.

The previously proposed prototypes are configured for elderly people during outings. If the bidirectional physical contact grows the trusting relationship between the user and the robot, both the accessibility and the acceptability of the wearable robot will be improved, which will lead to the continuous use of the robot. A deep understanding through emotional interaction with physical contact is expected to reduce the user's anxieties, which stop the user from taking further action.

The system requires the evaluation of the basic interaction with stepwise habituation and the internal state. In future work, the compositive design of the physical contact with other modalities should be further considered. From the viewpoint of the application for care receivers, a demonstration experiment in an elderly care house or nursery school should be held to clarify the effectiveness of the proposed design for elderly people or children.

Acknowledgement. This research was supported in part by JSPS KAKENHI 15H01698 and JSPS KAKENHI 25700021.

References

1. Duffy, B.R.: Anthropomorphism and the social robot. Robot. Auton. Syst. **42**, 177–190 (2003)
2. Yonezawa, T., Yamazoe, H.: Wearable partner agent with anthropomorphic physical contact with awareness of clothing and posture. In: Proceedings of ISWC 2013, pp. 77–80 (2013)
3. Yonezawa, T., Yamazoe, H., Abe, S.: Physical contact using haptic and gestural expressions for ubiquitous partner robot. In: IROS 2013, pp. 5680–5685 (2013)
4. Yonezawa, T., Yamazoe, H.: A structure of wearable message-robot for ubiquitous and pervasive services. In: Streitz, N., Markopoulos, P. (eds.) DAPI 2014. LNCS, vol. 8530, pp. 400–411. Springer, Cham (2014). doi:10.1007/978-3-319-07788-8_38
5. Yamazoe, H., Yonezawa, T.: Direction indication mechanism by pulling user's cloth for wearable message robot, In: ICAT-EGVE 2015, P2 (4 p.) (2015)
6. Yamazoe, H., Yonezawa, T.: Wearable robot with vital sensors for elderly care and support. In: RO-MAN 2015, IS-12 (2 p.) (2015)
7. Gineste, Y., Pellissier, J.: Humanitude: Comprendre la vieillesse, prendre soin des Hommes vieux (think old age, caregiving for old men), Armand Colin (2007). (in French)
8. Honda, M., Ito, M., Ishikawa, S., Takebayashi, Y., Tierney Jr., L.: Reduction of behavioral psychological symptoms of dementia by multimodal comprehensive care for vulnerable geriatric patients in an acute care hospital: a case series. Case Rep. Med. **2016**, 4 (2016). Article ID 4813196
9. Feil, N.: Validation therapy. Geriatr. Nurs. **13**(3), 129–133 (1992)

10. Giannopulu, I.: Enrobotment: toy robots in the developing brain. In: Nakatsu, R., Rauterberg, M., Ciancarini, P. (eds.) Handbook of Digital Games and Entertainment Technologies, pp. 1011–1039. Springer, Singapore (2017). doi:10.1007/978-981-4560-50-4_59

11. Yonezawa, T.: Stepwise Experience Design of Tactile Interaction in Children's Enrobotment. In: HAI Workshop of Enrobotment, 2 p. (2016)

12. Sidner, C.L., Kidd, C.D., Lee, C., Lesh, N.: Where to look: a study of human-robot engagement. In: Proceedings of the 9th International Conference on Intelligent User Interfaces, pp. 78–84 (2004)

13. Yonezawa, T., Yamazoe, H., Utsumi, A., Abe, S.: Gaze-communicative behavior of stuffed-toy robot with joint attention and eye contact based on ambient gaze-tracking. In: Proceedings of the 9th International Conference on Multimodal Interfaces, pp. 140–145 (2007)

14. Kim, H.H., Lee, H.E., Kim, Y.H., Park, K.H., Bien, Z.Z.: Automatic generation of conversational robot gestures for human-friendly steward robot. In: International Symposium on Robot and Human interactive Communication in RO-MAN 2007, pp. 1155–1160 (2007)

15. Walters, M.L., Dautenhahn, K., te Boekhorst, R., Koay, K.L., Kaouri, C., Woods, S., Nehaniv, C., Lee, D., Werry, I.: The influence of subjects' personality traits on personal spatial zones in a human-robot interaction experiment. In: Robot and Human Interactive Communication, ROMAN 2005, pp. 347–352 (2005)

16. Berns, K., Hirth, J.: Control of facial expressions of the humanoid robot head ROMAN. In: IROS 2006, pp. 3119–3124 (2006)

17. Thayer, S.: History and strategies of research on social touch. Nonverbal Behav. **10**(1), 12–28 (1986)

18. Haans, A., IJsselsteijn, W.: Mediated social touch: a review of current research and future directions. Virtual Reality **9**(2–3), 149–159 (2006)

19. Argall, B.D., Billard, A.G.: A survey of tactile human-robot interactions. Robot. Auton. Syst. **58**, 1159–1176 (2010)

20. Knight, H., Toscano, R., Stiehl, W.D., Chang, A., Wang, Y., Breazeal, C.: Real-time social touch gesture recognition for sensate robots. In: IROS 2009, pp. 3715–3720 (2009)

21. Wang, R., Quek, F.: Touch talk: contextualizing remote touch for affective interaction. In: Proceeding of the Fourth International Conference on Tangible, Embedded, and Embodied Interaction, pp. 13–20 (2010)

22. Cabibihan, J., Pattofatto, S., Jomaa, M., Benallal, A., Carrozza, M.: Towards humanlike social touch for sociable robotics and prosthetics: comparisons on the compliance, conformance and hysteresis of synthetic and human fingertip skins. Int. J. Soc. Robot. **1**(1), 29–40 (2009)

23. Mase, H., Yoshida, Y., Yonezawa, T.: An interactive stuffed-toy device for communicative description on Twitter. In: Proceedings of SCIS-ISIS 2014, pp. 1360–1363 (2014)

24. Kaminoyama, H., Matsuo, T., Hattori, F., Susami, K., Kuwahara, N., Abe, S.: Walk navigation system using photographs for people with dementia. In: Smith, M.J., Salvendy, G. (eds.) Human Interface 2007. LNCS, vol. 4558, pp. 1039–1049. Springer, Heidelberg (2007). doi:10.1007/978-3-540-73354-6_113

25. Tsuji, A., Yonezawa, T., Yamazoe, H., Abe, S., Kuwahara, N.: Proposal and evaluation of toilet timing suggestion methods for the elderly. Int. J. Adv. Comput. Sci. Appl. **5**(10), 140–145 (2014)

26. Asada, M., MacDorman, K., Ishiguro, H.: Cognitive developmental robotics as a new paradigm for the design of humanoid robots. Robot. Auton. Syst. **37**(2), 185–193 (2001)

27. Oudeyer, P.Y., Kaplan, F.: Intrinsic motivation systems for autonomous mental development. IEEE Trans. Evol. Comput. **11**(2), 265–286 (2007)

28. Yamazoe, H., Yonezawa, T.: A tactile expression mechanism using pneumatic actuator array for notification from wearable robots. In: Proceedings of HCII (2017 to appear)

29. Yamazoe, H., Yonezawa, T.: Simplification of wearable message robot with physical contact for elderly's outing support. In: HAI 2014, pp. 35–38 (2014)

30. Suzuki, N., Takeuchi, Y., Ishii, K., Okada, M.: Effects of echoic mimicry using hummed sounds on human-computer interaction. Speech Commun. **40**(4), 559–573 (2003)

31. Hess, U., Blairy, S.: Facial mimicry and emotional contagion to dynamic emotional facial expressions and their influence on decoding accuracy. Int. J. Psychophysiol. **40**(2), 129–141 (2001)

32. Kramer, N.C., Simons, N., Kopp, S.: The effects of an embodied conversational agent's nonverbal behavior on user's evaluation and behavioral mimicry. In: International Workshop on Intelligent Virtual Agents, pp. 238–251 (2007)

33. Weizenbaum, J.: Computer power and human reason: from judgment to calculation. W.H. Freeman and Company (1976). ISBN 0-7167-0463-3

34. Lader, M.H., Mathews, A.M.: A physiological model of phobic anxiety and desensitization. Behav. Res. Ther. **6**(4), 411–421 (1968)

35. Read, S.J., Miller, L.C.: Rapist or 'regular guy': explanatory coherence in the construction of mental models of others. Pers. Soc. Psychol. Bull. **19**(5), 526–540 (1993)

36. Russell, J.A.: A circumplex model of affect. J. Pers. Soc. Psychol. **39**, 1161–1178 (1980)

37. Russell, J.A., Mehrabian, A.: Evidence for a three-factor theory of emotions. J. Res. Pers. **11**, 273–294 (1977)

38. Mehrabian, A.: Measures of individual differences in temperament. Educ. Psychol. Measur. **38**, 1105–1117 (1978)

Author Index

Printed in the United States
By Bookmasters